THE ART OF BIOGRAPHY
IN EIGHTEENTH
CENTURY ENGLAND

THE ART OF BIOGRAPHY
IN EIGHTEENTH
CENTURY ENGLAND

BY DONALD A. STAUFFER

NEW YORK / RUSSELL & RUSSELL

CT
34
G7
S67
1970

COPYRIGHT, 1941, 1969, BY PRINCETON UNIVERSITY PRESS
REISSUED, 1970, BY RUSSELL & RUSSELL
A DIVISION OF ATHENEUM PUBLISHERS, INC.
BY ARRANGEMENT WITH PRINCETON UNIVERSITY PRESS
L. C. CATALOG CARD NO: 78-83850
PRINTED IN THE UNITED STATES OF AMERICA

For
Mart and Cariella

CONTENTS

THE ART OF BIOGRAPHY
IN EIGHTEENTH
CENTURY ENGLAND

"Men and women are always the same. Such a number of people are like their grandfathers!"

—LOUIS-PIERRE ANQUETIL

INTRODUCTION

BIOGRAPHY as a branch of literature has been too long neglected. Nevertheless, Waldo H. Dunn's pioneer survey of *English Biography,* Mark Longaker's more recent *English Biography in the Eighteenth Century,* brief critical discussions such as those by Harold Nicolson and André Maurois, have done much to establish biography as a literary form worth serious attention. This present study, by limiting its scope to a single century and considering all the biographical writings of that period may, I hope, contribute to the general knowledge of the art of biography. Such a purpose necessitates certain definitions and certain statements of the principles on which this book was written.

Biography is here taken to mean the more or less formal and conscious recording of the life, or of a respectable fragment of the life, of an actual individual human being. The raw materials for biography as so conceived—letters, for instance, or diaries; funeral sermons or eulogies or historical annals or brief biographical notices in periodicals—are therefore treated incidentally and only when they throw light on the development of more formal, more conscious, or more complete records of human careers.

A second principle of this study, reached only after extensive reading, is that the distinction between biography and autobiography is largely artificial. Many autobiographers, such as Benjamin Franklin, have the capacity to see themselves from the outside, almost as if the writer of a life and the liver of the same life were two different persons. Conversely, many of the great biographers, such as Boswell and Mason, pride themselves on the autobiographical elements in the shape of their subjects' private journals, letters, or other writings which make up a great part of the biographies of their heroes. Whether or not the reader accepts this conviction that no fundamental difference distinguishes biography from autobiography, few would deny that the two forms are interdependent. Since this book attempts to present as historically comprehensive a picture as possible, both biography and autobiography are therefore included. The history of either form cannot be fully understood without the other.

A third principle is that emphasis should fall upon biography as an art rather than as a science. Individual pieces are to be judged, in other words, according to their success in conveying the sense of a life being lived, rather than according to the quantity or the accuracy of the facts they contain. Great biographical collections such as the *Biographia Britannica,* therefore, are given less attention than a little known work such as the *Memoirs of Sophia Baddeley,* because however important the encyclopedists and antiquaries are to scholars and historians, they contributed little to life-writing as an aesthetic form. This bias toward biography as literature rather than as a storehouse for facts accounts, for instance, for the first three chapters, which relate the form to drama, the novel, and the newly developing romantic spirit. Nor is the absolute historical importance of a figure used as a criterion for surveying the biographies written about him. Pope, for example, stood first among the poets of his time, and the three Hanoverian Georges filled the English throne during most of the century; but their biographers are a sorry crew. George III must therefore give way before an obscure member of one of his Parliaments, John Elwes; and Pope is less important in a history of eighteenth century biography than a minor poet like Richard Savage.

Why, then, does Johnson's *Life of Savage* receive scant attention? Because of a fourth principle which has generally been followed in the ensuing chapters: that this work is not final and complete in itself, but supplementary to earlier studies. The full consideration of those works which are well known is not so imperative, therefore, as the presentation of obscure works that should be better known, and the presentation of obscure as well as famous lives in relation to the whole pattern of the century in English biography.

The organization of the material cannot be completely satisfactory. I have wished to make this book both readable and authoritative, and the two are not always compatible. The scholar may find that he prefers to skip the longer descriptive analyses of individual lives in favor of the biographies themselves; the average reader will brush over the attempts to support general assertions by quoting chapter and verse. A strict chronological survey would have made the book insufferable. It would also have proved very little, except that influences and currents in biography are not so much functions of chronology as tokens of kindred temperaments.

In manner of treatment, some of the chapters split in the middle. Such fission arises largely from the impossibility of simultaneously considering each work as a unit and as a small piece in the large historical pattern. In the main, the first parts of the several chapters contain general analytical discussions; the last parts are devoted to the most significant biographies that illustrate, in single works of art, the main positions of the chapter. The book as a whole also follows this plan, for Chapter VI considers, individually, the best-known biographies of the century, in their relation to biographical theory and practice as analyzed in the earlier sections.

The last chapter is a general critical and historical sketch. Certain repetitions—of ideas, if not of illustrations—have been inevitable. Overlappings in classifications are also inevitable throughout; the careful reader will soon discover that a biography which has been considered in the chapter on the drama, for example, might justifiably have been treated in that dealing with the novel or the romantic spirit. Certain readers will feel that I have done too much classifying, others too little. I apologize to them both.

American biography, insofar as it existed in the eighteenth century, has not been considered fully, but only casually in the illustration of general points or in circumstances where a life written by an American was of influence in England during the century. Franklin's autobiography, for instance, is practically omitted from the text.

Wherever possible, I have quoted copiously and directly, since often a paragraph or a phrase from the original biography will more exactly convey the temper of the writer than a page of description. Quotations within quotations are uniformly set off with a single inverted comma. Italics in the originals have usually been disregarded and no attempt has been made to retain the capitalizations as they appear on the original title-pages. Apart from these changes, the capitalization, punctuation, and spelling of the originals have been retained. Obvious misprints only have been silently changed. When a publisher prints "it" for "is" I have corrected his error; but if the reader comes across such words as "Goal" for "gaol," "imagionation," or "unparalled," I hope he will not suspect careless proofreading. I would rather be thought careless, however, than place a [sic] after every unusual word; if it occurs within quotation marks, I take refuge in the Nun's Priest's disclaimer:

"Thise been the cokkes wordes, and nat myne."

This present volume contains the critical and historical survey of biography in eighteenth century England. Its companion volume, the Bibliographical Supplement, lists alphabetically the biographies read in connection with this study. Cross-references to "Bibliography" in text and notes refer to this second volume.

At the end of the Bibliographical Supplement, the chronological table of the principal biographies, significant either because of their intrinsic worth or because of their influence, may be of some value in seeing the century as a whole.

The Bibliography describes briefly any important biography not considered in the text, and also distinguishes with a [T] those that are mentioned at any great length in the text of this first volume. The result is a rough triple classification: those biographers good enough to require separate consideration in the text, those good enough to warrant description in the Bibliography, and those lucky to be listed at all. A mere title in the Bibliography means that the work is conventional, or derivative, or third-rate as a piece of biographical writing.

In spite of its length, the Bibliography cannot pretend to completeness. Certain important biographies must have been overlooked entirely; many unimportant ones undoubtedly are missing. It ought to be taken for what it is: a book-list made as the result of twelve years of sporadic study in three libraries. It should represent a fair cross-section of eighteenth century English biography.

Any judgments on individual biographies I have tried to make while bearing in mind the course of biography and its achievements during the whole century. Such general knowledge, based on the reading represented by the titles in the Bibliography, is the only compensation I can make for failure to consider any individual work with the care and attention to scholarly detail which many of them merit.

I wish to thank the staffs of the Bodleian Library in Oxford, the British Museum in London, the University Library and University Press in Princeton for their unfailing courtesy in the face of heavy demands; the Council of the Humanities at Princeton for a travel grant; and the Committee on University Research, Princeton, for substantial assistance in the publication of the Bibliographical Supplement. Had it not been for generous grants from the John Simon Guggenheim Memorial Foundation neither the research which these volumes represent nor the volumes themselves would have been possible. Among many colleagues and friends who have helped me with their interest, their knowledge, or their advice, I am deeply grateful to David Nichol Smith, J. Duncan Spaeth, Hoyt H. Hudson, Robert K. Root, Gordon H. Gerould, Christian Gauss, Gilbert Chinard, Walter B. C. Watkins, Francis R. B. Godolphin, James M. Osborn, William Dighton II, and particularly to Charles Grosvenor Osgood.

D. A. S.

Princeton, New Jersey
September 9, 1940

CHAPTER I

BIOGRAPHY AND THE DRAMA

"They have their exits and their
entrances."   —SHAKESPEARE.

THE eighteenth century in England was an age acutely
aware of literary forms. Many of these forms—the verse
satire and verse epistle, the elegy and the pastoral, the
fable, tragedy, comedy, polemical pamphlet, history—had fairly
sharp edges. They followed accepted models and have subsequently been studied with care. No less than these, biography
as a literary form merits attention. Before the eighteenth century
began, biography had a long and healthy tradition in England;
during the period it developed in surety, in subtlety, and in range.
The urbanity of Augustan society, the Londoners' interest in
persons, the conversation of drawing-room and club and country-
house, encouraged biographers. The polite world was not their
sole domain. The period stretches out between two great struggles—the English Civil Wars and the French Revolution: the
severe Puritan spirit continues to afford material to the introspective autobiographer; the emerging middle-classes at last
achieve the expression of their ways of thinking and of living.
The chapters of this book will show, in repeated specific instances,
how the dominant characteristics of the century, social, spiritual,
economic, were given form in biography.

In such an age of fighters for new ideas and stalwart defenders
of old ones, the raw materials for biography were obviously at
hand. A sympathetic and varied audience existed. But excellent
subject matter and an attentive public together cannot make an
art. They can only increase the chances of its flourishing. Art is
the product of the artist. The writers in a period that set such
high store by literary forms could hardly fail to develop the particular form which would appeal so naturally to the eighteenth
century mind—biography.

Neither the extent nor the art of life-writing in the eighteenth century has been fully realized. The bibliography to this volume should convince the skeptic that the biographies of the century merit attention through sheer bulk. How much attention do they merit as art? The answer here is not simple. Biography possesses certain artistic qualities from the very nature of its subject matter: it is unified around a single central figure; birth, life, and death give to it Aristotle's artistic requisites of a beginning, a middle, and an end.

On the other hand, the mere fact that biography deals with historical material often leads us to assume that its artistic qualities are subsidiary. We may read a life for the data it gives us as sociologists, or psychologists, or political philosophers; we may read the life of Swift for the light it throws on Swift as an artist. Yet the life we read may itself be art, as is, for example, Johnson's life of Swift. The great biographies, read and re-read by each generation, have not survived because they present a mass of facts, but because they present a living person. The facts that Izaak Walton gives for his five heroes might be compressed into a few paragraphs in the *Dictionary of National Biography,* yet we continue to read Walton because he was an artist. Who bothers about the historical importance of Richard Savage or John Sterling? Today we remember these minor authors because Johnson and Carlyle are great artists in biography, as we remember Hallam because Tennyson was a great poet. Many personalities of the eighteenth century must have been more fascinating than Edward Gibbon's; few, however, are so clear in our minds, because Gibbon is an artist in self-portraiture. Dr. Johnson as a man was undoubtedly great; he would appear dry and small today were it not for the skill, as well as the industry, of Boswell. Art in biography, so evident in the acknowledged masterpieces, determines the worth of inferior works also, and of the more important lives which are still little known.

Nevertheless, too frequently we continue to judge a biography by the quantity and accuracy of its recorded information rather than by the purpose and success of its recording, as if a life were written for the use of the antiquary rather than for the pleasure of the critical reader. That the subject of a biography has lived does not make accuracy the sole, or even the main, criterion in appraising the book. Few readers would consider that *Paradise Lost* and *Henry IV* should be judged primarily as faithful records of the historical events on which they ostensibly rest. Biography, although more straitly bound by its materials than the epic or even than the history play, may legitimately be criticized by similar standards, as a work of the creative artist. It must necessarily try to state the facts, but it must also be moving, convincing. It must have life to be a life. The most insistent accuracy, the most complete assembling of details, cannot produce biography. To create the illusion of a career being lived over again requires art, art of the highest order, art akin to that of the dramatist and novelist.

Let us grant immediately the difficulty of writing lives. A completely successful biography is the rarest of literary phenomena; Carlyle justly says that it is harder to write a good life than to live one. The rigid accidents of historical existence are stony fare for the shaping imagination of the biographer. He must forever front the dilemma that Sir Philip Sidney proposed:

"Truly Aristotle himself in his discourse of poesy plainly determineth this question, saying that poetry is more philosophical and more studiously serious than history. His reason is, because poesy dealeth with the universal consideration, and history with the particular."

The biographer moves between the poles of poetry and history. He must record the particular by the very nature of his art; but he cannot refrain from appraisals and values based upon universals. The mere decision to write the life of a certain man, the selection and combination of details, imply judgments. The biographer is a chronicler who seeks import in his chronicle. The pure historian in him makes him write of life as it is; the pure artist, shaping, ordering, emphasizing, assessing, makes him consider life as it should be, life as significant. At one pole is the encyclopedist, dispassionately collecting facts; at the other pole is the "poet," the creator of significant fictions. In between lives the biographer. By profession he lives, as most of us do, uneasily aware of opposed worlds. Rarely, very rarely, he is able to strike a balance between antiquarian annals at one extreme and pure fancy at the other. Philosophy and history may be hostile in the Sidneyan sense; the biographer's dilemma is that he must not disregard either.

Though ideal biography is difficult if not impossible, it came closer to being realized in the eighteenth century than at any other period of its long history in England. It was cultivated naturally as a branch of literature, owing much to other forms and giving much in return. For this reason the first two chapters will consider it in its relations to drama and the novel, the two forms to which it is so obviously allied. The method of each chapter will be to present an illustrated analysis followed by a consideration as unities of the most important biographies germane to the subject. The third chapter is designed to support the thesis that biography, more easily, perhaps, than any other form of literature, reflects the new ideas of the time: the democracy, the commercialism, and the sentiment of nineteenth century England are to be found in English biography long before the French Revolution and the Romantic movement. The fourth chapter considers some of the varied biographical forms which the universal spirit of curiosity assumed in the eighteenth century. Chapter V centers on the growing subtlety and art of the biographer, both in portraying human beings and in judging them.

Only after such weaving of many threads are we justified in taking up the best-known biographies of the time. Often these famous lives are regarded as statues without pedestals. The first five chapters are more than pedestals, for they consider biographies which, though not so well known, are important in their own right. But in relation to the works of Johnson, or Boswell, or Gibbon, they may be considered as prolegomena, and may help to demonstrate that the masters of eighteenth century biography did not float in a void, but rested naturally upon a tradition of which they were perfectly well aware. What they owed to tradition, how they surpassed it, and what their original qualities were, may be more evident after a comprehensive survey of earlier biographies in the first five chapters. The great biographers, therefore, may be more justly appreciated in the light of all the material that precedes Chapter VI.

The various themes of this history are by no means clear and simple. If there are new experiments in theme and treatment stirring, there are also many biographies written in accepted patterns. The history of biography is not characterized by a steady development, a progress; there are cross-currents. It is not a study of growth followed by decay, but of growth *and* decay simultaneously existing, as the lower branches may fall from a pine tree while new needles appear at its top. Nevertheless, in an attempt to draw the pattern together, the final chapter presents a critical survey of the entire century, the old modes and the new, the sense of form and style, the instinctive practice and the conscious theory, the weaknesses and the strengths—the relationships of biography as an árt form, in short, to the century it looked at with its Argus eyes and to the literature of which it formed a part.

This immediate chapter, for instance, might begin with rather mechanical evidence of the close relation of biography to the drama. A new type of brief life arose, performing a unique function. In the first half of the century, if a play on a historical subject was produced, there was a fair chance that a brief pamphlet biography, presenting more fully or more exactly the career of the dramatic hero, might be put on sale. Such biographies, written for particular occasions, came into being solely because of the theater. They were biographical mistletoe growing on the tree of the drama. Sometimes they heralded a play in rehearsal; sometimes they were contemporaneous with a *première;* again they appeared belatedly in the hope that a popular production might continue in vogue. Lives of Cato, Jane Shore, Herod and Mariamne, the Sultan Solyman, Richard I, Themistocles, Scanderbeg, Regulus, Coriolanus, Cromwell, Boadicea, and Essex[1] would never have been written had it not been for dramatic works by Addison, Rowe, Fenton, Mallet, Sewell, Madden, Lillo, Havard, James Thomson, George Smith Green, Glover, and Henry Jones.

The drama, however, was destined to shape biography far more profoundly than through these superficial companions-to-the-playhouse. Shakespeare's influence during the century was, of

---

[1] See Bibliography. Also *Modern Language Notes,* April 1940, Vol. LV, D. A. Stauffer, "A Parasitical Form of Biography," pp. 289-92.

course, far-reaching, and the observations on conduct and morals scattered through his plays, the broad perspectives of life and the meditations on its significance, eventually became common property. Who can estimate to what extent the taste of the eighteenth century was rendered more delicate and sensitive by Shakespeare? The beauty of an Irish landscape at Ballyanan recalls to one biographer Othello's words:[2]

"If it were now to die, 'twere now to be most happy."

And another, to describe the sensations aroused by Venetian music heard at night, must again have recourse to Shakespeare:[3]

"Methinks it sounds much sweeter than by day.
Silence bestows the virtue on it—I think
The nightingale, if she should sing by day,
When every goose is cackling, would be thought
No better a musician than the wren."

A few lines from the Elizabethan dramatist are made the touchstones by means of which an autobiographer or memorialist may evaluate the actions of a whole life. Thus, James Annesley's *Memoirs of an unfortunate young nobleman, return'd from a thirteen years slavery in America where he had been sent by the wicked contrivances of his cruel uncle* (1743) revolves around the motto on the title-page:

". . . Foul Deeds must rise,
Tho' all the Earth o'erwhelm 'em, to Mens Eyes.
Spoken by Hamlet of his Uncle."

Or the *Memoirs of a younger brother . . . written by himself* (1789) not only quotes Horace's *Vitiis nemo sine nascitur* but defends this youthful production by including in the title:

"And little of this great world can I speak,
And therefore little shall I grace my cause
In speaking of myself; yet by your patience
I will a short unvarnish'd tale deliver
Of my whole course."

---

[2] *The real story of John Carteret Pilkington*, 1760, p. 89.
[3] Charles Burney, *The present state of music in France and Italy: or the journal of a tour through those countries*, 1771, p. 151.

A warning in biographical form against betting and racing is heralded by the ghost's words to Hamlet:[4] "I shall a tale unfold, whose lightest words would harrow up the soul, freeze the young blood." The sorrows of the consort of King George I are introduced by lines from *Henry VIII*:[5]

> " 'Tis better to be lowly born,
> And range with humble livers in content,
> Than to be perk'd up in a glitt'ring grief,
> And wear a golden sorrow."

The dubious career of a lady-in-waiting to Marie Antoinette is justified by:[6]

> "If little faults, proceeding on distemper,
> Shall not be wink'd at—how shall we stretch our eyes
> When capital crimes, chew'd, swallow'd and digested,
> Appear before us?"

An answer to a libel explains itself by "The reply churlish—'—if you said so, then I say so.' "[7] The *Genuine Memoirs of Mr. Charles Churchill* (1765) quotes, or misquotes:

> "He was a man, take him for all in all,
> I ne'er shall look upon his like again."

Perusal of title-pages, indeed, soon convinces one that the eighteenth century was swarming with men whose like their biographers will not again behold.[8]

The listing of such quotations from Shakespeare, which have here been confined almost exclusively to the title-pages of biographies, is of significance because it shows the widespread influence of Shakespeare upon eighteenth century biography, particularly in the estimation of character, the imaginative identification with other natures, and the passing of moral judgments. To read the memoirs of such biographers and autobiographers as

---

[4] *The Life of Dick En—l—d*, 1792, t.p.

[5] *Memoirs of the Princess of Zell*, 1796, 2 vols., t.p.

[6] *Memoirs of the Countess de Valois de la Motte*, 1789.

[7] *An answer to the memoirs of Mrs. Billington*, 1792.

[8] See *An essay on the character of the late Mr. William Bruce*, 1755, p. 31; *The Life of David Garrick*, 1779, t.p.; Joseph Cornish's *Life of Thomas Firmin*, 1780, t.p.

Anthony Pasquin,[9] Michael Clancy, Letitia Pilkington and her son, and George Stayley, is to see that in their understanding of life these writers are the disciples of William Shakespeare. Michael Clancy may be taken as representative. Clancy was an Irish dramatist of sorts himself. The career of the notorious Colonel Charteris, which others were turning into sensational biographies, he made into a play, *The Sharper,* which he says Dean Swift read and commended. His own *Memoirs* (1750) are full of theater: direct dialogue, oaths and characteristic speech, hostile characters drawn under assumed names, and whimsical and minute anecdotes. Continually Clancy draws upon Shakespeare for parallels and clarification, from sleepless Cassius to "Ann Page's Master Slender."[10] Most important, Clancy has absorbed some of Shakespeare's detachment, but little of his nobility, in his view of the whole of life. Human beings in their pursuit of wealth and power he sees as "Millions of short-liv'd Vermin bustling for Superiority" (p. 16); and the *Memoirs* are given some coherence from the mechanistic views expressed in the opening sentences (p. 13):

"The World is a Stage; Necessity and Self-gratification are the general Motives of every Action in the various Scenery. As the Desire of Happiness is implanted in the Breast of every Man, the Difference of Characters in Life, arises from the Diversity of those Means which every Individual pursues to attain to it."

Biographers evidently believed that a casual quotation from Shakespeare gave dignity and authority to their introductions. Mark Moore, for instance, opens his *Memoirs and Adventures* (1795) by asserting, in regard to his book "with all its 'imperfections on its head' ": "I have borrowed nothing from the wardrobe of fiction, I have extenuated nought, nor set down aught in malice."

This last echo from Othello's injunction immediately before his death is by far the most popular of all Shakespearean quotations among the biographers. Time and time again it appears in

---

[9] See, in the *Memoirs of Warren Hastings,* 1793, by Anthony Pasquin [= John Williams] the quotations, paraphrases, and allusions on pp. 1, 8, 11, 19, 35, 45, 51, 53, from *The Tempest, Measure for Measure, Macbeth, Lear, Hamlet.*
[10] pp. 86 and 113.

garbled forms on title-pages or in preliminary remarks;[11] and whether or not it strengthened the ideal of impartial life-writing, at least it was used to justify productions ranging from scurrilities and horseplay to tragic personal confessions.

The language and phrases of Shakespeare, as well as his manner of description and analysis, become part of the stock in trade of biographers who are connected with the playhouse. Miss Ambross in her memoirs of Ann Catley (1789, p. 10) introduces in a single scene two reminiscences from *Hamlet* and one from *Lear*, not to mention *Paradise Lost*:

"It was now rather late, the air was eager, nipping and damp— it was such a night, to adopt the language of Shakespear's fool in the tragedy of Lear, as would 'cool a courtezan'—but Nan was in the 'hey day of her blood' and her hand which the fortunate linen

---

[11] Some of the variants are:

Original anecdotes of the late Duke of Kingston and Miss Chudleigh . . . by Thomas Whitehead . . .

> ". . . nothing extenuate
> Or set down aught in malice." 1792.

Memoirs of the life of his Grace Philip late Duke of Wharton. By an impartial hand.

> "When you shall my unhappy Deeds relate,
> Speak of me as I am.—Nothing extenuate,
> But set down nought in Malice." 1731. Not only on the title-page, but once in the text and again as a conclusion the author uses Othello's famous phrase, which was also a favorite of Wharton's.

Genuine Memoirs of Mr. Charles Churchill . . .

> "Nothing extenuate
> Nor set down aught in malice." 1765.

The life and memoirs of the late Miss Ann Catley, the celebrated actress . . . By Miss Ambross. 1789. p. 3 states that the authoress "has followed the advice of Othello, when he desires those present, at his death, to speak of him as he deserves,

> ". . . Nothing extenuate,
> Nor aught set down in malice."

cf. the disguised quotation in Gilbert Wakefield's *Memoirs* (wr. 1792; 1804 ed., Intro., p. 8): "I can think and speak of myself, as well as of other men, without malice and without extenuation."

Also quoted in *Memoirs of Mrs. Letitia Pilkington*, 1748; *The Musical Tour of Mr. Dibdin*, 1788; *Memoirs of the Countess de Valois de la Motte*, 1789; Edward Topham's *Life of the late John Elwes*, 1790.

An essay on the debt of eighteenth century biography to *Othello* alone for phrases and ideas would form a small volume.

draper had pressed between his, communicated an amorous fire to his soul. . . . The kiss and the glass for some time went round, till the amorous draper being wound to the utmost pitch of impatience led her, 'she nothing loath' to a situation from which they soon returned to the bottle."

The ebullient young nobody who composed the *Memoirs of a younger brother* (1789) not only finds Milton, Butler, Pope, Thomson, Addison, Sheridan, Dryden, Chesterfield, Gay, Johnson, Goldsmith, and Young godsends in illustrating his life, but introduces into his elegant tessellation from British letters quotations from *Hamlet, Othello, Lear, The Tempest, As You Like It,* and *Much Ado About Nothing.* And the bookseller James Lackington acquires some of his success in presenting his *Memoirs* (1791) from his devotion to the stage. "I have also read," he confides (p. 239), "most of our best plays, and am so fond of the Theatre, that in the winter season I have often been at Drury-lane or Covent-garden four or five evenings in a week." Shakespeare and Dryden, Heywood, Beaumont and Fletcher, Middleton, and Rowe all help him to interpret his life in the words of the theater.

That astonishing character Mark Moore finds parallels to garnish his own *Memoirs* (1795) not only in Shakespeare but in many English playwrights and novelists. In a career that led him from Boston and the Caribbean to Smyrna and the court at Stockholm, knocking against specimens of humanity that ranged from General Cornwallis to a castaway Turk, Moore nevertheless has time to dwell upon his enthusiasm for Shakespeare (pp. 152-3):

"I was highly charmed one day, in a conversation which happened to turn on the merits of Shakespeare and Racine, to find a young Frenchman, who had lived many years in England, enter the lists as the champion of the British bard, which he did with so much ingenuity and success, that I swore if ever I should be so lucky as to meet him on the banks of the Avon, that he and I should not part 'till we drank a bottle under the shade of the mulberry-tree, which the poet had planted with his own hand. After this, perhaps the reader will pardon me, if I present him with the concluding part of the eulogy which he pronounced on our poet. . . .

[This eulogy fills a whole paragraph, ending:]

"Que si la nature humaine étoit détruite, & qu'il ne restât aucun monument, excepté ses ouvrages, d'autres êtres pourroient savoir, par ses ecrits, ce qu'étoit l'homme?"

At the conclusion of Moore's life, as his duplicity and recklessness lead him into more and more sordid country-fairs, waterfront taverns, and debtors' prisons, a quiet letter which he inserts from an acquaintance in Ireland strikes like a last ray of the sun (p. 255-6):

"The schoolmaster of the parish is my only companion, and if you wish to know his character, you'll find it in Doctor Goldsmith's Deserted Village. . . . I have a few books filled with wise laws and good remarks; Shakespeare is my favourite, but I have turned all his commentators out of doors."

The magic of Shakespeare, entering into the everyday life and thought and speech of actors and actresses, underpaid minions of Edmund Curll, adventurers and ambitious young University bachelors, bore fruit in the writing of biography.

The statement is not extreme that if it had not been for the Elizabethan and Restoration drama, and above all for Shakespeare, Boswell's *Life of Johnson,* for example, would have been less colorful, alive, and dramatic.

One of the most undeniable contributions of the drama to eighteenth century biography is lifelike and characteristic speech. If Shakespeare had never created Fluellen, to take one instance, how much buoyancy would depart from this crowded Adrian Brouwer tavern scene:[12]

"Our poet being thus turned cider-merchant, business flowed in apace. 'Parson! bring me a mug of the right sort,' cries one. 'This is excellent stuff, i' faith,' cries another. 'I pray you now, Mr. John Jones, I peseech you, and intrete you, now to tell me, look you, if you do not think this cider is better than Lewis Morgan ap Thomas's?' asked another. In short, they all agreed the parson's cider was excellent; and they swore, 'By Cot, there faz not such another coot liquor in Wales, look you!' "

[12] *Genuine Memoirs of Mr. Charles Churchill,* 1765, Dublin ed., p. 31.

This scene from Churchill's *Memoirs* may savor of fiction, but no one would doubt the truth of the episode in which Doctor Burney, using the same technique, reproduces the broken English of Handel when the old composer apologizes to the young Burney for a fit of rage:[13] "I pec your barton—I am a very odd tog:—maishter Schmitt is to plame."

Juliet's nurse and Dame Quickly (either directly or through Sterne) lie back of the helter-skelter monologue of such a biographical fragment as this early example of the "stream of consciousness":[14]

"His Mistress was much alarmed, and took on mightily: it was to be sure a vast Misfortune to be handsome,—the Monster did not hurt him,—shocking Wretches!—she'd see them get to Tyburn,—Jack was handsome to be sure,—Aye, he should swear—Here, take this Glass of Sack—Come, drink it up—Lord! how I tremble!—Oh! the filthy Monster! Here, take another I tremble so—he did not hurt you, Jack,—I am all I don't know how,—My Hand,—Come, Jack, here's your Health,—Feel me, how I shake with Anger."

And when Letitia Pilkington's Widow Warren writes to her:[15] "It is not in your Power to defamatonous my Corector in your wild Memboirs," she takes her place, a lesser Mrs. Malaprop, among the numerous offspring of Dame Quickly.

James Thomas Kirkman's *Memoirs of the life of Charles Macklin* show in summary what biography had learned from stage dialogue. Even mental musings are enlivened by being cast in the form of broken speech:[16]

"During this time, the eyes of the widow could not be accused of an entire abstinence from his person. She was imbibing a pas-

[13] *An Account of the Musical Performances in Westminster-Abbey . . . in commemoration of Handel*, 1785, which includes "Sketch of the life of Handel," p. 36.

[14] *The Life and Extraordinary History of the Chevalier John Taylor*, Dublin, 1761, p. 9. The Edinburgh life of Taylor—*Doctor Sartorius Sinegradibus*—n.d., contains two meditations which are patently modelled on Falstaff's catechism on honor (pp. 4 and 5).

[15] *Memoirs of Mrs. Letitia Pilkington*, 1748, Vol. I, p. 160.

[16] 2 vols., 1799. Vol. I, p. 37. cf. also George Stayley's *Life and opinions of an actor*, 1762, in such passages as pp. 158-65, a conversation between a gentleman and Stayley. Stayley was a practising playwright in Ireland.

sion for him, which self-interest, and the value he was to the house
[through singing, dancing, and mimicking] encouraged. If her
late husband, at times, broke in upon her thoughts, it was only in
a disadvantageous comparison with the superior merits of our
hero. She argued with herself in the following manner—'What
would the world say? What! to marry a beardless boy; a stranger,
and an Irishman too—after having had the best of husbands! it
would be too bad;—and as for any thing else, it would be worse!
—for who then could answer for his constancy?' Whenever a
conflict of this kind takes place in the mind of a woman, it requires no great sagacity to determine on which side victory will
declare."

Kirkman writes whole scenes, such as Macklin's quarrel with
his landlady (Vol. I, pp. 164-6), in the form of a dialogue and
stage directions:

"*Macklin,* (bursting into a fit of laughter). 'Madam, I beg your
pardon. . . .' "

No less meticulous than Boswell, Kirkman takes his aged hero,
who is akin to Dr. Johnson in wit, roughness, dogmatism, and
integrity, and painfully reconstructs his every word. In soporific
detail Kirkman recounts all the trivial remarks Macklin makes
to him one certain day in Macklin's hundred-and-sixth year (Vol.
II, pp. 416-24); and he will go to any length in repetitious rambling to get the exact accent of the stage veteran, who was nineteen years old when Johnson was born, as he narrates a quarrel
with James Quin (Vol. I, pp. 138 *ff.*) :

". . . we present it to our readers, nearly in the words of the
old gentleman, as he told it, in the year 1787, at the Rainbow
Coffee-house, in King-street, Covent-garden, to an acquaintance,
who asked him—if Quin and he had ever quarrelled? Many persons, in the adjoining boxes, attended to the veteran, who spoke,
as usual, in a very audible voice; but exhibited, in the course of
the narration (as the reader will perceive), strong proofs of the
rapid decay of his memory:—'Yes, Sir; I was very low in the
theatre, as an actor, when the surly fellow was the despot of the
place. . . .' "

In the lives and anecdotes in which David Garrick figures, his
swearing, his ejaculations, and his trick of halting speech in

ordinary talk are seldom left unrecorded. The importance of conversation in life-writing, the just proportioning of dialogue to narrative, cannot be reduced to rule; but there is no question that individual passages gain vigor and reality from the impact and accent of good talk. Imparting individuality through novel speech, long practised by the dramatists, came as a discovery in the field of biography; but once found, it was practised widely before Boswell learned to speak more like Johnson than Johnson himself.

Hardly less important than this sense of dialogue learned from the dramatists is the sense of visualization. The little gesture, the significant posture, the tiny detail in foreground and background —matters of which early English biographers were generally unaware—were now introduced with relish and with art.[17] The sudden death of the Earl of Barrymore affords a good example. Of this early cricketer, his biographer John Williams writes (1793): ". . . alas! Death bowled down his own wicket before his desires could be fulfilled." The Earl dies as the result of an accidental discharge of his fusee by his servant; he is riding in his carriage, he has just kissed a tavern hostess, and he is "pointing with his pipe, to shew his servant how plain the coast of France appeared in view."

Or again, Mary Robinson—Perdita to the Prince of Wales's Florizel—gives solidity to the scenes and figures in her *Memoirs* (wr. 1800) by sketching in the brilliant backgrounds which meant so much to her. Garrick watching her début as Juliet, the hissed première of *A Trip to Scarborough* when her curtsey saves the comedy, the first meeting with Florizel and the glances from the eighteen-year-old Prince—such episodes are made effective because she is keenly aware of her settings, at Ranelagh, at Vauxhall, or in the concert rotunda of the overpowering Pantheon.

John Carteret Pilkington, son of the notorious Mrs. Pilkington, shows also how the stage can improve the telling of a life-story.

[17] cf. scenes quoted later in this chapter between Colley Cibber and Mrs. Bracegirdle; George Anne Bellamy's first encounter with her mother; or Tate Wilkinson playing preacher as a young boy. cf. also the description of an Irish wake, pp. 61-5, in Anthony Pasquin's *Eccentricities of John Edwin*, 1791.

This young man, who had knocked about with strolling players, who quoted Shakespeare at the drop of a hat, who tried to submit his own play to David Garrick, not only catches Irish rhythms of speech in some of his humorous anecdotes, but even lights his stage and fills it with movement and humor as if he were a theatrical producer:[18]

". . . after passing thro' one of the gates of the city [Cork], and a variety of blind alleys, lanes and passages, we arrived just by candle-light at the spacious confines of a smoaky thatched cabbin; in which there seemed to be all imaginable harmony, as the swine, the wife, the pigs, and the children, lived very sociably together, and seemed to vie with each other in point of nastiness. When the light of a bullrush had discovered this delightful scene to me, I for the first time wished myself back in my father's kitchen."

The actor's habit of thinking in terms of the stage leads to a more effective division of the incidents of a life as scenes in a play. The old smooth-flowing formal narrative tradition breaks down before a conception of life as a series of important moments, of conflicts between personalities, which must be staged as little entities.

As an extended illustration, consider how the travelling showman Mark Moore sketches in, in leisurely fashion, a multiplicity of figures against the background of the prison in Worcester Castle:[19]

"My messmates were nine in number,—one a gentleman of eighty years of age, had been a prisoner in the rebellion of forty-five; another was a merchant from the Isle of Man; I called him Freeport, from the character of the English merchant [in the play by George Colman the Elder]; another was a young Oxonian; extravagance never led him to this place, his avarice being such, as seldom to allow himself a cheerful glass; he was the true emblem of a niggard; . . . the next was a dealer in horses, a quiet inoffensive man; when sober, he was prudent, but when he broke out, he was quite of a different turn to the Oxonian.

"To him followed one from Clowbent, a place famous for making nails, to which business he was brought up, but marrying

[18] *The real story of John Carteret Pilkington*, 1760, pp. 33-4.
[19] *Memoirs and Adventures*, 1795, pp. 204 ff.

a woman with money, it affected his brain so much, he grew
pedantic; his doggerly poetry, and half-starved Latin, would
sometimes help to dissipate the gloom which at times will over-
shadow the mind of the most unthinking . . . two brothers,
builders from Manchester, and a native of Denmark, made up
this eccentrical group. Hamlet, (for by that name I distinguished
the Dane) was as singular and remarkable a character as ever
came under my, or perhaps, my reader's observation:—A settled
melancholy seemed to have taken possession of his soul, and when
the mighty secret came out, it was love, that little invader of the
ease and peace of man, had rivetted an arrow in his heart, and
more troublesome than even imprisonment itself. He seldom went
out of the room; up to the knees in boots, he stuck close to the
fireside, smoking all weathers; he enjoyed a good state of health,
ate very hearty, but took no exercise."

Mark Moore proceeds to use this queer cast of characters for his
own ends. He lends the Dane *Tom Jones*. A Methodist vestal tries
to save him. A Manchester man, in prison for a three-thousand
pound debt, teaches the Oxonian boxing, who in return teaches
the Manchester man music and dancing. Finally the Oxonian
and the Wesleyan visiting angel who believes in Platonic love are
caught compromised. This part of the narrative moves with a
constant verve and humor which Moore picks up from his two
favorites, Fielding and Shakespeare.

In such scenes, it is true, the biographer may be learning directly from the novelist as well as from the playwright. This
hardly weakens the point, however, for the novelists themselves
had picked up many of their most successful tricks from the stage.
Letitia Pilkington, for instance, developed her ability for satire
under Swift, and, possibly, her rather shaky handling of sentiment
from Richardson, whom she admired and had met. But her greatest debt is to Shakespeare. This young lady, who as the pet of the
ferocious Dean of Dublin could cap Shakespeare line for line as
easily as Swift could cap *Hudibras,* studs her three volumes of
memoirs with quotations and recollections of the stage. It is not
remarkable, therefore, that when she comes to an extended scene
of pathos, as in the death of her father, where for ten pages she
must remain like Niobe all tears, her narrative owes much to

Shakespeare's dramatic conceptions for its credibility and firm outline.

One of the problems of the dramatist has always been to intensify certain traits in his characters and present those traits in concise, memorable utterance. In order to give his train of action aesthetic significance, he is compelled to interpret his characters' secret selves by means of their own speech—to judge, analyze, motivate, characterize them in speeches. The eighteenth century realized Shakespeare's mastery of this art, and in one case, at least, made out of it a parlor game. *The Modern Characters from Shakespear alphabetically arranged. Shew Virtue, her own Feature.—Scorn, her own Image. Hamlet,* was printed for E. Johnson in 1778. The anonymous author selects the appropriate lines from Shakespeare to describe contemporary churchmen, authors, actresses, soldiers, politicians, and, principally, aristocrats. His blanks may be filled in easily. In Doctor Johnson's circle, for instance, we find for Dr. J——n himself:

"You must borrow me Garagantua's mouth,
'Tis a word too great for any mouth of this age's size!"

Mr. B——ke has, appropriately, two quotations from *Julius Caesar,* the second being

"The posture of your blows are yet unknown,
But for your words, they rob the Hybla bees,
And leave them honeyless."

Mr. G——k is accorded, no less appropriately, two from his great vehicle *Hamlet:* "I saw him once . . ." and "An eye like Mars . . . ." And Sir Joshua R——ds is described as

"That rare master, who had he himself eternity, and cou'd put breath into his work, wou'd beguile nature of her custom. Winter's Tale, Act V."

As apt as any among his many hits is the author's selection for Mrs. M—nt—gue":

"For in her age
There is a prone, and speechless dialect,
Such as moves men! besides she hath prosperous art

When she will play with reason, and discourse;
And well she can persuade. Measure for Measure, Act I."

This amusing little pamphlet presents in less than a hundred pages a discovery that many biographers were making for themselves: that Shakespeare in his old plays could aid them in the interpretation of living persons. Pilkington draws the full portrait of his uncle more clearly because he sees him "like ancient pistol" (1760, p. 46); and George Stayley, comedian of Smock-Alley in Dublin, sets the whimsical tone of his *Life and Opinions* (1762) by disclaiming such omens at his birth as shook the world at the birth of Shakespeare's Owen Glendower. Even current politics may be illuminated by the clearly conceived figures of the drama: *Iago Display'd* (1730?) is an ephemeral tract in which William Pulteney as Cassio accuses Robert Walpole as Iago, of corruption, while Othello is metamorphosed into a Hanoverian monarch.

More and more, as the century progresses, the subsidiary figures in biographies take on an air of animation; they move and speak. Largely this is achieved through the intensification of one trait or peculiarity, making minor figures into caricatures whose foibles are insistently dwelt upon. The biographers, like the dramatists, are finding out that every man has his humor, and that artistic economy demands that this humor be emphasized. Even principal figures, under the influence of the drama, come to be thus considered:[20] in the life of Boadicea, the queen is presented to the public as *Female Revenge: or, the British Amazon* (1753); Topham's *John Elwes* (1790) gains its great power from his persistence in making the hero a fantastic English Harpagon; *The life of the late Earl of Chesterfield* (1774) appears with the subtitle, "or, the Man of the World," and the author centers it upon his portrait of "the omnis homo, or all-accomplished Chesterfield."

In such attempts, trifling though some of them are, biography is acquiring a new artistry in interpreting and criticizing life. Serious English drama from *Doctor Faustus* to *Irene* had made

[20] The biographies of Garrick afford the best examples of characterization through the speech of the principal figure; for subsidiary figures, see the many caricatures in Mrs. Steele's *Memoirs of Sophia Baddeley*, 1787.

some attempt to find significance in the life of its principal figure. English life-writing—aside from the conviction of religious biography, which too often dreamed of future worlds until this earthly life became illusory—leaves most to be desired, aesthetically considered, in its failure to set up standards for judging the careers of its heroes. If, then, the comic and tragic actors and playwrights contributed in any way to deliberate interpretation in recording individual lives, their influence upon biography is more important than has hitherto been suspected. The exact influence upon biography of Shakespeare as a philosopher can never be determined, but it is not too much to assume that a great part of the suppleness, tolerance, and skepticism in judgment that characterize eighteenth century biography stems eventually from him. "The Web of our Life is of a mingled Yarn, good and ill together," philosophizes an attendant lord in *All's Well that Ends Well,* and other life-writers had found that out as well as George Anne Bellamy who uses it to adorn the title-page of her *Apology* (1785). A certain flavor of Shakespeare's disciplined disillusion may be detected in the anonymous *Genuine Memoirs of Mr. Charles Churchill* (1765) from the opening appraisal (pp. 28-9): "Mr. Churchill was a man—a compounded being of flesh and spirit—neither a deity, nor a devil; as his friends and foes seem to insinuate. He had many virtues; and some vices."—to the deathbed letter (p. 174): "The curtain is almost drawn, and the farce is over." Gradually, eighteenth century actors acquire the ability to dramatize themselves. Under the influence of the stage, a writer is not so afraid to express emotions in recording his own life or interpreting another's; his feelings are more poignant, or at any rate his expression of them tends to be more unrestrained and frank.

Moreover, the dignity of an actor's career being in the eighteenth century slight, a more humorous, or cynical, or direct, or disillusioned analysis of motives and character is possible. In the written lives of stage luminaries, biography loses to some extent its earlier function as a solemn mausoleum and remembrancer for noble bones. The spirit of Falstaff begins to touch biography;[21]

[21] See, e.g., William Cobbett's *Life and Adventures of Peter Porcupine,* 1796; *Memoirs of Michael Clancy,* 1750; lives of Quin and Macklin.

and partly because of the popularization by Sterne, Yorick as a pattern for blending mirth and pathos influences the interpretation of men's careers.[22]

Through the Middle Ages and the Renaissance, existence had been either a testing ground preceding eternal rewards and punishments, or a grim tragedy. The seventeenth century managed to regard it occasionally with curious and practical eyes. But it was left for the eighteenth century to discover that life may be comic. Here again, the drama, particularly the comedy of the Restoration, was influential. Moreover, the stalwart host of comedians, actors, and managers—Quin, Macklin, Foote, Haynes, Wilks, Parsons, Cibber, Spiller, Stayley, Lewes, Edwin, Henderson—did their share in persuading the world to treat life as one of the lighter arts, with laughter and with grace. Teaching no longer precludes a smile. "My intention, my Lord," writes one theatrical biographer who assumes the significant pseudonym of Pasquin,[23] "was to make society merrier and better." The hero of a biography may now joke and make puns even upon his deathbed.[24] Quin or Macklin as Falstaff, Cibber as Shallow or Sir Fopling Flutter, Foote taking his "dish of tea," had delighted London audiences. Their perception of the ridiculous or the witty in life was no less keen offstage, and they imparted it to their biographers. The dinner-table anecdote and the carefully built story, at which so many of these comedians were adept, passed into the realm of biography and marked a great advance in the artistic shaping of episodes and stories so that they might have a beginning, a middle, and an end.[25] The long lives, now growing to two volumes or even more, ripple and glint with occasional laughter; and these informal anecdotes become so popular that collections of bon mots and wit-

---

[22] See *Memoirs of the Life and Writings of Samuel Foote*, ca. 1778. t.p. quotes "Where are now your Gibes? Your Gambols?", etc.

Memoirs of that celebrated comedian, and very singular genius Thomas Weston.—"*I knew him well;*
        He was a Fellow of infinite Humour." 1776.

[23] John Williams's *Eccentricities of John Edwin, comedian*, 1791, Dedication.

[24] cf. *Spiller's Jests*, ca. 1729.

[25] cf. *The History of the Stage*, 1742, which handles its subject in a series of anecdotes well written and connected; or the *Real Story* (1760) of John Carteret Pilkington, who has a flair for humorous and vivacious anecdote.

ticisms were issued separately or at the end of the memoirs,[26] much as earlier centuries had taken pleasure in gathering at the close of a biography, in a group of its sage subject's apothegms, the wisdom of the world. So closely were wit and the comic stage bound together that even given such a perfect subject as Doctor Johnson, the editor of *Johnsoniana; or, a collection of bon mots* (1777) was forced to fill up his jest-book with stories about Foote and Quin. Gay's "Life is a jest and all things show it" is the belief of many of these comedians and their biographers, so that many of their titles suggest that there is little difference between a man's life and a collection of anecdotes or witty encounters. *Spiller's Jests* (*ca.* 1729) has the alternative title of "the life and pleasant adventures of the late celebrated comedian Mr. James Spiller"; and *Memoirs of Charles Lee Lewes* (wr. p. 1793) is described by the subtitle: "containing anecdotes, historical and biographical, of the English and Scottish stages." The *res gestae* of the medieval hero have become the Jest-book of the eighteenth century comedian.

Much of this wit comes through to us with the freshness and the stamp of personality that is so astonishing in Boswell. So we find Samuel Foote, whom Johnson himself had found irresistibly funny, apologizing for greeting a roué at Bath by saying, "You know there's no turning one's back upon such fellows." Or again, as a direct hit in his perpetual duel with Garrick:[27] "Previously to Foote's bringing out his *Primitive Puppet-Show* at the Haymarket Theatre, a lady of fashion asked him, 'Pray, Sir, are your

---

[26] *The life of the late famous comedian, Jo. Hayns. Containing, his comical exploits and adventures, both at home and abroad,* by Tobyas Thomas, 1701.

Mrs. Pilkington's Jests: or the cabinet of wit and humour, 1759, gleaned from her *Memoirs,* 1748-1754, 3 vols.

Colley Cibber's Jests, or the diverting witty companion, 1761.

The life of Mr. James Quin, 1766, followed by *Quin's Jests: or, the facetious man's pocket-companion.*

The Eccentricities of John Edwin, comedian. Collected from his manuscripts, and enriched with several hundred original anecdotes, by John Williams, 1791.

Memoirs of Charles Macklin, comedian, with the dramatic characters, manners, anecdotes, &c. of the age in which he lived, by William Cooke, 1804.

Memoirs of Samuel Foote, Esq. With a collection of his genuine bon-mots, anecdotes, opinions, &c., by William Cooke, 1805, 3 vols.

See also the Bibliography for Thomas Davies, whose enthusiasm for, and diligence in, collecting anecdotes outdistanced his skill in presentation.

[27] *Memoirs of Samuel Foote,* by William Cooke, 1805, Vol. II, p. 58.

puppets to be as large as life?'—'Oh dear, Madam, no: not much above the size of Garrick!' "

The influence of the drama upon biography was not wholly fortunate. In the hands of the hack-writers, quotations at great length afforded an easy means of filling up space. The publisher Curll and his tribe use this device without conscience: the *Memoirs of Mrs. Anne Oldfield* (1741), between her amour with Maynwaring and various last wills and testaments, sandwiches in many long transcriptions from rôles she had played. In using quotations, frequently from Shakespeare and usually from a play of some sort, as the headings for each of the 107 letters into which Charles Dibdin divides his *Musical Tour* (1788), the game of finding apt phrases becomes a burden rather than a pastime. And in the jumble of documents strewn through Kirkman's *Life of Charles Macklin* (1799) the long speeches of Iago and Shylock and the inclusion in full of the death of Falstaff scarcely assist the reader in drawing closer to Kirkman's hero, the "father of the English theatre." Too often, in these reminiscences by actors who had played Shakespeare so frequently that they talked his language as a kind of natural patois, we feel the need for some such repentance as Letitia Pilkington's, when she apologizes for her frequent borrowings by borrowing once more:[28]

"I must beg my reader's pardon for these numerous quotations; but, as Swift says: 'those anticipating rascals the ancients have left nothing for us poor moderns to say.' "

In a few instances, moreover, both the actors themselves and their biographers lose their sense of life in their sense for the drama. The scenes that result are stilted, hollow. "To be followed by others," writes Edward Topham in his life of John Elwes (1790, p. 101), "we must follow nature. All acted character is a miserable thing; and the extravagant relation of it is less interesting still than the thing itself."

Yet in spite of occasional unfortunate hybrids, the union of biography and the drama was happy. The theater taught biographers the immense power of carefully wrought dialogue in

[28] *Memoirs*, 1748. Quoted fr. 1928 ed., p. 133.

delineating personalities; it helped them to visualize more clearly action, gesture, expression, surroundings; it taught them to construct scenes, to point stories, to group their figures and build up to their climaxes; it revealed some secrets in the economical delineation of character; it gave them a more just appreciation of the place of wit, humor, possibly of pathos, in human life; and, through Shakespeare, it made sweeter, more smiling, and more mature, man's judgment of his fellow man.

The new spirit and elasticity which the memoirs of actors brought into the practice of biography appealed to the public. The lives of the great actors—particularly of the actresses and comedians—were devoured. Because of popular demand, Colley Cibber records, "many hasty writers have been encourag'd to publish the lives of the làte Mrs. Oldfield, Mr. Wilks, and Mr. Booth, in less time after their deaths than one could suppose it cost to transcribe them."[29] Cibber's own *Apology* exhausted two editions in one year and was re-issued ten years later. Thomas Davies's life of Garrick (1780) went through four editions, ran up profits for its author, and occasioned other memoirs and collections of anecdotes. *An Apology for the life of George Anne Bellamy* (1785), although issued in five and in six volumes, appeared in three editions in one year, not counting a Dublin reprint and a shortened version; these offerings to the public came out so rapidly that the *Westminster Magazine* mentions that the third edition was on sale before it could review the first.

The reasons for such popularity are fairly obvious. Not only were the readers amused by the wit of the English comedians and fascinated by the erotic intrigues of its stage beauties; they also felt that they knew personally the men and women whom they had so frequently beheld on the boards. Earlier biography had appealed to family pride or the instinct for edification; this new type touched curiosity and fellow-feeling, drawing on the same springs of interest that keep alive today innumerable magazines that give the life-histories and intimate opinions of motion-picture and radio stars. The popular mind

[29] *Apology*, Chap. I, p. 6, Everyman ed., 1914.

today transforms such characters into national sweethearts and public friends; nor was biography in the eighteenth century slow to exploit such possibilities. "A man," Cibber writes (p. 6), "who has pass'd above forty years of his life upon a theatre, where he has never appear'd to be himself, may have naturally excited the curiosity of his spectators to know what he really was, when in no body's shape but his own." And later, after asking "of what importance can the history of my private life be to the public?" Cibber replies (p. 7): "To this, indeed, I can only make you a ludicrous answer, which is, that the publick very well knows my life has not been a private one; that I have been employed in their service, ever since many of their grandfathers were young men." One further reason for the popularity of actors' lives, as has already been pointed out in this chapter, lies in the fact that familiarity with the stage and the technique of the drama had actually taught writers how to tell a more entertaining and artistic story.

Among the numerous memoirs of the stage, certain productions are worth more than a glance. Five figures, at least—Cibber, Garrick, George Anne Bellamy, Sophia Baddeley, and Tate Wilkinson—have made themselves more than names. They continue to move with unmistakable life through old volumes.

In his provocative *Aspects of Biography*,[30] M. André Maurois propounds a theory for life-writing which he has elsewhere advanced for the novel: that the setting of pen to paper, the creating of some more ideal or more rational world of the imagination, affords an emotional outlet for the writer. This is particularly true of the autobiographer. The mistakes of his career may be extenuated; his virtues may be diffidently brought to the reader's attention; the whole of his life can be given a pattern and a purpose in the recording which may not have been present in the living. Confessions, as autobiographers have found from the days of Saint Augustine, are good for the soul.

[30] 1929, particularly in Chap. IV, "Biography as a means of expression."

Among the most entertaining of the mental purgations anterior to the classic example set by Jean-Jacques Rousseau, is Colley Cibber's apology for his own life (1740). His manner as he enters the autobiographical confessional is engaging. Where Rousseau is truculent in unmasking his weaknesses—they are no more glaring, he believes, than any man's would prove if they were known—Colley Cibber is playful. He is amused at himself. Every autobiographer, of course, tries consciously or unconsciously to create the impression of his impartiality as he records his own life; a strange duality appears: a man looks at *himself*, as do characters in the plays of Pirandello. Cibber is more successful than most in attaining this attitude of the impartial observer contemplating his own life. Naturally a comedian, with no exaggerated sense of his own dignity, he develops with evident gusto his unusual thesis: What a fool this mortal is! Against Pope's cruel and largely unwarranted lashings, there could have been no more effective defense than Cibber's own deprecatory smile. A solemn justification, or a retort in kind to the author of the *Dunciad,* would have been beyond his powers. But his confidences and anecdotes are so disarming that his two-volume apology continues to be rediscovered and republished, and as the reader progresses among its anecdotes and confidences, the caricature by Alexander Pope gives way before a three-dimensional figure, of the tribe of Izaak Walton and Oliver Goldsmith, who is by no means the fool that Pope—and Cibber himself—make him out to be.

Cibber dedicates his autobiography to the Right Honorable Henry Pelham, and talks to him direct in explaining his reasons for writing, since he finds that his genial nature throughout the book needs to unburden itself to a friend. "And now," he says,[31] "you will say the World will find me, under my own Hand, a weaker Man than perhaps I may have pass'd for, even among my Enemies.—With all my Heart! my Enemies will then read me with Pleasure, and you, perhaps, with Envy, when you find that Follies, without the Reproach of Guilt upon them, are not inconsistent with Happiness.—But why make my Follies publick?

[31] *An apology for the life of Mr. Colley Cibber,* 1740. Quotations fr. 1889 2-vol. ed., Vol. I, p. 2.

Why not? I have pass'd my Time very pleasantly with them, and I don't recollect that they have ever been hurtful to any other Man living. Even admitting they were injudiciously chosen, would it not be Vanity in me to take Shame to myself for not being found a Wise Man? Really, Sir, my Appetites were in too much haste to be happy, to throw away my Time in pursuit of a Name I was sure I could never arrive at."

Rousseau's argument that we are all sinners, though not all equally original in our sins, finds this tempered variation in his precursor (Vol. I, pp. 2-3):

"Now the Follies I frankly confess I look upon as in some measure discharged; while those I conceal are still keeping the Account open between me and my Conscience. To me the Fatigue of being upon a continual Guard to hide them is more than the Reputation of being without them can repay. If this be Weakness, *defendit numerus,* I have such comfortable Numbers on my side, that were all Men to blush that are not Wise, I am afraid, in Ten, Nine Parts of the World ought to be out of Countenance."

The *Apology* that ensues shows an old man, almost seventy, who chatters like a jay, looking back over his life to the distant time when at the free school of Grantham in Lincolnshire he wrote a funeral oration on the death of Charles II which won him simultaneously the headship of his form and the dislike of his fellows. "The passions of men and children have much the same motives, and differ very little in their effects," he tells us; certainly his memories of his own childhood betray from the first his fatal facility with the pen, his self-assurance, and his knack of inspiring disgust in others.

Practising as an infant for the future Poet-Laureateship, he follows the oration on the old king's death by writing an ode on the new king's coronation. Cibber also, therefore, must have lisped in numbers, and the mistake of turning poet he lists among his madnesses and follies, along with "Matrimony before I was Two-and-twenty," and "breaking from the Advice and Care of Parents to turn Player." Regret for this last of his errors, however, is hardly more than formal, for continually Cibber shows a passion for the stage and a joy in relating its stories. World history, from old

Rome to Blenheim, he considers a convenience to illustrate the history of Drury-Lane and its triumvirate. He has John Aubrey's jackdaw talent for picking up scraps and anecdotes, but he adds to this the power of generalizing, with just remarks upon writing, acting, and managing, upon stage censorship and the dignity and usefulness of drama. As one of the triple pillars of the stage, Cibber the actor-manager finds himself between the extravagant Wilks and the economical Doggett. Cibber is proud of his rise and success; his yearly takings as manager invalidate the first half of his *bon mot* on Doggett: "but as he had more Money than I, he had not Occasion for so much Philosophy."

Whether it was necessary or not, philosophy Cibber definitely possessed. The power to analyze character which in his fourth and fifth chapters he uses brilliantly in sketching the great actors of his youthful years, is even more sensitive when he applies it to himself. He is conscious of his exaggerated enthusiasms (Vol. I, p. 51):

"Whenever I speak of any thing that highly delights me, I find it very difficult to keep my Words within the Bounds of Common Sense: Even when I write too, the same Failing will sometimes get the better of me."

But his central trait is vanity, vanity tempered by humor, cultivated as a pleasant failing, and often disguised as humility. Repeatedly he refers to his humble mentality, or preens himself upon being a fool. He delights in quoting familiar tags of Latin, French, and Italian. Yet he is so self-conscious that he was afraid to play the part of a villain on the stage for fear the audience would think him villainous. The actor is always present in the autobiographer, but an actor so acutely aware of himself that in some of the passages from his *Apology,* English biography takes on a new subtlety. The first chapter, for instance, includes a long digression for the reader's pleasure, which springs out of an anecdote to prove that one should not poke fun at dull-witted people. This develops into "Rules for Raillery" and a defense of amusements and laughter; it ends with Cibber's laughing at himself (Vol. I, p. 27):

"So that all this my Parade and Grimace of Philosophy has been only making a mighty Merit of following my own Inclination. A very natural Vanity! Though it is some sort of Satisfaction to know it does not impose upon me. Vanity again!"

The second chapter continues with ridicule of the vanity of all autobiographers.

In his quest for the reasons that led him to write, Cibber sets aside one after another fame, profit, and the instructing or delighting of his readers. His own amusement he considers a sufficient reason for writing, and also his desire to prevent falsification by later memoir-writers and scavengers. "But behind all this," he says (Vol. I, p. 4), "there is something inwardly exciting, which I cannot express in few Words; I must therefore a little make bold with your Patience." In a passage which contains fine shading and the delicate drawing of a mind (Vol. I, pp. 5-6), Colley Cibber reveals that this "something inwardly exciting" is an actor's desire to show

"as true a Picture of myself as natural Vanity will permit me to draw: For to promise you that I shall never be vain, were a Promise that, like a Looking-glass too large, might break itself in the making: Nor am I sure I ought wholly to avoid that Imputation, because if Vanity be one of my natural Features, the Portrait wou'd not be like me without it. In a Word, I may palliate and soften as much as I please; but upon an honest Examination of my Heart, I am afraid the same Vanity which makes even homely People employ Painters to preserve a flattering Record of their Persons, has seduced me to print off this *Chiaro Oscuro* of my Mind."

This is excellent direct observation. Yet much of the feeling for Cibber as an original comes to the reader indirectly. His anecdotes are full, from the early story of how 1688 determined the fate not only of James II and the Prince of Orange but of "so minute a being as myself," to the final extended scene between Wilks, Booth, Mrs. Oldfield and himself. In the main, however, the incidents are of historical interest; about his own thoughts and life off the stage, Cibber is curiously reticent. There is mention of his early marriage on a salary of "twenty shillings a week from my theatrical labours, to maintain, as I then thought, the happiest young couple that ever took a leap in the dark!" Later, there is further joking about the number of his plays and the number of his children—"my muse and my spouse were equally prolifick." That is all. His relations with his daughter Charlotte Charke or his protégée Letitia Pilkington, we learn from their autobiographies, not from his. Colley Cibber was a gay dog in his day in London; yet his *Apology* is complacently vague on this score.

On one subject alone is he tremblingly alive—his good-natured vanity. In the light of Henry Fielding's theory of comedy—that the only source of the ridiculous is affectation, and that affectation proceeds either from vanity or hypocrisy—it is not surprising that Fielding makes Cibber's *Apology,* even more than Richardson's *Pamela,* the continual butt for his satire in that "biography," *Joseph Andrews.* But Cibber himself had anticipated Fielding. He is enough of an artist to make comedy out of his own vanity. Cibber is vain; but he is also good-natured. He constantly wishes the world to think well of him; he thinks well of almost everyone; naturally Pope's delight in hating puzzles him. In the quarrel with Pope he resembles nothing so much as a well-meaning, tail-wagging mongrel. He has done nothing to offend Pope, except wear the nation's laurels; he would like to be his friend; he does not answer Pope's attacks; and for reward, Pope places him on giddier and still giddier thrones of asininity. At last, as an old man, Cibber can keep silent no longer. He lets the secret pass. In spite of his protestations, he has been hurt by the jeers of the town; he shows it by being the first to satirize his own *Apology* (Vol. I, pp. 27-8):

"I presume the terms of Doating Trifler, Old Fool, or Conceited Coxcomb, will carry contempt enough for an impartial censor to bestow on me; . . . my style is unequal, pert, and frothy, patch'd and party-colour'd, like the coat of an harlequin; low and pompous, cramm'd with epithets, strew'd with scraps of second-hand Latin from common quotations; frequently aiming at wit, without ever hitting the mark; a mere ragoust, toss'd up from the offals of other authors: my subject below all pens but my own, which, whenever I keep to, is flatly daub'd by one eternal egotism. . . .

"Now I have laid myself at your feet, what will you do with me?"

It is as if there were something essentially hollow about Cibber's character. His very omissions, his apologies, his vacillation between vanity and humility, the determined cheerfulness that suffuses his writings, combine to give a faint air of sham to the principal actor. Perhaps Colley Cibber had been too long associated with the stage ever to throw off the actor's part; and certainly in his *Apology* he envisions himself as the Good-Natured Man. His judgments of others are charitable, from the splendid tribute to the Duchess of Marlborough near the beginning of his memoirs to the defense of Nell Gwyn near the end. He writes enthusiastically of everyone that he can, and, to repeat a characteristic remark of his, "Whenever I speak of any thing that highly delights me, I find it very difficult to keep my words within the bounds of common sense." What delighted him most was the theater, and himself in the theater. The paradox which makes his book fascinating is that in spite of his outward assurance, fundamentally he lacks conviction, certainty, standards. He lets others judge him; he does not know how to judge himself.

This peacock of a Cibber, then, who sets himself upon the stage and then laughs at his own finery, who blocks in his own character with bold strokes and proceeds to refine it in cunning detail, cannot be lightly dismissed as a biographer or as a man. When we remember that Pope and Fielding were his enemies, we must either consider them as triflers, or admit the importance, the annoying importance, of Cibber himself. What an early editor remarked is true:[32] "In short, Cibber not being a dunce, Pope could not make him one." It may be significant that one of Cibber's most famous parts was that of Justice Shallow; but his success must have been due more to quick perceptions of Shallow's foibles than to kindred inanities with the Gloucestershire justice. Doctor Johnson said that Cibber's *Apology* was well done, because Cibber had stooped to what he understood.[33] This dictum might well end our consideration of George II's Poet Laureate, for it

32 "Editor's Preface," 1826 ed., Hunt and Clark.
33 Boswell's *Life* for May 15, 1776.

focuses the attention on Cibber the artist rather than the comedian. His *Apology* is satisfying because it fulfills its purpose; it
treats a little subject in a little way; and Cibber's philosophy and
manner, his whimsical digressions and his certainty that the stage
and Colley Cibber are of overwhelming interest, fit well together.
In spite of his many amiable failings, Cibber never commits the
supreme folly of making himself ridiculous by taking himself too
seriously. Behind his homely face, his small pig-eyes, and the
innumerable posturings of the actor, there is a large fund of
common sense which gives his autobiography a humble harmony
lacking in many works which are more pretentious.

In the back room of a bookseller's shop in London, on that
momentous Monday in May, Boswell was introduced to the great
Johnson by Tom Davies, the proprietor. Davies was more than a
bookseller and a host for tea-drinkers. He had tried, unsuccessfully, to get a foothold in the theater, and his enthusiasm for the
stage continued unabated through his life, so that there trickled
from his tireless pen such works as an account of Mr. George
Lillo (1775), the life and theatrical transactions of Mr. John
Henderson, commonly called the Bath Roscius (1777), the life of
Philip Massinger (1779), and—after his death, as if the grave
could not stop his writing—*Roscius Anglicanus, or, an historical
review of the English stage* (1789).

But Davies's most important work is his *Memoirs of the life of
David Garrick,* which appeared in two volumes in 1780. Doctor
Johnson contributed the opening for the benefit of his worship-
ping friend: "All excellence has a right to be recorded. I shall
therefore think it superfluous to apologize for writing the life of
a man who, by an uncommon assemblage of private virtues,
adorned the highest eminence in a public profession."[34] Although
the biography does not proceed in Johnsonian phrases of balanced
magniloquence, Davies manages to give a pleasant and fairly

[34] The Johnsonian thought and rhythm may be detected in the opening sentence of Davies's life of Lillo, prefixed to Lillo's *Works,* 1775, p. 5: "There is no
passion more incident to our nature than the desire of knowing the actions of
men, whose genius has raised our admiration, and whose labours have given us
instruction or entertainment."

dependable account of his subject. He has acquired the knack of imparting life to an anecdote by means of realistic action and conversation, as in this story dealing with Garrick's crescent fame (Vol. I, p. 46):

"In a conversation which she [Mrs. Bracegirdle] had with Colley Cibber, who spoke of him with an affected derogation, she reproved his malignity, and generously said, 'Come, come, Cibber, tell me, if there is not something like envy in your character of this young gentleman. The actor who pleases every body must be a man of merit.' The old man felt the force of this sensible rebuke; he took a pinch of snuff, and frankly replied; 'Why faith, Bracey, I believe you are right—The young fellow is clever.'"

Though Davies had addressed his life of Lillo to Garrick and sincerely admired the actor, after Garrick's death he reveals many little weaknesses and secrets which Roscius alive might not have enjoyed. The reader sees the young David make his stage début in blackface, in the part of Aboan in *Oroonoko;* he speculates over Garrick's short stature and possibly bowed legs in such a phrase as "he would never willingly put on the Roman habit"; he witnesses an actor's death in Garrick's final blank-verse quotation applied against doctors. Yet Davies also imparts a sense of Garrick's career and character—his perpetual quarrels, his stage successes, his triumphs abroad, his vacillating, hesitant nature, his contradictory miserliness and bursts of generosity, and above all, the inordinate vanity of this Prospero who ruled over the fortunes of Drury Lane for so many years.

The full title of this biography states that it will be "interspersed with characters and anecdotes of . . . theatrical contemporaries. The whole forming a history of the stage, which includes a period of thirty-six years." Davies is here riding two horses; structurally he surmounts his difficulties by devoting separate chapters to Garrick's companions and rivals. There are thus not only complete sections for such actors as Rich, Foote, and Cibber, but for Smollett, Goldsmith, and Aaron Hill as well, while Johnson, Fielding, Pope, and Burke also cross the stage. Davies is at his best in such an extended story as the battle between the two rival theaters, as salient in eighteenth century

anecdotal stage history as the premières of *Cato* and *Irene*. For
twelve successive days, Mrs. Cibber and Mr. Barry at Covent
Garden, George Anne Bellamy and Garrick at Drury Lane,
clashed in simultaneous performances of *Romeo and Juliet*. At
last Mrs. Cibber fell ill, so that Garrick triumphed, but not before
London, disgusted and bored, had enjoyed such epigrams as this:

> "Well, what's to-night, says angry Ned,
>   As up from bed he rouses?
> Romeo again! and shakes his head,
>   Ah! pox on both your houses!"

At the end of the century, Arthur Murphy writes another life
of Garrick, following Davies closely, supplementing his account
with documentary appendices, and compressing Davies's stage
history into a more orthodox biography written in an entertaining
and more literate style.

Fanny Burney, at the age of twenty-one, surpasses both Murphy
and Davies in catching Garrick's peculiarities of speech and
phrasing, and setting them in a scene vividly visualized. Garrick,
visiting her father Charles Burney the musician, has just suggested that Burney rests his mind by listening to the "prattle" of
Fanny and her sister Susan:[35]

" 'Quite the contrary,' cried I, 'my father *exerts* his understanding to keep pace with us!'—He understood me, and getting up in a
violent hurry, he came to the table where I was making tea; and
with a thousand whimsical gestures, he cried, 'O! you quite mistake me;—I meant to make you the greatest compliment in the
world! I could not make you a greater!—what I meant was—to
say that—that when you were all about him, he could then most
delightfully'—

" 'Repose?' cried Sukey. 'Aye,' cried he, 'repose, and—and—
most delightfully—do this, and that, and the other.'

" 'Excellent, Mr. Bayes!' cried my father."

In the galaxy of eighteenth century actresses who recorded their
own lives—Manley, Charke, Mary Robinson—none had a greater
faculty for dispassionate self-observation than the little spitfire

[35] *Early Diary*, 1768-1778, 2 vols., 1907, Vol. I, p. 227. For the year 1773.

who, still in her teens, acted Juliet opposite Garrick's Romeo in the memorable theatrical duel of 1749: George Anne Bellamy. In her memoirs she coolly analyzes scenes that the novelists around her would have submersed in a warm flood of sentiment. Take, for instance, her account of the first time the maid servant conducts George Anne, then very small, to see her mother, who was playing at Covent Garden:[36]

"We were instantly ushered up stairs, where we found my mother in a genteel dress. Though I was too young to experience any attraction from her beauty, yet her fine clothes pleased me much, and I ran towards her with great freedom. But what concern did my little heart feel, when she rudely pushed me from her, and I heard her exclaiming, after viewing me with attention for some moments, 'My God! what have you brought me here? this goggle-eyed, splatterfaced, gabbart-mouthed wretch, is not my child! take her away!' I had been so accustomed to endearments, that I was the more sensibly affected at this unexpected salutation, and I went away as much disgusted with my mother as she could be with me."

Or again, she sets down another objective estimate of herself, also unfavorable, which she admits she heard through the keyhole of James Quin's dressing-room as he agonizes over which of his company shall play the heroine in *Tamerlane* (Vol. I, p. 127):

". . . hearing voices within, I stopped for some time, lest I should interrupt business, or be one too many. As I stood, I distinctly heard The Fox say (for Volpone was then exhibiting) 'Why, my Lord, we have Woffington at the receipt of custom, and who bids more!—Ward, flatter than a half-baked pan-cake—and little Bellamy as cold as ice, and as conceited as the devil.'"

Cold and conceited she was—reckless, brassy, headstrong, improvident, worldly.

But she was also beautiful. At the height of her career she had become in London (Vol. I, p. 255) "sole dictatress among the polite ranks in the article of dress." She could clear eleven hundred pounds at a single benefit performance, and journey to Dublin on the basis of a thousand guineas and two benefits for

---

[36] *An Apology for the Life of George Anne Bellamy*, 1785. Quotations from the Dublin ed., 1785, 2 vols., Vol. I, pp. 16-17.

herself. "I besides received," she writes (Vol. I, p. 256), "presents from Asia, Africa, and America, together with others the produce of our own climate. In short I was now in possession of every thing that could excite the envy of the world."

"And yet," she continues, "amidst all this, even in the very zenith of my splendor, I was not happy." All her objectivity and her saving sense of the ridiculous are required to shadow forth as convincingly as she does the dazzling and dismaying contrasts of her career. The striking qualities of this unique work lie in her power of psychological motivation, as firm and penetrating as most novelists', in her dramatically projected figures and conversations, and, unfortunately, in the fulsomeness of her prose.

A contemporary review, after stressing the exemplary lessons to be drawn from her life, makes the reservation that[37] "In many parts, however, there is an air of romance, which would be more proper for a novel, than a narrative of facts." Is it possible, for instance, that human beings act in life on such romantic notions, conventional enough in the cause-and-effect world of the drama or the novel, as George Anne sketched in her *Apology?* Did her mother, finding from the Earl of Blessington that her lover Lord Tyrawley was trying to repair his fortunes by marrying Blessington's daughter, send Blessington all Tyrawley's love-letters to her, in a passionate desire to break off the match? And did Mr. Bellamy marry her mother within two months of our heroine's birth but without any knowledge of its approach? And was her mother's motive for this marriage revenge against Lord Tyrawley and his new Portuguese love?

The quickness of George Anne Bellamy's mind, her power of assimilation, cannot be questioned. She is a little ape, and for her narrative technique she owes much not only to Colley Cibber in his *Apology*[38] but to Sterne and Richardson. One of the sentimental frontispieces to the volumes shows her in "Despondency on the Steps of Westminster Bridge"; and in narrating her despair at this stage in her career, she attains, to use the words of a con-

[37] *Westminster Magazine* for March, 1785. Quoted in "vol. 6" of the 3d ed. of her *Apology,* p. 178.
[38] Her *Apology,* for instance, like Cibber's, takes the form of letters, 102 in all, addressed to a sympathetic friend.

temporary,[39] "those frequent bursts of tenderness, anxiety, and passion, which captivate the reader so much; and which throughout these volumes, prolong an agitation that is at once melancholy and pleasing. Mrs. Bellamy knows how to communicate the exquisite tone of her feelings." As she contemplates suicide, that gloomy evening on Thames' bank, nearing her fiftieth year, friendless and in debt, "impatiently waiting for the tide to cover me," echoes from Shakespeare and James Thomson float through her mind and lead the episode at last to a beautifully narrated ending.[40] But if such successes in sentimental portrayal are infrequent, her psychological observations in passing are numerous. "How comes it," she wonders (Vol. II, p. 256), "that ignorance is more conspicuous in a man than in a woman? As drinking and swearing, though dreadful vices in themselves, appear more horrid in the latter than the former." Or, as she remembers the death of her first friend Miss Frazer, who succumbed to the measles, she observes, stumbling on Platonism (Vol. I, p. 21):

"There is, I believe, no impression that affects so strongly a young mind as the supposition of being dear to another. Though originating merely from self-love, it incites a reciprocation. The very idea that you are pleasing, stimulates you to render yourself really so, even though there be not that similarity of manners and disposition on which an union of souls is usually founded."

From such meditations her range extends to bitter and effective irony, as in the long appended letter to John Calcraft, which seethes with indignation over her six years of slavery to a man already married.

Yet Mrs. Bellamy is at her natural best in scenes that contain some element of the ridiculous. She prefers the hard road of common sense to the tundras of the heart. Even her most emotional scenes are in danger of ending in a burst of laughter. The writer of the *Apology* is the same person who, while playing Cleopatra, falls to giggling when another actress trails on to the stage with a kettledrum on her train. She can be funny even in describing a love scene with the despairing old Mr. Crump (Vol. I, p. 67):

[39] *English Review,* Feb. 1785, quoted fr. 3d ed. *Apology,* Vol. VI, pp. 171-2.
[40] Dublin ed., Vol. II, pp. 213-16.

"After prancing about the room for some time, he approached me, and with a deep-fetched sigh, which would have blown the boat we had lately entered over the river, without the assistance of the ferry-man, took hold of my hand."

Or she can set a neat trap to catch a detractor of her virtue (Vol. I, pp. 87-90). When Garrick pleads with her to play Jane Shore at his benefit, she makes the little man look ludicrous (Vol. I, pp. 75-7); and when he tries to prevent her from playing Constance in *King John,* she cleverly manipulates her friends in Dublin society to bring the English Roscius to his knees.

Probably because she is herself hard-headed, her most satisfying portraits are such full-length figures-in-action as that of brusque, bluff, witty, great-hearted James Quin, or her even more triumphant portrayal of the salty Duchess of Queensberry, who was for so many years her patroness and friend. Unquestioningly, the reader accepts her figures as actual human beings. George Anne Bellamy reveals the temper of a *grande dame* almost by accident, as in this sentence from an interview with the Duchess (Vol. I, p. 41):

"Whilst her Grace was talking in this manner to me, she was cleaning a picture; which I officiously requesting her permission to do, she hastily replied, 'Don't you think I have domestics enough if I did not choose to do it myself?'"

One of the reasons for the immediate success of Mrs. Bellamy's *Apology* must lie in the number of famous people who play their scenes with her. Her father Lord Tyrawley, in one of his infrequent paternal moods, had introduced her to Chesterfield and to Pope. Harry Fox was a close friend. Samuel Johnson gave her instructions in elocution. The notorious Lord Byron planned to abduct her. Sheridan hired her for his theater in Dublin. Cibber gave her a granddaughter as a legacy (Vol. II, p. 69). Quin and Tyrawley engage in high debate while she acts as bluestocking hostess (Vol. I, p. 142):

"Every word conveyed extatic delight to a mind fond of learning and the belles letters; to a person trembling alive to every rational enjoyment, as well as every delicate sensation."

To follow her life is to watch history as it unrolls (Vol. I, pp. 241-2):

"General Braddock, to whom I had been known from my infancy, and who was particularly fond of me, was about this period appointed to go to America. . . . Before we parted, the General told me he should never see me more; for he was going with a handful of men to conquer whole nations; and to do this they must cut their way through unknown woods. He produced the map of the country, saying at the same time, 'Dear Pop, we are sent like sacrifices to the altar.' The event of the expedition too fatally verified the General's expectations."

With such a famous cast of characters and such varied scenes and emotions to record, George Anne Bellamy tells her story. "Having now informed you with how little applause I made my first entrance on the stage of life" (Vol. I, p. 14), she continues from her unwanted birth through her years in a French convent; her easy success on the stage; her elopement with Mr. Metham, who promises to marry her, in order to escape marriage with the odious Mr. Crump; her diamonds and coaches; her son by Metham and her marriage contract with the rich young plebeian Jack Calcraft, whom she gradually grows to hate; luxury in London and penury in Antwerp; debts amounting to over ten thousand pounds; little thumbnail descriptions of Dublin, Brussels, the Hague, and Edinburgh, a city which she so detests that she cuts off her hair close to her head so that she will not be asked to appear in public; her reconciliation to Metham, now Sir George; a risible story of an old "mirror of knighthood"; robbery in a bedchamber; accounts of her children—one son by Metham, another by Calcraft—now full-grown, roisterers and gamblers, who drift off to Jamaica and the Colonies. She sinks further and further into debt. She cannot brook being crossed or commanded, and invariably she makes bad decisions—usually in a tantrum. Her temper becomes soured; she imposes on all her friends; but she never learns how to be a "good oeconomist." When at last even her old servant tries to lend her money, she bursts into tears and compares him to old Adam in *As You Like It.*

Suicide seems the only escape from the almost incredible monsters that batten on this prematurely old and defenseless woman. She learns of the death of her son in the West Indies. All her friends die. She lives under the name of West, and advertises for a position as housekeeper. Hating the common herd and remembering her own former largesse, her frequent Shakespearean quotations are now largely drawn—it is no wonder—from *Coriolanus* and *Timon of Athens*. And the *Apology* closes, as so many of the autobiographies of eighteenth century actresses were doomed to close, in warning gloom:[41] "And may Sterne's recording Angel drop the tear of pity and obliterate my faults."

Earlier she had written of her *Apology* (Vol. I, p. 79): "You must remember that it is the history of a weak woman, recited by the same weak woman." Here she is in error. The beautiful little actress may have been impulsive, selfish, and heartless. Her history may have been sordid at the close, but it was not weak. Her career had been crowded, active, unpredictable; notable events happened to her, and she gave them, thanks to her temperament, sharp outlines. And at the end, with some of her old indestructible vitality, she takes debtors' prisons, squalid quarters, and the ominous waters of the Thames, views them dispassionately, and shapes them into this pure expression of her spirit: "An apology for the life of George Anne Bellamy," one of the important biographies of the eighteenth century.

Commenting upon six little volumes fresh from the press in 1787, the *Monthly Review* observes:[42] "The success of Mrs. Bellamy's memoirs hath, no doubt, paved the way for these relative to her *professional* sister." The volumes referred to are *The Memoirs of Mrs. Sophia Baddeley. Late of Drury-Lane Theatre. By Mrs. Elizabeth Steele.* The contemporary reviewer treats them contemptuously as one further slanderous compilation; and they have been attributed to Alexander Bicknell, who is alleged to have had a share in the fashioning of Mrs. Bellamy's *Apology*.[43] To hold that Bicknell created these *Memoirs* is to believe him an unacknowledged imaginative writer of the first rank, for the stamp of life as it is lived is on every page, and the cumulative effect as volume follows volume, at times as inconsequential, bor-

[41] Vol. II, p. 261. For other evidences of Sterne as master, see Vol. I, pp. 117, 260; Vol. II, pp. 14, 133 and *passim*.

[42] Vol. 77 for 1787, p. 83.

[43] In Bicknell's *History of Miss Maitland*, a two volume novel, he is called the "Editor of Mrs. Bellamy's Apology" on the title-page.

ing, and pointless as existence itself can be, is one of truth. There seems little of conscious art here; but in the instinctive and exact presentation of the actual world, it is possible that biography, in one more instance, has accomplished what the novel had not yet learned to do. As in many of the great biographies, the personality of the writer as well as of the subject is vividly conveyed. No dramatist of the century had the power to suggest character so subtly, so indirectly, yet so completely as the personality of Mrs. Steele is suggested in these volumes. If the obscure Alexander Bicknell or some other ghost writer was engaged in producing these volumes, his task must have been limited to clothing Mrs. Steele's direct reminiscences in acceptable English.

Elizabeth Steele had known her Sophia Snow from those early years, when, the daughter of a sergeant-trumpeter, Sophia marries Baddeley at the age of sixteen in order to escape from her music lessons. Through most of Mrs. Baddeley's checkered career her friend and biographer acts as a kind of shocked duenna, trying repeatedly to reform the wayward Sophia, but in the end adopting for herself, without admitting it, the morals of the procuress. At the very outset, Mrs. Steele describes complicated relationships and emotional states as if they were the commonest occurrences in the world. Sophia has married Baddeley, whom she did not love, is deserted by John Hanger, whom she loves passionately, and is courted by Lord Melbourne even while the latter insists that he loves his wife, "dear Betsy," to whom, at the age of twenty-one, he has been married ten months. Few eighteenth century dramatists or novelists could take this casually as the opening situation in a long career. Many of the situations presented are left inconclusive and unresolved, as if life may have less definition and clarity than art. For instance, when John Hanger deserts Sophia, her heart almost breaks and she ruins her health by taking laudanum; yet when he tries to win her back, she spurns him, then wavers, half accepts him, and cannot make up her mind.

The quality which makes these memoirs unique and of first importance is the sense of unconscious development and change in minor as well as in major figures. No biography of the century can approach Mrs. Steele's *Memoirs of Sophia Baddeley* in this

sense of the effect of the passing years upon character. In leisurely
fashion, as if the actual time of the original events were again
flowing past, three figures emerge and grow older and change:
Lord Melbourne, who in his infatuation casts away upon Sophia
his father's fortune, which he might well have left to his own
more famous son; Sophia herself, with her enchanting voice, her
beauty, and her liking for handsome officers and undergraduates,
Sophia loved alike by lords and players, singing at Vauxhall, acting at Drury Lane, quarrelling with Garrick, Sophia flighty,
thoughtless, shallow, impulsive, warm; and Mrs. Steele, teller of
the story, with her love for her friend, her conventionality, her
homage to the proprieties, and her ruling passion—which she herself never admits—for money. Through Sophia's long progress,
Mrs. Steele never ceases her attempts to make her friend respectable; yet even in her failures she does not forget to notice whether
the bedroom door is locked when there are callers, and how many
hundred pounds each lord leaves Sophia as a token of his respect.
Steele sees and knows all of her friend's weaknesses, yet she never
deserts her.

Some portion of this character portrayal is conscious. "It was
an act of imprudence in Mrs. Baddeley," Mrs. Steele writes,[44]
"notwithstanding her anger, to shew Mr. Damer, Mr. Hanger's
letter; but this imprudence was general with her, and was one
of her usual weaknesses, she had unfortunately a babbling tongue
and could keep nothing a secret; the private conversation of one,
she would communicate to another; and though she felt not it's
effects at present, it was in the end very injurious to her." Mrs.
Steele can even give deliberate and extended notes on Sophia's
extravagance, her generosity, and her whims[45]: "No certainty of
her being in the same mind two days together. Apt to be struck
with new faces, in men, though not wickedly so." Yet even here
her desire for exact truth tempers her severity (Vol. I, p. 209):

"Having thought proper to mention a variety of Mrs. Baddeley's extravagancies, it is but justice that I should say a word or
two of her economy. In house-keeping she was far from expensive.

[44] Vol. I, p. 99. Quotations throughout are from the 1787 3-vol. Dublin ed.,
issued in the same year as the 6-vol. duodecimo London ed.
[45] Vol. I, pp. 181-3. Quotations fr. p. 183.

Though we had all sorts of French and Spanish wines, to entertain our noble friends with, when they did us the honour to dine
with us, and our table was set out with elegance; yet when we
dined alone, a single joint served us for dinner, and nothing was
drank but small beer. As lived our servants, so did we. Dinner was
ready regularly at three, and if we were not at home at that hour,
the cloth was removed and the joint served up below. For the
many years we lived together, we never opened a bottle of wine
for ourselves, nor had we any strong beer."

Yet frequently in these volumes character is more perfectly
described by indirect means; and the reader easily believes in
Sophia's extravagance when he learns that she spent three guineas
a day for flowers, when he reads of forty pounds laid out in cloth
for one mask ball, when he sees repeated instances of her passion
for diamonds and silks, or when he is presented with an itemized
account—surely an important document in eighteenth century
social history—of her outstanding bills after three years, amounting to 2666 pounds, four shillings, and sixpence (Vol. II, pp. 92-3).

The beauty of Homer's Helen, we have often been reminded,
is revealed not by direct description, but by narration of its effect
upon others. Has not Mrs. Steele arrived unconsciously at the
same method in her account of Baddeley's triumph at Samuel
Foote's presentation of *The Maid of Bath?*[46]

"About the middle of the piece, where Mr. Foote enlarged
much on the beauty of the Maid of Bath, he added, 'Not even the
beauty of the nine Muses, nor even that of the divine Baddeley
herself, who there sits,' (pointing to the box where we sat) 'could
exceed that of the Maid of Bath.' This drew a thunder of applause
from all parts of the house; he was encored, and Mr. Foote repeated the words three times. Every eye was on Mrs. Baddeley,
and I do not recollect ever seeing her so confused before. She rose
from her seat, and curtesied to the audience, and it was near a
quarter of an hour before she could discontinue her obeisance,
the plaudits lasting so long."

Mrs. Steele's own character is also indirectly revealed. Probably
the best example occurs in an amusing scene after Sophia's first

[46] Vol. II, p. 18.

assignation with the Duke of Northumberland—not in Mrs. Steele's house, for she will not permit it. Mrs. Baddeley brings back a glove as a peace-offering from the Duke (Vol. II, p. 16):

"Finding I would not take it up, she stooped for it, and pulled out from it three bank-notes of one hundred pounds each.—'They are,' says I, 'the price of your infamy, and you may keep them yourself; I will have nothing to do with them; you are the proper person to enjoy them, if they will afford you any enjoyment.' She said, if I did not take them, she would throw them into the fire, and, on my refusing them, actually did, and it was at the risk of my hands, that I rescued them from the flames. I then put them into a drawer, and locked it, saying, it was not times to destroy such a sum."

In this clash of personalities, Mrs. Baddeley's recklessness coupled with Mrs. Steele's greed gives the victory to Sophia, and the three hundred pounds are eventually used to pay off some of the mounting and menacing debts.

Many of the tricks of the stage Mrs. Steele employs. She has a knack at catching characteristic speech. Steele promises Sophia to set off on a journey in a week's time. "'A week!' exclaimed she, 'that's an age! Why can't we go to-morrow?'" (Vol. I, p. 126). And if Mrs. Steele remains impervious to the influence of Shakespeare or of the sentimental or heroic drama, she learns much from the comic stage in reproducing the speech of her characters (Vol. II, p. 242):

"The servant, who was a complete Irishman, swore by Jasus, that he believed his maister was mad for Mrs. Baddeley; that, he would not let them rest day or night, but was every where flinging about after her, and the devil-a-bit of ease could they get."

Critics of these memoirs have considered them primarily as an essay in extortion. "Many are the names introduced, and many the reputations that are 'hack'd and hew'd' past all mending."[47] Mrs. Steele uses the technique of caricature ingeniously enough in her campaign of slander. She imitates in dialect the little Jew Mr. Franco who, spurned by Mrs. Baddeley early in her career, is, in Volume III, frightened away by her debts. She imitates the speech

---

[47] *Monthly Review*, 1787, Vol. 77, p. 83.

of a Danish suitor (Vol. III). And, whenever it serves her purpose, she can twist speech maliciously (Vol. II, p. 262):

"On this gentleman's return to London, he came to me in a most violent rage, and swore he would larn his wife *description,* (he meant *scripture*) and would beat her, and make her obedient to his will."

This means of ridicule she uses for the written as well as the spoken word; when Lord Melbourne falls out of her favor, she includes, or invents, comically spelled letters with the comment (Vol. I, p. 125): "This letter is a literal copy of his Lordship's: his other letters were equally ill spelt, &c. but I have taken the liberty to correct them, that they may not hurt the eye of the reader."

The leisurely portrait contains many minute touches of scene and background and action that give it three-dimensional reality. If Dr. Johnson's cat Hodge brings the old man closer to us, Sophia's cat Cuddle similarly brings the actress nearer (Vol. I, pp. 158-9):

"We were now at home, after a ramble of some time, and spent our evening together, talking over the occurrences of the last month, with a placid satisfaction, that no place but home, with quiet, affords. Home, however, was at present something new to us, and we determined to spend a week here, with our birds and our cats, for no one knew of our being in town. Mrs. Baddeley was very fond of cats, and had one Grimalkin which she called Cuddle, and with which she would often take long journeys; and this cat was as much enquired about, by those who courted her favour, as herself. She had also a favourite canary-bird, which she brought all the way from Paris to Brighthelmstone, in a handkerchief, and from thence to Grafton-street."

Then follows an anecdote in which a coach full of people is overturned, but Baddeley is worried only over poor Cuddle's bones. In such rambling details, which, however, always cast light upon the character of the heroine, the narrative proceeds.

Gradually, the simple outlines in the inevitable prosecution of disgrace become clear. A series of scenes, fully developed and lighted and graced with dialogue, traces Sophia's progress. Nowhere in eighteenth century biography is human psychology presented with more subtle detail than in the scenes of quarrels, estrangement, and reconciliation between the two women.

"When I related to her what I had said respecting her situation in life, not entitling her to the honour of visits from men of such rank, she was rather hurt, and would not admit there was any disgrace in receiving them; and thought he might have been pre-mitted to have come. At this I replied with some warmth, 'that her visits and visitors had already caused me a great deal of un-happiness and I was determined, she should receive no more of them under my roof: that his offering me a bribe, was an insult of the highest degree, and that I was just on the eve of calling up my servant to turn him out of the house.' At this Mrs. Bad-deley laughed, said she was only in joke, and begged I would not be angry" (Vol. I, p. 102).

This last excerpt forms a small part of a longer scene, as detailed as Johnson's dinner with Wilkes or his conversation with the King, in which the talk, the callers, and the situations of a single day in Sophia's life are recalled in eleven pages. To illustrate Mrs. Steele's ability to construct a scene which might easily be trans-ferred to the stage, their dinner on board ship as guests of the British navy, when Sophia, with her perfect voice and her perfect beauty, was at her most brilliant, may be quoted at some length. Six admirals were present (Vol. II, pp. 50-1):

"Admiral Spry was happy and merry, and when dinner was over, bade the music strike up. Calling on Mrs. Baddeley for a sentiment, she took a glass of champaigne, and gave, 'May every engagement at sea, be attended with the loss of as few lives, as that of *this* day; but may we be ever victorious over the French!'

"This sentiment pleased; it went round, and was written down by a gentleman present. I was then called upon for mine, and gave, 'May there never be greater cause for engagements, than the cause of this day; and may all belonging to his Majesty's navy, enjoy the blessings of peace!' This was also penned down. After every sentiment we had a song. Admiral Spry sung

'Hearts of Oak, &c.'

and was chorused. When it came to Mrs. Baddeley's turn to sing, she begged their choice, and was requested to sing,

'Where little foolish fluttering thing, &c.'

from the *Padlock*. —She did, and when she came to that part,

'Where little wanton would you be,
Half so happy as with me?'

a gentleman present, cried out aloud, 'No where, by G—d,' which made her and the rest laugh so much, that she could not go on for some time. 'No more of your declarations, Captain,' said the Admiral, 'let's have the song.' 'Flesh and blood,' returned he, *'will* speak.' This caused a fresh laugh; however, having finished her song, a sentiment was given, and she called for another."

Life was not always so merry. Sophia, "little foolish fluttering thing," frightens away even her most opulent lovers by her extravagance; and at last, to avoid debtors' prison, lives with Stephen Sayer, sheriff of London and archpatriot, by whom she has a son. Sayer is the occasion of the separation between the two women, which Steele had threatened so many times. And now that Steele is no longer witness and confidante of every scene, the biography draws to a close rapidly. The dark and sordid years go by in fewer paragraphs than, earlier, an evening at Ranelagh's. Once, before Sophia's son is born, Steele visits her and finds her a hypochondriac who cannot endure the light and who thinks herself a supernatural being. Mrs. Baddeley is forced back to the playhouse, and lives with a succession of actors; the last of them, Mr. Webster, by whom she had two children, dies in her arms.

Then follows the final dramatic scene which is presented in full. Steele finds Sophia "in a small house in Pimlico, for which she paid twenty five pounds a year," and is ushered up by John, a footman who seems quite at ease with his lady. Steele is suspicious, and gradually gets the truth from Sophia (Vol. III, p. 228):

"She then begged me to promise, on her relation of John's story, not to forsake her for her folly. I told her, that if her folly would have led me to it, I should have forsaken her long since."

John had been footman to Webster, the actor with whom she was living; and when Webster dies, Sophia, finding consolation in unaccustomed brandy, and deserted by all but the faithful and well made footman, takes the inevitable step which accords with the story and her own character. The genteel Steele is no less true to her own disposition (Vol. III, p. 237):

"I found it was of no use to talk to her; therefore left her to act as she pleased. She never introduced this fellow to me, and as he did not presume to sit down where I was, I had no cause to complain on that account."

There is one last characteristic touch in this scene, as, for a moment, the paths of two celebrated actresses and London toasts cross in Steele's presence (Vol. III, pp. 232-3):

"Whilst we were in this conversation, we heard a loud rapping at the door; I went to the window, and saw a lady, in an elegant little phaeton, with four beautiful ponies, and two little post-boys, in blue and silver jackets: I mentioned this to Mrs. Baddeley, and she cried, 'Good God! John, who is it?' 'Ma'am,' said he, 'a lady wishes to see you, whose name is Robinson.' 'Desire her,' said Mrs. Baddeley, 'to walk up; this is,' continued she to me, 'the person the Prince of Wales is so fond of.'"

So Mrs. Robinson presents Sophia with ten guineas from the Duke of Cumberland and listens to her sad story. "When Mrs. Robinson heard, she cried out. 'Oh, the ingratitude of mand-kind!' And shed a few tears, unperceived by Mrs Baddeley" (Vol. II, p. 233).

Drury Lane no longer wants her. She sings in odd engagements in London, plays one season in Ireland, and finally drifts off to Edinburgh with "her paramour, John." There she dies of a consumption, in 1786, in her "thirty-eighth year" (though she was born in 1745); and her medical care at the end is paid for by a weekly subscription taken up by her fellow actors, "as she was much beloved by the performers."

These *Memoirs* are no less a work of art and a powerful moral lesson because so many of their best effects are unconscious. The volatile and warm-hearted Sophia, always attracted by handsome men and always in need of more money, is present in three dimensions. Mrs. Steele herself is equally solid, with her protestations of respectability as absurd in her circumstances as Mistress Quickly's, her worry and nagging and tears and account-books. Best of all is the change in the characters and the relationship of the two women as the years pass by and the scene gradually darkens. When Steele records the beginnings of Sophia's affair with Northumberland (Vol. II, p. 7): " 'Good God!' said I, to myself; 'the Duchess of Northumberland is still living.—How wicked is this fashionable world!—To me all this is dreadful.' " She continues, however, with an observation which in her case was profoundly true: "But like all other bad things, they become familiar at last; and we think nothing of them."

According to her own account, Mrs. Steele is not only eminently respectable; she also dissipates her little fortune in the service of her friend. Has she told the precise truth? Or has she learned to think of herself as she would wish to be? The *Gentleman's Magazine* for 1787 (p. 1033) records the death of "Mrs. Eliz. Steele, lately advertised for a forgery committed on a respectable house in the city, but better known by her having dictated the truly infamous 'Memoirs of Mrs. Sophia Baddeley,' who supported Mrs. Steele, during her affluence, in the capacity of a convenient woman." At the Dolphin Inn, then, in Bishopsgate-street, Mrs. Steele died, "attended by an old man, who called himself her husband." She "was buried in Bishopsgate church-yard, in a manner rather better than a common pauper." The tone of the *Gentleman's Magazine* is too harsh. It is better, and perhaps nearer the truth, to remember her as she creates herself: querulously loyal to her friend—to remember her as "my dear Steele" (in Sophia's phrase) who can say: "I told her, that if her folly would have led me to it, I should have forsaken her long since."

The year 1791, in which Boswell's lifework appeared, also witnessed the publication of another landmark in English biography, the culmination of the actors' memoirs of the eighteenth century. The title of the three-volume Dublin edition is *Memoirs of his own life, by Tate Wilkinson, Patentee of the Theatres-Royal, York and Hull.* For the development of a looser, more vivid and entertaining manner, English biography owes much to the two actor-managers Colley Cibber and Tate Wilkinson. Wilkinson himself derives largely from Cibber. There is the same naïve confession of pride,[48] the same tendency to shoot off upon tangents from specific anecdote, the same device of genially taking the reader into valued confidence, the same appraisal of actors and actresses.

But Wilkinson has a sense of pathos and sentiment which distinguishes him from Cibber and gives warmer tones, a more personal interest, to his life, particularly in its early years. He was born in 1739, the son of the King's chaplain at the Savoy, and recalls his youth in such anecdotes of tender reminiscence as this (Vol. I, p. 15):

"I being forcibly struck with my father's manner in several church services, was never easy unless I had an old surplice thrown over my shoulders, and my whole delight was in praying, preaching, burials, &c. I was generally locked up in a room, supposing it a church; and in a large chair, the bottom taken out, went through the morning or evening service as it happened to occur in the course of the day; then replacing the chair bottom, and throwing off the old surplice of my father's, that had just before occupied my shoulders, I mounted and leaned over the back of the said chair, and with mighty authority proceeded with the sermon; several of which discourses were my father's."

At the age of five, he sees a puppet-show, with a sea fight so terrifying that his father, several years later, is almost compelled to use force to get him into Covent Garden Theatre. He prefers church (Vol. I, p. 17):

"So, after my repeated refusals, my reverend dad at last grew really angry, and insisted on my going there, with this conditional salvo, that if I was not pleased, he pledged his honour he would never urge me to see another. I, choked with grief, assented to this cruelty, as I really thought it was."

His father might well have been appalled by the effectiveness of his discipline. The stage immediately absorbs Tate's mind, he attends all the rehearsals he can, he acts the plays in his own room, he collects several hundred old playbills. "The bills I have often produced, not as a proof of my sense, but insanity, or theatrical

---

[48] Pref., p. xi, Vol. I, 1791. Wilkinson, speaking of his own writing, says: "But, notwithstanding its ricketty origin, be it known to all men, that there is a secret pride, which, however I would endeavour to conceal, will burst out when I perceive *three volumes* in print—*By* TATE WILKINSON."

influenza." Harrow fails to hold his attention against such superior diversion; he runs away from the school, in spite of his success in acting the part of Lady Townley before the school *à la mode* Peg Woffington. This lady, and David Garrick, are destined to turn the course of his life more than once. Through Rich, the actor, he almost secures a place, but by bad luck, Mrs. Woffington scents an insult, and his chance vanishes. Yet his ability to mimic this celebrated actress later gives him his first real opportunity. His father, sentenced in 1757 to transportation for fourteen years for violating the marriage act, dies at Plymouth on the way to America, and Tate is left in penury at the age of eighteen with the task of supporting himself and his mother. The account of his hearing before David Garrick has therefore an element of real suspense. As if even in actual life Garrick could not escape the conventions of comedy, there is a curtain in the room, and a lady—"Mrs. Mouse"—behind it. She laughs audibly at Tate's imitation of Peg Woffington, and for him the battle is won. Wilkinson's analysis of motives in this incident which gave him his start is penetrating (Vol. I, p. 115):

"If it had happened otherwise Mrs. Mouse would not have appeared but kept snug in her hole. Perhaps female prejudice here might operate in my favour, as Mr. Garrick had previous to his marriage with Madam Violette, paid his devoirs to Mrs. Woffington."

His rise is not rapid. Garrick, as he believes, tricks him on a pre-dated contract, and, what seems worse, considers him a "d——d exotic." Foote does not take care of him when he is ill. Many of his stories, growing out of his sensitive nature, have to do with discourtesies, snubs, and boorish conduct. The incidents in his struggle to place himself are exciting, and his steady care for his widowed mother forms a tender sentimental background. Some of her letters to him, preserved for more than thirty years, he includes in his memoirs. His own self-pity is evident in such a scene as he stages in connection with his journey to Ireland with Foote, where, miserably seasick, he calls on his family's old friends, the Chaigneaus (Vol. I, p. 138):

"I had no sooner entered the room where they were sitting, than—than what?—why to proceed requires the *best* of novel

pens to present, fulfil, and do service to the scene that followed.
This generous Mr. William Chaigneau and wife, were on the
list of the few instances, where

> Mutual temper with unclouded ray,
> Could make to morrow welcome as to day.

"Their pleasures were the same—their affections were the same.
Their instantaneous recollection of me—the great intimacy between the families—my father's death and calamities being so
lately public, and now refreshed to their memory, revived the
idea of their own distress, from the loss of their darling child,
the infant-marriage between me and that daughter, my present
assured, unfortunate, helpless, situation, with a look of desponding
hope dependent on their feelings, all collected rushed on their
alternate sudden thoughts with such quick transitions, as made
them all combined too mighty for Mrs. Chaigneau's tender spirits; indeed so powerfully, that the fictitious distress of Lady
Randolph on the stage, was by no means equal to her poignant
sense of my misery and situation; and it was actually some
time before she could recover herself with any degree of composure to inquire what had brought me there, or what could be
done to serve me."

At the close of the third volume, after his checkered life and
at the venerable—to him—age of fifty-one, his thoughts turn
back to the sentimental center of his life, his mother. The wheel
has come full circle (Vol. III, p. 128):

"When I walk with my memory, I often get a pleasing hour, by
reflecting with gratitude, and bowing with adoration to my God
for his peculiar goodness, and his snatching me from the brink of
the grave, when sunk with poverty and ever threatening approach of misery, and then lifting me up with his own almighty
arm, and restoring me to instant health, accompanied with worthy
and benevolent friends, respect, and affluence, which prevented
at the same time the best of mothers from sinking with her grey
hairs into the grave with sorrow, and blessing me with the power
and the will to give comfort to her latter years and days; and
above all am consoled with my parent's confession to God, that

her son was the cause of that unexpected and uninterrupted happiness.—Here let me stop my career."

If there is something that verges upon the maudlin, upon self-
dramatization, in such a passage, it is nevertheless genuine; it
is the same quality which made him an actor. The re-enacting at
will of powerful feelings, which is an actor's chief talent, is not
an unfortunate trait for a biographer to possess, provided always
that he can keep his imagination from running beyond what
may strike the sympathetic reader as truth. And Wilkinson's
peculiar gift of mimicry—which won for him his first great
success in Dublin—stands him in good stead in creating entertaining and lifelike reminiscences. The influence of the drama
upon autobiography is everywhere apparent in his memoirs. The
presentation of characters, the organization by scenes, the language itself, are born of the theater.

Wilkinson, long familiar with the stage, naturally utilizes
caricature as a means of artistic economy in the presentation of
minor figures. There is something new and fresh in the ending
of such a brief scene as the following between Tate Wilkinson
and Rich, after Tate's failure in his part of the Fine Gentleman
(Vol. I, p. 102):

"Unfit for the stage, what could I do? My mother's existence
was procured by the sale or pawning every trifle that could raise
a few shillings; and she trembling to view the darkened prospect
when the last resources were expended, compelled me to wait
on Mr. Rich once more, and solicit him to retain me on any
trifling salary for the ensuing year; but I received a short and
peremptory 'NO! You are unfit for the stage, Muster Whittington, and I won't larn you—you may go, Muster Whittington;'
and he stroked his favourite cat."

The same sharp observation of the born mimic, the same centering upon peculiarities, are evident in an interview with Garrick
after Wilkinson's successes at Bath and Portsmouth (Vol. I, p.
198):

"My first words after my salutation were, 'Sir, what am I to
make my first appearance in, and when?'—for now I was not so
timid and afraid of this lord of lords and ruler of princes, as I
was the year before when I acted as his groom, and rode his

hobby-horse. He was on this easy question so full of hum-s and ha-s, and hey, why, now, yes, they, now really I think—that finding nothing could come from nothing, I very soon obliged him by retiring, as I was certain he wished my absence."

Each person's peculiar speech—Rich's pronunciation, Garrick's halting repetitions and foul language (Vol. II, p. 27), Sheridan's "grumbling and squeaking"—are reproduced with delight. Detesting the Methodists as much as the Methodists detested the theater, Wilkinson travesties George Whitefield's sermons most amusingly (Vol. II, pp. 149-51). This is the opening of his parody:

"The Rev. Mr. Whitfield (the first actor in the Methodist walk) was of a contrary cast [to John Wesley] entirely, and not without humour here and there. His dialect was very particular—*Lurd* instead of Lord, *Gud* instead of God—as, *O Lurd Gud!*"

This instinct for idiosyncrasies of speech, coupled with an ability to conceive a scene dramatically and carry it to a point,[49] may be shown in a final scene between Garrick and Doctor Johnson, in which Wilkinson as a narrator suffers little in comparison with Boswell for fullness and vividness[50] (Vol. I, pp. 225-6):

"Doctor Johnson, being with Foote, Holland, Woodward, and others, on a party at Mr. Garrick's villa at Hampton, as they were conversing on different subjects, he fell into a reverie, from which his attention was drawn by the accidentally casting his eyes on a book-case, to which he was as naturally attracted as the needle to the pole: on perusing the title pages of the best bound, he muttered inwardly with ineffable contempt, but proceeded on his exploring business of observation, ran his finger down the middle of each page, and then dashed the volume disdainfully upon the floor, the which Garrick beheld with much wonder and vexation, while the most profound silence and attention was bestowed on the learned Doctor; but when he saw his

---

[49] For further examples of biography conceived in terms of the drama, compare Garrick's denunciation of Wilkinson for his mimicry, Vol. I, pp. 227-32; or his caricatures of a young actress and her mother, Vol. II, pp. 39-43; or the moral and tearful story of Lucy Cooper, the reigning toast of the 1760's, Vol. II, pp. 89-93.

[50] Vol. I, pp. 225-6. This comparison cannot be extended to Boswell's and Wilkinson's styles. The reader is inclined to accept at face value Wilkinson's own motto for the volumes: "—If I had held my PEN but half as well as I have held my BOTTLE—what a charming hand I should have wrote by this time!"

twentieth well-bound book thus manifestly disgraced on the ground, and expecting his whole valuable collection would share the same victim fate, he could no longer restrain himself, but suddenly cried out most vociferously,—'Why d—n it, Johnson,— you, you, you will destroy all my books!'—At this Johnson raised his head, paused, fixed his eyes, and replied, 'Lookee, David, you do understand plays, *but you know nothing about books!*' which repartee occasioned an irresistible laugh at Garrick's expence, as well as that of his having given them a good dinner, with plenty of choice viands."

At one point in his *Memoirs* Wilkinson observes, with penetration, concerning Garrick (Vol. II, p. 37): "Mr. Garrick was an actor on the stage of life; and on the stage itself he was not the actor, but life's exact mirror he held to public view." The first part of this statement would apply equally to Wilkinson himself. All happenings he dramatizes, emotionalizes, intensifies; and his speech itself smacks of the theater. Doubtless his syntax could have been much improved if he had not run away from Harrow, but as if conscious of his own failings, he bolsters up his narrative most disconcertingly with patchwork and paraphrases from the dramatists. Echoes from Shakespeare may be observed in the passages already cited, or more strikingly in this plea for the reader's indulgence, in which the audience plays a passive Angelo to Wilkinson's Isabella (Pref., p. vii): "Good reader, Be kind, courteous, merciful, and forgiving; for how would you be, if HE, who is the top of judgment, should but judge you as you are? Oh! think on that, and mercy then will breathe within your lips like man new made."

Strong emotion brings quotations, apposite and inapposite, to his mind, and he ends his last volume, upon his assuming the managership of the York company and theater in 1766, with these melancholy reflections at the patriarchal age of fifty-one years (Vol. III, pp. 125-7):

"I . . . may add, that no boy was ever so weary of his tutor, girl of her bib, nun of doing penance, or old maid of being chaste, as I am with thirty-four years rolling about in a restless theatrical hemisphere. . . . If any pen of merit think these sheets worth an attack on my feeble and acknowledged *ignor-*

ance, I will receive the dart as a noble, unexpected, and an honourable extinction of nothing. But I will not, like melancholy Jaques, moral on the time more than to observe, I do not at this juncture perceive any extraordinary light or pleasing prospect to cheer my walk down hill, for I am truly weary, lame, and tired with service; though each month certainly presents the prospect of this world's lessening to my view, and the vast abyss more plain and ready to ingulph and swallow, where we shall all be enveloped, and imperceptibly view new lights for information, by the permission of a Superior Being.—

> Men must abide
> Their going hence, ev'n as their coming hither.

"The reader, I think, cannot, on a summary of my whole life collected, pronounce it has been solely that of pleasure.—Thanks to my God for my happy state of temper; for I can declare, that in the whole course of my days, in the tedious round of fifty-one years, I have not known nine out of the number to term those of misery or real grief: And though my life has been checquered by innumerable situations, in which I have been whimsically and variously placed, consequently no wonder, if I have often acted right, that I have also oftener acted wrong; and, like an eager child, have not only tasted but devoured the sweets, and now make faces at a few bitters, and wish and want to be secure of health and happiness on bond to the end of my days: for Adversity I do not like to get acquainted with, though at times I fear she will be sending me a card of invitation, and compelling me to dine with her Willy Nilly, and *perchance* without a clean table-cloth—and that is horrid, unless truly hungry. But alas!—

> Heaven doth with us, as we with torches do,
> Not light them for ourselves. . . ."

He had begun to write, he tells us, solely to pass the time while confined to his bed with a fractured leg, and he is mortally weary, at the end, of the theater. But there is more than a bit of Shandyism in Wilkinson, and the joys of recording his whimsical thoughts on plays and troupers cannot be put away. He views his own writing with a smile, and terms it (Vol. II, p. 239) "this complex—*what d'ye call it*—*something-nothing of a book*; for the work will certainly be allowed originality, and that no such hurlo-thrumbo production as to information of jumbled matter and anecdotes ever before appeared!" He lays aside his pen, then, with only a feigned relief, and almost before England had had a chance to read his first volumes through slowly, there appeared at York in 1795 in four volumes *The Wandering Patentee, or a history of the Yorkshire theatres.*

"I take the liberty to introduce," he writes (Vol. I, p. 26), "a kind of stage-journal, as Wandering Patentee; . . . the gliding appearance of heroes and heroines, kings and cobblers, queens, ladies of quality and no quality, chambermaids, and footmen, with the various *et caeteras,* will make such circumstances by many be read over with remembrance of pity, laughter, and regret."

He is still playing his self-imposed rôle of Uriah Heep—the Preface opens "I am of so little importance . . ."—and is more determined than ever to amuse, even if he must make himself ridiculous to please the reader, whom he hopes gratified by his "prittle prattle" (Vol. IV, p. 231). Now, at the age of fifty-six, he leaves his friendly reader with sorrow, for he presages death. Nevertheless, he goes off the stage with a health in a bumper of wine, as the Duke of Clarence, in Edward IV's reign, chose to "make his exit in a hogshead of Madeira" (Vol. IV, pp. 232-3). Always he has at his penpoint a parallel drawn from the other world of the theater.

From an ever-widening cornucopia, therefore, since his memories multiply as they approach the present, Tate Wilkinson pours out reminiscences of actors and actresses, revenues, programs, and benefit performances, with himself as poor Yorick generally in the foreground—slightly harassed, tangled in his own weird syntax, and full of a great self-pity.

CHAPTER II

BIOGRAPHY AND THE NOVEL

"Pilate saith unto him,
'What is truth?' "

IN the first half of the eighteenth century, the rise of the novel radically altered the art of English biography. Conversely, the established biographical tradition affected the development of the novel to an extent not yet fully realized. During this period, neither form can be fully understood without the other.

Biographers by definition treat the actual. Many novelists, seeking credence, followed the existing biographical patterns. They imitated the exact details, the matter-of-fact tone, the enumeration of dates and places, the unconscious personal biases, the meditations and apologies, even the ineptnesses, which they found in earlier biographers. The art of writing lives, therefore, helped definitely to turn fiction from the artificiality of heroic romance to the observation of life as it is lived in the world about us.

The nature of his material makes it more difficult for the novelist than for the biographer to effect a "willing suspension of disbelief." Generally the reader is aware in advance that the novelist's subject matter is fictitious. It is easier to make the reader believe in the birth of Laurence Sterne, who demonstrably lived, than in the birth of Tristram Shandy, who demonstrably did not. Because of the very difficulty of their tasks, therefore, the novelists who wished their creations accepted as genuine men and women had to improve or invent techniques of narration and description. Art must make imagined characters seem, during the moments of reading, at least as actual as historical persons. Sterne, for instance, perfects the daydream with its associational broodings and side-excursions; he perfects the half-expressed thought—suggestions, ejaculations, reticences; he notes down postures and actions as running commentaries on his dialogue and narration. Such devices produce magical illusions, and his puppet-characters, governed by his mind, appear to move and think as autonomous, authentic individuals. If the novelist must be a magician, the biographer must be a necromancer. Art is no less necessary in trafficking with the dead in order to make them live again. Biography here borrows from the novel. Every technical discovery in fiction is immediately appropriated by the biographer, as this chapter will try to demonstrate. If Sterne, to continue with our example, had not developed his peculiar technique of fiction, then his own actual death—the one gesture, the one melodramatic short phrase—could never have been told so convincingly in the memoirs written by his imitator John Macdonald.

The gradations between actual and fictional narratives are infinite. Many of the authors, and more of their readers, probably could not have drawn the line between the imaginative and the historical worlds. Sarah Fielding argues that biography is more informative and just than fiction, which, "like false Coin, is rather calculated to deceive, than profit us." But her long panegyric on biography comes in a preface to *The lives of Cleopatra and Octavia* (1757), in which she records what that pair of noble dames tell her on her trip to the underworld. The more strange and wonderful the tale-spinning becomes, the more the title-pages swear authenticity and seek to document what follows.[1] Such solemn protests constitute the homage that second-rate fiction paid to biography. Sometimes the provenance of a "surprising, authentic" history is so circumstantial that only the most cynical or practised reader will raise his eyebrows. And Edward Kimber, who wrote eight novels in the form of biographies, is most ingenious of all in belittling the "fictitious lives and histories of persons that never have existed" before presenting his own novel, *The life and adventures of Joe Thompson* (1750).

The strange hybrids that fill the period demonstrate that neither biography nor the novel had attained artistic certainty. Half-fiction and half-fact, they are acceptable neither to the historian nor to the literary critic. Sometimes writers of romances will cen-

---

[1] cf., in Bibliography, titles under: Dudley, 1706; Sethos, 1732; Grigg, 1733; Berington, 1737; Ephraim Bates, 1759; and Wilkins, 1783.

ter their "memoirs" upon some notorious foreign name, in the hope that popular curiosity about genuine characters will sell their weak inventions.[2] This procedure, however, is reversed in a more popular type, in which the lives of real people are told under romantic pseudonyms. Disguise of this sort, in cases of current scandal or of political acrimony, may have been necessary. Secret histories soon became a habit; keys were issued to identify the baffling initials, the Mirabels or the Hilarias; and the public, delighted by mysteries, almost assumed that the more "secret" the history, the more certain its truth.[3] The most bewildering variant of all is the pseudo-biography which introduces both historical and imaginary personages, who laugh and frown at each other, and converse.[4] Few of these mongrel productions possess literary value. They show, nevertheless, that the boundary between biography and the novel was not fixed in the eighteenth century, and that changes in one form might easily and quickly affect the other.

The fictional impulse came into eighteenth century biography through two main channels: through the French romance and the English pamphlet of travel.[5] The interminable volumes of *Le grand Cyrus* and *Cléopâtre* lie back of one great group of self-styled memoirs in the early eighteenth century; hardly less important in the development of a new type is the Anglo-Saxon instinct for adventure that is imbedded in Hakluyt's *Voyages* and in *Robinson Crusoe*. Far back of these new fictional biographies, then, loom the medieval court of love and the Elizabethan adventurers and voyagers; close at hand, the two prime exponents

---

[2] cf., in Bibliography: Ormonde, 1741; Du Barry, 1771. cf. also Curll's technique of publishing potpourris as the memoirs of any conveniently dead celebrity.

[3] cf., in Bibliography: Zarah, Mirabel, Pomponius, Aristides, Zell, Katty N————, Foley, and particularly Aulnoy, Curll, and Manley.

[4] cf., in Bibliography: Haywood's *Mary Stuart*, 1725; *Mr. Cleveland*, 1735; Mainvillers, 1751; Beauval, 1754; *Memoirs of a baroness* for the picture of Henry IV of France; G. A. Stevens, 1785; Godwin's *Jane Grey*, 1791; Clara Reeve's *Roger de Clarendon*, 1794.

[5] For fuller treatment of peripheral material than the scope of this volume warrants, cf. Bibliography, Part II, particularly Johanna Birnbaum, Frank Wadleigh Chandler, and John Campbell Major.

of fierce wars and faithful loves are Daniel Defoe and Mrs. Manley, author of the *New Atalantis.*

Most of the little biographies of the bedchamber were written by women. The English learned to deal with sighs and whispers and intrigue and passion from their neighbors across the Channel, for they order such matters better in France, and there, already, had reduced all possible tender sentiments to charts.

Because of the growth of free-lances of all sorts—in letters, on the stage, and in the shifting circles of London society around the Court—and particularly because of the attitude of insouciance and gaiety imported from France at the Restoration and fashionably dominant through the Age of Anne, a new type of pseudo-biography attained some popularity in England during the first years of the new century. Fiction mingled strangely with fact; *contes scabreux* alternated with the most delicate problems of etiquette and romantically conceived conversations; the prime requisite was always entertainment—never truth or edification. Many of the memoirs in this loose group resemble in spirit and conception the novels of the pamphleteers, Nashe, Greene, and Deloney; but their actual ancestors are foreign, and they form the brood, shrunken in size, of the French *romanciers,* made witty and worldly somewhat after the fashion of *The Rape of the Lock.* In this class of fictional biography the boundaries between England and France are practically non-existent; memoirs are announced as translated from the French or Italian which were written in English;[6] or the lives·of English courtiers with astonishing names in phonetic French—the Duc de Bouquinkam, the Comte de Candisch, or the Comte de Vvarvvick—are presented in French and often never translated.[7]

---

[6] cf. Mrs. Manley, *Memoirs of Europe, towards the close of the eighth century. Written by Eginardus . . . And done into English,* 1710; *Adventures of Rivella,* 1715; and *Secret memoirs . . . from the New Atalantis . . . Written originally in Italian,* 1709. Vol. II of this last title adds: *and translated from the third edition of the French.*

[7] cf. Madame d'Aulnoy: *Travels into Spain,* 2d ed., 1692, French ed. 1691; *Histoire de Jean de Bourbon,* 1692; *Mémoires de la cour d'Angleterre,* 1695, tr. 1708; *Mémoires secrets de M*[r]*. L.D.D.O.* [le duc d'Orleans] 1696; *Histoire d'Hypolite, Comte de Duglas,* 1699; and Anthony Hamilton, *Mémoires de Grammont,* 1713, tr. 1714.

One of the chief perpetrators of this new brand of piebald biography was Marie Catherine Jumelle de Bernville, comtesse d'Aulnoy. Between 1690 and 1700 she published a number of volumes,[8] which dealt almost solely with the *affaires du coeur* of high-born historical personages in France and England. When one volume[9] can begin with Henry VII and jump as far as Zephire in love with a disdainful rose, or another[10] can close with a Voltairean stinging and brilliant prayer to Saint Remy, "mignon des Anges," the connection of Madame d'Aulnoy with English biography may seem obscure. But in spite of her fancy and in spite of her frequently conventional treatment, with its *déguisements*, its *bergers amoureux*, its *soupirs languisants*, and its *plaisirs un peu plus criminels*, she has the knack of entertaining. She introduces to England in wholesale quantities the intimate lives of the great, and her scandalous chronicles offer a new approach to aristocrats and kings, salted with *un peu de malice*, after the medieval moralizing on the falls of princes and the Elizabethan encomiums of sovereigns and patrons.

Besides being a writer of fairy-stories and of biographies which partake of fairy-stories, Madame d'Aulnoy is a distinguished autobiographer. The *Memoirs of her own life*[11] may well have furnished the model for the confessions of injured females which poured out from eighteenth century printing-presses; it is only regrettable that more of her successors did not have her power of delicate psychological analysis. Yet what part of her confessions is literally true? Can the reader take seriously a work in which occurs an incredibly romanesque mistaken-identity assignation between a magistrate and his own son, escaped from prison and masquerading as a woman; in which a lover disguised as a valet gains access to the heroine; in which swordplay over her ends in death beneath her windows; in which her second husband breaks off his duel with a calumniating lover in order to rescue him from enemy troops?

And if such incidents are doubtful, what is to be said of her defense of her career in love? "Indeed," she declares (p. 2),

---

[8] See preceding note for titles of her principal works.   [9] *Hypolite.*
[10] *Memoires secrets de Mr. L.D.D.O.*
[11] pp. 1-135 of *The diverting works of the Countess D'Anois*, 2d ed., 1715.

"there are none who have done more Injustice to their Sex, than they who have written the Memoirs of their Amours, and dispers'd into the World, Letters for which their Passion and Debauchery found Materials." After such prefatory circumspection, a reader may be surprised to find her first lover, the Marquis of Blossac, followed by d'Aulnoy, and d'Aulnoy by the Marquis of Sauveboeuf, and Blossac again, and Sauveboeuf, and the Duke of Candale, the Abbot Fouquet, the Marquis of St. Albe, Montalzac, the Duke of Savoy and the Marquis of Fleuri, "withouten oother compaignye in youthe." In her conduct, she laments, no one will believe her innocent, and it is hard to see how anyone could. Yet she writes, not to excuse herself, since her ill fame is sent by God to punish her for vanity, but "to justify by my Example such Persons of my Sex as have of late been made the Objects of common Reproach." Such conviction that the world is wrong and that the outcast autobiographer is suffering unjustly after impeccable conduct, will not be uncommon among other unfortunate women who turned an honest penny, at last, by writing their memoirs. At the close of her autobiography, Madame d'Aulnoy's attitude is still the same (p. 135):

"I hope to continue the Design I have begun in justification of Women. I have known several who have been as little spar'd by publick Report as my self; and I shall shew by the recital of their Adventures more clearly than by my own that outward Appearances are frequently deceitful, and that there is more misfortune than Irregularity in the Conduct of Women."

The purpose of the memoirs, then, is to furnish a cautionary tale as to how to preserve one's reputation.

"Outward Appearances are frequently deceitful." The woman who had realized that had also cut deeply enough into her own inner life to record it convincingly. Her account of painful first love, its griefs and its blind or oblique impulses, is very fine. When her letters to the Marquis of Blossac, written in the passionate style of the romances she had been reading, are discovered by the abbess of her convent, the young girl Marie convinces her superior of her intention to reform (p. 9):

"She knew not that Pride was the cause of it, and that this Pride proceeded from no other Reason, but because I would not be despis'd by Blossac. It never came into her Thoughts that a Girl of no more than Thirteen years of Age should be capable of such a refin'd piece of Cunning."

Still mistress of duplicity and of its analysis, she later shows marked attention to the Marquis of Sauveboeuf in order to hide from her husband her real love for Blossac; the result is that (p. 21) "all three took me for the Arrantest Cocquet in nature." She retires to a convent, but this teaches her (p. 3) "that of all the Resolutions that a Woman, whether guilty or innocent, can take, the worst is to leave her Husband's House." The description of her state of mind, as she returns to d'Aulnoy after Blossac rebuffs her, is a rare and nice achievement in autobiography. And her account, whether it is false or not, rises to heights of abnegation when she forces her true lover Saint Albe to marry another instead of deeding her his inheritance, and when he acts towards her with unselfish nobility. She is glad she has found such a lover, and even more glad, when, as in a fairy-tale, her husband and his wife conveniently die and, united at last, she and Saint Albe may live happy ever after.

A recent editor considers that Madame d'Aulnoy is much more accurate in her books than Anthony Hamilton in his *Memoirs of the Count de Grammont*. She further adds justly of Madame d'Aulnoy's writings that "though the morals are of the time, the manners are irreproachable, and there is not one sentence that is indelicate. This is more than can be said of Hamilton's sprightly masterpiece."[12] In her autobiography, Madame d'Aulnoy furnishes an example of self-justification, amorous intrigue, and noble sentiment that will be frequently turned to account in the eighteenth century; most important of all, she has presented some incidents that are so beautifully imagined that if they did not exist it is fortunate that Madame d'Aulnoy found it necessary to invent them.[13]

---

[12] *Memoirs of the Court of England in 1675,* 1913 ed., p. xvii. Edited by Mrs. William Henry Arthur.

[13] For other contributions from France to subtle psychoanalysis, cf. the translated lives of Madame de Maintenon, 1753, 1757, 1760; and C. Pineau-Duclos's *Course of Gallantries; or, the inferiority of the tumultuous joys of the passions to the serene pleasures of reason: attested by the confession of a nobleman who had tried both,* 1775.

The defense of dubious virtue which Madame d'Aulnoy—and others, such as Courtilz de Sandras and Eliza Haywood—perfected, became immediately popular in England. In a list that would extend from the anonymous life of Aphra Behn (1692) to Mary Robinson's autobiography (1801), an important early interpreter of such *vies amoureuses* is Mary de la Rivière Manley. Unhappily married at an early age to her own cousin, successful on the stage in *The Lost Lover,* following Swift as editor of the *Examiner* in 1711, quarrelling with Steele, Mrs. Manley is almost as swashbuckling in her career as Mrs. Behn. Of her ability as an author, Swift said that she wrote "as if she had about two thousand epithets and fine words packed up in a bag, and that she pulled them out by handfuls, and strewed them on her paper, where about once in five hundred times they happen to be right."[14]

Whatever the faults of her style may be, her *New Atalantis,* first published in 1709 anonymously, created a furor, and rapidly ran through seven editions. It purports to be "Secret memoirs and manners of several persons of quality, of both sexes." Wisely it was issued under the masks of anonymity and foreign authorship, for it is little more than defamatory satire, with actual personages and their luxury barely hidden beneath classical names. It is told as a conversation between the figures of Astraea, her mother Virtue, and their female guide Intelligence. On the island of Atlantis these three form an allegorical vice-investigating commission, which manages to bring to light a gallant *Hecatommithi.* The stories vary from a forerunner of *La nouvelle Héloïse*[15] to the tale of Marlborough's climbing up the backstairs to influence via the boudoir of the Countess of Castlemaine. The *New Atalantis* might be described not so much as a series of short biographies as of character sketches of the heart—a history of desire and voluptuousness. Mrs. Manley's accounts are made fictional or are intensified for dramatic purposes, but sufficient authenticity attaches to them so that it might be said that the

[14] Letter to Addison, August 22, 1710. Quoted from the *Dictionary of National Biography.*

[15] 1709, 2d ed., Vol. I, pp. 105-30: a pure passion, a baron friend, a trusting Monsieur St. Amant. The lady dies for love.

New Atalantis introduces into English that faintly uncharitable approach, so common in modern biography, which makes puppets of the principal figures—examples to titillate the biographer's and the reader's sense of amused superiority.

Whether or not Mrs. Manley herself wrote it, her own biography, published as *The adventures of Rivella. . . . With secret memoirs and manners of several considerable persons her cotemporaries* (1715, 2d ed.), is done in her manner, and comes closer to being biography than the *New Atalantis* itself. To give it color and interest, the adventures open with a framework which in this type of fictional biography became increasingly popular. The young Count D'Aumont is walking with Sir Charles Lovemore in Somerset House Garden, eagerly trying to learn the history of Rivella, whom he considers the world's mistress in the art of love. As the story progresses, it is made lively by D'Aumont's interruptions and questionings. The account of Mrs. Manley's— or Rivella's—early training and first love affairs is truth and biography told under the guise of romance.[16] The psychology is sound and delicate, if at times sentimentalized. Mrs. Manley can dismiss one person as (p. 67) "a sort of an insignificant Gentleman," or excoriate another (p. 66): "Calista . . . was the most of a Prude in her outward Professions, and the least of it in her inward Practice, unless you'll think it no Prudery to allow Freedom with the Air of Restraint." Worldly wisdom is mixed with ridiculous interludes in which Christopher, the son of General Monk (under the name of Tim Double), figures in escapades that might have come from Thomas Nashe's *Unfortunate Traveller*. The argument which justifies scandal under pretense of reform, almost invariably introduced into such pseudo-biographies, may be discerned in an interview between Cleander, who is telling the story, and Rivella. He finds her (pp. 108 *ff.*) "in one of her Heroick Strains":

"She told me that her self was Author of the *Atalantis*, for which three innocent Persons were taken up and would be ruin'd

---

[16] The 1715 edition is followed by a "Compleat Key" to the fictitious names. cf. "Mistress Delariviere Manley's Autobiography," by P. B. Anderson, in *Modern Philology*, Vol. XXXIII, Feb. 1936, pp. 261-78.

with their Families; that she was resolv'd to surrender her self into the Messenger's Hands, whom she heard had the Secretary of State's Warrant against her, so to discharge those honest People from their Imprisonment: I stared upon her and thought her directly mad; I began with railing at her Books; the barbarous Design of exposing People that never had done her any Injury; she answer'd me she was become Misanthrope, a perfect Timon, or Man-Hater; all the World was out of Humour with her, and she with all the World, more particularly a Faction who were busy to enslave their Sovereign, and overturn the Constitution; that she was proud of having more Courage than had any of our Sex, and of throwing the first Stone, which might give a Hint for other Persons of more Capacity to examine the Defects, and Vices of some Men who took a Delight to impose upon the World, by the Pretence of publick Good, whilst their true Design was only to gratify and advance themselves."

Yet in spite of such a politically acrid defense, Rivella's adventures end more sweetly with the pleasures of the bed—flower-strewn, for she will use no perfume. Swift has described her as fat and homely, but the fictitious Chevalier D'Aumont has other ideas. He cannot wait to be received by her. "*Allon's,*" he says at the close, "let us go, my dear Lovemore."

By far the most entertaining, the best known, and, according to most recent criticism, the most authentic, of the *chroniques scandaleuses* is Anthony Hamilton's *Memoirs of the life of Count de Grammont*. Written probably before Grammont's death in 1707, the memoirs were published anonymously in French in 1713 and translated in 1714; a key to identify the characters appeared in 1715. The general lines of the stories are corroborated by contemporary evidence. The early pages in the English version assert that Anthony Hamilton and his brother were persuaded to write these memoirs of their lively relative by Saint-Evremont. Interspersed with gay rhyming tetrameters, the introduction professes amusement as the goal of the ensuing pages, speaks in suave, mocking panegyric of the "indefinable brilliancy" of the hero, proclaims that "the order of time and disposition of the facts" will be disregarded, and justifies such procedure by means of laughable examples from the patron saint of biographers:[17]

"The celebrated Plutarch, who treats his Heroes like his Readers, begins the Lives of the one where he thinks fit, and diverts the Attention of the other, either to curious Antiquities, or agreeable Passages of Literature, which have not always a Coherence with his main Subject.

"Demetrius Poliorcetes for instance, as Plutarch tells us, was not, by much, so tall as his Father Antigonus. On the other hand, he acquaints us, that his reputed Father Antigonus was but his Uncle: But all this he relates, after he has begun his Life with a short Account of his Death. . . .

"I would not be thought in all this to have an Intention to find fault with the Historian to whom, of all the Ancients, we are most obliged: This was only meant to authorize my manner of Writing a Life, more extraordinary than any he has transmitted to us."

Hamilton is adept at narration. The second chapter, for example, opens with Grammont and a friend penniless at the siege of Trino, and uses Grammont's bewailing of his situation as an excuse to turn from the middle of things to his early life.[18] Episodes of love, war, and wit at the courts of Turin and of London center around the gay count, this impudent, brilliant, gaming, cheating Lothario. The interest of narrator and actor alike might be briefly defined as breeding, modified by good breeding. Scandalous histories flow from Anthony Hamilton's pen so merrily and inexhaustibly that one may easily understand Saint-Simon's belief that even Grammont's worst enemies would not have dared to publish them. Yet the total impression left by the memoirs is that they are merely reminiscences, long ago and far away, of gay uncles and ancestors, in which every event is interpreted with a witty lack of charity. The verve and finesse of

[17] 1714 ed., tr. Abel Boyer, pp. 2-3.

[18] "In those Days," Grammont's account begins, "things were not managed in France, as at the present time." Even in Boyer's clumsy translation, the parallel here to the famous opening of *A Sentimental Journey* is obvious. Laurence Sterne's debt to Hamilton is a profitable subject for speculation; it is amusing to note in passing, among odd literary genealogies, that Sterne for his informal, digressive, confiding, fantastic style has Plutarch as grandfather.

the turns in thought is almost breath-taking, from Lord Robarts—who[19] "under the pretence of a pilgrimage to Saint Winifred the virgin and martyr, who was said to cure women of barrenness . . . did not rest, until the highest mountains in Wales were between his wife and the person who had designed to perform this miracle in London, after his departure"—to the comic wedding-bells that conclude the whole (p. 320): "and the Chevalier de Grammont, as the reward of a constancy he had never before known, and which he never afterwards practised, found Hymen and Love united in his favour, and was at last blessed with the possession of Miss Hamilton."

The French memoirs and romances, then, through Mrs. Manley and Anthony Hamilton, infuse into life-writing in England a certain leaven, a gaiety and intimacy and witty malice which this brace of writers probably carried too far, but which acted as much-needed correctives to the solemn and somnolent tones affected by their graver forebears.

Madame d'Aulnoy and Mrs. Manley, prolific themselves, have numerous imitators. "Secret history," "Secret memoirs," or "Life and amours," in the first third of the century, become almost compulsory titles for commercially profitable pseudo-biographies.[20] One anonymous writer combines at least four fashions in biography in a single title: *Modern Amours: or, a secret history of the adventures of some persons of the first rank. Faithfully related from the author's own knowledge of each transaction. With a key prefixed.* (1733).

The other great group of stories in the form of biography is made up of the accounts of lives spent in strange lands and far

[19] 1846 ed., p. 171. Boyer's 1714 ed. differs in phrasing.

[20] cf. *Polish Manuscripts: or the secret history of the reign of John Sobieski*, 1700; *The secret history of the most renowned Q. Elizabeth and the E. of Essex*, 1708; *A secret history of one year* [1688], 1714; *The secret history of the White-Staff, being an account of affairs under the conduct of some late ministers*, 1714; *The secret history of the Prince of the Nazarenes and two Turks*, 1721, 3d ed.; *The Persian anecdotes: or, secret memoirs of the Court of Persia*, 1730; *The secret history of Mama Oello, Princess Royall of Peru. A new Court novel* [about Ann, eldest daughter of George II], 1733; *The secret history of Zeokinisul* [Louis XV], 1761; *The secret history of the Green Rooms*, 1790. A similar list could be made for the "Life and amours" type. There is a sharp decline in biographies with such titles in the last two-thirds of the century.

travels. One writer, Penelope Aubin, exactly combines the two forms of life-and-amours and life-and-adventures.[21] Like Daniel Defoe and the modern cheap newspaper, she attains popularity by assuming a rigid moral attitude while narrating immoral acts at which she ostentatiously shudders. She gives a pessimistic picture of the age in England, and rails against those qualities she so well exemplifies; then she turns her hand to writing her romances of salaciousness blended with preaching, and bitterly proclaims that they will not be believed because some of the characters are virtuous. For her ability to spin a flimsy web anew, to weave a complicated tissue from the very threads she has so often used before, Mrs. Aubin was well christened Penelope.

By this time it is sufficiently evident how much the new trends in biography owe to France.[22] Richard Steele had already ridiculed the authenticity and provenance of current memoirs in 1709, when Isaac Bickerstaff writes from the Grecian Coffeehouse on October 21:[23]

"The first whose merits I shall inquire into, are some merry gentlemen of the French nation, who have written very advantageous histories of their exploits in war, love, and politics, under the title of memoirs. I am afraid I shall find several of these gentlemen tardy, because I hear of them in no writings but their own. . . . There are others of that gay people who (as I am informed) will live half a year together in a garret, and write a history of their intrigues in the court of France. . . . I do hereby give notice to all booksellers and translators whatsoever, that the word 'Memoir' is French for a novel; and to require of them, that they sell and translate it accordingly."

If Steele is correct in making the French responsible for the blurring of the bounds between memoir and novel, he has yet not told the whole truth. The archculprit was to be found at

[21] For a list of her interesting titles, cf. Bibliography.

[22] cf. d'Aulnoy, Manley, Hamilton, Aubin, Prévost, "Peter Marteau," and later in the century *Memoirs of a noble foreigner* (1752), Charlotte Lennox, Susanna Dobson, and Pineau-Duclos.

[23] *The Tatler,* ed. G. A. Aitken, 4 vols., 1898, Vol. II, pp. 248-9.

home, and his name is Daniel Defoe. What the French accomplished in rendering fictitious the biographical *genres* of memoirs, secret histories, and amours, Defoe achieved for the life-and-adventures type. More than any other novelist of the century, with the possible exception of Laurence Sterne, he changed the direction of biography, and it may as well be admitted at once that his influence was bad. Through Defoe's mastery of the technique of biography and his application of it to fiction, the art of the novel was greatly advanced. But, in the opposite direction, his genius led biographers astray. He is the great master in the art of telling a lie; this gift is no fit legacy for biographers. Almost to the same extent that novels written in his school seem more credible than earlier romances, so biographies written under his influence arouse more doubt, skepticism, or sheer bewilderment as to their authenticity. In the strange and authentic adventures, the faithful and surprising histories that fell from the press between 1700 and 1750, the boy has cried Wolf once too often, and all the asseverations in the world cannot dislodge our doubt regarding their truth.

Yet no figure serves better than Daniel Defoe's in showing how interdependent are the two forms of biography and the novel. He himself, after scrutinizing the artless memoirs of the late seventeenth century, copied even their artlessness. In this game of making his own fabrications more believable than another man's truths, he imitates reality so exactly that at times he seems to vanish as a creative personality. Arthur Wellesley Secord remarks of him:[24]

"He writes in imitation of true records. If the narratives of the military careers of the Cavalier and of Carleton are to pass as authentic, they must resemble history; if *Robinson Crusoe* and *Captain Singleton* are to receive credence they must resemble the genuine accounts of travellers and adventurers. Obviously these genuine records, whether of military activity or of travel, have little to offer as models of well designed plot.

"*Robinson Crusoe,* as others have remarked, imitates life in its very shapelessness."

[24] *Studies in the narrative method of Defoe,* University of Illinois, 1924, p. 232.

Defoe mimics the actual accounts and biographies of the seventeenth century even in his titles. *Robinson Crusoe* was published as *The life and strange surprising adventures*; *Colonel Jack* as *The history of the most remarkable life, and extraordinary adventures, of the truly honourable Colonel Jaque, vulgarly call'd, Colonel Jack*; and *Jonathan Wild* with the title-page, indignant against imposture, of *The true and genuine account of the life and actions of the late Jonathan Wild; not made up of fiction and fable, but taken from his own mouth, and collected from papers of his own writing.* Very seldom indeed, and then almost as if by accident, does Defoe drop the mask in this game of meticulous authenticity:[25]

"Nor is it of any Concern to the Reader, whether it be an exact historical Relation of real Facts, or whether the Hero of it intended to present us, at least in part, with a moral Romance: On either Supposition it is equally serviceable for the Discouragement of Vice, and the Recommendation of Virtue."

Disconcertingly enough, Defoe's art that conceals art conceals also the artist. The attempt to establish a corpus for his work is doomed to failure, for he is most himself when he is least discoverable. We need not stop to argue, therefore, as to whether Defoe or George Carleton wrote Carleton's *Memoirs* (1728). Here it is enough to call by the name of Defoe that ability to present history, geography, politics, horror, or argument in biographical terms, making a bare account vivid by living a life over in the imagination in its most minute and exact details. This is the gift that can take the conventional *vie-et-amours* type and create, if not in *Roxana*, at least in *Moll Flanders*, a masterpiece in the form of realistic autobiography.

The productions attributed to Defoe, varied though their purposes may be, fall in a surprising number of cases into the biographical mold. Genuine "memoirs," in the sense of contemporary history observed by an individual, he presents in *Memoirs of John Duke of Melfort* (1714), *Memoirs of a cavalier* (1720) and *Memoirs of an English officer . . . by Capt. George Carleton* (1728). His flair for the analysis of politics and diplomacy at

[25] *Colonel Jack,* 1741 ed., Pref., p. iv.

home and abroad, which has never received adequate notice, is evident in the *Memoirs of publick transactions in the life and ministry of his Grace the D. of Shrewsbury* (1718), *Some account of the life . . . of George Henry Baron de Goertz* (1719), and *Memoirs of the life of Prince Menzikoff* (1727). In *An impartial history of the life and actions of Peter Alexowitz* (1723) he turns Russian military history into a fast-moving, crisp narration of battles and campaigns. Political satire also he casts into biographical form in *The glorious life and actions of St. Whigg* (1708) and *The political history of the devil* (1726). He experiments with public curiosity in such productions as *The history of the life and adventures of Mr. Duncan Campbell,* the deaf-and-dumb London prophet (1720) and *The Dumb Philosopher: or, Great Britain's Wonder . . . Dickory Cronke* (1719). This last-named work takes full advantage of the traditions of ecclesiastical biography in its detailed account of the religious death and pious meditations of its hero; and if we can believe that the *Remarkable passages in the life of a private gentleman* (1708) is the work of Defoe, we owe to him an important experiment in subjective life-writing.

In contrast to such devout soul-searching are the numerous sensational tracts ascribed to him. From the lives of the pirates Captain Avery (1719) and John Gow (1725), from the biography of a converted thief (1728) or the lives of the famous robbers John Sheppard (1724) and Jonathan Wild (1725), it is the easiest of transitions to *The life, adventures, and piracies of the famous Captain Singleton* (1720).

As soon as Defoe had perfected his technique, it became the common property of all the professional scribblers of London. Defoe's devices—it seems fair enough—were turned even against himself, as in *The life and strange surprizing adventures of Mr. D—— DeF—, of London, Hosier, who has liv'd above fifty years by himself, in the kingdoms of North and South Britain. The various shapes he has appear'd in, and the discoveries he has made for the benefit of his country* (1719), in which Crusoe and his man Friday upbraid him for portraying them as he does, and Defoe is trounced for being a turncoat in politics and religion.

Among the numerous biographies and pseudo-biographies which deliberately or accidentally resemble Defoe's productions, few warrant detailed consideration. It is enough to remember that he helped to teach biographers—and he himself learned from biographers—the manner of presenting geography and history entertainingly by means of a thread of personal narrative,[26] that his inventory method of listing small and exact details became common technique in giving solidity to real as well as to imagined histories,[27] and that the success of his works undoubtedly inspired many genuine soldiers, sailors, and adventurers, in the subsequent fifty years, to publish their own actual stories.[28] Defoe gave a voice to the eighteenth century Londoner; by producing works that exactly reflected middle-class tastes and outlook, he taught them to express themselves.

Two or three artisans in the life-and-adventures school of Defoe, however, stand out from the mass.[29] By far the best biography of the sort that Defoe might have written is *The life and surprizing adventures of James Wyatt, born near Exeter, in Devonshire, in the year 1707. . . . Written by himself. Adorn'd with copper plates* (1748). The life is composed because the hero is tired of recounting to all his friends how he escaped from the Spaniards. Wyatt is ingenuous, cheerful, disarming. He admits that his ability to blow the trumpet and beat the drums, his good looks and his good

[26] cf. *Life of Sethos*, 1732; *Memoirs of the Count de Forbin*, 1731; *Travels of Edward Brown*, 1739; and *Memoirs of Major Edward McGauran*, 1786. cf. also in connection with life-and-adventures, the first half of Chap. IV, *passim*.

[27] James Sutherland, his latest biographer, says in *Defoe*, 1937, p. 245: "He can still look facts in the face. There is nothing that he better likes doing. . . . He took a quite un-puritanical delight in experience for its own sake." cf. in this connection *The Hermit: or, the unparalled sufferings and surprising adventures of Mr. Philip Quarll*, 1727; John Drummond's *Memoirs of Sir Ewen Cameron*, wr. 1733; *The travels and adventures of James Massey*, 1733; *The life and adventures of Matthew Bishop*, 1744; and particularly *The life and surprizing adventures of James Wyatt*, 1753, discussed later in this chapter.

[28] cf. *A short history of the life of Major John Bernardi*, 1729; *Memoirs of Mr. George Fane, a London merchant, who suffered three years of slavery in the country of Algiers*, 1746; *Memoirs of Capt. Peter Drake*, 1755; Henderson's *Memoirs of James Keith, Field-Marshal*, 1758; *The Sufferings of William Green, ca.* 1774; *Memoirs of the life and gallant exploits of the old Highlander, Serjeant Donald Macleod*, 1791; *A narrative of the sufferings of James Bristow*, 1793.

[29] cf. particularly Ambrose Gwinett, *post* 1730; Gilbert Langley, 1740; Hannah Snell, 1750.

disposition, get him out of some tight scrapes. In two years (1741-1743) he manages to crowd in several lifetimes of adventures as a sailor on the privateer Revenge, a prisoner in Spain, a fugitive in a small cockleshell-boat trying to make Madeira from the Canaries, and a prisoner among the infidels on the Barbary Coast. The reader is inclined to agree with him when he writes (p. 175):

"The Hardships I endur'd among the Moors, (which were exceeding great, and such as I believe so many Men hardly ever underwent before) being added to the Sufferings before-mention'd, I believe I may venture to affirm, that no one Man ever went through such a Variety of Hardships besides myself."

Through it all he is cheerful and light-hearted. In the game of privateering hide-and-seek, the sailors make all sorts of reckless sallies for the sake of a little wine or adventure. After chasing a Portuguese vessel which thought them Algerine pirates, they climb aboard and are rewarded with a cask of wine by the relieved Portuguese (pp. 19-20):

"Our Ship came up to us in less than an Hour, and we took our Boat and went aboard. Our Captain, finding one of us missing, said, I hope none of you are hurt by the Shot, where is Jones? for he saw the Portuguese fire at us. Our Master answer'd we are all safe but him, and he is dead at the Bottom of the Boat. As we came along Side, our Ship's Company look'd over the Gunnel of the Ship and began to pity him, saying he was the first Man that had the Misfortune to be kill'd.

"They let down the Tekel to hoist him in, and the Man who took him in his Arms to lay him on the Deck, said, he was sure he was not quite dead, for he could perceive he breath'd. After he had laid him on the Deck, he turn'd him over, to see where he was wounded; but our Master coming over the Ship's Side, said, Pox take him, don't trouble yourself any more about him; it is the Portuguese Wine, and not their Balls, that has made him in this Condition; he is only dead drunk: Which made our Ship's Company laugh heartily."

War on the Spanish peninsula James Wyatt ordinarily treats as a pleasant hit-or-miss affair. The Spaniards they meet simply throw rocks at them (p. 34):

"As soon as we landed, the Men that had thrown Stones at us ran away. We march'd up in very good Order to the Cellar where we thought to have found the Wine; but, when we came there, it was all taken away. There were several Womens Shifts in the Place, which we took, and put on over our other Apparel, which caus'd us to make a very comical Appearance."

And no Defoe hero could be more exact in listing his booty (p. 36):

"I brought on board, for my Part of the Plunder, a new Smock, a Bell-metal Pestle and Mortar, two Pewter Plates, and a few Onions, which was more than was got by any other Person."

He is no less detailed with regard to his wounds (p. 46):

"As soon as they saw me they began to fire at me from every Side. I was inform'd, after I was taken Prisoner, that they fir'd above three Hundred Shot at me, though they wounded me but in nine Places, *viz.* five Small-Shot lodg'd between my Shoulders, three in the Poll of my Neck, and one Ball graz'd on my Left Shoulder; besides the Ball which I had before receiv'd in my Right Shoulder, and had almost gone through it."

Wyatt sees the world with some of that rare matter-of-fact clarity that is Defoe's and Boswell's secret (pp. 39-40):

"We kept rowing for our Lives, till we thought we were out of Danger; then we lay upon our Oars, and threw our Deep-Sea-Line over board, to try if we could find any Bottom, but found none. When we had haul'd in the Line, the Master order'd me to sound, BRITONS *strike home,* which I did [on the trumpet]: But while I was sounding, a Ball came from the Castle and graz'd in the Water about fifty Yards astern of us. It rose again, and came in at the Stern of the Boat, between the Master and myself. We being all in our Shirts, it took off the Belly of mine, but did me no other Damage. It shot off the Sleeve of one Thomas Pennyston, whose Mother kept a Poulterer's Shop at Kensington; and took off the Leg and Thigh of another Man, who row'd at the Bow Oar. He liv'd about two Hours after we got on board, and then expir'd."

His naïveté is sometimes indistinguishable from humor (p. 12):

"When I came to our Ship, I found one of our Midshipmen (whose Name I have forgot) was drowned in *Catwater,* in endeavouring to swim ashore. He was buried very decently in the new Churchyard, in Plymouth; and those of our Men that made the best Appearance, and which we were sure would not run away, attended at the Funeral."

With no introspection, no sentimental passages, no descriptions of personal relationships, he presents the story of a true-born Englishman in straightforward style. Action was in his blood: he was a woolcomber and dyer near Bath for three years (p. 9):

"during which Time I married, and liv'd very well: But Mr. Motet coming into the Town with his Collection of wild Beasts, and wanting a Trumpeter, I agreed to go with him, and travell'd near four Years in that Capacity."

Thanks to luck, practical accomplishments, and a sunny disposition, he survives all his hardships and returns to England to tell about water-monsters in African lakes, called Pesiengoni, which, when captured, "fetch heavy Sighs, and cry with a mournful, yet charming Tone, very musical, and something resembles the Voice of a Woman" (p. 169). Nor does Wyatt forget, any more than Robinson Crusoe, to thank Providence in occasional afterthoughts (p. 175): "But, far be it from me to mention my Sufferings with Murmuring or Discontent; that were to be dissatisfy'd with the Dispensations of the Divine Being, whose Mercies to all his Creatures, and me in particular, are numberless as the Sand on the Sea Shore!"

So, with his phonetic spelling and bad grammar, James Wyatt brings his strange adventures to a close. At the end he is about to sail for Jamaica to exhibit a new-fangled electrical machine, promising to print the future adventures which he is confident will happen to him. To such a choice spirit, following his star with a merry heart, further exciting incredibilities must certainly have occurred, and he must have met them with a casual competence. It is as if Sancho Panza were to experience and recount the wanderings of Ulysses.

A very small distance indeed lies between the real world of James Wyatt and the imaginary world of Edward Brown. *The travels of Edward Brown*[30] has been attributed to John Campbell.

[30] 1739. Quotation from 1753 2-vol. ed.

If this attribution is true, Campbell is to be complimented on his skill in building the illusion of reality, for the reader is soon persuaded to accept the actual existence of the adventurous Brown. As he drifts further from his English moorings, and Rouen, Geneva, Venice, even Malta, fade to the northwest, his character changes. His adventures in Africa are interesting in themselves and are well described; nor does he pass over perfunctorily the characters of his friends—Hassan the Arab prince, the French surgeon in Ethiopia, Johnson his faithful body-servant, or Signor Ephraim the Armenian merchant-philosopher.

"He is equally an Admirer of Men and Things," writes his editor (Pref., p. ix), who may also have composed the narrative that follows, "examines both candidly, and wherever he can be suspected of erring, it is on the right Side. He had it seems a great Delight in collecting scattered Pieces of History of all sorts, and was as well pleased to contemplate the Steadiness and solid Prudence of a Dutch Skipper, as the wonderful Variety of Adventures which have happened to Princes, Publick Ministers or Favourites, of which however we find Instances in his Writings."

Alexander Pope was fond of this biography of romantic adventure, and with good reason. *The travels of Edward Brown* should be better known, not only because it is an amusing book, but because it reveals a man who is a philosopher, an adventurer, a virtuoso, almost a poet; above all, a man of the world, of an open and pleasant temper.

Along with Defoe and John Campbell, a third writer should be named to contend for the title of *fabricator maximus*—William Rufus Chetwood. Interested in the theater, he wrote a slipshod life of Ben Jonson, and paragraph lives of playwrights to prefix to old plays which he published; in various editions of compilations of theatrical history, he twitted the laborious historian Gerard Langbaine for inaccuracy at one time, and on his own account passed on hearsay anecdotes at another. But his best work fitted into the Defoe pattern. *The voyages, travels and adventures of William Owen Gwin Vaughan, Esq; with the history of his brother Jonathan Vaughan, six years a slave in Tunis* (1736) is ascribed to Chetwood. It is a novel, so well told and realistic that one is inclined to accord to its author the honor of having also written what ranks among the *chefs-d'oeuvre* of this whole species of tall stories made credible: *The voyages and adventures of Captain Robert Boyle, in several parts of the world* (1726). Boyle—or Chetwood—convinces the reader by introducing into his wildest yarns some arresting little touch of local color that makes it impossible to doubt his experience. How unusual is his dedication to Sir William Young, which says in part:[31]

"The People of Mexico, every Year, offer'd something to their Emperor in Token of Vassalage: and frequently, among other Things worthy the Notice of a King, he receiv'd even Sacks of Common Earth, from those Persons that could not afford a nobler Offering.

"But they, like me, did what was in their Power, with an Expression in their Language, which signified, I would it were more worthy of your Acceptance."

As the story of thrilling escapes and separated lovers unfolds in Africa, Brazil, and all parts of the known world, the hero frankly admits his inventive powers in scenes so well conceived that the reader accepts them as actual. The Irish renegado captain of Barbary pirates, who captures him, "shook his Head, and with a Smile, said I was very ready at a Lie" (p. 20). Yet even when the Irish captain is quite aware of Boyle's gift, his prisoner can escape from his difficulties by flattery and fabrication. "As soon as I saw your Honour upon Deck giving Command," Boyle tells him (p. 20), "I thought you had the look of a Gentleman, (tho by the By he had a damn'd Tyburn Face.)" And later, Boyle—or Chetwood—blends the admitted lie with the lie concealed to gain credibility for his story (p. 41):

"Our Story brought us to Town, and I was very much pleas'd, for I was both tir'd in inventing Lies to amuse him, and riding after the Moorish manner, with one's Knees almost to one's Mouth; and there's no altering the Stirrups."

Few genuine travellers can record details as convincing as those which Chetwood has picked up from some source or other and woven into his romance (pp. 254-5):

---

[31] Quotations from 1744 Liverpool ed.

"As we approach'd the Town [Antwerp], he and my Indians were surpriz'd to see the manner of begging. The Boys and Girls would run before you, and of a sudden stop short, stand upon their Heads, and clap their Hands, saying their Prayers all the while."

[p. 102] "I could not forbear smiling to see the Providence of the Moors, Walking one Day about a Mile from Mequinez, it began to rain prodigiously; I got under a Tree to shelter my self from the Tempest. But I observ'd several of the Natives undress themselves with a great deal of Precipitation, make up their Cloaths in a Bundle, and sit on 'em stark naked; and all their Care was to keep them from the Wet, leaving their Naked Bodies expos'd to the Fury of the Storm. When it ceas'd, they walk'd a little Way till their Bodies were dry, and then dres'd themselves. If a Man were to do so in England, he would be counted a Madman, or a Fool, yet I must own I thought 'em in the right; for be the Storm ever so violent, yet when it's over, they pursue their Journey with dry Cloaths on their Backs."

Thanks to the theatrical knowledge of his creator Chetwood, Captain Boyle quotes Shakespeare smoothly, and it is possible that the influence of Shakespearean comedy accounts for the ingenuity in plot construction and the neat tying up of all threads at the end in a series of melodramatic coincidences, recognitions, and long-lost children. Robert Boyle's adventures are therefore much nearer perfection in formal structure than, for example, most of Defoe; and their blending of romance with travel, of *Moll Flanders* with Hakluyt and *Captain Singleton,* so exactly hit the popular taste that they ran through at least six editions during the century.[32]

[32] No more than passing mention need be accorded to the biographical framework used to support voyages into imaginary countries, philosophical romances, Utopias and satires. *Gulliver's Travels* is the obvious example here, but Swift had many followers and a few predecessors. cf. *The improvement of human reason, exhibited in the life of Hai Ebn Yokdhan. . . . Translated from the original Arabick by Simon Ockley, 1708; The life of Sethos. Taken from private memoirs of the ancient Egyptians. Translated from a Greek manuscript. . . . By Mr. Lediard, 1732; The travels and adventures of James Massey. Translated from the French, 1733; The memoirs of Signor Gaudentio di Lucca, 1737,* and *Memoirs of the life and adventures of Tsonnonthouan, a king of the Indian nation called Roundheads, ca.* 1763. Verisimilitude in such accounts was at last entirely

The interplay between Defoe's productions and the popular biographies of the first part of the century is obvious. The relationships between biographers and the other important novelists of the period are more difficult to trace.[33] Yet if their impact was not so immediate and direct as that of Defoe, their influence was in the main less harmful to biography as an art and even as a science.

Samuel Richardson obviously impinges upon biography in the *Memoirs of the life of Lady H—— the celebrated Pamela* (1741), which assumes standard biographical form and gives an account of Pamela's upbringing, her conduct as a servant, her marriage, her children, and her acceptance by society. This biography of an imaginary character must, of course, be fictitious; but James Parry publishes his own actual memoirs as *The true Anti-Pamela . . . In which are inserted, his amours with the celebrated Miss —— of Monmouthshire* (1742). This curious title is explained by the actions of Parry's lady-love. In bringing a lawsuit against him, he maintains, for kissing her, she is the exact opposite of Richardson's Pamela. Parry's Parthenissa "is rich, and kept me for her Pleasure several Years, still leading me on with the Thoughts of marrying me, till I was almost ruin'd, and then she jilted me."

Such obvious debts to Richardson as these two productions show are of little importance. More significant is the influence of his epistolary form and his psychological insight. By writing *Pamela* as a series of confidential letters, Samuel Richardson undoubtedly popularized an admirable vehicle for the confessions

abandoned. Inanimate objects were made to narrate their own life-histories, so that Doctor Arbuthnot sketched in biographical form, from birth and education to death, the chapter headings for *The life and adventures of Don Bilioso de L'Estomac;* and largely under the influence of Charles Johnston's popular *Chrysal; or the adventures of a guinea* (1760), autobiographical in form, within the space of twenty-five years the biographical chorus was swelled by the piping voices of a bank-note, a corkscrew, a black coat, a rupee, and a pin.

[33] Isolated instances of interrelationships, such as the debt of the autobiographer Silas Told to Bunyan, or the parallel between Fawcett's *Life of Oliver Heywood* (1796) and *The Vicar of Wakefield,* are not here considered. Goldsmith as biographer will be found in Chap. VI.

and analytical autobiographies of the century.[34] A series of letters written to a close friend naturally sets a tone of intimate revelation; and the hypothesis of a sympathetic reader may have made easier the unburdening of the heart. Moreover, *Pamela* is in some ways a declaration of independence for feminine sensibility; although his influence here cannot be established precisely, Richardson must have been partially responsible for the unusual number of eighteenth century autobiographies by women, with their leisurely and delicate self-analysis, their elevated sentiments, and their tender emotions.

Smollett also had his little circle of imitators, although here again it is difficult to determine what, exactly, Charles Dibdin owes Smollett for his vivid description of Bath, or Jane Elizabeth Moore for the collection of caricatured guests who crowd the pension at the spa where she was taking the waters, or John Macdonald for the impudent buoyancy of his picaresque career as a gentleman's valet, or Charlotte Charke for the sordid vitality of her scenes as sausage-seller and puppeteer.[35] What relations, for instance, exist between *The expedition of Humphry Clinker,* the travel chapters in *The history of Tom Jones,* the stagecoach expeditions to Oxford and elsewhere in Boswell's *Life of Johnson,* and such an accomplished and good-natured account as the following, drawn from Charles Dibdin's *Musical tour?* The chapter title itself—"Containing a journey to Oxford—with a description of a musician with good sense, and a clergyman without pride"—shows how much the author has learned from the novel-

[34] cf. Charlotte Charke, Mary Robinson, Charles Dibdin, Thomas Amory, George Anne Bellamy, Fanny Burney. See also Orrery's *Swift* and the Rev. John Martin's autobiography. Frances Sheridan's *Memoirs of Miss Sidney Bidulph. Extracted from her own journal, and now first published* (1761) was published under Richardson's aegis, is in diary form, though addressed to "My dear and ever-beloved Cecilia," and is circumstantial in its attempts to establish authenticity. But cf. also Evelyn's *Margaret Blagge Godolphin* (ca. 1680), *Prince Mirabel* (1712), and Colley Cibber's *Apology* (1740), written as letters before *Pamela* (1740-1741).

[35] These four biographers are separately considered elsewhere in this volume. See Bibliography and Index. Also cf. Mark Moore, discussed later in this chapter; and *The life of T. Smollett, M.D.,* 1797, by Dr. John Moore, the author of *A view of the commencement and progress of romance.*

ists. For economy, wit, and style his own travelogue suffers little in comparison with theirs or with Boswell:[36]

"On the seventeenth of March, 1787, I left the regions of smoke for the regions of accomplishment. Nothing passed on the road worthy your notice. The conversation of the passengers in the stage-coach was in the usual stile. Almost every object brought with it some remark. We admired, as usual, the entrance of Sion-House, the convenient situation for star-gazing of Mr. Herschel —we sighed, as usual, to think on human depravity, on contemplating the gibbets upon Hounslow-Heath; and we lamented their fate who were poisoned at Salt-Hill. The very dinner was as usual—some soup which might have been mistaken for a dose of salts relished with leeks, and a boiled leg of mutton scarcely warmed through. At length the majestic view of lofty steeples, towers, and turrets demanded our admiration—and we presently arrived at Oxford."

The autobiographical element in Smollett's own novels is marked enough to have received the doubtful honor of German monographs.[37] If Smollett's personal acquaintance with surgeons and sailors imparts a certain hard-headed coldness to his fictions, much the same philosophy, derived from much the same background, is found in the actual *Memoirs of his own lifetime* (1747) by Dr. William Houstoun. Houstoun is a Scot, the youngest of fifteen children, who studies medicine in Holland under Boerhaave and follows that with midwifery in Paris; he leads a wild life in London among the nobility and the wits (Arbuthnot is his good friend), and finally, to avoid being jailed for debts, he goes to Sierra Leone as the colony doctor. The memoirs end with Houstoun in Jamaica, engaged in various trades, and embroiled

---

[36] 1788, pp. 15-16. cf. also James Lackington's coachride, partially quoted in Chap. III, or his treatment of a runaway on the road near Durham (*Memoirs*, 1791, pp. 287-93); J. C. Pilkington's detailed journey to Scotland (*Real Story*, 1760), which may stand beside Smollett's account in *Humphry Clinker*; and the account, in Letitia Pilkington's *Memoirs* (1748, opening of Vol. II), of the journey from Chester to London with a Member of Parliament, two gentlemen of the law, and a Welsh parson who "made me a present of a gingerbread-nut curiously wrapped up in white paper."

[37] cf., e.g., *Autobiographisches in Smollett's "Roderick Random,"* Max Leuschel, Leipzig, 1903.

in lawsuits.[38] He and Smollett might well have been twins. Tough, straightforward, uncouth, independent, a quoter of scraps of Latin, Houstoun is cynical in his attitude; he thinks that pride and money make the world go round; and he can tell a story with the detached brutality and swift action of his Scottish compatriot. Here is a passing incident during a period when Houstoun was in hiding for his debts (pp. 125-6):

"At this Juncture I withdrew into a solitary, but pleasant, little Retirement near Sunbury, by myself, revolving in my Mind what had passed, which seemed to me still more like Dreams than Realities; when one Day the Lords Hervey, Drogeda, and Johnstone found me out, and made me a Visit; but I could not entertain them at my little Hut, so we went to the Tavern at Sunbury. After drinking hard, Lord Drogeda called a Fidler, who was noisy enough with his Fiddle, which my Lord seemed to like greatly, caress'd the Fellow, and gave him several Shillings and Halfcrowns; when all of a sudden, without any Provocation that we knew of, he stuck the Fellow dead on the Spot [Houstoun himself had "stuck" an attorney earlier in his career, and had laid him up in bed for a month], which could not possibly be foreseen, or prevented by any of the Company, having no such Suspicion. This sad Accident gave me great Trouble, and much more so, as my Name was again brought on the Carpet, that was sinking into Oblivion. In short, had it not been for my Lord Falmouth's (Drogeda's Father-in-law) Interest and good Conduct, we all of us had certainly been obliged to have taken our Tryals for it: But all Affairs were made up, and the Widow handsomely provided for."

The most startling hybrid of the century, in the mixing of biography and the novel, occurs in the works of Smollett. Chapter 88 of *The adventures of Peregrine Pickle* (1751), by far the longest chapter in the whole work, consists of the "Memoirs of a lady of quality" which the original title-page had promised. Peregrine, while succoring a widow in distress, meets "the celebrated lady ———" who tells him this story-within-a-story of her life. The *Memoirs* are tailored to fit into the story of the hero's life as well

[38] The *Dictionary of National Biography* account of Houstoun seems unaware of this important autobiography as a source for his life.

as usual, for the eighteenth century novelist spent little pains over the joining of a story-within-a-story to the main narrative. When the lady finishes her tale, Peregrine and the company express their pleasure, though some of them say that she has not told everything (here the lady blushes) about her benefactions and generosities. Peregrine himself decides not to precipitate an affair with her, because her sentiments are too delicate and she insists upon too great devotion from her lovers, all of whom, he observes, act as if they had been bewitched.

Yet the imaginary Peregrine is here contemplating making love to a woman of flesh and blood—Frances Anne, Viscountess Vane (1713-1788), who paid Smollett to insert these *Memoirs* in his novel. *The history of a woman of quality: or, the adventures of Lady Frail* (1751) embroiders on her notorious career in 227 lubricious pages; and in the same year *An apology for the conduct of a lady of quality, lately traduc'd under the name of Lady Frail,* professes to answer the above libel. But little can be done to save the reputation of Viscountess Vane, least of all by the *Memoirs* which she, possibly with the aid of a compiler, turned over to Smollett. Her cold sneers at her husband's sufferings and shame, her sadism and nymphomania are obvious enough. The best that can be said for her shocking *Memoirs* is that once again biography outstrips fiction in its recording of truth, and that certain of her amazingly delicate psychological—or psychopathic—analyses surpass anything that is recorded for her gallant listener Peregrine Pickle.

Apart from Defoe, the two novelists who are the most influential in the development of English biography are Henry Fielding and Laurence Sterne. For Fielding, at any rate, this seems natural enough, for his technique as novelist adapts or parallels biographical methods in many ways. His titles are obviously modelled on the biographical tradition. *The history of Tom Jones* contains in its critical chapters much speculation and theory applicable to biography;[39] *Joseph Andrews* parodies Colley Cibber's *Apology* as

---

[39] cf. also Fielding's own biographer, Arthur Murphy, himself quite a theorist upon life-writing, who calls *Tom Jones* "fictitious biography" (p. 87, *Works*, 1762, Vol. I).

much as it parodies *Pamela; Jonathan Wild* assumes in the reader familiarity with the current criminal biographies that flooded London; and *Amelia* also refers to brief sensational lives. Fielding's tolerance toward peccadilloes, his flippant descriptive chapter-titles, his satirical methods, some of his later crusading zeal, and even his interjected confidential chapters to the reader, find their parallels in eighteenth century biography.[40]

For example, the *Memoirs of a young lady of family. Being a succinct account of the capriciousness of fortune, and an accurate survey of the heart of that incomprehensible animal, called man* (1758) begins with a preface to end prefaces. The authoress is disgusted with their custom of "forewarning thee that thou wilt find nothing astonishing, the utmost that is aimed at, is the being natural." She is glad that the public has outgrown airy romances; she defends the satiric novel; she points out that every character need not have a living original. And yet "the subject of the ensuing pages," she assures the reader, "is drawn principally from common life, and . . . the lady was an intimate acquaintance of the author's." The novelist, and particularly Fielding, may be detected in the descriptive chapter-heads, in the interjected Latin quotations, in the narrative in the first person although author and heroine are separated in the preface, and finally in Chapter I of Book II: "A bone for the criticks," which is an inept attempt at the interchapters of *Tom Jones*.

George Stevens acknowledges his borrowings openly:[41]

"The authors of *Joseph Andrews* and *Tristram Shandy* wrote themselves into reputation, and I believe got money by what they did; and really deserved it.—Ever since I have engaged in this work, I have endeavoured to copy one or both of their stiles, manners, or maxims; but I cannot fancy myself quite so clever."

[40] cf. *Memoirs of a young lady of family*, 1758; *The history of Tom Fool*, 1760; George Alexander Stevens's *Dramatic history of Master Edward, Miss Ann, and others*, 1785; Charles Dibdin's *Musical tour*, 1788; John Macdonald's *Travels*, 1790; and Dibdin's *The younger brother*, 1793.

[41] *The Dramatic History of Master Edward*, 1785, p. 126. The scene, for example, in which an author is browbeaten by a rich booby-squire who pretends to learning (pp. 167-81) is a subtle piece of rancor worthy of Lucian or any of the eighteenth century satirical novelists.

Frequently the biographies and pseudo-biographies of the period refer in admiration to Fielding or imitate him;[42] sometimes whole narratives will be modelled more closely upon Fielding than upon fact.[43]

Stevens is not confined in his enthusiasms to Henry Fielding alone. His *History of Tom Fool* (1760), which the *Dictionary of National Biography* calls "concealed autobiography," he had published with a dedication "To Tristram Shandy, Esq;" which begins: "Sir, The World waits with Impatience for your coming into it." And Charles Dibdin apologizes for his dilatory opening by writing:[44] "As Tristram Shandy was a long while employed on writing his history before he was born, so I shall be some time getting on with my MUSICAL TOUR before I set out." The long-delayed birth of Tristram Shandy was not wholly fortunate for biography.[45] Improvisation in the hands of a master is delightful; but when Sterne's style fell among imitators it frequently

---

[42] *Memoirs of the Count Du Beauval*, 1756, translator's preface; Dralloc's *Life of James Molesworth Hobart*, 1794. cf. the clergyman, Mr. Harvest, in Gilbert Wakefield's *Memoirs*, 1792 (1804 ed., pp. 52-8), consciously done in comparison with "the ever-memorable Parson Adams."

[43] *The life of Mr. John Van, a clergyman's son, of Woody, in Hampshire*, n.d., by G. S. Green. A novel in imitation of *Tom Jones*, this nevertheless contains an interjected chapter, "A brief account of the life and death of John Earl of Rochester," which follows historical fact. See also *The life and memoirs of Mr. Ephraim Tristram Bates*, 1756, which refers to *Joseph Andrews*.

[44] *Musical Tour*, 1788. Also, Dibdin's description of Calais, particularly of M. Dessein's inn, in *The professional life of Mr. Dibdin* (1803, Vol. I, pp. 186-7), is simply a rendering in biography of the material Sterne turns to more artful or fanciful use in the opening pages of *A sentimental journey*.

[45] cf. *An authentic detail of particulars relative to the late Duchess of Kingston*, 1788, which quotes Yorick, p. 74, and includes boisterous anecdotes in his style, as on pp. 77-81; the *Apology*, 1785, of George Anne Bellamy, who quotes and copies Sterne so enthusiastically; George Stayley's *Life and opinions*, 1762, and Charlotte Charke's autobiography, 1755, discussed later in this chapter. John Macdonald's *Travels*, 1790, should not be forgotten, for they contain the firsthand account of the death of Sterne.

The following titles should be added to show the surprising importance of Sterne in the development of biography: *The life and memoirs of Mr. Ephraim Tristram Bates*, 1759; *Genuine memoirs of Jane Elizabeth Moore . . . Her sentimental journey through Great Britain*, 1786; *The life, adventures, and opinions of Col. George Hanger*, 1801; and *Memoirs of the life of the Rev. Dr. Trusler, with his opinions*, 1806. At least three of these four titles precede genuine memoirs; all of them are Shandean.

resulted, as in *Tom Fool,* in something bubbling, maggoty-pated, and disguised past all recognition.

As the most flagrant example of theft from Laurence Sterne, the following passage from *The life and opinions of . . . Mr. George Stayley* (1762) should be compared with the birth of Tristram Shandy (p. 7):

"All I know of the matter is (and I only know that by information) that my mother, in the midst of her labour (or rather my labour; for I worked, they say for birth, like a Mole under ground) exclaimed with great vociferation,—Now, God bless thee, my child, but thou strugglest hard to get into a troublesome world!—And even with the word, as if she had uttered an oracle, —I dropped into the midwife's arms."

After justifying his typographical tricks by references to Yorick's tombstone and to Tristram Shandy's marbled page, and after "A digressive chapter, with a remark: Proper to be bound with Tristram Shandy; a work which every body reads and nobody understands," Stayley bites the hand that feeds him in his final judgment that Sterne is a disgrace to the clergy.

The influence of Sterne is much more fortunate and much less direct in *The real story of John Carteret Pilkington* (1760). Pilkington's account of his Irish great-uncle, Dr. Vanlewen in Cork, finds a predecessor in Uncle Toby, and it is hard to believe that the delicate and humorous touches in the description of the doctor's crotchets—his odd speech and the manner in which he lolls out his tongue, his potations and his confidences to his young relation when he is far gone in his cups—could have been handled with such delicate humor if Sterne had not first pointed the way.

Sterne's effusive tenderness, as it found expression in biography, is noticed elsewhere,[46] but it would not be possible to quit him without mention of the biography in which his sentimentality found fullest expression, the *Memoirs and anecdotes of Philip Thicknesse* (1788). Sterne's world is so real for Thicknesse that he uses its values as standards for judging incidents that happen to him. He had met John Wesley on a ship in a stormy passage between Savannah and Charleston. Fifty years later, crossing the Severn in a boat, he again meets the great revivalist who had led

[46] See particularly Chap. III.

him to forsake profanity; Thicknesse reminds Wesley of their earlier meeting (probably with the transports of a Sterne), but Wesley acts with cool indifference (Vol. I, p. 37) : ". . . now uncle Toby would not have done so; would he courteous reader? this was not Shandean indeed Mr John Westley. . . ." When, regarding the Reverend Dr. Dodd, on trial for the capital crime of forgery, Thicknesse retails the cruel remark of a certain Lord who "said he was going *'a parson hunting.'* . . . I hope therefore he was in at *the death,"* he concludes with (Vol. I, p. 230) "but Uncle Toby would not have said so—would he Yorick?"

In a wilderness among the American Indians, which he has refined into a Utopia worthy of Chateaubriand, a sudden revery of his mother's "departed shade" leads him to return to England. But it is in the natural nobility of the Jamaican slaves and the savage treatment of them by their white masters that Thicknesse's sentiment finds freest play. "The assembly of that Island," he writes (Vol. I, p. 82), "allowed seventy pounds for every pair of wild Negroes ears which were brought in." He thanks God that he himself "never gathered a single pair." To balance this, there is a sentimental story, of the finest water, of the slave on a sugar plantation killed by the first and last blow his master ever gave him. The slave's body cannot be buried until a negro, speaking for it, has said (Vol. I, p. 288, note) : "Good bye Massa, good bye Misiss, good bye gemem, me always serve you true Massa, my heart burn true Massa, and you never beat me no more than once, me sorry to die before me boil the crop; so Massa and Misiss went crying away. . . ."[47]

The biographers and autobiographers who learn most from romance and the novel are also tempted to write novels themselves. In this group may be placed Madame d'Aulnoy, Mrs. Manley, Sarah Fielding, Charlotte Lennox, Charlotte Charke, Thomas Amory, Charles Dibdin, George Alexander Stevens,

[47] cf. also the macabre anecdote of the "sentimental Soldier," Vol. I, pp. 240-9, an old sergeant shot for desertion, whose skull Thicknesse digs up; or the long "Story of the Wooden Gun" in Vol. II. Tracing of literary debts is usually profitless business, but one wonders whether the Sterne of the *Sentimental Journey* had himself ever read the *Life of Major John Bernardi,* 1729, with its little biographies of the brave Major General Mackay (p. 64) or of the ninety-year-old Colonel Anselm who is disgraced, and is found serving as a private sentinel.

Fanny Burney, Dr. John Moore, and Mary Robinson.[48] Nor should the genuine biographies written by Defoe and Goldsmith be forgotten in any complete consideration of the relations existing between biography and the novel. To separate romance from reality in the complete works of all of these authors, no less than the skill and data of the recording angels would suffice. As illustrations of the novelist's technique applied to biography, a few salient lives will here be considered at greater length.

Elizabeth Montague, after reading the first volume of Letitia Pilkington's *Memoirs* (1748), wrote characteristically:[49] "I am sorry to say the generality of women who have excelled in wit have failed in chastity." This combination, however, is not wholly unfortunate in biography. Any attempt to reduce Mrs. Pilkington to ethical consistency will end in Mrs. Montague's puzzled regret. The heroine of her own memoirs was wild and unpredictable; she delighted Dean Swift and disgusted him; she was moved by Milton and by low jests; she was desperate, treacherous, ungrateful, but she dreamed of sleeping in the Poet's Corner of Westminster Abbey, between the monuments to Shakespeare and Rowe; petty and spiteful, her last thought was to protect her son.

In a century which developed satire as an art, Letitia Pilkington was not behind in hate. The thread that runs through all three volumes of her memoirs is an unwavering loathing for her husband—"one of the greatest villains, with reverence to the priesthood be it spoken, that ever was wrapped up in crape." He was "ever rash, obstinate, and self-willed, and should I add treacherous, cruel, and ungrateful, I should not wrong the truth," she declares, and calls on Shakespeare to witness that she has set down naught in malice. To this monster, then, because of the "capricious temper" of her mother and the indifference of her father, a Dutch man-midwife, this young girl is married. Pilkington himself had hastened the match, if we may trust his wife's novelizing of her own life, by threatening to stab himself in despair if she refuses him. She resigns, therefore, her reading in

[48] See Bibliography for titles.

[49] Bibliographical note by J. Isaacs, 1928 ed. *Memoirs*, p. 472, ed. with Intro. by Iris Barry.

Pope and Shakespeare and Dryden—she particularly admired *Alexander's Feast*—to take over Pilkington's worldly goods: they consist of a harpsichord, a cat, and an owl.

Through the medium of Letitia's original poems, the young couple meet Patrick Delany, and through Doctor Delany they meet Swift. The anecdotes about Swift are vividly caught; they are recorded with that same curiosity and love of life which Fanny Burney infuses into *Evelina* and her own diaries. Swift treats her as a child, and, at their first dinner in the Deanery, before complimenting her for letting him make the coffee, he calls her "a damned, insolent, proud, unmannerly slut."[50] She is a little baffled by his rudeness, but esteems him nevertheless "polite." Later she recounts the scene at dinner when Swift calls a certain woman the nastiest old bitch ever seen, adding "except the company, Ladies!" (p. 237). And in the last volume she gives in convincing detail a raw and slanderous story of Swift's brutality to her. Her Dean Swift may not be a strictly historical copy, but her stories about him, with their dialogue and sharp detail, must have increased greatly the popular demand for her *Memoirs*.

One of the rarest merits in these *Memoirs* (as the gradations in the Swift anecdotes show) is the presentation of the change in the character of the heroine, the slow deterioration from a girl of high spirits and talent to a blackmailing, venomous, querulous prostitute. The sense of the passage of time is no less difficult to achieve in life-writing than it is necessary to the biographical illusion; Letitia Pilkington captures it. Her vivid pictures, characters, and conversations show conscious artistry: in attempting a full portrait of Cibber, she says (p. 207), "I think I cannot do it in a better manner than I have used in describing Doctor Swift— that is, to give him to my readers in his words and actions, as near as I can recollect them." Drama[51] and the novel have taught her to make her Irish landlady speak like an Irish landlady on the stage (p. 140)—"Arah, by my shoul (said the old dame)"— and to reveal a Bishop not only by making him talk phonetically, but by accenting his "make-up," like Pistol or Chaucer's Sum-

[50] 1928 ed., p. 53.

[51] e.g., she compares her husband, at various times, to Mr. Fribble and Sir Paul Plyant; and she quotes Shakespeare on all occasions.

moner: his countenance (p. 194) "was full of bubuckles and knobs and flames of fire," and he looked like the Spanish Friar.

In Dublin Swift adopts the young Pilkingtons as his protégés. Letitia pastes his letters from all the great men in a fine binding of Horace's *Epistles,* translated. More than once, and not unsuccessfully, she breathlessly matches wits with the Dean (p. 66 or p. 88). And after a walk in his garden, during which she catches him at his furtive charity, she reveres him as "the angel of Ireland" (p. 65). Swift introduces Pilkington to Alderman Barber in London, and uses him as a catspaw to bring out his poems directly instead of through Pope. According to the memoirs, Pilkington is finally arrested for publishing Swift's treasonable verse, but not before Letitia has joined him in London and has had an affair with the painter-critic James Worsdale—an affair which she blames on her husband, who, she says, played Pandarus in order to get grounds for a divorce. When this charming couple returns to Ireland, Pilkington again tries to compromise her by leaving her "undressed" in a summer-house with a fine gentleman, who (p. 122), "laying hold of my hand . . . began to address me in a most bombastic style, with fustian from exploded plays." This same gentleman assures her that her husband "begged I would be so kind as to make him a cuckold, so that he might be able to prove it, in order to a separation from you" (p. 124).

The world begins to fall away from her. Her father dies, and in a scene of Gothic emotionalism, when the sheriff's officers start their inventory and lay hold upon her father's coffin (p. 119): "I, almost wild with grief, ran after them: the coffin was open, and I raised my dear father in my arms, and, as if he could have heard me, asked him: 'Would he not protect his family?'" Dean Swift about this time also gives her up in contempt, for no reason that Letitia is ever capable of imagining; and Pilkington, now sure that she will inherit nothing, deserts her for the Widow Warren, locking up the garden of their little house, the library, and the tea chest, in order to spite his wife. "So I was left like a tame cat." She does not like "buxom Joan," as she calls the Widow Warren,[52]

[52] Was the figure, or the name, of the Widow Warren in Sterne's mind when he created the Widow Wadman?

and her desire to degrade her husband makes her confess—almost—that she has been unfaithful to him. Here are twisted passions (p. 133):

"But whether he is entitled to the horn or not must always be a secret: I hope some curious commentator will hereafter endeavour to find out the truth of it, for my mind gives me that

> I, like the classics, shall be read
> When time and all the world are dead."

She is now rapidly going down hill. Twelve watchmen break in her chamber door at two in the morning to find her reading a book with a gentleman. She takes lodgings, where, in a graphic scene, she is tempted to turn prostitute (pp. 136-7). Another gallant she knowingly distrusts because of "the various medicines in his apartment." And now the lovers come so thick and fast—churchmen and counsellors and travellers and lords—that as subscribers to her libellous memoirs they will keep this broken-down woman out of debtors' prison (p. 141):

"And if every married man who has ever attacked me does not subscribe to my *Memoirs,* I will without the least ceremony, insert their names, be their rank ever so high or their profession ever so holy."

Ireland is not enough for her; she journeys to London, where she lodges opposite White's chocolate house, so that she may send over notes to the friends whom she sees enter. And she continues to try her hand at writing, not only furnishing Mr. Worsdale with verse, interminable and competent, which he passes for his own; but actually persuading Dodsley to print her *Trial of Constancy* (p. 175) "by which I got above five guineas, and a very much greater happiness, the favour and friendship of the Poet Laureate."

Colley Cibber and the Earl of Chesterfield figure in the memoirs of notorious women in the eighteenth century so frequently that they almost become stock characters for the fatherly friend and the dangerous man of the world. Under Cibber's protection, Letitia's London career for a time becomes gay. There are subscriptions to be taken for her forthcoming volume of verse, and impromptu poems to be written for her friends, and visits from noblemen, especially "a pleasant droll gentleman, who was so old that he had been page to King James when he was Duke of York," and the handsome young Duke of Marlborough who gives her fifty pounds, and Mr. Rooke who told her really funny stories about Robert Walpole and the next day "fell down in an apoplectic fit, and instantly expired," and Dr. Turnbull, the Earl of Winchelsea, Sir John Ligonier, Chesterfield, and a petition to be presented to the Archbishop of Canterbury in the House of Lords on Christmas Day.

Time passes. Summer in London is hard on her, so she moves to cheaper lodgings in Grosvenor Square, where on Sundays she eats with the principal servants of many fine establishments, and learns much that may have helped her in writing her *Memoirs*. Then she is found living—innocently, of course—in the house of a procuress, and meets the future Lord Chief Justice Eyre. Increasingly, insensibly, she becomes immersed in the stews of London. "I have been a lady of adventure," she writes (p. 289), "and almost every day of my life produces some new one."

But her own adventures no longer suffice to fill her volumes, and she is forced to narrate the scandalous amours of others when her own begin to run out. Edmund Curll tries to enlist her as one of his purveyors of filth; and somehow—she is not very definite about it—she is suddenly in prison for debt. After a stay of nine weeks, she is liberated through Colley Cibber's efforts to get subscriptions for her; and after a memorable scene, through the help of Cibber, the young Marlborough, and the novelist Richardson, she is finally set up in a print-and-pamphlet shop in St. James, where (like Richardson) she will write letters for twelvepence on all subjects except the law, and will draw up petitions at the same rate. One of her first patrons is "Tom Brush," a nobleman in disguise, who has her write a love-letter for him; Lord Kingsborough is also generous. Yet most of London is miserly, and is also not sufficiently intimidated by her recriminations, so that her second volume ends with Billingsgate against bishops, cozeners, and people who give her no more than a guinea on petition. Yet her third volume will be even more exciting than the first two, she promises on pain of drowning her book "deeper than did ever plummet sound."

The third volume appeared posthumously. Letitia Pilkington died in 1750, an old woman who had not yet reached the age of forty. "Truly," she says (p. 345), "I mean to give both pleasure and offence: Lemon and Sugar is very pretty." In this third volume, a last impulse toward decency and fairness takes the shape of a split personality, as if the bright, gay girl she had been were surveying dispassionately, with wonder, the harridan she had become. She begins to speak of herself as "poor Letitia" and finally laments that "poor Letitia is become the football of fortune" (p. 424). She is even aware of her reputation as a blackmailer (p. 347): "I was very well diverted with Mr Woodward's *Coffee* [like Foote's "Dish of Tea" and his "Chocolate"], and humorous description of me, crying: Subscribe, or else I'll paint you like the Devil!" And in the midst of invective and wild literary criticism she observes her own style and moods (p. 359): "I am no Methodist either in writing or religion. Sometimes irregularities please; shapeless rock, or hanging precipice, present to the poetic imagination more inspiring dreams than could the finest garden. . . . I am, in short, an heteroclite, or irregular verb, which can never be declined or conjugated."

Earlier, also, in an odd conversation between "I" and "Myself" (evidence again of her split personality), she had defended her borrowings, quotations, and recriminations in a passage that ends with this bit of satirical self-criticism (p. 341):

"Madam, your story has nothing in it either new or entertaining; the occurrences are common, trivial, and such as happen every day; your vanity is intolerable, your style borrowed from Milton, Shakespeare, and Swift, whom you pretend to describe, though you never knew him; you tell us a story of his beef being over-roasted, and another of a mangy dog—fine themes truly!"

Sometimes her mind wanders; she speculates on a man hanging on a gibbet for rape, though he had been a good Catholic; she develops wild theories—that the earth's spinning will turn it into a comet, or that the ocean is bottomless. Even at the end, back in London after another trip to Ireland, with "her boy" John Carteret Pilkington helping her out in the little shop, certain traits remain steady with her. She is still bitter against Pilkington (p.

397): "Sooner shall lambs make love to lambs, tigers to tigers, and every creature couple with its foe [This is a quotation from Congreve's *Double Dealer*], as the poet wittily expresses it, than I unite with thee." And, characteristically, the life finishes in a quarrel with her generous friend Lord Kingsborough, in which, as usual, she shifts treacherously from promised dedications and panegyrics to libel.

And yet: when she feels she is dying, she leaves her poor son this legacy of the third volume and begs Kingsborough to protect him. "My mother," her son John observes (pp. 464-5), "who possessed a pretty manner of writing, was apt to fall too hard on those whom she imagined herself injured by." His account of her last days is moving and detailed: she can joke and hate even on her deathbed, as when she tells her son she will forgive her husband, but *only* if she dies.

"Thus died Letitia Pilkington," warns the *Gentleman's Magazine*,[53] "—the Companion of Swift yet the tool of Worsdale; betray'd like many others by wit to folly and by pride to meaness. To those who read her life she cannot surely have lived in vain since she has scarce related a single incident which does not concur to prove that no natural excellence can attone for moral defects nor any power of pleasing others secure an equivalent for the chearful independence of honest industry."

Yet some of her readers may agree with her that (p. 424) "a woman who has suffered in reputation knows not what to do"; and, instead of her moral defects and her lack of honest industry, may choose to remember Letitia walking in the walled garden with the Angel of Ireland, or her real understanding of Falstaff, or her dreams in the pulpit when she was locked in Westminster Abbey among "the solitary mansions of the dead," or her occasional speculative asides (p. 58): "I have often been led to look on the world as a garden, and the human minds as so many plants . . ." (p. 373): "I have observed that the scent of a flower, or the tune of a song, always conveys to remembrance the exact image of the place in which they were first noticed."

[53] Quoted on flyleaf, Bodleian 1749 Dublin copy.

She cudgelled her brains for bread. She wrote a novel out of her experiences; but because they were her own experiences, the result is as vivid and inconsistent as life itself.

Identical twins are rare in biography, but one case may be recorded in the publications of Letitia Pilkington's *Memoirs* and of *An apology for the conduct of Mrs. Teresia Constantia Phillips*. They both were born in the same year, 1748, and as writers they both had Mrs. Manley for a mother and Colley Cibber for a father. But if Letitia Pilkington has some agreeable traits, Con Phillips has none. The reader is inclined to agree with the Gentleman of the Inner Temple, who, in *A familiar epistle to the celebrated Mrs. Con. Phillips, on her Apology* (n.d., p. 5), speaks of "making the People accessary to your Faults after the commission," and believes it possible that her subscribers give her "a larger Encouragement for a Detail of your Gallantries, than,—perhaps they originally afforded: Which must be a very dangerous Precedent, and terminate in the Ruin of numbers of your Sex, who will need no great Persuasions, to give up their Virtue, when convinc'd the History of its loss will yield a Profit, after the Sweets are gone." He suggests only one practical use for her *Apology*.

Mrs. Phillips's prefaces foam at the mouth against injustices and plots to get her into Newgate for wine debts. Her *Apology* appeared in successive numbers, before its three-volume publication in the two editions of 1748 and 1749. Such a method of airing her dirty linen in as many installments as she pleased offered magnificent opportunities for extortion. The narrative proceeds as though written by a friend who has known of her for twenty years and has been a close acquaintance for three. "Mr. Grimes," who, it would seem, is the future Fourth Earl of Chesterfield, tries to seduce her when, at the age of thirteen, she is living by her needle because she cannot endure her stepmother, previously a family servant. Finally she escapes to private lodgings, visits Grimes to see the fireworks, and drinks "Barbadoes water" which he calls wine. After he has tied her to a chair and stripped off her clothing, she says she will "pass over in Silence what follow'd."

But Mrs. Phillips does not pass over incidents in silence frequently enough for readers of delicate stomachs. "You Bitch!" strews the pages, and sensational brutal passages gave her *Apology* a wide sale.[54] Before she is fifteen years old, Mr. Grimes has deserted her, she has gone through a wedding ceremony with a man already married, so that she may escape debtors' prison, and has succeeded also in marrying Mr. Muilman, a rich young Dutchman.

Much of what follows is in the form of letters and legal documents in the eternal wrangle between Con and the Muilman family. The tangles in the law-courts are so intricate and interminable that the perusal of this book, at a much later date, inspired Jeremy Bentham to seek the reform of the English courts. Yet her five-year prosecution of Muilman does not seriously interrupt the accounts of her affairs with Mr. B——, the Count Charleroi, Sir H—— P——, and Lord F——, in scenes that shift from *grand luxe* in London and Bath to a convent in Ghent.

"The Life of a Lady," says its recorder (Vol. I, p. 314), "which will appear to have been almost but one continued Campaign of Love and Gallantry . . . has been rather fill'd with Hostilities and Defiance, with Jarrs and Devastation, than with the Indolence and soft Allurements of that dangerous and bewitching Passion." Con can icily record Sir H—— P——'s stabbing himself because "dearest Conny" is to leave him. Sir H——'s jealousy, rising almost to madness, is surveyed with the detachment of Proust and the phraseology of the eighteenth century novel (Vol. II, p. 33): ". . . in an Extasy of Grief, scarce possible to be described, Oh! my Conny, said he. . . ." It is not remarkable that Fielding could class Con Phillips, "last, not least," with Dalila, Agrippina, and Lady Macbeth among strong-willed women contemptuous of the male sex.[55] She severs her connection with Sir H—— P—— in order to become the mistress of Lord F—— over whom she acquires such a firm hold that a scene may be introduced in which a female emissary from Lady H—— pleads with

---

[54] cf. 1748 ed., Vol. I, pp. 122, 127, 129; or the incident, pp. 143-7, in which a lover stops her chair on the street, and with some ruffian friends strips her and sends her home almost naked.

[55] *Amelia*, Book I, Chap. VI.

Connie to allow a marriage between Lord F—— and Lady H——'s daughter.

But Con Phillips's triumph in distilled poison is "The Amours of Tartufe" inserted in the second volume (pp. 119-224). It opens with an amusingly scandalous caricature of this gentleman with whom she had a five-year liaison, and closes with a sneer at his Roman Catholic fear of damnation for adultery when he "had not less than three or four such Vehicles of Damnation upon the Wheel." Many of his letters to her are included—even numbered. She is with child by him at one time, and he swears he will always help her, to which she subjoins a frigid footnote that he is now worth a hundred thousand pounds. One of her best inventions is the embarrassment which results when letters to two of Tartufe's mistresses cross in the post. Tartufe—he should have been named Harpagon—is summed up finally by a debit and credit accounting of how much he owes Connie in cash.

This "History of Tartufe" shows, as do other sections of the *Apology,* how the whole work was brought out piece by piece, almost a work *extempore*—and probably only after Connie had found it more profitable to print than to suppress. As was true for Mrs. Pilkington's *Memoirs,* Mrs. Phillips's *Apology* deteriorates in the third volume into pointless and sordid stories. She, too, needs a larger stage, and journeys to Jamaica and the Colonies. Always, however, she returns to England. Even her compiler now seems using her career for profit; but she is undoubtedly a disagreeable creature, and it is no wonder that Grimes and Tartufe and Muilman wanted to get her out of England—to France, America, Jamaica, anywhere. And finally, in 1754, years after her *Apology* had done its worst, Muilman bribes her to leave the country for Jamaica. She dies abroad, though not before she has married an Irishman, then a Scot, and last of all a Frenchman.

To the end she is sure she can do no wrong. She complains of her critics who say the earlier parts are written (Vol. III, p. 309) "in a ludicrous, obscene, immoral Stile," whereas she claims for them "Decency and Modesty of Stile." "Law, Equity, Justice, Humanity" (Vol. III, p. 250)—all are against her, and the third volume closes in snivelling. The change and fall, the sense of injured merit, and the loss of personal self-respect until she becomes a puppet mouthing her old arguments and complaints, make the *Apology*, viewed as a whole, gloomy and grimy.[56] Her work has the spirit of domestic tragedy with everything domestic left out. Moll Flanders is a noble character when set beside Con Phillips. And in this one instance, perhaps, the argument of the usefulness of biography in furnishing warning examples may hold true, for the figure of Con Phillips is indeed direful.

A more masculine adventuress produced, shortly after Constantia Phillips's *Apology, A narrative of the life of Mrs. Charlotte Charke, youngest daughter of Colley Cibber*, evidently patterned on the narratives by Cibber, Pilkington, and Phillips. Like Mrs. Phillips's *Apology*, it appeared in installments, so that a later section opens with the remark to her father Colley Cibber:[57] "I doubt not but you are sensible I last Saturday published the first number of a Narrative of my Life." Comparable in self-appraisal to Letitia Pilkington's dialogue between "I" and "Myself" is Charlotte Charke's dedication: "The Author to Herself." With humorous self-consciousness she assures herself that "Your exquisite taste in building must not be omitted: the magnificent airy castles, for which you daily drew out plans without foundation" make her only rival "in oddity of fame" "that celebrated knight-errant of the moon, George Alexander Stevens."[58]

This capricious dedication gives a fair sample of what is to follow. Charlotte Charke writes in a crotchety, eccentric style which well reflects her moods. "I confess myself an odd mortal," she writes (p. 54), and speaks complacently (p. 16) of "my whimsical head." She preens herself upon her singularity. "I have promised to conceal nothing that might raise a laugh," she says (pp. 12-13), and in consequence she opens her *Narrative* with such pranks as her dressing up in her father's wig at the age of four, or her setting up as a doctor until poor Colley has to pay the bills for the free drugs she has dispensed. She should have been born a boy; as it is, her brash independence and recklessness is continually

---

[56] cf. the glitter followed by gloom in the memoirs of Letitia Pilkington, Sarah Gooch, Charlotte Charke, George Anne Bellamy, Sophia Baddeley, or Mary Robinson.

[57] p. 72, 1827 ed., Vol. VII of *Autobiography. A collection*.

[58] See Bibliography and Index for Stevens.

leading her into scrapes. She protects the household as a child against a discharged gardener; she turns gardener herself; she tries her hand as grocer and tea-merchant and later as sausage-seller; she sells pork and poultry, but she will not sell fish. She is married young to Charke—a musician who wishes to become Cibber's son-in-law in order to advance himself, as she records in disillusionment. Her husband, after betraying her with many mistresses, finally dies in Jamaica. She contracts a secret alliance, but her lover also dies and leaves her in debt, so that for a day she is even in custody until she is released by the kind hearts of female friends who take up a purse for her.

As a true daughter of Colley Cibber, she cannot keep the stage out of her narrative for any length of time. Cibber had tried to give her a good education in spite of herself; and the remnants of her early studies and her later associations are present in her autobiography in the form of quotations. Like a magician pulling rabbits from a hat, she displays many quoted parallels from dramas, generally from comedies; and she has a genius for choosing undistinguished lines. She first plays Mademoiselle in *The Provoked Wife,* and is vain in the account of her per-formance. But the teamwork of the stage is irksome to her erratic spirit, leading her to set up her own puppet show, in which she won whatever fame has since been accorded her. In brief flares against a murky background, the reader glimpses this queer mortal as a superior domestic in the Irish Lord A——a's house-hold, where she is friendly with his mistress; as an actress with her brother Theophilus in the Haymarket; training her niece for the stage; planning a speaking and acting academy which she will shortly advertise; helping a Mr. Russell with his Italian puppets for a guinea a night (the next flashes show Mr. Russell in debtors' prison at Newgate; then in his coffin at the Fleet); being hoodwinked by sharpers; presenting *The Beaux' Stratagem* in a country town; trying to give herself a benefit performance of *George Barnwell* at Bristol with actors from Wells, among them her daughter Kitty, now three years married; acting as prompter during the season at the Bath Theatre; and finally returning to London to publish her novel, *The history of Henry Dumont, Esq; and Miss Charlotte Evelyn.*

She received ten guineas for her novel; her autobiography, she hopes, will be even more profitable, for it was written primarily to effect a Lear-and-Cordelia reconciliation between Colley Cibber and herself. The very old man—he was in his eighties —is now under the domination of a "cruel monitor"; and it is characteristic of Charlotte Charke's mental processes to think that she may win her father's forgiveness by ridiculing his second marriage.

Her narrative is quite in the manner of Smollett; it is a picaresque novel, full of sordid vitality. Among the female autobiographers of the century, Charlotte Charke stands out rude and brusque. To avoid creditors, she had learned to masquerade as "Mr. Brown," and she frequently appears more at home in breeches than in skirts. As Captain Plume in *The Recruiting Officer* she breaks the heart of a sixty-thousand-pound heiress; she serves in disguise as a waiter at Mrs. Dorr's tavern in "Mary-la-bonne"; but in spite of her adventures and intrigues, the mystery of her being in breeches, she tells us (p. 84), must always remain a secret.

"This daughter of Colley Cibber, the late Poet Laureate," writes an acquaintance,[59] "was a lady of surprising singularity; but the oddities of the human mind are unaccountable." Her narrative pays no attention to time, place, or character. She likes stories; she likes fun; she likes adventures. Wanderlust seizes her and leads her bewilderingly through country jails and playhouses and law-courts and inns. But though the scenes shift so fast that she never bothers to describe any of them, Charlotte Charke remains the same strolling-player, careless, wild, irresponsible even in her quotations. The effect produced by her narrative is one of undirected power, thunderous and murky, masculine. It is difficult to forget the two figures of the lunatics her grandfather the statuary had set up above the gates of Bedlam: the "Raving" and the "Melancholy." If Alexander Pope had lived longer and had sought heirs for Cibber's throne in the dusky kingdoms of the *Dunciad,* he would have found ready-made to his hand Colley Cibber's two eccentric children Theophilus and Charlotte! But

[59] G. A. Stevens, *History of Master Edward,* 1785, p. 135.

although Charlotte Charke might rule with a certain fitness over a kingdom of fools, she could never have reigned in an empire of dullness.

Hardly less eccentric than Charlotte Charke, and with an utter incapacity to draw the line between fact and daydream, is Thomas Amory. His *Memoirs: containing the lives of several ladies of Great Britain* (1755) plainly starts out from a biographical impulse, since it is designed to correct Ballard's collection which had appeared in 1752 with a similar title. Amory can even show disgust with his rival's lack of knowledge (p. xxx): "As to Mrs. Grierson, Mr. Ballard's account of her in his *Memoirs of some English Ladies,* lately published, is not worth a rush. He knew nothing of her." Amory's plans are grandiose (p. xxxi): "Note farther, that the whole the author has to offer to the Public, under the title of Memoirs, will be comprized in Eight Volumes in Octavo." *A Table of the Lives* which Amory intends to produce extends to twenty. Yet his *Memoirs* never got beyond the first volume and the first life, that of Mrs. Marinda Benlow. Amory is even aware from the beginning that he may wander, for he says (p. xxv): "the work might have been named *Pandecta,* as it contains a great variety of matter, and . . . the narrations relative to the ladies are the least Part of the performance." Nevertheless, "because the illustrious women therein mentioned are the choicest things in the collection," he believes his title is justified. He follows this defense with ridiculous reasons for relegating to the second volume his history of the Romans in Britain and his refutation of Tritheism.

The life of Mrs. Benlow, when it finally gets under way, is written in the form of a letter to "dear Jewks," and starts off a mad ramble on all topics. Amory wanders, with apparent seriousness, from comedy to a discussion of religion and simple faith, and couches his reflections on life, death, and Methodism in unacknowledged translations and paraphrases from the Latin poets, or from Milton and Shakespeare. For Amory is a learned man, and is willing to discuss with owlish gravity John Locke, or Richard Baxter, or Thomas Chubb. His brain effervesces with imaginations, philosophical arguments, and straws of learning from the past. Most of this "life" of Mrs. Benlow is devoted to her journal, "Transactions and observations in a voyage to the Western Islands: in the year 1741," which is full of romances and histories like a nest of Chinese boxes, with further ornamentation drawn from geography and natural history. In 1749 a storm blows them from the Hebrides to the Cape Verde Islands. Among such happenings, it is natural enough that even Thomas Amory's fictitious characters are puzzled by the heroine's adventures (p. 267): "Zulima replyed: Mrs. Benlow, your discourse hath astonished me."

This early *Journey to the Western Islands* may also be parallelled with *Rasselas,* though Amory has a feeling for natural scenery that Johnson rarely shows. Page after page Amory devotes to chorographical descriptions of "the Green Island" or of Scalpa, "an amazing frightful rock" the inhabitants of which constitute a Utopian society. Amory is fond of Greek quotations in the text, and of scholarly notes,[60] sometimes in French. He is completely unaware of form: one moment Mrs. Benlow is narrating her escape like the Lady in *Comus*; and shortly after, without any clear transition, Amory in his own person is proving to poor Jewks that "the religion of Jesus is that natural truth, which is older than the creation." Amory principally resembles Sterne in that he never arrives at the point he sets out for.

Imagination is here close to insanity. Nor are the bounds between biography and the novel, or between the novel and mere raving, more sharply defined in Amory's *Life and opinions of John Buncle* (1756), which has analogues in Rabelais, Sterne, Fielding, and Samuel Butler. With its pompously phrased wit and its scholarly inanities, *John Buncle* is a mad and fascinating hodgepodge, completely without order, in which John Amory himself plays the rôles of many kinds of conscious fools.

If Amory may be taken somewhat arbitrarily as a forerunner of Shandyism in the field of life-writing, Mark Moore's autobiography may be similarly compared with Smollett's histories, and John Macdonald's travels with Fielding. The full title of

---

[60] One digression, for instance, compares, quotes, and translates Vergil's and Lucan's descriptions of storms.

Moore's production is "The memoirs and adventures of Mark Moore, late an officer in the British Navy. Interspersed with a variety of original anecdotes, selected from his journals, when in the Tuscan, Portuguese, Swedish, Imperial, American, and British Service, in each of which he bore a commission. Written by himself" (1795). With such a career behind him, Mark Moore can describe, with Smollett's clear-sighted lack of sentimentality, his disposal of his little black slave Ranger (p. 47):

"My boy Ranger, was killed with a musket ball; he was on the main deck, handing along powder; with the most heartfelt regret and sorrow, I ordered him to be thrown overboard, for, though not quite dead, he was shot through the bowels, so that he was absolutely irrecoverable, and, if he had lived for a few hours, his excruciating torments must have been dreadful; and, not being able to see him in his dying agonies, with piteous looks, kissing my feet at his last moments, my fondness for the boy, quite unmanned me to see him suffer. . . ."

No wonder he can record that (pp. 47-8) "the Captain said, privateer fighting was dog eat dog, and nothing to be got but hard blows and rags."

Somewhere, in the course of his knocking about the world, Mark Moore has picked up a balanced and dignified style which is rare among eighteenth century biographers; not only his phraseology, but his manner of writing about himself must have been learned from the novels written in the first person:

"In a few moments, I fell into a profound sleep, and, when I awoke, I found myself so much refreshed, that I began to reflect on my situation; a thousand images rushed on my imagination, but young as I was, I had sufficient knowledge of human nature, to select the most pleasing, and to amuse myself with them . . ." (p. 9).

"My curiosity was raised on tiptoe, to visit the emporium of the British empire, of which I had read and heard so much. The immense population of the city, the magnificence of its build-ings, the richness of its shops, and the beauty of the ladies that led ambrosial lives, and breathed the purer air of the west end of the town, scarce permitted my imagination to repose; but the theatres, above all, filled my mind with the highest hopes of being fully gratified. The doctor and I having settled our affairs with all the dispatch imaginable, set out for London, in the situation of Archer and Aimwell, in the Beaux Stratagem" (pp. 22-3).

From the novelists also he learns to tell a complete history with a racy economy, as in the story of his acquaintance in Ireland, a dissipated country squire who has reformed and is (pp. 84-5)

"determined to chuse his wife from a much humbler class; he informed me of his unalterable resolution; and in order to put it in practice, he went to a tenant on his estate, who kept a public-house, and desired him to get a shift, to decorate it with ribbons, and display it in a conspicuous manner, and inform all the young women in the vicinity, that on such a day the smicket would be ran for; and he informed me, he was resolved to make the girl who won the race his wife. At the day appointed, five started; the girl that won did not win his fancy, but the second; in consequence of which he prevailed on me to set aside (as Judge) the claim of the first, on the ground of not starting fair, and award the prize to the second, whom he afterwards married, and who was really a very fine girl. He had her instructed in the French language, and all the polite accomplishments; she had a quick capacity, and improved considerably: he then took her to France, where they lived a year, and when I saw her last, which was in 1790, she was, in every respect, a woman of polished and refined education, and has been the instrument of reforming my friend from that listless round of pleasures in which he was involved, to the calm pleasures of a retired and social life."

Mark Moore's career led him into so many places and such diverse walks of life that even Smollett or Defoe could have found in his life material for several novels. He is born in Boston in 1739, goes to college, but takes French leave from Harvard at the age of fifteen, because he is so fascinated by a visiting company of players that he must follow them to Barbadoes, where he plays the part of George Barnwell. A Colonel Dowling who sees him perform persuades him to forsake the stage for the navy. Wounded in a skirmish with the French, and participating in various hot encounters on privateers, he finally works his way from St. Kitts to England, being paid off with thirty guineas before he goes, to keep him from testifying about a duel in which a Welsh surgeon kills an Irishman.

He now goes as mate-and-surgeon on a slave ship to Africa and the Caribbean; then on a Dutch ship; then to Sweden; then on a Mediterranean cruise under his Swedish friend Captain Delbourg. He sees the Doge wed the Adriatic, he has a duel in Algiers, he quotes *Paradise Lost* to show his contempt for superstition in Sicily; after sailing to Constantinople and through the Black Sea, he experiences romance and a fit of the gout in Leghorn; and at Gibraltar, though his ship is in quarantine, he visits a lady on shore in a complicated intrigue. Presentation at court in Stockholm follows, in chronological though not in causal sequence; then the Mediterranean again; a terrible duel at Gibraltar; a practical-joke ghost that crazes and kills poor Ramsey, the mate of his ship; plague at Smyrna, and recovery in the house of a Jewess; dinner with General Cornwallis at Gibraltar; cruising in a xebec, which nets him much prize money; entrance into the Portuguese service and trouble at Lisbon; a journey to America on a disreputable sloop.

Yet the adventures which are here outlined occupy only the first quarter of his autobiography. Mark Moore did not believe in leisurely dallying, either in life or in letters: he meets a young lady at a public ball and gives her until eleven the next morning, in the College green, to marry him. She cannot resist such a courtship. The young couple go off with a travelling company on a salary of four shillings a week for the two of them, and there follow incidents of penury and cunning in provincial theaters, such as strew the pages of Charlotte Charke and Tate Wilkinson. His wife passes as a singer, "Signora Morini," and he is Signor, the musician-husband. At Wells, where they "performed three nights under the roof of the cathedral," he is bearded as an Englishman, but his Italian saves him and wins him an apology and a ball in reparation. Their tour in Scotland and England is so successful that they buy a phaeton; but shortly after, only the help of Kemble Senior and Mrs. Siddons can bring Moore victory over his theatrical rivals in Tewkesbury, and later he finds himself imprisoned at Dudley on a robbery charge, and again in Worcester Castle. Bristol makes him long for the sea; he sails for Leghorn, tries his hand disastrously as a merchant at Ostend, and finally, captured as a French spy upon the English fleet, he thinks he is to be hanged. But he lands on his feet as usual, and even recoups his fortunes at Bartholomew Fair by exploiting a stone-eater, "honoured with the presence of the King, Queen, and Royal Family," whom he pretends to have found on a desert island while cruising in the Levant.

His career goes down hill rapidly. For three years he is with a travelling company of comedians at country fairs; his wife dies, and his only child also, a boy in the Emperor's service. He leads an inactive life in London for three years more, until in 1790 he is commissioned to convey pressed men for the navy. He re-marries, this time a lady in "the liquor business" near Liverpool. But even the tendernesses of a barmaid cannot keep him out of jail, and he is sucked down at last into the maelstrom of debtors' prisons, against which the whole conclusion of this autobiography is a powerful and conscientious plea. The tragedy of age is upon him, so that he is at last persuaded not to go to sea again on the *Hercules,* merchantman (pp. 266-7):

"Old age, with all its concomitant evils, began to stare me in the face. I consoled myself with the hopes that I had made some friends, but my mind revolted at the idea of pecuniary dependance. I began seriously to think of what I could do, and I now find that I adopted a line for which I am exceedingly ill calculated— Biography.—When I took up my pen, I flattered myself that I should have it in my power to do justice to the generosity of some, the courage, patriotism, &c. of others, and that I should not be entirely the hero of my own tale;—but sickness, disappointment, and chagrin continued to cloud my prospects, and arrest my feeble pen. To attempt an apology, would almost be vain, as every line would require one. On the theatric boards, I have often known the *will* taken for the *deed,* and if I am so lucky as to experience the same indulgence on *paper,* I shall then have it in my power to say, that a British audience, and British readers, never fail to pardon, even where they cannot praise.

FINIS."

He is fifty-six years old; he has travelled as widely and viewed the world as ingenuously as Voltaire's Candide, whose tutor's famous creed he translates approvingly as "All is for the better." In his own distinctive style, with its mixture of nautical terms and quotations from the theater, he unfolds a career in which he candidly committed most of the seven deadly sins, besides others of his own invention. He is the true philosopher of the picaresque, for he does not even find it necessary to defend his actions. But in spite of his frank duplicity, he has the gift for making friends in his roving life—friends, moreover, who will subscribe to his forthcoming volume, and, if he were better known, it is safe to say, friends also in the twentieth century.

In the course of his work Mark Moore refers to Tristram Shandy and to Partridge in *Tom Jones*. Moore himself had visited Fielding's grave in Lisbon. He had lent a fellow-prisoner his favorite volume, *The history of a foundling*. He himself is quite like Tom Jones in his ingenuous and open nature, like Roderick Random in his matter-of-fact acceptance of life. But he is like Tom Jones or Roderick Random with a difference: it was Mark Moore's misfortune that the war with the French came to a close, for he shows up better on the deck of a privateer than in the later scenes in the crowded prisons. His life has no neat and happy ending. He is Tom Jones in actual life, and there is no creator to step down like a god from the machine, "interpose at the difficult minute," and, at the end, save the creature he has grown to love.

Even more cocky, impudent, and picaresque than Mark Moore is John Macdonald, whose *Travels, in various parts of Europe, Asia, and Africa, during a series of thirty years and upwards* is of enduring freshness.[61] The patronizing original preface asserts that only a few alterations from Macdonald's own account have been made, for the sake of intelligibility, and is aware of some of Macdonald's sarcastic powers, for the writer says:[62] "The simple

---

[61] 1790. John Beresford reprinted it in 1927 as *Memoirs of an Eighteenth-Century Footman*.
[62] p. 1, 1927 ed.

strokes of truth and nature with which he paints the caprices, the vanities and vices of others, possess all the force of satire." The writer of the preface justly compares Macdonald to Gil Blas, but is on more doubtful ground when he maintains that the book is unified by Macdonald's belief that his whole life is an example of "the beneficence of an all-ruling Providence." Macdonald's religious belief seems much closer to being a bold assurance in his lucky star. Thus he writes about his early reading of the Bible in order to keep out of Hell (p. 32):

"I have prayed a hundred times that I might die, having heard so much about heaven. . . . I had a great desire to see the Devil; and often looked behind me to see if I could see him, that I might rebuke him; for I was confident he could not hurt me."

His mother died when he was two years old; when he was four, in September 1745—year of the Young Pretender—his fourteen-year-old sister with her three younger brothers set out from the parish of Urquhart to seek their soldier father in Edinburgh. They never found him. In two months they cover a hundred and fifty miles, begging, eating little but oatmeal, encountering a lunatic. His sister tells him all this, for at four-and-a-half he was too young to remember. His childhood he spends as a beggar in Edinburgh, and it is a happy one. For four months he is attached to a blind fiddler. Finally he becomes the littlest postilion in Scotland, and goes a-courting with his master to the Laird of Craig-Leith's.

In his various occupations, he is quick to pick up such accomplishments as reading, curling hair, and making himself attractive to the ladies. His fellows tease him about fourteen-year-old Sally Macrath, but soon his reputation as a lady-killer is no laughing matter and he can complacently note (p. 58):

"I have often heard the ladies say, as they were walking along the streets of Edinburgh, one to another: 'Is that him?' 'Yes,' says another. . . ."

Or, as self-righteous as Joseph, upon one of the few occasions when he withstands a serving-maid who is smitten with him and who obliges him to undress her, he observes (pp. 76-7): "What a terrible thing is lust! How terrible when disappointed!" John Macdonald's immense self-satisfaction, which stops just short of boasting, is the most amusing quality in these most amusing memoirs. He prides himself particularly on his ability to make Queen of Scots soup, and this famous dish, which he prepares in France, in London, and in India, appears repeatedly as a kind of *motif* throughout his travels.

He has the knack of detailing conversations in their essence, and of convincingly presenting whole scenes, as in the dinner in Clifford Street, when among those who sat down at table were the Duke of Roxburgh, the Earls of March and Ossory, the Duke of Grafton, Garrick, and Hume. " 'John,' said my master, 'go and inquire how Mr Sterne is to-day' " (p. 92). When Macdonald the footman gets access to Sterne's lodgings, he finds Yorick dying, sees him hold up an arm as if to stop a blow from an invisible enemy, and hears his last words: *"Now it is come."*

Macdonald rarely troubles himself with analysis or motivation. He presents the outside of things. Here, for instance, is part of his passage to India (p. 99):

"Sometimes one died, and the burying was always before breakfast. At other times a man or boy would fall overboard and bury himself. A lieutenant going out passenger to India, wanted to do the same; but was caught hold of by the legs, and stopped from that rash action, and taken care of. Something troubled his mind."

In his Eastern adventures, Jack acquires a turban, and describes the life of India in great detail, with all its tigers and elephants, its big dinners in Bombay, its strange rites and visits to princes. He inducts the reader into the servant problem as seen by the servant: he never knows whether to dress elegantly or plainly in applying for a position, and he always guesses wrong (p. 180). Later, in his journeyings in the Iberian peninsula, his accounts give practical advice to travellers (p. 194):

"From the time I left Lisbon till I returned to England, I became, or travelled, as a Roman Catholic. I have seen many different religions, and found it was best to pay respects to the people and conform to their religion. In the morning we packed up our baggage, and paid our bills."

Now his panorama embraces Cadiz, bullfights, wayside shrines to the Virgin, Madrid, Bordeaux, and London again.

When he returns to Spain, he finds that Malilia, the girl in
Toledo whom he remembers vaguely, has a four-months child
which she says is his. He is aware that he is so handsome that no
woman can resist him; in gallant compensation, he is rarely able
to resist a woman. Even in Africa, when a black Prince entertains his English guests by presenting them with two fine girls,
Macdonald writes (p. 107): "I declare they were like a diamond:
they made my hair stand on end to see them." So now, in Toledo,
he marries Malilia. She is eighteen, he thirty-eight, and since she
would regret leaving her mother for London and its foreign
tongues, he genially winds up his narrative by going to Toledo.

Throughout his travels, John Macdonald reveals himself as
spiritually akin to Robert Burns, a man of self-sufficiency and
good nature, delighting in living, loving, eating, and dressing
well, warm-hearted but satirical, independent enough to give
warning when he finds his position embarrassing or boring. He
wins our sympathy as Tom Jones wins our sympathy: he is full
of faults, but never ungenerous or calculating; he falls into
errors, but he always means well.

The record by this sunny-tempered valet stops tantalizingly
when the French Revolution is just over the horizon. And it
closes, more artistically than many novels, with a return to his
wife and a return to the central theme of his irresistibility. Sterne
might have envied Macdonald one of his last lines, as the book
ends with Malilia bearing him another man-child (p. 249):
"I said to myself: 'The Macdonalds grow in Spain.'"

In contrast to the bold and brassy independence of most of the
women autobiographers of the century, Mary Robinson's dreamy
and sensitive nature is refreshing. She had some pretensions as
novelist, and the titles of her works show that she was preoccupied with such subjects as the false friend, a domestic tale;
or with the dangers of credulity, or with a hero who is a pupil
of nature. She was also an enthusiastic poet, and her poems, published in two volumes late in the century under the patronage of
the Duchess of Devonshire, exhibit Byronic sentiments clothed
in Augustan diction. She has, for instance, two long books on
The Progress of Liberty; she writes *Golfre. A Gothic Swiss Tale*

in five parts; and most interesting of all, her poems in blank verse, *The Alien Boy* and *London's Summer Morning,* seem—if such a thing were possible—a combination of Wordsworth and Walpole.

Born in 1758, Mary Robinson wrote her *Memoirs* in 1800, although it was left for her daughter to finish and publish them in 1801. The first paragraphs of her account show her as one of the school of Walpole. After her novel *Walsingham,* an incredibly melodramatic story of murder and disguise and hysterical sentiment, the opening of her own life is fortunately held in check by the reality of the Bristol that she (no less than Chatterton) knew well. Yet sensitivity to the Gothic and the novel of mood or atmosphere here undoubtedly breaks in upon the writing of lives:[63]

"In this venerable mansion there was one chamber whose dismal and singular constructure left no doubt of its having been a part of the original monastery. It was supported by the mouldering arches of the cloisters, dark, Gothic, and opening on the minster sanctuary, not only by casement windows that shed a dim midday gloom, but by a narrow winding stair-case, at the foot of which an iron-spiked door led to the long gloomy path of cloistered solitude. . . .

"In this awe-inspiring habitation, which I shall henceforth denominate the Minster House, during a tempestuous night, on the 27th of November, 1758, I first opened my eyes to this world of duplicity and sorrow. I have often heard my mother say that a more stormy hour she never remembered. The wind whistled round the dark pinnacles of the minster tower, and the rain beat in torrents against the casements of her chamber. Through life the tempest has followed my footsteps, and I have in vain looked for a short interval of repose from the perseverance of sorrow."

Some of her early essays had been signed "Tabitha Bramble," and Smollett's influence, which may seem inexplicable in the light of her melting femininity, is present side by side with Walpole's. Her portrait of Meribah Lorrington, her drunken and brilliant schoolmistress at Chelsea (p. 21), "one of the most

[63] pp. 2-3, 1894 ed., Philadelphia. Ed. J. F. Malloy.

extraordinary women that ever graced, or disgraced, society," is effective because it is heightened almost to caricature, even while it remains objective; and the scene is dramatic indeed (p. 27) when later, a hooded, filthy beggar-woman turns out to be Miss Lorrington. In the fashion of a practised novelist, Mrs. Robinson lays a train of plot when she introduces the young lawyer who looks out of the window across the street, pale, languorous, and handsome: he is to become her husband. Her characters are more than names; they move through space and time, they need to be clothed in "chip hats" and ribands, or surrounded with silks and bedspreads and colors. As a complete success in Smollett portraiture, her meeting with her husband's father Mr. Harris and her husband's sister Miss Robinson shows how pleasingly the technique of the novel may unite with genuine autobiography (pp. 58-60):

"Mr. Harris came out to receive me. I wore a dark claret-coloured riding habit, with a white beaver hat and feathers. He embraced me with excessive cordiality, while Miss Robinson, my husband's sister, with cold formality led me into the house. I never shall forget her looks or her manner. Had her brother presented the most abject being to her, she could not have taken my hand with a more frigid demeanour. Miss Robinson, though not more than twenty years of age, was Gothic in her appearance and stiff in her deportment; she was of low stature and clumsy, with a countenance peculiarly formed for the expression of sarcastic vulgarity—a short snub nose, turned up at the point, a head thrown back with an air of *hauteur*; a gaudy-coloured chintz gown, a thrice-bordered cap, with a profusion of ribbons, and a countenance somewhat more ruddy than was consistent with even pure health, presented the personage whom I was to know as my future companion and kinswoman!

"Mr. Harris looked like a venerable *Hawthorn*; a brown fustian coat, a scarlet waistcoat edged with narrow gold, a pair of woollen spatter-dashes, and a gold-laced hat, formed the dress he generally wore. He always rode a small Welsh pony, and was seldom in the house except at eating-time from sunrise to the close of the evening.

"There was yet another personage in the domestic establishment, who was by Mr. Harris regarded as of no small importance: this was a venerable housekeeper of the name of Mary Edwards. Mrs. Molly was the female Mentor of the family; she dined at the table with Mr. Harris; she was the governess of the domestic department; and a more overbearing, vindictive spirit never inhabited the heart of mortal than that which pervaded the soul of the ill-natured Mrs. Molly."

Among her other effective scenes are those in which Garrick watches her début as Juliet; or Mary Robinson, with a curtsey, saves the hissed première of *A Trip to Scarborough*; or Marie Antoinette, who has given *la belle Anglaise* a mesh purse, probably for rejecting the advances of the Duc d'Orléans, dines opposite her; or the Prince of Wales meets her alone for the first time that dark night before the iron gates of old Kew Palace. He had first seen her in the *Winter's Tale,* and to the Prince she is always Perdita, as he is Florizel to her.

The moods of the memoirs are various. At times they can assume the conventional motivation of the life-and-amours type, as when Lord Lyttelton tries to persuade her to avenge herself for her husband's infidelities by paying him back in kind, or Fighting Fitzgerald almost abducts her. They can shift to cool psychological judgment:[64] "I do not condemn Mr Robinson; I but too well know that we cannot command our affections. I only lament that he did not observe some decency in his infidelities." And they can become objective and cynical, as in the account of her return to her father-in-law's in Wales (p. 91):

"I was consulted as the very oracle of fashions; I was gazed at and examined with the most inquisitive curiosity. Mrs Robinson, the promising young actress, was a very different personage from Mrs Robinson who had been overwhelmed with sorrows, and came to ask an asylum under the roof of vulgar ostentation."

Yet the principal mood is that of romantic nostalgia presented in night-pieces whose soft and mysterious shadows waken memory and allow her heart to overflow. One of her works, *The Maniac,* she had dictated in delirium, in a laudanum stupor; and

---

[64] 1826 ed., p. 87.

the recollections of her own life also possess the qualities of a dream. She revisits Bristol:[65]

"The house in which I first opened my eyes to this world of sorrow, the minster, its green, the school-house where I had passed many days, the tomb of my lost relatives in the church of St Augustine, were all visited by me with a sweet and melancholy interest. But the cathedral, the brass eagle in the middle aisle, under which, when an infant, I used to sit and join in the loud anthem, or chaunt the morning service, most sensibly attached me. I longed again to occupy my place beneath its expanding wings, and once I went, before the service began, to gratify my inclination."

Or again:

"I cannot help mentioning that, shortly after my marriage, I formed an acquaintance with a young lady, whose mind was no less romantic than my own; and while Mr Robinson was occupied at chambers, we almost daily passed our morning hours in Westminster Abbey. It was to me a soothing and a gratifying scene of meditation.—I have often remained in the gloomy chapels of that sublime fabric, till I became as it were an inhabitant of another world. The dim light of the Gothic windows, the vibration of my footsteps along the lofty aisles, the train of reflections that the scene inspired, were all suited to the temper of my soul: and the melancholy propensities of my earliest infancy seemed to revive with an instinctive energy, which rendered them the leading characteristics of my existence."

Mary Robinson possessed such beauty that she was not allowed to indulge the melancholy propensities of her mind. Like George Anne Bellamy, she set the style for London; her portrait was twice painted by Reynolds, and by Cosway, Romney, and Lawrence as well; she aroused such infatuations that one man, George Brereton, tried to seduce her by getting her husband in his power through gaming, though rather than yield to him she spends ten months with Robinson in a debtors' prison. She is so accustomed to adulation that her desertion by the Prince of Wales leads her to write a bitter letter:[66]

[65] pp. 39 and 38.
[66] Molloy's preface, 1894 ed., p. xiii. For Oct. 5, 1794. To John Taylor.

"Have I not reason to be disgusted when I see him to whom I
ought to look for better fortune lavishing favours on unworthy
objects, gratifying the *avarice* of *ignorance* and *dulness,* while I,
who sacrificed reputation, an advantageous profession, friends,
patronage, the brilliant hours of youth, and the conscious delight
of correct conduct, am condemned to the scanty pittance bestowed on every indifferent page who holds up his ermined train
of ceremony?"

Yet these transient moods and incidents do not go well with
the broad-browed and wistful face that looks out from her portraits. "Indeed," she writes (1826, p. 38), "the world has mistaken
the character of my mind; I have ever been the reverse of volatile and dissipated; I mean not to write my own eulogy, though
with the candid and sensitive mind I shall, I trust, succeed in
my vindication." The meetings with Florizel on the banks of
the Thames are too much for her poetic sensibility or her sense
of decorum, and the autobiography breaks off in some confusion
about the time she first received the advances of the Prince. In its
continuation by her daughter Maria, we catch glimpses of the
beauty who had been the friend of Garrick, Sheridan, Fox, and
Reynolds in her little salon in London, set up with the help of a
five-hundred-pound pension from Prince George. The Prince of
Wales and the Duke of York condescend to visit her there; possibly the pension explains her change of sentiment toward the
Prince, so that the autobiography itself (in spite of her caustic
letter of 1794) may say that he is a fine, generous, sensitive prince,
and that any coldness or cruelty on his part is due not to him
but to his counsellors.

The worldly outcome of her career is not the important thing
in the life of Mary Robinson. She has never been very practical;
what happens to her mother, her father, or her husband she does
not bother to record. And the reader will longest remember the
trance-like idyls in her memoirs, her appearances as Shakespeare's
youngest heroines, or her efforts to help Colonel Tarleton out of
his money troubles, or her ecstasy in the face of "the wild luxuriance of nature" among the Welsh mountains, or her dressing a
doll three months before her marriage, or her little daughter's
first words during one of their night walks in the prison grounds,

or her return to the Gothic minster-house at Bristol, with its dark pinnacles and moldering arches. The Perdita who was lost in a succession of fashionable London gatherings and plots to seduce her grows insubstantial, unreal, in contrast with another Perdita, lost in her own meditations in Westminster Abbey as the dim light pours through the Gothic windows and she hears the faint sound of her own footsteps echoing among the lofty vaults.

No one except Boswell in the eighteenth century, biographer or autobiographer, achieved a more complete revelation of character than did Fanny Burney. She is completely natural. To open one of the volumes of her diary is to have a living person in the room. In periodic prose, Macaulay excuses her for her confessions by saying:[67] "If she recorded with minute diligence all the compliments, delicate and coarse, which she heard wherever she turned, she recorded them for the eyes of two or three persons who had loved her from infancy, who had loved her in obscurity, and to whom her fame gave the purest and most exquisite delight." Her confidences and outpourings were not always written even to her dear sisters Susan and Emily. Her early diary, for instance, is "Addressed to a Certain Miss Nobody"—the only one, save her sisters, in whom she can confide completely; it was written "to have some account of my thoughts, manners, acquaintance and actions, when the hour arrives in which time is more nimble than memory." And her diary for 1773 is entitled (1907 ed., p. 189) *My Life and Opinions—addressed to Myself.*

Fanny Burney defies all categories. Her diary is not the usual ordered succession of dry jottings; it is her life, written as easily, as naturally, as it was lived. Her letters to Daddy Crisp are the same as her diaries, and the scenes and conversations of her novels are little different from the scenes and conversations of her journals. Paul Elmer More, in a delightful essay, says that her novels "are properly mere excursions in the more realistic transcript of life,"[68] and it would not be incorrect to say that her never-ending

---

[67] *Edinburgh Review,* January 1843, p. 539, quoted from Austin Dobson's ed. of Madame d'Arblay's *Diary and Letters,* 1904-1905.

[68] *Shelburne Essays,* Fourth Series, 1906.

habit of recording her own life gave Fanny Burney her distinctive style as novelist.

Spontaneity and a dizzying sense of vitality are the distinguishing qualities of her writing: the words tumble and multiply so fast that Miss Fanny and her reader are left breathless:[69]

"It would be miraculous had I power to maintain the same glowing enthusiasm—the same—on my word I can *not* go on, my imagionation is rais'd *too* high, it soars above this little dirty sphere, it transports me beyond mortality—it conveys me to the Elysian fields—but my ideas grow confused. . . ."

"I cannot express the pleasure I have in writing down my thoughts, at the very moment—my opinion of people when I first see them, and how I alter, or how confirm myself in it. . . ." This immediate and copious reproduction of what happens is her secret. A perusal of her diaries may even convince a reader that in the generous recording of a scene complete with conversation, Fanny Burney surpasses her bitter rival James Boswell.[70] "We passed the most curious evening yesterday," she writes (Vol. I, p. 39). "Never sure did any conversation seem more like a scene in a comedy." To prove her contention, she spreads out the entire evening before her reader. Some of her scenes, indeed, are almost too full of unselected talk, faithfully recorded, to be presented on the stage.

No one ever had more ebullient spirits than Fanny Burney. Nor does she shine alone. In the household of their social and music-loving father Doctor Burney, her sisters Susan and Emily do not fall behind her in gaiety and intelligence. Susan's letter to Fanny about *Evelina*[71] is good criticism in the effusive tradition of the Burney family, and Charlotte Ann Burney's letters and journal[72] are almost sharper and cleverer than Fanny's. Her vocabulary is racier, full of Split me's, My cot!'s, and Stuck in his gizzard's.

[69] *Early Diary*, 1907, Vol. I, p. 7, and pp. 14-15. Ed. A. R. Ellis. Year 1768. She was then sixteen.

[70] cf. her conversation with Mr. Seaton, detailed on pp. 33-8, *Early Diary*, 1907, Vol. I; or the *genre* picture of the New Year's masquerade at M. Lalauze's, pp. 70-7; or the scene in which Garrick apologizes to Fanny, Vol. I, p. 227, after she had rebuked him for talking down to young ladies (quoted in part in Chap. I).

[71] Vol. II, pp. 222-7, Dobson.   [72] Vol. II, pp. 277-320, Dobson, 1777-1787.

Charlotte outshone Fanny at Doctor Burney's gatherings; she was a particular favorite of David Garrick's, who would imitate for her Doctor Johnson with[73] "his see-saw, his pawing, his very look, and his voice! . . . 'Yes, yes, Davy has some convivial pleasantries in him; but 'tis a futile Fellow. . . . No Sir; I'm for the musick of the ancients, it has been corrupted so.'" Charlotte's hectic and brilliant wit, approaching to genius, and her early death give her the rôle of Emily Brontë to play opposite Fanny's Charlotte Brontë; indeed, this eighteenth century family of three girls, with their vivid literary interests and their circle of great friends, need not fear comparison with the Victorian family of the Brontës.

Fanny Burney moved in the gay world and enjoyed it. Few journals are so vivacious, readable, quotable, and coherent as hers. She gives with gusto her accounts of balls and operas and plays, her raptures over the singing of Signora Agujari, and her meeting with Omai, the native from the Society Islands, "this lyon of lyons, for such he now is of this town." And yet this chatterbox aspires to the sublime. The principal theme of her early diary is the surreptitious growth and publication of her first novel *Evelina*. What a jig there was around the mulberry tree in Mr. Crisp's garden when she learns of Johnson's approbation! Her pride in its success is so droll and jubilant that the reader cannot help sharing in her joy:[74]

"This year [1778] was ushered in by a grand and most important event,—for at the latter end of January the literary world was favoured with the first publication of the ingenious, learned, and most profound Fanny Burney!—I doubt not but this memorable affair will, in future times, mark the period whence chronologers will date the zenith of the polite arts in this island!"

Fanny's own beaux, her family and acquaintances, had served as models for the characters in her novel; now, when Edmund Burke sits up all night to finish it, and Mrs. Thrale receives her as an addition to the Streatham *salon*, Miss Burney's world expands to even wider horizons. Her conversations were written like speeches from a play—"I think I shall occasionally theatrical-

73 Vol. II, p. 282, Ellis ed.
74 Vol. II, p. 212, Ellis ed.

ise my dialogues," she writes[75]—and the cast of characters now includes Mrs. Montagu and Mrs. Cholmondeley, Reynolds, Sheridan, Burke, and Dr. Warton.

In an account of a dinner at the Thrales as fine as such scenes from Boswell, her Doctor Johnson is presented in an unusual rôle when he pays one of his most ingenious compliments simultaneously to Fanny Burney and Mrs. Thrale by saying:[76] " 'Tis a terrible thing that we cannot wish young ladies well, without wishing them to become old women!" Again, Johnson breaks out in delighted disapproval of his protégée: "Oh, you little character-monger, you!" The relations between this girl in her twenties and the old man of seventy are so intimate that Fanny unconsciously picks up some of his famous phrases (Vol. I, p. 59): "Sir John [Hawkins] was a most *unclubable* man!" And correcting to some extent Boswell's jealous estimate, Miss Burney's portrait of "my sweet, naughty Mrs. Thrale" reveals a fine woman, intelligent, generous, as Miss Burney sees her, tolerant, and tactful.

Johnson's "towering superiority of intellect" is such that she cannot endure, after his death, Boswell's assiduous recording of the Doctor's faults and foibles. For her, the Laird of Auchinleck becomes "that biographical, anecdotical memorandummer."[77] After the publication of his great work, she writes of Boswell:[78]

"I felt a strong sensation of that displeasure which his loquacious communications of every weakness and infirmity of the first and greatest good man of these times have awakened in me, at his first sight; and, though his address to me was courteous in the extreme, and he made a point of sitting next me, I felt an indignant disposition to a nearly forbidding reserve and silence. How many starts of passion and prejudice has he blackened into record, that else might have sunk, for ever forgotten, under the preponderance of weightier virtues and excellences!

"Angry, however, as I have long been with him, he soon insensibly conquered, though he did not soften me: there is so little of ill design or ill nature in him, he is so open and forgiving for

---

[75] Vol. I, p. 111, ed. Dobson. This was written in 1778 at Streatham when Johnson and Mrs. Thrale were persuading her to write a play.

[76] Vol. I, p. 56, ed. Dobson, and p. 90.   [77] Vol. III, p. 219, ed. Dobson.

[78] Vol. V, pp. 83-4, ed. Dobson. Year 1792.

all that is said in return. . . . before we parted we became good friends. There is no resisting great good-humour, be what will in the opposite scale."

This last quotation shows a thoughtful maturity and justice in weighing complex evidence that were not apparent in the earlier diaries. It is now much later, the year is 1792, and Fanny Burney has at last grown up. In her early diaries, little evidence of the progress of her mind can be found; Miss Burney at the age of twenty-six is not different from Miss Burney at sixteen. She is almost piqued when the family call her "feeling Fanny," and indeed in these early years there is little indication of anything more than great good nature and bubbling spirits. The 1768-1778 journal lacks deep personal emotion throughout; its heroine is never moody, never seems to have suffered growing pains.

But by 1792 she is forty years old. Her great and good protector Doctor Johnson has died, and she has recorded, before his death:[79] "I am thankfully happy in hearing that he speaks himself now of the change his mind has undergone, from its dark horror,—and says—'He feels the irradiation of hope!'"

And after his death she confides to her secret pages:

"In the evening I went to Mrs. Chapone. . . . But I was very sad within; the loss of dear Dr. Johnson—the flight of Mrs. Thrale—the death of poor Miss Kitty Cambridge, and of poor, good Miss Strange,—all these home and bosom strokes, which had all struck me since my last meeting this society, were revolving in my mind the whole time I stayed."

By this time, too, she has known another of the most admirable characters of the century—Mrs. Delany—, has planned to write Mrs. Delany's life with her, and has seen death defeat those plans (Vol. III, p. 484):

"Yet then, even then, short as was her time on earth, the same soft human sensibility filled her for poor human objects. She would not bid us farewell—would not tell us she should speak with us no more—she only said, as she turned gently away from us, 'And now—*I'll go to sleep!*'—But oh, in what a voice she said it! I felt what the sleep would be; so did poor Miss P——."

[79] Vol. II, p. 279, ed. Dobson; also p. 283.

And as maid of honor at court, Fanny Burney, now moving in the highest and stupidest circles, has disciplined herself to withstand ennui, has observed Queen Charlotte so closely that she makes of her one of her most successful portraits, has undergone stormy interviews with that "Cerbera" Madame Schwellenberg, and in Kew Gardens has been pursued by the mad King George III. When, terrified and panting, she is overtaken by the now subdued monarch, he kisses her benignly, "though something still of wildness in his eyes."[80] The Rosalind and Beatrice of the earlier volumes now looks at life, though only at times, through more experienced eyes.

The French Revolution casts its débris of *émigrés* upon the shores of England, and one of these, a Monsieur d'Arblay, aide-de-camp to Lafayette, she marries. More humbly now, in a little cottage, she writes her novels and presents them, as well as her husband, at Windsor. They are becoming stiffer, more sententious and grandiloquent in style, as though her admiring love for Doctor Johnson had in the end determined even her manner of writing. But she writes on. As late as 1832 she publishes her memoirs of Doctor Burney, though the three volumes of anecdotes do not hold together very well. The last forty years of her long life (1752-1840) are recorded in only fragmentary fashion among her voluminous papers.

Austin Dobson speaks of her "lynx-eye for the ridiculous" and her "unfeigned admiration for goodness";[81] in her memoirs it is difficult to say which gives greater pleasure to the reader. Her life is all before him, from the time her first suitor gives her "a most ardent salute!" to the touching death of her husband and his last words, *"Notre réunion!"*[82] And as the complete presentation of the life of a young girl, with all its actions and exclamations and speeches and emotions and impulses, Fanny Burney has given a full-length portrait which is almost without rival in the history of biography, or, for that matter, in the history of the novel.

[80] Vol. IV, pp. 242 *ff.*, ed. Dobson.   [81] Vol. VI, p. xviii.
[82] *Early Diary,* Vol. II, p. 48; and Dobson, Vol. VI, p. 368.

In reconstructing and recording life, a certain amount of imagination is necessary to the biographer no less than to the novelist, for the process is that of bringing into the actual present what does not exist. If biographers taught novelists how to imitate nature by imitating actual memoirs, the novelists reciprocally exercised a fortunate influence upon the writers of lives: they showed them that the record of human life may be an art; that the attempt at interpretation and appraisal may be of more significance than the setting down of dates, facts, and actions; and that in reviving the dead, the prevalence of the imagination is less dangerous than its absence.

CHAPTER III

BIOGRAPHY AND THE ROMANTIC SPIRIT

"These strong passions, these quick nerves, this universal glow, this thrilling of the blood. . . ."
—HOLCROFT, *Life of Baron Trenck.*

BEFORE the eighteenth century in England, the prevailing ideas of a hierarchy in Church and State had determined the main course of biography. The lives of ecclesiastical and temporal princes were worthy of record; the lives of their subjects were not. The annals of the Third Estate had been short and simple. Piety, patriotism, and family pride produced biographies; when the life of a person humbly born was set forth in print, almost invariably that person was a cleric, and the motive back of the biography was not to present an individual but to present a typical example for the edification of Christian communicants. To the corporate society of the Tudors and Stuarts, of Hooker's *Ecclesiastical Politie,* of Hobbes's *Leviathan,* and even of Milton's *Of Reformation in England,* Doctor Johnson's dictum that there has rarely passed a life unworthy of record would have been met with raised eyebrows or flat denial. The breath of *égalité* and *fraternité* had not yet blown over England, and there was little speculation in the actual churchyards of the seventeenth century over the village Hampdens, the guiltless Cromwells, and the mute Miltons that might possibly rest beneath the stones.

The social changes between 1700 and 1800 have been so frequently analyzed that they need no recounting here; but it will be of some interest to see what exact parallels are furnished, in the limited field of biography, to those tendencies which have often been noticed in other fields of literature, history, and sociology.

The ecclesiastical and civil strife of the seventeenth century, with its multiplication of sects and parties, had taught the English that several opinions might be held on the same subject and that even if an individual had discovered the ultimate truth, it was dangerous to force it down another man's throat. The age of the archbishop who slit dissenters' ears and of the king who prorogued Parliament in a fit of pique had definitely passed. A cat might now look at a king; he might even scratch. Partly because of this growing spirit of freedom, partly because of the laxity of censorship, satires, libels, and veiled histories of the great flourished in the first half of the eighteenth century as they never flourished before or since. The combined influence of Pope, the Duchess of Marlborough, Mrs. Bracegirdle, and Arbuthnot, it is said, was not sufficient to suppress Curll's scandalous *Memoirs of the life, writings and amours of William Congreve* (1730). And if Pope and his friends could do nothing to muzzle Grubstreet, neither could Grub-street do anything to suppress Pope. Marlborough at the height of his power, Sarah, his Duchess, when she ruled England through Queen Anne, Robert Walpole himself during his long ascendancy, the notorious Duchess of Kingston, were unable to keep from the bookstalls vituperative grotesques which were labelled lives.[1] From the days when such poisonous fabrications might pass unpunished, it is a far cry back to the time when Queen Elizabeth had John Hayward imprisoned for publishing a seemingly innocent and historical biography of Henry IV.

That in themselves these satiric and slanderous memoirs are of little value is beside the point. They did much to free the biographer from a predetermined attitude of unquestioning reverence. "There is at least as great a fondness," writes one biographer,[2] "for lowering exalted characters as there is for raising obscure ones." And in their denigration of famous men, writers suggested unconsciously that if the great are no better than the common herd, then the career of the common man may conversely be as worthy of record as the career of a king. If Walpole's life may be presented thinly disguised as *"The life of Mr. Robin Lyn, very noted in Great-Britain for his large dealings in foreign commodities: containing, his birth and parentage; his rise from a petty trader to a wealthy merchant; the way of his transacting*

---

[1] See Bibliography for titles.

[2] Thomas Martyn, "Life of John Martyn" before his *Dissertations upon the Aeneids*, 1770, p. ii.

private business, tho' contiguous to public trade, and the pros-
perity of his sovereign's subjects; an account of his places of profit,
badges of honour, and skill in state-physick and golden-specif-
icks; and the particulars of his management as sub-governor and
treasurer of an impoverished company" (1729), why may not the
result be the exalting of the merchant and physician as well as
the debasing of the statesman? Fielding's *Life of Jonathan Wild*
may unintentionally magnify the career of a highwayman in spite
of its primary purpose of satirizing the unscrupulous great.

At any rate, whether or not as the result of the astonishing
popular demand for the lives of criminals and for satirical, sensational, and cynical biographical tracts,[3] the English attitude
toward the life of the ordinary man changed. So long as the prime
purpose of biography is edification, artistic economy demands
that the subject be definitely good or bad. But when biographies
are written principally to gratify or to tease curiosity, a grotesque
or an amoral subject may serve; the common reader may view
with complacence men more wicked or more unfortunate than
himself; or he may view with sympathy men like himself, neither
saints nor demons, but a mixture of good and bad.

> "Learn from this proof, that, in life's tempting scene,
>   Man is a compound of the great and mean;
>   Discordant qualities together tied,
>   Virtues in him and vices are allied."[4]

The popularity of *The Beggar's Opera* in spite of indignant
outbursts against its morality demonstrates well enough that a
gay or flippant attitude toward existence can now exist in England side by side with the older conception of life as an exemplification of ethical principles. The picaresque spirit has come into
its own. The flavor of the following excursion from *The memoirs
of Major Alexander Ramkins* (1719) could hardly be duplicated
before the eighteenth century. The gallant Major had just been
robbed on Hounslow Heath, after which he and his companion,
meeting a merry landlord (pp. 150-1),

---

[3] See Chap. IV and Bibliography.

[4] Quoted by Edward Topham in his *Life of John Elwes*, p. 98, 12th ed., 1805,
copied from the *Chelmsford Chronicle* and following Topham's discussion of
Elwes's gentle manners combined with miserliness.

"sat down, and made our selves most immoderately drunk. The Landlord discanted very copiously upon the ancient and modern Practise of Robbing upon the Road, and seem'd very much inclin'd to lessen the Crime. Formerly, said he, no Body robb'd upon the Road but base scoundrel Fellows; but now 'tis become a Gentlemanlike Employment, and young Brothers of very good Families are not asham'd to spend their time that way; besides the Practise is very much refin'd as to the manner, there's no Fighting or Hectoring during the Performance, but these Gentlemen approach you decently and submissive, with their Hat in their Hand to know your Pleasure, and what you can well afford to support them in that Dignity they live in: 'Tis true, says he, they often for Form sake have a Pistol in their Hand, which is part of their riding Furniture; but that is only in the Nature of a Petition, to let you know they are Orphans of Providence just fallen under your protection."

Major Ramkins in this passage is moved neither by the avowed moral indignation of many writers of the lives of criminals, nor by the serious if somewhat patronizing pity of later philanthropists. His spirit is one of sympathetic raillery. We are all brother-rogues, from Louis XV to the men of Hounslow Heath, and the Major does not except himself.

The salt of malice, therefore, leads to plainer speaking, more tolerance, and less didacticism in life-writing. It opens up also whole new galleries of figures whose lives may be recorded for the amusement they may afford or the curiosity they may satisfy. "The lowest and most contemptible vagrants, parish-girls, chambermaids, pickpockets, and highwaymen, find historians to record their praise, and readers to wonder at their exploits. . . . Even the prisons and stews are ransacked to find materials for novels and romances."[5]

Closely allied to the satirical, sensational, and defamatory lives and similar in their effect upon the practice of biography are the narratives of adventurers and travellers. Here again a new class of human beings, hitherto silent about their personal affairs,

---

[5] Francis Coventry, *History of Pompey the Little,* 1750. Quoted from 1820 ed., p. 10.

gradually becomes articulate.[6] They themselves may be of no importance, they imply, but the places they visit, the historical battles and political struggles they witness, the natural catastrophes and strange panoramas that they have been privileged to behold—these are worth recording. Caste, position, and birth are no longer necessary for the hero of a biography; gratification of the Englishman's delight in adventure and of his curiosity about far places tends to render biography more democratic in its choice of subjects. Robert Drury is no more than a waterfront boy in his teens swimming in the Ganges, but his *Pleasant and surprising adventures* (1729) in Madagascar during fifteen years commend him to the attention of the reading public. George Psalmanazar may be a charlatan masquerading under an assumed name, but his tall stories about travels in Formosa (1704) arouse wide enough interest to justify much later the publication of a repentant and more veracious account of himself (1764). An audience came into being which accepted eagerly, and frequently in more than one edition, the account of John Williams (1707) during his two years of privation as slave among the Indians of Canada; or the adventures of John Creichton (1731) among covenanters and conventiclers on the Scottish border; or the life of Job (1734) in his journeys on three continents; or James Bristow's privations in India (1793); or John Macdonald's experiences in Europe, Asia, and Africa (1790). The above-mentioned individuals were, respectively, an obscure preacher in the Colonies, an octogenarian Scottish pauper, a runaway slave, a common soldier, and a gentleman's valet equally at home on a coach-box or in a kitchen. But one had witnessed torture and death in the Deerfield massacre, another had gone tiger-hunting, and a third, after ten years' captivity under Hyder Ally and Tippoo Sahib, had made his almost unbelievable escape. When strange adventure strikes, all men are equal.

A further phenomenon that increased the range of biographical subjects was the mercantile expansion of England. The possession of money gave more than one individual a sense of his own im-

---

[6] Other aspects of biographies in this group are treated in Chaps. II and IV.

portance; more than that, money offered a means, if a successful merchant or a wealthy recluse wished to print privately, of acquainting the public with one's life and opinions.[7]

Money does a great deal, for instance, in the case of Thomas Pennant. Independent means give Mr. Pennant the sense of possessing an independent mind, as well as the complacent belief of the well-to-do dilettante that his slightest opinion on any subject is worth the attention of the world. Like many leisured amateurs, he develops an erratic whimsicality which he mistakes for strength and brilliance of mind. He publishes his memoirs as *The literary life of the late Thomas Pennant, Esq.* (1793), on the grounds that although he is still alive in the flesh, he has died, he says, as an *author*. What follows is principally an account of his works—how he wrote his British zoology, then his Indian zoology, and then decided to include the fishes. This small landholder and widely read eighteenth century antiquarian gentleman is bustling and cocksure somewhat in the manner of Boswell. He details his friendship and correspondence with Buffon and with Linnaeus, his visit to Voltaire, his honors, travels, and occasional verse, and—to make sure that he omits nothing—his epitaph for a friend, which (p. 33) "may be seen on a small brass plate in Whiteford church." He published many of his own writings at a loss, and in his constant travels he took with him an engraver or artist hireling so that later the world might enjoy his experiences even more completely. In quick succession were issued his tour of Scotland, his tour to the Hebrides, and his matured thoughts on quadrupeds. He is the original public-spirited citizen who reforms society by letters on all subjects from mailcoaches to militia laws. And although the compass of his little trips had never extended beyond Germany and the farthest Hebrides, he is not averse at last to recording for posterity his meditations on the Patagonians.

Economic influences shape English biography in another somewhat unexpected way: the printers, publishers, and book-sellers,

[7] Among the biographies and autobiographies printed for the authors are Pennant's, David Stewart's, Whiston's, Lackington's, George-Monck Berkeley's, Hollis's, and the *Memoirs of a Printer's Devil.* And, of course, Horace Walpole's productions.

who usually determined what books were to be printed, more than once decided that the biographies that would interest the public were the biographies of themselves. *The life and errors of John Dunton* (1705) is discussed at length in the fifth chapter of this volume. It is unique in its hero and in its form, but one may venture to assert that it would not have appeared when it did if the author had not also been one of the most active publishers of London.

Another biography in this group is *Memoirs of a Printer's Devil* (1793), in which the anonymous author justifies the publication of his humble life by quoting from Lyttelton's *Letters*: "The political history of great men is useful and necessary to many; but the domestic history of all men is useful and necessary to all." Perhaps Lord Lyttelton exaggerated. After an introduction that defends the value of printing, these memoirs ramble, and in pointless, moon-gazing anecdotes the hero falls in love, or doesn't, takes a journey, quotes Pope, or tells in several pages how a pocketbook is restored to its owner, until he has successfully revealed a thoroughly undistinguished mind.

James Lackington is a man of larger calibre. The *Memoirs of the first forty-five years* of his life (1791) constitutes a vigorous autobiography of a self-made man. He is sure of his own importance, and rightly convinced of the interest of his story. "Slow rises worth, by poverty depressed," he quotes in his introduction, and the ensuing memoirs are written not only to exemplify Johnson's bitter observation, but to gratify the requests of friends, refute the slanders of enemies, and demonstrate Lackington's "upright conscientious demeanour in trade towards the public" and his ability "to emerge from obscurity, by a proper application of those talents with which Providence has favoured him."[8]

Lackington does not underrate his own worth. He is aware of John Dunton's *Life and errors* as a prototype for his own venture, but considers it "a whole volume of dullness." He prefers to compare himself to Pope attacked by Grub-street writers, or to Shakespeare's low-born Thomas Cromwell. He loves to quote tags of poetry, and he draws helter-skelter upon Herrick, Dryden, Mid-

[8] 1791 ed., p. xvii.

dleton, Shakespeare, old ballads, Horace in translation, Cowley, Butler, Rowe, Pomfret, Thomson, Pope, Daniel, Gay, Blair, Milton, Prior, Young, and Aaron Hill to adorn his work. This flow of borrowed numbers seems natural enough in one who taught himself reading when almost a grown man and who learned to write after he was twenty-two. And just as John Bunyan had intensified his early sins in order to magnify God's saving grace, Lackington dwells upon the penury and meanness of his boyhood because its low scenes render his later success more dazzling.

The university of hard knocks has made him cynical, and proud to call a spade a spade. He tells the reader that his grandfather was found dead in a ditch, drunk; that his father was a shoemaker; that his own early career was that of a restless bad boy, in which he throws snowballs at citizens, or "serpents and crackers into their houses" (p. 17), teases idiot Molly, saves a down-at-the-heel baker by teaching him a new method of crying "apple-pies," experiments with infectious yawning and with ghosts and even "ghostesses" (p. 34).

At the age of fourteen, he is apprenticed to an Anabaptist; his memoirs contain what is probably the most valuable realistic picture of the bourgeois religious life of the century, for although he continued to help a Methodist chapel until his death, his accounts of his brethren, even of himself in a religious rôle, are disillusioned and sharp. The pious family circle of "the dipping Community" at Taunton is thrown into dismay by the son's conversion by "one of Mr. Wesley's Preachers, who had left the plow-tail to preach the *pure* and *unadultered* Gospel of Christ" (p. 41).

"I also," Lackington observes (pp. 47-8), "went to the Methodist meeting, to hear one Thomas Bryant, known in Taunton by the name of the *damnation preacher;* (he had just left off cobling *soles* of another kind.) His sermon frightened me most terribly. I soon after went to hear an old Scotchman; and he assured his congregation, that they would be damn'd, and double damn'd, and treble damn'd, and damn'd for ever, if they died without what he called *Faith. . . .* At last, by singing and repeating enthusiastic amorous hymns, and presumptuously applying particular texts of scripture, I got my imagination to the proper pitch, was born again in an instant, became a very great favourite of heaven, and was as familiar with the Father, Son, and Holy Ghost, as any old woman in Mr. Wesley's connection."

The young James Lackington coolly continues to record his disparate triple existences as young rake, Methodist convert, and literary amateur. He reads his current love, passages from the Bible justifying faith; she replies by quoting verses concerning "works." His career in Methodist meetings between the ages of sixteen and twenty-one is followed by his escapade in Bridgewater with "the beautiful Nancy Trott." Betty Tucker confides that she is with child by him, but he notes cheerfully that it was (p. 77) "a still-born child, so that I was never troubled for expences." He thereupon turns his attention to Homer and Epictetus. But when he hears the voice of Wesley himself from the pulpit, he returns to Methodism, converts the entire Jones family in Bristol, and buys many godly books. Also, he records, there are "a few of a better sort, as Gay's Fables; Pomfret's Poems; Milton's Paradise Lost" (p. 93), which he follows by Plato, Plutarch's Morals, and Confucius.

This ambitious shoemaking Lothario now decides to settle down. He goes back to his idyllic first love Nancy Smith, the milk-maid, to whom (as well as to Hannah Allen) he had given spiritual advice when he was seventeen; and they take up married life with a joint fortune of "one halfpenny to begin the world with" (p. 114).

Long before Lockhart wrote his *Life of Scott,* Lackington realized how important money affairs, to the last farthing, can be in the record of a life. Almost incredible poverty and sickness and starvation lie ahead of the young couple. Since his wife is usually ill, he sets off alone from Bristol bound for London, where he arrives with half a crown in his pocket. He sends for his wife. He inherits ten pounds from his grandfather, but he knows so little about the methods of finance that he travels in person to his old home to get the bequest, losing sixteen shillings on the way back —a catastrophe for him—spending almost five pounds on the journey, and nearly freezing to death in the winter weather. His wife is glad to rip open his clothes for the remnant of the inheritance sewed inside. With their last half-crown James Lackington buys Young's *Night Thoughts* instead of their Christmas dinner, and explains to Nancy how food for the mind is superior to food for the body. "My wife was convinced" (p. 136). She did not have to remember his arguments for long, however, for within ten pages she is dead, and her husband's funeral tribute changes into an anecdote about his second wife, Miss Dorcas Turton, "still more valuable" than his first, and closes with a description from Ovid of the "celebrated nymph Anna Perenna" (p. 150).

The reader is never sure whether James Lackington is himself aware of the moral blemishes in his own portrait. Possibly he delights in his own hardness, coarseness, and self-sufficiency. Certainly he can rise superior even to his own superiority, as when he remarks, in connection with the godlessness of London (pp. 125-6): "However I at length concluded, that if London was a second Sodom, I was a second Lot; and these comfortable ideas reconciled me to the thought of living in it." And here is a picture of himself, a callow Methodist youth on a December stagecoach, which is a masterpiece of humorous objectivity (pp. 131-2):

"But a more dreadful misfortune befel me the next morning; the extreme severe weather still continuing, in order to keep me from dying with cold, I drank some purl and gin, which (not being used to drink any thing strong) made me so drunk, that the coachman put me inside the carriage for fear I should fall off the roof. I there met with some of the jovial sort, who had also drank to keep out the cold, so that I found them in high glee; being asked to sing them a song, I immediately complied, and forgot that I was one of the holy brethren, so that I sung song for song with the merriest of them; only several times between the acts, I turned up the whites of my eyes, and uttered a few ejaculations, as 'Lord forgive me!' 'O Christ! What am I doing?' and a few more of the same pious sort."

Reading Amory's *Life of John Buncle* had destroyed Lackington's Methodist enthusiasm, he tells us; and side by side with graphic accounts of the death of Wesley or objective appraisals of Methodism crop up scurrilous tales and anecdotes. Peter Pindar in his "Ode on Finsbury Square," where Lackington later had his enormous bookshop, hints that the spicy and picaresque stories in this autobiography were written for him by a friend.

But such alluring fiction is not necessary to insure the publication of thirteen editions of his memoirs before his death. The story of his success is sufficient. His hobby of books proves his making. When he sets up his shop as a master-cobbler in 1775, he displays a few old calf-bindings as a sideline. The business grows. He and John Denis go into partnership, and publish catalogues. He starts the idea of selling books cheap and for cash. He buys up remainders, and cuts the prices to a half or a fourth of what they originally were. One of his smoothest devices is to appraise any library for five per cent of what it brings if it is sold to a competitor; if it is sold to him as appraiser, he magnanimously waives the commission. Small wonder that his profits rose to as much as four thousand pounds a year! He buys a carriage, on which he has inscribed, as his substitute for a coat-of-arms (p. 234): "Small Profits do great things."

He is sure of himself now. He sees himself mirrored in "The Progress of Ned Drugget" in Johnson's *Idler;* he can say authoritatively that (p. 249) "among all the schools where the knowledge of mankind is to be acquired, I know of none equal to that of a bookseller's shop." He feels himself partly responsible for the fourfold increase in the sale of books in England within the preceding twenty years, and he even dares to launch a quip sarcastic against the editors of the *Biographia Britannica*: he is writing and publishing his own life because he is not sure that they will ever reach the letter *L*. He travels over the British Isles and makes independent observations on Scottish washerwomen treading barefoot on the linen in their tubs, or on the Newcastle invention of an iron cage fastening over the head and into the mouth "to punish notorious scolds." He remembers just in time that he must not grow excited about the French Revolution, and writes his last letter about watering-places, from a watering-place. He is failing in health; he will soon marry a third time and retire from business; but not before he presents a final glimpse of himself revisiting youthful haunts—the homecoming of a Dick Whittington. The wheel has come full circle.

Lackington had observed (p. 239) that in some cases novels "have given us a more genuine history of Man . . . than . . . History, Biography &c." In his own work, written by a man with a flair for drama and the picaresque novel, he presents the dynamic career of a youthful satiric puritan who hardened at the end into a skeptical and hard-headed money-maker. The portrait betrays immense self-gratulation. Lackington need not have gone to such trouble on his own account, for many of his readers will be inclined to acknowledge his great ability to present realistic scenes in a life not without distinction, force, and purpose.

Of all the recorded careers in which money or financial success plays an important part, by far the best is Edward Topham's *Life of the late John Elwes* (1790). Like Lackington's *Memoirs* it was immediately successful. This life of Elwes is almost without ancestors in English biography in its masterly concentration on a single theme. Its hero, its tone, and its purpose render it unique, and Topham's skill in presenting and grouping anecdotes gives him a place among the best biographers of the eighteenth century. The appendix to the 1805 copy speaks of eight editions published in other countries as well as the dozen that had appeared in England, and tells this story about Walpole and Topham himself (pp. 99-100):

"It was my fortune some years ago, at the private theatricals of Richmond House, to find myself placed by the side of the late Horace Walpole, who was pleased to tell me, amongst other observations, that he considered *The Life of Mr. Elwes* 'as the best piece of biography in this country.'

" 'Laudari a laudato' has long been held very estimable commendation. . . ."

Edward Topham was hardly the man whom one would have picked offhand as an accomplished biographer. Nor was John Elwes an obvious subject for an overwhelmingly successful biography. Yet this hard-riding Beau Brummell, the friend of the Prince Regent and the protector of Perdita Robinson, increased the circulation of *The World* at an unprecedented rate and made Elwes a national figure by publishing in twelve installments the life of a retiring and inoffensive country gentleman who cut no figure in history or the arts and sciences, a lonely bachelor who died in 1789 at the age of seventy-five.

The secret of Topham's art becomes apparent in the very opening of his preface:[9]

"During the lifetime of Mr. Elwes, I said to him more than once, 'I would write his life.' His answer was—'There is nothing in it, Sir, worth mentioning.'

"That I have been of a different opinion, my labours will shew; and if I have any knowledge of history, or human nature, it will form an epoch in the biography of the eighteenth century, that such characters lived as those of Sir Hervey, and Mr. Elwes, his nephew—men voluntarily giving up all the blessings of life to save money, they knew not why; embracing poverty and mortification as the best lot of existence; and dying martyrs to that wealth, whose accumulation afforded no enjoyment."

Topham's *Life of Elwes,* in spite of his prediction, did not form an epoch; it was left for Lytton Strachey, more than a century later, to popularize the possibilities of grouping selected anecdotes, written in a suave and polished style, around a simple theme—an innovation which Topham had practised more than a hundred years before.

Only gradually does Topham build up that portrait of his hero on which he fixes his eyes so unwaveringly at the end. Young John Elwes was educated at Westminster School, where he was a fine classical scholar, though he never afterwards opened a book. His schooling was completed at Geneva, where Voltaire, whom he met, did not remain in his memory half so vividly as the horses which Elwes rode so superbly. Young Elwes had great charm of manner and a certain selflessness which he used assiduously in order to ingratiate himself with his skinflint uncle, Sir Harvey Elwes, by copying his niggardliness in the most minute particulars. Number II in Topham's serial publication is devoted entirely to the portrait of Sir Harvey, done in masterly strokes to show how a man may become "little else but Vegetation in a human shape."[10]

[9] 1805 ed., pp. [v]-vi.
[10] pp. 5, 7, and 11-12.

"At all times, he wore a black velvet cap much over his face—a worn-out full-dressed suit of clothes, and an old great coat, with worsted stockings drawn up over his knees. He rode a thin thorough-bred horse, and 'the horse and his rider' both looked as if a gust of wind would have blown them away together.

"When the day was not so fine as to tempt him abroad, he would walk backwards and forwards in his old hall, to save the expense of fire."

"To those who are continually courting the bustle of society, and the fever of public scenes, it may be curious to learn, that here was a man, who had the courage to live nearly seventy years alone!

"That this was done without former scenes to afford matter for reflection, or books to entertain; but in pursuing one ruling passion—the *amassing unused* WEALTH."

And now, as Elwes gains control of a great fortune which he was to spend his life in increasing, Topham shifts to an insistence on his miserliness which he does not forget until the whole story is told. The transition from Elwes's able and attractive youth to his avaricious manhood is made by a reference to his gentlemanly bearing and conduct (p. 16): "In this part of his character, nothing could be more pleasant than was Mr. Elwes; it was the pecuniary part which ruined, as the Dramatist would say, 'the stage effect of the whole thing.'"

Topham makes his painting doubly effective by allowing his protagonist not only pleasant manners, but also complete disinterestedness during his three terms in Parliament, and even generosity—upon occasions. By such devices he convinces the reader that his hero is more than a creation of his own mind, a caricature glaringly centered on the one corroding vice of penurious living. "While holding the pen of a faithful biographer," he writes (p. 31), "I am forced to recount . . . that his avarice consisted not in hardheartedness, but in self-denial." Consequently Elwes is portrayed as a man in whom penury is united with occasional bad business judgment: he lost a hundred and fifty thousand pounds in bad loans, which, Topham assures the reader, was the way of Providence to keep him from acquiring all the wealth of England.

Such a portrayal enables Topham to develop a balanced paradox, marvelling at the enigmas of human conduct (p. 61):

"These pleasant acts, of endangering his neck to save the payment of a turnpike, and starving his horse for a halfpennyworth of hay, happened, from the date of them, at the time he was risking the sum of twenty-five thousand pounds on some iron-works across the Atlantic Ocean, and of which he knew nothing, either as to produce, prospect, or situation!

"Strange man! whose penury and prodigality, whose profusion and meanness, all so mixed together, puzzle me still more and more, as I detail them to the public!"

Whenever John Elwes rode after the foxhounds—is it not probable that Topham met him at the hunt?—he carried hard-boiled eggs in his greatcoat pockets to save the expense of a meal during the day. This one habit Topham mentions three times in the course of his narrative; usually he has such a fund of stories and traditions that his memory, or his ingenuity, seems inexhaustible. Topham has a genius for grotesque anecdotes: his hero patches windows with old glass and brown paper to save the expense of new panes; he gleans corn in his tenants' fields after their harvest; he pulls down an "extravagant" crow's nest for firewood; he rides on the turf to lessen the expense of horseshoes; when a stable-boy leaves hay before a visitor's horse, he steals it back; he eats putrefied fish and "meat that walked about his plate"; he goes to a neighbor's to save his own fuel. "In short, whatever Cervantes or Molière have pictured, in their most sportive moods, of *avarice in the extreme,* here might they have seen realized or surpassed!"

One of the most admirable qualities in this biography is the sense of the aging and hardening of Elwes's character which Topham conveys without departing from anecdotes which always concentrate on the miser. Near the beginning one of his two natural sons falls off a ladder (pp. 24-5):

"The boy had the precaution to go up into village to the barber, and get blooded: on his return, he was asked where he had been, and what was the matter with his arm? He told his father that he had got bled—'Bled! bled!' said the old gentleman, 'but what did you give?'—'A shilling,' answered the boy:—'Psha!' returned the father, 'you are a blockhead! never part with your blood!' "

From such laughable stories, Topham gradually shifts to a more sordid portrayal (p. 72):

"He, one day, during this period, dined upon the remaining part of a moor-hen, which had been brought out of the river by a rat! and, at another, ate an undigested part of a pike, which a larger one had swallowed, but had not finished, and which were taken in this state in a net! At the time this last circumstance happened, he discovered a strange kind of satisfaction, for he said to me,—'Aye! this was killing two birds with one stone!' In the room of all comment—of all moral—let me say, that, at this time, Mr. Elwes was, perhaps, worth nearly *eight hundred thousand pounds!* and, at this period, he had not made his will; of course, was not saving from any sentiment of affection for any person."

Topham reflects his love of the stage in his conception of his hero as a man of an overpowering Jonsonian "humour," in his quotations from the drama, and in his frequent use of carefully selected dialogue to enliven his anecdotes. The author's favorite mark of punctuation is the exclamation point, as if to emphasize the incredibility of Mr. Elwes's behavior, and never does he seem more shocked than in learning that Elwes has never been at the theater (p. 70): "And Mr. Garrick, Mrs. Siddons, Mrs. Jordan, and Mr. Kemble, all sunk before—*five shillings!*"

Dramatically, then, the career of Elwes unfolds. He serves in Parliament, where (p. 48) "he had the very singular quality of not determining how he should vote, before he heard what was said on the subject." The danger of a royal reward for his services comes perilously close (pp. 38-9): ". . . he was unhappy for some days on hearing that Lord North intended to apply to the King to make him a peer. I really believe, had such an honour fallen unexpectedly upon his head, it would have been the death of him. He never would have survived the being obliged to keep a carriage, and three or four servants, all, perhaps, better dressed than himself!"

And he grows older (p. 41). "At this period of his life Mr. Elwes wore a wig. Much about that time when his parliamentary life ceased, that wig was worn out—so then (being older and wiser as to expense) he wore his own hair, which, like his expenses, was very small."

His restless loneliness is intensified by sketching in the nightmare figure of a single old serving-woman, a worthless human chattel against the chiaroscuro of his London mansions (pp. 32-3):

"He was frequently an itinerant for a night's lodging; and though master of above an hundred houses, he never wished to rest his head long in any he chose to call his own. A couple of beds, a couple of chairs, a table, and an old woman, were all his furniture; and he moved them about at a minute's warning. Of all these moveables, the old woman was the only one that gave him trouble, for she was afflicted with a lameness that made it difficult to get her about quite so fast as he chose; and then the colds she took were amazing! for sometimes she was in a small house in the Haymarket; then in a great house in Portland Place; sometimes in a little room and a coal fire; at other times with a few chips which the carpenters had left, in rooms of most splendid and frigid dimensions, and with a little oiled paper in the windows for glass. In truth, she perfectly realized the words of the Psalmist—for, though the old woman might not be one of the wicked, she certainly was 'here to-day, and gone to-morrow.' "

In one of these empty houses, his nephew, Colonel Timms, finally finds him dying and his servant dead.

And now Topham begins to paint his portrait with more intense shadows as he draws his moral (pp. 70-1):

"Thus, in every trait of his character, came forth the *evil genius* of money, and spread its influence over all. In the close of that life to which I am hastening—well will it be, if the passion which undermined all the happiness of Mr. Elwes, proves the means of destroying such a second passion in others!"

(pp. 82-3) ". . . *money* was now his only thought . . . and as his capacity sunk away from him by degrees, he dwindled from the real cares of his property, into the puerile concealment of a few guineas. This little store he would carefully wrap up in various papers, and depositing them in different corners, would amuse himself with running from one to the other, to see whether they were all safe."

As he contemplates Elwes's deterioration, Topham interjects what he remembers of Hamlet's words—"Rest! thou perturbed spirit!—rest!" But the tragedy deepens. Elwes's attorney, staying with him in Berkshire, is waked "by the noise of a naked foot." Elwes has stolen five and a half guineas and half a crown, which are found later in a corner behind the window-shutter. His early good manners have given place to forgetfulness, querulousness, and suspicion, and worst of all, to those insane and trivial acts in which the sin of avarice walks embodied in senescent flesh. On the twenty-sixth of November, 1789, the old miser dies, as easily as a child goes "to sleep on the breast of its mother, worn out with" the rattles and the toys "of a long day."

The spirit of the biography, as this last quotation shows, is not less sentimental than it is satiric. Topham could not write a cold, defamatory life, for his own spirit was too warm, impulsive, and generous—he was a spendthrift even with his dashes, italics, and exclamation points. And although he cannot help delighting in the exercise of his wit and his genius for story-telling, Topham seems fairly sincere in his professed purpose of showing how a single vice may corrode the most promising character. He is no less aware of the possibilities than of the failures in human life, and he pleads with as much eloquence as anyone during the century for the portrayal of man as man, neither devil nor angel (p. 100):

". . . as I have long been sensible of the weaknesses of human nature, in knowing my own, and never had the honour of meeting a gentleman without some folly or other—I must be content to take things as they are, and to speak of man as he is. What kind of painter would he be, who, in his portraits, concealed every thing that was not beautiful? What kind of biography would that be, which represented nothing but what was good, generous, brave, tender-hearted, full of talents, and full of virtues? It must be the biography of an angel: and, I confess, I am not qualified to write any biography of that kind. A very ingenious man used to say, 'that had it fallen to his lot to live near such a man as Richardson's Sir Charles Grandison, he would have got out of the country as soon as he could.'"

For vividly realized scenes, flowing informality of style, a sense of the growth of character, seemingly dispassionate judgment, economy of purpose, vitality, humor, and originality, Topham's *Life of Elwes* deserves a far more honorable place in English biography than it has hitherto been accorded.

The career of John Elwes shows that money may be the blood of life, and the popularity of Topham's and Lackington's biographies indicates a growing public which finds commercial transactions and the power of money absorbing topics. Although these two lives may be the best in the field, they were not the first:[11] the great prototype of subjects for biography in which economics plays a major rôle is John Law, whose financial genius, more than any other man's, led France and England into the Mississippi Company and the South Sea Bubble; lives of Law were published in 1721 and 1791.

Although the lives of merchants seemed of great importance to the merchants themselves, and when recorded in print may have been read with eagerness by their fellow-merchants, it is interesting to observe how many biographies of money-makers were written and laid aside, published only in the still more mercantile nineteenth century.[12] The ingrained humility of the English tradesman was not lightly to be overcome in a few decades.

"The number of the laity whose lives are writ," observes a city father of Newcastle,[13] "bears no proportion with those of divines

---

[11] cf. *The memoirs of John Ker, of Kersland, in North Britain, Esq; relating to politicks, trade, and history. . . . With an account of the rise and progress of the Ostend Company in the Austrian Netherlands. Published by himself.* 3d ed., 1727. This might possibly be considered the first full biography of commerce; fittingly it comes from the North. Also cf. *Memoirs of the life and times of Sir Thomas Deveil,* 1748, for the account of a hero raising himself by his own merits; and *Memoirs of a younger brother,* 1789, for the life of a hero "constrained to dabble in dirty grocery, and piddle in petty haberdashery." *The Life and distresses of Simon Mason, apothecary,* ca. 1754, is a whining story of a failure in business.

[12] cf. 1820 and 1885 reprints of the scarce 1776 *Memoirs of Sir John Barnard, Alderman; A family history begun by James Fretwell,* wr. 1739, pub. 1877; *Autobiography of William Stout, of Lancaster, wholesale and retail grocer and ironmonger,* wr. ca. 1744; pub. 1851; *The birth, education, travels, and life of Henry Lamp,* apothecary, wr. 1711, pub. 1895. In certain respects, Benjamin Franklin's autobiography also falls into this group.

[13] *Memoirs of the life of Mr. Ambrose Barnes, late merchant and sometime alderman of Newcastle upon Tyne,* wr. 1716; published abridged in 1828, in full in 1867. Ded., p. 3.

whose eulogies and encomiums are coming out every day. . . .
To accomodate this defect in our Nonconformist Martyrologie,
have I by your direction made this beginning."

Yet the "Life, fortunes, and opinions" which follow such a modest dedication lay in manuscript through the whole century. Ordinarily diffident about publishing their own lives, the burghers
contented themselves with the business triumphs of other lands
and other centuries.[14] The principal bourgeois character in the
drama, George Lillo presented as a warning example of the
tradesman who aspires beyond his class; and the autobiographies
of Mark Moore and Charlotte Charke attest the popularity, if
any proof were needed, of *George Barnwell, or the London Merchant*;[15] this same interest in the rise or fall of Mr. Worldly
Wiseman is shown in the actual career of Alderman Barber,
though a closer parallel from the stage would probably be Simon
Eyre in *The Shoemaker's Holiday. The life and character of
John Barber, Esq; late Lord-Mayor of London, deceased,* printed
in 1741 to sell at a shilling, contains all that the burgher reader
desires. Not only are "His amours and gallantries" promised on
the title-page, but "The methods he made use of to establish
himself in business, worth the perusal of every young beginner,"
and "His death, burial, and last will, or his disposal of his estate."

[14] cf. *The life of Mr. Thomas Firmin, late citizen of London* and philanthro-
pist, 1791, repub. from the ed. of 1698; or *The life and adventures of John
Christopher Wolf,* 1785, self-educated German who attains moderate affluence in
Ceylon.

[15] For the influence of the drama and of Lillo's play in particular, in calling
forth a novel cast in the guise of biography and possibly containing some historical
truth, see Charlotte Charke's *The Mercer, or Fatal Extravagance: being a true
narrative of the life of Mr. William Dennis. Mercer, in Cheapside, London. The
Occurrences herein related, are well worthy the observation of the reader, and
proper to be regarded, by every mechanick in Great Britain,* n.d., *ca.* 1740?
"The strongest Motive that could possibly induce me to publish this Melancholly," she writes, pp. 31-2, "was an Observation I have made for many Years
of the presumptiae [*sic*] Vanity daily increasing and prompting many Persons in
Trade to live up to the State of those, whose Birth and Fortune might justifie
the running into such Expences, as must naturally terminate in the Ruin of
Trading Families, and be the unhappy cause of Multiplying the numerous Indigent, who but for this failing in Parents might live comfortably to themselves
and be generally beneficial to the World." The ruin of aspiring tradesmen was
borne in upon her less from the failures of actual life than from the ruin of
George Barnwell as he is pursued by the Nemesis of the counting-house.

The anonymous author is certain that interest in (p. 1) "the Life of one, who, tho' not born, yet died a Gentleman . . . will more than justify the following Publication to the Town." The reader is assured that this friend of Swift, Pope, and Bolingbroke was *not* born in Newgate—he was just brought up there. His father was a barber; he was apprenticed to a widow in the printing business; and—important lesson for the readers of this type of biography—"He . . . always kept the main Chance in View, thro' the whole of his Servitude" (p. 5).

The writer of Barber's life caters to the appetite of his particular public by detailing John Barber's affair with Mrs. Manley, when he "remained in Possession of the Fort for several Years; and even till a merciless, and a more powerful Conqueror took Possession of it, and laid it level with the Ground" (p. 12), and by insinuating that the Lord Mayor had secretly married his residuary legatee, Mrs. Sarah Dovekin. But apart from such stories in the school of Edmund Curll, the biographer's main theme of the rise of a 'prentice is developed with some skill. Money transactions are recorded, and Barber's success is analyzed by showing his complaisance, his shrewdness, his dependability, loyalty, and business dispatch. As printer for the government and the Tories under the ministry of his great patron Bolingbroke, while making the most of his financial opportunities, Barber remained self-controlled at the height of his career. The height? Not yet (p. 23): ". . . all this was very far from what his good Stars intended him, and Fortune had yet in Store for him: No, she set him upon a much loftier Pinacle afterwards, to which she mounted him by just Gradations, and not in a Moment of Time; so that he never grew giddy with the Height, or was ever in any Danger, but once, of tumbling, or being tumbled down."

And the story which follows—the career of a man who could reap profits even from the South Sea Bubble; who could begin as an orphan in the London gutters and end with a town-house and Sir William Temple's former estate near Richmond; who, although he had been the loyal friend of Atterbury, Oxford, and Bolingbroke, could yet become Sheriff of London and in

1733 Lord Mayor—such a story is most edifying in showing what fortune will do for its favorite, provided always, of course, he keeps the main Chance in View.

At the end of the century, as a fitting coda in which are caught up for the last time the themes of the rising bourgeoisie, of the power of money, of peculation and public service set forth in topical anecdotes, with a spice of malicious gossip, appears *City Biography, containing anecdotes and memoirs of the rise, progress, situation & character, of the Aldermen and other conspicuous personages of the Corporation and City of London.*[16]

Even the feminine autobiographers are touched by the love of lucre and commerce. Thus, the third volume of Jane Elizabeth Moore's *Genuine memoirs* (1786) becomes "A comprehensive treatise on the trade, manufactures, navigation, laws and police of this kingdom, and the necessity of a country hospital." In the earlier volumes, though Mrs. Moore is more personal, she is not less commercial. Her favorite theme is "accumulation," by which she means money-making; and she seems to have been trusted with affairs by her father, who has a manufactory at Woking. Even chivalric terms turn ludicrously practical under her un-tutored pen, as when she refers to her mother's romance as (Vol. I, p. 26) "a night errand scene in a strange country." In what she calls (Vol. II, p. 64) "My search after knowledge in the trading line," she travels over the British isles, appraising power-sites and buying mills, until she becomes so tangled in speculations in wool, silk, and leather that she ends in a debtors' prison.

The moral of her career she has tagged in a couplet:[17]

"In town and country golden streams I sought,
And with accumulation sorrows bought."

She declares that she submits to God, but is certain that he has never tried any individual so much as she has been tried. And when she makes her final inventory of sorrows, characteristically enough all of the crosses she bears are material, and most of them monetary (Vol. II, pp. 338-9):

---

[16] 1800, 2d ed. cf. also *Memoirs of the late Sir John Barnard, Knt. and Alderman of the City of London,* 1776.
[17] p. 5 of her introductory "Index," written in rhymes

". . . from Michaelmas 1784, to Christmas 1785, being only the space of fifteen months, I endured the very extraordinary experience of being robbed once on the high road, had once my own waggon robbed, once lost a large quantity of linen and other things out of a neighbour's waggon, which was likewise robbed, sustained damage in trade to a large amount, suffered a great loss by horses, had nine different accidents at the risk of my life, by attending my occupation, had a confirmation from Jamaica of the loss of near a thousand pounds, lost the sale of my premises, was six weeks under a surgeon, with a contusion in my left shoulder, (which will never I believe be again as before) was arrested by Mr. Moore's executors, and lay six weeks in a spunging house, and from thence was obligated to remove to the King's Bench Prison."

Life, to Jane Elizabeth Moore and to many of the practising biographers of her time, is not primarily spiritual or emotional or rational; it is economic, and biography may best be written on the debit and credit pages of a ledger.

One of the sincerest and most affecting of the biographies of self-made businessmen is *The life of William Hutton,* principally written in his seventy-fifth year in 1798. "I have lived," he writes (1816 ed., p. 231), "to see one person an infant, and his son an old man! . . .

"When I consider that within my memory the surface of the earth is totally altered, that the old buildings upon that surface have disappeared, and the new become old, that the former inhabitants have given way to the present, whose opinions and manners are different, I may say with Dr. Young, 'This is not the world in which I was born.' "

And just after the turn of the century (p. 237): "My year runs round like a boy who beats his hoop round a circle, and with nearly the same effect, that of a little exercise." The "little exercise" took the shape, when he was seventy-eight years old, of a six-hundred-and-one mile walk through the Lake Country.

Yet William Hutton did not become such a happy and hale peripatetic sage without years of endurance and self-discipline. Walking—walking mentioned continually in his autobiography—

becomes a symbol of his spirit; his walk was a long one, it was uphill, and he never turned his back. In his memoirs the style is the man; the sentences are short, crabbed, shrivelled, direct, sometimes sarcastic. He says in the Preface:[18]

"I must apologize to the world, should this ever come under its eye, for presenting it with a life of insignificance. I have no manoeuvres, no state tricks, no public transactions, nor adventures of moment, to lay before my Readers. I have only the history of an individual, struggling, unsupported, up a mountain of difficulties. And yet some of the circumstances are so very uncommon, as barely to merit belief. A similar mode of a man ushering himself into life, perhaps, cannot be met with.

"If I tell unnecessary things, they are not told in unnecessary words. I have avoided prolixity."

Hutton's remarkable memory recalls four incidents for the year 1725, when he was two years old. One of them is (p. 3): "I set fire to my petticoats, frock, and bib." But a more extended anecdote in his third year shows his knack of telling a story as if he were re-living it in a hallucination (p. 4):

"1726. Every class of the animal world associates with its like. An old couple, Moses Simpson and his wife, who lived at the next door, took great notice of me, but I shunned them with horror; had they been young, I should probably have sought *them,* but I was fully persuaded they would kill me. I stood at the top of a flight of stairs, and this woman at the bottom, coaxing me to come to her. She might as well have intreated the moon. I instantly tumbled to the bottom. She took me in her arms, endeavoured to pacify me, dandled me on the knee, and I was surprized that I escaped with life."

Later he walks home from a public house with an aunt who has got completely drunk, and tells the story as a puzzled child would see it. The background of his family and elders is Hogarthian or Dickensian (p. 5):

"At Mountsorrel I had an uncle who was a Grocer, and a bachelor; also a grand-mother who kept his house; and at Swith-

[18] 1816 ed., pp. v-vi.

land, two miles distant, three crabbed aunts, all single, who re-
sided together as Grocers, Milliners, Mercers, and School-mis-
tresses."

His schoolmaster, Mr. Thomas Meat, used to knock his pupil's
head against the wall; his mother dies when he is seven; his father
he portrays as follows (pp. 18-19):

"Though my father was neither young, being forty-two, nor
handsome, having lost an eye, nor sober, for he spent all he could
get in liquor, nor clean, for his trade was oily, nor without
shackles, for he had five children, yet women of various descriptions courted his smiles, and were much inclined to pull
caps for him.

"On my birthday at night my father treated us with a quart
of twopenny beer; and observed, that the life of man was divided into seven stages of ten years each, and that I had now
completed the first."

Even in this first decade of his life, young William had seen a
deal of hardship. He had been set to work in the silk mills while
he was still so small that he had a pair of high pattens tied to
his feet to enable him to reach the machines. Being sent as a
'prentice to his uncle's at Nottingham must therefore have come
as a relief; when at the age of seventeen, however, he is thrashed
by his uncle so soundly that his cries are heard by all the girls of
the neighborhood, his shame is so great that he runs away. A long
separate section follows, entitled *The History of a Week*,[19] detailing his sufferings and adventures.

Yet all these sordid and painful details are buoyed up by
Hutton's hopes and by the reader's knowledge of his eventual
success. He conveys a sense of the passage of time, and keeps
these far-away incidents in their frame by repeated contrasts with
later scenes. Thus he records that before he left the silkmill (p. 24)
"I cut, with a pen-knife, upon one of the top rails of the seventh
mill above, W. H. 1737, which I saw in 1790, fifty-three years
after." Or again, when he comes to Mr. Grace's house in Birmingham (p. 43):

"I appeared a trembling stranger in that house, over which,
sixteen years after, I should preside. I stood like a dejected culprit

[19] pp. 31-50. Written in 1779.

by that counter, upon which, thirty-eight years after, I should record the story."

After his reconciliation with his uncle, the idle apprentice becomes industrious. Soon he is the second best stocking-maker in Nottingham, then an independent shopkeeper, a bookbinder in Birmingham, a dealer in paper, a manufacturer of paper, an overseer of the poor, a commissioner of the Court of Requests, a businessman so tangled in purchases and debts and finance that "like Sterne's starling, 'I was caught in a cage, and could not get out'" (p. 132). The account of his rise in business is interwoven with his progress in literature, from his first purchase of three volumes of the *Gentleman's Magazine* to the publication of his *History of Birmingham* and his election as Fellow of the Antiquarian Society of Scotland. He also recalls one dark night, when he was standing in a doorway with Miss Sarah Cock; the succeeding pages, recounting "the happy effects of reciprocal love," form a beautiful and unaffected tribute to his wife. He buys a new house, then a coach, for Sarah Hutton and the children. And suddenly, on Bastille Day, 1791, in the midst of these family joys, bursts "that most savage event," the Birmingham Riots. Through sixty pages the reader is given flashes of the furious mob sacking his home in the name of patriotism, burning his country house, shouting for "Church and King" until one hundred thousand pounds worth of damage had been committed by "our black sovereigns." Just fifty years before the riots, to a day, he had entered Birmingham as a runaway apprentice.

From this catastrophe he recovers very slowly. The riots almost ruined him, and shortened his wife's existence. "The nature of the human species," he writes bitterly (p. 215), "like that of the brute creation, is to destroy each other." He resigns the public office he has filled for nineteen years, and turns over his business to his son. His autobiography closes with tolerant religious views and skeptical or pragmatic political opinions. Only in his later annals has he learned to say (p. 247): "A *happy man?* That man is myself. Though my morning was lowering, my evening is sunshine." He has health, property, affectionate children, a taste for reading; moreover, he has memoirs of the Huttons to write, in which he includes some fascinating stories of a middle-class burgher family. It is left for his daughter Catherine to record, after his death, that his foremost trait was the love of peace.

Not only the men of trade, but the men of science were accorded increasing recognition in the biographies of the eighteenth century. Here again, when popular curiosity concerning the field of knowledge which they explored was first awakened, the lives of the scientists followed as a natural corollary. Lives of men connected with all sciences and arts and professions were given to the public. The antiquaries had always been able to take care of themselves; but the eighteenth century witnessed, for instance, lives of almost all of its foremost physicians—Sir Robert Sibbald, or Mead, or Radcliffe, Fothergill, Pott, Alcock, Monsey, or Freind—of painters, architects, musicians, scholars,[20] learned ladies, and mathematicians. If in England an officer or a fellow of the Royal Academy, the Society of Physicians, or the Society of Antiquaries stood a fair chance of having a memorial written upon his death by a member of his association, in Scotland in the last quarter of the century he was practically sure of it. During that period the intellectual capital of the British isles, one is tempted to assert, shifted from London to Edinburgh, and in the lives and memorials of the economist Adam Smith, the philosopher David Hume, the historian William Robertson, and others of almost equal brilliance, written by their admirers, particularly by Dugald Stewart, Scottish *pietas* established the principle that intellectual achievement deserves its memorial no less than party politics, pulpit oratory, and skirmishes of horse.

One of the most enthusiastic younger members of this Edinburgh group was David Steuart Erskine—David Stewart he styles himself on title-pages—Earl of Buchan. His national pride led him to conceive a series of lives, far outsoaring the ambitious *Biographia Britannica* of Dr. Kippis, in which every great man of Britain was to be commemorated in a separate quarto volume. He began by publishing at his own expense *An account of the life, writings, and inventions of John Napier* (1787), in which he,

---

[20] cf. that unusual work, John Ward's *Lives of the Professors of Gresham College: to which is prefixed the life of the founder, Sir Thomas Gresham*, 1740.

as the "young man of quality" he calls himself, supplies a fulsome opening, and his 'obscurer collaborator supplies the logarithms into which Napier's life rapidly disappears. In 1792 the self-conscious Earl issues one further volume, *Essays on the lives and writings of Fletcher of Saltoun and the poet Thomson,* in which he is still to be found exclaiming Bravo! as critical comment on Fletcher's opinions. After this volume, the fine flame of his enthusiasm flickered out.

The Earl of Buchan is representative, however, of a class of people who are responsible for a new group of eighteenth century lives. The same spirit which led the bluestocking Mrs. Macaulay to defend equality until Doctor Johnson floored her by suggesting that her footman sit down at table with them, resulted in a series of biographies sponsored by the intelligentsia. Buchan's essay on the poet James Thomson is all enthusiasm, no industry; and leaves the reader with the principal impression that Buchan's carriage upset on his way to deliver a panegyric at a centennial celebration in Thomson's honor. Other charitable patrons are caught in equally awkward postures in their condescension. Hannah More's "Prefatory letter to Mrs. Montagu" before *Poems ... by Ann Yearsley, a milkwoman of Bristol* (1785) sketches the life of the milkmaid poetess and defends native genius. Ann Yearsley replies with praise of *Stella,* which, in view of a subscription list for her poems that covers fifteen pages in double columns, seems no more than adequate. Yet by 1787, Lactilla "has unfortunately had a dispute with her original patroness which was carried, on both sides, to a disgusting excess,"[21] and, in an episode whose obvious moral is "Don't help the poor," the milkmaid of genius shows herself more skilled as a debater than a poet, and makes her patroness appear spiteful, changeable, and ridiculous.

Like Hannah More stooping down above her milkmaid, Joseph Spence had already adopted a patronizing, superior attitude toward the thresher poet, Mr. Stephen Duck, who diverted Queen Caroline much as John Taylor the water-poet amused Charles I. After detailing how Duck, sweating from field labor, discovers

---

[21] *Catalogue of living authors,* 1798, Vol. II, p. 400.

Milton, Shakespeare, the *Spectators,* and *Telemachus,* his biographer deigns to observe: "With these Helps Stephen is grown something of a Poet, and something of a Philosopher."[22]

High on the throne of Poetry at Oxford, the Reverend Joseph Spence evidently enjoyed his rôle as herald to the world of humble and neglected genius. In 1754 he sponsors *An account of the life, character, and poems of Mr. Blacklock; student of philosophy, in the University of Edinburgh,* in which, although Mr. Spence seems unaware even of Thomas Blacklock's first name, he is sure the young man is worthy because the young man is blind. And in 1757, from the Strawberry Hill press, Spence issues *A parallel: in the manner of Plutarch: between a most celebrated man of Florence: and one, scarce ever heard of in England.* The Florentine is Antonio Magliabecchi, librarian to Cosimo III, and the Englishman is Robert Hill, humble, self-schooled, but hardly a great scholar. Spence notes complacently that Hill is unknown outside Buckingham and its ten-mile circle, and seems to take principal delight in calling forth from obscurity a human mole.

Equality and brotherhood, then, are fashionable. Not only does an insignificant clerk consider that he must publish his life to rescue himself from the accusation in some newspaper that he is the worst pulpit reader in London,[23] not only does a whining woman in prison in the Fleet defend her conduct in three volumes,[24] a self-made scientist narrate his desolate boyhood in a cottage in Banffshire,[25] and a nameless Dubliner devote five-hundred-and-forty pages to a career of pointless travels and trivial incidents,[26] but also the literary bigwigs and sentimental aristocrats feel their hearts so overflowing with fraternal affection that they raise to the dignity of biography humble lives as yet unconscious of their own importance.

[22] *Poems of Stephen Duck,* 1753, 3d ed., p. xxii.

[23] *My own life, by C.[Charles] Este,* 1787.

[24] *The life of Mrs. Gooch. Written by herself,* 1792. Also *An appeal to the public, on the conduct of Mrs. Gooch. . . . Written by herself,* 1788.

[25] *Life of James Ferguson,* before his *Select Mechanical Exercises,* 1773.

[26] *The life and history of a pilgrim.* By G—— W——, Dublin, 1753. The preface says the author would dedicate it to a noble lord, but he is afraid the noble lord would be ashamed of it. Nevertheless, he publishes. cf. also the lives of eccentrics in Chap. IV.

But the greatest single cause of the prevalence of biographies of the Third Estate lies in the revivals of religious enthusiasm. The almost innumerable Quaker lives of the first half of the century and the Methodist lives of the latter half are with few exceptions lives of the lowly. Where, before, the career of the pastor had been worth recording, now the experiences of each lamb in the flock become of importance. The undistinguished careers of serving-maids, for example, can be presented under the Wesleyan aegis, almost as if their humble position and negligible place in society afforded additional reasons for recording their pious lives.[27] The "brethren and sisters" of George Fox and Charles Wesley is more than the opening phrase for an exhortation; it represents an active belief; and its result in the field of biography is the multiplying of exemplary lives, minutes of God's mercies, journals of spiritual conflict and desolation. With the Quakers, the record of one's own life for the possible edification of friends became a customary act of devotion; and the Wesleyans, in the *Arminian Magazine* and in published sets of volumes which extended well into the next century, developed an efficient system for the dissemination of saintly biographies. It was not sufficient that God had numbered the very hairs on their heads; these zealous biographers and autobiographers number them over again. James Lackington gives a vivid account[28] of the scene in the Chapelyard and its vicinity, immediately after the death of Wesley, when accounts of his life, hastily run off the press, are hawked abroad by peddlers who bawl out that their particular pamphlet constitutes the only true and faithful biography.

Yet although as a whole, these Christian memorials are inept and dull and over-serious, they rendered a great service to biography in fascinating individual exceptions,[29] and in their emphasis, through sheer number, on the possibility of recording the

[27] cf. the popularity of the *Life of Armelle Nicolas, commonly called The Good Armelle; a poor maid servant in France, who could not read a letter in a book, and yet a noble and happy servant of the King of Kings,* 1772; *Letters wrote by Jane Cooper: to which is prefixt some account of her life and death,* 1764, 2d ed. A servant girl, who did plain-work in London.

[28] *Memoirs,* 1791, pp. 188-9, Letter xxv.

[29] See Chap. V, the first section, on subjective life-writing.

life of the spirit as well as the life of action, the life of a cobbler as well as the life of a king.

If all men are brothers, and yet are living in a society which does not suggest that such a truth is obvious, philanthropic and professional reformers may develop. The last half of the eighteenth century records the lives of such sociological crusaders.[80] Sometimes this new *motif* is introduced almost accidentally into a biography, as in Alderman Barber's effecting an important prison reform (1741, p. 54), so that an acquitted prisoner can no longer be detained in Newgate until he pays his imprisonment fees—he is now instantly discharged on acquittal. The brief life of Captain Thomas Coram, purely philanthropic in purpose, is issued with the title *Private virtue and publick spirit display'd* (1751), and shows him so interested in the welfare of the state that he loses all his own wealth and must finally depend upon his friends for support. His projects range from the development of Nova Scotia or the granting bounties on naval stores from the colonies in order to make Great Britain independent in foreign wars, to the institution of a Foundling Hospital, realized only after seventeen years of exertion, or of a Christian school for Indian maidens. Richard Rawlinson's *Short historical account of the life and designs of Thomas Bray*[81] shows a missionary to Maryland, an agitator for public libraries, and a prison reformer who possibly gave General Oglethorpe the idea for the colonization of Georgia. The best of the lives of pure philanthropists is John Aikin's *View of the life, travels, and philanthropic labors of the late John Howard*,[82] which follows him through all his travels and visits to prisons until his death from fever in the Chersonese shortly after he reads of the fall of the Bastille. Nor are the tributes to his character by Burke and Erasmus Darwin,

[80] See Alexander Cruden's *History of Richard Potter*, 1763; *The life and writings of the Rev. William Dodd*, 1780; John Pugh's *Remarkable occurrences in the life of Jonas Hanway*, 1787; and as a forerunner, the life of Walter Moyle prefixed to his *Works*, 1727.

[81] Printed by B. C. Steiner for the Maryland Historical Society, Baltimore, 1901. Written about 1746, according to the *Biographia Britannica*, which published an account of Bray, evidently derived from Rawlinson.

[82] t.p. of Philadelphia edition, 1794; 1st ed., 1792, London.

William Hayley's ode, and Aikin's careful character-sketch necessary to convince the reader that Howard was a man of sinews
and of practical benevolence.

One other philanthropist, William Whiston, sums up in his own
person many of the qualities and tendencies which opened up
these new fields in biography. His individuality and conceit do
not stop far short of madness; yet he was also a distinguished
mathematician, a theological controversialist, and a pugnacious
humanitarian long before Godwin and Tom Paine. Writing in
his eightieth year and after,[38] the old man evidently considers
that his motto—*Ne quid falsi dicere audeat, ne quid veri non
audeat*—gives him leave to say what he pleases. In unbelievably
smug and self-centered pages about his early years, he explains
why he abandons the Cartesian philosophy for the Newtonian,
recounts Newton's confiding in him that he arrived at his theory
of gravity through calculating the moon's attraction toward the
earth, and includes the meditations and sermons he composed
as an undergraduate. He even wrote a chronology of the world,
based on a study of Isaac Newton. Finally he becomes a substitute
for Newton as professor of mathematics at Cambridge, and then
his successor. Yet science was never enough for his restless mind.
To him, for instance, as he looks back upon his life, the eclipse
of 1715 "appears now to have been a Divine Signal for the End
of over-bearing Persecution in two of the ten idolatrous and
persecuting Kingdoms, which arose in the fifth Century, in the
Roman Empire, the Britains and the Saxons." He rummages
around in antiquity until he discovers and embraces the Eusebian
doctrine—"then called the Arian heresy"—and is condemned and
expelled by the University because of his unorthodoxy.

The break with Cambridge merely gives him more windmills
to tilt at, more people to annoy with his militant righteousness.
He helps break up a Hell-Fire Club; he publishes his scruples
against the Thirty-nine Articles; he fulminates against Lady
Calverly, living in fornication; and he takes up the case of the
Earl of Essex and a debauched virgin in a letter to the Prince

[38] *Memoirs of the life and writings of Mr. William Whiston*, 1749.

of Wales and his Princess. Dangerously pig-headed, he "discovers" new sacraments and rites merely by turning over the Fathers, and he administers them himself while his trial for heresy hangs fire. He characterizes the bishops individually and bitterly in thirty pages; he declares that Newton has prevented his election to the Royal Society because of Whiston's independence; and he points out Richard Steele's venial sins because Steele (p. 303) "has given a Character of me in his Address to the Pope, but tis too ludicrous to appear in this Place."

He writes letters to everyone and on every subject; he explains the faults and merits of the Baptists in an epistle addressed to them; he abhors execution for robbery, he abhors gaming, and he abhors the practice of administering the sacrament when inducting civil officers. After including countless scraps, he writes on page 632: "I could easily add a great many other Passages in the Course of my long Life. But that I may not render this Account too large, and of too great a Price, I forbear. Only I desire my Reader to observe that I have said very little of the Royal Family, for peculiar Reasons." But four years later there appeared a final outburst, which scarcely fulfills its title of memoirs of his life by reprinting his tracts: *Lectures on the late remarkable meteors and earthquakes, and on the future restoration of the Jews,* and *The liturgy of the Church of England reduced nearer to the primitive standard.*

It is unfortunate that such a strong intellect as his should have gone astray; and that energetic and generous-hearted projects for reform should be so inextricably tangled with sheer bad temper and fanatical vaporing. At the end of his memoirs, he is still convinced that he, and he alone, has seen all the truth. He compares himself to Milton's Abdiel who sole among Lucifer's hosts dared stand for God (p. 283): "It may not be amiss to take Notice here of the Consolation I used to receive by Milton's Character of the Seraph Abdiel. . . . It so near fitting my Case, who have almost alone attempted to restore Primitive Christianity, . . . that I could not but frequently solace my self with it." Whiston entrusts the reader with his discovery that the Millennium will begin A.D. 1766. He himself, however, in a London so wickedly deaf to truth, does not bother to wait for it, and on the twenty-second of August, 1752, unshaken, unseduced, unterrified, William Whiston turns his back

"On those proud towers to swift destruction doomed."

It is time to offer apologies and explanations for including the lives of criminals, adventurers, travellers, tradesmen, scientists, Methodists and milkmaids in a chapter which purports to deal with Romanticism. The sense in which that difficult and ambiguous term is used in this discussion may be expressed simply: Romanticism is taken to indicate the dominance of imagination, in contradistinction to the dominance of reason implied in classicism. And the imaginative act, as Coleridge discovered and described it, consists in the sudden grasping, as if by a flash of insight, of complex existence. The act of the imagination is an act of synthesis; the act of the reason is an act of analysis. Reason reduces all things to its own terms; it disregards, or selects, or takes to pieces, or simplifies, until the dead components with which it deigns to deal are easily understandable, or may at least be reduced to words or syllogisms; reason seeks for common denominators. The imagination, on the other hand, makes no claim to explain existence. One will not go far astray in identifying the imagination with *complete, individual consciousness,* where the reason plays a dormant rather than a dominant part in a complex which includes physiological, emotional, and spiritual states. Newton formulating the laws of motion is behaving as a rationalist; Newton standing on the seashore by starlight and meditating that all our mortal knowledge is as a grain of sand upon a beach, is behaving as a romanticist.

Slowly, during the eighteenth century, imagination supplanted reason. Neither the world, nor man in the world, could be explained easily and completely by rational processes. "Whatever is, is right" was answered by a gradual reversion to a belief that there are more things in heaven and earth than are dreamt of in philosophy. The rational satisfaction of Deism gave way before the mystical experience of Methodism. The "renaissance of wonder" was at hand, as the complex and multiplex worlds of the imagination supplanted the homogeneous and explicable world of reason. And because each man came to be considered as an unpredictable bundle of mysterious forces, in which infinite permutations and combinations were possible, the growth of genuine biography, which is the record of an individual life, was natural enough during the eighteenth century. With the dominance of the imagination, it is equally natural that the motive for writing lives should change from an ethical purpose based on the presentation of typical virtues and vices in a typical example of the species Man, to the hedonistic aim of gratifying curiosity by presenting the idiosyncrasies of an individual who is interesting precisely because he does *not* resemble anyone who had lived before, or during, his lifetime. Because of this conception of the romantic spirit, the new subjects for biography included in the first half of this chapter, disparate though they are in other respects, have been introduced.

Certain of the lives already dealt with may seem pre-romantic, or even Augustan, in many of their characteristics; but all of them show novel, non-rational interpretations of life; all of them conceive new possibilities in experience—a fundamental belief at every historical recurrence of the romantic temper.

Moreover, an important feature of romanticism is that it tends toward democracy as opposed to the aristocracy of classicism. The imagination takes account of the whole man; reason disregards, or tries to discipline, many parts of his nature. Evidently the average man leads an economic, and an emotional, even a spiritual life; it is not so certain that he reasons. In early English biography, there is no excuse for presenting the life of any man who has not figured in the development of the body politic or who does not exemplify virtues and vices which our reason can comprehend. The medieval and Renaissance theories of biography are based upon Aristotelian ethics: that is, upon the exemplification *in action* of rational decisions. But when the individual becomes increasingly important for his own sake, when the right to independent existence is secured not only for his significant thoughts and actions, but for his tears and velleities, his slightest movements, his daydreams and the sudden silent flash of God's forgiveness upon his soul, the spirit of romanticism increases the number of possible subjects for biography until it equals the number of human beings in the world, and also multiplies in each case the possibilities of treatment.

Romanticism, in sum, makes all men important in the social system; its motto there is *égalité, fraternité*. And in each individual that makes up the social aggregate, romanticism insists upon the importance of all parts of his consciousness; its motto there is *sensibilité*. If Wordsworth should be invoked to protect the first half of this chapter, the demon of Coleridge must be propitiated to watch over what remains.

"My morning walks from thence," writes Sarah Gooch of her days at Evian on Lake Geneva,[34] "were generally directed to the rocks of Meillerie, from whence I gazed pensively down on the little peaceful town of Vevay; Rousseau's Eloisa was my constant companion in them; and often did my heart vibrate to the sorrows of these faithful and unfortunate lovers!"

Such a spirit in writing of one's life is found only accidentally before the eighteenth century; but between 1750 and 1800 the qualities evident in this passage are evident in scores of biographies—the sympathy with the unfortunate which amounts almost to an appetite for the pathetic, the luxuriating in tender emotions, the intuition of mysterious and almost sentient trees and rocks, the freeing and expanding of the spirit by dwelling upon memories of far-off things.

The increasing exercise of the imagination tended to make man independent, self-sufficient. All good and evil, all greatness and triviality, he finds within himself. He can say with John Donne, "I am a little world made cunningly of elements," or with Shakespeare, "I could be bounded in a nutshell and count myself a king of infinite space." He is no longer the subordinate and obedient cog in Pope's and Bolingbroke's celestial machine. And with this centering on self comes the need for a belief in the capacities and native goodness of man. *La bonté naturelle*, with its trust in instinct as opposed to artificial social refinements, seems an almost inevitable early romantic doctrine.

An anonymous schoolmaster, writing *The Life of Commodus* (1789) largely to discourage the brutal sport of boxing, asserts

[34] *The life of Mrs. Gooch. Written by herself*, 1792, Vol. II, p. 121.

(p. 4): "I hope, and am myself persuaded, that no one is by *nature* inclined to vice or cruelty; and that on the contrary, virtue and the love of our species, benevolence and *humanity* are congenial to the human mind." This theory was put into practice. Hannah More and Mrs. Elizabeth Montagu take up subscriptions for a milkmaid, Queen Caroline assures the advancement of a rustic thresher, George II presents an African slave with a gold watch (to be sure, the slave is possibly the son of a high priest), and the lives of all three of these humble or unfortunate persons are recorded because of the belief that genius and true worth are instinctive rather than acquired, that a savage is noble because he is a savage. "True dignity," writes Miss Ambross,[35] "must spring from the heart alone, and can only be illustrated by the actions of the individual."

The *Life, sentiments, and character of John Mort* (1793) is brought to a conclusion with sixteen lines of Mrs. Barbauld's very blank verse written to this undistinguished dissenter (p. 47):

"Happy old man! who stretch'd beneath the shade
Of large grown trees, or in the rustic porch. . . ."

Here again, simple country life develops—almost compels—instinctive virtue. As an extended instance in which actors, writer, and reader revel together in the unrestrained exercise of benevolence and generous feeling, consider the episode which John Fawcett sketches so lovingly in his *Life of the Rev. Oliver Heywood*,[36] and which the biographer finds "well authenticated." In his reconstruction of the past, Fawcett shows how this dissenting but holy minister was persecuted in the hard days after the Restoration. At one time, when his children are starving in his sight, he tells Martha Bairstow, a maid-servant, to go to town and borrow five shillings from Mr. N, the shopkeeper, in order to buy food. Afraid to accost Mr. N, Martha walks up and down opposite his shop until he spies her, calls her to him, and gives her five guineas which some friends had collected to relieve the Reverend Heywood's distress. She hurries home with food (pp. 37-8):

[35] Miss Ambross's *Life and memoirs of the late Miss Ann Catley*, 1789, p. 5.
[36] 1796, pp. 35-8. The tone and accent in this anecdote and others is Fawcett's own; it is not to be found in the autobiography and diaries of Heywood, pub. 1882-1885, 4 vols,

"When she knocked at her master's door, which now must be kept locked and barred, for fear of constables or bailiffs, it was presently opened, and the joy to see her was as great as when a fleet of ships arrives, laden with provisions, for the relief of a starving town, closely besieged by an enemy. The children danced round the maid, eager to look into the basket of eatables, the patient mother wiped her eyes, the father smiled and said, 'The Lord hath not forgotten to be gracious; his word is true from the beginning; the young lions do lack and suffer hunger, but they that seek the Lord shall not want any good thing.' Martha related every circumstance of her little expedition, as soon as tears of joy would permit her; and all partook of the homely fare, with a sweeter relish than the fastidious Roman nobles ever knew, when thousands of pounds were expended to furnish one repast. Had you been present while this pious family were eating their bread and cheese, and drinking pure water from the spring, you might perhaps have heard the good man thus addressing the wife of his bosom, 'Did I not tell you, my dear, that God would surely provide for us?' "

In the lines quoted above by Mrs. Barbauld, the belief that the common man close to the soil is naturally good stands out as clearly as in Wordsworth or Goldsmith or the Gray of the *Elegy*; the *Heywood* is not far in spirit from scenes in *The Vicar of Wakefield* or those among the Bourbonnais peasants of the last sections of *A Sentimental Journey*. For natural goodness is no esoteric doctrine during the latter half of the eighteenth century, and men's tears flowed easily at the thought of their own fine feelings.

The heart rules, not the brain. The warm fountains of emotion inundate the formal parterres of exemplary biography.

The lives of philanthropists and reformers already discussed in this chapter show how sympathy with suffering could be made almost into a profession in the latter half of the eighteenth century. *The life and writings of the Rev. William Dodd,*[37] for instance, adds up a very high philanthropic score for its hero, who "reclaimed and converted upwards of 1000 unfortunate Fe-

---

[37] 1777. Also see John Pugh's *Remarkable occurrences in the life of Jonas Hanway,* 1787.

males," "released, from the dreary Walls of a Prison, 4468 wretched and confined Debtors," and, through his society for reviving persons, apparently dead from drowning, "snatched from the Grave 127 Objects." This biography itself is humanitarian in purpose, since it was issued in an attempt to save Dodd from being hanged for forging a bond.

Doctor Dodd was not only compassionate himself; he inspired compassion in others. Thus, Philip Thicknesse[38] mentions his last glimpse of the condemned man in sentences of real poignancy:

". . . the last time I saw him, was in a situation, neither to be described nor conceived, it was after he knew his *certain fate,* and when Mrs. Dodd was taking her everlasting farewell of him; they were alone; and at the upper end of a long room, I walked up to them, and found their hands locked in each others, and their minds as much departed, as if they had been both dead; after being almost as *lost* as they were for about a minute, and plainly perceiving, that they neither saw me, nor one another; I quitted the room."

Doctor Johnson himself strenuously tried to defend the saintly forger against such mechanical justice, and even wrote brief memoirs for Doctor Dodd which Dodd's wife suppressed. But the Reverend Mr. Dodd, who had succored so many others, could not save himself. He was hanged June 27, 1777; and the reformer who had believed so thoroughly in his own reforms that he had married one of his rescued Magdalens, carried his convictions beyond the gates of death by deeding his body to experimenters in scientific resuscitation.

Earlier in the century the prisons, the courtrooms, and the public hangings had afforded opportunities for "hymning Tyburn's elegiac lines" in periodically published lives and confessions.[39] Lingering over these blood sacrifices in print offered an English equivalent for the Roman circus; the lurid accounts sold steadily among the curious. But *The Ordinary of Newgate* began to fall off before mid-century, and in Alexander Cruden's *History of Richard Potter* (1763) the deadening monotony of those annals of the gallows gives way to honest indignation and desire for re-

[38] *Memoirs and anecdotes of Philip Thicknesse,* 1788, Vol. I, pp. 222-3.
[39] cf. Chap. IV.

form. Potter, the title-page states, "was tried at the Old-Bailey in July 1763, and received sentence of Death for attempting, at the instigation of another Sailor, to receive Thirty-five Shillings of Prize-money due to a third Sailor." This account contains "a modest Attempt to shew the necessity and expediency of our gracious King George the Third's acting the part of an Hezekiah in reforming his People." Although Cruden is self-assured, he steps softly (p. 13):

"I am very unwilling to say any thing to offend. . . . But it hath been said that too many have been hanged lately, and some for small crimes, tho' with a good intention, I suppose, to make others fear to commit the like: But we find that it hath not had that effect."

Cruden cuts a rather ridiculous figure in the journal he writes, as he walks through the prison-rooms taking snuff and cinnamon and rapee-leaf tobacco to guard against the stench as well as against infection. He attempts to soften the wholesale horrors by giving a poor woman a penny to leave off cleaning shoes on Sunday, or by instituting a system of black marks in order to stop swearing in the prisons. Yet in spite of his maiden-aunt tendencies, he is a well meaning, enthusiastic, determined reformer, and the picture he creates of "jail-distemper" and injustice, of callousness and degradation, is a nightmare of pity and fear.

Personal experience and observation often kindle into a crusading zeal for general reform, as in Jane Elizabeth Moore's *Genuine memoirs* (1786), which in the third volume contains a chapter "On arrests and imprisonment for debt" and in which the career of the harassed debtor is intensely realized (pp. 188-9):

". . . thus perplexed, and alternately adhering, he yields to the unpleasant reception of a prison, where by the corroding progress of despair, and its concomitants, he is lost in a reversion of confused ideas; where after being a long series of time in the most awful suspense, he exhausts his strength, loses his health, debases his morals, corrupts his principles, spends unavoidably the money which would have paid his creditors, to the best of his ability, tires out his friends, disposes of his clothes for needful support, and after all, which is too often the case, dies for want of the necessaries of life . . . yet still the prevailing hardness of man's heart calmly sits down under those poignant reflections."

Even the ludicrous image in the final sentence cannot blunt Mrs. Moore's sharp resentment. Such humanitarian sympathy increased during the century. Liberty, equality, and fraternity combine to illuminate *The interesting narrative of the life of Olaudah Equiano, or Gustavus Vassa, the African. Written by himself*,[40] an indictment ostensibly written by a freed slave and charging the whole white race with cruelty to the subjected negroes. This telling abolitionist tract may or may not be genuine: the important point here is that within five years (1789-1794) it ran through eight editions.

Love which embraces all humanity is perhaps best shown in a judgment on Pitt which closes Pitt's biography by that early pacifist William Godwin (1783, pp. 296-7):

"PATRIOTISM itself however was the source of some of his imperfections. He loved his country too well: or, if that may sound absurd, the benevolence, at least, that embraces the species, had not sufficient scope in his mind. He once stiled himself, 'a lover of honourable war'; and, in so doing, he let us, into one trait of his character. The friend of human kind, will be an enemy to all war."

The fashion of sensibility did not insure that the English biographers, offhand and immediately, would acquire a sympathy at once delicate and controlled. Many instances of the new spirit seem no more than exercises in current jargon;[41] yet occasionally and with growing frequency, the quality of mercy, and above all the capacity to enter imaginatively into the lives of others, touched the writing of lives with a new beauty and a new nobility.[42]

---

[40] t.p. from 4th ed., 1791.

[41] cf. Nathaniel Wraxall's *Memoirs of the Kings of France*, 1777, opening of Vol. I: "The history of France may be considered as abounding more in those interesting scenes which touch the heart, than any other. . . . The little weaknesses of the heart, the trespasses of passion, how infinitely do they engage! We contemplate ourselves, we pity, and we forgive. . . ."

[42] As a single example, see Langworthy's defense, or rather explanation, of the criticisms levelled against George Washington by his disgraced and embittered subordinate (*Memoirs of the life of the late Charles Lee, Esq. Lieutenant-Colonel*, 1792, pp. 61-70): "Humanity will draw a veil over the involuntary errors of sensibility, and pardon the sallies of a suffering mind. . . ."

Indignation against injustice, sympathy with the unfortunate and with those who suffer unnecessarily, inspired such literary giants as Johnson and Voltaire to take up their pens; their forceful accounts of Richard Savage and Jean Calas are characteristic biographical products of the eighteenth century.

And if biographers are made pregnant to good pity through the art of knowing and feeling sorrows in others, autobiographers also become increasingly sensitive to the pathos of their own lives. A convict on the eve of execution writes, and the public reads, an ode of which this is the last stanza:[43]

> "Lo! descending from above,
> Mercy hov'ring like a Dove:
> Drive, my Soul, each Care away,
> Quit, oh! quit, this shameful Clay;
> Spring to the Skies: Lord, Lord, I come,
> Oh! take me, Angels, take me Home."

And with equal self-compassion, Mrs. Elizabeth Gooch after a wandering and dubious career, surveys herself [44]

"In every stage of my life I have been uniformly unfortunate; nor have I ever known a felicity in the respective characters of daughter, of wife, of mother, or of friend. Disappointed in a first, and real attachment—hurried into a precipitate marriage—torn from my children, who have never since been suffered to hold any converse with me—and without ever possessing *one real friend!*—yet I have a soul that is formed to fill up all these connections with the truest tenderness. I have bitterly to lament that I never was blessed in the objects of them."

Such virtuosity in playing upon the heart-strings would have been well nigh impossible a hundred years before; yet almost all the feminine autobiographers of Mrs. Gooch's times are dexterous in handling their own piteous desolation. The writer whose life affords the most unrelieved example of pathos and

---

[43] *An authentic account of the life and manners of Mr. William Smith, an unfortunate convict, executed at Tyburn, on the 3d of October, 1750, for forgery,* 1750, p. 39.

[44] 1792, Vol. III, pp. 127-8. See also *Memoirs of an unfortunate young nobleman, return'd from a thirteen years slavery in America,* 1743.

despair remains, unfortunately, anonymous. Ann W———
published her memoirs as *The life of Lamenther: a true history.
Written by herself. In five parts. Containing a just account of
the many misfortunes she underwent, occasioned by the ill treatment of an unnatural father* (1771). Such a title closely parallels
some of the spurious concoctions of the times, but a subscription
list for her miscellaneous poems, headed by the Duchesses of
Queensberry and Marlborough, tends to establish its authenticity,
and the work that follows has the ring of truth throughout.

When Ann was two years old her father hit her with "some
Part of a Bedstead," from which she received "a Hurt that can
never end but with my Life." The crippled author, however, con-
soles herself by quoting her favorite author Pope: "Whatever is,
is right." In her case, this consists in living, she and her sister,
with their father, his mistress, and two brats by yet another
mistress. In heart-tearing detail she narrates how she is shut up
in a closet where she almost dies of hunger, even though she
surreptitiously steals scraps of food by night. When her aunt
finds how she is treated and threatens to take her case to court,
Mr. W——— leaves his two girls and one boy in a country
house to starve. One loaf of bread and no water suffice them for
a fortnight, she says. She escapes, is brought back from a gypsy
camp, scourged with a rod of nettles, horsewhipped, and kicked
downstairs. No wonder her relations do not wish her to publish
her memoirs.

The brutal breaking of her ribs seems a minor catastrophe in
her narrative, as it continues with escapes, ill luck, sordid poverty, and the horror of the inevitable returns to her sadistic father
and his "Deviless." She turns seamstress, lives from hand to
mouth, often without a place to sleep, throws herself on the
parish—on many parishes—and is committed to St. A———'s
workhouse. Her father gets her out in order to sell her to a
procuress, but she escapes from a horrible den to become a mil-
liner. At the close she seems to be staying with her cousin George,
writing her account out of indignation against her father, who is
still living. The whole sordid melodrama, which affords a good
bridge between Defoe and Dickens, is nicely gauged to rouse
the fashionable emotions of mercy, charity, and pity. When she is

still almost a baby, her young sister dies and Ann wishes that she might die instead. "But the unfavourable Archer took the fairest Flower" (p. 17). In such conventional and mixed metaphors she couches her ugly story of torture and penury. "Let every one who is blest with a tender Sensibility, judge." This is her plea throughout, and before the reader has finished her five installments, he may well be convinced that Ann W——— wisely chose as her *nom de plume*: Lament her.

The biographical production which plays most obviously upon the newly discovered sympathy for the weak and unfortunate is the *Memoirs of the celebrated dwarf, Joseph Boruwlaski* (1788). At the age of thirty Boruwlaski was three feet three inches high; he never grew taller. He writes to prove (p. 43) "that the smallness of our stature does not prevent us from experiencing the power of the passions."[45] And in detailing his popularity, as if he were some kind of animated doll at the courts of Poland and France, particularly in recounting his love affairs, one disastrous and one successful, with women of normal size, Boruwlaski undoubtedly throws himself upon the mercy of the English public. His unfortunate size only increases his sensitivity (p. 71):

"I not only mean to describe my size and its proportions, I would likewise follow the unfolding of my sentiments, the affections of my soul; I would speak openly; rather tell what I felt than what I did, and demonstrate that, if I can upbraid nature with having refused me a body like that of other men, she has made me ample amends, by endowing me with a sensibility, which, it is true, displayed itself rather late, but, even in my wantonness, spread a teint [French: *teinte*] of happiness, the remembrance of which I enjoy with gratitude and a feeling heart."

As a child he had wept when, in his presence, courtiers had heartlessly made fun of the idea of marrying him to his two-foot-high sister. But in the end, he learns that he can live only by appealing to the compassion or the curiosity of others. In order to support his wife and his children, he gives concerts, he travels,

[45] cf. William Hay's semi-biographical essay on *Deformity,* 1794.

he shows himself for a guinea and at last for a crown. "Am I doomed," he cries (p. 245), "to be for ever the sport of necessity, the slave of the moment?" The Baron de Breteuil, French ambassador to Vienna, cruel only to be kind, had earlier given him advice (p. 169):

"'Do not think, my little friend, that concerts will always be sufficient to answer your expenses, and to procure you a support; you must needs give up pride, or choose misery; and if you do not intend to lead the most unhappy life; if you wish to enjoy, in future, a state of tranquillity, it is indispensable you should resolve to make exhibition of yourself.'"

This sentimental autobiography is the dwarf Boruwlaski's final exhibition. The long list of aristocratic subscribers shows that it must have been fairly successful. In the inconsistent and paradoxical eighteenth century, with its malicious and melting moods, its crowds at public hangings and its tears over a dead ass, its hardness and its tenderness that protests almost too much, is it unreasonable to believe that England may have been more generous-hearted than her Continental neighbors? Certain widely travelled biographers thought that she was. "O beneficent and generous nation!" this same Polish dwarf apostrophizes (p. 247), "should I sink under my griefs, I recommend to you my wife and children." And the Armenian patriot Joseph Emin (1792) becomes almost inarticulate in his fervent admiration of English generosity and fine feeling.

The lives of Boruwlaski, Lamenther, and Sarah Gooch contain studied and melodramatic poses, inept or exaggerated. The appeal for public sympathy and the analysis of one's own sorrows were novel undertakings. A sure and subtle art had not yet been developed. In at least one case, however, an autobiographer speaks of his grief naturally and without constraint. Anguish is not forced when Arthur Young writes of the death of his daughter:[46]

"I think I feel that this deep regret, this calm sorrow will last my life, and that no events can happen that will ever banish her from my mind. Ranby called and I conversed with him about her

---

[46] *Autobiography*, wr. 1797. Quotation from 1898 ed., pp. 295-6. cf. also the poet James Beattie's restrained emotion in his biographical tribute to his son, 1794.

till tears would, had I continued it, [have] stopped my speaking. I hate and pity those who avoid talking to the afflicted upon the subject which causes their affliction, it argues a little trifling mind in one party or the other."

Love, no less than pity, dilates the heart. "Persons of the most generous, open, and good-natured dispositions," writes one biographer,[47] "are of all others the most subject to this passion; . . . persons of a sour, ill-natured turn of mind are seldom or ever engaged in it." Another biographer inveighs even more warmly against the light of common day:[48]

"But say, ye cold and phlegmatic definers of love! was it to the accomplishments of the mind that Petrarch paid such tender and fervid devotion? Could such warm and enthusiastic raptures, such expressions of love (by some deemed metaphysical), be wasted on mere mental talents, however useful and excellent, in a woman? It was indeed a passion as lasting as it was vehement."

And the biography explodes in phrases of which the following fragments are typical: "ardent transports . . . impetuous . . . animated . . . Petrarch breaks forth with raptures the most expressive of his short and momentary happiness . . . poignant sensations of love . . . stifle a passion . . . fostered with the tenderest hopes . . . the language of the heart. . . ."

For better or for worse, therefore, late eighteenth century autobiographers, their imaginations expanded and warmed by the tender emotion, frequently record such passages as the two following:

"One evening, at their house, after we had been playing some tunes on the harpsichord and eating our tarts, the time approached for my departure, Miss Gould drew from her bosom a visiting ticket, on which was engraved, 'Mr. Temple Luttrell.' She kissed it, and replaced it there; telling me, at the same time, she was resolved never to marry any other man.

[47] *Autobiography of Thomas Wright, 1736-1797,* 1864, p. 59.
[48] *A sketch of the life and writings of Dante and Petrarch,* 1790, p. 52. The lives of Héloïse, Petrarch, and Madame de Guion were of great influence in determining the attitude toward love assumed by derivative eighteenth century biographers.

"Some years after my misfortunes I inquired what was become of these friends of my infancy? and I learned, with much satisfaction, that Miss Gould really *was* married to Mr. Luttrell, in defiance of many more splendid offers that had been made her."[49]

"It was during one of these night walks [within prison walls] that my little daughter first blessed my ears with the articulation of words. The circumstances made a forcible and indelible impression on my mind. It was a clear moonlight evening; the infant was in the arms of her nursery maid; she was dancing her up and down, and was playing with her; her eyes were fixed upon the moon, to which she pointed with her small forefinger; —on a sudden a cloud passed over it, and the child, with a slow falling of her hand, articulately sighed, '*all gone!*' . . . These little nothings will appear insignificant to the common reader; but to the parent whose heart is ennobled by sensibility, they will become matters of important interest."[50]

This last selection suggests also the importance of surroundings in determining moods. Mary Robinson was particularly sensitive to the places in which she passed her days, varying from a cloistered Gothic minster-house to the brilliant rotunda of the Pantheon, or this moonlit prison-yard. Whatever freed her imagination, whether it was the gloomy vaults of Westminster Abbey or the splendor of the Welsh mountains, led her to insert rhapsodies in her memoirs. In the following passage she is at Trevecca in the Wales she describes so well (p. 63):

"Here I enjoyed the sweet repose of solitude: here I wandered about woods entangled by the wild luxuriance of nature, or roved upon the mountain's side, while the blue vapours floated round its summit. O, God of Nature! Sovereign of the universe of wonders! in those interesting moments how fervently did I adore thee!"

Here is a passage from the *Secret journal of a self-observer* :[51]

[49] *The life of Mrs. Gooch,* 1792, Vol. I, pp. 20-1.

[50] *Memoirs of Mrs. Robinson,* wr. 1800. Quoted from 1826 ed., Vol. VII of *Autobiography, a collection.*

[51] Peter Will's translation from the German of J. C. Lavater, 1795, Vol. II, p. 344. cf. J. Berington's *Abeillard and Heloisa,* 1787, p. 57.

"At six o'clock I took a walk to the water with Pf. [Pfenninger] and his wife. The lake was as smooth as a mirror; the town was covered with a soft darkness; the steeples and country-houses along the lake were still encircled with light; and the sailing vessels seemed to emerge from a dark ground. The chain of snow-mountains was embroidered with silver, and their edges distinctly delineated."

As easily as in Rousseau's *La nouvelle Héloïse,* such sensitive descriptions of natural surroundings blend with the subtle mental analyses which form the bulk of these personal confessions. Thomas Amory, to mention one further example, though he dates his dedication from the Barbican, addresses it in hyperboles to a sequestered widow "of Paterdale, on the Banks of the River Glenkroden, in Westmorland," and recalls with nostalgia the virtuous simplicity and beautiful surroundings of rural life. The descriptions of nature in his memoirs range from Gothic to Arcadian landscapes.[52]

Compassion for mankind mingles with admiration for natural scenery in William Matthews's *A short tour of observation and sentiment through a part of South Wales* (1786). His somewhat clumsy imitation of Sterne is evident in the first sentence:

"And is it impossible, said I, (as I went on my way from Bath to Bristol) that this same journey into Pembrokeshire, having for its main object a common concern of business, can be made a journey also of reflection and sentiment?"

Mr. Matthews observes a great deal, he feels a great deal, but his remarks are trite and over-serious. Some of his topics are: Entrance into Wales; Welch Cottages; The Spendthrift, with Reflections; The Lunatic; Village Inn. Here is a specimen of this sentimental traveller, this moralizing Yorick, as he meditates on the indigence of the Welch Curate (pp. 193-4):

"Indeed when I afterwards cast my eyes on the dejected countenance of the poor man, to whom these few books belonged [his curacy yielded less than ten pounds a year], I could not repress

---

[52] *Memoirs: containing the lives of several ladies of Great Britain,* 1755. cf. his descriptions of Scotland, or of "the valley of Wells," p. 450. cf. also possibly the finest scene of man-in-nature in all biography before the time of Wordsworth: Petrarch on Mount Ventoux, Dobson's *Petrarch,* 1799 ed., Vol. I, pp. 75-83.

the rising of indignation, at the inequality of allowance among the clergy, so long, and so justly complained of, without redress. Against such fruitless feelings, however, a traveller through Wales must guard himself as well as he can—and must remember, in aid of himself, and the miserable people whom he compassionates, that a period will soon come, when the luxury and wantonness of many rapacious dignitaries will be humbled, and recompensed; while the crying miseries of their more virtuous dependants will be ended and balanced, according to the mercy of Him who judgeth righteously in the earth."

The miseries of the poor, the tender stirrings of affection, the contemplation of instinctive bounty, the sight of ruined monuments of the past, or of the grandeurs, asperities, and softnesses of natural scenery—all these provided means of freeing the imagination and the heart, transporting the sensitive soul into expansive regions of generous emotion or mysterious realms of melancholy. One further device—the appeal to memory—sheds romantic nostalgia over many lives. Here the imagination is free to rove through far-off places and through far-off days, and life becomes rather like a dream than an assurance. Even such a hard-bitten man of affairs as William Hutton, as we have seen earlier in the chapter, seems lost in trance-like sentiments while he contemplates the initials he had carved above his place in the silk-mill fifty-three years before. The reader is touched, in the midst of exceptionally trivial memoirs, when a mother, writing the life of her dead son, pauses to think far back into her own childhood to a time when her own mother had disciplined her four-year-old daughter:[53] "She can almost fancy that her wrist, when she thinks of it, feels the grasp of her mother's elegant long fingers." Many of the finest effects in Mary Robinson's autobiography come from her sense of the vista of time, as she glances ahead—"Gracious heaven! How should I have shuddered, had I then contemplated the dark perspective of my destiny!"[54]—or mournfully gazes back at the decaying mansion where she was born, the school-house,

[53] Preface, by Mrs. Eliza Berkeley, before George Monck Berkeley's *Poems,* 1797, pp. dxxiv-dxxv.
[54] p. 60, 1827 ed. Wr. 1800.

the tombs of relatives, and the cathedral with its lectern under which, when an infant, she had sat and joined in the anthem. She longs to turn back once again and occupy her place beneath its expanding wings, and once, before the service begins, she steals alone into the cathedral to re-enact this remembered scene of childhood.[55]

Mrs. Gooch, who has figured several times in this chapter, and whose narrative in general is either humdrum or definitely unpleasant, displays real emotional power when she recalls her first love affair with Dr. Crawford, their clandestine correspondence, and their planned elopement which was abandoned because of her tenderness for her mother. If she had married Crawford, she persuades herself as she writes down her memories, she would have been happy, he would not have been lost. "This idea will never forsake me: it is twisted round every fibre of my heart, and will only be renounced with its last sigh" (Vol. I, p. 41).

In her last paragraphs, in spite of rodomontade which crosses Rousseau with the style of a funeral sermon, her narrative comes to a close that is not without pathos, as her thoughts turn back to her first lover waiting in the rain to carry her away (Vol. III, pp. 140-1):

"My FIRST attachment will be my LAST. Perhaps (though I dare not hope it!) in some corner of the universe still exists Dr. Crawford!—Oh! if he does, may these pages catch his eye, and when I may be buried in my long-wished-for grave, may he (if it be possible he lives!) give a tear to my hard fate!—But if he is, as I have every reason to suppose, removed from this world of woe, and become an inhabitant of the regions of eternal peace, may my first love be permitted to 'look with an eye of pity down,' and await the arrival of that soul, congenial with his own, which, purged from its body of infirmities and error, may partake, with him, a joyful RESURRECTION!"

[55] For additional remarks on Mary Robinson, see Chap. II. Her extremely romantic memoirs should also be compared with her poems, which bear such titles as "The Cavern of Woe," and "Solitude," and contain such lines (*Sappho and Phaon*) as

"Recalls the scenes of past and happier years," or
"If bliss from coldness, pain from passion flows,
Ah! who would wish to feel, or learn to love?"

More than any other device, such deliberate recollection gives poignant reality to memoirs. A whole life is comprehended in an instant; our days, as in Wordsworth's haunting thought, are bound each to each by natural piety; and we experience what Proust, in his search for times that are lost, so exactly describes: the union, in one living moment, of the past and the present. Only occasionally does the eighteenth century come to the verge of shaping such sentiments into a conscious theory, as in such a passage as this:[56]

"Come forth then, ye enchanting images of youth, though the pictures ye exhibit scarcely seem to bear any resemblance to my present self! Come forth! delude my fancy, ye beloved shadows! —ascend, ye sweet hours of infancy, as a thin vapour from the ocean of the past, and float once more before my eyes!—I stand upon the brink of the stream of time. . . ."

Yet the remembrance of a happy time in days of misery is scarcely less poignant because it is unconscious, and one may look far in biography without finding a more moving emotional passage than the following, in which Arthur Young lives simultaneously in the past and present, after the death of his adored fourteen-year-old daughter Bobbin:[57]

"On Monday, the 17th [July, 1797], I arrived at Bradfield, where every object is full of the dear deceased.

"On going into the library the window looks into the little garden in which I have so many times seen her happy. O gracious and merciful God! pardon me for allowing any earthly object thus to engross my feelings and overpower my whole soul! But what were they not on seeing and weeping over the roses, variegated sage, and other plants she had set there and cultivated with her dear hands. But every room, every spot is full of her, and it sinks my very heart to see them. Tuesday evening, the 18th, her remains arrived, and at midnight her brother read the service over her in a most impressive manner. I buried her in my pew,

[56] *Sketch of the life and literary career of Augustus von Kotzebue*, 1800, tr. by Anne Plumptre, pp. 5-6. A somewhat similar sentimentally reminiscent attitude toward his childhood is to be found in William King's *Political and literary anecdotes of his own times*, 1818, wr. *ca.* 1761.

[57] *Autobiography*, 1898 ed., p. 281. Wr. 1797.

fixing the coffin so that when I kneel it will be between her head and her dear heart."

Tentative and faltering as its experiments were, the eighteenth century imagination nevertheless conceived, and attempted to record, new modes of living. The lives of action, of common sense, of reason, or of Christian orthodoxy no longer offered all conceivable patterns. Memory of unconscious associations, sentiment, evanescent and almost indescribable emotion, now played their parts; each now had its rights. The life of sensation, the influence of natural environment and of the experiences of youth in the formation of character, were recognized. Not only were man's senses, emotions, and imaginings set beside his reason and his religious faith as legitimate guides in rendering his character comprehensible; the importance of his driving will was reasserted. Not only did all men have similar and complex possibilities; but also each individual man had the right (at least in comparison with earlier tradition) to exercise his possibilities as he pleased. Not only equality for all men, but liberty for each. The cult of eccentricity in English biography during the last half of the eighteenth century is a notable result. Again and again, moreover, liberty for the individual, maintained in theory or illustrated in action, is bound up with the idea of liberty as a political principle. The numerous sympathetic translations of memoirs of leaders in the French Revolutionary years—even in an England politically unsympathetic—the lives of Madame Roland or of Jean-Baptiste Louvet or of Dumouriez, the effusions of Joseph Emin (1792), Boswell's own *Journal of a tour to Corsica,* and, of course, innumerable incidental passages, show how powerful the idea of liberty became in eighteenth century biography.

As illustrative of this admiration for the human will, coupled and connected with an admiration of political liberty, the climax in William Godwin's account of Pitt—his comment upon Pitt's fatal seizure on the floor of Parliament—may be selected:[58]

"But the last scene of his life, is of all others, the most unparalleled. In whatever other views, we may consider; and, in whatever views, condemn it: as an example of never-ebbing spirit,

---

[58] *The history of the life of William Pitt,* 1783, pp. 291-2.

we cannot but admire. His infirmities had now rendered his every limb, the rebel of his will. The couch of lassitude seemed all, that remained to him. The situation of his country too, was arduous, hopeless, and untried. The inexhaustible genius of a Chatham, was forced to confess, that he knew not, how we were to be extricated. Yet, in these circumstances, with his lifeless, nerveless hand, he was willing to have grasped the helm. It was improbable; it was impossible, he should have succeeded. But these impotent efforts of immortal man; these instances, in which the soul bursts the bands of earth, and stands alone, in confessed eternity; are the most beautiful, the most pathetic, the most sublime exhibitions, of which the mind of man is adequate to conceive."

Sensibility, then, as the above pages testify, was introduced into eighteenth century biography in diverse forms and in numerous instances. Many writers of lives vaguely anticipated, or eagerly followed, the emotionalism, delicate or harrowing, of Richardson, of Rousseau, and of Sterne. Three of these new biographies of the generous heart are worth separate extended notice. Two of them, and the most popular two, came originally from the Continent, though they were introduced to English audiences by translators with minds of their own; the third writer was deeply influenced by Goethe and Rousseau.

When Mrs. Susanna Dobson published her *Life of Petrarch* (1775), she did not translate literally the full and scholarly memoirs of the Abbé de Sade.[59] His initial two quarto volumes, for instance, she condensed to her first volume in octavo, transforming a documented chronicle into a readable book. She is more didactic and decorous than Sade: she omits such Gaulois anecdotes as the account of Laura, surprised by Petrarch while bathing, splashing water in his face. Mrs. Dobson's strong moral sense is in continual conflict with her warm heart; and this clash is so

[59] Amsterdam, 1764-1767, 3 vols. cf. *Monthly Review* for 1775, Vol. 53, p. 223: "Mrs. Dobson's easy, natural, and unaffected manner, gives it, indeed, much of the air of an original work; her abridgment of the French Memoirs, too, is very judicious."

marked that her production may justly be considered an original
work.

The tearful tales of thwarted love, of Eloise[60] and of Tristram,
have always excited the romantic impulse, and the sad but true
story of Petrarch and Laura, presented to a susceptible public in
1775 in two volumes, was so immediately popular that Mrs. Dobson's ample two-volume work ran through six editions within
thirty years, and even produced dependent essays.[61] Mrs. Dobson's
energy met with no success in her attempt to break into Mrs.
Thrale's *salon,* but it more than sufficed to produce a biography
quivering with sensibility and filled with ethical judgments. "To
susceptible and feeling minds alone Petrarch will be ever dear,"
she ends by admitting in her preface,[62] after condemning his love
for Laura because it was immoderate, all but incredible, and
therefore wrong. Following Sade, Mrs. Dobson declares that she
will center on the "secret folds" of Petrarch's heart which he revealed in his letters to friends (Pref., pp. xi-xii):

"And I have the rather guarded against all such prolix and in-
trusive digressions, that I might have room to dwell minutely
upon every part of Petrarch's private character, and his admirable
letters; thus to exhibit him encircled with his friends, and in the
familiar circumstances of life. It is in these situations the heart
discloses itself without disguise or reserve; all its intricacies are
laid open, and we are enabled to form a true judgment of its

[60] With Dobson's *Petrarch* should be compared Joseph Berington's *The history
of the lives of Abeillard and Heloisa,* 1787. The Preface shows it was written with
her work in mind (p. xxi): "A few years ago, I remember, the Memoirs of
Petrarch were in every body's hands, and the general interest they excited was
great." Berington's work, which was not the first treatment of the medieval lovers
in the eighteenth century (see Bibliography), illustrates in a single volume many
of the qualities touched on in this chapter: the romantic use of natural scenery,
enthusiasm for "unexampled sensibility" and "disinterested magnanimity," and
imagination and subtlety in the interpretation of character. Berington is faintly
hostile to Abeillard, sympathetic to Heloise, in whom (p. 198) "love and nature
would sometimes prevail; and we shall see how reluctantly they surrendered a
heart, which seemed made to be possessed by them alone."

[61] *Essay on the life and character of Petrarch,* 1785, probably by A. F. Tytler.
This is largely a sentimental treatise, which proposes this *question d'amour:* is it
possible to love a married living woman twenty-one years and her memory
twenty-six more years, without sin? See also *A sketch of the lives and writings of
Dante and Petrarch,* 1790; *Petrarch's View of Human Life. By Mrs. Dobson,* 1791.

[62] 1799 ed., p. xiv.

character; an object which, next to the great Author of nature, is certainly the most important to contemplate, as a warning, or as a pattern, to the human mind."

Such a strong declaration of the independence of the heart needs a subject like Petrarch and a biographer like Mrs. Dobson to carry it to fruition. Petrarch is indeed a perfect subject for a biography of sensibility. Few men have felt more piercingly the tears of things or have lived more intensely in their emotions, their enthusiasms, and their dreams. More than that, Petrarch is a great artist at sketching and analyzing his friends' characters and his own moods. Petrarch's autobiographical writings and the Abbé de Sade's collections give Mrs. Dobson a good start. She does not neglect her opportunities. From the time when as a boy he climbs Mount Ventoux and discovers for the world the heart-shaking beauties of savage nature, to the last meditations by the fountain of Vaucluse, the biographer minutely records his career. The background is competently sketched with its contrasting brutality and intellectual enthusiasm. By her care in giving the reader the atmosphere of the times, Mrs. Dobson contrives to make it seem natural that Petrarch should be crowned with laurel in Rome amid wild rejoicings, or that the life of Rienzi should be spared, in spite of barbarous political vendettas, simply because he was a poet.

"What do you think of our lawyers, and our physicians?" Petrarch writes (Vol. II, p. 133). "They no longer consult Justinian or Esculapius: deaf to the cries of the sick, and of their clients, they will listen to none but Virgil and Homer." His friends—the Colonna, Boccaccio, Socrates, his young secretary Malpighi about whom Petrarch writes (Vol. II, p. 342) "He acts from feeling, and not from interest"—are given a just share in the biography. Petrarch's last letter was to Boccaccio concerning the *Decameron*. "Soon after this he was found dead in his library, July 18, 1374, with one arm leaning on a book" (Vol. II, p. 391). The life is well organized and well written. Although the biography is largely made up of Petrarch's own words, it seems more than a patchwork in its presentation of a living and gradually aging individual.

In creating this lifelike figure moving against a rich and varied background, Mrs. Dobson centers upon his relations with Laura. In the account of their first meeting, the lady appears like the conventional heroine of an old romance (Vol. I, p. 26): "When she opened her mouth, you perceived the beauty of pearls and the sweetness of roses." But the long description of Laura's death and character throbs with sensibility (Vol. I, p. 386):

"How touching is it to view this amiable woman sinking under distresses from an unhappy marriage, from imprudent children [Laura had six sons and four daughters], and inwardly pining at heart with an attachment that in a state of liberty would have been her felicity and glory, continually to behold the object of this affection a prey to the agonizing sensations of this fatal and tyrannic passion!"

Petrarch's capacity for suffering because of his love is no less than Laura's, for after her death (Vol. I, p. 387) "He lived several days without eating or drinking, nourishing himself with his tears." With these words Mrs. Dobson ends her first volume, and at the conclusion of the second she returns to her central theme (Vol. II, p. 399):

"We have now finished the account of Petrarch: and when a life (if I may so speak) paints itself, it would be a reproach to the reflection of the writer, and a very ill compliment to the penetration of the reader, to attempt to draw it over again by a summary of insipid assertions. I shall therefore only remark one particular, which, with all feeling hearts, will apologize for that unfixed and variable temper so justly ascribed to Petrarch, and this was his tender and ardent passion for Laura, which entirely unsettled him for twenty years, and produced a restlessness in his mind (not formed, perhaps, by nature, in the calmest mould) through every succeeding period of life."

The biography closes, like the *Nouvelle Héloïse,* with the triumph of self-discipline over turbulent passions (Vol. II, pp. 400-1):

"His heart was formed for tenderness; but, alas! it fixed where its affections could not be sacredly confirmed. . . .

"From youth to manhood he was a prey to the keenest sensibility; from manhood to old age he was struggling to recover a calm and virtuous state of soul. . . .

"Those readers who have been interested in the fortune of Petrarch, will pity his fate, admire his sublime and exalted genius, and revere his humble piety, which their candour, penetration, and sensibility, will draw out to life from this faint and imperfect representation."

The passionate quest for liberty, no less than the pathos of star-crossed love, can rouse the imagination. To reconstruct the deep emotions that the very sound of the words freedom or tyranny could call up in the years between Sterne's caged starling and *The Prisoner of Chillon* or *Prometheus Unbound,* one could not do better than to read *The Life of Baron Frederic Trenck.*[68]

"The man of feeling, and the friend of freedom," Holcroft writes in the Preface (p. vii), "will read this work with sensations perhaps too strong: it will remain an eternal monument of the dreadful, the detestable, the diabolical effects of despotism."

Even such a short quotation will show that the translator possesses convictions and a style of his own. Thomas Holcroft is aware of the liberties he takes in reshaping and compressing Trenck's explosive autobiographical tract against tyranny (Pref., pp. vi-vii):

"The author's haste, his daring spirit, his lively imagination, and his sensibility of heart, were qualities so ill adapted to the cool and clear explanation of affairs . . . that his repetitions, complaints, remonstrances, appeals to the heart, execrations

---

[68] *The life of Baron Frederic Trenck; containing his adventures; his cruel and excessive sufferings, during ten years imprisonment, at the fortress of Magdeburg, by command of the late King of Prussia; also, anecdotes, historical, political, and personal. Translated from the German, by Thomas Holcroft,* 1788, 3 vols. Possibly some of this passion for liberty, as well as the general liking for exciting stories, is to be found in the popularity of biographies of thrilling escapes. In addition to Trenck's narrative, cf. *Narrative . . . by John-Baptist Louvet,* 1795; *A narrative of the sufferings of James Bristow,* 1793; *Memoirs . . . of . . . Count de Benyowsky,* 1789; and best of all in this connection, *Memoirs of Henry Masers de Latude, during a confinement of thirty-five years in the state prisons of France. Of the means he used to escape once from the Bastile, and twice from the dungeon of Vincennes,* 1787.

against injustice, and the desponding consolation he found in his own honour and honesty, are unceasing. Surely, however, they are not unmoving: they are often beautiful, often sublime; and, therefore, have often been retained. Sometimes they are omitted or contracted."

Holcroft is no less in sympathy with Trenck than Mrs. Dobson is with Petrarch, and the resulting English version retains the vitality of the original autobiography while it adds a more chastened form.

"In this gloomy history of my life," the hero asserts (Vol. I, p. 27), "I would paint myself to the world such as I am, and, by the recital of my sufferings, afford a memorable example, and interest the heart of sensibility." Then follows the career of the young Cornet of Horse in Frederick's entourage, who, because of an innocent connection with an Austrian blood relation, is suspected of treachery and clapped into prison at Glatz. He is not even told that his sentence will terminate in a year, and ironically, therefore, he makes his escape only a few days before he would have been freed. A series of breath-taking flights and captures succeeds his first attempt, and each time he gets deeper and deeper into dungeons. He is more clever than Jean Valjean; he outdoes the Count of Monte Cristo. When, after more than a decade of imprisonment, he is finally pardoned, he shows his jailers how he was about to escape from the underground dungeon at Magdeburg where he had been trussed up with wrist, ankle, and neck chains, not to mention an iron belt bolted around his waist. Trenck envisions himself as the principle of liberty, and judges all others in their relation to his own career (Vol. I, pp. 82-3):

"Unhappy people! where power is superior to law, and where the innocent, and the virtuous, meet punishment instead of reward. Unhappy land! where the omnipotent SUCH IS OUR WILL supersedes all legal sentence, and robs the subject of property, life, and honour."

Yet such indignation against the Prussian Frederick only balances his gratitude toward the Austrian Emperor, with whom he had an interview after his release (Vol. II, pp. 222-3):

"I spoke with freedom; the audience lasted more than an hour. At length the Emperor was so moved that he rose from his seat, and retired into the next apartment; I saw the tears drop from his eyes. With sympathetic enthusiasm, I fell at his feet, embraced his knees, and wished for the presence of a Rubens, or Apelles, to preserve a scene so highly honourable to the memory of the monarch, and paint the sensations of an innocent man, imploring the protection of a great, a just, and a compassionate prince."

Incidents of intrigue and diplomacy are detailed in these memoirs, and even a love episode, to which Holcroft is careful to add a note warning the reader of Trenck's "mixture of good and bad morality." The death of the unhappily married seventeen-year-old girl with whom, upon his escape to Moscow, he was plotting to run away, "was the severest trial," he writes (Vol. I, p. 268), "I had ever felt." Yet memory of this love helps him to support the ten years at Magdeburg. Even when he takes up his pen at the age of sixty, remembrance of things past gives him new fire (Vol. I, p. 269):

"Enough of this. My blood again courses swifter through my veins as I write! Rest, gentle maiden, noble and lovely as thou wert! For thee, ought Heaven to have united a form so fair, animated as it was by a soul so pure, to ever-blooming youth and immortality."

The first half of the memoirs is the best. It tells a story of a man with the spirit of an eagle, a story in which indomitable will, courage, and resourcefulness are pitted against an impassive military system and the thick stone slabs of impregnable fortresses. It is quite typical of Trenck that as a joke he should allow forty peasants to shoot at him while wolf-hunting, after he has secretly loaded their guns with blank cartridges (Vol. II, pp. 277-9).

The Baron's reckless force is dissipated in the endless litigation that clouds the last half of Trenck's autobiography; after forty-two years he is restored to his Prussian estates and finally to his Austrian estates as well. When he records his life, he has become a gray-haired man, the father of eleven children; and he has developed the fixed belief, almost the monomania, that he is a symbol of persecution by tyrants. Yet even the diffuse third volume harks back to his exciting early career, in the *Anecdotes of the life of Alexander Schell* with whom he escaped from the fortress of Glatz. Part of the dying Schell's letter to Trenck, when they are both men worn out by life, mixes pathos and laughter as his epilogue (Vol. III, p. 295):

"Repine not, weep not, rather laugh; let the last moments of the crazy Schell be a subject of mirth; he himself has laughed, on the world's great theatre, beholding the deepest tragedies; laughing he quits the scene, and the curtain for ever falls."

Trenck fulminates so bitterly against the injustice he finds on every hand that even Holcroft, the friend of Paine and Godwin, is forced to defend the English law courts against Trenck's charges. False men, Holcroft says, may lead justice astray; they do not make it impossible. Yet the least hint of tyranny or oppression wakes the old spark in the heart of the intrepid Baron, like steel striking flint, and he is at his most characteristic in the prayer "Dated at the Castle of Zwerbach, December 18th, 1786" which closes the second volume (p. 345):

"Thou, oh God! my righteous judge, didst ordain that I should be, that I might remain, an example of suffering to the world; thou madest me what I am, gavest me these strong passions, these quick nerves, this universal glow, this thrilling of the blood, when I behold injustice."

Such words are not empty air; they express passionate conviction and offer a standard for action. Trenck wrote them in Austria in 1786; Holcroft translated them in England in 1788; in 1789 they tottered the towers of the Bastille.

A career as meteoric as Trenck's must end melodramatically. "Volume the fourth, and most important," of his *Life* appeared in English in 1793. His life had not been uneventful (Pref., p. xiv):

". . . fate has not inserted my name in the page of rest: it has enrolled me in the number of knights errant, doomed incessantly to wander throughout the earth, without ever tasting the cup of fortune."

This Byronic hero, therefore, moves restlessly through the turbulent and changing world (p. xviii): "Before the door of my prison in Magdeburg I have seen grass growing. . . . In Paris I beheld the Bastille, the tomb of virtue and freedom, taken and destroyed."

The English reader of 1793 could read the final fulminations of this irreconcilable and truculent fanatic, martyr to his own extreme conceptions of liberty. The next year, at Paris, two days before the execution of Robespierre, Trenck's head fell beneath the guillotine. With such a spirit as his, Trenck at last may have had his chance to test his motto:

Flectere si nequeo superos, Acheronta movebo.

Holcroft's friend and Shelley's father-in-law, William Godwin, produced in 1798 a brief life of Mary Wollstonecraft which distills the fine essence of eighteenth century romantic biographies into one hundred and seventeen small pages. It has all of Godwin's blindnesses, prejudices, and attempted rational philosophy; it has also his idealism. Turning its leaves, the reader understands more easily Godwin's dominance over Shelley, and realizes that Godwin's temper fitted him admirably to mirror the proud, generous, sensitive spirit of his wife.

"We not infrequently meet with persons," he observes (p. 65), "endowed with the most exquisite and delicious sensibility, whose minds seem almost of too fine a texture to encounter the vicissitudes of human affairs, to whom pleasure is transport, and disappointment is agony indescribable. This character is finely pourtrayed by the author of the Sorrows of Werter. Mary was in this respect a female Werter."

Goethe and Rousseau are his two mainstays as he writes this memorial to his dead wife. *Werther* repeatedly furnishes parallels in the analysis of Mary Wollstonecraft's thoughts, and Rousseau gives him comfort—Rousseau, who, in his understanding of human nature, Godwin ranks next to Homer as "the abstract and deposit of every human perfection."

Yet though he can thus kindle his mind by the contemplation of magnanimous human spirits rising above their sufferings, he is writing so close to Mary's death—she died in September, 1797—that his control in this biography is the more remarkable (p. 27): "While I thus enumerate her more than maternal qualities, it is impossible not to feel a pang at the recollection of her orphan children!"

The little memorial is written with a beautiful sense of proportion, a unique standard of values, and a combination, difficult to achieve, of sympathy with absolute frankness.

The high terms in which Godwin describes their first embrace may arouse the smile of a sarcastic reader, but his language does not conceal the truth and depth of his feeling (p. 90):

"Mary rested her head upon the shoulder of her lover, hoping to find a heart with which she might safely treasure her world of affection; fearing to commit a mistake, yet, in spite of her melancholy experience, fraught with that generous confidence, which, in a great soul, is never extinguished. I had never loved till now; or, at least, had never nourished a passion to the same growth, or met with an object so consummately worthy.

"We did not marry. . . ."

And again, he presents the domestic idyl of a philosopher in which, whatever may be said of the phrasing, the psychology is subtle. Nor had these emotions found adequate expression, before Godwin, even outside the field of biography (pp. 97-8):

"She was a worshipper of domestic life. She loved to observe the growth of affection between me and her daughter, then three years of age, as well as my anxiety respecting the child not yet born. . . . A little ride into the country with myself and the child, has sometimes produced a sort of opening of the heart, a general expression of confidence and affectionate soul, a sort of infantine, yet dignified endearment, which those who have felt may understand, but which I should in vain attempt to pourtray."

The unshakeable love and trust that must have existed between Godwin and Mary is perhaps best shown by his complete knowledge of her past life, and his unwavering analyses as to what she felt at the time of her attraction toward this man or that, and what changes in her were effected by each relationship. He explains her *liaison manquée* with Fuseli by saying (p. 53):

"The delight she enjoyed in his society, she transferred by association to his person. What she experienced in this respect, was no doubt heightened, by the state of celibacy and restraint in which she had hitherto lived, and to which the rules of polished society condemn an unmarried woman."

To escape Fuseli, Mary Wollstonecraft fled to France, where she had a long affair with the tepid-spirited American writer Gilbert Imlay. Their relationship Godwin describes as "that species of connection, for which her heart secretly panted, and which had the effect of diffusing an immediate tranquillity and cheerfulness over her manners." Her cheerfulness was short-lived. She has a child by Imlay; she lives in an agony of doubt as to his love; she journeys to Norway on his account; at last she is certain, or almost certain, that he will not come back. But in a subtle description of her heart, Godwin shows how her despair, in 1795, was both kept alive and increased by the half-hope that Imlay still loved her. Godwin gives a painful picture of death imminent in the night rain at Putney bridge, recounts her two attempts at suicide, and then describes his own first meeting with her, their double establishment, their brief moment of happiness and tranquillity before the hideous and protracted nightmare of her death in giving birth to his child.

The delicate psychological portrayal[64] which is one of the best features of this biography would not have been possible if the incidents had not been (p. 2) "principally taken from the mouth of the person to whom they relate." This gives the memoirs a quality of vivid personal reminiscence which is rare in biography, as in the account of Mary's childhood when the future author of "A Vindication of the Rights of Woman" characteristically tries to save her mother and other defenseless domestic animals from her father's blows (p. 6), lying "whole nights upon the landing-place near their chamber-door."

In reliving Mary Wollstonecraft's life, with all its despair and enthusiasm, William Godwin at times permits bitter reflections to escape (p. 17):

"The last words her mother ever uttered were, 'A little patience, and all will be over!' and these words are repeatedly referred to by Mary in the course of her writings."

He sums up the long account of her last illness with stony pessimism (p. 113): "These were the amusements of persons in the very gulph of despair." And from the pen of the notorious re-

[64] Page 64, for instance, summarizes the mental states and disasters in her career to the year 1793 and the Imlay ménage in Paris.

former such ironic phrasing as this falls unexpected (p. 19): "For ten years, from 1782 to 1792, she may be said to have been, in a great degree, the victim of a desire to promote the benefit of others."

Yet the best passages in the biography occur only when one headstrong idealist describes another, as in the distinction Godwin draws between Mary's character and that of her friend Fanny Blood (p. 23):

"There were some essential characteristics of genius, which she possessed, and in which her friend was deficient. The principal of these was a firmness of mind, an unconquerable greatness of soul, by which, after a short internal struggle, she was accustomed to rise above difficulties and suffering."

At the close of his brief work Godwin almost forgets his purpose of rendering "justice . . . to the illustrious dead" in the poignant sense of his own loss. "This light," he notes (p. 117), "was lent to me for a very short period, and is now extinguished for ever!" Short though the period of their happiness was, it was enough to call forth from the pen of this free-thinker the noblest subjective record of a life to be found in the eighteenth century outside the field of religious biography. Even there, few lives concentrate with such beauty, understanding, and power on the simple, passionate actions of the spirit, the candor of the heart.

CHAPTER IV

KNOWLEDGE INFINITE

ECCENTRICS AND ANTIQUARIES

"Every singular character merits some notice from posterity."
—SHAFTESBURY.

MAN'S almost boundless curiosity concerning his fellows furnished the mainspring for diverse biographical productions of the eighteenth century. This curiosity might take the form of a delight in stories, sensational but true, of brutality and horror, of pirates and highwaymen; it might find satisfaction in gossiping or malicious memoirs; it might inspire the biographers of current statesmen and rulers at home and abroad, or of great men of the past for whom modern parallels were sufficiently obvious; it might survey with satisfaction the lives of those who had just died, or of soldiers of fortune, or of travellers in strange lands, or of any man who had broken from the common highway and led a life without pattern or counterpart. Higher, or at least superficially less frivolous than such inquisitiveness, is the curiosity of the antiquary, the patient determination to learn everything that may be learned of great ancestors and contemporaries, and to set forth their biographies in permanent collections and ordered records. From the memoirs of gamesters and courtesans to the *Biographia Britannica,* eighteenth century England shows its eager interest in preserving the lives of men.

To begin with the ridiculous and ascend to the sublime, one should consider first the ephemeral tracts that fluttered daily from the printing presses to gratify the public appetite for the horrible and the strange. A single volume in the Bodleian Library[1] contains a fair cross-section of such early eighteenth century pamphlets: *The life and history of Sarah, Dutchess of Marlborough* with a cut showing her as pockmarked; accounts of Newgate

---

[1] Shelfmark: 2702.2,1.

criminals; taunts against the French king; prophecies of James Ussher, Archbishop of Armagh; stories of fires, Quakers and impostors; of coronation ceremonies, ghosts, and sextuplets; of devils which appeared to old bawds and of unnatural and cruel fathers, sons, daughters, and uncles; a life of the murderer Edward Jefferies and another of the adventurer Captain Avery. The value of such productions, considered as biographies, is almost nonexistent, except in showing avid public curiosity for anything new and extraordinary.

A single example among sensational biographies may be drawn from the productions of the publisher Edmund Curll, adept in promising more on title-pages than his scribes could ever perform. In 1710 he republishes a pamphlet that had appeared in 1640 as *The penitent death of a woeful sinner, or, the penitent death of John Atherton, executed at Dublin, the 5th of December, 1640.* Curll gives this topical pamphlet the lurid new title of *The case of John Atherton, Bishop of Waterford in Ireland. Who was convicted of the sin of uncleaness with a cow, and other creatures, for which he was hanged at Dublin, Decem. 5, 1640.* Counting on continued popular curiosity, a pamphlet appears in the same year 1710, ostensibly a correction of Curll's publication, called *The case of John Atherton, Bishop of Waterford in Ireland: fairly represented against a late partial edition of Dr. Barnard's relation, and sermon at his funeral.* With the righteous indignation which these catchpenny biographers of the early century so well knew how to assume, the writer of this latter pamphlet speaks of Curll's use of "Capitals, to render the most remarkable and odious thing more observable. And as if that were not enough to make it sufficiently known, the Publick Papers must be filled with this Modest Title Page to carry it far, and near on the Wings of an Advertisement." The reader is assured that this retort is hastened from the editor because of a new advertisement, this time reproduced not from the *Tatler* but from the *Post-Man:* "This Day is Publish'd the 2d Edition of the Cases of unnatural Lewdness, Viz 1. The Tryal of the Lord Audley for a Rape committed on the Body of his Lady, and Sodomy with his two Servants, for the which he was Beheaded, and they Hanged 1631. 2. The Case of Bishop Atherton. . . ." The ingenuity of such writers in gaining publicity needs no further notice here, except to remark that it was no less common than it was diabolical. In modified form, the sensational appeal to sensuality occasioned the life-and-amours type of biography that flourished in the first years of the century and gave way later to the serially published numbers of feminine autobiographers, exploiting the same desires while using more nearly genuine biographical materials.[2]

The fascination of scenes of cruelty, deliberate brutality, and suffering, made evident by the success and frequency of biographical productions that gratified such cravings, might tend to establish the dictum of Anatole France that man is a torturing animal. *Anecdotes concerning the famous John Reinhold Patkul* (1761) can be marketed because Charles XII had Patkul broken on the wheel alive. *The life, and various vicissitudes of fortune, of Peter Williamson* (1759) is published by a canny bookseller with the leading title of *French and Indian cruelty*.[3] "The life and sufferings" is one of the common titles for eighteenth century biographies.

Possibly the best account of pure horror brought about by human cruelty is *The memoirs of a Protestant, condemned to the galleys of France, for his religion. Written by himself* (1758).[4] The original was by Jean Marteille of Bergerac in Perigord, published in Rotterdam in 1757 with blanks for proper names; this translation is the work in which Goldsmith made his bow to the world as a man of letters. Goldsmith did not bother with a close rendering; he enjoys introducing classical allusions and patriotic comparisons between France and England; but his elegance cannot change the shocking story of adventures and privations, from

[2] See the first three chapters on the drama, the novel, and the romantic spirit, *passim*. cf. Manley, Haywood, Charke, Gooch, Phillips, Catley; a fair sample is *The life of Lamenther*, 1771.

[3] cf. also *The redeemed captive returning to Zion or the captivity and deliverance of Rev. John Williams of Deerfield*, 1707; and *The history of the life and sufferings of Henry Grace, of Basingstoke. . . . Being a narrative of the hardships he underwent during several years captivity among the savages in North America, and of the cruelties they practise to their unhappy prisoners*, 1764.

[4] cf. Trenck's memoirs, 1788; and *An abstract of the history of the cruel sufferings of the blessed French martyr Louis de Marolles, from his condemnation to the gallies, to his death in the dungeon*, 1713; other editions in 1712, 1788, and 1790.

the bloody tortures in Perigord under the Duke de la Force to the winter march of the chained galley-slaves from Le Havre to Marseille. Life in the ghastly Tournelle prison in Paris is described without mincing words—eighteen prisoners are frozen to death, naked—and existence on board the galleys is no less completely recorded, from the terrors of the bastinado to the awful powers of the *comités* or the galley-officers. This humanitarian tract leaves the reader with a new realization of the unsuspected capabilities in the human animal both for cruelty and, as if in compensation, for moral endurance.

Hanging was the most nearly certain way to immediate biographical fame in the eighteenth century. A good life did not insure a memorial for posterity; but a violent and public death usually produced a pamphlet. Everyone knows the name of Jonathan Wild, largely because both Defoe and Fielding contributed to the biographical facts and fiction that sprang up around his name. But each famous pirate or highwayman of the times—Captain Avery, John Gow, Cartouche, Dick Turpin, Sixteen-string Jack Rann, James Maclean, or Mandrin the smuggler —had his biographer or corps of biographers. The stories sell better, journeymen writers evidently found, if the hero has just been hanged or is about to be; stories assembled by a craftsman in fiction are more eagerly read if they may be ascribed to a recently condemned criminal with such a title-page as: "Written by himself in Maidstone Goal, whilst under Sentence of Death."[5]

Occasionally, moreover, the repentance, or brutality, or stupidity, or fear, of a criminal about to die is made more impressive by the shadow of the gallows. One does not easily forget the *Authentick account of the life of Paul Wells, Gent.* (1749), the young man of Oxford, with his capital offense of altering a figure 2 to a 3 on an old receipt, his fainting when sentence is passed against him, his terrible leave-taking from his father, and his final collapse so that he cannot mount the ladder to the platform where he is to be executed.

As the reading public became more and more familiar with the lives of savage lawbreakers and their punishment by an

---

[5] *The life and surprizing adventures of Gilbert Langley,* 1740.

equally savage society, the accounts were formalized in periodical publications, as in *The Ordinary of Newgate his account of the behaviours, confessions, and last dying words of the malefactors that were executed at Tyburn on Friday the 29th of January 1719-20*. These pamphlets were published upon the execution of each batch of criminals, regularly, for a series of years;[6] they sold for twopence, and were signed by the prison chaplains, who usually had become so case-hardened that they simply went through their official functions and observed " 'em," as they refer to the prisoners, hang for their watch-stealings or forgeries. The sentiments of narrator, prisoner, and audience seem to the modern reader deadening and hopeless. "One Thing above all," writes James Guthrie, the Ordinary in 1743, "stuck for sometime terribly in his Stomach, namely, that he should suffer Death for only breaking into a House, when he did not carry any Thing off. . . ."

The spirit in which the public received such productions in the Augustan Age is sufficiently betrayed in the title-pages. Captain Alexander Smith issued in 1714 *The history of the lives of the most noted highway-men, foot-pads, house-breakers, shop-lifts and cheats, of both sexes, in and about London, and other places of Great-Britain, for above fifty years last past. Wherein their most secret and barbarous murders, unparallel'd robberies, notorious thefts, and unheard of cheats, are expos'd to the publick*. The preface proclaims that its purpose is "to recount the Actions of Criminal and Wicked Persons, that by the dreadful Aspects of Vice, they may be deterr'd from embracing her Illusions." Captain Smith, though he maintains that all his accounts of criminals are "penn'd from their own Mouths," shows unexpected delicacy in substituting dashes for oaths. As in certain of the *Canterbury Tales*, naturalism is here in conflict with decorum; yet the conscientious captain cannot give up entirely the suggestion that criminals do swear; his blank spaces enable him "to paint them in their proper Colours; whose Words are always so Odious, De-

---

[6] I have examined such productions in more or less regular series from 1719 to 1744; a similar production for the year 1824 shows wholesale numbers still sentenced to death or transportation for life—23 to death in one short session, most of them for stealing in dwelling-houses.

testable, and Foul, that some, as little acquainted with a God as they, would be apt to conclude that Nature spoil'd 'em in the Making, by setting their Mouths at the wrong end of their Bodies." Smith does not condemn his subjects; he simply reveals their practices and their actions—chiefly, if one accepts his avowals, for the benefit of those amateurs who are dangerously like the criminals themselves, and for the protection of honest citizens, travelling or at home, against cozenage. To render his volumes more practical, they are preceded by an alphabetical table of incidents and characters. Some of the tricks of the cheats and sharpers are extraordinarily cunning and amusing;[7] and some of Captain Smith's sooty anecdotes are no less extraordinarily broad. In a preface, Smith confides to the reader that he gave up divinity for the sword. Yet his career in promoting virtue still ostensibly continues in these volumes of collected scabrous and hilarious stories.

Immensely popular, variations on Captain Smith's productions, as well as on those by his rival and successor Captain Charles Johnson,[8] came steadily from the presses in the early decades of the century. Sometimes they took the form of extended rogue-biographies, as in Smith's *Memoirs of the life and times, of the famous Jonathan Wild, together with the history and lives, of modern rogues* (1726), which employs Defoe's technique of giving a trellis of facts, dates, and actual places on which to twine romanesque and fantastic anecdotes. Sometimes they take the form of redactions with an appendix to bring the whole up to date; sometimes they swell to a three-volume affair[9] with copious indexes and a preface that opens "The Clemency of the Law of England is great," and reveals a few pages later that grand larceny, punishable by death, is defined as stealing goods worth more than

---

[7] cf. Theophilus Lucas, *Memoirs of the lives, intrigues, and comical adventures of the most famous gamesters and celebrated sharpers*, 1714, 2d ed.

[8] Among these assiduous "Captains" might be mentioned Captain Charles Walker, whose *Authentick memoirs of the life, intrigues and adventures of the celebrated Sally Salisbury. With true characters of her most considerable gallants* (1723) learnedly sketches, in bare-faced stories, a career in which Sally outdoes all the famous courtesans of antiquity.

[9] *The lives of the most remarkable criminals*, 1735, containing well over 1300 pages.

twelvepence. Here the Newgate annals are crossed with the picaresque novels to inculcate morality by narrating a series of shocking brutalities on the part of both criminals and law-courts. The growth of a new reading public for such productions is evident even on the opening page:[10]

"I flatter myself that however contemptible the *Lives of the Criminals,* etc., may seem in the eyes of those who affect great wisdom and put on the appearance of much learning, yet it will not be without its uses amongst the middling sort of people, who are glad to take up with books within the circle of their own comprehension."

Among the biographies written by semiliterate citizens for their fellows, one of the most amusing is Thomas Whitehead's *Original anecdotes of the late Duke of Kingston and Miss Chudleigh, alias Mrs. Harvey, alias Countess of Bristol, alias Duchess of Kingston: interspersed with memoirs of several of the nobility and gentry now living* (1792). The Duchess of Kingston made the mistake of trying to cut off Whitehead, who attended the Duke in his last illness, from his legacy of two hundred pounds: these memoirs are the result. They are the clumsily told, malicious anecdotes of a butler; but they reveal, with some degree of success, an eighteenth century household as seen from below-stairs—the family régime of an amiable, hen-pecked nobleman; the snowy winter months in the country, with the gossip, the guests, and the dancing; the account of a sporting lord's life in contrast to the ludicrous picture of an uncomfortable valet on horseback. Most of the stories about Miss Chudleigh will not bear repeating in the sober pages of this history; but it may be permissible to pass on her invention for keeping her feet warm while fishing. She liked (p. 54) "plenty of rum . . . to put in her shoes. I have known her use two quarts in a day; being obliged to change her clothes twice or thrice during that time; standing from morning till evening in the wet; sometimes too without catching a single fish."

Pirates and royal prostitutes, cullies and conny-catchers are brought upon the stage to gratify the curiosity of the vulgar.

[10] Quoted from 1927 reprint of the above, 2d paragraph of preface, ed. A. L. Hayward.

Malicious memoirs of the great, scandalous stories of gentle-women of fashion, serve the same purpose. The secret story of the rise of Marlborough is at the disposal of every London chair-man and body-servant. The Duchess of Marlborough, Chancellor Jeffreys, Doctor Sacheverell, Robert Walpole, John Wilkes, Thomas Paine, or any outstanding controversial figure is fair game for friendly and unfriendly biographers.

In recording, or inventing, incidents that will satisfy the public demand, these hostile life-writers attain a certain skill. The biog-rapher of Paine, for instance, accuses him of filial ingratitude, conjugal cruelty, coldness, impotence, and mercantile conduct unbecoming a tradesman and a maker of corset-stays. George Chalmers (if he was the author of this clever tract) writes with wit and style, as in his description of the reception in the Colonies of Paine's pamphlet, *Common Sense.* "But, who wrote it was the wonder. It must be Adams, said the Bostonians; it must be Franklin, said the Philadelphians; it must be Washington, said the Virginians."[11] And in criticizing Paine's "mutilated brat" *The Rights of Man,* Chalmers finds fault not only with its mis-representations and egotism, but with its "Bad Grammar, Sole-cisms, Barbarisms, and Balderdash." Chalmers is small-minded, but he is neither inefficient nor dull as he rises to this final curse:[12]

"Biography treats only of the past: prophecy can alone reveal the future: what may be our author's subsequent course or fate, it is impossible to foretel. But without the spirit of prophecy, it may be foretold, that whether Pain fight with Fayette, in Europe, or wander through America, to Washington, he will carry this genuine history of his life along with him, as a badge upon his back, which will announce to all, that as a man, Pain has no *moral* character; and as a writer, that he is entitled to no *literary* fame; that wherever he may be, his great aim is to incite anarchy;

[11] p. 33, 1792, 5th ed.

[12] pp. 165-6, 5th ed. Such vituperation is catching. A later biographer, in 1797, ends his brief life of Paine with (p. 60): "Whenever and wherever he breathes his last, he will excite neither sorrow nor compassion; no friendly hand will close his eyes, not a groan will be uttered, nor a tear will be shed. Like Judas he will be re-membered by posterity; men will learn to express all that is base, malignant, treacherous, unnatural and blasphemous, by the single monosyllable, *Paine.*"

but that his power of performance is not always equal to the vigour of his will."

Such orations against Catiline, particularly when accompanied, say, by a "vignette of Paine surrounded by apes" or an engraving of John Wilkes in which his crossed eyes are hideously exaggerated, seem satisfactorily to have purged high political passions. Even biographies of men long dead—particularly of Romans— might be sold if parallels could be imagined with engrossing events and figures of the present. To any student of English history, the dates of the following biographies will be significant: *The lives of Roger Mortimer, Earl of March, and of Robert, Earl of Oxford, &c. Prime Ministers in the reigns of Edward the Second, and Richard the Second* (1711); *The life and history of Belisarius, who conquer'd Africa and Italy, with an account of his disgrace, the ingratitude of the Romans, and a parallel between him and a modern heroe* (1713); *The life of Sir Robt. Cochran, Prime-Minister to King James III of Scotland* (1734: this was issued just before the elections to demonstrate the evils of a minister who is too powerful); *An impartial history of the life and death of James the Second* (1746, Dublin); and Mark Noble's monitory *Lives of the English regicides* (1798), with its dedication "to the Regicides of France." The dramatic years following the Rebellion of 1745 and the career of the Young Pretender bring forth their quota of topical political biographies.[13] Later, the French Revolution offered a rich opportunity for biographers to impart fresh news, or codify information, or express sheer prejudice.[14] Even a general philosophical difference of

---

[13] See *An account of the behaviour of the late Earl of Kilmarnock. . . . By James Foster*, 1746; *The genuine dying speech of the Reverend Parson Coppock, pretended Bishop of Carlisle, who was drawn, hanged and quartered there, Oct. 18, 1746, for high treason and rebellion*, Carlisle, 1746; *A candid and impartial account of the behaviour of Simon Lord Lovat, from the time his death-warrant was deliver'd, to the day of his execution*, 1747; *The female rebels: being some remarkable incidents of the lives, characters, and families of the titular Duke and Dutchess of Perth, the Lord and Lady Ogilvie, and of Miss Florence M'Donald*, Edinburgh, 1747.

[14] See *Life and anecdotes of General Pichegru*, n.d. but *ca.* 1792; *The life of J. P. Brissot, Deputy from Eure and Loire, to the National Convention. Written by himself*, 1794; *Biographical anecdotes of the founders of the French Republic*, probably by John Adolphus, 1797 and later editions; *Biographical sketches of some of the leading men at the head of affairs in France*, Edinburgh, 1792; *A narrative*

opinion, though it culminate in no definite crisis, may produce controversial biography, as in *The true nature of imposture fully display'd in the life of Mahomet. With a discourse annex'd for the vindication of Christianity from this charge. Offered to the consideration of the Deists of the present age. By Humphrey Prideaux* (1723).[15]

The great modern newspapers have prepared in their files biographies of famous living people, so that life-histories of any one of them may appear on the day of his death or the following morning. If eighteenth century publishers had not developed such efficiency, they knew at least that the appeal of their popular tracts directly depended upon the speed with which they could record current sensational careers. Charles Price, a notorious forger, hanged himself in April 1786. The "sixth edition" of his history, though it ran to 344 pages, appeared in the same year. The author of the life of Robert Ramsey (1742) apologizes for publishing his work "so long after the Execution of the unhappy Subject thereof," although this biography comes out in the very year of Ramsey's death.

Profit-seeking printers, catering to public curiosity, powerfully influenced biographical productions; their catchpenny lives served much the same purpose and public as do the cheap modern newspapers which emphasize personalities and scandal. A bloody death, an aristocrat in trouble, a mystery, above all a prolonged legal struggle, could always be padded out into a profitable pamphlet, thrown into the biographical mold so that additional facts might fill its pages, and published while the subject was on every one's lips. Authentic and fictitious, decked out with black-bordered elegies, dying confessions, and shorthand accounts of trials, such productions kept the presses busy and afforded entertainment to "the middling sort of people." Two lords kill each other in a duel in Hyde Park (1712); "the Rape-Master-General of Great Britain" is finally condemned in the only instance when

---

of the sufferings and escape of Charles Jackson, late resident at Wexford, in Ireland, 1798, 3d ed. 1799; *The Revolutionary Plutarch*, 1804; *The Female Revolutionary Plutarch*, 1803, 3d ed.

[15] This was the 8th ed. of a work the preface to which is dated 1697. cf. the Roman Catholic *Life of Saint Wenefride*, 1700, and the several retorts upon its publication listed in the Bibliography.

he may have been innocent (1730); a girl, later convicted of per-
jury, accuses a gypsy woman of abducting her and sees the old
woman convicted (1754); a brilliant self-taught scholar is hanged
in chains for a murder which he may or may not have committed thirteen years before (1759); a dissipated young nobleman
wilfully shoots and kills one of his servants and is tried for it
before the House of Lords (1760); two Frenchmen and the wife
or mistress of one of them, accused of forgery, try to save themselves from the gallows by reciprocal accusations and degrading
recrimination (1776); a minister of the Church of England is
found guilty of forgery and is hanged in spite of wide public
protestation (1777); the late Master of Ceremonies at the Pantheon is convicted of poisoning his brother-in-law in order to inherit an estate (1781); the peers of Britain rise one by one in the
House of Lords, after the trial of a duchess for bigamy, and pronounce sentence (1788).[16]

Such sordid and savage episodes in a nation's history may seem
of little significance in themselves; yet a correct perspective of
eighteenth century biography cannot be attained until it is realized that such careers resulted in more biographical compilations
than did the lives of most statesmen, scientists, artists, or benefactors of mankind; that the happenings in the lives of most of
the lawbreakers cited above were recorded by more than one
biographer and appeared in several editions; and that although
the subject matter may be disgusting or trivial, the execution of
many of these pamphlets is competent and trustworthy. One point
they have in common: their interest is topical; a successful commercial publisher and his journeyman biographer must record
a nine-days wonder within nine days.

Edmund Curll popularized another ephemeral species in his
true and authentic copies of the last wills and testaments of famous people—Gilbert Burnet or Thomas Sprat, John Partridge
or the Marquis of Wharton. In 1722, for instance, Curll advertises for sale, separately published or in one volume, the last wills

[16] See Bibliography under the respective names of Lords Hamilton and Mohun,
Francis Charteris, Elizabeth Canning, Eugene Aram, Lord Ferrers, Margaret Rudd
and Robert and Daniel Perreau, William Dodd, John Donellan, and the Duchess
of Kingston.

of eleven men—men of family and poets, astrologers and historians, antiquaries and ecclesiasts. The wills of very rich men and of public benefactors seem to have been in particular demand.[17] The growing mercantile classes, with their interest in the extent of any man's fortune as well as in his disposal of it, made such ventures profitable. The pamphlets sold for sixpence or a shilling. Curll occasionally advertised a life followed by a last will; in these instances the tail usually wagged the dog.[18] When too much trouble was required to secure a faithful copy of the real will, a hoax might suffice.[19] Curll had countered Pope's satire against him by complacently promising to publish the last will and testament of Alexander Pope as soon as Pope had the grace to die. Curll did not execute his threat, but the practice had become so prevalent by the time of Pope's death in 1744 that Pope's will was actually published in the same year.[20]

In Curll's copy of the last wills of Thomas Tenison and Dr. George Hickes he advertises, at one pound three shillings, *The lives of the most eminent persons who died in the years 1711, 1712, 1713, 1714, 1715, in 4 vols. 8vo.* This novel means of grouping biographies was never systematically carried out.[21] Two volumes, however, appeared, of which the first bears the title *Memoirs British and foreign, of the lives and families of the most illustrious persons who dy'd in the year 1711. . . . To be continued yearly.* In 1714 two further volumes appeared, covering the years 1711 and 1712. John Le Neve, the author, shows his industry in the initial collection of 557 pages followed by an index. He notes

---

[17] See the lives and published bequests of Thomas Gresham and Edward Alleyn, or of Sir Hans Sloane, 48 pp., 1753. Also *A true copy of the last will and testament of Thomas Guy, Esq; late of Lombard-street, bookseller: containing an account of his publick and private benefactions*, 1725, containing 55 pp.

[18] e.g., *London's wonder: or, the chaste old Batchellor: Being, a faithful account of the family, life, and legacies of Mr. Samuel Wright, of Newington-Green, in the County of Middlesex, Gent. With a true copy of his last will and testament*, 1737. One shilling. 20 pp. plus 24 pp. of will and testament.

[19] e.g., *An authentic copy of the last will and testament of the Reverend Dr. Swift*, Dublin, n.d. The will is dated 1745.

[20] Printed for A. Dodd. cf. the life of Pope, 1745, by Curll's henchman, William Ayre.

[21] cf., however, at the other end of the century *The annual necrology, for 1797-8; including, also, various articles of neglected biography*, 1800, printed for R. Phillips; 2d ed., 1805, in which the purpose is similar.

with satisfaction that (p. iv) "That Cruel Tyrant Death, having in the Compass of the last Year, exercised his Dominion over the Great, in a more signal manner than usual, has afforded a large Field to Range in, and Copious Subjects to Work upon." And though he worships titles and estate, and depends too much upon county histories, genealogy and heraldry, his compilation is more conscientious and full than one might expect from Curll's hireling. In spite of the title, an antiquary rather than a journalist is writing. Throughout the century, in fact, the line between legitimate antiquarian interest and vulgar curiosity was seldom drawn, and it is consequently not drawn very seriously in this chapter. Were Hakluyt's *Voyages,* for example, collected in order to give permanent form to the chorographical and geographical discoveries of Tudor seamen, the history of the Spanish Main and the seven seas; or were they published to gratify the Englishman's native sense of adventure? This question is no more easily answered categorically with regard to many of the memoirs of eighteenth century travellers. They tell thrilling stories; they acquaint the reader with new regions and the strange customs of foreigners who are nevertheless men; they develop, directly or indirectly, the characters and careers of the narrators; above all, they show the almost infinite capacity, resourcefulness, resilience, and indomitable courage of the human spirit in dangerous and difficult new worlds.

These biographies of wanderers have their settings in most of the countries of the globe. Wales[22] and Portugal[23] are not too close and familiar to warrant descriptions, nor are Patagonia[24] and Kamchatka[25] too far away. Travelling and adventure—the

[22] William Matthews's *Short tour of observation and sentiment, through a part of South Wales,* Bath, 1786.

[23] *The history of Thomas Aram, Commander of the Fancy, in the Rhoan trade . . . written by himself,* 1776, gives a very fine picture of his runaway youth in Portugal.

[24] *The narrative of the Honourable John Byron . . . containing an account of the great distresses suffered by himself and his companions on the coast of Patagonia, from the year 1740, till their arrival in England, 1746, 1768.* As an exciting picture of brave men fighting almost overwhelming hardships for years, this surpasses *Robinson Crusoe.*

[25] *Memoirs . . . of . . . Count de Benyowsky,* 1790, discussed later in this chapter.

unexpected events of the road, the disasters, ludicrous incidents, grotesque companions, and changing panoramas—may
reveal character as well as accounts in which direct portrayal of
a subject is the avowed purpose. The close similarity, in spite of
their titles, between Boswell's *Life of Johnson* and his *Tour to
the Hebrides* attests this sufficiently, if any proof is needed; in
this connection Fielding's *Voyage to Lisbon* should not be forgotten, nor the travelogue form by means of which Swift, Defoe,
and Johnson, Fielding, Smollett and Sterne develop their fictitious characters. And in the authentic narratives of travel, the
titles themselves are not invariably informative; "strange, surprising adventures" may reveal a personality, while the "memoirs" or the "life" of another may be almost entirely geographical.[26] Biographical details and psychological observations may
be presented even in a fictitious work with such apparent truth
as to lead an unwary reader to accept them without reservation.[27]

For sheer enthralling narratives of action, the actual accounts
of their own lives by Lowellin, Drury, and Benyowski cannot be
surpassed by fiction. David Lowellin's account of his adventures
in Africa[28] offers the reader a *Captain Singleton* yarn told in
straightforward fashion. If we can believe Lowellin (and the
comical misprints and Malapropisms seem genuine enough), he
was blown ashore in a derelict on the Slave Coast of Africa, lived

[26] A list of the best travel-and-adventure biographies would include: North
America, J. Carver, 1778; John Williams, 1707; Peter Williamson, 1759; David
Brainerd, 1749; Russia and Siberia, Peter Henry Bruce, 1782; John Howard, 1792;
Jonas Hanway, 1787; Count Benyowsky, 1790; Africa, Edward Brown, 1753;
Bluett's *Job*, 1734; Annamaboe, n.d.; Thomas Jenkins and David Lowellin, 1792;
Robert Drury, 1729; India, Stanhope, 1784-1785; Macdonald, 1790; Japan,
Psalmanaazaar, 1704; La Perouse, n.d.; the Seven Seas, Kippis's *James Cook*,
1789; John Newton, 1764; Mark Moore, 1795. Also see Mrs. Margaret Calder-
wood's amusing adventures nearer home, 1756.

[27] On first reading *The travels of Edward Brown*, 1739, for instance, ascribed
to John Campbell, I accepted it as in part genuine. It is some comfort to know
that this biography of romantic adventure met with Pope's approval; but one
wonders with some trepidation how many works of fact and works of fiction are
incorrectly listed in this present volume.

[28] *The life, voyages, and travels, of Thomas Jenkins, & David Lowellin, through
the unknown tracts of Africa. With the manner how Lowellin lived eight years
on an uninhabited spot; and, having sustained many dangerous attacks from the
wild beasts and savages, returned safe to London, in September, 1784, after having
been fourteen years in those extensive regions*, 1792.

with the blacks, escaped northeast into the desert, spent seven years in an isolated oasis where his one companion died, and finally was rescued and convoyed blindfolded to Cairo.

Yet good as is Lowellin's story of a rolling stone, it is surpassed by one less questionably authentic adventure in Africa, which forms one of the best travel narratives that has ever been written. This is *The pleasant and surprising adventures of Robert Drury, during his fifteen years' captivity on the island of Madagascar. Written by himself* (1729). Shipwrecked on the way back from India when he was about fifteen years old, Robert Drury is made a slave in a Madagascar tribe. Life on the island he describes in matter-of-fact detail, with its treasures of honey and bullocks, its wild panoramas, its raids and guerilla warfare, its savage tribal chieftains whose actions and characters Drury differentiates so vividly. At one time young Drury escapes, living off the country for weeks, swimming a river with a torch in his hand to keep off crocodiles. Finally he is sold to the captain of a ship that touched at Madagascar, and he returns to England in 1717 to write a narrative of adventure that indicates throughout the biographer's cool and resourceful courage.

Some fifty-odd years after Drury left the island of Madagascar, another adventurer, the Count de Benyowsky, arrived there to found a French colony. Benyowsky was always arriving in the most unlikely places. During the crowded forty-five years before he was killed in a guerilla skirmish (1786), this strange Pole had traced a dizzy course from Hungary and Poland to Russia, had made the epic journey across Siberia, had escaped from Kamchatka, married a Tonquin wife in the Japanese archipelago, travelled in China, and accepted a commission to occupy Madagascar in the name of France. His English editor, William Nicholson, tries to establish the authenticity of his memoirs,[29] the French original of which he says he is presenting to the British Museum; and his attempt is laudable, for they form one of the most enthralling and convincing of all adventure and travel books. The account of the great trek of the exiles across Russia and Siberia would alone give Benyowsky's memoirs a high place

[29] *Memoirs and travels of Mauritius Augustus Count de Benyowsky . . . written by himself*, Dublin, 1790, 2 vols.

among the biographies of wanderers; and his machinations to escape beyond the farthest eastern boundaries of the hated Russian empire form a masterpiece of intrigue and excitement. Whether Benyowsky is narrating facts or not—and if they are fabrications, his imagination was astounding—to read his account is to believe it, for he is punctilious in recording numbers, dates, and *les petits faits significatifs*.

The travellers who write their own memoirs rarely philosophize about their lives; action for them is reality. If as a class they may be said to have any philosophy of existence, it might take the form of the ruminations of battered old Thomas Aram, commander of the *Fancy* in the Rouen trade. One of his wives died and left him with two children; a second wife is unsympathetic; his daughter-in-law is no good; one son drowns—"his head stuck in the mud." Yet Aram keeps on with his commerce, his smuggling, and his fighting, through the French war and through the French peace. At the age of seventy he is still working, and has found "that the only real and permanent bliss springs from a contented mind."[30] He ends by saying that he is "perfectly satisfied that my troubles were necessarily inflicted; and that 'Whatever is is right.'" He is proud of his motto: *Endure, and conquer.*

Closely allied to the foot-loose and restless travellers are the fighters, the soldiers of fortune.[31] Records of their careers were popular in the eighteenth century. Jonathan Swift helped out one such adventurer to the extent of two hundred pounds when he drew up and digested the memoirs of eighty-three-year-old Captain John Creichton (1731). And a nameless author profited from popular approval of life-histories true yet strange by writing *The life and adventures of Mrs. Christian Davies, commonly called Mother Ross; who, in several campaigns under King William and the late Duke of Marlborough, in the quality of a foot soldier and dragoon, gave many signal proofs of an unparallell'd courage and personal bravery. Taken from her own mouth* (1740). This production shows some of Defoe's cleverness in picking up jour-

[30] *The history of Thomas Aram . . . written by himself*, 1776, p. 66.
[31] Further similar biographies of travellers and soldiers are considered, in their relation to the novel, in Chap. II.

nals, histories, memoirs, and oral accounts, and giving them coherent and convincing autobiographical form.

One of the earliest and most deservedly popular of the lives of
adventurers is *The memoirs of Maj*ʳ. *Alexander Ramkins, a
Highland-officer, now in prison at Avignon. Being an account
of several remarkable adventures during about twenty eight years
service in Scotland, Germany, Italy, Flanders and Ireland; exhibiting a very agreeable and instructive lesson of human life,
both in a public and private capacity, in several pleasant instances of his amours, gallantry, oeconomy, &c.* (1719). Sharply
drawn in his own biography, Major Ramkins stands out almost
as distinctly as his compatriot Lismahago or his fellow-soldier
and military theorist Uncle Toby, although his common sense
exceeds theirs and keeps his portrait from being a caricature. His
crotchets and prejudices are evident from the first. "It seems,"
says the publisher, "the Gentleman had been sour'd by French
Practises, and was willing that the World should be no longer a
Stranger to what was the ground of his distast." He thinks of
himself as a political philosopher throughout, and his unvaried
position is that the French have been making fools of the English
for a century, that James II in exile at Saint-Germain was the catspaw of Louis XIV, and that Louis was playing the old game of
weakening an opponent by fostering internal strife, as Richelieu
had done so well with Charles I, whom he could have saved.
Major Ramkins's hard-bitten, cynical remarks and analyses make
his narrative as interesting as Defoe's *Memoirs of a Cavalier* or the
life of *Mrs. Christian Davies*. Written half a century later, the
Major would have bulwarked his observations by quoting Fielding or Smollett, occasionally even Richardson.

His story opens with young Alexander, a seventeen-year-old
student at Aberdeen, joining the Stuart soldiers after Killie-
crankie. He draws a sarcastically objective picture of three hundred soldiers roaming the Highlands (p. 6):

"Our commanding Officer was Romantickly Loyal, and look'd
upon every little Hill we scrambled over, as an impregnable
Fortress, from whose Summit he often took occasion to Harangue
us, as if the Eyes of all Europe were upon us, and the Fate of
the Three Kingdoms hung at our Swords Points. But the Truth

was, I believe, we were unknown to all Mankind, and if those Villages we march'd by cou'd but secure the Cattle from us, the State was in no great Danger from our Quarter."

Ramkins learns his seasoned politics from an old soldier whom he adopts as master and who advises him to sell his share of his estates and look for service abroad. He realizes fifteen hundred pounds from his inheritance, twelve hundred of which he lodges with an Amsterdam banker. This money, which he successfully harbors against cardsharpers, forgers, and everyone except his wife, gives a pleasant glow to all his adventures and lifts them above the penury of the picaresque. On the Continent, he escapes from the Rhineland campaigns, where his greatest danger was from his gaming friends, only to fall foul of the authorities in Paris, where he is mistaken for his brother who had just fled after killing a lady's cousin in a duel over her honor. The ensuing trial costs Ramkins money, as had his training among the French cadets at Strasbourg. He likes Paris, but he prefers war. This is his account of the Battle of the Boyne, which is quoted at length because it shows vividly the difference between the autobiographer, who risks his neck, and the omniscient historian, who risks only his opinion (pp. 55-8):

"My Post was to Head a Company of Fingalian Granadiers, who were plac'd in an Orchard which hung over a Defilee, through which we expected the Enemy would march after they had pass'd the River. I make bold to stile my Company Granadiers, because they were design'd to be so when first rais'd, but were now arm'd rather like Pioneers than Grenadiers; we had not above a dozen Granadoes, no Bayonets, and several without any Fire-arms; and if the Chief Men of the Action were no better equipp'd, 'tis easy to guess how the Gross of the Army was provided. According to our Expectation, a Party of the Enemy fell into the Trap, and what Shot we had, we let it successively fly at them out of the Orchard; in the mean time, we heard a great Noise behind us, and turning my self about, I saw the Orchard almost surrounded with Horse, which I expected were some of our own Party coming up to support us, but found them to be a Squadron of the Enemy, who immediately summon'd us to yield, or we must expect the last Fate of War. There was no

time to Parley, upon which I made a Sign to the Commanding
Officer of the Enemy not to proceed to Slaughter, and so out
of Twenty Two Men with which I defended that Post, Nine
of us fell into the Enemies Hands, the rest dying bravely in the
Engagement. . . .

"'Tis not a being in a Battle that makes a Person a capable
Judge how to describe it; every Officer has his Post which he
must not depart from, and though he may be able to describe
the Scituation of the Troops before an Engagement, yet afterwards during the Fight, there is so much Noise, Smoak and
Confusion, that for my part, I scarce can give a true Narration
of what happen'd within a dozen Yards compass."

Parolled in Dublin, where the canny Scot in him had already
arranged money matters in case of a defeat at the Boyne, he
cannot keep from bitter reverie upon Louis XIV's perfidy (pp
60-1):

"But in the midst of all the Disasters I met with, nothing
affected me with a more sensible Grief than the Thoughts of
Lewis the XIVth's Insincerity, for though it only rid my Mind
in the Nature of a Scruple or first Impression, yet I found it grew
daily more and more upon me, and often in the height of my
Diversions it lay upon my Stomach like an indigested Meal. . . ."

He does not speak, however, for he has heard of the Bastille. He
contents himself with the generalization (p. 82): "All Masters
in Politicks look one way and Row another."

But if the political and military reflections of this gentleman
adventurer are original, his observations on the fair sex are no
less so. And his satirical, objective accounts of his affairs of the
heart, unique in biography, are many years ahead of such technique in the novel. He tells his story so well that he should be
allowed to repeat it (pp. 68-73):

"A general Whining, and Pining away for a Trolloping Girl,
was to me a very awker'd and inconsistent Piece of Pageantry;
however, I had been often told by Persons of Experience, that no
Man had so just an idea of the World, as he that had been well
hamper'd and sower'd by a Love Intrigue. . . .

"I had at my first entrance upon the Stage of the World made
a double Promise to my self, the one was never to hearken to a

Love Affair till I had acquired a Stock of Experience, and Money to make that Passion Serviceable and of real Use in an honourable Way; the other was not to graft upon a Foreign Stock; but I was forc'd to humble my self under a violation of both these Purposes; for the Object of my Passion was a Spanish young Lady though of Irish Extraction. . . .

". . . in all the Skirmishes and Sieges I had been at, they never threw me into such a Consternation and Absence of Thought; and accordingly I met with an old Adept in these Affairs. When he heard my Case, after two or three Turns he approach'd me with the serious Air of a Physician, and I thinking he had Design to feel my Pulse, I offer'd him my Hand, which he only shook very gently, saying, Young Man, all the Comfort I can give you is, that you must buy your Knowledge by Experience as I and many others have done before you. . . .

"While the old Gentleman was entertaining me with this Lesson, my Head grew so dizy, as if some invisible Hand had turn'd it round like a Gigg, so I left him abruptly, and went directly to my Lodgings to Bed, but to this Day I cannot tell, whether I went a Foot or in a Coach my Head was in such a Confusion."

Young Ramkins confesses his feelings to the Spanish lady, and in his courtship is under a (pp. 73-4) "constant Charge of Presents, Treats, and now and then a Serenade according to the Spanish Customs." During one of these serenades, jealousy and suspicion first assail him (p. 74): ". . . drawing up my Musick under the Lady's Window, besides her Face, which was at the Casement wide open, I saw the Reflexion of a Periwig move toward the Corner of the Window." And later, in the chocolate house, he sees a snuff-box which he had given the Spanish damsel manipulated by a gentleman, he believes, in the same periwig (pp. 75-7):

". . . vid. a flat Top, neither rais'd nor parted in the Middle, which spoke it to be a Piece of English Furniture. The Sight of the Snuff-box drew all my Blood into my Heart, and left my pale Cheeks to account for the Consternation, wherefore not able to contain my self had I kept my Ground, I flung out of the Chocholate House, not unobserv'd by the Company to be in some Disorder; but when they look'd out of the Window and saw me stand gazing in the middle of the Street, (for my Motion thither was purely Animal, having no thought whither I was going) it encreas'd their Surprise. However, at three Steps I was got again into the Chocolate House, and with a galliard Air, addressing my self to the Gentleman with the Snuff box, Sir, said I, I confirm the Gift, and may all sniffling Fools that are in Love be serv'd like me. I allow'd no Time for a Reply, but bolting again into the Street, it came into my Head that perhaps two Snuff-boxes might be so much alike, as not to observe the difference without confronting 'em. This Thought gave me a Curiosity to step into a Toyshop, where I desired to have a Sight of the newest fashion'd Snuff-boxes, and when among others, I saw above half a Dozen exactly like that I had made the Lady a Present of, a Secret Confusion spread it self over my Soul to have given way to such Suspicions."

Hereupon, Ramkins tries to throw off both love and jealousy, luckily favored in his attempt by the lady's setting off for Spain (pp. 77-8), "so that I had in Election either to throw up all my Expectations in France, and follow her, or Moralize a Week or two upon the Disappointment, and so recover my self again to my Senses, which I quickly did by spending my Time in a Treatise of Algebra and Fortifications." The affair concludes with his sense of mortification that "what I had made a Study and Business of, was only her Diversion and Amusement."

As a result of such discipline, Major Ramkins is a seasoned veteran by the time of the courtship that leads to his marriage and ruin (pp. 160-3):

"There liv'd in Paris a Collonels Widow, neither very young, nor very handsome. . . . The Method I took with her, was quite different to what I observ'd in pursuing my Spanish Mistress. There was no Balls, Treats, nor Serenading, we both knew the World too well, either She to expect, or I to offer her such Entertainments. In a Word, our whole Discourse when I visited ran upon Oeconomy and Morals. . . .

"In conclusion, I put on the Trummels, and never question'd but I had made the most prudential Choice that any Person could do; but there is something in Woman-kind which can never be found out by Study or Reflection. 'Tis only Experience that can

School a Husband, and can give him a true Idea of that mysterious Creature; for in less than Twelve Months my Thousand Pounds which I had so carefully kept unbroke at Amsterdam was all dispos'd of, my Soldiers Pay being my only Subsistance for my self and Family, my Wife reserving her own Income for Pinmony; my Credit very low, my Days very irksome upon many accounts, and I who had hitherto appear'd with Assurance in Company, because of my Money-merit, was now Neglected; for every Tradesman began to smell out my Poverty. I am of Opinion it would do Posterity no kindness, if I shou'd discover how I came to be ruin'd by a Prudent Wife, for no Body wou'd Credit me."

He therefore solaces himself with political observations at the end, developing his position as a Roman Catholic submissive to George I.

Major Ramkins has not only sarcastic humor and an objectivity rare among autobiographers; he has an even rarer power of construction. His incidents are presented, as the selections from his wooing of the Spanish lady may have shown, with full detail, but they are selected with artistic economy and they invariably build up the picture of Ramkins in his dual rôle of philosophical soldier and philosophical lover. A single passage will suffice to show how he can collect the themes and incidents he has narrated, in a paragraph of retrospect, a *tour de force* similar to the justly famous close of Lytton Strachey's *Queen Victoria*. Wounded in Flanders, Ramkins drinks too much Lorraine beer (pp. 119-20):

"I was delirious above three Days, which though it was but a melancholly Sight in it self, yet I behav'd my self so various in my rumbling Discourse, that it occasion'd no small Diversion to such as were present, and had no immediate concern in my Welfare. I besieg'd Towns, rally'd scatter'd Forces, accepted Challenges, wandred over the Alpes, and pass'd over several Seas without Ships; I was in the Orchard at the Boyne, under the Walls of London Derry, and diverted with the fine Rode to Lions, and what I thought I should never have in my Head again, some amorous Ideas, though very faint ones, discover'd themselves, and I was heard to talk of Snuff-Boxes, Periwigs, and Spanish Ladies."

When to truth, autobiography can learn to add such art, few forms of literature can afford equal pleasure.

Major Ramkins, according to the *Dictionary of National Biography,* may have died in jail at Avignon. If he did, poetic justice was asleep; his spirit was so independent and outspoken, his hatred of Bourbon politics so intense, and his study of womankind so assiduous that it seems unfair for him to have ended his career alone, without a penny and without an audience, among the foreign rats of a French prison.

Almost as much as military careers, religious convictions could bring adventures in their train: witness the narratives of the persecuted Quakers and the Wesleyan evangelists. In the two cases of Colonel James Gardiner[32] and John Newton, however, sudden religious conversions, instead of initiating careers of rude action and danger, marked their ends.

The co-author, with William Cowper, of the Olney Hymns, who ended his evangelical life as the rector of Saint Mary Woolnoth's, is hardly recognizable as the writer of *An authentic narrative of some remarkable and interesting particulars in the life of xxxxx* (1764). The first of the fourteen letters in which it is written does, to be sure, declare that Newton's purpose is to show how Christ, "our adorable Redeemer," has plucked such sinners as Saul, the late Colonel Gardiner, and the writer as brands from the burning. But the letters that follow, written in a sturdy, simple prose adventitiously reminiscent of Daniel Defoe, and not over-puritanical in thought or phrasing, reveal a normal, active, bold young man, strong in mind and body. The son of a pious dissenting mother and a father who commanded a vessel in the Mediterranean trade, John Newton takes after both parents: before he is sixteen, he has made several sea-voyages and has also repented of his sins and reformed several times, usually after some sobering accident. But when he is pressed for his Majesty's Navy, deserts at Plymouth, is captured, stripped, whipped, and sent on a five-year voyage to the East Indies, his life becomes more abandoned. At Madeira he is transferred to a ship bound for Sierra Leone. He is made lieutenant of a slave-trader; and the persecutions of a black mistress who appropriates him alternate incongruously with his mastering the first six books

---

[32] Discussed in Chap. V.

of Euclid under great difficulties. Deliverance, storm, England, hardship, repentance, a new voyage to Africa in the slave trade, South Carolina, England again, marriage. At last an apoplectic fit causes him to give up slaving, and he is left, in his last letter, studying for a life in God's work. Thirty years later John Newton wrote a pamphlet against the slave trade; but this early account seems singularly free from scruples as to its moral status. The letters are held together by Newton's belief that God watches over him and saves him from many deaths; they are also unified by his steadfast love for the fourteen-year-old girl he had met so long ago in Kent—a love which remained in his memory through all peril, a "dark fire" (p. 21). The character portrayal by direct means is weak; the story lacks the final drive of Bunyan; and yet in some fashion, the adventures, the communing with God in the open air and hot sun of the tropics, the single devotion to a far-off girl, are so well told as to bring up the illusion of Newton himself on the deck of his slave-ship.

A Scot who, like Ramkins and so many of his countrymen, led the career of professional soldier is Peter Henry Bruce. Bruce's memoirs[33] are almost too good to be true. One anecdote follows another, and the characters range from Indian chiefs to the Czar, from nomadic Tartars to thirty giant grenadiers hand-picked for the King of Prussia. Bruce, who treated the world as a plaything "for to admire and for to see," tells his story in such admirable fashion that it is difficult to credit his prefatory apology (pp. 1-2): "The following journal was originally written in the German, my native language; but as I have lately enjoyed the leisure of a country retirement, I have, in this year 1755, translated it into English (to me a foreign tongue), for the entertainment of my friends, and the information of my family." This Scotsman, who had been born at Detring-Castle in Westphalia, died in 1757 at the age of sixty-five, leaving his gracefully written memoirs to be published for the benefit of his widow.

---

[33] *Memoirs of Peter Henry Bruce, Esq. a military officer, in the services of Prussia, Russia, and Great Britain. Containing an account of his travels in Germany, Russia, Tartary, Turkey, the West Indies, &c. as also several very interesting private anecdotes of the Czar, Peter I. of Russia*, 1782.

In this group of reckless gallants belong the American Mark Moore, the Scot John Macdonald, and the Austrian Baron Trenck, all of whom have been discussed elsewhere. An Irishman, it would seem, might naturally be found in such company, and the most likely candidate is Theobald Wolfe Tone, the patriot who was captured by the English on his third expedition to free Ireland and who died by his own hand in a dungeon, in 1798, while soldiers erected a gallows for him before his windows. His memoirs,[34] dated from Paris, August 7, 1796, "may amuse my boys, for whom I write them, in case they should hereafter fall into their hands" (Vol. I, p. 11). The autobiography and the diary which follows it are written with the impulsive gaiety of youth and the Irish. Tone comes from a reckless family; the three brothers and one sister whom he sketches have all "a wild spirit of adventure" (Vol. I, p. 16), a liking for travel and fights. "So," he later writes of one of them (Vol. II, p. 340), "there is one more of our family dispersed. I am sure if there were five quarters of the globe, there would be one of us perched on the fifth."

His own character shows a warmth of spirit and lightness of heart. He is lazy, brilliant, courageous. He elopes with a sixteen-year-old girl whom, later in his career as patriot, he almost deserts. He attends Trinity College in Dublin desultorily, and drifts to London, where, after two years in the Middle Temple, he writes (Vol. I, p. 28): "As to law, I knew exactly as much about it as I did of necromancy." He has a resilient style and spirit (Vol. I, p. 26):

"At length, after I had been at the Temple something better than a year, my brother William, who was returned a few months before from his first expedition to St. Helena [where he was in the garrison for six years], joined me, and we lived together in the greatest amity and affection for about nine months, being the remainder of my stay in London. At this distance of time, now eight years, I feel my heart swell at the recollection of the happy hours we spent together. We were often without a

[34] *Life of Theobald Wolfe Tone . . . written by himself and continued by his son; with his political writings, and fragments of his diary,* Washington, 1826, 2 vols. Also ed. by R. B. O'Brien, 1912.

guinea, but that never affected our spirits for a moment, and if ever I felt myself oppressed by some untoward circumstance, I had a never-failing resource and consolation in his friendship, his courage, and the invincible gaiety of his disposition, which nothing could ruffle."

After supporting himself by writing reviews for the magazines, Tone becomes increasingly involved in Irish affairs, journeys to America, and at last arrives in France, where he spends much of what is left of his short life in plotting the freedom of Ireland. He was ideally gifted to see France in the stirring years from 1796 to 1798. Youthful, a friend of freedom, sentimental, humorous, alert, he presents the revolutionary beehive with all its vitality and movement. The emotions and convictions of the new France are before our eyes in the heart-stirring scenes which he witnesses, the massed enthusiasm for liberty in a French theater (Vol. II, pp. 9-11) or the interview he secures with Napoleon. Against this background Tone carries on his political writings and helps organize French expeditions to aid the Irish. He even spares the time for a brief reunion in Holland with his wife and children. At the end, his son, who showed he inherited his father's spirit by serving in Napoleon's armies until 1815, takes up Wolfe Tone's story and describes his capture, his trial, and his gallant and terrible death in prison. Yet in spite of this finale, perhaps because of it, the memoirs as a whole comprise the most exciting of diaries, written by an impulsive boy. The entries are long for each day, with interjaculated endearments of his friend Thomas Russell, his wife, and his children, and many apposite and racy quotations from Shakespeare and other poets. Tone's life had possessed significance and fire. He himself considered it as "adventures." It was lived not only with courage, but with frankness, grace, and joy, so that the reader feels that a close friend was lost in the diarist who can dash off the entry (Vol. II, p. 221):

"A furious penury of beds. Privat and I, to show a good example, lay rough on a mattress on the floor. Lay awake half the night, laughing and making execrable puns. We were not much crowded, there being only nine of us in one small room. I like this life of all things. There is a gaiety, and a carelessness about military men, which interests me infinitely."

Soldiers, sailors, travellers, rich men, poor men—the voracious reader was eager to learn what happened to them all. And if a man lived who was unique, absolutely without parallel, he stood a good chance of rising phoenix-like from his own ashes, in memoirs which carefully emphasized his peculiarities. This cult of individuality, which may be identified in some particulars with romanticism, was sedulously nursed by certain biographers—by Charlotte Charke, for instance, or George Alexander Stevens, or Amory, or Topham in his *Life of Elwes*. Relish for fantastic variants from the careers of ordinary mortals produced such biographical grotesques as the various lives of Duncan Campbell, of Fighting Fitzgerald, Old Patch the forger, the spendthrift Earl of Barrymore and the skinflint John Elwes, William Fuller the impostor and the gallivanting oculist the Chevalier Taylor, the racing Count O'Kelly and Bampfylde-Moore Carew, King of the Beggars. And since some of these gentlemen discovered new possibilities in living, and all of them offer thoroughly satisfying material for entertainment, they must be accorded their niche in this study of the infinite ways of passing a life which Englishmen managed to fall into during the eighteenth century.

At the end of his autobiography William Fuller records with some disgust that his uncle had "cut me off with Mourning and a Shilling." Yet after surveying Fuller's own apology and the various lives written about him,[35] the careful reader will conclude that the uncle's bequest was twelvepence too large. The spotlight of history shone most glaringly upon William Fuller when he gave anti-Jacobite testimony in 1690-1691 at the instigation of such prompters at Titus Oates. He was largely instrumental in spreading the story of the changeling Prince of Wales. He admits brazenly that (1703 ed., p. 132) ". . . as to what I writ and published concerning the pretended Prince of Wales, and of one Mrs. Mary Grey [who he swore was the baby's mother], I must own, That all my Assertions did not amount to any Proof of the Matter." Yet his only excuse for his many perjuries and far-reaching inventions is (p. 131): "I was not then above twenty

---

[35] *The life of William Fuller, Gent. . . . Written by his own hand,* 1701; *The life of Wm. Fuller . . . an Impostor,* 1701; *The whole life of Mr. William Fuller,* 1703; life of Fuller by Abel Roper, 1692; two anonymous lives in 1700 and 1701

Years of Age, so that the thoughts of Greatness, and such Prompters . . . were sufficient to set and spur me on."

A moralist would find abundant material in the career of William Fuller to show how duplicity rots away all pretense to character, until in reading his confessions, one gains a glimpse into the consciousness of a white worm. Stubborn upon the stand, he publishes his memoirs not from any genuine repentance but from mixed motives of braggart pride in his own cunning and of resentment against his former fellows.

"I assure you," he writes in his preface dated August 2, 1703, "That my Ends in writing this present Narrative, are plainly and impartially to tell the World, how I came to endeavour to impose on both Houses of Parliament, how it was that I deceived the World; all which, neither Parliaments, nor any other Power, could extort from 'me, until now that I plainly see my own Folly, the Villany of those that impos'd upon me, and artfully led me into the Snare; so that I must justifie those who Censur'd me, and say, my Punishment was due for my Stupidity."

He seems at ease only in acts of stealth or deceit. He takes pleasure in hanging curtains in front of the windows before he lights candles and turns to his Roman Catholic devotions. And he enjoys the hidden life of the hunted (1701 ed., p. 11):

". . . at that time came out several Warrants against us both, so that we durst not stir out of our Chamber for many Days; only the Night we us'd to crawl like Cats over the adjacent Houses, and meet behind a handsom Stack of Chimneys to consert measures in order to our getting abroad."

This skulking on the housetops was necessary because Fuller, who began life as a page attached to the court of James II, served as a messenger and spy after the flight of the King. He is apprehended in England on one of his missions from France, and describes graphically his progress to prison (1703 ed., pp. 22-3):

". . . being observed by some busie Fellows, the Ship was stopt, and all the Passengers brought back, and landed at St. Catherine's, under a Guard, to be by them conveyed to the Tower; and the hellish Mob of the Place being in an uproar, cried-out, *Jesuits, Papists, Devils, Blood-suckers, Murderers,* and what not; and so pelted us with Dirt, Turnip-tops, and all manner of Filth that lay in the way, that before we came to the Tower, both Men and Women were in such a Pickle, that we could hardly be known or seen what we were made of, only as we had Life, we might otherwise be taken for a dumb St. Taffy, on the first Day of March."

It is at this point that under pressure from Archbishop Tillotson, and in a dramatic interview with William of Orange, he doubles his duplicity, gives his enemies the fifty letters which they had been unable to find and which were sewed up inside the buttons of his clothes, and while still acting ostensibly as a servant of the Stuarts, actually becomes the instrument for William and Mary. Conscience flickers only feebly in his breast, but cowardice can cause him to repent his treachery in scenes which he describes vividly. On his return to France (pp. 41-2), "The Queen commanded me to go to Monsieur Lovoy, as heretofore, and I thought with my self, if he knew but on what account I came, I suppose I might go to the Rack, or be broke on the Wheel, instead of kissing the King's Hands. In plain, I was forced to make my self half drunk, whenever I appeared about Business."

Unconscious of the full extent of his self-revelation, Fuller unfolds the grim story of a base action and its consequences. He even condemns to death his friend Crone by becoming an informer. His double-dealing, apparent on every page, is not his only fault. Extravagance and love of ease lead him to throw his sister downstairs because she will not support him, or to become affianced to a young lady worth twenty thousand pounds (p. 72): "but unfortunately she fell sick of the Small Pox and died, and I was a faithful Mourner a long time for her; for if I knew my own Heart, I valued her Person more than her Fortune, but both together was too great a Blessing for me." And finally, because of his slanderous and filthy publications, he is to stand three times in the pillory, to receive thirty-nine lashes at Bridewell, to serve a sentence at hard labor, and to pay a thousand mark fine. The biography concludes with Fuller again in jail, making abject apologies to all and sending through the prison bars his best wishes to the Queen. He is willing to swear anything, to admit anything, that will secure his freedom. He prefers, however, to be banished to one of her Majesty's plantations, for he is afraid of Jacobite poisoners and assassins (1703 ed., p. 110):

"I . . . am now a Prisoner in the common side of the Queen's Bench; lodg'd under Ground in close nauseous holes, such as a Gentleman would hardly put a Dog into that he loved; we have no Air, nor is there any thing but Misery to be seen: I have been also kept in Irons, tho' only a Prisoner for Debt, and all my usage, in the Execution of my Sentence, has been barbarous beyond comparison, which makes me, with holy Job, cry out, Pity me! pity me! O ye my Friends; for the hand of the Lord is upon me."

Fuller's autobiographies are notable for more reasons than this inadvertent revelation as to how low a human being may sink. His very defects—his drunkenness and gluttony and passion for high living—contribute to the vividness of his biography. He has a knack for describing low life in London and abroad (1703 ed., p. 35): ". . . but just as the Fowls were taken from the Spit, I by chance, stood in a Passage looking into the Kitchen, where I saw the Woman cram her Mouth full of Salt and Water, which she gargled up and down her Throat and Mouth for a while, then squirted the same through the Body of the Fowl, and this she put into the Dish for Sauce, and my Stomach was satisfied before I sate down." Few writings can equal Fuller's confessions in presenting a convincing picture of crowded London, its prisons and public-houses, the Ax-Yard, the One Tun Tavern in the Strand and the Three Tun Tavern, the Punchhouse in the Blackfriars and the Haunch of Venison in the Palace-yard, the Young-man's Coffee house at Charing Cross, the Lodging at Mr. Leopars, and a Coffin Shop, at the corner of Fleet-lane in the Old-Bailey, from which William Fuller looked out on the honest citizens whose actions and motives he could never thoroughly understand.

Just as a small group of hostile tracts clustered around the figure of Fuller the impostor, or another group of merry, magical, and bawdy anecdotes grew up around the person of the notorious Duncan Campbell, the deaf-and-dumb gentleman, who was gifted with the powers of second sight and of commercializing his visions, so the Chevalier John Taylor becomes the subject of no small group of life-histories.[36] Like Fuller and Duncan Campbell, John Taylor turns autobiographer in self-defense; the accounts of his life that are abroad annoy the Chevalier.

The fulsomeness and flamboyance we find in his autobiography might be guessed from the style of a later admirer,[37] who dedicates his work—at the close of the volume—"To the Prime Genius Of this Age, Professor of the Art of Teaching the Passions, and unparallelled Adventurer." The dedication ends in such horseplay as this:

"Therefore, to the Importance of your Mightiness, Prostrate at the Threshold of your Munificence, Do I Asiatically bow my Head; Hallelujahing your Honour, and Honours; And may your scientific Brow, Nod Benignly, On the Insignificancy Of your most humble, And most submissive Servant, and Slave, The Author."

Taylor's notoriety grew very largely out of the overwhelming oratory in which he proclaimed his knowledge of the diseases of the eye; one of the lives of Taylor[38] caricatured his "true Ciceronian" by reproducing a mountebank's harangue and his "Oration at Oxford" on the eye. Not only in his speech, but in his life and his writings, Taylor was lavish. He is an Elizabethan born too late, overflowing with energy and self-confidence. He dedicates his memoirs not only to his son but to David Garrick and the Merchants of London, and follows the dedication with an address to his readers, and high-flown panegyrics saluting the Pope and "ye Imperial—Oh! ye Royal—Oh! ye great masters of empire."[39] There had been an eclipse of the sun at Taylor's birth at Norwich,[40] "A city memorable for many great events in our

[36] *The English impostor detected*, Dublin, 1732; *A faithful and full account of the surprising life and adventures of the celebrated Doctor Sartorius Sinegradibus*, Edinburgh, n.d. but possibly *ca.* 1744-1746; *The life and extraordinary history of the Chevalier John Taylor*, Dublin, 1761, 2 vols.; *The history of the travels and adventures of the Chevalier John Taylor, ophthalmiater . . . written by himself*, 1761, 3 vols.

[37] George Alexander Stevens, *The dramatic history of Master Edward*, 1785, pp. 183-6.

[38] *The life and extraordinary history*, Dublin, 1761, Vol. I, pp. 32-42, and Vol. II, pp. 108-20.

[39] *The history of the travels and adventures*, 1761-1762 [Pref., p. vii], Vol. I.

[40] Vol. I, p. [1], "Address to my Readers," 1761-1762 ed.

English annals; and it is possible, that its having been the place of my birth, may not one day be judged unworthy the notice of posterity." .

His youthful years he passes over as too trivial to record, for he wishes to haste into the midst of things and tell of his interviews with the Pope and the honors paid him by foreign courts. A more conceited coxcomb can hardly be imagined. The Chevalier Taylor makes Boswell an amateur at pursuing and capturing famous lions. Taylor has visited *all* the towns of *all* the European countries (Vol. I, p. 6): "I have been also known personally to every man of distinguished character now living, or has lived in all Europe, in the present age, in every science, and in every part of useful knowledge." *Quid plura?* A dozen pages are devoted to the chronological listing of his travels between 1727 and 1760. Twenty more are necessary for him to catalogue by countries the great personages he has known. Interminable notes bulwark his boasts or give in full translation proclamations of approval from European princes.[41]

Yet since conceit is not an unfortunate quality in an autobiographer, the reader progresses with amusement through the Chevalier Taylor's verbal fireworks; for beneath all this ebullience, these journeyings from Persia to Sweden, these opinions on the peace of mind which superstition confers, on tyranny and duelling, dancing and jealousy, Platonic love and inoculation, on beauty, dress, tenderness, suicide, and the force of prejudice, the Chevalier is found to be a cosmopolitan physician of advanced and sophisticated opinions.

An equally original figure is Bampfylde-Moore Carew, who, the son of a clergyman, gives up his schooling and his distinguished family connections to become the King of the Beggars. Carew was induced to impart his memoirs, the preface states,[42] by his vanity and his hope of profit; the accounts that follow seem to have been taken down by an amanuensis literally as they fell

[41] Vol. I, pp. 77 to 135 carry a single running "footnote"; Vol. II, pp. 1-86 another.

[42] *The King of the Beggars,* Oxford, 1931, ed. by C. H. Wilkinson, reprints *The life and adventures of Bampfylde-Moore Carew,* Exeter, 1745, and *An apology for the life of Bampfylde-Moore Carew,* n.d. but *ca.* 1749.

from his lips. The short, repetitious anecdotes do not build up
to any climactic effects, nor are they told with marked skill, in
spite of the author's consciousness of the eighteenth century novel.
Yet the social background and the descriptions of England and
America cannot fail to be of interest; and occasionally Carew's
cool roguery and vagabondage kindle even his uninspired an-
nalist. The following is one of the racier of its picaresque anecdotes:[43]

"There was at this Time a very hot Press in Bristol, wherein
they not only impressed Seamen, but all able-bodied Landmen
that they could any where meet with, which made one fly one
Way and another another, putting the City into a great Rout and
Consternation; and Bampfylde, among the Rest, knowing himself to have a Body of a dangerous Bigness, was willing to secure
himself as effectually as he possibly could, greatly preferring his
own Ease and Pleasure to the Interest and Honour of his King;
he therefore sets his Wife and Landlady to Work, who with
all Speed and Cleanliness made a great Number of small Mutton
Pies, Plumb-Puddings, Cheese-Cakes and Custards, which
Bampfylde, in an ordinary Female Habit, hawks about the City,
making *Plumb-Pudding, Plumb-Pudding, Plumb-Pudding, hot
Plumb-Pudding, piping-hot, smoaking-hot, hot Plumb-Pudding,
Plumb-Pudding, Plumb-Pudding,* eccho in every Street and Corner, even in the Midst of the eager Press-Gang, some of whom
spent their Penny with this masculine Pye-Woman, and seldom
failed to serenade her with many a complimental Title of Bitch
and Whore."

By the end of the century the devices for writing a life in a
series of entertaining anecdotes had become common property.[44]
The genuine memoirs of Dennis O'Kelly (1788) competently
narrates his backstairs rise from sedan chairboy to gigolo, gamester, and officer in the militia during the War with the Colonies,
up to the time of his death, a rich man in Piccadilly, married to
a noted prostitute and owner of an even more noted race-horse.
Or *The life and political opinions of the late Mr Samuel House*
(*ca.* 1785) tells the breezy history of a precursor of the Populists, a

[43] Wilkinson, pp. 46-7.
[44] Besides those mentioned here, see Moore, Trenck, Price, Elwes.

rough, bold, blasphemous tavern-keeper who jumped off Westminster Bridge on a bet, married a bibulous barmaid, and swore
by Wilkes, Fox, and LIBERTY.

One of the best of the memoirs of eccentrics is *The life of
George Robert Fitzgerald* (1786), which tells in a series of anecdotes the story of a bravo—almost a murderer by profession—
from his schooldays to his execution for a cold-blooded killing.
His desire to amuse leads the author to give up the orderly
arrangement of the usual biography (p. 186): "All chronological
order and distinction have been sacrificed for the purpose of
variety and contrast." Yet the diverse anecdotes are grouped
tellingly around Fighting Fitzgerald seen as a duellist and as a
gamester. Even the customary *motif* of gallantry is subordinated
to this double picture of a hot-tempered killer and a reckless
player for high stakes. Two anecdotes illustrate in such striking
fashion the fever for gambling in the eighteenth century that
they deserve to be better known (pp. 118-21):

"Accordingly [in order that a certain nobleman might pay
Fitzgerald a gaming debt], next day, about noon, the noble
Lord called upon Mr. Fitzgerald at his lodgings, in a hackney
coach, and having taken him in it, proceeded down the Strand
in their way into the city; but being prevented going through
Temple Bar, on account of a stoppage occasioned by a number
of carriages promiscuously meeting together, just at the same
moment of time, Mr. Fitzgerald, whose invention was ever on
the rack, proposed to pull the longest hair out of the seat of the
coach for a hundred. The noble Lord agreed, and won upon
the first pull. The bet was laid a second time, and afterwards
repeated so often, and so successfully in favor of his Lordship,
as to win back every farthing of the money he had lost to Mr.
Fitzgerald; upon which he put his head out of the coach, and
told the coachman to turn round, and drive home again.

"The other bet, pronounced to have been of so whimsical a
nature, and which terminated more fortunately for Mr. Fitzgerald, was produced in the following manner. A great deal of
play had been at Brooks's, and Mr. Fitzgerald and the late Lord
L———n, after it was over, found they had been very successful.
They could, each of them, count their winnings, which they

laid before them on the table, at little less than eight thousand pounds. 'Here goes, (cried Mr. Fitzgerald) odd, or even, for the whole sum,' and laid hold, at the same time, of a bowl in which a bishop had been just made. In short, he proposed, that he would throw the bowl, with its contents, against the wall, and upon picking up the pieces and telling them, his Lordship should have odd, or even, whichever he pleased for the whole money. 'Done (cried Lord L———n) I'll have even.' Mr. Fitzgerald immediately cried, 'here goes then!' and instantly flung the bowl with all his force against the wall. Upon the pieces being counted by a couple of tellers appointed for that especial purpose, they were declared to be odd, and Mr. Fitzgerald swept away the whole of the money."

The anonymous author holds his anecdotes together by considering the riddle of existence (pp. [3]-4):

"In the vast fund of speculation to be met with in the chain of human events, nothing seems more adapted to give employment to a contemplative mind, than that we should so frequently find instances of individuals, as eminently formed by nature, as they are completely blessed by fortune, to enjoy every happiness of life, passing through it branded with every mark of obloquy and contempt: or, at length, cut off from society by a shameful and ignominious death."

Characteristically, at the hour set for his execution, Fitzgerald jumps so recklessly off the scaffold that the rope breaks, and, as if he had at last learned the virtue of patience, he prays for an hour before making his second exit from the world.

This survey of the unusual lives of unusual individuals could not end more fittingly than with Anthony Pasquin's *Life of the late Earl of Barrymore. Including a history of the Wargrave Theatricals, and original anecdotes of eminent persons* (1793). Its hero, who died at the age of twenty-four, is notable because of his genius for squandering money. Pasquin compares him to Rochester and the Duke of Wharton, but in his spending three hundred thousand pounds in five years he may be entitled to a pedestal of his own. With Pasquin playing a somewhat priggish rôle as monitor and friend in the front of the picture, Barrymore is shown as "a janglere and a goliardeys," associating with the

Prince of Wales and Mrs. Fitzherbert, roistering at the Claret
Club and the Jockey Club, buying a filly from Colonel O'Kelly
at the Newmarket Races, erecting a gigantic private theater in
the country, hunting, drinking, soldiering, playing at cards, making love, patronizing "the bruisers of the day," and promoting
the novel game of cricket.

Pasquin shows ingenious refinement when, after narrating a
vulgar story about the Lord Chief Baron and Lord Thurlow
(pp. 71-2), he says that he did not laugh himself because "coarse
language and coarse manners never failed to disgust me." And
like so many of the biographers of eccentrics, Pasquin seems
moved to write largely out of a sense of wonder at the incongruous amalgams that may constitute a human being. The familiar paradox of vice and virtue coexistent in one man he repeats
(p. 50):

"It was a celebrated axiom with an antient prince, that we have
two souls, one leading us to vice, and the other to purity. . . .
Lord Barrymore has frequently exhibited all the imbecilities of
youth in the morning, and all the goodness of a reflecting sage in
the evening."

This section may close with Pasquin's speculation on the enigmas of life and death (p. 8):

"Like some beneficial preparation in chymistry, half finished,
what he was to have been, in the conclusion, was not universally
understood—his passions had been thrown too hastily into the
resolving crucible of action, when the fire was too intense and
too consuming."

Sheer inquisitiveness about the present may easily turn into
sheer inquisitiveness about the past, so that William Tytler
neatly sums up the eighteenth century in one aspect when he
describes it as "this age of curiosity, when whatever seems to
throw light upon the history, literature, or manners of our
country in ancient times, is anxiously sought after."[45]

The two seemingly disparate halves of this chapter are held together by the belief that the journalistic biographer and the
antiquary are brothers under the skin. Neither seriously attempts

---

[45] *Poetical remains of James the First, King of Scotland,* 1783, p. 1.

to interpret life; the presentation of action is enough. For both of them the truth lies in the unadorned fact; the more numerous the facts, the greater the truth. Yet if moral values are to be disregarded, the difference between the Thirty Years War and the nine-days-wonder is only quantitative. Antiquarian knowledge is of no more demonstrable value than complete familiarity with the latest criminal prosecution. The lives of today's adventurers and criminals and eccentrics, as tomorrows flow over them, become the bright threads and gay colors in the pattern of the past.

Whatever may be said theoretically for the consanguinity of the journalist and the scholar, pragmatically their paths frequently crossed in the eighteenth century. The scholarly passion for exact detail, indexing, and methodical presentation in the development of the *Newgate Calendars* and the *Tyburn Chronicles* might support a monograph. If the 1705 and the 1726 collections of *The lives of the highwaymen* are contemptible, Alexander Smith in his 1719 volume has given them order, uniformity, and narrative coherence; and in 1734 Charles Johnson, in *A general history of the lives and adventures of the most famous highwaymen,* a fine folio volume of 484 double-column pages with distinguished copperplates, has really elevated his material until it constitutes a *Biographia Britannica* for all rogues from the days of Falstaff.

Before the close of the century, the lives of highwaymen, robbers, and pirates had been gathered with assiduity and edited with considerable scholarship. Nor are the highwaymen unique. The uninspired historian W. H. Dilworth gratifies the popular desire for bloodshed with his biographical collection, *The royal assassins* (1759). Sensationalism and research are combined in the collection called *The history of female favourites* (1772). And most striking of all, to commemorate the thirtieth day of January, anniversary of the beheading of Charles I, an enterprising publisher issued *The history of king-killers . . . containing the lives of thirty one fanatick saints, famous for treason, rebellion, &c. being one for every day in the month* (1719). Evidently this terrifying collection was successful, for it resulted in *The fanatick martyrology containing the lives of three hundred sixty five hellish saints of that crew* (1720), a work arranged like a saint's calendar and showing, in its way, the same sort of industry and scrutiny of the past for relevant material which may be found in the genuine hagiographical volumes of Moreri or the Bollandists.

Sheer curiosity is systematically exploited in *Memoirs for the curious,* a periodical which in its first numbers (1701) contains such choice accounts as that of a Dutch child with Hebrew and Latin characters around the pupils of its eyes, or of a serpent found in the left ventricle of a man's heart. But in the rat's nest of information contained in its volumes for 1707 and 1708 it includes "the Lives of the most Eminent Men Deceased within that Time." This wedding of curiosity and methodical antiquarianism is balanced at the other end of the century in such works as *Eccentric biography; or, sketches of remarkable characters, ancient and modern. . . . The whole alphabetically arranged; and forming a pleasing delineation of the singularity, whim, folly, caprice, &c. &c. of the human mind* (1800), or James Caulfield's *Portraits, memoirs, and characters of remarkable persons* (1794-1795). In three volumes Caulfield gives portraits and life-histories of astonishing freaks—Turkish rope-dancers, "posture-men" or contortionists, Mother Damnable, Popish plotters, Merry Andrews, dwarfs, and bearded ladies. In his Advertisement, he says of a predecessor's collection: "Of the twelve different classes of Engraved Portraits arranged by the late ingenious Mr. Granger; there is not one so difficult to perfect, with original prints, as that which relates to persons of the lowest description." And in the three volumes that follow, the penny-dreadful popular pamphlets of the earlier centuries are dignified by the interest of the systematic collector and antiquary.

The inquiring mind, then,

> "Still climbing after knowledge infinite
> And always moving as the restless spheres,"

does not pause to differentiate between scandal and scholarship. In what category, for instance, should William Rufus Chetwood be placed? He wrote novels and travelogues which he passed off as genuine; he collected and republished old plays during the same decade as Robert Dodsley; he gathered industriously many ephemeral bits about the British theater and the lives of actors. Yet in his effort to catch the popular eye, he concocts undoubtedly the best *non sequitur* among the titles of collected biography: *Memoirs of the life and writings of Ben. Jonson, Esq; Poet Laureat to King James the First, and King Charles the First. With an abstract of the lives of their favourites, Somerset and Buckingham* (1756). Even this, slipshod as it is, contains interesting scraps about Jonson—"contributions to knowledge." The antiquary Anthony Wood owes much to the gossip John Aubrey. Is Boswell himself actuated by the spirit of scholarship, or by the spirit of inquisitiveness, or by both?

The publisher Edmund Curll may be taken as a final illustration. Ever since the time of Pope he has been considered as the vilest of commercial publishers, lining his pockets by pandering to popular taste with lies and libels. No man can be so bad as Curll is painted. A defense of this publisher, who seems ubiquitous in the first third of the century, would take disproportionate space. But, in regard to the theme of the close relationship between antiquarian zeal and pure vulgar curiosity, a few points may be brought forward. First, Richard Rawlinson, Oxford recluse, and as quintessential an antiquary as may be conceived, knew Curll, wrote for him or supplied him with information, and even took a chorographical trip with him, inspired by their joint interest in possible county histories. Second, some of Curll's lieutenants are more than negligible scribblers: Le Neve, Des Maizeaux, and particularly his foreign correspondent Le Clerc, have respectable claims as antiquaries or historians. Third, even granted that many of his productions are worthless, that some of them may be feigned, that all of them are formless, and that they were issued solely to make a profit, nevertheless the fact remains that considerable biographical material would have been lost if it had not been for Curll's mania for publishing. No one has ever established a case that Curll did not print all the authentic biographical material he could lay his hands on. The publication of last wills and testaments, for example (since they were almost immediately available), may show his respect for authentic documents combined with his cunning appeal to the public through topical biographical titles. The publishers John Nichols and

Richard Phillips at the end of the century rendered definite and acknowledged service by their antiquarian interests; yet their predilections and even their methods were largely anticipated by Edmund Curll. These remarks on the antiquarian merits of the most lurid and sensational of publishers may close with a note by an eighteenth century editor of one of the men whose character Curll is supposed to have blackened:[46]

"The memory of Edmund Curll has been transmitted to posterity with an obloquy he ill deserved. Whatever were his demerits, they were amply atoned for by his indefatigable industry in preserving our national remains. Nor did he publish a single volume, but what, amidst a profusion of baser metal, contained some precious ore, some valuable reliques, which future collectors could no where else have found."

The same restless eagerness to know about other men which produced the lives of criminals, travellers, adventurers and eccentrics inspired the diligent searchings of the antiquaries. If for the eighteenth century the proper study of mankind was man, that study could be conducted in various ways: strange and novel types of human existence could be explored, or the recognized types could be collected, grouped, and catalogued, or the lives of single great individuals in the past could be rewritten and reinterpreted with the help of new data or a less distorted perspective. As a general rule, the antiquaries were not so much pioneers, experimenters, and artists in life-writing as they were consolidators, traditionalists, and scientists.

Francis Bacon, who at the beginning of the seventeenth century, had lamented the paucity of English biography and definitely indicated its relationships and its future, might have been almost satisfied at the progress made in the eighteenth century in systematizing and organizing biography, in increasing the numbers of subjects treated as well as the types of lives and the manner of presentation, and in making biography more accessible to the common reader.

All classes of people received the dignity of biographical record; none were too exalted or too lowly. If the lives of thieves

[46] John Nichols, in his Advertisement, before the 4-vol. ed. of Francis Atterbury's *Letters*, 1783.

and pirates were collected, so were the lives of lord chancellors and admirals.[47] The principles on which such groupings were made are often novel: there exist collected lives of botanists, of ancient philosophers and of those who died in the year 1711, of professors at Gresham College; royal and noble authors, English regicides, and learned women; of Roman empresses and pious foreigners; of Etonians and converted American Indians; of Parliamentary leaders, of London aldermen, and of those individuals whose portraits happened to hang in Knole House; there are collections of women because they are women and of Scotsmen because they are Scotsmen.[48]

Though some of these subjects may seem of limited scope and special interest, quarto-size or two-volume works were frequently published to cover adequately particular fields. "What a figure must science make," Joseph Priestley exclaims,[49] "advancing as it

[47] *The lives of all the Lords Chancellors, Lords Keepers, and Lords Commissioners, of the Great Seal of England*, 1708, 2 vols.; John Campbell's *Lives of the British Admirals*, 1742-1744, 4 vols., frequently reissued, revised, pirated, and condensed.

[48] To obviate clumsy footnotes in the rest of this chapter, notes are not given for many statements in the text where verification and illustration are immediately available in the Bibliography. For respective illustrations of the various classes mentioned in the last sentence of the text, see, e.g.:

Pulteney's *Historical and biographical sketches of the progress of botany*, 1790, 2 vols.;

The lives of the ancient philosophers, 1702;

John Le Neve's *Memoirs . . . of the most illustrious persons who dy'd in the year 1711*, 1712;

John Ward's *Lives of the professors of Gresham College*, 1740;

Horace Walpole's *Catalogue of the royal and noble authors of England*, 1758, 2 vols.;

Mark Noble's *Lives of the English regicides*, 1798, 2 vols.;

George Ballard's *Memoirs of several ladies of Great Britain*, 1752;

George James's *Lives and amours of the empresses*, 1723;

Select lives of foreigners, eminent in piety, 1796;

Thomas Harwood's *Alumni Etonenses*, 1797;

Experience Mayhew's *Indian converts*, 1727;

George Chalmers's *Parliamentary portraits*, 1795;

City biography, 1800;

H. N. Williams's *Biographical sketches*, 1795;

Biographium Faemineum. The female worthies, 1776, 2 vols. [See also Anne Thicknesse, Thomas Gibbons, and Mary Hays.]

For Scottish collected biography, see Pinkerton, Crawfurd, Mackenzie, Dalrymple, Howie.

[49] *A description of a chart of biography*, 1777, 3d ed., p. 24.

now does, at the end of as many centuries as have elapsed since the Augustan age!" Such enthusiasm bore fruit in biography. Just as the medieval hagiographers honored a monastery or a see by publishing the lives of its abbots or bishops, so scientific amateurs paid tribute to the leaders in their field of study. Thus Richard Pulteney issues in two volumes *Historical and biographical sketches of the progress of botany in England* (1790) with a preface which declares (p. x):

"In tracing the progress of human knowledge through its several gradations of improvement, it is scarcely possible for an inquisitive and liberal mind, of congenial taste, not to feel an ardent wish of information relating to those persons by whom such improvements have severally been given: and hence arises that interesting sympathy which almost inseparably connects biography with the history of each respective branch of knowledge."[50]

Ecclesiastical lives were not neglected by the compilers: witness the Anglican collections of John Walker and John Le Neve, the Nonconformist and dissenting volumes of Edward Calamy and Daniel Neal, the lives of the Scottish reformers by Robert Wodrow, the Methodist collections inspired by the Wesleys. Antiquarian diligence took various directions; it extended itself in vast county histories, with biographical materials imbedded in them, such as the *Danmonii orientales illustres: or the worthies of Devon* (1701) by John Prince, whose delightfully mellow, discursive spirit makes the pioneer among county historians seem also the last of that learned company that numbered Burton, Browne, and Fuller. Or it produced the *Royal genealogies . . . from Adam to these times* (1736) by James Anderson, and the various many-volumed editions of the *English Baronage* and the *Peerage of England* by Arthur Collins, as well as his documented memorials of such families as the Sidneys and the Cecils. Collins was not alone in his peering into peerages. The great families of the Cavendishes and the Boyles, the royal houses of Brunswick,

---

[50] In this one field of botany, for instance, see also G. C. Gorham's *Memoirs of John Martyn, F.R.S. and of Thomas Martyn. . . . Professors of Botany in the University of Cambridge*, 1830, which reprints Thomas Martyn's 1770 life of his father; the memoirs of Thomas Pennant, discussed earlier in Chapter III; *Memorials of John Ray* by William Derham, 1760; Duncan's *John Hope*, 1789; and Mason's *Thomas Gray*, 1775.

Windsor, Orange, and the Stuarts—all have their memorialists. Lesser families also had their monuments, as in *Parentalia,* a volume of memoirs of the family of the Wrens (1750); it is compiled by Sir Christopher Wren's son, published by his grandson, and prepared for the press by a "Fellow of the Royal Society and Secretary to the Society of Antiquaries." Such monuments to family pride and antiquarian diligence are common. Their value as literature, except for *The Lives of the Norths,* is negligible.

Moreover, many public-spirited gentlemen with a flair for history and a position of their own, realizing that past eras are very largely reconstructed from individual journals and annals and diaries, consciously recorded the history of their own times. Their view is most clearly stated by Dr. Matthew Maty in his essay before Lord Chesterfield's works (1777), entitled *Memoirs of his life, tending to illustrate the civil, literary, and political history of his time.*

"It is from the number and variety of private memoirs," Maty writes, "and the collision of opposite testimonies, that the judicious reader is enabled to strike out light, and find his way through that darkness and confusion, in which he is at first involved."

Maty regrets that the world lacks a *Cato* and an *Anti-Cato,* that Caesar's *Commentaries* are incomplete, that Pompey's sons did not write memoirs for their father or Cicero for himself. In preferring contemporary biographical records to second-hand compilations, he commends the *Agricola,* and says that (pp. 2-3):

"Cornelius Nepos, Suetonius, and Plutarch, convey more exact representations of persons and facts, than compilers, or writers of abridgments, such as Paterculus, Florus, and Justin; and to come nearer to our times, the Comines, Sullys, Clarendons, and Ludlows, will continue to survive the Daniels, D'Orleans, Oldmixons, and Guthries.

"But besides this general utility, which public history derives from private authorities, other advantages, perhaps no less important, may be obtained from them. It is from observing different individuals, that we may be enabled to draw the outlines of that extraordinary complicated being, man. The characteristics of any country or age must be deduced from the separate characters of persons, who however distinguishable in many respects, still preserve a family likeness. From the life of almost any one individual, but chiefly from the lives of such eminent men as seemed destined to enlighten or to adorn society, instructions may be drawn, suitable to every capacity, rank, age, or station." Maty's practice justifies this perspicuous statement of his theory. The reader gains not only a picture of Chesterfield made convincing by anecdotes selected to display his courtesy, wit, or tact, but also a background of the politics and personalities of the times. Illustrative notes, original letters, characters of Addison, Vanbrugh, Garth, Arbuthnot, Gay, and Pope, of George I, Queen Caroline, Pulteney, Hardwicke, Pitt, and—brilliantly done—of Robert Walpole, give the "life and times" amplitude.

To theories or predilections similar to Maty's respect for contemporary memoirs, the world owes such diverse productions as Boyer's annals of the reign of Anne, issued yearly for over a decade; the memoirs of Ulick de Burgh, Marquis of Clanricarde, published in 1722; the translated "history of his own time" by Bishop Parker, published in 1727; George Bubb Dodington's astonishing Pepysian diary (1749-1761, published in 1784) of a time-serving politician, vain and greedy; Matthew Prior's *History of his own time* (1740); and John Nichols's voluminous and super-annotated biographical and literary anecdotes of William Bowyer, printer (1782), which is only the first volume of an inexhaustible collection of literary trivia that appeared from time to time for well over half a century. But the focus in all these productions is so diffuse as to leave the resultant minutely recorded and scattered facts scant claim to consideration either as stories of lives or as works of art.

There are two exceptions: Hervey and Walpole. Lord Hervey's *Memoirs of the reign of George the Second from his accession to the death of Queen Caroline*[51] presents a secret history of motives and hidden causes as seen from his vantage point at the ear of Eve. Yet the personality of the writer is hardly that of Pope's "familiar toad, half froth, half venom." It more closely squares with Hervey's own estimate of his son as "invaluable,

[51] They cover the period 1727-1737, with later supplements. Wr. before 1743; ed. by John Wilson Croker, 1848, 2 vols. Again in 3 vols., 1884; 3 vols., 1931.

constant, and dutiful."[52] Hervey's editor speaks of him as "the Boswell of George II. and Queen Caroline—but Boswell without his good-nature."[53] Hervey is sharp and witty on the inevitable partiality of all memoirs and on the unimportance of his own place in the sun. "I leave," he writes at the start, "those ecclesiastical heroes of their own romances—De Retz and Burnet—to aim at that useless imaginary glory of being thought to influence every considerable event they relate." Photographic impartiality may result when a writer holds such disillusioned theories as this:[54]

"Let Machiavels give rules for the conduct of princes, and let Tacituses refine upon them . . . let those pretend to account for accidental steps by premeditated policy, whilst I content myself with only relating facts just as I see them, without pretending to impute the effects of chance to design, or to account for the great actions of great people always by great causes; since the highest rank of people have as many and the same passions as the lowest; and since the lowest have five senses, and none of the highest that I know of have six. I look upon the world, and every incident in it, to be produced as much from the same manner of thinking, as I do the operations of kitchen-jacks and the finest repeating watches from the same laws of motion and the same rules of mechanism: the only difference is a little coarser or finer wheels."

If Hervey's judgments are uncharitable and his philosophy pessimistic, the fault frequently seems to lie at another's door, as when the King says (Vol. III, p. 162): "Chesterfield is a little tea-table scoundrel, that tells little womanish lies to make quarrels in families"; or when Queen Caroline, now a grandmother, rushing to St. James on the birth of Prince Frederick's daughter (Vol. III, p. 171), "kissed the child, and said, 'Le bon Dieu vous bénisse, pauvre petite créature! vous voilà arrivée dans un désagréable monde.'" These intimate revelations of royalty may be unethical; they are certainly good reading. In such an atmosphere, Hervey's own delicate, polished, and merciless analyses are not out of place (Vol. II, p. 91): "The Princess Emily wished Lady

---

[52] *The diary of John Hervey . . . 1688 to 1742*, Wells, 1794, p. 85.
[53] Croker, 1884 ed., p. lvii.   [54] Croker ed., Vol. II, p. 376.

Suffolk's disgrace because she wished misfortune to most people."
Moreover, if he makes Princess Emily hateful, he is capable of
portraying a likeable Princess Caroline; if his portrait of Bolingbroke is damning, then the balancing study of Walpole by this
master of "vile antithesis" is sympathetic. Hervey is aware that
Bolingbroke, Chesterfield, and Carteret are also writing memoirs;
and, as if in conscious competition with such noble lords, he produces his own amusing work of art. His royal portraits are more
in the spirit of Goya than of Van Dyck; the boorish and ob-
streperous Prince of Wales and the fine full-length of Queen
Caroline with her surface flippancy, her perpetual stream of
"My God's," her chatter that shifts between French and English,
are portraits of living people. And in one corner of this large
Court-painting, among its many petty, feminine, irritable, sophisticated figures, stands the *Hic pinxit* of Lord Hervey himself,
faintly smiling, a subtle and disenchanted courtier.

Close agreement exists between Hervey's annals and Walpole's
Reminiscences, as well as his *Memoires of the last ten years of the
reign of George the Second.*[55] Writing for the amusement of
Miss Mary and Miss Agnes Berry, the aging dilettante spreads
out a vast collection of amusing historical anecdotes. He fills
whole museum shelves with sharply modelled figurines of Swift,
Chesterfield, and Robert Walpole, of the Duchess of Marlborough
and Mrs. Howard. His royal portraits, like Thackeray's four
Georges, are witty and cutting sketches. Like Hervey, Walpole
does not exaggerate his own importance. He finishes a neat
appraisal of himself by suggesting his own "worthlessness,"
adding: *J'aye dict le mot, pour ne frustrer la posterité.* And no
less skilfully, Walpole plays his own variations on Hervey's theme
of the littleness of life. "Here," he writes,[56] "are no assassins, no
poisons, no Neros, Borgias, Catilines, Richards of York! Here
are the foibles of an age, no very bad one; treacherous ministers,
mock patriots, complaisant parliaments, fallible princes. So far
from being desirous of writing up to the severe dignity of Roman
historians, I am glad I have an opportunity of saying no worse—
yet if I had, I should have used it."

[55] Wr. in 1788, pub. 1805; *Memoires,* 1822, 2 vols.
[56] *Memoires,* Vol. I, Postscript, pp. xxxix-xl.

The example most famous in its day of "the severe dignity of Roman historians" was Dr. Conyers Middleton's *History of the life of Marcus Tullius Cicero* (1741). The young Samuel Johnson was one of the subscribers to the original two-volume edition; Fielding in *Joseph Andrews* takes exception to its preface, its translations, and its dedication to Lord Hervey; Lord Lyttelton is inspired by it to write a philosophical and political psychograph on Cicero;[57] Cibber does the same; and the biographers of the period continually refer to it as a landmark. Middleton's *Cicero* had also a certain adventitious importance; its position in the history of biography is analogous to Addison's *Cato* in the drama, for the career of the Roman orator afforded opportunities for stormy Whig and Tory arguments as to what constitutes patriotism, freedom, and just government. Yet Middleton's life deserves praise, absolutely considered, as a model for stately history; it strives for impartiality, and is conscientious in its dates, notes, indexes, and use of source-material. Middleton even italicizes all passages directly translated from his sources, and includes the Latin originals at the foot of the page. He makes extended use of Cicero's letters; the death scene is a model of biographical narration; and the whole forms a dignified and beautiful formal history in which antiquarian diligence makes the figure of Cicero seem actual.

In contrast with Middleton, the other attempts to reconstruct antique glory—Smith's *Scipio Africanus* (1713), Leland's *Philip of Macedon* (1758), Schomberg's *Maecenas* (1748) and his *Pindar and Horace* (1769), Blackwell's easily flowing *Court of Augustus* (1764, 3d ed.), Clayton's rendering of St. Croix's *Alexander the Great* (1793), or the numerous lives and criticisms of Homer— though they are generally painstaking, seem rather heavy and pedantic. Middleton's closest rival as historian and stylist is David Mallet, whose perspicuous *Life of Francis Bacon* appeared in 1740. Writing with Tacitus as a model, Mallet broadly handles the historical background and the court intrigues, and presents a searching analysis of the humiliations into which ambition leads.

[57] *Observations on the life of Cicero*, 1774 ed. of his *Works*, pp. 1-28. Earlier eds., 1731, 1741.

The prose is impressive; and Fielding is well justified in speaking of Mallet's careful judgment and his "nervous, manly style."[58]

Regarding this work, that eager *précieuse,* the Countess of Hertford, wrote to her friend, the Countess of Pomfret:[59] "Mr Mallet has published a life of my lord chancellor Bacon: which is not ill-written, though with an apparent design to make the reign of queen Elizabeth appear a contrast to the present; and, by every invidious method, endeavouring to represent that of James the First as its parallel." Such use of antiquarian methods for current controversial purposes was frequently practised during the eighteenth century, and even more frequently suspected. Thomas Phillips's extensive and painstaking *History of the life of Reginald Pole*[60] seems to the modern reader to be a conscientious, luminous, and impartial portrayal of a great and firm soul; yet an eighteenth century critic refers to its author as "an English Papist, writing with a view to excite in us a favourable opinion of himself and his party."[61] And the same critic (who may himself be prejudiced) speaks of Fiddes's extensive *Life of Wolsey* (1724) as being written by "a Protestant-Papist . . . to prepare us for Popery and the Pretender."[62]

Yet the biographers' avowals of detachment are, of course, insistent; and outside the realm of ecclesiastical history, success in achieving impartiality is not infrequent. In the tempestuous times of Queen Anne, the self-assurance of an ecclesiastical dignitary is needed to bring out the three folio volumes that comprise *A complete history of England: with the lives of all the kings and queens thereof* (1706). Even here, White Kennet tries to insure himself against the charge of passion by reprinting in his first volumes earlier authorities such as Milton, Daniel, More, Buck, Camden, Bacon, and Clarendon. The documentation is full, and the controversial material for more recent years, the reader is assured, is "new Writ by a Learned and Impartial Hand." Yet Bishop Ken-

---

[58] *Joseph Andrews,* Book III, Chap. VI.
[59] *Correspondence,* 1805, 3 vols.; Vol. II, p. 21.
[60] 1767 ed., 2 vols. 1st ed., 1764, Oxford.
[61] Jortin, *Tracts,* 1790, Vol. II, p. 43.
[62] *ibid.,* p. 38. cf. also Bibliography under R. Pole.

net's bias, so carefully concealed, provoked a storm of pamphlets from even more biased opponents.

Historians, however, continued to strive for impartiality. William Wynne's *Life of Sir Leoline Jenkins* (1724), secretary of state under Charles II, is a conscientious record in two ponderous volumes; Isaac Kimber's frequently reprinted life of Cromwell[63] makes a fairly successful attempt to be dispassionate, and draws on many sources; Coxe's admirable life of Robert Walpole (1798) is far enough removed from its subject to present a comprehensive view; William Harris's moralizing lives of Cromwell, James I, Charles I, and Charles II (1753-1765) are heavily documented after the manner of Bayle, and their industry is guided by a burning sense of justice and an intense sensitivity on questions of national honor; and Lyttelton's elegantly phrased *Henry II* (1767) is written deliberately to establish royal biography as a more respectable branch of literature. Many of these historians—Gilpin, John Lewis, Mallet, Middleton, Lyttelton, Bolingbroke—rendered a service to biography by showing that a career, even in its trivial and anecdotal aspects, might be narrated seriously in elevated prose.

In writing the lives of men long dead, style is often the only contribution a biographer may make. Gibbon abandoned his project to rewrite the life of Raleigh because he realized that all he could add was the dubious merit of style. And John Urry, scholar and editor rather than amateur in *belles lettres,* has the clarity of vision to see that a life of Chaucer cannot be written. He reproduces the few documents and facts that are extant (1721), much as an archaeologist might gather together the broken columns and shards found on an ancient site; but he refuses to hide his ignorance under speculation, irrelevancies, and fine writing. He sacrifices readability to truth. To the perfect antiquary, the fact in itself suffices. Samuel Pegge, a prebendary in Lincoln Cathedral, even dedicates himself with joy to the ascetic search for truth.

"Those that read merely for Amusement and Diversion," he writes in his *Memoirs of the life of Roger de Weseham* (1761),

[63] 1724; 5th ed., 1743.

"must certainly be disappointed in turning into these Memoirs, which, as they concern a Prelate of a studious Temper, and but little engaged in public Business, can afford no Entertainment to such as are Hunters after Pleasure, and want only to kill Time.

"Embellishment is a Thing they are in their Nature incapable of; but still there is an Accuracy and Precision in these Matters, that are pleasing to many, and which by some are thought to have their Use; and this is what hath been chiefly aimed at in making the following Collection of Facts, and throwing them into a regular Series of Time."

The life from which this is quoted is no more than a trial balloon of sixty painstaking quarto pages. Thirty-two years later, exemplifying some of the whole-souled devotion to *minutiae* of Browning's Grammarian, Pegge published his life's work: *The life of Robert Grosseteste* (1793).

The most solid and imposing of these antiquarian histories of Englishmen is Thomas Carte's *History of the life of James Duke of Ormonde . . . wherein is contained an account of the most remarkable affairs of his time, and particularly of Ireland, under his government* (1736). Although it extends to two huge folio volumes with a third volume of letters, Carte never allows himself to be buried under his materials. The preface shows that the work had been digested from an enormous mass of documents—"153 bundles" supplied by Ormonde's grandson the Earl of Arran, "fourteen wicker bins" of papers from the castle of Kilkenny, seven thousand folio pages in Latin written by an Irish priest, besides innumerable other manuscript fragments. Carte is so painstaking in his search for truth that he must have worked under pressure to complete his task in six years. The Irish question is handled on a vast scale; it has some of the sweep and breadth of Clarendon, plus the stiffer style of Sprat or Fell; and Carte is undoubtedly indebted to the great seventeenth century historians for the scope and manner of his work, and possibly for some of his material. Some of his character sketches are very fine, though they seem buried in such a long work. And Carte has the good sense to include telling details in portraying his hero (Vol. II, p. 551 and p. 554):

"His dress was plain, but very elegant and neat: no body wore his cloaths better, but he still suited them to the weather. For this end, in our uncertain clime, he had ten different sorts of waistcoats and drawers, sattin, silk, plain and quilted, cloth, &c. His first question in the morning was, which way the wind sat; and he called for his waistcoat and drawers accordingly."

"He used frequently to hunt, but used it as a diversion, and for the sake of exercise; so that he always returned home to dinner, and the hounds knew it so well, that when upon hearing the dinner-bell ring at the castle of Kilkenny, the Duke hath turned his horse homewards, the dogs all followed him, and quitted the hare, though in view. . . ."

"Once in a quarter of a year, he used to have the Marquis of Hallifax, the Earls of Mulgrave, Dorset and Danby, Mr. Dryden, and others of that set of men at supper, and then they were merry and drank hard. . . . Whenever he had drank hard, he never went to bed, but wrapped himself up warm, sat all night in an easy chair, and after a nap, got on horseback, rode for three or four hours, and then came home fresh and fell to business."

In spite of the admiration which Carte felt for his noble subject and which his diligence as biographer shows, the life of Ormonde is not written by a sycophant or panegyrist. The complex relationships between Ormonde, his mistress Lady Isabella Rich, and her friend Elizabeth Preston (who, the ward to Lady Isabella's father, is also Ormonde's cousin and his wife) are handled delicately but frankly by Carte. One of the most unusual scenes in eighteenth century biography occurs when letters written by the Duke to these two women unfortunately are mixed in the post. Lady Isabella immediately visits the Duchess of Ormonde, and though the Duchess now knows that Lady Isabella has a promising son by Ormonde, nevertheless (Vol. II, pp. 555-6) "The Duchess desired of her old friend that this mistake might not occasion any breach between them; nor indeed did it."

The whole work is an admirable and stately history in which Ormonde shines a gigantic, magnanimous courtier in a world bigger than our own. One can understand the enthusiasm of Mrs.

Delany when she writes:[64] "I am quite charmed with the Duke of Ormonde, his is the *completest* character of a truly great man I ever read!"

The dignified historians of great Englishmen were rivalled by the English biographers of Continental heroes. Among their most noteworthy productions should be mentioned: Farneworth's *Pope Sixtus V* (1754), an anecdotal account of a Machiavelli in the Vatican, who found Rome pagan marble and left it Christian; Harte's polished and weighty military life of Gustavus Adolphus (1759), Samuel Johnson's brilliantly stylized sketch of Charles Frederick of Prussia, published with a continuation in 1786; Joseph Towers's *Frederick the Great* (1788) and Tooke's *Catharine II* (1797); Susanna Dobson's *Petrarch* (1775) and William Roscoe's *Lorenzo the Magnificent* (1795).[65] The numerous lives of Frederick the Great, for instance, run the gamut from scandalous or anecdotal compilations gathered around a figure of current interest, to sincere attempts at history; and it would be difficult to determine whether the lives of Eastern monarchs published at this time were issued because of genuine historical interest or because of curiosity and delight in the new, the exotic, and the strange.[66]

Christian tradition also became a legitimate field for antiquarian excavations.[67] The skeptical scholarship of the great encyclopedist Bayle, the "higher criticism" of eighteenth century Deists and free-thinkers, and the answering justifications by Christian

[64] *Autobiography and correspondence,* 1861 ed., Vol. III, p. 8. Wr. Jan. 19, 1751.

[65] As good a combination of history with biography as the century produced was written in France and translated in five volumes in 1726. It is Madame de Motteville's *Memoirs for the history of Anne of Austria.*

[66] As examples of earlier Eastern rulers, cf. in the bibliography Genghiz Khan and Tamerlane or Timur-Bec. For eighteenth century monarchs, see the conqueror of Persia and India, Nadir Shah or Kouli Khan, and the great opponent of England in India, Hyder Ally. Nadir Shah, at any rate, had two distinguished biographers in William Jones and James Fraser.

[67] See the lives of the Fathers popularized by Richard Allen in *Biographia Ecclesiastica,* 1704, 2 vols.; Fleetwood's lurid and discursive *Life of Christ, with the lives of his holy evangelists, apostles, and disciples,* 1792, 2 vols.; and particularly Alban Butler's scholarly *Lives of the fathers, martyrs, and other principal saints,* 1756-1759, 4 vols.; 2d ed., 12 vols., 1779-1780.

ministers, produced biographical studies of Scriptural characters in which every shred of evidence was carefully considered.[68]

Truth lies neither in malicious blackening of character nor in pious whitewashing. The important point here is that both attitudes, and all the prejudiced gradations separating the two, stimulated the study of antiquity. And out of the fierce wars between antiquaries—witness the battle of the books over the Epistles of Phalaris—truth may finally emerge, and may emerge even more sharply and immediately than if there were no rancor and no provocative retorts. The bibliography of this book, for such figures as Cicero, or Cromwell, Reginald Pole, Richard III, or David, sufficiently shows how controversy may promote the cause of truth, somewhat in the manner which Milton outlines so ingeniously in the *Areopagitica*.

The antiquaries, with laudable *esprit de corps,* recorded the lives of their fellows, so that a new class of subjects may be observed in such biographies as that of Bayle (1708), Ashmole (1717 and 1774), Hearne (1736), the Elstobs (1784), Dugdale (1793), and Ruddiman (1794). Antiquaries are even grouped, as in William Huddesford's two-volume *Lives of Leland, Hearne, and Wood* (1792). As the anonymous writer of an undated life of Anthony Wood points out, among all classes of men the immortalizing biographer most justly deserves immortality for himself. This argument is less charitably paraphrased from Pope beneath an engraving in Curll's memorials of Thomas Hearne:[69]

> "Hernius behold! in Closet close y-pent,
> Of sober Face, with learned Dust besprent;
> To future Ages will his Dulness last,
> Who hath preserv'd the Dulness of the past."

Dull or brilliant, the antiquarian labor is without end. Not only individual lives grow longer and longer, with footnotes even upon footnotes,[70] but also learned collections of all sorts appear,

---

[68] cf., e.g., the lives of David considered in Chap. V.

[69] Vol. III of *Mr. Pope's literary correspondence,* 1735.

[70] The ultimate in footnotes, reminiscent of Swift's fleas with other fleas to bite 'em, is to be found in William Harris's lives of the Stuarts, which consist principally of footnotes. Footnotes on footnotes are regular occurrences with him,

carefully authenticated, with all their sources placed clearly at the disposal of the public.[71] *Biographia* became a familiar word on title-pages. During the century there appeared not only the *Biographia Britannica,* but the *Biographia Classica, Dramatica, Evangelica, Ecclesiastica, Gallica, Literaria, Medica, Nautica and Navalis, Philosophica, Scotica and Scoticana.* And for their limitless patience in collecting and publishing biographical material and encyclopedias, such writers as John Aikin, Alban Butler, Richard Challoner, John Nichols, Joseph Towers, Erasmus Middleton, Thomas Flloyd, Stephen Jones, and Jeremy Belknap deserve at least the tribute of a roll call to their memories.

The outstanding work, the collection of collections, is the *Biographia Britannica.* For almost half a century (1747-1795), in successive volumes and editions, with such editors, contributors, and assistants as William Oldys, Andrew Kippis, Joseph Towers, Dr. Campbell, and Dr. Johnson, this noble experiment in systematizing English biography continued. Yet under the editor of the second edition, Dr. Kippis, the scheme becomes too ambitious for completion, and when after fifteen years the fifth and final volume of this edition is issued,[72] the alphabetical progression has gone no further than the letter *F.* In seeking to make the *Biographia Britannica* exhaustive, the editors made it exhausting. It becomes a magpie's nest, in which every new attractive thing is brought in, as, for instance, the leisurely letters about Vesuvius that are included in the account of the philosophy of Bishop Berkeley, or the endless journey through a coal-mine and the dissertation on canals introduced under the name of James Brindley, or the final article on John Fastolff containing a long discussion of Shakespeare. To cover the lives of Beaumont and Fletcher, two lines at the top of each folio page usually suffice for the text,

and if the type had permitted him (as in his *Life of James I,* 1753, repr. 1814 ed., Vol. I, pp. 283-4), he would have had a footnote on a footnote on a footnote.

[71] As illustrations, cf. Cibber's, Johnson's, and Anderson's lives of poets; Cumberland, Graham, Strutt, Beckford, Matthew Pilkington, Barry, Vertue, Buckeridge, and Walpole for lives of painters and engravers; Rivers, Marshall, and Rider for living authors; John Campbell, Kent, and Charnock, for the admirals; the various histories and biographical dictionaries of the stage by Theophilus Cibber, "Betterton," Baker, Davies, Chetwood, and anonymous authors.

[72] 1778-1793. Part of a sixth volume appeared in 1795.

while the rest of the page is occupied by double-columned notes quoting verbatim and at too great length from Jacob, Langbaine, Rymer, Dryden, the *General Dictionary,* and the dramatists' own works.

Kippis tries to justify his fatal passion for byways and side-tracks by appealing to "the example of such Biographers as a Tacitus and a Plutarch, a Bayle and a Johnson."[73] The preface to the second volume of the second edition of the *Biographia Britannica* shows Lilliputians struggling with a gigantic task. They apologize for not having got through the letter *B,* but point out that "*B* is a letter which furnishes a larger number of names, and those too of importance, than several other letters will do united." They hope to complete their undertaking in nine volumes, provided busybodies keep their suggestions for additional lives to themselves, and also provided too many great men do not die in the interim. Almost with a note of despair the editor observes (p. vii): "The mortality of human life is continually adding to our task."

Even in this great work, the harassed editor forgets at intervals scholarly methods:[74]

"With respect to the Life of Cruden it must be mentioned, that having happened to put it into a wrong drawer, it slipped my memory when it should have been introduced in p. 544. I have, therefore, annexed it to Chatterton, in the Appendix to Letter C."

And in his chatty, discursive opinions about eighteenth century civilization presented under the guise of biography, Dr. Kippis is not unlike his friend Boswell.

Yet the first editor, William Oldys, had nobly announced a program which might be considered as expressing the purpose and method of all true British antiquaries:[75]

"The *Biographia Britannica* was undertaken . . . in order to collect into one Body, without any restriction of time or place, profession or condition, the memoirs of such of our countrymen as have been eminent, and by their performances of any kind deserve to be remembered . . . a British Temple of Honour, sacred to the piety, learning, valour, publick-spirit, loyalty, and

---

[73] Pref., p. ix, Vol. II, 1780.   [74] Pref., p. viii, Vol. IV, 1789.
[75] Pref. to 1st ed., 1747, Vol. I, p. viii.

every other glorious virtue of our ancestors, and ready also for the reception of the Worthies of our own time, and the Heroes of Posterity. . . .

"We saw that multitudes of Lives were already written, in different manners and from different motives, which varied widely as to almost all the facts that are common to them, and which would not admit of any reconciliation. We saw that general characters, high-flown panegyricks, or outrageous satires, had very frequently appeared under the appelation of Lives, without any regular series of facts, with little or no respect to dates, and digested rather according to the whim and fancy of the writer, than in obedience to the laws which reason, and the practice of the best authors have established, in reference to this kind of writing. We saw that most general Collections were too short, and that many particular Lives were too prolix, that some were trifling, others tedious, and very many so carelessly and incorrectly written, as to be of very little, if of any, service, towards such a work as we proposed."

Of Oldys's first edition of the *Biographia Britannica,* the opinion expressed in the *Monthly Review*[76] on the appearance of the fourth volume may still be quoted as just:

"To rescue, therefore, the characters of the Great and Worthy, from misrepresentation; to place their actions in a proper point of light; to determine the share of merit or demerit due to each; appears to be one intention of this work:—a plan highly deserving the attention and encouragement of the public, and of the utmost importance to those who wish to be truly acquainted with the transactions of past ages; which can by no means be so well elucidated, as by the personal histories of the principal actors in those transactions."

The great biographical dictionary issued by the Frenchman Pierre Bayle at the end of the seventeenth century occasioned similar productions in England.[77] One of the principal of these

[76] Vol. 17 for 1757, p. 578.

[77] cf. *An historical and critical account of the life and writings of the evermemorable Mr. John Hales . . . being a specimen of an historical and critical English dictionary,* 1719, possibly by Des Maizeaux. The author hopes to surpass Bayle; but his ambition seems to have ended with this solitary sample. See also

is "A general dictionary, historical and critical: in which a new and accurate translation of that of the celebrated Mr. Bayle, with the corrections and observations printed in the late edition at Paris, is included; and interspersed with several thousand lives never before published . . . by the Reverend Mr. John Peter Bernard; the Reverend Mr. Thomas Birch; Mr. John Lockman; and other hands." This appeared in ten volumes between 1734 and 1741; its industry is only paralleled by its stupidity, lack of proportion, and absence of critical sense.

The skeptical and indefatigable Bayle, the enthusiastic, industrious, and methodical Oldys, the followers and imitators of both men, and the large number of collectors and amateurs who touched the skirts of biography,[78] rendered accessible vast quantities of biographical material and tended to establish, at least, the minimum standards for biography and to emphasize the virtue of dispassionate chronicling. As a last mark of erudition, in order to make their works permanently accessible in the great commonwealth of scholarship, all through the eighteenth century collections appeared written in Latin.[79]

For unwearied diligence and a certain success in resurrecting a figure from dusty records and a minimum of facts which must be extended with labor and interpreted with caution, particular notice should be given to William Stukeley's quaint but gallant attempt, which would have delighted and convinced Sir Thomas

Bibliography under Jeremy Taylor, Joseph Towers, John Nichols, Dalrymple, Belknap, Flloyd, Noorthouck, Stephen Jones, Aikin, Ladvocat, and the *New and general biographical dictionary*, 1761-1762 and subsequently.

[78] See, as instances in the Bibliography, Le Neve's inscriptions on monuments, his ecclesiastical calendar of names and dates, and his annual obituaries; Francis Peck's *Desiderata Curiosa*, 1779, 2 vols., which reprinted scarce biographical tracts; Winwood's *Memorials*, 1725; *Biographical collections*, 1766, 2 vols., reprinting nineteen seventeenth century lives; Edmund Lodge's *Illustrations of British history, biography, and manners*, 1791, 3 vols.; John Berkenhout's *Biographia literaria*, 1777; *The biographical and imperial magazine*, 1789; *The biographical magazine*, 1794; John Nichols's select collection of wills, 1780; and Phillips's *Necrology* for 1797-1798.

[79] See the eight *Vitae quorundam eruditissimorum et illustrium virorum . . . scriptore Thoma Smitho*, 1707; *Vitae antiquae sanctorum qui habitaverunt in . . . Scotia . . . quasdam edidit . . . Johannes Pinkerton*, 1789; *Bibliotheca Britannico-Hibernica: sive, de scriptoribus . . . commentarius: auctore . . . Thoma Tannero*, 1748.

Browne, to reconstruct the life of Carausius, Emperor in Britain, from Roman coins (1757, 1759); to Thomas Warton for his *Life of Sir Thomas Pope, founder of Trinity College Oxford* (1772); to Robert Lowth for his *William of Wykeham* (1759); to Malone for his amply and admirably documented life of Dryden (1800); to Edward Thompson for his *Andrew Marvell* (1776); to Samuel Knight for his impartial and integrated histories of John Colet and Erasmus (1724 and 1726); to Ralph Churton for his lives of the founders of Brasenose College (1800); and to Thomas Comber for his memoirs of the life of his great-great-grandfather Sir Christopher Wandesforde, a fine country gentleman under the Stuarts (1778).[80] Yet these partial successes after disproportionate years of labor only serve to emphasize Thomas Warton's remark in his *Life of Ralph Bathurst:*[81]

"It is difficult to collect the circumstances of a life which is not conspicuous in history. The researches of the biographer are necessarily multiplied, in proportion to the privacy of the character he describes. Facts and anecdotes relating to persons who have rendered their names illustrious in public and national stations, are commonly recorded at large in obvious books, and are easily reduced into a comprehensive detail. But the lives of scholars, and of those who have shone in the confined circle of unambitious, but not inglorious, leisure, retain but few memorials; and unless seasonably transmitted to posterity by the provident diligence of some cotemporary friend, soon become obscure and forgotten."

In view of their assiduity and the reputation of some of them in their own day, it seems almost unjust to dismiss with only a word and a fingerpost-suggestion that the list of their works be consulted in the Bibliography, such writers as John Lewis, whose lives of Wicliffe, Pecock, and Bishop Fisher lucidly develop the history of the English Reformation in a homely, vigorous style

[80] cf. also Burigny's *Grotius*, 1754, a translation of a very fine original, John Lewis's *Wyllyam Caxton*, 1737, written with the county patriotism of a Kentish dilettante; and Samuel Pegge's thorough *Robert Grosseteste*, 1793, mentioned earlier in this chapter.

[81] 1761, p. v. Bathurst lived 1620-1704.

that is almost Elizabethan in certain of its qualities; or Richard Fiddes, who strives for force and beauty of style in his folio life of Wolsey (1724); or William Gilpin in his lives of great church-men, and particularly in his readable psychological biography of Cranmer (1784); or William Oldys, whose masculine life of Sir Walter Raleigh (1736) set a new standard as the most thoroughly documented and careful piece of biographical research that had so far been achieved. Andrew Kippis, John Strype, and Thomas Birch, conscientious, official, self-appointed biographers, should be mentioned if for no other reason than to marvel that such great industry could exist side by side with such utter absence of art.

A less readable style could hardly be imagined than is to be found in the characteristic cluttered sentences that the Secretary of the Royal Society constructs. "Dr Tillotson," Birch writes as part of one sentence (1752, pp. 37-8), "was desir'd to preach the ser-mon on Sunday the 15th of November 1668, in the chapel in Ely house, at his consecration to the Bishopric of Chester, vacant by the death of Dr. George Hall, on the 23d of August preceding, of a wound received by a knife in his pocket, in a fall from the mount in his garden at the rectory house at Wigan." A lifetime does not seem long enough or unimportant enough to write down the inexhaustible pages that were published over the name of Dr. Thomas Birch; it is no wonder, therefore, that he had no moments to arrange and condense his materials or to set them forth in acceptable English.

Yet while we praise the industry of the antiquaries, and realize the solidity and dignity of their contributions to biography and the worth of occasional productions, we are reminded too often, in turning over their volumes, of Voltaire's pronouncement: *Il ne faut point d'esprit pour s'occuper des vieux événements.*

This chapter has surveyed many of the forms which biograph-ical curiosity assumed in the eighteenth century, varying from the vulgar interest which produced sensational tracts to the patriotic sense of duty which created the great encyclopedic collections.

Different in degree these impulses are, but who can say that the same ingrained inquisitiveness is not present in *The Ordinary of Newgate* and the *Biographia Britannica?* Gregarious and inquiring man instinctively desires to know anything and everything about his fellows and his ancestors. And in the excursions of human curiosity, who can draw the line between trivial gossip and significant history? Carried away by his enthusiasm, James Granger writes of his *Biographical History:*[82]

"I have, perhaps . . . extended the sphere of it too far: I began with monarchs and have ended with ballad-singers, chimney-sweepers, and beggars. But they that fill the highest and the lowest classes of human life, seem, in many respects, to be more nearly allied than even themselves imagine. A skilful anatomist would find little, or no difference, in dissecting the body of a king and that of the meanest of his subjects; and a judicious philosopher would discover a surprising conformity, in discussing the nature and qualities of their minds."

From some such conviction as Granger's, that all men are essentially one, spring many of the philosophical justifications of biography during the eighteenth century. "It is from observing different individuals," writes Matthew Maty in his life of Chesterfield (1777), "that we may be enabled to draw the outlines of the extraordinary complicated being, man." Biography, then, enables the amateur philosopher to generalize soundly from observed particulars. And many of the readers, as well as the writers, of biography felt that they were exercising, as Doctor Johnson exercised,

"The keen research, the exercise of mind,
And that best art, the art to know mankind."[83]

This was the reward of biography at its best. Even at its most trivial, the curiosity of the biographer, as John Prince smilingly informs his audience,[84] furnished "an innocent way of Raising

---

[82] 1769. Vol. IV, p. 567.

[83] From John Courtenay's *Poetical review of the literary and moral character of the late Samuel Johnson*, 1786.

[84] *The Worthies of Devon*, 1701, "Epistle to the Reader."

the Dead without going down to Endor, or applying your selves to Necromantick Spells." The Grub-street chronicler of whores and pirates, the country rector writing of Renaissance churchmen, and the don at Oxford recording the lives of medieval scholars may all alike have felt with Horace Walpole: "Books and past ages draw one into no scrapes, and perhaps it is better to know little of men until they are dead."

CHAPTER V

THE LIFE WITHIN

I. THE BIOGRAPHER AS PSYCHOLOGIST

"... and oh! that my Heart could be seen to all mankind!"
—WILLIAM FULLER.

ONE of the distinguishing characteristics of both biography and autobiography before 1700 is a tendency toward objectivity. A man's life was equal to the sum of his actions. Even the character of a great churchman or saint would be revealed through what he did: witness such works of biographical art as Adamnan's *Columba*, Bede's *Cuthbert*, or Walton's *Donne* or *Herbert*. The prevailing assumptions explain the rarity of biographies of literary figures and the conventional apologies, when such lives were written, for attempting to record careers in which few external happenings and no changes in Church or State could be appropriately noted.

The eighteenth century changed all that. Various literary forms —particularly the drama and the novel—familiarized Englishmen with the recording of mental states which had hitherto been disregarded, and gave them, as well, more varied modes of expression. This shift in emphasis to include the contemplative as well as the active life became more pronounced in the latter half of the century. A straw to show which way the wind blew may be seen in the difference between the policies of the first and second general editors of the *Biographia Britannica:* William Oldys consciously formulates his intention not to include too many literary figures; Andrew Kippis speaks almost with contempt of men of action and statecraft and assures the reader that the literary men will be amply and generously commemorated.

Interest in literary men and literary methods, then, is one great cause for the increase in subjective biography. Two further causes are the growth of autobiographies among various classes, and the increase in the biographies of Christian protestants.

Earlier than the English, the French had shown capacity for self-analysis in their memoirs, which were widely read in England in the eighteenth century, and most of which appeared without much delay in English translations. The letters of Madame de Sévigné, the essays of Montaigne, the autobiographical memoirs of the Duchess of Mazarin, Madame D'Aulnoy, the Sieur Pineau-Duclos, Cardinal de Retz, and Madame Roland, enabled the English better to realize and express delicate mental states. *The Memoirs of the Dutchess of Mazarin* (1713) afford the subtlest account of mental cruelty and incompatibility in print at that time in England; Madame D'Aulnoy shows great power to present her moods and dreams as a girl and as a young matron in a complicated aristocratic society; Duclos dispassionately observes his meanest and noblest thoughts in the light of his final philosophy. "The French," Horace Walpole muses,[1] "have the merit of anatomising the whole of human nature, while our hypocrisies mutilate the figure, and destroy all its truth."

If foreign subtleties advanced subjective biography, native innocence, though unaware, was at times equally helpful. Ingenuousness in an autobiographer frequently serves the same purpose as the most sophisticated self-knowledge, and, as in Cellini or Pepys or Bunyan, the autobiographer stands revealed in spite of himself. An eighteenth century critic summarizes this well when he says:[2] "The writers . . . very often, draw their own native characters without at all designing it."

Native and foreign, the increase in personal memoirs tended, by sheer weight of number, to influence the development of biography as a whole. In the Middle Ages, while biography predominated, autobiography tended to follow the objective methods of biography. With the increase of autobiography, however, the biographers more and more adopted the autobiographer's position and wrote as if they were inside their subject's mind and knew its workings. Biographers also came to realize that the inclusion of their hero's letters, diaries, journals, or meditations offered a legitimate means of presenting his life. The growing fashion for pub-

---

[1] *Walpoliana*, 2 vols. [1799], Vol. II, p. 63.
[2] Edmund Calamy's *Historical account of my own life* [1671-1731], 1829.

lishing collected correspondence, and the greater informality and intimacy of the letters themselves, were not without effect upon biography. Mason's *Life of Gray* and Boswell's *Life of Johnson* afford well known examples of the conscious utilization of letters and personal documents; but long before Mason and Boswell, a biographer was writing:[3] "With respect to the Interior of any Person, so as to come to the Knowledge of what Manner of Spirit he is of. . . . This may be best discern'd by his private and Familiar Letters." And later, Job Orton in his preface to the *Memoirs of the life, character and writings of the late reverend Philip Doddridge* (1766) announces that (p. vi):

"I have made such Extracts from his Diary and other Papers, written solely for his own Use, and his Letters to his intimate Friends in which he laid open his whole Heart, as I judged most proper to give my Readers a just Idea of his inward Sentiments, and the grand Motives, on which he acted thro' Life. . . . I am sensible, it hath been objected, that 'what was principally written for a Person's own Use, ought not to be made public.' "

But after all, Orton decides, what are David's Psalms and the writings of Marcus Aurelius but private meditations made public?

If, in the sphere of politics, the formation of the Anglican Church in the sixteenth century may be compared to the creation of an independent monarchy, and the Presbyterian dominance in the seventeenth century to the rise of an oligarchy or limited republic, then the revivalist movements of the eighteenth century resemble the growth of democracy. Obviously the Church had always emphasized the spiritual life; but with the rise of the dissenting sects, particularly of the Quakers and Wesleyans, the importance of individual experience was felt as it had never been felt before. Such a belief was of immense importance in the development of biography. With regard to the Quakers alone, a

---

[3] *Two select and exemplary lives* of Bernard Gilpin and John Rawlet, 1728, attributed to Dr. Thomas Bray. cf. also the life of John Abernethy prefixed to his *Sermons,* 1748, in which the anonymous author draws largely upon the six large quarto volumes of Abernethy's diary (p. xiv): "The discipline of the heart, is the great business which he appears in the whole of this diary to have pursued." cf. also Eadmer's *Anselm* and Adam of Eynsham's *Hugh of Lincoln* for twelfth and thirteenth century examples.

recent scholar writes:[4] "Before 1725 they had published over eighty religious confessions and journals, a number probably greater than all the non-Quaker autobiographies printed in England during the preceding 75 years." The author makes the further point that, whereas many other memoirs remained in manuscript, the Friends published their autobiographies; and she justly observes that: "In seven decades they succeeded in carrying the doctrine of the inner Light to the English-speaking world and beyond. . . .

"The Friends addressed their appeals to the 'inward' eye and gave expression to their inner states. Their habits of mind resulted in the elevation of intuitive and the subordination of reasoning powers. Nearly a fifth of the writers have left autobiographical accounts in which they have detailed their struggles in finding and in keeping the inner Light."

What the Quakers accomplished during the first half of the century, the Methodists carried on during the second half, largely through a single act of John Wesley. "Mr. Wesley," writes Thomas Jackson,[5] "requested many of the Itinerant Preachers who were employed under his sanction to give him in writing an account of their personal history, including a record of their conversion to God, of the circumstances under which they were led to minister the word of life, and of the principal events connected with their public labours. Several of these accounts he inserted in the early volumes of the 'Arminian Magazine'; where they have been greatly admired for their simplicity, and the edifying views which they present of personal religion."

The danger, of course, with the autobiographies of both Friends and Wesleyans was that in such enthusiastic corporate communion the writing of lives might be reduced to a formula, and the resultant products might turn out to be conventional exercises couched in a special jargon. Unfortunately, in most cases this was true. Professor Wright finds that the Friends made no great contribution to English literature because of their neglect of scholarship and their preoccupation with sectarian positions; in auto-

---

[4] Luella M. Wright, *The literary life of the early Friends 1650-1725*, 1932, pp. 110 and 237-8.
[5] *Lives of early Methodist preachers*, 1838, 3 vols., Pref., Vol. III, p. iii.

biography, it may be added, they failed to reach the first ranks because the religious experiences they described and the language in which they described them had been conventionalized into insipidity.[6] In exceptional cases, nevertheless, the memoirs of these dissenters present the frank, clean temper of the English yeoman in the language of the King James Version.

With these prefatory generalizations, we may turn to the analysis and illustration of the devices by which the eighteenth century made invisibles realities.

Some of the most fascinating passages in eighteenth century lives occur when the writer unconsciously describes his thoughts and difficulties in detail. Take the state of mind of William Fuller, traitor and spy, while he is trying to decide whether to serve the exiled James II or the new King William:[7]

"I was mighty uneasie in my Mind, and loved extremely to be alone, contemplating with my self, I said, What am I doing! I am in the Service of three Kings, how shall I behave my self, and have a good Conscience? I resolved at last upon this expedient, to keep a strict Fast three Days together, to spend all the time I could in my Devotion, to make an humble Contrition for my past Sins, and to resolve, by God's Grace, never to commit them again; after this was done, to put two Names, James and William into a Book, to Blind-fold my self, and then lay the Book down, afterwards walk three times round the room, then take the Book up, and shake it, and that Name which fell nearest to me, that King would I serve; and doing this, William fell as close to me as might be; this, how foolish soever, strengthened my Resolutions a little; however, I constantly pray'd to Almighty God, to direct me in the right, and preserve me therein."

The biographer of Alderman John Barber[8] shows the novelist's or the autobiographer's complete certainty as to what is going on in his hero's head, in an unusual episode in which, as Boling-

---

[6] To see how quickly such patterns in narration can grow up, cf. the monotonously similar accounts in John Howie's *Biographia Scoticana* (1796, 3d ed.), a martyrology for "Reformation principles"; and Patrick Walker's stalwart, recriminatory, scriptural, foreboding, fanatical accounts of hateful persecutions reprinted in *Biographia Presbyteriana*, Edinburgh, 1827.

[7] *The whole life of Mr. William Fuller*, 1703, p. 42.   [8] 1741, p. 29.

broke's ministry totters, Barber wonders whether or not he should desert to the other side. Such decisions can be made into the theme of a whole biography, as in the *Memoirs of the life of Mr. John Kettlewell* (1718), which is an extended case of conscience with regard to taking the Oath of Allegiance after 1688. Long letters and memoranda of Kettlewell's are included in dramatizing this inner struggle of a country vicar, resulting in his refusal to take the oath. And in the case of the Methodist missionary William Black, the Manichean principle so dominated his mind that he records long dialogues carried on between his better nature and his inner tempter and accuser. Anecdote, mental reconstruction, documentation, dialogue—here are four methods of presenting internal conflict.

The most interesting of these methods is probably the assumption of omniscience on the part of the biographer. Two definite statements may be made at the outset: first, the deliberate assumption of omniscience as a narrative device belongs to the eighteenth century in biography; second, biography adapts this device from the novel, or, more properly, from the French romance. Thus, *The secret history of the most renowned Q. Elizabeth and the E. of Essex. By a person of quality* (1708) is of the same school as the artificial novels of Madame D'Aulnoy, Mrs. Manley, or Penelope Aubin, which, in their turn, stem from the seventeenth century French writers of romances. Part of this *Secret History* is told as direct discourse by Elizabeth; part takes the form of direct narratives by others; and the whole is moulded into a romantic story, credible mainly because it is coherent. Some of the characters—the Duchess of Essex, the Duchess of Nottingham, and the Earl of Southampton—are recognizable, their principal traits being deduced from actual historical incidents.

Eliza Haywood's *Mary Stuart, Queen of Scots: being the secret history of her life* (1725), is similar. The introduction is careful to acquaint the reader that what follows "is not a Romance, but a True History." Yet Mrs. Haywood uses her technique as a novelist in describing psychological states, or the little events that happened in private interviews—"bursting into a flood of tears," and the like. She does not need to invent facts or situations, however, in dealing with Mary of Scotland,[9] and for the occasional liberties with history which her exuberant imagination takes, she soothes her conscience by recording that she has quoted more than a dozen historical sources and has relied particularly upon Elizabeth's antiquary, William Camden.

Another novelist, the Abbé Prévost, creator of Manon Lescaut, likewise turns his hand to biography; in the translated preface to his *History of Margaret of Anjou, Queen of England* (1755), he shows himself well aware of the distinctions between novelist and biographer as well as between biographer and historian.[10] This artist in psychology also shows himself preoccupied with plot, order, and proportion when dealing with biographical material.[11] After admitting that most histories follow the chronological order, he continues:

"yet I have experienced, that without any violation of truth, there may be such a happy arrangement of the circumstances, as by making them reflect more force and lustre upon each other, will render them much more interesting. My opinion is not to be a rule to my readers; but if this work meets with success, I am confident it will be owing to the care I have taken to reconcile all the advantages of truth, with that agreeable illusion which arises from surprize, from suspense and impatience, and which, in point of amusement, will make this history differ little from the most interesting works of imagination."

To show the persistence of novelized biography by citing an example from the last quarter of the century, Sarah Draper's *Memoirs of the Princess of Zell, consort to King George the First* (1796) may be mentioned. Supposedly this is translated from a manuscript of unknown provenance. Filled with imaginary con-

---

[9] cf. also Freebairn's *Life of Mary Stewart*, 1729, p. 1: "The Life of Mary Stuart, Queen of Scotland and France, has something so extraordinary in its Conduct, and so fatal in its End, that without swerving from the Truth, the plain Narrative of it will appear no less surprising, than the Fictions of any modern Romance." And Thomas Robertson's *The history of Mary Queen of Scots*, 1793, a penetrating analysis, Pref., pp. xiii-xiv: "The two principal objects in view, have been, To ascertain, what was the real character of that Princess; and, To explain, what were the actual principles of her conduct."

[10] See Chap. VII for further discussion of his biographical theory.

[11] Vol. I, pp. 8-9.

versations, tender court history, and exalted personal relationships and sentiments, it tells the romantic story of Count Königsmark; and makes up for scantiness of facts by oracular certainty in interpreting them.

Psychological analyses and speculations regarding motives came naturally to the novelist turned biographer; they were acquired by the antiquary and the formal historian. When a writer attempts the dignified and leisurely history of a career for which few dependable details or documents are available, he is forced back upon guess-work to round out his account; and hydra-headed hypotheses take the place of one lost fact. He may qualify his surmises with a scholarly "perhaps," but such caution cannot disguise his using the technique of the novelist. The historians of Christianity in particular were compelled, in the absence of certainties, to assume omniscience; and there is scarcely one of the lengthy and eagerly purchased lives of Christ that does not partake of fiction. Take, for example, one biographer's account of such a brief incident as Simeon's beholding the infant Jesus in the Temple:[12]

"Methinks one sees this venerable old man—his body bowing under a weight of years—his hair silvered with age—his countenance strongly marked with dignity and piety—methinks one sees this good old man advance towards the altar—approach the Virgin—gaze in a flood of transport upon the lovely babe—then taking the child from its parent, who readily yielded it to so aged and good a man—methinks one sees the old man folding the child in his arms—looking up to God with gratitude, while tears of joy streamed down his cheeks, and at last breaking forth into these expressions: *Lord! now lettest thou thy servant depart in peace!*"

An imaginary speech in direct discourse is given to Simeon; into its tissue the biographer works further actual quotations from the Gospel narrative. In another instance, by concentrating on psychological speculation and historical background, the author of *The life of Pontius Pilate* (1753) produces a respectable

[12] *The life and character of Jesus Christ delineated. By Edward Harwood,* 1772, pp. 17-18.

work of sixty pages without letting the reader perceive that the facts about Pilate's life total little more than zero.[13]

By the end of the century, the more complex and satisfying novel form, with its realistic handling of scene, character, and conversation, had affected biography so that no longer were the attempts at psychological omniscience so obvious and unconvincing as many of those detailed above.[14] Joseph Berington's *History of the lives of Abeillard and Heloisa* (1787), for example, plausibly analyzes Fulbert's emotions as he receives Abelard as a guest in his house (p. 73):

"The old canon swallowed the bait with eagerness. Money, and with it the prospect of benefiting Heloisa, accorded with all the feelings of his heart. It was no trifling circumstance either, that Abeillard should put his foot over his threshold, and that he should be permitted to sit down at table with a man, whom the world admired. Thus vanity, which never dies in the human breast, hung her bias also on the side of his ruling passions."

Surpassing the above passage in subtlety is Berington's delicate sketch of Abelard's attitude when he revisits Heloïse in the nunnery, for this ironically hostile reconstruction of what passes in his mind is to some extent assembled from Abelard's own letters (p. 93):

". . . Heloisa might propose, as the only way to end all troubles, to consecrate herself to religion.—He would never compel her to so severe a choice; but should she herself first suggest it, it would not become him to oppose her holy purpose. Liberty and independence would be again in his possession; and he might reach from fortune's wheel to the proudest objects of his ambition. The sight of his fair nun would, I know, dispel this airy castle; but when the gay hour was over, and reflection returned, his imagination would rebuild it perhaps in gaudier colours."

Most happily irresponsible of all eighteenth century biographers in conjuring up scenes that could not have been witnessed and would not have been recorded is the notorious Parson Weems. Everyone knows that his brazen invention of George-Washing-

---

[13] cf. the lives of David, quoted later in this chapter.
[14] cf. examples quoted in Chap. II.

ton-and-the-cherry-tree has given American folk-lore its most popular anecdote; and his life of Washington throughout makes fresh, imaginative, joyous reading, mixing anecdote and ethics in a prose style that runs easily from slang to rhetorical periods. The young George Washington's cosmogonic questioning of his father illustrates Weems as novelist. "High, Pa," George exclaims,[15] "an't you my *true* father?" and he receives the answer that his true father is God.

William Gilpin and Thomas Gibbons may furnish two final examples of biographers assuming the novelist's technique of omniscience. Gilpin, reconstructing the life of Archbishop Cranmer (1784) analyzes not only the motives of Cranmer's enemies, but the Archbishop's own emotions (p. 203):

"His soul they had damned: his body they were determined to burn; and to compleat their triumph, they wanted only to blast his reputation. . . . After the confinement of a full year within the melancholy walls of a gloomy prison, this sudden return into social commerce dissipated the firm resolves of his soul. A love of life, which he had now well mastered, began insensibly to grow upon him. A paper was offered him, importing his assent to the tenets of popery; and in an evil hour his better resolutions giving way, he signed the fatal snare."

Gilpin, who should be better known, has a sense of style that invents and compresses, changing dry documents into short vivid scenes, in his attempt to invest them with significance. This is his version of Cranmer's attempt to save Sir Thomas More, about to be beheaded for failure to acknowledge Henry VIII's supremacy in the Church. It might have been written yesterday (p. 41):

"With More he had lived on terms of great familiarity; and was prompted to employ even casuistry to save him. 'On one hand, said he, you are *doubtful* as to the point in question. On the other, you are *certain,* you ought to obey your prince. Let *doubt* then give way to *certainty.'*—More smiled, and laid his head upon the block."

A further attempt at reconstruction of a mood is afforded by Thomas Gibbons in his rather rhetorical *Memoirs of the Rev.*

[15] *Life of George Washington* [*ca.* 1800], quoted from 1810 Philadelphia ed., p. 16.

Isaac Watts (1780). He supports the following imaginative and Miltonic paragraph with a footnote in which his authorities include several named friends of Watts, the poet's works in general, and one poem in particular:

"When he went abroad," Gibbons writes (p. 141), "among the scenes of rural verdure, beauty, and fruitfulness, like the bee in its industrious ranges for celestial sweets, he was solicitous to gather fresh food for heavenly contemplation, or fresh materials and ornaments for future compositions. The pastures covered with flocks and herds, the fields waving with the ripening harvests, the groves resounding with the melody of the birds enlivened his praises, and he saw, heard, and confessed his God in all. The skies by day struck his soul with admiration of the immense power, wisdom, and goodness of their divine Author, the moon, and starry train by night increased his conceptions of Deity, and in the open manuscript of God, the wide extended heavens, he read the letters of his great and wonderful name with profound homage and veneration."

Thomas Stackhouse states that diving into the depths of his subject's mind is one of his devices in writing his *Memoirs of the life, character, conduct, and writings of Dr. Francis Atterbury:*[16]

"I thought, that to give some Account of a Man, who had made Noise enough here, and was likely to make Figure enough Abroad, might not only be some Entertainment to the Curious, but that, to consider him likewise in his several Capacities; to remark his Learning and other Abilities; to trace the Springs and hidden Motives of his Actions; and to disclose the Temper and predominant Passions of his Mind, might be of collateral Use."

Stackhouse finds Bishop Atterbury's prevailing passion to be pride, and for clarification quotes a section from one of Young's sermons on "the proud Man" which is in reality Theophrastus delivered from the pulpit. Stackhouse's biography in structure is indeed little more than a clever, hostile character sketch. It should be noted here that the character sketch, which had become an accepted device in biography long before the eighteenth century, represents a formal attempt at subjective interpretation. Ordi-

---

[16] 1727, pp. iv-v.

narily, however, these sketches were so perfunctory, conventional, laudatory, and generalized that they seldom conveyed the sense of a hero's temper, and even more infrequently any of the incidents in his inner life. Possibly the most graceful remark on the character sketch as a particular form of subjective biography occurs in the anonymous "Imitations of the Characters of Theophrastus":[17]

"Prometheus is said to have been found fault with by Momus for having neglected, when he made his men of clay, to fix a window in their breasts; but Theophrastus in the present work seems willing to supply this defect, by opening a window, through which we may clearly see the nature and operations of the human heart."

Interest in the analysis of personality is shown by the great number of eighteenth century editions of Theophrastus and his brilliant successor La Bruyère.[18] The discoveries which the Greek or the French temper recorded as general observations on human types, the native English genius was not slow to transform into the specific appraisal of specific individuals.

Autobiographers themselves became increasingly aware of their own minds and of the complexity of human consciousness.[19] Colley Cibber, for instance, in a passage quoted in the chapter on the drama, is not only vain, and aware of his vanity, but knows that he is vain of his awareness. A similar example of subtle self-analysis is to be found in the extended preface to Charles Dibdin's *Professional Life* (1803) in which he says (p. ix):

"In the following work, which contains my professional life, I have related circumstances and events. In the present address, its

[17] 1774. Pref., p. xx, where it is quoted from Duport's Pref. to Theophrastus's *Characters*.

[18] The Bodleian Catalogue, for instance, lists editions of Theophrastus, appearing in Great Britain in Greek, Latin, or English, for the following years: 1702, 1707, 1712, 1739, 1743, 1744, 1748, 1754, 1758, 1790. Other editions, with La Bruyère, appeared in 1700, 1709 (the "5th ed."), 1713, 1714, 1718. This list of editions is probably far from complete, and takes no account of such derivative productions as *The English Theophrastus*, 1702, or the *Imitations*, 1774, quoted above.

[19] cf. the memoirs of Lady Anne Vane, inserted in *Peregrine Pickle*, considered in Chap. II.

proper harbinger, I shall enter into a consideration of motives and inducements. The first is a history, the result of the mind; the second an examination of the mind itself."

Dibdin's preface contains so much of that Socratic ignorance which is the necessary prelude to an understanding of one's own mental processes, that some of the more profound and skeptical of his apothegms may well be quoted (pp. x-xiii):

"We see nothing before us; we pretend to a knowledge of what we can never understand; we affect to grasp objects beyond our reach, and are insensible to those within our power; and we are covetous to perfect what it is not in our nature or capacity to comprehend. . . .

"A man's mind may, sometimes, be better penetrated at first sight than after long experience. This is a bold declaration I confess, but it is truth; and it might, with great facility, be proved in detail. We form the minds of men not from their qualities, but from our judgments. We seldom look into their motives such as they are, but such as we wish them to be. . . .

"How many worlds, says a writer, does this world in which we live contain! . . .

"To know others, however, we ought to know ourselves, for nothing is farther removed from us than our own minds. . . .

"The character of your mind is in danger of altering without your knowledge; in which case you are lost to yourself."

The self-scrutiny which lay back of Dibdin's delicate observations produced at the beginning of the century a biography unique in its method, the *Life and errors of John Dunton* (1705). The later years of this bookseller were tinged with insanity; and even in this work, there is something wild, original, unbalanced, mixed with profound psychological observations on himself and others. "I love to know the inside of a man," he writes (1818 repr., Vol. I, p. iii); and this passionate curiosity dominates his writings. His autobiography, for instance, also claims to present "The Lives and Characters of a Thousand Persons now living in London." Stationers, printers, licensers, customers, great lords— everyone from Queen Anne to Daniel Defoe and Dunton's personal friends is sketched in swiftly. Dunton delights in characterization by single adjectives, as in "Understanding Locke, satirical Oldham, celebrated Congreve, Almanack Partridge," or for the more humble, "Wiveing R——ns, single-eyed Norton, Purgatory Turner, Anabaptist (alias Elephant) Smith," and he carries on this feat for pages (pp. 291-4). His longer etchings also make the most of words (pp. 355 and 358):

"Genteel Bettisworth. His garb and gesture is free and natural, and his eyes sparkle like any thing."

"Mr. Bury, my old Neighbour in Redcross-street: He is a plain honest man; sells the best Coffee in all the neighbourhood; and lives in this World like a spiritual Stranger and Pilgrim in a Foreign Country."

His description of an entire ship's crew, whom he observes during a long voyage to New England, is of the same family as Chaucer's *Prologue*. Here is one of them:[20]

"The next Man was the Purser, an old, dull, sleeping Fellow, and so abandon'd to obstinacy and self-will, that there was no perswading of him; And if one had a mind to have him do a thing, the only way was to declaim against it."

His mind is absorbent, and he carries out the promise of one of his title-pages in giving "Particular Characters of Men and Women, and almost every thing He saw: or conversed with."[21] Dunton, though he chatters like a jay, is no fool. He has an ever-present sense of humor, and can see through most men's pretensions, including his own. This, for example, is his opinion of Grub Street:[22]

". . . the Learning itself of these Gentlemen lies very often in as little room as their Honesty; though they will pretend to have studied you six or seven years in the Bodleian Library, to have turned over the Fathers, and to have read and digested the whole compass both of Human and Ecclesiastical History—when, alas! they have never been able to understand a single page of Saint Cyprian, and cannot tell you whether the Fathers lived before or after Christ."

The anecdotes of his childhood with which he opens his account include his badnesses, his "signal deliverances," and his first love-

---

[20] *John Dunton's Letters from New-England*, published for the Prince Society, Boston, 1867.

[21] *ibid.*, t.p.   [22] *Life and errors*, 1818 repr., Vol. I, pp. 61-2.

affair at the age of thirteen. Later he gives a humorous account of the three Sarahs, any one of whom he might have married. In church he meets "a young lady that almost charmed me dead"— so he proposes to her sister. The memory of his wife Elizabeth (he writes after her death) tinges his memoirs with emotion; and indeed, John Dunton had no more control over his feelings than over his imagination or his style.[23] During his courtship, he wrote to Elizabeth Annesley at Tunbridge, declaring that letters from her "will give poor languishing Philaret all the transports that a Lover can imagine"; she cautions him in reply: "please to deny yourself a little luxuriance in your Letters, lest my Father should find them, and be offended with them." And the closing prayer of his *Life and Errors* is: ". . . when my breath is gone, grant, O Lord, that I may see and know *her* again, who died praying for my ever-lasting happiness."

His reveries are likewise unchecked. "My head is pregnant," he writes, "with agreeable and everlasting inventions." Dunton was the bookseller who was largely responsible for that early periodical, the *Athenian Mercury,* that grew out of his Athenian Society, and for the hodgepodge of questions and answers on divinity, history, philosophy, mathematics, love, and poetry which he published as *The Athenian Oracle.* As a young man, he had conceived the idea of voyaging to the colonies with a trunkful of books and of disposing of them there. Again, at one time he planned and almost finished (p. xv): "The Funeral of Mankind; or an Essay proving we are all dead and buried, with an Elegy upon the whole Race: To which is added, a Paradox, shewing what we call Life is Death, and that we all live and discourse in the Grave." To such an enterprising young man, whose mind is always crowded with fantasies, the ordinary events of life assume

[23] For style, see his elegant description of seasickness, taken from his *Letters from New-England,* 1867, p. 23:

"For now the Sea began to work upon me; and the fighting of my Humors with Each other, soon made it evident the Harmony of Nature was quite out of Tune, which made as great a Tempest in my Microcosm as on the boyling Gulf on which we floated. And had I not been comforted by some experienced Passengers, that I should be the better for it afterwards, I should have fear'd the Dissolution of the Bodies League had been at hand. For I was so disorder'd by it, that at every heave, it set me on the Borders of the other World, and made me sensibly to touch the Extremities of Life."

strange forms. When he leaves for America, he is pleased to imagine the parting is his funeral:[24]

". . . and accordingly, Octob. 14, 1685, I took my solemn leave of the good Doctor, (my Reverend Father in Law,) his wife and family. And now, my Dear, methought 'twas a little representation of a Funerall, to see thee and my severall friends, (like so many mourners) marching with me to the water-side; for I now fancyd my selfe as 'twere a Herse and Coffin upon their shoulders, and my weeping spouse decently attending the Ceremony; but we wanted Torches; and besides, it's not usuall for any to waite upon their own Coffins."

The last phrases of this quotation show the practical John Dunton criticizing the dreamer. This dual nature is continually present in his writings, most strikingly in the structure of his *Life and Errors* itself. This production grows out of a feeling of remorse as he looks back on a misspent life. "The review of my busy life," he confides to his "impartial Readers" (p. xi), "put me sufficiently out of humour with it: there were very many passages I could easily recollect, which wanted both repentance and amendment. I found the world and myself had very different thoughts of John Dunton." Consequently he originates the idea of parallel chapters, one dealing with a certain phase of his past career, and the next with how he should have lived that phase, or how he would relive it. Thus Chapter VII is entitled "The Life and Errors of John Dunton, from the day of his marriage to Mrs. Elizabeth Annesley, till the day of her decease," and Chapter VIII: "The Idea of a New Life, or, the manner how I would think, speak, and act, might I live over again my married state with dear Iris." His split personality is evident in such chapter headings even in the pronouns, which suggest that he sees his past life objectively, and then reshapes it in an ideal world of his own, in which his wife Elizabeth lives as Iris and he himself as Philaret. And his final words, when, after much agonized piety, he contemplates his own *Vita Nuova,* show him still conscious of a divided personality (p. 413): "So that, if I practise my own *Idea of a New Life,* I may say, as the converted gallant once said to a strumpet

that tempted him after three years' absence, 'Ego non sum Ego.'
—'Do not you know me?' said she; 'why, it is I!' 'Yes,' said he,
'but I am not the same Man.' "

Dunton's public penitence is extreme, self-conscious, and purposeful. "Candid Reader," he writes in his introduction (p. xix):

"It goes hard with the *pride* of human nature, and the principle
of self-love, to take a Review of our past Lives, and to make a
Collection of Mistakes and Errors; though it would certainly be
the ready way to amendment, and I am resolved to give the
world a precedent of this nature. St. Austin informs us, that he
who repents is almost innocent; and I may add, that Confession
is the best companion of sincere Repentance."

Later he writes (p. 383): "I find more real joy in one penitential
tear than in all the sins I ever committed."

After such avowals of himself as the chief of sinners, it may
seem paradoxical to find him truculently using a *tu quoque* argument in the spirit of Rousseau's *Confessions* (pp. 408-9): "I have
not an acquaintance in the whole world, I will scarce except the
reverend Sam. Wesley [father of Charles and John], but may
find enough in his own life to damp his censuring me." Such
inconsistencies are the stuff of his innermost nature. He is
humble, yet he resents Swift's criticism in the *Tale of a Tub*. He is
satirical, yet he plans to publish, and publishes, elegies of seventeenth century dissenting divines. The touching letters between
himself and his wife during her last sickness; the death of Iris,
who expires, as she had lived, with 'O this Eternity!' on her
wondering lips; their wish to sleep in the dust together and his
own vow never to marry again—these are immediately followed
by his wrangling over his second wife's estate which he wants to
use to pay his debts. Like Job, he frequently curses the day that
he was born; but he no less frequently repents and admits that
he has felt this thought "too often." And he can express with
equanimity two such jangling sentiments as "The Life which I
here *un-live,* has been an amusement to me forty years" (To the
Readers, p. xii), and "Life . . . at best, is but a dull repetition of
the same thing" (p. 411). John Dunton was unlike most of his fellows in that he possessed the gift of realizing his transient moods,

as indistinct as water is in water, and of expressing them. His psychological insight is at times subtle and universal (p. 300):

"I think it is scarce possible to meet a man, could we but look within him, exactly in the same humour this, that he was the last hour: in this sense, every man is no less than a Proteus to himself and to all the world. We are so much governed by the laws of Mechanism, by every new tone of the blood and spirits, that there can be no consistency in ourselves; how much less can we always harmonize with another person!"

Scribbling, rambling, generous, flighty, weak-willed, over-emotional, scatter-brained, garrulous, he nevertheless succeeds in presenting a living self-portrait (p. 329):

"Thus, with the Pelican, have I dissected my breast, to shew the Reader where the defects of humanity reside. . . . Having now made the whole world my Confessor, I shall here hang out a flag of defiance to all my Enemies, to prove me either better or worse than I here declare."

At the end, the reader takes leave of John Dunton, plagued by diseases, "disorders of mind," by financial and dowry troubles, by the jealousy of his new wife at St. Albans, so unlike his Iris, by his enemies Sir Gnaw-post and Squire Vinegar, and by the slanders and suspicions of the world. Yet even here he can subtly observe in passing (p. 404): "And every man thinks, be he never so scrupulous in other respects, that to *be-rogue* another is to *be-saint* himself." In the final chapter, which he calls "The After-Thought," reviewing his whole past life, he is not sure that he could make a better job even if he might relive it. At any rate, in his confessions, he has revealed himself as a forerunner of Colley Cibber and Rousseau, a journalist-adventurer of the school of Deloney and Greene, a self-made philosopher who writes his own *Religio Bibliopolae* and chooses for his motto "Out of the frying-pan," an individual of a flickering double nature, aspiring and active, a close observer and subtle psychologist, a penitent as proud as John Bunyan.

More ordered than Dunton in his self-revelation is Thomas Scott, Morning Preacher at the Lock Chapel in London, whose *The Force of truth: an authentic narrative* appeared in 1779.

Dunton's occasional fits of humility are continually present in Scott, who constantly remembers the quotation from Job which adorns his title-page: "Vain man would be wise, though man be born a wild Ass's colt." He professes that his autobiography (p. iii) "contains little more, than the history of my heart, that forge of iniquity: and my conscience, that friendly, but too often neglected monitor." In consequence, the whole of the short little volume is an inner drama, full of struggle, despair, exaltation, and Scott's "extempore cries for mercy." Scott pitilessly dissects the skeptical and sordid reasons that led him to enter the ministry; yet soon, because he cannot credit the eighth article of the Creed, the coequal Trinity, he declares his belief and gives up his preferment. To such a decision, however, he cannot accord unqualified praise; his awareness of the prick of conscience he considers commendable, but he also finds mingled in his action (pp. 31-2) "self-sufficiency, undue warmth of temper, and obstinacy." Much of his short account is devoted to the adventures of his soul among books. He pays a tribute to Locke, discriminating between his valuable *Treatise on Toleration* and his harmful *Reasonableness of Christianity*; he admires Bishop Burnet and analyzes his *Pastoral Care*; he records his reading minutely and chronologically, and states how his mind was changed by reading Hooker, Soame Jenyns, Beveridge, Dr. Evans's *The Christian Temper,* Venn, Hervey, Witsius, Bishop Hall, and Dr. Reynolds. A purely spiritual and intellectual life so dispassionately observed is rare in any century. Scott may truthfully conclude his account with the words (pp. 87-8) : "And now, as in the presence of the heart-searching God, I have given without one wilful misrepresentation, addition, or material omission, an history of the great things God hath done for my soul." His final "Observations on the foregoing Narrative" seek to establish a case, by objective self-analysis, that his final Christian attitude "hath been effected under the guidance and teaching of the Holy Ghost," since i. he was "a most unlikely person, to embrace this system of doctrine," ii. "this change in my sentiments was very gradual," iii. the change was coolly accomplished "without any teaching from the persons, to whose sentiments I have now acceded"; iv., v., and vi. the change was brought about by reading the Scriptures, by prayer, and without the transient hysteria of the enthusiasts.

This addendum by the Reverend Thomas Scott merits notice here because the workings of God in delivering the soul from sin can hardly be overemphasized as a *motif* in eighteenth century biography. The theme may manifest itself in countless trivial paragraphs such as the following:[25]

"In the same year [1703], he was nearly choked by a pin which he swallowed at dinner, and which he did not fail to record in his memorandum book, as amongst the many mercies which he had received. 'Let them give thanks,' he adds, 'whom the Lord has delivered.'"

It may afford the organizing principle for such a popular collection as Samuel James's *An abstract of the gracious dealings of God, with several eminent Christians, in their conversion and sufferings* (1774).[26] It may furnish the drive of a long biography such as the *Memoirs of the Rev. Thomas Halyburton* who writes:[27]

"This being the design of this narrative, namely, to give some account of the Lord's work with me, and of my own way towards him, as far as I remember it, from my birth to the present time; I shall proceed in it."

Halyburton's narrative centers upon God and the sinful autobiographer. Halyburton recounts his slow attaining of grace and his many lapses into sin; even when he speaks of his wife, even when he writes of his dying children, there are only two actors present: the Lord and Halyburton.

Or again, the theme of God's mercies may afford an ostensible text for an autobiography which, as is the case with Symon Patrick (written in 1706), though it professes to be "a thankful remembrance of God's mercies to me," is actually a straightforward, practical journal of an octogenarian bishop whose conscience had always guided him to the parties in power and the most profitable preferments.

---

[25] Weeden Butler's *Mark Hildesley*, 1821 ed., p. 13; 1st ed., 1799.

[26] t.p. 4th ed., 1774; 1st ed., 1760; 9th ed., 1824.

[27] p. 58, 1833 ed. Princeton. Halyburton, 1674-1712. cf. also *Some memoirs of the life of John Glover, late of Norwich: intended to display the Glory of God . . . Written . . . by himself*, 1774.

Sincere and intense gratitude for the goodness of God as the cause for writing memoirs shines in the following preface to a Quaker autobiography, which also shows an evaluation of life characteristic of all these autobiographies:[28]

"Beloved Friends, Remembering the Lord our Gracious God in His Ways, and Merciful Dealings with me from my Youth; how He found me among His lost and strayed Sheep, on the barren Mountains of Fruitless Professions, and how He drew me to an inward Experience of His Power and Sanctifying Work in my Heart, and to know His Teaching and Spiritual Ministry; thereby to enable me by Degrees, experimentally to minister to others, and oblige me to live accordingly; as also to suffer patiently, with Resignation of Liberty and Life for Christ's Sake, when called thereunto, and being supported by His Power, and chearfully carried thorough many great Trials and deep Sufferings for His Name-Sake, and having had many eminent Deliverences and Preservations, even from my young Years; I say, considering these Things [plus his compassion for other Friends and his success in securing greater toleration for them] . . . a Concern hath long been upon my Spirit, to leave some Remarks and Footsteps (by an Historical Account) of my Progress under the Lord's Help and Conduct, in His Work and Service."

Realization of the grace of God, important in all Christian philosophies, becomes doubly important in the individualistic and experiential sects, particularly among the Wesleyans. An ordinary man is transformed into one of God's chosen through a sudden permeating of his consciousness by an awareness of God—a flooding, an illumination, of the spirit. This single and unexpected moment was of overwhelming significance to him. William Cowper, for instance, in his sketch of his brother John, writes of him (1802, p. 34): "directing his speech to me, he said; 'Brother, I was going to say I was born in such a year; but I correct myself: I would rather say, in such a year I came into the world. You know when I was born.'" The writers of their own lives or the lives of others, familiar with "the nature of salvation by grace, when it is truly and experimentally known"

[28] *The Christian progress of that ancient servant and minister of Jesus Christ, George Whitehead,* 1725, Pref., A2, *recto* and *verso.*

(*ibid.,* p. 31), frequently produced biographies of great dramatic power through their concentration on the single great crisis of spiritual illumination.

Some remarkable passages in the life of the Honourable Col. James Gardiner (1747), by Philip Doddridge, may be singled out as the best example of this type, for it ran through many editions and had great influence in the century. The life cannot be illustrated adequately by quotations, for Dr. Doddridge was not a stylist; but taken as a whole, the tract is as impressive as Bishop Burnet's *Life of Rochester,* and for the same reason: it is written purposefully from a single point of view. Colonel Gardiner was born in 1688, the year of the Glorious Revolution; he died defending it at the battle of Prestonpans in, 1745. Doddridge includes the realistic death on the battlefield as told by a servant who witnessed it. A bullet had gone through Gardiner's mouth and neck at the battle of Ramillies in 1706; he was almost bayoneted by the French soldiers on the field of battle. If the life of a soldier here appears vivid, so does the courtier's life in the first section of the biography, when Gardiner at the French Court, under the protection of the Earl of Stair, engages in a "series of criminal amours" between his nineteenth and thirtieth years. He is known as "the happy rake," which Doddridge considers "a dreadful kind of compliment." And then, in intense and minutely detailed pages, Doddridge narrates his conversion. Waiting for a midnight assignation, Gardiner reads Thomas Watson's *The Christian Soldier.* Christ appears to him, and he feels that he is damned. Three months later, aided by the nonconformist antiquary Edmund Calamy, he is saved. In contrast to his early years, the latter part of the biography is devoted to Gardiner's subsequent exemplary life, his attempts to convert others, his patience under the loss of his children, his domestic character as master, father, husband, and friend, his almsgiving, gentle discipline, theological opinions, meditations on eternity, and above all, his admirably realized spirit of resignation.

Interesting in connection with Doddridge's influential biographical tract is his *The Christian Warrior animated and crowned: a sermon occasioned by the heroick death of the Honourable Col. James Gardiner* (1745). Since Doddridge says: "I purpose publishing, in a distinct Tract, Some remarkable Passages of his Life," the sermon remains a generalized consideration of the Christian Soldier. But although at the time he delivered it Doddridge did not know the details even of Gardiner's death, he already realized in its general outlines what a striking didactic example he had at his command in the contrasting two halves of Gardiner's life and their link in the sudden conversion of a libertine (pp. 26-7):

"He was, in the most amazing and miraculous Manner, without any Divine Ordinance, without any Religious Opportunity, or peculiar Advantage, Deliverance, or Affliction, reclaimed on a Sudden, in the Vigour of Life and Health, from the most licentious and abandoned Sensuality, not only to a steady Course of Regularity and Virtue, but to high Devotion, and strict tho' unaffected Sanctity of Manners: A Course, (in which he persisted for more than Twenty-six Years, that is, to the Close of Life,) so remarkably eminent for Piety towards God . . . that when I consider all these Particulars together, it is hard to say where, but in the Book of God, he found his Example, or where he has left his Equal."

This fervent spirit of edification comes out clearly in the favorite hymns quoted in the biography of Gardiner, and also in its general tone; but Doddridge is meticulous in including Gardiner's letters and in authenticating all his remarks and anecdotes by giving sources. This determined accuracy should be noted particularly, because the crucial episode in the life is one of purely subjective revelation.[29]

The list of biographies in which such illumination is important or central is long; and, as Gardiner's biography demonstrates, this exaltation was not limited to the clergy alone. "David Lowellin," a runaway at an early age, who spent part of his life adventuring in the Americas and many years of it alone in an African oasis, records an experience similar to Gardiner's (1792 ed., p. 11):

[29] Its authenticity is questioned in an interesting passage in the autobiography of Dr. Alexander Carlyle (1722-1805), 1910, p. 22. A trance recorded by William Grimshaw himself is compared to Gardiner's experience in John Newton's life of Grimshaw, 1799, p. 36.

"After this I remained pretty well composed for several days, though not entirely satisfied in mind concerning my own salvation; till one day, when leaning back in a great chair, and falling into a kind of dose, but whether asleep or awake I do not pretend to say, because I really thought myself awake, I observed a person of nearly my own stature gradually approach me, concealing all the way of his features from my view; when near he pronounced these words, 'Believe and be saved.' Then he vanished from my sight like a shadow. This unexpected favour entirely convinced me that I was not out of the reach of mercy. My hopes therefore increased, and I became very thankful for having been thus happily prevented from putting a period to my existence."

The frequency of such experiences as an important part of life cannot be forgotten in surveying eighteenth century biography as a whole. There is the "Early conversion to serious piety" of Increase Mather as recorded by his son (1724); Thomas Scott's description of the Satan with whom he wrestled as a real and powerful figure, objectively observed (1779); *An account of the remarkable experience of Mary, the wife of James H——— in her conviction, faith, and repentance on her death-bed, in the 45th year of her age* (*ca.* 1768); and the sudden conversion of William Howard as recorded by Joseph Milner (1785). Moreover, the accounts of native Englishmen are generally far more detailed and convincing than this statement from a translated life of Emanuel Swedenborg (1787, p. 7):

"The Lord . . . was graciously pleased to manifest himself to me his unworthy servant, in a personal appearance, in the year 1743, to open in me a sight of the Spiritual World, and to enable me to converse with Spirits and Angels, and this privilege has continued with me to this day."

More characteristic is this episode in the life of Mr. John Haime, late soldier in the Queen's Regiment of Dragoons (1799, p. 5):

"I was violently tempted to blaspheme, yea, and to hate God: at length, having a stick in my hand, I threw it toward heaven, against God, with the utmost enmity. Immediately I saw in the clear element, a creature like a Swan, but much larger, part black, part brown. It flew at me, and went just over my head. Then it went about forty yards, lighted on the ground, and stood staring upon me. This was in a clear day, about twelve o'clock: I strove to pray, but could not. At length God opened my mouth. I hastened home praying all the way, and earnestly resolving to sin no more. But I soon forgot my resolution, and multiplied my sins, as the sands on the sea-shore."

The style and matter of the above quotation indicate obviously enough that John Haime was a Wesleyan; and indeed, the best accounts of spiritual struggle and revelation of the century are written by Methodists. The *Arminian Magazine,* in which many of them first appeared, states in its first issue (1778) that one of its aims is to justify the Wesleyan central doctrine of salvation by "Particular Redemption" which Arminius is made to stand for as opposed to the "Absolute Redemption" of Romanist-Thomists and Calvinists. The *Magazine* also promises in each issue "An extract from the life of some holy man, whether Lutheran, Church of England-man, Calvinist, or Arminian," and "Accounts and Letters, containing the experience of pious persons, the greatest part of whom are still alive." The treasure trove of Christian biography that grew up out of these avowed purposes is made up mainly of the accounts of Methodist ministers. These narratives resemble each other in recording the deep conviction of sin, the blinding flash of redemption, the flushing and irradiation of the spirit by God's love, the fear of this world, hardships and travels easily born. Together they give a complex picture of middle-class England; almost all of these itinerant preachers were the sinful sons of artisans. Certain of the best or the most typical accounts may be singled out to represent them all.

The absolute dependence of the Wesleyans upon their Saviour is best shown by a typical epitaph, which sums up, for its own composer, the significance of life:[30]

"Here lies The earthly Remains of John Berridge, Late Vicar of Everton, And an Itinerant Servant of Jesus Christ, Who loved his Master, and his Work; And, after running on his Errands many Years, was caught up to wait on him above. Reader! Art thou born again? No Salvation without a New

---

[30] *A short account of the life and conversion of the Rev. John Berridge,* 1794; 1st ed. 1760. Epitaph wr. by Berridge.

Birth. I was born in Sin, February 1716. Remained ignorant of my fallen State till 1730. Lived proudly on Faith and Works for Salvation till 1754. Admitted to Everton Vicarage 1755. Fled to Jesus alone for Refuge 1756. Fell asleep in Christ January 22, 1793."

Not even the man of faith *and* works, therefore, is godly, for he is not attributing to Christ alone the full source of salvation. In a preface to a *Life and Death,* John Wesley generalizes concerning the typical illumination or conversion:[31]

"The general Manner wherein it pleases God to set it [his Kingdom] up in the Heart is this. A Sinner, being drawn by the Love of the Father, enlighten'd by the Son ('the true Light which lighteth every Man that cometh into the World') and convinced of Sin by the Holy Ghost; through the preventing Grace which is given him freely, cometh weary and heavy laden, and casteth all his Sins upon him that is 'mighty to save.' He receiveth from him, true living Faith. Being justified by Faith, he hath Peace with God: He rejoices in Hope of the Glory of God, and knows that Sin hath no more Dominion over him. And the Love of God is shed abroad in his Heart, producing all Holiness of Heart and of Conversation."

Since Wesley himself says of the life of Haliburton,[32] "This Work of God in the Soul of Man is so described in the following Treatise, as I have not seen it in any other, either antient or modern, in our own or any other Language. So that I cannot but value it next to the Holy Scriptures," it is interesting to note its proportions and emphasis: out of a total of 92 pages, pages 21 to 56 are occupied by Haliburton's doubts, strugglings, temptations, convictions, mistakes, discoveries, and deliverances; and from page 68 to the end his death-speeches are detailed. The Wesleyan biography, then, becomes very largely the story of slow awakening to light and life, followed by an exemplary death scene.

The theological doubts and mental sufferings of these autobiographers are often set forth in all their intricacies, as in this

---

[31] *An extract of the life and death of Mr. Thomas Haliburton,* 1741.
[32] *ibid.,* Pref.

paragraph written by John de la Fléchère, one of the gentlest and noblest of all the Wesleyans:[33]

"When I saw that all my endeavours availed nothing against my conquering sin, I almost gave up all hope, and resolved to sin on and go to hell. Yet I had a strange thought, 'If I do go to hell, I will praise God there. And since I cannot be a monument of his mercy in heaven, I will be a monument of his justice in hell.' But I soon recovered my ground. I thought, Christ died for all. Therefore he died for *me*. He died to pluck such sinners as I am out of the devil's teeth."

William Black opens his autobiography[34] without wasting words:

"I was born at Huddersfield in Yorkshire, in the year 1760. When I was about six years old, I had serious impressions on my mind; and the thoughts of my state so distressed me, that I frequently said within myself, 'O that I were a toad, a serpent, or any thing but what I am! O that I had never been born, or else had been greater than God! and then he could not have punished me for my daring sins.'"

Black shares the Wesleyan sensitivity to certain sins, a sensitivity that led one man to drown himself because he played cards[35] and another to reform because a young girl died after attending a dance.[36] Black is guilty of both dancing and card-playing (p. 119):

"I grew in wickedness, as I advanced in age, turning the grace of God into lasciviousness; spending whole nights together in the ridiculous practice of shuffling spotted pieces of pasteboard, with painted Kings and Queens on them; and dancing for four or five nights in the week."

But Black is helped by John Newton, and gradually his straightforward and dramatic account of spiritual conflict gives way before the account of his missionary work in Nova Scotia. The

[33] *A short account of the life and death of the Rev. John Fletcher,* 1786, by John Wesley, p. 19.

[34] In Jackson's *Lives of early Methodist preachers,* Vol. III, p. 117. Black dates his MS. June 1, 1788.

[35] See Jackson, Vol. I, under Christopher Hopper, pp. 3-50.

[36] See Jackson, Vol. III, under George Shadford, p. 185.

juxtaposition of soul struggles and rough, dangerous actions[37] may seem incongruous; but it forms the ordinary stuff of life to these Wesleyan autobiographers: their inner battles resulted in intense convictions, and their convictions led them confident and fearless through riots and floods.

George Shadford, for example, in his brief account[38] tells what he remembers about killing a duck when he was small, how he ran away from a preacher who tried to stop his playing games on Sunday, how he read Ovid's *Metamorphoses* and his *Art of Love* until he enlisted in the militia and reformed, how he converted his father and mother, how he impressed, or was impressed by, such diverse figures as a hermit in the Jerseys, a visionary in Philadelphia, a chained lunatic near Baltimore, and a dancing-master in Virginia. In his colonial travels, his spiritual contact with such people is for him the reality, and it is only casually that the reader finds that the Revolutionary War is drawing on, that Shadford is menaced for praying for the King, and that he managed to return to England only after the war itself had begun.

Silas Told's autobiography deserves mention, not only because it presents an admirable man, but because it records his life, rich in action and spiritual adventure, with something of Bunyan's magic touch. Told describes the inner and outer worlds with equal sureness. In his early childhood "my sister Dulcybella and self"—"I was then in petticoats"[39]—wander into a wood and lose themselves. Twice a dog that does not bark appears in order to drive them to safety, and then silently, mysteriously, vanishes. "This was the Lord's doing," writes Told, "and it was marvellous in our eyes." Throughout, the two worlds of spirit and sense blend as if they were one. At the age of fourteen Told goes down an "apprentice to the seas," and the ensuing eleven years of brutality and seasickness are mixed in his narrative with speculations on the appearing and disappearing land of "Old Brazille" which Atlantis-like was swallowed up by the Atlantic hundreds of

---

[37] cf. John Wesley, William Bromfeild, Thomas Rankin, Sampson Staniforth, Patrick Walker.

[38] See Jackson, Vol. III, pp. 175-214.

[39] *An account of the life, and dealings of God with Silas Told,* 1786, pp. 8-9.

years ago. The stories of the shockingly barbarous Captain Tucker, the poisoning of Captain Roach, the Africans trying to cure Told's headache, the lurid and bloody accounts of slave-traffic, fever in Jamaica and death by thirst, are told to an accompaniment of rats and Spanish pirates, of chicken-turtles and shipwrecks that would make Smollett envious, or Defoe. Yet when Told is almost drowned in learning to swim, he has a vision (pp. 78-9): "I rushingly emerged out of thick darkness into a most glorious city." The agony of winning his way back to life "was as through a devouring ocean of blood and fire." His escape from drowning, coupled with his reading of *Pilgrim's Progress* (which so evidently influenced his style), sets his mind toward a religious life. After scenes of torture in Jamaica, he finds Boston relatively pious and pleasant; and finally, associating with Methodists, he goes to hear "the Reverend Mr. Wesley at the Foundry," and in 1740, between four and five in the morning, in a ruined building, he is converted. He has a knack for making all things vivid; he can suggest a scene and introduce scraps of direct talk so successfully as to make his almost the best of the Wesleyan autobiographies. Even when he is thoroughly domesticated—he had two wives— and has settled down in London as a clerk, his early life of action prevents him from becoming over-righteous or torpid in withdrawal from the rough life of the city. A fine apocalyptic vision which dispelled his last religious doubt is immediately followed by descriptions of the most remarkable Newgate criminals, for he has now turned his vitality to the task of rescuing others. He converts his wife; he teaches charity-children; he visits prisons and comforts the condemned criminals, so that on their way to the gallows "they appeared like giants refreshed with wine."

John Nelson's *Journal* (*ca.* 1749) is probably the most vital and simple of all the Methodist biographies. It also is written in the style and spirit of Bunyan. Nelson did not easily arrive at spiritual certainty. This Yorkshire stonemason marries at nineteen to keep himself from sin; but when he is over thirty years old, though he is successful in his trade and the father of two children, he is unsettled and almost desperate; at last, though not easily, he is saved by John Wesley in an episode which can be paralleled in many of the other Wesleyan narratives. Despair and exaltation alternate in him. "But O! the hell I found in my mind when I came to be alone again . . ."[40] is followed in a few pages by: "That moment Jesus Christ was as evidently set before the eye of my mind, as crucified for my sins, as if I had seen him with my bodily eyes: and in that instant my heart was set at liberty, from guilt and tormenting fear, and filled with a calm and serene peace." His vivid remembrance of moods extends back to his childhood, as in this intensely realized vision (p. 3):

"When I was between nine and ten years old, I was horribly terrified with the thoughts of death and judgment, whenever I was alone: one Sunday night as I sat on the ground, by the side of my father's chair, while he was reading the twentieth chapter of the Revelation, the word came with such light and power to my soul, that it made me tremble, as if a dart was shot at my heart; I fell with my face on the floor, and wept till the place was as wet where I lay, as if water had been poured thereon. As my father proceeded, I thought I saw every thing he read about, though my eyes were shut: and the sight was so terrible. I was about to stop my ears, that I might not hear, but I durst not; for as soon as I put my fingers to my ears, I pulled them back again. When he came to the 11th verse, the words made me cringe, and my flesh seemed to creep on my bones, while he said, 'And I saw a great white Throne. . . .' O what a scene was opened to my mind!"

Nelson is no less realistic in narrating in Biblical prose such emotional scenes as the following, in which his unconverted wife first turns toward his opinions (p. 25):

"She then said, 'Nay, my happiness with thee is over; for according to thy words, I am a child of the devil, and thou a child of God.' Then she wept and said, 'I cannot live with thee.' I said, 'Why so? Thou shalt never want while I am able, by honest endeavours, to provide for thee. Nay, I continued, if thou wilt not go to heaven with me, I will do the best I can for thee; only I will not go to hell with thee for company; but I believe, God will hear my prayer, and convert thy soul, and make thee a

[40] 1810 Leeds ed., pp. 4 and 11-12.

blessed companion for me in heaven.' After this, my wife began to be concerned about the salvation of her soul."

His wife sickens, Jesus touches her as she falls, she wakes, is cured, and praises him. And Nelson, though eventually he is forced to take up stone-cutting again in order to support his family, now begins his career as a preacher. A story of prisons, fasting, and persecution follows. He is pressed for a soldier, but he refuses to fight against those he prays for. Yet in spite of an atmosphere of drum-beats and privations, his dreams are his reality:[41]

"In the night I dreamed I was in Yorkshire, going from Gomersal Hill Top to Cleck Heaton; and about the middle of the lane, I thought I saw Satan coming to meet me in the shape of a tall black man, and the hair of his head like snakes."

Eighteenth century biographers, no less than medieval writers and the most modern authors, believed that dreams and visions formed an important part of life. Colonel Gardiner's figure of Christ, Haime's brown swan, Lowellin's mysterious messenger, John Newton's vivid dream of perdition and divine aid, Nelson's terrifying glimpse of the great white throne and of his Medusa-like Satan—these are the equivalents in the eighteenth century of the devils that tormented Guthlac and Dunstan, the angelic visitations to Columba and Anselm, the vision of Dante. More homely they may be, but no less significant in the dreamers' lives. The young Baptist Samuel Pearce learned Bengalee and determined to go as a missionary to India largely because of his visions and experiences of grace. He records in his diary:[42] "Oct. 18. I dreamed that I saw one of the Christian Hindoos. O how I loved him!" Long after the reader has forgotten Letitia Pilkington's actual everyday actions, he will remember her dreams (when she is locked all night in Westminster Abbey) of her blessing the phantom of Henry V clad in armor, and of the

---

[41] p. 23, 1810 Leeds ed. Nelson has many dreams that give him information about the future. cf. all the biographies by Patrick Walker (Edinburgh, 1724-1732), whose heroes, because they were God's chosen, are addicted to prophecies which are invariably fulfilled.

[42] *Memoirs of the late Rev. Samuel Pearce . . . Compiled by Andrew Fuller,* 1801, Boston. 1st ed., 1800, Clipstone.

royal inmates of the Abbey, "these shadowy crowned heads passing by me, like those in Macbeth."

The gradations from daydreaming through trances, visions,
dreams, and hallucinations to temporary or permanent insanity
are almost infinite. Thus, at one extreme, as an instance of pure
subjective biography with the rational mind in control, consider
General Dumouriez's account of his mental state during the trial
of Louis XVI, when he meditates abandoning the now frantic
republicans. He writes of himself in the third person:[43]

"During the whole of that month, he was a prey to chagrin
and indignation; he left his apartments but seldom, and remained plunged in the bitterest reflections. Such was the life
of the man who had saved France in Champagne, and conquered
Belgium. It was then that he meditated on the following saying
of Plutarch in the life of Cleomenes: 'When a thing ceases to be
honourable, it is time to see its turpitude, and renounce it.'"

As the next step toward the irrational or suprarational, when
emotion and association replace logic, consider Elizabeth Cairns.
This humble Scottish spinster, a servant and a schoolmistress
with the soul of a poet and a beautifully rhythmic style, records
her intuitions quite simply:[44]

"There was one day, when this light was absent [the light
derived from praying with neighboring shepherds on the Sab-
bath], I was going by a corn field; I stood up by a stalk of corn,
and it was higher than I, at which I fell a weeping, when I
considered, how short a time it had been in the earth, and yet
had come so great a length, and I had made so little progress, in
my way to heaven."

Yet there is no sharp boundary between the poignant imagination of Elizabeth Cairns and the self-induced trance of Philip
Thicknesse as he leads an idyllic life on his own island in the
Carolinas and even contemplates wooing an Indian maiden of
the Creek tribe:[45]

[43] *The life of General Dumouriez*, 1796, 3 vols., Vol. III, p. 428.
[44] *Memoirs of the life of Elizabeth Cairns*, 1762, p. 17.
[45] *Memoirs and anecdotes of Philip Thicknesse*, 1788, 2 vols., Vol. I, p. 51.

"Walking upon the margin of my creek, & playing upon the Flute; such was the effect of an affectionate, and warm imagination; that I had a transient, but as perfect a sight of my Mother, as if she had actually been before me, in *Propria Persona*. Strongly possessed with the talk and idle [sto]ries which children hear, & many men cannot overcome, its no wonder that a Boy, as I then was, concluded it was my mother's departed shade; my Squa;— my Island;—and my Robinson Crusoe plan, instantly lost all their charms."

Self-induced hypnotism would also be the modern explanation for one of the trances of the mystic Jakob Boehme:[46]

". . . he was in the Beginning of the 17th Century, viz. 1600, being in the 25th Year of his Age, enraptured a second Time with the Light of God, and with the astral Spirit of his Soul, by Means of an instantaneous Glance of the Eye cast upon a bright Pewter-Dish, (being the lovely Jovialish Shine or Aspect) introduced into the innermost Ground or Center of the recondite or hidden Nature."

Yet the reader is moving into a world of special values when mysterious strangers and apocalyptic symbols of future grace are introduced by such a sentence as (p. 5):

"Nor is the Supposition improbable, that even externally, and by Means of a certain Magic-Astral Operation of the constellated Spirits, a Kind of secret Tinder and Glimmer might have been laid for, and at the same Time have concurred and contributed unto, this holy Love's Fire."

A Quaker autobiographer describes the state in which he writes, almost automatically, his fearful Solomonic visions in terms which suggest Urania appearing to Milton:[47]

"And, about the same Time the next Evening, being alone in the same Room, the same Mind returned, and filled me with great Consolation; which rested upon me for some Time with perfect Content, which nothing but himself can give; and, from the Center of that Mind, a Concern arose in me to write again; and, from that Fulness I perceived resting in me, was apprehensive I

---

[46] *Memoirs of the life, death, burial, and wonderful writings, of Jacob Behmen,* by Francis Okely, 1780, pp. 7-8.

[47] *A journal of the life of Thomas Story,* 1747, p. 24.

might write much; and therefore took a Quire of Paper, and began to write, as Matter began to appear, and with full Assurance, in Manner following: . . .

"Flow down, as Wax before the Sun, O ye Mountains of Pride; for the Prince of Meekness has overcome you. . . ."

The *Dictionary of National Biography* records as a matter of fact that George Trosse was at one time a prey to delirium tremens. It did not seem so to him. And as George Trosse tells of his frivolous "atheistical" youth, his travels in France and Portugal, his sins—particularly drinking—and his breaking of the Ten Commandments, the reader is caught up by his terrible simplicity and feels with him the real temptation by a real devil and the sudden snapping of his frayed sanity. The reader lives within Trosse's mind. The workaday world pales before the intense actuality of his hallucinations. Delusions have never been more vividly described. After years of roistering, Trosse falls off his horse one day, is carried home drunk, wakes, and hears voices. He kneels, and a voice says: "Yet more humble,"[48] until he has taken off all his clothes, put his head in a hole in the planking, and sprinkled dust on his hair. It is the voice of the devil. "Sometimes I was sollicited to dash my Head against the Edge of the Board near which I sate; at other times, I was tempted to dash out my Brains against the Walls, as I walk'd." He eats nothing. "While I thus lay upon my Bed, with such a wild and troubl'd Fancy, Night and Day, I seemingly heard many Voices and Discourses; which I attributed to Fairies, who, I thought, were in the Wall, and there convers'd and were merry together. And I fancy'd I saw upon the Wall a great Claw, for a long while together; but what the Meaning of that was I could not tell. Thus was I continually haunted with Multitudes of such Whimsies." In order to be conveyed to Glastonbury for treatment, he must be bound to a stout man on horseback. "All this while I was full of Horrours and of Hell within: I neither open'd mine Eyes nor my Mouth. . . .

---

[48] *The life of the Reverend Mr. Geo. Trosse,* 1714, pp. 47-63, for the following quotations.

"As I rode along, I fancy'd many Devils flying in the Air just over me, and by my Side as many Firy Flying-Dragons, expressing their Rage against me.

". . . And when they put a Glass into my Hand to drink of it, methought I saw in the Glass a Black Thing, about the Bigness of a great black Fly, or Beetle; and this I suppos'd to have been the Devil; but yet would drink it; and, methought, the Devil went down my Throat with the Liquour, and so took possession of me. At which desperate Madness of mine, it seem'd to me that all were astonish'd; and I fancy'd, that every Step I stepp'd afterwards, I was making a Progress into the Depths of Hell. When I heard the Bell ring, I thought it to have been my Doom out of Heaven; and the Sound of every Double Stroke seem'd to me to be, Lower down; lower down; lower down; (viz.) into the Bottomless Pit. This to me then was a dismal dejecting Sound. Whatever Noises I heard as I past by, my Fancy gave them Hellish Interpretations: For I was now perswaded that I was no longer upon Earth, but in the Regions of Hell. When we came to the Town, I thought I was in the midst of Hell: Every House that we pass'd by was as it were a Mansion in Hell. . . .

"All was Hell and Horrour to me!"

Visions of Purgatory and his suffering friends follow. One of his attendants, who rebuffs him, he takes for Christ. "And my very external Senses were deceiv'd, for I well remember, that applying my self to read in a Book I had taken up, I saw, as I apprehended, horrid Blasphemies in it; which made me presently lay it aside."

His attempts to wound himself, to break his bones, even to commit suicide, his hallucinations, his recoveries, and his sinking back three times into the kingdom of lost men, make heart-breaking reading.

But in the end he wins back to sanity and a state of grace, writes his memoirs after he has kept steadily on in the ways of God for nearly forty years, and orders his wife to publish this account of the single great action of his life after he is dead (Preface): "For the terrifying of Presumptuous and Secure Sinners, for the encouraging and perswading of such as are sensible, and humble, to make a Return to God thro' Christ; and for the comforting Converted, but Dejected Christians, that they may not be overwhelm'd with Sorrow." The citizens of Exeter might well have said of George Trosse, as the Italian women said of Dante, "There goes the man who has been in hell." His account is repetitious, but it is powerful and sincere; few men have been where he has been and returned to this world to give an account of their wanderings.

One further Dantesque pilgrimage cannot be overlooked. It is the account of a Frenchman who lived his last forty years in Pennsylvania, but it was of wide enough interest to warrant publication in London. George De Benville's visions were so much a part of his life that he himself seems unaware of the transitions from the ordinary to the extraordinary world. The title-page promises to record what he saw and heard, in the regions of misery and happiness, during the forty-one hours after his apparent death from a consumption.

"I felt myself die by degrees," he writes,[49] "and exactly at midnight I was separated from my body; and seeing the people occupied in washing me, according to the custom of the country [he was in "Mons, in Hainault"], I had a great desire to be freed from the sight of my body; and immediately I was drawn up as in a cloud, and beheld great wonders where I passed, impossible to be written or expressed. Presently I came to a place which appeared to my eyes as a level plain."

George De Benville thereupon journeys through the seven habitations of the damned, where he sees "a man whom I had been acquainted with upon earth," and the five habitations of the elect, before he reassumes his body in a scene as weird as may be found in biography (p. 36):

"Then my guardians took me up, and re-conducted me to the house whence I came, where I perceived the people assembled to my funeral, and discovering my body in the coffin, I was re-united with the same, and found myself lodged in my earthly tabernacle. And coming to myself, I knew my dear brother Marsay, and many others; who gave me an account that I had been 24 hours in the coffin, and that I lay 17 hours before they put me in

---

[49] *A true and most remarkable account of some passages in the life of Mr. George De Benville,* 1791, pp. 24 and 36.

my coffin; which altogether made 41 hours; but to me they seemed as many years."

From the frenzies of George Trosse and the two-day trance of De Benville, the distinction is quantitative rather than qualitative in passing to the fixed delusions of eighteenth century prophets. In the accounts of John Lacy, Alexander Cruden, and Richard Brothers, subjective biography is carried to its extreme, for the heroes of these accounts live in a world entirely their own. *The prophetical warnings of John Lacy* (1707) were "Pronounced under the Operation of the Spirit; and Faithfully taken in Writing, when they were spoken." They were issued in at least three separate parts, carefully dated, describing Lacy's contortions while "the voice" was speaking, and breathing fire and brimstone. Prophecy was in the air, and for this novel biographical form, as for others, England may have turned to France. Elias Marion, for instance, one of the commanders of the Protestants that had taken up arms in the Cévennes, uttered prophetical warnings in London between September 1706, and March 1707, "under the Operation of the Spirit" which fill 192 closely printed pages. "The Devil's Destruction is near," Marion's voices admonished. John Lacy himself admits that he had "been present divers Times at the Ecstasies of Mr. Marion, Mr. Fage, and Mr. Cavalier," but he maintains that he has not been inspired by them but by God.

The adventures of Alexander the Corrector, issued in three parts in 1754 and 1755, is the autobiography of a madman. Alexander Cruden was employed as a corrector of the press, and had published a concordance to the Bible. Suddenly these two parts of his life coalesced fantastically in his brain, and he imagined that God had appointed him corrector of public morals; he was especially designed to prevent swearing and to secure a more regular observance of Sunday. Twice at least, he was committed to a lunatic asylum, once for making unwelcome advances to a young lady. Once, also, he escapes from his imprisonment. Some of these happenings he details in his autobiography, but the focus is distorted and he rarely deviates into sense. The accounts of the cruelty and punishments of his confinements make gloomy reading, without parallel in biographical literature; for to him, of course, the real world is topsy-turvy and godless, and he is tortured for trying to save it. His two confinements in lunatic asylums he speaks of as the "campaigns of Bethnal-Green and Chelsea" (Vol. I, p. 10). He was first incarcerated for beating a blasphemous workman with his own spade. The nightmare story continues, always told in the third person; and "Alexander," after his commitment, tries to get his character cleared in the eyes of the law—unsuccessfully, for even his sister testifies against him. A certain Forbes he hates so intensely that he says—the reasoning is characteristic of the whole autobiography—he will call him by the "emblematical title" of Moonland.

The dreams and the visions of power crowd in upon him—always, pathetically, in a world which he finds intractable. The second part of his adventures ends with the suggestion that King George appoint him "The Corrector of the People" (Vol. II, p. 40), and the Appendix admits, still more pathetically, that "It was also foretold in a wonderful manner March 22, 1738, sixteen years ago, That the Corrector would be Sir Alexander Cruden, twice Lord Mayor of London, and Member of Parliament for the said City." Even in Alexander Cruden's own mind, the pattern of destiny was not always clear (Appendix 3 to Part II): "The designs of Providence in relation to the Corrector are yet somewhat mysterious, but are thought to be of very great importance to his Majesty and his People."

Part III becomes the love story of a lunatic. It is dedicated to Mrs. Elisabetha Whitaker, whom he woos by carrying on "the War" against her by "praying Bullets." He tries so hard to be made a knight; he is involved in another law-suit; his courtship takes the form of a "declaration of war" from "Alexander the Conqueror" to "the Lady Elisabetha." But it is no use. The adventures trail off inconclusively, indeterminately, in the wisps and tatters of his injured mind.

Yet only some such suffering rebel against society could feel the stupid and brutal rigidity of the eighteenth century social system. It is Alexander Cruden who writes *The history of Richard Potter* (1763), in an effort to commute a death-sentence passed against a sailor for attempting, when drunk, at the instigation of another sailor, to receive thirty-five shillings of prize money due to a third sailor. Cut to the brains by a society he has tried to

help, Cruden has some of the wavering humility of the mad King
Lear when he writes such sentiments as (p. 15): "I am very unwilling to say any thing to offend. . . . But it hath been said that
too many have been hanged lately." And so the feverish dream
continues, with the sailor Potter, not yet twenty-one, almost dying
of jail-distemper, with piety, officiousness, disease, injustice, callousness, and pity mingled together, and Cruden's ludicrous attempts at petty reforms inseparable from his deep sense of social
wrongs. But Cruden's brain was cracked; and no one had time
to distinguish between his follies and his prophetic glimpses of
a more humane state. At the end, nearly seventy, he died on his
knees at prayer.

As the last side-panel in this triptych of madmen comes Richard
Brothers. His vision of this life was the most grandiose of all.
The title-page of his autobiographical writings proclaims him
God's anointed King, and Shiloh of the Hebrews, and (as if
treading in the footsteps of Alexander the Corrector) he includes
not only prophecies, but letters to the King and to Mr. Pitt, and
a letter to Miss Cott, "God's Recorded Daughter of King David,
and Future Queen of the Hebrews." To insure the authenticity
of his writings, they are printed only for George Riebau, "Bookseller to the King of the Hebrews." A sympathetic Governor of
the Poor, in appraising Brothers's character,[50] frees him from the
charge of being an impostor. The prophet was sane and shrewd
on most subjects, benign as well; but always, when the one string
of religion was touched, he jangled. "He spent most of his time
in reading books of controversy, and which I conclude has had
the same effect upon his brain that romances and books of chivalry is feigned to have had upon that of Don Quixote." In 1791
the entire wicked city of London would have been sunk beneath
the sea if Brothers had not prayed; and as a result of this salvation of the city, the Lord God was angry with Brothers for three
days for making him reverse his expressed determination to
annihilate London.

In spite of such public service, and in spite of several printed
defenses by his followers, Brothers was committed for insanity

[50] *Anecdotes of Richard Brothers, in the years 1791 and 1792, with some
thoughts upon credulity*, by Joseph Moser, 1795, p. 22.

in 1795, and his last letter is dated from Islington Mad-House, March 18, 1798. Yet he had been frequently rapt up to Heaven, where the Holy Ghost, a beautiful silver bird, keeps between him and the devil. Earlier in his career, he had had luck in prophesying the deaths of Louis XVI and the King of Sweden, and the 1794 title-page of his *Prophecies and times* confidently announces that it was "Wrote under the direction of the Lord God, And Published by his Sacred Command." But when the foretold destruction of the world in 1795, dreaded by many believers and half-believers, did not take place, the influence of Brothers waned; and his self-recorded career, the ultimate in idiosyncratic views of life, closes, like Cruden's, wavering and indeterminate.

In a survey of subjective techniques in life-writing, the transition from lunatic to lover is not necessarily an abrupt one. Both are indeed compact of imagination; and the important events in their lives take place within their minds. The fervent spirit of John Wesley himself furnishes possibly the most intense authentic love-story of the eighteenth century. "An account of an amour"[51] is a detailed story, almost frightening in its directness, of the passionate suffering of three people: Grace Murray, John Wesley and his helper John Bennet, the two men she had promised to marry. While she is torn to pieces in trying to decide where her obligation lies, Charles Wesley appears suddenly on the scene, and, to save the Wesleys' joint cause of revitalizing the Church, contrives to get her married to Bennet. Such, in brief outline, is the story; but in telling it, John Wesley attains almost the proportions of a tragic hero. "If these things are so," he writes (p. 98), "hardly has such a Case been from the beginning of the World!" And the journal of his love is a living autobiography, showing his changing emotions from the ardent and spiritual devotion to a woman at the beginning to the noble renunciation and acceptance of

---

[51] Printed in *Wesley's last love,* Dent, 1910. Its possessor in June 4, 1788, called it a "Diary," but later substituted the title "An account of an amour." The editor, Augustin Leger, brings psychoanalysis to bear in interpreting Wesley's career. Earlier ed., 1848.

God's will at the end. He opens with a quotation from a poem occasioned by this experience:

"What Thou dost, I know not now
but I shall know hereafter!"

and plunges immediately into the story. Few autobiographies concentrate so artistically on a single important episode, or present emotional crises with such sustained power. He describes his own state, on first hearing of Miss Murray's marriage (p. 87):

"I felt the Loss both to me & the People, which I did not expect could ever be repair'd. I tried to sleep: but I tried in vain; for Sleep was fled from my Eyes. I was in a burning Fever, & more & more Thoughts still crouding into my Mind, I perceiv'd, if this continued long, it would affect my Senses. But God took that matter into his Hand; giving me on a sudden, sound & quiet sleep."

And this is his analysis of his feelings on first meeting with Charles Wesley after his brother had taken it upon himself to act the rôle of Providence (p. 88):

"Thurs. 5. about 8. One came in from Newcastle & told us, 'They were married on Tuesday.' My Brother came an hour after. I felt no Anger. Yet I did not desire to see him. But Mr. Wh. [Whitefield] constrain'd me. After a few Words had past, He accosted me with, 'I renounce all intercourse with you, but what I would have with an heathen man or a publican.' I felt little Emotion. It was only adding a drop of water to a drowning man. Yet I calmly accepted his Renunciation, & acquiesced therein. Poor Mr. Wh. & J. Nelson burst into Tears. They pray'd, cried, & intreated, till the Storm past away. We could not speak, but only fell on each other's neck."

Yet he never can entirely forget his brother's action, and, of course, never can entirely recover from this painful fever of the heart. The climax had come in October 1749. He was then forty-six years old. Sixteen months later he married Mary Vazeille, a widow with children. It was not a romance. And, almost forty years later, three years before his death, he sees his first love again. He controls himself.

Here are the last two stanzas of a thirty-one-stanza poem which he composed when the flare of his devotion had sunk to embers; in these lines the sublimation of his emotions brings the story to a close:

> "What thou hast done I know not now!
> Suffice I shall hereafter know!
> Beneath thy chastning Hand I bow:
> That still I live to Thee I owe.
> O teach thy deeply-humbled Son
> To say, 'Father, thy Will be done!'

> "Teach me, from every pleasing Snare
> To keep the Issues of my Heart:
> Be thou my Love, my Joy, my Fear!
> Thou my eternal Portion art.
> Be thou my never-failing Friend,
> And love, O love me to the End!"

The intensity and sincerity of Wesley's feelings, manifest throughout this remarkable journal, help to explain the great personal influence of the evangelist. The outpouring of warm and noble emotions is dominated, under the influence of necessity, by an even greater abnegation and childlike humility. Permeating the whole may be felt a desolation and loneliness of spirit, but a loneliness which John Wesley never allowed to change into despair.

Although John Wesley's account of his thwarted love is magnificent self-revelation, it does not stand alone. Others, less successful, were even more conscious of presenting the contemplative rather than the active life. One biography, written in Latin, was cited more than once as a model for sketching a life subjectively. It was George Garden's *Viri Reverendi Joannis Forbesii à Corse, vita exterior, & vitae interioris brevis idea*, with his *Vitae Forbesianae interioris, sive exercitiorum spiritualium commentaria*, published before the two folio volumes of Forbes's works in Amsterdam in 1703. The spiritual exercises of Forbes, who was Professor of Theology at the University of Aberdeen until his death in 1648, exhale and exude peace, but Garden's summary of their purport is even better. Garden builds up his "brief idea" by some such statements as: "Tota ejus vita, continua fuit praeparatio ad mortem, de ea quotidie meditabatur, ut in Domino et ejus pace decederet quotidie orabat" (p. 89), which he proves by quotations in the rest of a paragraph from Forbes's diaries and meditations. His letters, controversies, and subtle religious opinions are given in full, and it is unusual to see a competent biography organized definitely from such mystical materials as this (pp. 75-6):

". . . Inter opera vero Dei alia sunt extra nos in hoc mundo. . . . Alia sunt opera Dei intra animam, operatio nempe divinae gratiae cor purgans, illuminans, roborans, consolans, ubi Deus animae bonitatem, misericordiam ac immensam suam erga nos dignationem, propriâ experientiâ sentiendam & gustandam praebet, & tunc concipitur non tanquam in supremo coelo regnans, & longe a nobis remotus, sed in animâ nostra, in interiori spiritus nostri praesens, in corde nostro inhabitans, suaviter movens, excitans & inclinans, ut eum velimus, quaeramus & desideremus, cujus operationes divinae sentiuntur, & purae affectiones cordis inde excitantur. . . . Deum intra se [Forbes] sentiebat, non per modum objecti cogniti, sed per modum primi principii operantis voluntatem ad amandum per tactum suum immediatum, & intellectum ad quaerendum faciem & praesentiam ejus, quem cor ita tactum diligit, moventis & applicantis."

Somewhat similar in scope and purpose to the *Vitae interioris brevis idea* is *An account of some remarkable passages in the life of a private gentleman; with reflections thereon. In three parts. Relating to trouble of mind; some violent temptations; and a recovery*. It has been attributed to Defoe, evidently for no better reasons than that it is anonymous and appeared in 1711; for its attempts to show how a cultivated but melancholy gentleman may attain true faith are written with more sincerity than Defoe could muster on such a topic. The biography is purely spiritual, almost mystical; the exact details of the private gentleman's mental temptations are not always given, but his fear of hell fire and his gratitude to God for not yet being consigned there are constant, even when he makes little excursions in favor of public worship or against the presentation of plays. One paragraph describing a spiritual tempest upon hearing a sermon may be quoted, for its parallel may be found in half the religious biographies of the century (p. 103):

"But now such an awe was struck on my Spirit, as tho' I had heard a Voice from Heaven, till Terror and Astonishment possess'd every part of me. The greatest part of the Discourse I apply'd to my Self, which came with such irresistible force upon my Mind, as I ne'er felt before or since. I concluded God spoke to me by the Preacher's Mouth, and sign'd the Destruction of my Soul and Body by some expressions, then providentially made use of: They were very Emphatical, suitable to my Circumstances, portending peculiar inflictions of Punishments, with terrible aggravating circumstances, both as to Loss and Pain; but above all, the Power with which they press'd in upon me, was strangely singular."

And yet, though the confessions deal with such tenuous experiences as this, their authenticity is self-evident and does not require the accompanying attestations of its truth by a physician "F.S." and a chaplain, Richard Mayo, who was himself a biographer. It well fulfills its purpose—"to awaken the Presumptuous, convince the Sceptick, and encourage the Despondent"—in its portrayal of an intelligent gentleman placed at the beginning of a century when rational and religious forces were in conflict (pp. 76-7):

"Thus far have I endeavour'd to traverse the Windings of the subtle old Serpent, with those of my own Heart, thro' the different Stages of my Life, toss'd with so many Storms of Temptations, that often threatned to overset me, and must, had not a kind Hand of Providence continually trim'd the Vessel. . . . I overlook'd Sin, the Wrath of a holy God, and Satan the Executioner: I resolv'd all into Mechanism, the Disorders of the Blood and Spirits, Philosophising on the Subject, as usually do the Sons of Art."

A natural subject for spiritual biography is Henry More, the Cambridge Platonist, who found a fit biographer in Richard Ward. Ward's production (1710) cannot hope to equal the graceful and imaginative autobiographical fragment which Henry

More left of his own youth; but it succeeds in presenting an extended soul-sketch which is bulwarked by quotations from More's writings and by classical *sententiae,* and is indexed in the margin with the qualities of More's mind. Even in the ordered and minute account of More's life, Ward stresses his states of mind and his opinions, never forgetting that (p. 60): "He liv'd and died a private Fellow of Christ's-College in Cambridge." At times, Ward attains More's own rippling and sinuous prose rhythm (p. 68): "He passed in short, like a deep and calm-moving Water, more silently and flowingly; his Course here, yet leaving still as he went (on all sides of him) the rich Tracings of his Passage, all along in those fruitful and admirable Labours he left behind him to the World." To the memory of the bland and dream-rapt author of the *Life of the Soul,* Ward has produced in tribute this more personal *Psychozoia.*

Biographies or autobiographies of Thomas Shepard (1749), John Sharp (*ca.* 1758), Joseph Williams (1779), Philip Henry (1697, corrected in 1712), and John Martin (1797) continue in various ways the deliberate recording of mental life. Lives are conscientiously built up again from the original words and writings of their subjects: Thomas Sharp, for example, devotes a generous part of the life of his father to what he calls "His social virtues and interior life," modelled on Garden's *Forbes;* and Matthew Henry puts together piece by piece a lovingly laborious mosaic to express his father's personality, as he tends his orchard, in sequestration and out, at Broad Oak.

Benjamin Fawcett's *Extracts from the diary, meditations, and letters of Mr Joseph Williams of Kidderminster* (1779) is edited with such intelligence and artistry that it deserves wider recognition. The table of contents is descriptive, making the little book a readable manual of practical devotion. It centers on the reconcilement of a spiritual life with a commercial life and possesses some of the naïve, straightforward self-revelation that is to be found in the autobiographies of seventeenth century dissenters. John Williams, merchant of Kidderminster, is a sincere, somewhat self-righteous Christian, much given to rumination. A great part of his diary (though the entries are arranged chronologically and in full, businesslike detail) is a discourse with his own soul, or advice to himself. Williams's diary covers an extensive period, for the first entry he records dates as far back as 1710, when he was a young man; and the last entry, "His dying comforts" in a letter to his wife, was written only a fortnight before his death in 1755. But mingled with such subjects as "Prosperity in trade," "Promoting piety in a young clergyman," "The religious tradesman," and "His benefit from Bath waters" are other sections vivid and in a class by themselves, such as the exhortation to an old drunken servant whom he meets in a graveyard and who is afraid his tippling and swearing will damn his four children who are there buried, or his "Thoughts on apparitions," or "The death of a child," or "Meditation [on the Last Judgment] among the tombs." His letters are carefully and chronologically interspersed, so that the whole work is outstanding for painstaking integration of character and for power of selection.

The influence of Samuel Johnson is apparent in John Martin's autobiography, written in a series of twenty-one letters and dated March 1797. In addition to two more famous opinions of Doctor Johnson regarding biography, Martin quotes Johnson's (p. 3): "I do not think the life of any literary man in England well written.—Beside the common incidents of life, it should tell us his studies, his mode of living—the means by which he attained to excellence, and his opinion of his own works." Beginning his career a tapster in his father's public-house and ending a sincere, hard-headed Baptist, John Martin writes down his own life as controversialist and preacher without blurring the focus for a moment. His style is direct and simple; he has learned much from the favorite authors of his boyhood, "Pomfret and Pope, Swift and Addison, Shakespear and Dryden, Richardson and Gay" (p. 22); at the age of fifteen he criticizes Young's *Night Thoughts* as boring and "strangely rhapsodical" in comparison with *Paradise Lost*. He is at his best in the analysis of his own instincts. After turning over the religious autobiographies of the century, in which passages similar to the following are characteristic, a reader cannot doubt that the conviction of original sin is fundamental in human nature (p. 10):

"But I had very early, deep notions of my own internal depravity; and from what I have since observed, I now think, that every child is a law to himself, before he is acquainted with any written rule of action. . . .

"This moral law I daily transgressed [i.e. instinctive morality]; and my knowledge of that fact, brought me into bondage. What I suffered on this account, and from my ill state of health, led me to suppose, that I was more polluted than other children; nor could I always think well of my parents, who had, as I imagined, brought a poor child into this world, born to be unholy and unhappy."

Possibly his best bit of self-analysis is his description of day-dreaming, which he refers to as "this mental influenza" (p. 12):

"One thing, while yet a child, I cannot forget. I mean the pleasure I then had in being quite alone, especially in bed, on purpose to indulge a thousand foolish imaginations. In this situation to buy, sell, get gain; to build, plant, travel; to assume what character I pleased, and as I grew up, to act the part of Romeo, Hamlet, King Lear, George Barnwell, or some other theatrical exhibition; to dispute with my equals, and to debate like Nestor and Ulysses, before my superiors; to chastise Thersites, and send him howling to the fleet, and then to be applauded by Agamemnon in the camp; these ambitious whims, and many worse than these, were my delight. How wonderful, said I, is the secret power of the human mind! How amazing the range of human thought! Have all boys this ability in the same degree? If they have, they possess those pleasures of which they cannot be deprived.

"By often indulging such reveries, I discovered somewhat of the grandeur of the human mind; but its extravagance and folly escaped my notice."

In these studies in the imaginative re-presentation of the inner life, the lunatic Alexander Cruden, and the lover, John Wesley, have been considered. There yet remains the poet. This section on subjective life-writing may well end with the *Memoirs of the early life of William Cowper, Esq. written by himself* (1816 ed., wr. *ca.* 1765), the flowering into art of the evangelical autobiographies of God's mercies. Poignant and humble in its tone, in this narrative the reader sees the clouds approach, the storm break, and Cowper desperately overwhelmed in his first seizure of madness. Then, at the last, and for a time, there is the blessing of faint sunlight. The prose is simple and direct, but, as one might expect from Cowper's unsurpassed letters, it records subtle mental experiences with amazing clarity. At the outset, Cowper states that he intends what follows as the "history of my heart, so far as religion has been its object." He is quite aware of his innate timidity. He remembers, when he was six years old, at school in Bedfordshire, the cruelty of an older boy (p. 2): "he had, by his savage treatment of me, impressed such a dread of his figure upon my mind, that I well remember being afraid to lift up my eyes upon him, higher than his knees. . . . I knew him by his shoe-buckles, better than any other part of his dress." He tries to find comfort in his mind by remembering the words of the Psalmist, "I will not be afraid of what man can do unto me." Even in childhood, thoughts of death and the grave alarm his conscience.

But his great struggle came in early manhood when he was preparing himself for examinations. In his dejection as a student in the Temple, he writes (p. 9): "At length I met with Herbert's Poems; and, gothic and uncouth as they were, I yet found in them a strain of piety which I could not but admire. This was the only author I had any delight in reading. I pored over him all day long." As the day which he found so fearful approached, when he must stand a public trial for the clerkship of the journals in the House of Lords, he admits that he looked upon madness as his only means of escape (p. 26):

"My chief fear was, that my senses would not fail me time enough to excuse my appearance at the bar of the House of Lords, which was the only purpose I wanted it to answer. . . .

"Now came the grand temptation; the point to which Satan had all the while been driving me; the dark and hellish purpose of self-murder."

There succeeds, in Cowper's limpid phrasing, the account of grisly psychic sufferings, as he turns over in his mind the possibilities of laudanum, the knife, the halter (p. 34):

"Distracted between the desire of death, and the dread of it, twenty times I had the phial to my mouth, and as often received an irresistible check; and even at the time it seemed to me, that an invisible hand swayed the bottle downwards, as often as I set it against my lips."

With shuddering fascination he describes the horror before he pours the laudanum into foul water and throws the whole away. The night before his appearance at the bar he wakes at three (p. 39):

"Immediately I arose, and by the help of a rush-light, found my penknife, took it into bed with me, and lay with it for some hours directly pointed against my heart. Twice, or thrice, I placed it upright under my left breast, leaning all my weight upon it; but the point was broken off, and would not penetrate."

At seven o'clock, resolving that there shall be "no more dallying with the love of life," he hangs himself with his garter, which breaks after he has lost consciousness.

As a sequel to such humiliation, impotence, and despair, Cowper's calm prose presents mental horror in trivial external actions (pp. 49-50):

"I never went into the street, but I thought the people stood and laughed at me, and held me in contempt; and could hardly persuade myself, but that the voice of my conscience was loud enough for every one to hear it. They who knew me, seemed to avoid me; and if they spoke to me, seemed to do it in scorn. I bought a ballad of one who was singing it in the street, because I thought it was written on me.

"I dined alone, either at the tavern, where I went in the dark, or at the chop-house, where I always took care to hide myself in the darkest corner of the room. I slept generally an hour in the evening; but it was only to be terrified in dreams; and when I awoke, it was some time before I could walk steadily through the passage into the dining-room. I reeled and staggered like a drunken man; the eyes of man I could not bear; but when I thought that the eyes of God were upon me, (which I felt assured of,) it gave me the most intolerable anguish."

Both his brother and Mr. Madan try to save him, but he approaches nearer and nearer to the dizzying edge, and at last falls into the abyss of madness. Even this experience, which seems beyond the reach of autobiography, is caught up in the beautiful sentences that flow on with the unimpassioned impersonality of great art (pp. 58-9):

"While I traversed the apartment, in the most horrible dismay of soul, expecting every moment, that the earth would open her mouth and swallow me; my conscience scaring me, the avenger of blood pursuing me, and the city of refuge out of reach and out of sight; a strange and horrible darkness fell upon me. If it were possible, that a heavy blow could light on the brain, without touching the skull, such was the sensation I felt. I clapped my hand to my forehead, and cried aloud, through the pain it gave me. At every stroke, my thoughts and expressions became more wild and incoherent; all that remained clear was the sense of sin, and the expectation of punishment. These kept undisturbed possession all through my illness, without interruption or abatement." This illness of desolation and despair was to endure for months.

"The happy period which was to shake off my fetters" (p. 67) comes when, in Romans iii:25, he reads of: "Whom God hath set forth to be a propitiation through faith in his blood, to declare his righteousness for the remission of sins that are past, through the forbearance of God" (p. 67). Yet, as he sinks again into despair, when the hope of living with his friends the Unwins touches him, he is so shrinking, humble, and lonely, so naked on the sharp shingle of the world, that (p. 81): "From the moment this thought struck me, such a tumult of anxious solicitude seized me, that for two or three days I could not divert my mind to any other subject."

But the Unwins rescue him, and the simple account closes with Cowper in (p. 83) "my new abode, Nov. 11, 1765." Possibly it was written at the request of Mrs. Unwin, who, at any rate (p. 80), "will be one of the first who will have the perusal of this narrative." The fever had been prolonged; now a sick soul turns toward convalescence. Only out of great trust in some friend, only out of a deep love of God, could such memoirs be written, neither abject nor full of spiritual pride, narrating without hysteria the descent into darkness and the return to light. The autobiography is written by the poet who could treat of the castaway among the Atlantic billows, drowning in darkness as his ship sails on, and who could end his poem:

> "But I beneath a rougher sea,
> And whelmed in deeper gulfs than he."

The despair is the same, and the art is comparable. In no biography has the terror of desolation been more perfectly recorded than in Cowper's account of his early life; the darkness and the fever have been so prolonged that few readers can avoid a sigh of relief when at the end, like false-fire glimmering in a dark wood, there appears the uncertain gleam of hope as a sick soul turns toward convalescence.

In shaping a life, the importance of intangible conviction, though it may vary from steady purpose to hallucination, is evident in the biographies of the time. The cast of mind that led to William Cowper's tragic belief that he was damned, a belief that threw such terrible shadows on his own life, is present also when he writes the life of John Cowper (p. 1770). Here is a scene between the brothers (1802 ed., p. 14):

"At night, when he was quite worn out with the fatigue of labouring for breath, and could get no rest, his asthma still continuing, he turned to me, and said, with a melancholy air, 'Brother, I seem to be marked out for misery; you know some people are so.' That moment I felt my heart enlarged, and such a persuasion of the love of God towards him was wrought in my soul, that I replied with confidence, and as if I had authority given me to say it, 'But that is not your case; you are marked out for mercy.'"

An intuition of salvation which he could never long experience for himself, William Cowper experiences for his dying brother (pp. 15-16):

"I thought I could discern, in these expressions, the glimpses of approaching day, and have no doubt at present but that the Spirit of God was gradually preparing him, in a way of true humiliation, for that bright display of gospel-grace which he was soon after pleased to afford him."

In eighteenth century lives, the visions of Blake and of Christopher Smart were closer to many men than they are today, for biography had not gone far from Arise Evans, the wild Welsh prophet of Cromwell's day who pricked his jailer with a piece of glass because if you bleed a Witch, the Witch can't hurt you, and who could write (1653 ed., p. 9): "And seeing the Sun at its rising, skip, play, dance, and turn about like a wheel, I fell down upon my knees," or (p. 33): "there came in at the window a round Cloud, in colour like unto the Rain bowe, and it covered me, abiding upon me about a quarter of an hour, and when it came upon me I was so revived as if I had eaten all the delicates in the world; and after a quarter of an hour the Cloud departed out at the window in the same manner as it came in, untill it ascended out of my sight."

Cotton Mather presents in his *Life of Sir William Phips* (1697) not only the wars in Quebec and the treasure hunts in the Bermudas, but also "war with the invisible world" in the Salem witch trials. Duncan Campbell records in his *Secret memoirs* (1732) with perfect certainty (p. 6):

"I very well know, that from my Birth I have had the constant Attendance of both a good and bad Angel: I am confident of it, and have such undeniable Proofs, that the Being of a Sun, Moon, or Stars is not more certain to me, nor do I ascribe any thing extraordinary to myself in this: It is my Opinion, that great Numbers of People, especially in the first Ages of the World, have been thus attended."

The gradations from such primitive ideas, through John Macdonald's desire to see the devil, to Cowper's tragic conviction, John Martin's fantasies, or Major Ramkins's *tour de force* as he recollects in delirium all his past life, are often difficult to mark. The human mind is a chameleon. Dream and truth, the subjective and the objective, cannot be separated. The unquestioned realities of one age become the absurd superstitions of the next. And the best generalization which may be made in this chapter is that the eighteenth century at least began to realize that truth is not necessarily or wholly discoverable in outward action.

2. THE BIOGRAPHER AS MORALIST

After analysis and discovery, judgment.

To what end, it is reasonable to inquire, did eighteenth century biographers turn their greater knowledge of human consciousness, their record of man's thoughts and intentions as well as of his actions? The answer, naturally enough, is ethical. In no branch of literature is moral judgment more important than in biography, dealing as it must with the actions of actual men. It is therefore necessary to set down and illustrate the ethical beliefs, conscious or unconscious, of eighteenth century biographers.

As usual, theory did not keep pace with practice. The records of the purely contemplative (as opposed to the active) life increased greatly as the century progressed. Yet contemporary theorists rarely notice, and do little to explain, this unquestionable fact. The improved status of the artist and philosopher, the popular respect for writers, the increased interest in all the sciences, the greater conscious familiarity with psychological processes which this very chapter has illustrated, the Age of Reason itself—any or all of these may help to account for the greater number of biographies that center on mental states rather than on external events. The point remains that whether such a shift in interest was caused by the foundation of the Royal Society or the Society of Antiquaries, by the regular appearance of the *Gentleman's Magazine* or by the currency of Locke's conception of the human understanding, by Frederick the Great's admiration for Voltaire or General Wolfe's supposed remark about the author of the *Elegy written in a country churchyard,* the contemporary critics of biography overlooked the change almost entirely.

This disregard applies only to the records of *mental* life and growth. The value of the spiritual life as opposed to the life of action had long been a commonplace in biographical forewords, so that the following paragraph may be taken as typical of a belief often expressed during the century:[52]

"We are apt to gaze with admiration on the mighty conquerors of the world, and celebrate the praises of those, who through toil

[52] Sollom Emlyn's life of his father, before Thomas Emlyn's *Works,* 3 vols., 1746; Vol. I, p. v.

and danger have gained some signal victory, and triumphed over potent enemies; but surely the victory over the flesh and the world, over all temptations to betray our integrity from the allurements of earthly honours and riches on the one hand, or the terrors of reproach and sufferings on the other, is a no less difficult and arduous task, requires no less pains and steady courage, and is therefore no less illustrious, nor merits less our applauses; for whoever would triumph in this warfare, must endure hardships as a good soldier of Christ."

Only gradually, and it would seem almost accidentally, the possibility of biography as the record of a mind is realized, as in these sentences:[53]

"Family Pictures have always been in much Esteem, because they represent to us, the Face and Countenance of our Ancestors. A Family History is a Picture of their Minds, and represents to us the noble Qualities thereof, by which they were enabled and pusht forward to atchieve great and heroick Actions; and so the one is as much to be preferr'd to the other, as the Virtues of the Mind are to the Features of the Face."

The worth of the record of mental life is stated even more clearly in the translation of Condorcet's *Voltaire* (1790), and it is more than probable that much of the growing ability in mental analysis was introduced from France (p. 2):

"Every circumstance relating to such a man promotes the study of the human mind; with which we cannot hope to become acquainted if we do not observe its properties as they exist in those to whom Nature has been prodigal of her riches and her power, and if we do not seek in such minds what they possess in common with others, and in what they are distinguished."

Apart from the belief in the value of the life of the mind, a belief made evident by practice rather than theory, the development of the ethical theory of eighteenth century biography might be summarized as follows: the time-honored statement that biography is of use to the reader in helping him to imitate virtue and avoid vice was widely accepted, illustrated very neatly in many individual productions, questioned by some, and finally replaced

[53] *The history of the ancient, noble, and illustrious family of Gordon*, by William Gordon, 1726-1727, 2 vols. Ded. pp. v-vi, to Vol. I.

by ethical beliefs not formulated so simply or clearly, but tending toward a conception of life which was more complex, based on understanding, sympathy, and tolerance rather than on mechanical or melodramatic justice.

The ethical beliefs of the century, and particularly the importance of new theories which to the twentieth century reader seem familiar enough, cannot be fully grasped unless the prevalence of the old doctrine of biography teaching by example is emphasized. The conception of biography as the dispassionate record of fact is of relatively recent growth. The antiquarian spirit and the biographical collections did much to promote it; religious skepticism and social curiosity helped it along in the eighteenth century; the encyclopedic tendencies and the prevalence of the scientific method during the nineteenth century have now made it a commonplace. Yet only rarely during the eighteenth century does one come across such remarks as: "This being Design'd only as a Narrative of Facts, we do not pretend to enter upon his Character,"[54] or: "It becomes the moralist to advance, as the biographer retires."[55] Colley Cibber is not reflecting either the general opinions or the practice of the century when he writes of Middleton's *Cicero*:[56] "What is Cicero to him, or he to Cicero, that he should fret for him? The Merit of a Biographer is not at all concerned in the Virtues or the Imperfections of his Hero; Truth only is the Regard that ought to govern him." Far more typical is the remark of Robert Bisset:[57] "Biography involves in it not merely fact, but also reflection and discussion."

[54] George Smith Green's *Oliver Cromwell*, 1752. The biography here, however, was designed as a supplement to an accompanying historical play.
[55] George Dyer's *Memoirs of Robert Robinson*, 1796, p. 404.
[56] *The character and conduct of Cicero, considered*, 1747, p. 278.
[57] "A biographical sketch of the authors of the Spectator," Vol. I, 1793, p. x. before 8-vol. ed. of *The Spectator*. cf. also the opening of the Preface to *A brief account of the life and writings of Terence*, 1799: "It is generally expected in writing Biography, as in Travels, instead of copying the relations of those who have handled the subject before us, we should produce a series of our own observations, such as an attentive survey of the facts and places suggested to our own minds. Such is generally expected from Biographers. . . ." Yet cf. also Robert Bisset's *Edmund Burke*, 1798, p. 12: "To narrative biography only (accord-

Granted, then, that the aim of the biographer is to interpret as well as to record, how shall his interpretation prove most efficacious? Only if it inspires to righteous living, was the generally accepted answer. Vicesimus Knox, who theorizes at some length about biography, phrases this belief as follows:[58] "Biography is the species of history best adapted to teach wisdom in private life. There are many lives of English worthies, which cannot be attentively read by an ingenuous young man, without exciting an ardour of virtue."

And for a complete statement of the theory of the didactic function of biography, nothing better can be chosen than the preface to the 1762 abridgment of Plutarch's *Lives,* probably written by Oliver Goldsmith:[59]

"Biography has, ever since the days of Plutarch, been considered as the most useful manner of writing, not only from the pleasure it affords the imagination, but from the instruction it artfully and unexpectedly conveys to the understanding. It furnishes us with an opportunity of giving advice freely, and without offence. It not only removes the dryness and dogmatical air of precept, but sets persons, actions, and their consequences before us in the most striking manner; and by that means turns even precept into example: Whence arises the propriety of placing these volumes in the hands of youth. . . .

"An ingenious gentleman of my acquaintance, when asked what was the best lesson for youth? answered, *The life of a good man:* being asked, what was the next best? replied, *The life of a bad one;* for, that the first would make him in love with virtue, and teach him how to conduct himself through life, so as to become an ornament to society, and a blessing to his family and friends; and the last would point out the hateful and horrid consequences of vice, and make him careful to avoid those actions which appeared so detestable in others."

ing to Lord Bacon's distinction) does the author pretend, and arrogates to himself no qualities beyond those which it requires:—knowledge of important facts, veracity and impartiality in recording them."

[58] *Winter evenings,* 1790, 2d ed., Essay XXI, "On imitation of a model for the conduct of life."

[59] In 5 vols. Vol. I, pp. [iii]-iv, and vi.

All the familiar arguments are to be found in this quotation: that example is a better teacher than precept, that the biography of a good man inculcates virtue, and that the biography of a bad man renders vice hateful. One point that the writer makes—the usefulness of biography in educating children—should be emphasized. This function for biography became common before the end of the century. Mrs. Mary Hopkins Pilkington issues her *Biography for boys; or, characteristic histories, calculated to impress the youthful mind with an admiration of virtuous principles and detestation of vicious ones* in 1799, and her *Biography for girls* with a similar title in the same year. Each one of this baker's dozen of lives is a complete biography in form, ending with the exact year of its subject's death, his or her age, place of burial, and a didactic epitaph in ballad stanzas. Yet the imaginary histories are so fanatically and unswervingly moral that they should be reprinted as amusing curiosities. Here, for the improvement of twentieth century youth, are the contents of her *Biography for girls:*

> "Louisa Harrington; or, the Victim of Pride
> Emily Manley; or, Gratitude Displayed
> Sally Bowman; or, Filial Fondness
> Emma Hamilton; or, Human Vicissitudes
> Lucy Lutridge; or, Vanity Punished
> Frances Hindos; or, the Amiable Orphan."

Mrs. Pilkington was not a pioneer in this teaching the young idea how to shoot through the medium of didactic biography. In 1798 had appeared *The British Nepos,* a popular collection designed for the youth of the nation, which presented its half hundred subjects, ranging from King Alfred to Captain Cook, because they "have distinguished themselves by their virtues, talents, or remarkable advancement in life." The spirit of this sententious work is made manifest in the frontispiece, which shows "The Genius of Biography" with a torch, leading two children up a hill which is crowned by a Pantheon adorned with the busts of great men. As early as 1773 William Cooke had published, particularly for youth, *The way to the temple of true hon-*

our and fame by the paths of heroic virtue; exemplified in the most entertaining lives of the most eminent persons of both sexes.

Such professional didacticism seems to have grown out of the *Spectator* and the *Rambler* papers. Addison's moral observations are given cogency by biographical anecdotes, character sketches, or even careers in detail; and Johnson uses this technique even more frequently in the *Rambler* and *Idler* essays, which, in the manner of the other Jonson, indicate the "humours" of his characters with obvious names, or give life-sketches of actual persons under thin disguises. A transitional title between Addison and the didactic biographers for the very young is *Modern characters: illustrated by histories in real life, and address'd to the polite world,* which appeared in 1753. These cautionary tales, which number twenty-five in two volumes, may be represented by the twelfth: *Of the Distresses that may attend an obstinacy of temper. The fate of Flavia.* They are of such a nature that their neo-classic heroes and heroines seem to be the productions of Eliza Haywood, author of the *Female Spectator* and of the *History of Miss Betsy Thoughtless*—an edifying novel cast in biographical mold.[60]

The titles quoted so far have, in the main, introduced semifictional biographies, because in that field the imagination, untrammelled by actual happenings, more easily shapes material in accord with biographical theory as to the function of recorded lives. Yet actual careers may be cast in the pattern of a moral essay. Major James George Semple Lisle was an adventurer and traveller, eventually transported from England to Australia for defrauding tradesmen, although both Burke and Boswell wrote letters interceding for him. Yet when this soldier, Lothario, and cheat writes his *Faithful narrative of his alternate vicissitudes of splendor and misfortune* (1799), he gives the world a *Rambler* essay, in which the moral he advances is the result of the bitter experience of his whole life. Even the style is Johnsonian. Here, for instance, is his generalization as he looks back over his career (pp. 369-70 and 367):

[60] It may be noted that Haywood's *The fortunate foundlings: being the genuine history of Colonel M———rs [Manners], and his sister, Madam de P———y,* 1744, has as subtitle: "The whole calculated for the entertainment and improvement of the youth of both sexes."

"But where a youth sets out with high spirits, conspicuous talents, indulgent friends, and a small fortune, his ruin is next to inevitable; life is to him a perpetual ambuscade, with a thousand masked batteries ready to play upon him at every turn; his vanity is flattered, his senses amused, his companions press him to become the partaker of their pleasures, his enemies endeavour to entice him to destruction; he yields himself up to gaiety and expence, till at length he falls, and dunces rise on his ruin."

"Violent passions, the almost inseparable companions of a vigorous constitution, call upon youth, with an importunity nearly unceasing; experience, the surest guide, is inevitably wanting; example invites, splendour displays its allurements, fashion leads the way, and ruin too often follows. Gay, honest, unsuspecting, and generous, the young man rushes on to pleasure, and considering interest as trash, is apt to weigh the property of others as lightly as he does his own; amusements incur expence, and expence degenerates into prodigality. To supply those pleasures now become almost necessary to his existence; he contracts debts, which he cannot pay; he shifts from his creditors; his gay companions forsake him, as an incumbrance on their joyous moments; poverty stares him in the face, and actions, at which his soul recoils, become the only possible means of subsisting. If an accidental supply falls in his way, his relish for pleasure returns; he embraces it with an appetite sharpened by abstinence; he is again involved, and disgrace succeeds to ruin."

The belief in the power of biography to teach by means of example, therefore, was widely and sincerely held. The sins of others might enable a reader to keep from making his own life worse; the virtues of other lives would help him in bettering his own. This ideal has seldom been phrased more beautifully than by William Jones, chaplain to George Horne, Bishop of Norwich, whose life he writes:[61]

"All good men are walking by the same way to the same end. If there are any individuals, who by the shining of their light render the path more plain and pleasant, let us agree to make the

[61] 1795. Quotations from 1818 ed., p. 197.

most we can of them, and be 'followers of them, who through faith and patience inherit the promises.' "

The phraseology here is Biblical; in religious circles biography came definitely to be regarded as a moral exercise. The striking development of Quaker and Wesleyan memoirs furnishes the best illustration of the power of biography to guide and inspirit others.[62] But biography was studied and collected for edification outside these religious movements. Of unique interest are the pages prefatory to *Two select and exemplary lives, of two paro-chial ministers* (1728). The compiler here lists more than a score of "Lives of several Excellent Persons, worthy the Perusal of a Divine." "It will be generally agreed by all who are conversant in Books, that there is no Part of History more Useful and Enter-taining, than Biography." For parochial ministers, the author believes the lives of ecclesiastics who triumph over error and ob-stacles, and especially the "Lives and Sufferings of Confessors and Martyrs," are most useful; in the production which follows he reprints Carleton's seventeenth century life of Gilpin and a brief account of the Reverend Mr. John Rawlet.

Moreover, one good life inspires another. The Journals of George Fox and John Wesley set many private pens at work; and the perusal of various individual biographies led to imitations in life or in life-writing. Dr. Theophilus Lobb is not alone in this. "As it was with Dr. Lobb," records his biographer,[63] "on his reading the life of the Rev. Matthew Henry, so it should be with all, into whose hands these papers may fall; 'Through the grace of God, says he, I perceive the usefulness of such practice, and, ac-cordingly, depending on the assistance of the Holy Spirit, I now apply myself to the imitation of that eminent servant of Jesus Christ.' "

But the recording of exemplary lives has obvious drawbacks. Simple truth may be sacrificed in favor of a powerful lesson. If the lives of their heroes are less perfect, biographers fear they will

---

[62] As a single example, see *Piety promoted, in brief memorials, of the virtuous lives, services, and dying sayings, of some of the people called Quakers, formerly published in eight parts.* 1789 t.p., 3 vols. Other editions during the century were 1703 (the 2d ed.), 1711, 1721, 1723, 1759-1771.

[63] *The power of faith and godliness exemplified, in some memoirs of Theophilus Lobb,* by John Greene, 1767, p. 2.

lose their didactic force. Usually these efforts to twist, train, or suppress the truth for the sake of simple teaching are masked in some way, but John Greene is frank enough to admit (p. 7): "It is not my design to write the Life of Dr. Lobb, but only to give an account of his piety." And William Enfield is equally frank when he writes:[64] "The Author of these Discourses thinks it necessary to inform his readers, that he means to assume the character of the Biographer, only in subordination to that of the Preacher."

A second danger in the biographies for Christian edification is that the unblemished ideal which the heroes exemplified or which their biographers claimed for them may make their lives uninteresting and uniform in monotony. There are thousands of foibles, weaknesses, and idiosyncrasies; there is only one perfection: If "all good men are walking by the same way to the same end," the account of the journey, retailed for the twentieth time, may seem dull. Such ennui must be felt at times by all dispassionate observers of the multitudinous Methodist and Quaker biographies.

A more serious danger is that in the definite desire to create pious monuments to the goodness of God, the personality of the Christian hero may vanish almost completely. The evangelical encyclopedist Erasmus Middleton realizes this, though it is significant that his attempt to set up pious memorials destroys the possibility of biography:[65]

"There is also an additional difficulty, which attends the Christian Biographer, when he aims to describe the characters of extraordinary men, and which the writers of others lives are generally allowed to forget:—He must so represent the motives and actions of the persons he offers to view, as to remind his Readers, that they, no less than himself, are to consider the uncommon excellencies of some characters, not as resulting from the mere force or acumen of natural ability, but as flowing entirely from the Divine Bounty for purposes of his own appointment. Otherwise, instead of rightly placing them in a view for an imitation,

[64] *Biographical sermons: or, a series of discourses on the principal characters in Scripture*, 1777. Advt.
[65] *Biographia evangelica*, 1779-1786, 4 vols. Vol IV, pp. 294-5, under Jonathan Edwards.

attainable in any degree only through grace, or for an encouragement, reviving to the soul through the same grace; we should only set up idols, though idols of more worth than gold, and lead others astray, as well as ourselves, from the One great Object of the christian life, which is Jesus Christ and his fulness which filleth all in all."

The hostility between the biographical ideal and the Christian didactic purpose is nowhere more evident than in casual remarks dropped by the Reverend William Romaine in his life of the Reverend Thomas Jones:[66] "Of what related to God's gracious dealings with his soul," he writes, "I have given an account in his funeral sermon; and as to other particulars of his life, it is of no consequence to lay them before the public. However I shall repeat two or three things, which tend to exalt the glory of God." And later: "He had many precious graces, but don't mistake me. Whatever Mr. Jones had, except sin, he had it from Christ; whose love to him I would magnify from the greatness of the blessings bestowed." The brief life ends with: "Reader, this is a little sketch of Mr. Jones's christian life and death. And what thinkest thou of him? Is thy life like his?" Hortatory throughout in its presentation of its spiritual-theological exemplar, Romaine's *Jones* is not a biography but a manual of devotion.

To magnify God's goodness, accidents and every-day happenings are exaggerated, until the world becomes a maelstrom of dangers from which only the saints escape with their lives. Many biographies of the period were issued with titles hardly less lurid than the following, which had run through six editions by 1787: *God's protecting providence, man's surest help and defence . . . evidenced in the remarkable deliverance of Robert Barrow, with divers other persons, from the devouring waves of the sea; amongst which they suffered shipwrack: and also, from the cruel devouring jaws of the inhumane canibals of Florida* (1700). The records of such deliverances, in which the number of escapes determines the favor of the Lord to his elect, cannot be considered as the revelation of individual personality.

---

[66] Prefixed to Jones's *Works,* 1764, 3d ed., pp. vi, xv, and xix.

The more serious the didactic purpose, the less effective was this revelation of individual personality. This may be taken as an almost invariable rule. The Reverend Mr. Richard Pearsall presents his *Power and pleasure of the divine life: exemplify'd in the late Mrs. Housman, of Kidderminster* (1744) so that his readers may contemplate her life and triumphant death, as he phrases it, "in order to an Assimulation." And playing a variation upon one of the new popular images of the century, he introduces an Egyptian parallel in the following words (p. xvii):

"The ancient Egyptians embalmed the Bodies of their deceased Relations, and thus preserving them from Putrefaction, placed them standing upright in their Sepulchres or Houses; that by often viewing them they might be put in mind of their Virtues in order to a pious Imitation. This is the Reason that I have attempted to embalm this excellent Person, that you might have her in your Houses."

Unfortunately, too often in these pious biographies, that was exactly the effect secured: of something without life, an uncomfortable admonition to virtue, stiffly and awkwardly embalmed, and only faintly suggesting the spirit which had once inhabited dry bones.

The eighteenth century was to some extent aware of the defects inherent in purely exemplary biography, and viewed with occasional skepticism the lives of the unco guid. Thus, the *Monthly Review* dismisses *The power of faith and godliness exemplified, in some memoirs of Theophilus Lobb,* which has been quoted earlier in this chapter, with neat sarcasms which sufficiently show the prevalence of evangelical biographies:[67]

"From these Memoirs we learn, that the late Dr. Lobb was born; that he suck'd in non-conformity with his mother's milk; that he was himself a Dissenting minister (in Somersetshire and elsewhere) before he became a physician; that in the year 1713, when he was 35 years old, and eleven years after his commencing preacher, the Devil and the Doctor grew very intimate . . . that notwithstanding the power of faith and godliness were thus manifested in this good man, something or other was still the

[67] Vol. 36, pp. 244-5, for 1767.

matter, so that he and his congregation frequently disagreed, particularly about his sermons; that in 1722, he lost his 'godly and loving wife' and prayed to God to provide him another in her stead; that 'God graciously heard and answer'd his prayers,' and that the Dr. was very thankful; . . . that Fees not coming in very fast at first, he prayed to God for a comfortable supply of Patients, and that 'in kind answer to his prayers, God was pleased to procure employment for him as a physician;' that, finally, the Doctor lived to the age of eighty-four,—and then experienced, that he was himself as mortal as his patients, tho' he probably outlived most of them:—and here ends our Summary of the principal events recorded in this *edifying* 'exemplification of the Power of Faith and Godliness.' "

The crude belief in biography as a help in imitating virtue came to be examined critically in the eighteenth century. What can be said of the other side of the coin, biography as a guide in avoiding vice? At the beginning of the century, the numerous biographies of criminals, with almost complete unanimity, and, one cannot help feeling, with equal hypocrisy, proclaimed their moral purpose. The *Tyburn Chronicle,* with the effective subtitle of "Villainy display'd in all its branches," states: "If we reflect on the strong propensity of mankind to evil, and on the force of bad examples, we shall be at no loss to account for the great number of executions which disgrace our age and nation"; and yet can continue on the same page, with no apparent sense of inconsistency:[68] "This work is therefore offered to the public, and especially to the younger part of the world, as a *warning-piece* to avoid the fatal snares by which others have been deluded." After such a declaration of purpose, the sordid lives, the robberies, murders, prison scenes and hangings are presented with the determination "to blend the useful with the agreeable"! Although the majority of the sensational biographies offer no more than conventional lip-service to the ethical ideal, individual works are filled with the zeal of the genuine reformer. There can be no doubt, for instance, of the moral purpose back of George Trosse's amazing revelation of his hallucinations and despair. And from

[68] Pref., p. vi, Vol. I of 4-vol. ed., n.d. but *post* 1768.

such phrasing as: "The best and greatest Assemblies, were his greatest Delight; Balls, Opera's, Comedies, Hunting, Gaming, Feastings, and all Sorts of Diversions his chief Employment; nice in his Dyet, curious in his Dress, vain in his Equipage, profuse, and prodigal in his Expences,"[69] one can predict without much trouble the simple lines of the narrative, in which a wild young man is gradually tamed and brought to a Christian life.

The most thoroughgoing of these biographies which were to promote reform through the presentation of a horrifying example is *Memoirs of the life of Mr Josiah Tomkins, late student of medicine in the University of Edinburgh. Exhibiting his fatal seduction to vice, his sincere conversion, his awful warnings to his companions in iniquity, and his joyful and triumphant death. Collected by James Nassau, Esq; his companion in sin and repentance* (1774). Both subject and biographer lead parallel lives; they turn from their studies to drinking, gay companions, and light women; they become diseased, contract consumption, cough, repent, and die. Dissipation in Edinburgh sounds rather decorous and philosophical, as in the temptation scene in which Tomkins entices Nassau astray (p. 6):

"Mr N——u, you will find it to be greatly advantageous to you, to frequent our company at certain times, and indulge the pleasure of an enlivening glass. Man is a sociable creature. . . ."

Nassau's burning seriousness, however, leads him to present his convictions, gained through the observation of two lives, in full and flowing periods of pulpit oratory (p. 16):

"Lust and ebriety indulged to excess, will waste the firmest strength, and enervate the strongest body. Poor T——s must sigh out a farewell to lust and wine; his fine constitution, his blooming face, and charming air, must give place to weakness, to paleness, and ghastly looks! the enlivener of conversation, the favourite of the ladies, the eloquent, accomplished lover, the charming youth, must bid adieu to all pleasurable scenes, groan on a sickbed, and die! Who can bear the thought! Death! How melancholy is the sound! What! must the gay youth! the fine gentleman! the man who gloried in his excellent constitution! the man

[69] *A short discourse upon the life and death of Mr. Geo. Throckmorton,* 1706, p. 17.

who seemed to be the pride of human nature! and formed to
please, whom? the ladies, the elegant, the polite ladies, who triumph in their charms, their bewitching beauty, their graceful
shape, their transporting air, their musical voices, their sparkling
eyes, their ———, be no more! must he be numbered among the
dead, and reckoned among those who have been?—A consumption at last seized Mr. T——s."

Overdidactic and rhetorical as this is, its youthful sincerity is so
intense in its design "to repress Levity and Lewdness" that one is
hardly tempted to smile even by the dedication, which runs in
part: "To All Atheists and Infidels, The Sons of Vice and Dissipation, The lewd Offspring of pious or graceless Parents, All
thoughtless and secure Sinners, Every Hater of God and Religion, and All self-righteous Pharisees. . . ."

Yet such determination to reform the world by teaching men
to shun its wicked courses is not common; and criticism of
those who prefix moral justifications to obviously immoral tracts
is soon vocal. The dedication of *The adventures of John Le-Brun*
(1739) declares:[70]

"My whole Design is to divert an idle Hour; and as there are
Thousands in this Town who have nothing but idle Hours, I
doubt not but I shall have a large Number of Readers:—and if
the many Examples of Vice and Debauchery I have inserted,
shou'd any ways contribute to their Reformation, I shall think
my Book has more Merit than ever I thought it had."

This statement is, of course, a frank recognition that the
biographer's purpose is to amuse, rather than to improve, the
reader; and such a purpose, increasingly held during the century, has slight place in this discussion of biography as a guide
to life. But a modified attitude toward the record of iniquity
should be mentioned here. This theory does not assume that one
reads the horrible life of a hanged robber in order to avoid
being hanged oneself; it records weaknesses or vices so that the
reader may understand more fully the possibilities of human life,
so that he may avoid being duped by cynicism and idealism alike,
or by convention, stupidity, or superficiality. Thus the comedian

---

[70] pp. ii-iii. This is a novel in autobiographical form.

Samuel Foote issued early in his life the memoirs of his uncle Sir John Dinely Goodere, murdered by the contrivance of Sir John's own brother (1741). He publishes this account because he wishes to show the world how erroneous its judgments may be.

" 'Tis a great Misfortune," he writes (pp. 5-6), "that we seldom or never hit the true Characters of Men, which is very often as much owing to the Artifice of a Knave, who knows how to cloak his Vices, as to our own Prejudice, Ignorance, or Uncharitableness; hence it is that Captain Goodere, was counted a Man of Honour till he murder'd his Brother, and Sir John Dinely, a plain honest Gentleman, was reckoned a very sad Fellow, lived almost universally hated, and died unlamented."

Similarly, Thomas Nugent, in the preface to his translation of Benvenuto Cellini, ingeniously apologizes for his rascally subject (1771, p. viii):

". . . we should endeavour betimes to know human vices . . . wisdom in a great measure consists in avoiding those dangers, which too often take their rise from weakly believing in the goodness of the human heart. . . . Should the following history contribute to this end, that is, to promote the knowledge of human nature, and to supply the place of experience, I shall think myself very happy."

Here, certainly, biography is tending toward a new ideal: it will have served its purpose, and a moral purpose, if it increases our understanding of human nature, if it helps in seeing life steadily and seeing it whole.

Yet the acknowledgment of the complexity of life was not easily or immediately granted; before accepting it, the eighteenth century tested to the full a simpler, clearer, more rational interpretation of a man's career: the belief in a ruling passion.

Whether it sprang from Theophrastus, medieval allegory, or Latin and Elizabethan comedy, the idea of the ruling passion resulted in many instances in simplified biography. According to Pope's enthusiastic explanation in his *Moral Essays,* Number IV, every man is dominated by a single passion, often hidden; determine this mainspring of his being and all his actions and his secondary characteristics may be clearly interpreted. Following this theory, which becomes a commonplace of the century, biographers selected and arranged their details in order to present a career with complete economy. Topham's life of John Elwes the miser (1790) is an outstanding example. Another is Coxe's *Walpole* (1798), in which the cult of the ruling passion can be seen shaping a long career into a comprehensible whole (p. 744):

"The portrait of a Minister is to be traced from the history of his whole administration. Candour therefore requires that we should not judge by the selection of detached parts, but combine the whole in a connective series, and referring his conduct to one grand principle of action, judge of it as critics do of an epic poem, by comprehending, in one point of view, the beginning, the middle, and the end.

"Did the administration of Walpole present any uniform principle, which may be traced in every part, and gave combination and consistency to the whole?—Yes.—And that principle was THE LOVE OF PEACE."

Robert Walpole's son is also subjected to similar analysis by his biographer John Pinkerton (1799) in his *tour de force*, the *Biographical sketch, in fugitive crayons, of Horace Walpole, Earl of Orford,* one of the most charming and delicately done of all short biographies. Pinkerton finds Walpole's ruling passion in his sense of caste; the judgments of Pinkerton may have been acidulated by Walpole's failure to remember him in his will. The biography abounds with such observations as the following, cunningly adjusted to the text and making up the fine lines of the portrait:[71]

"He at all times hated democracy, which he considered as a theory too refined for human nature: and subordination of ranks was with him the golden chain of Homer. . . . With him there remained no doubt that the mass of mankind were, of absolute necessity, doomed to ignorance; and that the new mirrors of reason might dazzle the populace by a few flashing beams, but never could distribute a regular, continual light. . . .

"The pride of birth and rank, which the *philosophes,* and Rousseau in particular, attempted to level as adventitious and

[71] *Walpoliana,* in 2 vols. [1799], Vol. I, pp. xxi, xxxiii, xxxvii, and xxxix.

absurd, were ever in Mr. Walpole's eye far paramount to the fame of arts, letters, or philosophy. Alcibiades was, with him, a personage greatly superior to Socrates: angels, and people of rank, were created; vulgar people, vulgar painters, vulgar authors, were made, God knows how, on the fifth day of the creation, though the event was beneath the notice of any bible, richly bound and gilt. . . .

"Modesty also forbad his making presents, or doing any essential services, to artists or authors, who might perhaps, in their idle emotions of gratitude, have proclaimed the benefits received. . . .

"The ruling passion, repeatedly elucidated above, is strongly marked in his last will. Though he had many ingenious friends, not one slight memorial appears of his love of genius or talents."

Although Pinkerton's sketch of a "person of quality"[72] may be unfair, without question his use of the ruling passion gives it artistic structure and certainty. Almost invariably such narrow and definite interpretations result in clearer, more easily remembered, portraits. Sir William Young gives dignity to his "life without adventures" of Brook Taylor (1793) because he finds his subject to be one of those men who "personify, as it were, *learning itself*" (p. 4). Condorcet's *Voltaire* (tr. 1790) drives forcefully throughout, because the first paragraph states so clearly "the long war which in his youth he declared against prejudice, and which he maintained to the day of his death." The best of the many pamphlet-lives of the highwayman James Maclean[73] is made so by its concentration on "one predominant Foible, that is, an extraordinary Itch for a gay Appearance, and . . . to maintain this, he had from his Infancy proposed to himself no other Scheme but by seducing some Women of Fortune to marry him . . . in short, he had a strong Passion for nothing but fine Cloaths and a rich Wife." And Hird's *Fothergill* (1781) is knit together around the theme:[74]

[72] cf. the portrait of Lord Chesterfield, presented as *The man of the world* in an anonymous biography, 1774.

[73] *A complete history of James Maclean the gentleman highwayman* [1750?], p. 65.

[74] *An affectionate tribute to the memory of the late Dr. John Fothergill,* by William Hird, 1781, pp. 25-6.

"There was one great leading principle which prevailed in the Doctor's mind, at his first entrance into public life, and continued to its close.—He thought the great business of man, as a member of society, was to be as useful to it as possible, in whatsoever department he might be stationed.—Opulence was not his object; but it appears to have flowed upon him as the designation of Providence, to cherish and give activity to this principle."

One of the best theoretical justifications of the use of the ruling passion in life-writing is the anonymous "Essay on the character of the author" prefixed to the Reverend James Duchal's *Sermons*. This essay makes the difficult attempt to reconcile individuality with the doctrine of the necessarily simple dominant passion. After speaking of the biographer's obligation to treat of "natural complexion, habit, education, profession, many complicated circumstances," the writer continues:[75]

". . . through all these, the original cast of genius will predominate: . . . still the ruling principle will strongly mark the general character. See how endlessly the human face is diversified, by the combination of a few simple elements! while, in a general sameness, some prominent striking turn of feature stamps the peculiar character of countenance. Now, it is the seizing this characteristic distinctive mark, and producing it to light, which reflects the true image of the individual: This omitted, or unskilfully taken off, the particular man is lost, in the vague resemblance of the species at large. However, this individuating principle itself, is not always obvious: it may not be called out by any corresponding scene of action; it may go on to operate uniformly, through a still recurring sameness of life; like an equable motion proceeding from the same continued impulse. . . ."

In such sentences, rational or generalizing theory seems to combine with direct observation, much as it does in the best work of Doctor Johnson, dictator of eighteenth century theory and practice in biography. It is enough to point out here how many of the figures whose lives or characters Johnson sketches in the *Rambler* are perfect exemplifications of the ruling passion: Turpicula, who tells falsehoods; Leviculus, the fortune-hunter;

[75] 1765, Vol. II, p. x. 2d ed.

Dicaculus the unbounded railler; Misella the prostitute; Tetrica the peevish and Nugaculus the curious. The *Idler*, if it has perfect Theophrastian characters such as Sophron the prudent, becomes gayer in its names and analyses of Dick Minim the critic, Whirler, Linger, and Betty Broom; Molly Quick and Dick Shifter, Sam Softly and Sophia Heedful. Some of Johnson's portraits are as simple as Tranquil and Heartless; others as searching and sarcastic as Number 31: "Disguises of Idleness. Sober's Character." Johnson's strong ethical interests and his power of generalization compelled him towards these seeming simplifications around a central passion; yet his sense of reality was as strong as his didactic gift, and in view of his telling introduction of exact and minute details, it is not surprising to find that there were life-models for some of his portraits which at first glance seem generic.[76]

Most of the examples so far mentioned have been conscious adaptations of the theory of the ruling passion. Even more frequently biography acquired a strong ethical drive through the unconscious simplification of life-histories until they represent only one quality. This tendency is most apparent in collected biographies. The didactic purpose, fortified by the selective treatment of whole careers, is plain in the titles of such works as *The unfortunate Court-favourites of England, exemplified in some remarks upon the lives, actions, and fatal fall of divers great men*,[77] *The history of king-killers* (1719), the ominous *Lives of the English regicides* (1798) which the Reverend Mark Noble dedicates "to the Regicides of France," and Experience Mayhew's *Indian converts: or, some account of the lives and dying speeches of a considerable number of the Christianized Indians of Martha's Vineyard, in New-England* (1727).

Individual lives can likewise be issued with titles that almost save one the trouble of reading what ensues. Thus, Major Semple's life (1786) runs through eight editions as *The Northern*

[76] cf. R. Duppa's note to Johnson's *Diary of a tour into North Wales* in 1774, pub. 1816, p. 184, that Mr. Coulson, Fellow of University College, is designated under the name of Gelidus in the *Rambler*, No. 24. Johnson himself must have been the original for Sober.

[77] Issued by R. Burton, 1706 t.p.; 1st ed. 1695; 6th ed. 1729.

impostor; or prince of swindlers; Thomas Lurting gives the
public his autobiography (1710) as *The fighting sailor turned
Christian*; W. H. Dilworth issues his biography of Peter the
Great (1758) as *The father of his country*; the anonymous author
of a biography of Boadicea (1753) gives it the title of *Female
revenge: or, the British Amazon;* Joseph Jefferson writes *The
young evangelist; exemplified in a view of the life of the late
Rev. John Savage* (1798?); John Smith, the somewhat heartless reforming Vicar of Westham, publishes the life of the suicide
George Edwards (1704) as *The judgment of God upon atheism
and infidelity*; and John Dunton states his complete case in the
title *Death-bed-charity, exemplify'd in the life of Mr. Thomas
Guy . . . Madam Jane Nicholas . . . and Mr. Francis Bancroft . . .
proving that great misers giving large donatives to the poor in
their last wills is no charity* (1728).

Furthermore, a surprising number of the memorable biographies of the period focus upon a single action. These can hardly
be called examples of the Ruling Passion; the Overruling Accident would come closer to describing many of them. Yet the sole
and salient event in a long career is usually presented with appropriate moral observations. John Gordon (1734), although he
cannot have been over thirty years old when he writes, records
his escape from thirteen years of Roman Catholic education on
the Continent in order to show "the absurdities and delusions
of Popery"; Lewis Maximilian Mahomet considers his own life
worth recording (1727) because he is a Turk who turns Christian; Joseph Boruwlaski (1788) because he is a dwarf who nevertheless possesses normal feelings; and William Hay (1754) because he feels his being deformed has advantages as well as drawbacks. Joseph Spence and Gilbert Gordon narrate the life of
Thomas Blacklock (1754) not because he wrote verse, but because he was blind. Most of the criminal biographies and the
lives of eccentrics also center on single actions or single traits. To
render a biography amusing, one need not fulfill Aristotle's
requirements for tragedy: that it treat of an action which is serious and of a certain magnitude. It is enough if the hero of the
life, like Shakespeare's Coriolanus, is seen "not to be other than
one thing." Many a biography was popular in the eighteenth

century, and even now, once read, cannot be easily forgotten, because it recorded how an individual met a single stroke of fate.

One of the most unforgettable examples of unswerving purpose is the life of the great anatomist John Hunter, written by his helper and brother-in-law Everard Home (1794). Afflicted with angina pectoris, remaining at one time for forty-five minutes without pulse or breathing, though fully conscious, Hunter for the last twenty years of his life records all the symptoms of his sufferings, unemotionally, for the benefit of the medical profession. For page after page the minutest actions and sensations of his heart are carefully set down, until at last the reader sees, in another sense, what was deepest in his heart—the passion of a scientist.

Deliberately or unconsciously, then, the career of an individual may be presented primarily as a lesson in living.[78] An admirable example of what can be done with a dominant *motif* is the translation of Pineau-Duclos's autobiography published as *A course of gallantries; or, the inferiority of the tumultuous joys of the passions to the serene pleasures of reason: attested by the confession of a nobleman who had tried both* (1775, 2 vols.). The narrative is full of subtle observations (Vol. II, p. 46 *et passim*):

". . . he saluted me with that kind of timidity, which is observed in every honest man, who has either a favor to ask or receive. . . .

"Lovers would be very happy if there were continual obstacles set in the way of their desires; it is no less essential to your happiness to preserve and keep up desires, than to satisfy them."

The Sieur Duclos consciously centers on the actions of his own heart when he is in love. "I will therefore," he declares,

[78] A few further specimen titles may be given: *The faith of the true Christian, and the primitive Quakers faith,* printed in 1725 for its author William Bromfeild; *Private virtue and publick spirit displayed* in the life of Captain Thomas Coram, 1751; the *Life and errors* of John Dunton, 1705; *Faith triumphant, exemplified in the death of Mrs T. . .,* 1772; and Prideaux's *The true nature of imposture fully display'd in the life of Mahomet . . . offered to the consideration of the Deists of the present age,* 1723.

"confine myself only to distinguish the different characters of the women with whom I have had any amours." And after delicate analysis of his minor affairs, he concentrates on his one great love for the widowed Madame de Selve, and places in contrast to her the flighty, vulgar Madame de Darsigny. His gradual steps to marriage with Madame de Selve are masterfully presented; and if the narrative is closer to the *Princesse de Clèves* than to the ordinary autobiography, at least its form is well chosen and thoroughly successful. It is written as a confession to a young relative, in order to justify a retired monogamy by lusciously detailing its opposite. Mature and sophisticated, it balances two modes of life so neatly that the reader feels its final philosophy, far from being conventional preaching, represents the convictions of an experienced man of the world (Vol. I, pp. 2-3):

"I am not yet forty years of age, and I have exhausted those pleasures, whose novelty makes you think inexhaustible; I have wore out the world; I have wore out love itself; I have subdued the tumultuous and blind passions; they lye dead, and motion-less in my breast. If, I have lost some pleasures, consequently I am free from those troubles which accompany them, which are great both in number and degree. This tranquillity, or, if you will, according to your idea, this insensibility, is an advantageous amends, and perhaps the only happiness within the reach of man in this life."

Parallels in the manner of Plutarch afford one further method of simplifying human careers by means of balanced contrasts or comparisons, as in the *Two dialogues; containing a comparative view of the lives, characters, and writings, of Philip, the late Earl of Chesterfield, and Dr. Samuel Johnson* (1787), probably by William Hayley; or the *Curious particulars and genuine anec-dotes respecting the late Lord Chesterfield and David Hume, Esq. with a parallel between these celebrated personages* (1788), pos-sibly by Samuel Pratt. The tendency to select significant qualities may result in a generalized "biography": in *The character of a generous prince drawn from the great lives of heroick fortitude* (1703), James Gordon builds up heroic fortitude traditionally around courage, justice, prudence, and temperance, with many examples to show how each quality, or its absence, has affected actual careers.

Once at least—for imagination coupled with detachment is rare—a complete life was viewed symbolically by a great lady and recorded by her biographer:[79]

"Looking on her own Picture, drawn at large, with her Sister as two Sheepherdesses. The Posture in which she found her self drawn, with her right Elbow leaning on a Rock, carelessly stretching forth her Hand to a Stream of Water, which gushed out of a Grot, fell on her Hand, & immediately fell off; This Represented to her the Hieroglyphick of her Life: she had found Earthly comforts unstable as water; and therefore not much to be regarded, but to be let come and go without concern. And her only support under all the Variety of troubles and disappointments, had been her leaning on that Rock of Ages. . . . These few instances give a sufficient Specimen of her contemplative Genius, and shew how happy she was in her Spiritual Reflections."

Most of the ethical assumptions that have so far been considered—the inculcation of virtue, the detestation of vice, the moral lesson sugar-coated for the very young, the ruling passion, the career centering on a single event, the Plutarchian balanced lives—have tended to interpret life simply. Controversial biography, superficially considered, would also seem to lead to simplification; in its ultimate effects, however, if for no other reason than that it takes two to make an argument, disputatious life-writing taught men the complexity of truth.

The use of biography to drive home some moral lesson is naturally evident in controversial writings. If the writers of encomiums and the preachers of funeral sermons have a case to prove in reviewing the lives of their subjects, so have the satirical biographers. More effective than a hundred conventional presentations of the life of a criminal as a deterrent from vice is Doctor Arbuthnot's masterly satirical epitaph on Colonel Francis Charteris. Widely quoted in its century, it deserves reproduction here

[79] *The life of the Lady Halket*, Edinburgh, 1701, pp. 57-8.

in one of its variants as a demonstration of the moral possibilities in the satirical record of a life:[80]

"Here lieth the body of Colonel Don Francisco; Who with an inflexible constancy, And inimitable uniformity of life, Persisted, in spite of age and infirmity, In the practice of every human vice, Excepting prodigality and hypocrisy; His insatiable avarice Exempting him from the first, And his matchless impudence From the latter. Nor was he more singular In that undeviating viciousness of life, Than successful in accumulating wealth; Having Without trust of public money, bribe, Worth, service, trade or profession, Acquired, or rather created A ministerial estate. Among the singularities of his life and fortune Be it likewise commemorated, That he was the only person in his time Who would cheat without the mask of honesty; Who would retain his primaeval meanness After being possessed of 10,000 pounds a year: And who, having done, every day of his life, Something worthy of a gibbet, Was once condemned to one For what he had not done. Think not, indignant reader His life useless to mankind: PROVIDENCE Favoured, or rather connived at, His execrable designs, That he might remain To this and future ages, A conspicuous proof and example Of how small estimation Exorbitant wealth is held in the sight Of the ALMIGHTY, By his bestowing it on The most unworthy Of all the descendants Of Adam."

When a grossly disproportionate panegyric or philippic appeared in print, it frequently generated its opposite; biography affords little more than a forum for displaying debating skill in the successive black or white lives of the Duke and the Duchess of Marlborough, of Robert Walpole, or Cromwell, or Thomas Paine. Horace Walpole prints his *Historic doubts on the life and reign of King Richard the Third* (1768) largely to counteract the popular impression which Sir Thomas More's hostile biography had so skilfully built up. But in his enthusiasm, Walpole transforms his doubts into a practical certainty of Richard's innocence. His ingenious arguments call up three further opinionated answers, in the same spirit of forensic speculation, by F. W.

---

[80] Quoted as reproduced in *The new Newgate calendar*, 6 vols., 1796-1800, Vol. II, pp. 217-18.

Guidickins (1768), Robert Masters (1772), and George William Lemon (1792).

Or in the one case of David Hume, contrast on the one hand George Horne's *Letter to Adam Smith* (1777), which is clever devil-baiting of Hume by "one of the People called Christians," and on the other hand the apology for Hume's life and writings by Samuel Pratt (1777), which is a saint's life written about a skeptic, and Adam Smith's letter to William Strahan, a restrained panegyric which closes with:[81] "Upon the whole, I have always considered him, both in his lifetime and since his death, as approaching as nearly to the idea of a perfectly wise and virtuous man, as perhaps the nature of human frailty will permit." The controversial temper of both Hume's praisers and dispraisers is even more marked if they are compared with the cool, objective spirit of his own autobiography (wr. 1776). Hume is succinct, self-conscious, penetrating, good-humored. Yet the unity which his defenders and detractors had gained through partisan emotion, Hume secures for his brief memoirs by concentrating on (p. 32) "my love of literary fame, my ruling passion."

In one case, the spirit of inquiry applied to the Old Testament produced a sustained general scuffle. The biographies of David might be outlined here as a warning instance of the difficulty of attaining the biographical ideals of truth and impartiality. The industrious and influential encyclopedist Bayle might be considered the first scholar of importance who turned the light of the "higher criticism" upon the career of David. To refute him, Patrick Delany, Swift's good friend, published in 1740-1742 his *Historical account of the life and reign of David King of Israel: interspersed with various conjectures, digressions, and disquisitions.* The three books constitute a leisurely labor of love in which Delany quotes the original Hebrew with his own transliterations, translations, and comments. With such paraphernalia to establish its authenticity, Delany proceeds to interpret David's astonishing career as a revelation of divinity:[82]

"Here he [the reader] will see, not only the ordinary occurrences, revolutions, and events, which pass before a common eye,

[81] Quoted from the *Life of David Hume, Esq. Written by himself,* 1777, p. 62.
[82] Pref. to Vol. I, pp. vi-vii.

upon this stage of the world; but he will also behold the secret and unseen springs and movements, the whole machinery by which they are brought about: and from a careful observation, and right application of what he here learns, he will be able to contemplate the whole history of the world, the lives of princes, and the revolutions of empires, in a very different light from that in which they present themselves to careless observers."

With such cosmic ambitions, the amiable Doctor Delany ties himself up in embarrassing convolutions to explain David's actions. He delights in probing for causes and in justifying God. His case summarized is that whatever evil David did, he eventually was sorry for it; furthermore, the divine punishments were not inconsiderable. Doctor Delany is sufficiently convinced by his own presentation to write in peroration:[83]

"By birth a peasant, by merit a prince! In youth, a hero; in manhood, a monarch; in age, a saint!

"This is David: What his revilers are, their own revilings tell."

If Delany had remained content with panegyric, all might have been well. But he made one dangerous innovation: he attempted to reconstruct David's mental processes, to explain a barbaric king to the average eighteenth century Englishman; and in so doing, in replacing the word of the Bible by the exercise of the individual imagination, he opened wide gates to future historians. Here, for example, are Delany's psychological speculations when David on the house-roof sees and covets Bathsheba (Vol. III, pp. 4-5):

"I shall not take upon me to account for this quick impetuous passion, (the starts of passion are perhaps the strangest phaenomena in our frame) and much less will I presume either to excuse, or insult it: one thing only we know, that whatever in any degree impairs the power of reason, adds so much to the power of passion; and possibly that numbness of reason, that stupidity which never fails to attend an afternoon's sleep, upon a full meal, might have been one ingredient, or some way or other an addition to the extravagance of this; at least, the humane

[83] Vol. III, p. 358, 1742 ed.

reader will pardon me the weakness of wishing to alleviate it."

If Delany can explain David's lust as promoted by the torpor following a heavy meal, David's next biographer continues such speculative motivation but diverges from Delany in charity. *The history of the man after God's own heart*[84] (1762) is the first serious extended attempt at "debunking" biography—the stripping of glory from the great by means of hard-headed or disillusioned assumptions. Peter Annet, probably its author, was a truculent free-thinker who has been considered as a link between the early eighteenth century Deists and such men as Paine and Godwin. Annet speaks of Delany's *Life* as containing "gross palliations, puerile conjectures, and mean shifts."[85] His own biography may not be freed entirely from such charges. The following specimen of his popularization occurs when he is interpreting the state of mind of Nabal's wife Abigail (p. 34):

"Her own curiosity also might not be a little excited; for the ladies have at all times been universally fond of military gentlemen: no wonder therefore that Mrs. Abigail, the wife of a cross country-clown, was willing to seize this opportunity of getting acquainted with Captain David."

After displaying a certain ability in psychoanalysis and much more in invective and casuistry, and after his own powerful summation, in the worst possible light, of the damning array of evidence against David, Annet ends his cynical tract with a somewhat incongruous plea for truth, a parody of Delany's eulogy of David (p. 105):

"These, Christians! are the outlines of the life of a *Jew*, whom you are not ashamed to continue extolling, as a man after God's own heart!

"This, Britons! is the king to whom your late excellent monarch has been compared!

"What an impiety to the majesty of Heaven!

"What an affront to the memory of an honest prince!"

Yet his ostensible attempt to rescue George II, "our good old king," from a parallel with David did not keep Annet out of

---

[84] Halkett and Laing assign it to Archibald Campbell; others to Peter Annet. I assume in the text that Annet is the author.

[85] Pref., p. xxiv, 1764 ed.

trouble. "An honest desire to obtain truth," he writes (Preface, p. xi), "will sanctify the most rigid scrutiny into every thing." Annet's scrutiny of the life of Moses led him to two appearances in the pillory in 1763, a month in Newgate, and a year at hard labor in Bridewell. Yet he allows his preface to stand before the second edition of his *History of David* (1764), still unwavering in his homage to truth as he sees it (p. xx):

"The intention was, without any regard to remote objects, or heed of future consequences, which in fact ought *never* to be considered in investigating any point; to give a fair and undisguised narrative of the life and transactions of David king of Israel."

He enumerates three causes for the difficulty of his undertaking: the pious inclination toward accepting the story without reasoning about it; the bias that results from consulting Jewish historians, almost the only sources of our knowledge of Jewish history; and the fragmentary state of the unconnected records of those historians. His enumeration of the reasons for David's fame is cynically calculated to soothe neither Anglicans nor monarchists (pp. xvii-xviii):

"In what manner David first acquired, and has ever since maintained, this extraordinary reputation, is not difficult to deduce: he was advanced, by an enraged prophet, from obscurity to the Hebrew throne; and taught by the fate of the unhappy monarch who was raised in the same manner, whom he supplanted, and whose family he crushed; he prudently attached himself to the cause of his patrons, and they were the trumpeters of his fame. The same order of men, true to their common cause, have continued to sound the praise of this church-hero from generation to generation, unto the present time: in like manner the grand violator of the English constitution [Charles I] obtained the epithet of *holy Martyr*."

In the light of such purposeful writing it is easy to see why, as Annet records (p. xix), "this little squib . . . produced so much bustle in the clerical hives."

Annet's principal antagonist was Samuel Chandler, with whom he had had tiffs as early as 1744 over *The history of Joseph considered*. Chandler, a staunch authoritarian and opponent of the Deists, wrote a long *Review of The history of the man after God's own heart; in which the falsehoods and misrepresentations of the historian are exposed and corrected* (1762). Annet retorted with *A letter to the Rev. Dr. Samuel Chandler: from the writer of The history* (1762) and with his ironic dedication of the 1764 edition of the *History of David* to Chandler. The elegant Beilby Porteus, later Bishop of London, entered the lists in defense of David, and the Vicar of Lakenham near Norwich, John Francis, contributed *Reflections on the moral and religious character of David . . . wherein the aspersions thrown upon him by a modern author, are proved to be false and malicious* (1764). Finally, though the effort appears to have been so great that he was in his grave before it was published, Samuel Chandler produced a two-volume *Critical history of the life of David: in which . . . the chief objections of Mr. Bayle, and others, against the character of this Prince . . . are examined and refuted.* Aristophanes, Terence, and Tacitus furnish quotations on the title-page to suggest that it is easier to attack than to defend *any* character; and Chandler valiantly attempts to offer palliation for David's dancing before the Ark, the two hundred foreskins of the Philistines, and even the Uriah-Bathsheba episode. In Chandler's learned, Hebrew-quoting, dull, slow, strained attempt to uphold David in all his actions, contrary to the writings of the "little, undisciplined, unfledged, ignorant sciolists," the wheel has come full circle and the reader is back with Doctor Delany.

The various lives of David have been treated at such length[86] to furnish examples of the ethical bias which could invade even antiquarian works, and particularly to illustrate the difficulties, which the continued controversy itself made evident, of establishing a simple (and therefore a one-sided) truth.[87] "Among the many bad effects of controversy," writes William Enfield,[88]

[86] A voracious reader might also consult *The history of the life and death of David, with moral reflections,* 1741, which is a fairly straight story translated from the French; and *A view of the life of King David . . . By W. Stilton, horologist,* n.d., which quotes Bolingbroke with approval, wishes to supplant superstition by reason, and maintains that Moses, David, and Solomon "were after all no better, but rather worse then the generality of mankind" (p. 33).

[87] See also the various biographies of Reginald Pole.

[88] *Biographical sermons,* 1777, pp. 159-60.

"this is one, that characters which are supposed to be connected with the question in dispute, are liable to be misrepresented by zealots on either side; so that between the extravagant encomiums of the panegyrist, and the ridicule and obloquy of the satirist, it is extremely difficult for the impartial enquirer to discover the truth. This hath been remarkably the case with respect to the character of David."

And yet even if this argument be granted, Enfield's ensuing life of David is better proportioned and closer to the truth because of the diverse interpretations, exaggerated and partisan though they were, which had preceded his own.

For as the century progressed, biographers more and more tended to become skeptical or impatient of over-simple interpretations of human life. One after another the facile ethical theories in life-writing were analyzed and their weaknesses subjected to critical scrutiny. Confident snap-judgments, the forensic exaggeration of virtue or vice in order to hold naïve auditors, gave way to a desire for greater understanding before passing any judgment at all, and to a realization of the complexity of each individual personality and of the world which he inhabits. Criticisms of the theories of biography as a help in seeking the good life and shunning the evil life have already been mentioned. The theory of the Ruling Passion came under fire as well. Henry Hunter attacks the very basis of it, the belief that from innumerable external actions the analyst may deduce the single mainspring for such actions:[89]

"Men, who only see the outside, must of necessity infer the principles of human actions from the actions themselves. And yet no rule of judgment is more erroneous: for experience assures us, that many, perhaps the greater part of our actions, are not the result of design, and are not founded on principle, but are produced by the concourse of incidents which we could not foresee, and proceed from passions kindled at the moment."

[89] *Sacred biography*, 1792, 6 vols., Vol. I, pp. 9-10. (1st ed. 1783-1792.)

And Sarah Scott is equally aware of the complexity and irrationality of human actions in her attack upon glib historians:[90]

"When we read general histories, great actions appear to arise from great motives; kingdoms seem to quarrel with kingdoms, and every thing is represented as the effect of the foresight of wisdom, the rage of ambition, the arts of the acute politician, the passion of an head-strong prince, or the imbecillity of a weak one. One of these is laid down as the characteristic of the monarch; and though his actions are inconsistent, and appear to spring from contrary motives, yet the author endeavours, with all the subtilty of his understanding, to reconcile these contrarieties, tho' it lead him to attribute to the prince such political refinements, as were, perhaps, foreign to the thoughts of any politician in that century.

"The Biographer enters into a detail which more properly developes the human mind. He shews us, that kingdoms are often set at variance by trifles, scarcely worthy the contention of simple particulars. . . .

"From the Biographer we learn, that the same prince shall at one time wear the martial appearance of an hero, at another all the horrors of a bloody tyrant, and, in his turn, assume the dissolute character of the most abandoned voluptuary; and all this variety, not from any change in his disposition, or from political views, but from being the tool, at different times, of an ambitious minister, an unworthy favourite, and an abandoned mistress. Consistently governable, he is the same easy dupe through life, though his actions wear a continual appearance of contradictions, which the historian, whose mind is elevated by a view of the extensive plan he has laid down for himself, endeavours to reconcile by refined reasoning, and imaginary schemes."

In this apprehension of existence as accidental and complex rather than rational, it is a final proof of the amusing inconsistency of human nature that Mrs. Scott cannot abandon entirely the conception of the Ruling Passion which she is attacking: she accounts for the inconsistent, contrary actions of her imaginary

[90] *The history of Gustavus Ericson, King of Sweden*, 1761, Pref. pp. iv-v, vi-vii.

prince by assuming that he is "consistently governable," and then hands her weakling over to those old and familiar types, the "ambitious" minister, the "unworthy" favorite, and the "abandoned" mistress. Yet if her argument is not particularly noteworthy for its coherence, it shows, at any rate, an impatience with the simple rationalizations of courtly biographers and official historians.

In the interpretation of human life, the greatest single conception which gained wide currency in eighteenth century biography was the idea that in most mortals good and evil, strength and frailty, were inextricably tangled. Rarely expressed before 1700, this notion becomes such a truism in the eighteenth century that it would be a monotonous task to record here all the instances in which it was consciously stated. Where, before 1700, can an admiring biographer be found who dares to speak of his hero in such words as Vicesimus Knox uses with regard to Doctor Johnson?[91] "He was indeed a great man; but mortal man, however well he may deserve the epithet Great, comparatively, is absolutely, but a little being; and the example of Johnson is additional proof of this obvious, but humiliating conclusion." Here are three further ethical reflections on human life which could hardly be considered part of the common cultural heritage before the late eighteenth century:[92]

". . . such is the unaccountable mixture, of good, and bad, in the composition of that wonderful being, MAN. . . ."

"It is an undeniable fact that frequently, in the dispensations of her gifts, Nature, as tho' actuated by a species of caprice, blends in the same individual the most opposite, and, sometimes, the most ridiculous extremes. . . .

"Voltaire, or some other author, in noticing a being of this description says, 'this man was endowed with a graceful form, a charming address, and possessed the most exhalted sentiments;

---

[91] *Winter Evenings*, 1790, No. 11, "On the character of Dr. Johnson, and the abuse of biography," p. 110.

[92] *Memoirs and anecdotes of Philip Thicknesse*, 1788, 2 vols., Vol. I, pp. 229-30, *re* Dr. William Dodd; *Authentic memoirs of James Molesworth Hobart*, 1793, p. 31; *Life of Major J. G. Semple Lisle*, 1799, p. 368.

but somehow or other he could never be prevailed upon to entertain any *just* notions of the distinction of property.' "

". . . the man who is without vices is also, for the most part, without virtues; and . . . prudence is very often nothing better than low selfishness in disguise. . . ."[93]

Such paradoxical subtlety in the evaluation of life as is evident in the last quotation may well have been learned from Shakespeare. Anthony Pasquin uses as a motto for his defense of Warren Hastings Shakespeare's statement of the same paradox:[94]

> "Your virtues, gentle Master,
> Are sanctified and holy traitors to you;
> Oh! what a world is this, when what is comely
> Envenoms him that wears it!"

The irony of *Measure for Measure,* the alternating cynicism and idealism of *Hamlet,* the sympathy learned through suffering of *Lear,*[95] above all, the unswerving truthfulness coupled with Shakespeare's ever-present admiration for nobility, of *Othello,* deeply tinged English biography.

This blending of the good and the bad, this realization that even the greatest hero is weak because he is mortal, this sympathetic acceptance of *pauvre humanité* for what it is, sounds a new note in the century and was not therefore universally present; but because it marks a distinct contribution to the ethical beliefs expressed in biography, a few more examples should be set down. Sometimes the realization that the web of life is of a mingled yarn is stated in hyperbole, as in L. D. Campbell's life of Hugh Boyd (1798, p. 22): "Thus ended the life of this great and extraordinary man, at once remarkable for the most brilliant talents,

---

[93] cf. Chaudon's *Voltaire,* 1786, translator's Advertisement, p. vii: "No man, during his life, had, at different times, been so much or so little a philosopher; and could any instance have proved the opinion that man is composed of two natures, a good and an evil, it would have been M. de Voltaire."

[94] *Authentic memoirs of Warren Hastings,* 1793, p. 1.

[95] cf. in these same *Memoirs of Hastings:* "Could great men thunder," p. 19; "Use every man according to his deserts, And who shall escape whipping?" p. 35; "Tremble, thou wretch," p. 45; "be you as chaste as ice," p. 53. cf. also "The quality of mercy," pp. 51-2 (14 lines are quoted) in *An authentic narrative of the life of Miss Fanny Davies,* 1786; or "Rest! thou perturbed spirit!—rest!" in Topham's *John Elwes,* 1790, quoted from 1805 ed., p. 83.

and the most sublime virtues, darkened by the greatest follies."
Sometimes man's laughable irrationality may be illustrated by an
anecdote, as in the account of the duel between a Scots Highlander hero and a German officer at Lisle:[96]

"He, therefore, finding that he was fully master of his man,
determined to proceed by degrees. He first cut off a part of the
calf of his large and thick leg. The Captain still persevered in
the combat—the Serjeant wounded him smartly in the sword-
arm.

"He gave up the contest on this, and said, 'It is enough.' The
officer was assisted to his quarters; and, wounded as he was,
he insisted on Macleod's accompanying him home, and drinking
with him; which they did very plentifully. They both cried, and
kissed at parting.—Such is the nature of man, divided by selfish
and social passions, according to various situations!"

And sometimes the new conception may take the form of a delicate psychological observation which admittedly cannot be reduced to logic. Thus, George Dyer (1796) draws a fine but true
distinction, when, after admitting that his hero Robert Robinson
was vain, he adds (p. 408): "Notwithstanding the conclusions
that may be drawn from these apparent concessions, Robinson
was a man of humility. I leave casuists to settle this apparent con-
tradiction. They have reconciled greater."

No longer, then, is man a creature of a single nature which
may be praised as good or condemned as evil. He has a dual
nature. Sometimes even that is not sufficient. Mrs. Griffith, in her
Memoirs of Ninon de L'Enclos (1778), makes life even more
complex (p. 27): " 'Tis said that most people have two characters; but I believe Ninon is the first that ever had three." Human
life is so tangled, the mystery of personality so insoluble, that
another biographer, after presenting various judgments on Madame de Maintenon, refuses to estimate her character himself:[97]

"Mankind have hitherto been divided in their Opinions of
Madam de Maintenon. Some have looked upon her as a designing
Coquette; others have taken her for a Woman of precise affected

---

[96] *Memoirs of . . . Serjeant Donald Macleod,* 1791, pp. 36-7.
[97] *The letters of Madam de Maintenon . . . to which are added, some characters. Translated from the French,* 1753, Pref. to the French ed., pp. iv-v.

Piety. But I can't think that these Characters will be found in her Letters. Some may say, that she was a Person of an unsettled Mind, whilst others maintain she owed her Elevation rather to Chance, than to her own good Sense and Virtue. The Coxcomb will assert that she was but a narrow Genius: The pensive Man will look upon her great Piety as only a political Finesse, and fancy he can deduce Proofs of Dissimulation from her devout and mystical Stile.

"For my Part, who esteem nothing but what appears worthy of Esteem, I must admire Madam de Maintenon, leaving more forward Wits to pry into her Heart, and pass Judgment on it."

And in a third of the biographies which came to England from across the Channel, Corancez shows the ultimate in skepticism and suspended judgment, for he is not even sure as to the way in which his hero Rousseau's life ended.[98] Did he die quietly reassuring his wife? Or by his own pistol? Or of apoplexy while in a watercloset?

Here, and in many similar cases, the current is away from hasty judgment. Life is no longer as simple as *A B C.* "It has often been said by the wise and learned," one writer remarks,[99] "that when the lots of human life were shuffled together, he who drew the best of them had but a bad purchase. With all due submission to their maxim, it may be observed, that in some men's fortunes the shades are so exquisitely mingled and varied, so strangely and abruptly cast, that even at the end of a moderate long life, it is a disputed point in which class their lot should be arranged."

Many others observe, almost for the first time, the strangeness of human life:[100]

"Accordingly we find in them surprizing Mixtures of Devotion and Tenderness, of Penitence and remaining Frailty, and a lively Picture of Human Nature in its Contrarieties of Passion and Reason, its Infirmities and its Sufferings."

[98] *Anecdotes of the last twelve years of the life of J. J. Rousseau,* 1798.

[99] *The adventures of a Jesuit: interspersed with several remarkable characters, and scenes in real life,* 1771, Vol. I, p. 1. Picaresque novel in biographical form.

[100] *Letters of Abelard and Heloise. To which is prefix'd, a particular account of their lives,* by John Hughes, Pref., 1722—an early date for such an observation.

Or again:[101]

"After all, it is certainly strange, that a man, evidently possessing an uncommon portion of humour, whose writings are frequently interspersed with sallies of true wit, and who was in some respects constitutionally cheerful, should become the prey of so morbid and malignant a species of melancholy."

And one further illustration:[102]

"A person needs but little knowledge of human life, to see, that strange inconsistencies are often combined in the same character. It often happens, that the same man is, by turns a rake and a pious, temperate christian, a spendthrift and a miser, liberal and narrow-minded, tender-hearted and unfeeling."

As life becomes increasingly complex and unpredictable, as the admirable and the mean are seen mingled in human conduct, the ethical tendency of biographers is to observe rather than hymn or condemn, to set up the standards of sympathy and understanding above Mosaic justice, and to let the heart rule rather than the head. Harsh moral judgments and fanatical righteousness now make biographers impatient; and John Lewis writes his long and learned lives of Wycliffe, Pecock, and Fisher in order "to convince men of the falshood of those absurd and dangerous fancies, that the fierce wrath of man worketh the righteousness of God; or that truth may be imprinted on men's minds with the points of naked swords, and their understandings enlightened, so as to perceive the truth, by making bonfires of their bodies."[103]

The mingled judgments, in which the biographer plays the dual rôle of prosecutor and attorney for the defense, may be seen in Pinkerton's appraisal of Horace Walpole:[104]

"If biography did not operate as an example of reproof, as well as of approbation, it would be useless to mankind. An academician may pronounce an *eloge,* and a schoolboy an exercise, but a just and candid delineation of human character must ever 'smell of mortality,' to use an expression of Shakspeare. A faultless

---

[101] *Poems by Wm. Cowper . . . with a life of the author,* Newcastle [1800?], p. xvii.

[102] Robert Heron's life of James Thomson, 1793, p. xxv. .

[103] *Life of Reynold Pecock,* 1744, Pref., p. xv.

[104] *Walpoliana,* 2 vols. [1799], Vol. I, p. xxxviii.

character is the creature of imagination, while the chief object of biography is truth. And, with his faults, how much superior does Horace Walpole appear to thousands of his rank and wealth, whose faults and pursuits are alike beneath the notice of biography?"

With the possible exception of the writings of Rousseau, the *History of Tom Jones* probably did more than any single work to render current the idea of the natural man as opposed either to saint or villain. It was so immediately influential that we even find one biographer revolting against the conception in the ironical close of his *Apology for the life of Bampfylde-Moore Carew:*[105]

"Here we shall put an End, for the present, to this true History of our Hero, and, we hope, the gentle Reader is convinc'd, that he has as good, if not a better Claim to Fame and Immortality, than most of the present Heroes of the Age. We acknowledge he has his Faults, but every Body knows a perfect Character is quite out of Fashion, and that the present excellent Writers of the Age, hold it a Solecism and Absurdity to draw, even a fictitious Hero without a Plenty of Faults: To draw after Nature is the grand Criterion, that is, an equal Quantity of Virtue or Vice; or if the latter preponderates a little, no matter, so their Heroes do not fall without Temptation, and feel some Compunctions of Repentance when their Passions are cool'd; this is Perfection enough, for this is pure Nature: Upon this Account, we acknowledge, we have been at no little Pains in writing this true History, to throw a Veil over some of the Virtues of our Hero, lest he should be found to exceed the present Standard of Heroism, and be thought a Character out of Nature."

As a single final example of the vice-and-virtue philosophy applied in a character sketch, consider the following extracts from John Courtenay's *Poetical review of the literary and moral character of the late Samuel Johnson* (1786). The tendency of the heroic couplet toward antithesis is utilized in the scornful opening pages:

"Lost is the man, who scarce deigns Gray to praise,
But from the grave calls Blackmore's sleeping lays . . .

[105] 1749; repr. fr. 1931 ed., pp. 272-3.

At zealous Milton aims his tory dart,
But in his Savage finds a moral heart;
At great Nassau despiteful rancour flings,
But pension'd kneels ev'n to usurping kings. . . ."

After such just condemnation, Courtenay's later praise becomes even more powerful, and conveys the impression of severe impartiality; the twenty-seven-page poem is particularly interesting because it has forty-eight footnotes giving documentary proof, from Johnson's writings and Boswell's *Tour,* for the statements made in the text. Part of the conclusion is given below, since it shows Courtenay determined, like so many eighteenth century theorists, "to paint man *man,* whatever the issue":

"Thus sings the Muse, to Johnson's memory just,
And scatters praise and censure o'er his dust;
For through each checker'd scene a contrast ran,
Too sad a proof, how great, how weak is man!
Though o'er his passions conscience held the rein,
He shook at dismal phantoms of the brain:
A boundless faith that noble mind debas'd,
By piercing wit, energick reason grac'd:
A generous Briton, yet he seem'd to hope
For James's grandson, and for James's Pope:
Though proudly splenetick, yet idly vain,
Accepted flattery, and dealt disdain.—
E'en shades like these, to brilliancy ally'd,
May comfort fools, and curb the Sage's pride."

In the refined moral judgments which are to be found in the biographies of the last quarter of the eighteenth century, popular ethical theory had moved a great way from the days when the spirit of biography might be summed up in a crude woodcut in which a preacher encourages five criminals by pointing up to heaven on the left, while at the right is hell-mouth.[106] The biographies quoted or described in this volume sufficiently illustrate the increasing subtlety and accuracy of psychological and moral

---

[106] This was the usual cut reproduced again and again before at least a score of pamphlets, 1719-1724, published as *The Ordinary of Newgate, his account of the behaviours, confessions, and last dying words of . . . malefactors.*

presentation; all that need here be done is to record a few of the
conscious statements of the newly realized duty of the biographer
to etch the fine lines that reveal a personality, and to achieve on
his own part, before passing judgment, sympathetic identification
with his hero.

"Biography derives its principal advantage," writes Robert Bisset,[107] "from the minute knowledge it affords of moral causes,
their operation and effects; by enabling us to trace action to mind;
the modifications, habits, and affections of mind to their sources,
whether original or factitious; and thence deducing lessons of
moral conduct. It is interesting, from displaying situations and
passions which we can, by a small effort of the imagination, approximate to ourselves,—the feelings of the father, son, husband,
wife, and friend."

Again:[108]

"Sentimental works and books which tend to promote the
knowledge of the human heart, being, at present, read with so
much avidity, the subsequent Journal may hope to be not entirely
unacceptable to many a feeling and sensible heart.

"Thus much, at least, is certain, and it has frequently been repeated by keen-sighted observers, that a faithful and circumstantial moral history of the most common and unromantic
character is infinitely more important, and fitter for improving
the human heart, than the most extraordinary and interesting
Novel."

And finally, in the life of Burns, whose career affords such pit-
falls to the amateur moralist:[109]

". . . it is the proper business of the biographer; to trace the
gradual developement of the character and talents of his hero,
with all the changes which these undergo from the influence of
external circumstances, between the cradle and the grave; and at
the same time, to record all the eminent effects which the display
of that character, and the exercise of those talents, have produced

---

[107] *The life of Edmund Burke*, 1798, p. 4.

[108] *Secret journal of a self-observer . . . the Rev. J. C. Lavater*, 1795. Translated
from the 1770 German ed., by Peter Will. Pref., p. [iii].

[109] *A memoirs of the life of the late Robert Burns*, by Robert Heron, 1797, p. 2.
Heron considered his theory important enough to run the first sentence quoted
here in capitals.

upon nature and on human society, in the sphere within which they were exhibited and employed. The writer's wishes will be amply gratified; if this trifle shall be found to afford any exposition of the nicer laws of the formation and progress of human character, such as shall not be scorned as data by the moral philosopher, or as facts to enlighten his imitations, by the dramatist."

The consciousness of the weakness as well as the strength of human nature had a definite effect upon autobiographers. Humility had been an acknowledged virtue, of course, among earlier Christian autobiographers; but too often, in the mere assumption that the cosmos revolves around one's own errors, such humility seems hollow, and frequently it can hardly be distinguished from inverted pride. Bunyan in his *Grace Abounding* is content with nothing short of being the chief of sinners, and Jonathan Edwards in his autobiography writes, almost truculently:[110]

"I have greatly longed of late, for a broken heart and to lie low before God. And when I ask for humility of God, I cannot bear the thought of being no more humbled, than other christians. It seems to me, that, though their degrees of humility may be suitable for them; yet it would be a *vile* self-exhaltation in *me,* not to be the *lowest* in humility of all mankind. Others speak of their longing to be humbled *to the dust.* Tho' that may be a proper expression for *them,* I always think for *myself,* that I ought to be humbled down *below hell.*"

Yet if such exercises in self-abasement partake of fanaticism, the genuine (though often unconscious) conception of one's self as an odd tissue of frailties and good intentions is almost demonstrably responsible for the great increase in "apologies" and "confessions" during the century. Not only do such titles become more frequent, but the spirit which they represent becomes more and more evident in biography; so that from John Dunton and Colley Cibber to William Cowper and Mary Robinson, autobiography is tinged with a new humor and a new pathos, as the littleness as well as the grandeur of human life is set before our eyes.

[110] *Some account of the conversion and experiences of the late Rev. Jonathan Edwards* [1760?], p. 16.

The old moral lessons strike with doubled force when conventional prepossessions have been removed. Few can read the long succession of the memoirs of actresses—Connie Phillips, Charlotte Charke, George Anne Bellamy, Sophia Baddeley, Mary Robinson —without a fresh realization that an irresponsible and immoral life leads inevitably to disaster. The attitudes of the heroines may be brazen, or innocent, or sentimental, or sordid, or injured, or self-righteous, or rationalizing; but Nemesis sees through all disguises. And the impressive fact here is that this glaring and obvious moral lesson, as simple as the moral in a medieval *exemplum,* is not put forward openly by the subjects of their biographers; it emerges in spite of them. The *Gentleman's Magazine* may write of Mrs. Pilkington's *Memoirs* (1748) with justice:

"Thus died Letitia Pilkington;—the Companion of Swift yet the tool of Worsdale; betray'd like many others by wit to folly and by pride to meanness. To those who read her life she cannot surely have lived in vain since she has scarce related a single incident which does not concur to prove that no natural excellence can atone for moral defects nor any power of pleasing others secure an equivalent for the chearful independence of honest industry."

And similarly, the emancipated and witty young Oxford scholar who wrote *"The parallel; or, Pilkington and Phillips compared. Being remarks upon the memoirs of those two celebrated writers"* (1748) comes to the conclusion of the most reverend and hoary moralist after his survey of the popular reminiscences of these two notorious ladies (pp. 23 and 62-3):

". . . whatever their Author's Intention may be, they are compelled by an invincible Necessity to make their Writings of some Use. The Business of them is generally to relate their own Misfortunes, and this consequently obliges them to confess their own Faults. They may, indeed, palliate and soften them a good deal, but as this is very perceptible, it can do no great Harm; and shewing, as they must do, that Slips in Morality are attended with the most dreadful Tales of Fortune, their Readers are made so much the wiser and better in spite of their Teeth."

"In the next place, if these Memoirs [Connie Phillips's] are read by any who are of a serious Disposition, they will clearly

collect from them, that the only way to be safe is to be innocent.
. . . Providence frequently shews its Remembrance of our Sins
when they have escaped our own. There was a Notion (when
Christianity prevailed amongst us) that Repentance availed little
without Restitution, and that the only way to expunge Guilt, was
to atone for it. Now I am afraid that something of the same Kind
might be collected from our Lady's Tales."

A whole philosophy may be developed explicitly or implicitly
in a biography. Christian doctrine is made the background for
innumerable biographies; and the various Protestant sects afford
rigid trellises on which to train exemplary lives. Conventional
stoicism may be presented in Stanhope's *Life of Epictetus,* frequently issued in this century, or in the generalized *Doctrine of
morality; or, a view of human life, according to the stoic philosophy. Exemplify'd in one hundred and three copper-plates* (1721),
translated by T. M. Gibbs. More individual beliefs may tinge a
biography, such as the skepticism of Walpole in his *Richard III*
(1768), the alternate bitterness and idealism of Godwin's *Mary
Wollstonecraft* (1798), or the disillusionment felt by the author
of the *Memoirs of a younger brother* (1789), who can set down,
as he looks back over his career from the advanced age of thirty-
five (p. 21): "What Dr. Johnson said of old Macklin's conversation I think may be said of life, 'a perpetual renovation of hope
with a reiteration of disappointment.'"

Doctor Johnson himself is the great exemplar of the philosophical biographer. His mournful and sometimes Christian stoicism
tinges all his writings; and he is of first importance in the history
of biography for his genius at reading convincing moral truths
from the accidents of individual existence.

What should be a *locus classicus* in considering moral interpretations in biography is to be found in John Wesley's *Extract of
the life of Madam Guion* (1776). Here two noble and generous
souls come into conflict, and the tragic sense of life behind
Madame Guyon's quietism meets the joyous and positive illumination of Wesley's evangelical spirit:[111]

111 Pref., pp. vii and viii.

" 'Tis true," Wesley writes of Madame Guyon, "she wrote many volumes upon the scriptures. But she then read them, not to learn, but to teach. And therein was hurried on by the rapid stream of her overflowing imagination. Hence arose that capital mistake, which runs thro' all her writings, That God never does, never can purify a soul, but by inward or outward suffering. Utterly false! Never was there a more purified soul, than the apostle John. And, which of the apostles suffered less? Yea, or of all the primitive christians? Therefore all she says on this head, of 'darkness, desertion, privation,' and the like, is fundamentally wrong.

"This unscriptural notion led her into the unscriptural practice, of bringing suffering upon herself. . . .

"And yet with all this dross, how much pure gold is mixt! . . . So that upon the whole, I know not whether we may not search many centuries to find another woman, who was such a pattern of true holiness."

Not only do biographies reflect conventional and unconventional views of life; they may even contribute to philosophy. Adam Smith's *Theory of the moral sentiments* (1759), which accounted as much for his contemporary reputation as his *Wealth of Nations,* maintains as its central argument that morality results from the observation of the actions of others, which gives our intelligence the necessary data for integrating our own actions in society. A man becomes moral only when he has sympathetically reconstructed within himself the actions and attitudes of others and has also imagined the effects of his own actions upon others. How much this ethical theory owes to the standard statement of the value of biography in furnishing incentives to virtue and deterrents from vice—as well as to the refinements upon the statement which have been discussed in this chapter—cannot be determined. It is worth observing, however, that biography held much interest for that brilliant little Edinburgh group, including Hume and Robertson, in which Adam Smith moved. Certainly Smith's idea was adumbrated in partial form by many theorists on biography; in the following sentence, for instance, opening George Crawfurd's *Lives and characters of the Officers of the Crown, and of the State in Scotland* (1726), the embryonic doctrine of Adam Smith in the first phrases almost prevails over the traditional purpose of biography as stated at the end:

"It is a general Observation, That the moral and intellectual Conduct of Men's Lives, is in a great Part owing, to the Observations and Reflections which they make, either upon the Vertues or the Failures of others; and accordingly, as they imitate these, so they prove either more vitious, or more vertuous: Hence it is, that all, or most of the wise and polite Nations in the World, have with Care and Diligence, transmitted to Posterity, the Lives of the great and illustrious Men of their Country, that they seeing the Rewards and Honours, bestowed on such, might thereby, be excited to imitate those, in such laudable Actions."

The most comprehensive contemplation of man which takes its start from the view of individual lives is Joseph Priestley's *A description of a chart of biography* (1777). On a large chart which is to represent spatially the period from 1200 B.C. to A.D. 1800, Priestley plans to include, in parallel columns for various classes, lines to represent the lives of great men. Over the implications of this tablet of fame, his speculative mind dilates until he seems to hold eternity in his hand (p. 24):

"Time is continually suggested to us, by the view of this chart, under the idea of a river, flowing uniformly on, without beginning or end.

"Labitur et labetur in omne volubile aevum.

"If we compare the lives of men with that portion of it which this chart represents, they are little more than so many small straws swimming on the surface of this immense river; strongly expressing the admirable propriety of those lines of Dr. Watts, concerning the eternity of God,

> "While, like a tide our minutes flow,
> The present and the past;
> HE fills his own eternal NOW
> And sees our ages waste."

CHAPTER VI

THE GREAT NAMES

> "Never heed such nonsense. . . . A blade
> of grass is always a blade of grass. . . . Let us
> if we *do* talk, talk about something; men and
> women are my subjects of inquiry; let us see
> how these differ from those we have left behind."
> —JOHNSON.

AN INDISPENSABLE part of this chapter is the apology at the start. A few pages for each cannot adequately describe or criticize the biographical writings of such men as North, Gibbon, Goldsmith, Mason, Johnson, and Boswell. Furthermore, their recognized importance has already occasioned valuable and numerous criticisms of their works. Every major writer considered in this chapter has inspired students and biographers to assess his worth, insist upon his importance, and cherish his reputation. Assiduity has combined with sympathy and enthusiasm. So many good and so many true remarks gather around these great names that much may be taken for granted. Because of the adequacy and excellence of critical scholarship on, say, Boswell, or Johnson, or Gibbon, or Mason, it will be wise to devote to them here less space than their absolute worth entitles them to.

An apology is also necessary because a general historian of biography cannot hope to know, concerning any one of these important writers, what any special student of that writer might take as a matter of course. This chapter, therefore, does not attempt to present any one of its subjects in full; the observations it contains are fragmentary, supplementary, designed to add details to, or change emphases in, pictures whose main outlines are already well known. Any value it may have will derive precisely from the general rather than the limited approach: the great life-writers considered here are viewed not as isolated phenomena, but as figures in the history of biographical art; the famous works are considered in relation to the general questions—of style, form, purpose, and effect—which are considered in other chapters of this book. Popular and familiar biographies, therefore, will be used to illustrate further the principal statements that have been advanced in earlier sections. Conversely, the earlier chapters may now appear as prolegomena before a consideration of the acknowledged masters, or as the background necessary to bring out clearly the large figures in the foreground.

The first of the great names in eighteenth century biography is that of Roger North. Here, for once, the chronological and the logical patterns coincide: North's connections with what precedes and what follows him are obvious. He is the last of the great seventeenth century biographers; but also in many ways he anticipates the theory and practice of the late eighteenth century. In style, vocabulary, mood, and subject matter he is akin to Walton; yet his definite and individual ideas about life-writing constantly foreshadow Boswell's. Chronologically, too, he bridges the two centuries. His writings can be dated only with difficulty, for his superb disregard of the time element is not surpassed even by Izaak Walton's.[1] A great part of his autobiography seems written between 1691 and 1696;[1a] while his masterpiece, the *Life of Francis North, Baron of Guilford*, is later than 1706, since it repeatedly refers to Roger North's *Examen*, which he had written in reply to the third volume of White Kennett's *History of England* (1706). The order of the production of his *Lives*, however, is not important, for he added and tinkered and revised to the end of his long life in 1734. The histories of the four North brothers, like Walton's *Lives*, are not so much separate works as parts of one extended record of reminiscences and recollections. Like Walton, Roger North repeats himself. He assumes that if the reader enjoys hearing a story once, he will not mind hearing it again. There is always, in North, plenty of time.

[1] Augustus Jessop, for instance, who edited North's *Autobiography* in 1887, shows (note on pp. 143-4) Roger North's "strange disregard of chronological sequence in writing," in a passage in which North follows the events of 1685 with those of 1672-1674 without mentioning dates at all.

[1a] Jessop, however, dates it as a whole later than Roger's lives of his brothers.

Although Roger North has little sense of time as a mechanical measure, he is keenly aware of the difference between the past and the present; and much of the beauty of his work comes from his conscious summoning up of old happenings to the sessions of his present thought. The haze of distance is on many of his pictures, the patina of the past. It is almost as a grandfather in a chimney corner that he interjects his typical phrases: "He used to say," "I shall never forget," or "I have heard him say more than once." Reminiscent in key, his stories also gain some of their unique flavor from the mellow generalizations North makes on the basis of his wide experience. He lived vicariously through his brothers. Far more of a rambler than Doctor Johnson ever was, he resembles the Doctor in the delight he takes in using the incidents of daily life as raw material from which to draw up the laws of human conduct. And like Johnson, he has a great respect for the small individual fact. Boswell and Johnson would have understood and fully sympathized with the attitude North expresses in this paragraph:[2]

"Some may . . . alledge that I bring forward Circumstances too minute, the greater Part of which might be dropped, and the Relation be more material, and, being less incumbered, easier understood and retained. I grant much of that to be true; but I fancy myself a Picture-Drawer, and aiming to give the same Image to a Spectator, as I have of the Thing itself which I desire should here be represented. As, for instance, a Tree, in the Picture whereof, the Leaves, and minor Branches, are very small and confused, and give the Artist more pain to describe, than the solid Trunk and greater Branches. But, if these small Things were left out, it would make but a sorry Picture of a Tree. History is, as it were, the Pourtrait, or Lineament, and not a bare Index or Catalogue of Things done; and, without the How and the Why, all History is jejune and unprofitable."

And again (p. 11):

"And, if some things are set down which many may think too trivial, let it be considered, that the smallest Incidents in the Life

[2] *Life of Francis North*, 1742 ed., pp. 249-50.

of a busy Man, are often as useful to be known, though not so diverting, as the greater: And Profit must always share with Entertainment."

Like Boswell and Johnson, North feels that continuous association with a man best fits a biographer to write his life (p. 9):

". . . if I am not the best instructed of any Man living for it, it is my own Fault; because I passed almost all the active Time of my Life in his Company."

He has Johnson's rare ability to see that the permanent human values and problems and decisions may be studied in the humblest life as easily as in the most exalted: after telling a story about his own family, North remarks that only the setting distinguishes it from royal or imperial histories, where, of a similar story (p. 28), "the whole may be seen sprout up into the Altitude of State Intrigues." The distinction between history and biography he draws as sharply as Johnson (p. 77):

"If the History of a Life hangs altogether upon great Importances, such as concern the Church and State, and drops the peculiar Oeconomy and private Conduct of the Person that gives Title to the Work, it may be an History, and a very good one; but of any Thing rather than of that Person's Life."

Roger's plan in writing the life of his brother Francis bears resemblances to Boswell's: he intends to insert "in their proper Places throughout this Work" (p. 37) the original rough notes and memoranda of the Lord Keeper. In other words, Francis is to speak for himself whenever he has left materials, and his life is to be presented in its proper order. If this did not mean for Roger North Boswell's strict year-by-year chronology, at any rate he saw his brother's life as a progress, he divided it into four epochs in the career of the Lord Chief Justice, and he is more aware than Boswell that character may vary with the years.[3] Young men, he observes,[4] "suppose the greatest Absurdity, viz.

___

[3] cf. his statement, *Francis North*, p. 95: "I cannot vary his Character much, in this Stage [when Francis was Attorney-General], from that subjoined to the former, only. . . ." Also cf. his penetrating remarks on the difference fatal sickness made in his brother's character.

[4] *Dudley North*, pp. 39-40, 1744 ed.

that they shall be always of the same Mind, which one would think a few Years would disprove."

Just as Boswell's *Johnson* opens windows on the literary history of half a century, so North's life of his brother Francis discloses the important happenings in law and politics of the Restoration, seen by a single individual. As a first-hand source for the study of the origins and development of cabinet government, it has rarely received due appreciation. The character sketches which Roger inserts in the life of the Lord Keeper, and repeats in his own memoirs, are more finished and thoughtful than the comparable side-panels in Boswell. The Lord Chief Justice Hales is admirably done, in spite of obvious bias; and the careful portrait of Francis North's archenemy, Jeffreys of the Bloody Assizes (pp. 219-21), shows Roger's gifts at their best. He presents the deranged, intense, and terrible lawyer in grotesque nightmare flashes until the last scene, in which Jeffreys in disguise, in the obscure quarters of London, is recognized by a scrivener who could not forget, from an earlier encounter, that frightening face. All this is given with some of the redundant and undisciplined power of the Elizabethan dramatists; its nearest parallel in English biography is Sir Thomas More's handling of the figure of Richard III.

Although Roger North is not afraid to air any of his prejudices and hatreds, he is best seen in the expression of his loyalties. Even more strongly than in Boswell's *Johnson,* the interest in the *Life of Francis North* centers on the warm relationship between the biographer and his hero. It is the story of a great family, and of a great man in that family. Roger realizes his theme clearly (p. 309): "I have here shewed how an half-decayed Family, with a numerous Brood, and worn-out Estate, of the Norths, by the auspicious Character of one Child of ten, was re-edified; . . . no one of the whole Pack miscarried." Among the six brothers, with their varied talents, Roger has chosen for Francis the Homeric epithets of "best Brother" and "the Chief." His hero worship is unmistakable; his life is locked in that of his elder brother; he realizes that his position and revenues have come to him through the influence of this best brother; and he feels that without him he would be nothing. Roger's dependence leads to a scene of some pathos:[5]

"And it may truly be said that this Brother [Roger himself] was as a Shadow to him, as if they had grown together. . . . Once he seem'd more than ordinarily disposed to Pensiveness, even to a Degree of Melancholy. His Lordship never left pumping, till he found out the Cause of it: And that was a Reflection what should become of him, if he should lose this good Brother, and be left alone to himself: The Thought of which he could scarce bear; for he had no Opinion of his own Strength, to work his Way through the World with tolerable Success."

Yet Roger is treating of a seventeenth century family, where sentiment expresses itself naturally in manipulating settlements, estates, and dowries; so that the scene ends typically when Francis sells his brother a two-hundred-pound annuity in order to give him some feeling of that "independence" he was always seeking. In the autobiography, this episode is followed by a nice touch: the adoring younger brother, after standing Francis's slights and jocularities for ten years, rebels just when his big brother is made Lord Chancellor (p. 91). "I . . . could scarce brook the many mortifications, by little contempts my brother, sometimes in jest and often in earnest, would put upon me." He declares his independence in the presence of the new Keeper of the Great Seal, and happily records that ever afterwards Francis "was tender of my countenance."

The Norths might well be proud of making the best of whatever came to them. Six sons and four daughters there were in the family, "and," writes Roger, "no one scabby Sheep in it." He himself, who depended so much on others, had to head the North family for much of his life, and to watch over many nieces and nephews. Three of his elder brothers died in quick succession, leaving him their families to bring up. Family solidarity and a practical acceptance of the inevitable were in their blood. When

---

[5] p. 305. cf. *Autobiography*, 1887 ed., p. 90: "I was all the while under great diffidence of my success in the profession, and looked on my fortune to depend on my brother's life, and that if he should die I were lost. Sure I felt in myself defects to cause this despondence, and I could not work my mind to a better courage, which diffidence even to despair sat on me. . . . My brother observing it, to keep up my spirits, sold me an annuity of £200."

Dudley, for instance, realizes he is dying, he curbs his swearing, and contrary to his habit, he no longer rebels against the physicians, but swallows his medicine:[6]

"I thought Religion, as well as Reason, whispered him that his Time was his Friends, and not his own, and that he should not add Affliction to them by any averse Singularity on his Part, which he might prevent by his entire Resignation."

Slight wonder, then, that Mr. St. Amand, their neighbor and acquaintance, can say, and Roger can record with pride, upon Dudley's stoical death: "Well, I never saw any People so willing to die as these Norths are."

Family pride, then, causes Roger to write. The same impulse toward life-writing that made the Duchess of Newcastle and Lady Anne Fanshawe and Lord Herbert of Cherbury pick up their pens in the seventeenth century, led Roger North belatedly to preserve, almost in the teeth of time, these four last portraits of English gentlemen under the Stuarts. The family resemblance is in all of them, but the brothers had enough individuality to make each likeness distinct. Roger's self-portrait is perhaps the least successful. His modesty was so genuine that he did not consider himself important enough for close observation. There are few passages in which the reader participates in Roger's life while it was being lived, as in this description of one of the few times when he was well "fox't"—his own expression for drunk (p. 172):

"And I made my way like a wounded deer to a shady moist place, and laid me down all on fire as I thought myself upon the ground; and there evaporated for four or five hours, and then rose very sick, and scarce recovered in some days."

The immediate passage of time—life while it is being lived—does not usually interest Roger North; he prefers the philosophic judgment when experience is recollected in calm. Thus a transient sickness is important to him only because it leads to meditations on "When life is worth living" (pp. 152-3) or "Whether suicide be justifiable" (pp. 153-6) and because his speculations afford him permanent comfort:

"I have ease and repose in my mind so as if ever I am overwhelmed in irremediable calamity and pain, I may, if I find I

[6] *Life of Dudley North,* 1744 ed., p. 208.

cannot bear them, put a period to free myself, and in this thought
I have great comfort, and have had and shall continue to have all
my life long."

His best observations are general, or are related to other persons
than himself. He observes with great delicacy, for instance (pp.
164-5), how his brother Francis in anger attributes his passion to
the wrong stimulus; he enters imaginatively into the minds of
the two crazed old persons who have confessed to witchcraft, for
both he and his brother hate the trials of witches and "wizzerds";
here his subtlety in psychology leads to compassion (p. 132):

"It is not strange that persons of depauperated spirits should
be distract in their minds, and come to a faith of mere dream and
delusion. What hath been the discourse of the sleepy chimney,
with silent dull thinking, takes place as if the stories were realities,
and then pride and self-conceit translates all to their own persons."

Some of his profoundest remarks are casual (p. 117): "And the
things of this world [by which he means business and bodily
activity as opposed to the scholarly life] may possibly hinder
contemplation, but nothing else produceth humility, charity, and
peace in depraved mankind."

Yet since there is relatively so little self-observation in this
autobiography, Roger North appears only accidentally, and his
memoirs are most entertaining when they give bits of the world
about him, much as Pepys's diary and Boswell's journals are entertaining. The reader is well contented simply to learn of yacht-
ing to Harwich, and of the great fire at the Temple in 1678, and
of a steer that gets loose near the law-courts, and of the dust and
crowds and obscenity of the Greengoose Fair at Bow, and of the
game of ombre, its terms, rules, and fascination.

The *Life of John North* is the only one of the four that seems
written from a sense of family duty rather than from pure delight. "The moral Intent here," writes Roger,[7] "is to do Justice
to the Person, and Service to his Family." Ordinarily Roger was
too interested in his subject to bother about the moral intent. But
John he never really liked. He found him too studious, too with-
drawn, and too timorous; besides, brother John did not like
puttering about with his hands. As a boy, John had a "non-natural

Gravity," although Roger is fair enough to concede that such solemnity argued only "Imbecillity of Body" and not of mind. "He had a very researching Spirit," Roger remarks (p. 242) with no great approval. But Roger finds it more difficult to excuse his brother's congenital timidity. John's mistaking his tutor for "an enorm Spectre" and raising a great outcry may make a good story, but Roger is not proud of it; and John's timorous nature Roger believes may explain even his avarice and his short life.

Around the ruling passion for scholarship Roger economically constructs the career of his brother, from childhood, through the election to the Mastership of Trinity College, Cambridge, at an early age, to the paralytic stroke and mental breakdown that his less bookish biographer attributes to too much study and thinking. Since Francis North was sixteen years older than his brother, Roger does not give many pictures of Francis as a child. One of the brief glimpses, however, shows Roger's characteristic humor and his habit of seeing his brothers, not only set far off in time, but viewed from a psychic distance. Francis when very young is placed under the care of a Mrs. Willis, a "furious Independent," who is the wife of a schoolmaster:[8]

"She used to instruct her Babes in the Gift of praying by the Spirit; and all the Scholars were made to kneel by a Bed-side and pray: But this petit Spark was too small for that Posture, and was set upon the Bed to kneel with his Face to a Pillow."

A similar humorous portrait of the chancellor-to-be shows him after a drinking-bout, asleep in the saddle on his runaway horse in the middle of a pond. Ordinarily Francis did not drink much, but when he did (p. 50), "he used to sit smiling, and say little or nothing; so harmless a Thing of a petit good Fellow was he." Roger's admiration quite evidently stopped short of awe; his portrait is as faithful and full as he can make it, for it is to include all of Francis's concerns and reflections, such as (p. 77) "Matching, Residences, Fortunes, Entertainments, Reflections, Doubts, Melancholies, Confidences, with his Arts of governing himself and his Passions."

By "matching," Roger means seeking a suitable marriage, and again he is humorous in narrating the various matrimonial over-

---

[8] *Life of Francis North*, 1742 ed., p. 12.

tures Francis makes after he has decided in favor of domesticity because (p. 77) "he thought it would be an Ease to his Mind to know continually, after his Business done, what was to become of him." So we see Francis (p. 79) "held in a Course of bo-peep Play with a crafty Widow"; and wooing an heiress; and presiding over the country festivities for "the new-married Folks"; and getting on in the law until business "flow'd in upon him like an Orage" and his meals had to be eaten "like the Harpies Supper, by Snatches"; and carrying a Dutch Bible to church in order to pick up the language without wasting time; and travelling on circuit in Cornwall or on the "hideous" roads of Northumberland; and serving the interests of the Crown in stormy days. Then comes the last illness in the country, with Roger and Dudley trying to cheer their brother with music or with plans for developing the estate; and finally death, after which the two brothers drive back to London to return to the King (p. 268) "that pestiferous Lump of Metal," the Great Seal of England, which had made Francis so unhappy.

For Francis, in spite of his fine qualities, had no great sense of humor. He became angry at the report that as Lord Chancellor he had ridden upon a rhinoceros belonging to the friend of his brother Dudley. Dudley, on the other hand—the adventurer-traveller of the family—would have been quite at ease on a rhinoceros. He and Roger had much in common, and in many ways the *Life of Sir Dudley North* is the best of the series. Dudley's youthful exploits, such as swimming down the Thames and through the whirlpools below London Bridge, soon give way to exotic accounts of Archangel, Smyrna, and Constantinople, whither he goes as merchant. Dudley speculates on the "Burning Mountains" of "Strombolo" and Aetna, or on the aerial causes of earthquakes, but he is at his best in action: learning how to get along with the Turks, or "almost lamed with sitting cross-legged" (pp. 63-4), or swimming in the Hellespont, in water "so rigidly cold, that it almost congealed the Fat of his Belly" (p. 5).

The haphazard merchandizing of the East teaches him to curb his temper, and from the number of cases he lost in the Turkish courts (p. 48), "he had learnt a most useful Principle of Life; which was, to lay nothing to Heart, which he could not help. . . . I have known, when the rebellious Spirit hath risen, he hath conjured it down, by saying in great Zeal, The Pope hath not his Will, the King of France hath not his Will, the King of England hath not his Will, the Devil hath not his Will, and by G— I will not have my Will."

"Our Merchant," as Roger usually refers to his brother, "after he found his Heart's Ease at Constantinople . . . began to grow fat, which increased upon him, till, being somewhat tall, and well whiskered, he made a jolly Appearance, such as the Turks approve most of all in a Man" (p. 65).

The description of the homecoming of the much-travelled brother is in Roger's best vein. The housekeeper, who "was a pthisical old Woman, and could scarce crawl up Stairs once a Day . . . flew up Stairs, to tell the News, as if she had been a Girl of sixteen" (p. 144). With his "Mustaccio's" and his "Cordubee Hat," he looks "drest up to act Captain Dangerfield in the Play"; and Roger observes that "it was pleasant to observe his Figure; so bizarr was his Face and Dress." After shaving off his moustache, Dudley still sips his upper lip and tries "with his Fingers to part away his (then) no Beard. . . . The greatest Part, of what we act in our Lives, is more Machinery than the Effect of either Will or Reason." Roger participates with zest in the re-acclimatization of his brother, and sees all London anew through the eyes of the returned traveller. The coffee-houses had not been there when Dudley had sailed away.

"When he came first to England, all Things were new to him; and he had an infinite Pleasure in going about to see the considerable Places, and Buildings, about Town. I, like an old Dame with a young Damsell, by conducting him, had the Pleasure of seeing them over again myself" (p. 196).

They walk up the Monument; they climb around Bow Church; they visit Saint Paul's—"then well advanced"—and talk to Christopher Wren. "We had conversed so much with new Houses that we were almost turned Rope Dancers, and walked as familiarly upon Joice in Garrets, having a View, through all the Floors, down to the Cellar, as if it had been plain Ground." The two brothers philosophize on the littleness of life from the top of Bow Steeple, and in a similar passage, Roger typically views men—himself included—as tiny and humorous creatures—"petit Sparks" in his own phrase. This time Roger and Dudley are up on the leads at Whitehall, where they start the cheers upon the proclamation of James II:[9]

"And we two on the top of the balustres were the first that gave the shout, and signal with our hats for the rest to shout, which was followed sufficiently. And here I had the reflection of the fable of the fly upon the wheel, we animalcules there fancying we raised all that noise which ascended from below."

When they are not engaged in such metropolitan mountaineering, Roger and Dudley are happy in many other ways. Roger had always been fond of "manufactures and gimcracks"; and the corpulent Dudley likes any manual occupation he can sit down to. "I have . . . found him very busy in picking out the Stitches of a dislaced Petticoat." In the blacksmith shop at Wroxton which the two of them have fitted up and from which they emerge black as tinkers, Dudley likes to hew and carve, while "He allowed me," Roger records (p. 202), "being a Lawyer as he said, to be the best Forger." In such occupations, Dudley sings all afternoon (p. 203) "like a Cobler, incomparably better pleased than he had been in all the Stages of his Life before." Both of them like sailing (p. 203):

"When first he came over, I kept a Sailing-Yatcht upon the Thames; and the first Time we took his aboard, he claps himself down upon the Seat by the Helm, and, taking the Whipstaff in his Hand, By G—d, said he, I'll be Admiral; and there he sat, and steered, with all the Delight imaginable."

Long before this point, quotations from Roger North must have made it clear that he wrote as no man has written before or since. Much of the delight and much of the difficulty of the Lives comes from the style; Roger North himself was aware of many of its peculiarities and of the close connection between his man-

---

[9] Autobiography, p. 179. cf., for this humorous objectivity, his dropping into the third person in telling the story of his own childhood, when he falls in debt to the amount of half a crown: "which was a burden so heavy to a little man of honour, that he declined ever after to be in like circumstances," p. 12.

ner of writing and the cast of his mind. "And as to the Style aimed at here," he writes,[10] "I intend it not polite; if it be significant, it is well." And again:[11]

". . . my discourse was confused, and from thence I inferred my thinking was so too. . . . And, generally speaking, men who think well either speak or write well, and that according to the power and measure of justness in their thinking."

In a long passage of self-scrutiny which uncannily anticipates many of the points Boswell makes concerning himself in his journals, Roger North analyzes his weaknesses and merits with no uncertainty (p. 21):

"Next, I have observed in myself somewhat of confusion and disorder of thought. . . . And this did not appear to me more in speaking than in writing. For I was ever pleased to be writing somewhat or other, and striving at method and clearness, but could not attain so as to perfect any one design. . . . But I had from all that pains no other profit than a discovery that I did not understand so much as I thought I did, and that my style (if it might be called such) was unnatural, affected, and obscure. I have been most sensible of my defects of this kind, and particularly in the practice of my profession; for it took away my assurance, and often when I have made a motion I could have gladly received an arquebusade for an answer. . . . I find my knowledge to have had a share of everything, but not very deeply of anything. This has made me propense to talk and babble. . . . And all the content I have in remembrance of these things is that I used all along a sincere mind; and, busy as I was, it was in prosecution of truth, and no false unjust projects."

Yet even here, while talking about his inability to express himself, his image of the arquebusade conveys, obliquely but perfectly, his mortification at speaking ineffectively. Roger North's mind thronged with figures; his imagination was powerful, original, and undisciplined; he lived over past events in all their visual concrete detail; and his verbs of action enliven his narrative:[12]

---

[10] *Life of John North*, pp. 234-5.   [11] *Autobiography*, p. 22.
[12] *Life of Dudley North*, p. 2. cf. his description, *Life of John North*, p. 244, of a spider tying up "a great Master Flesh Fly."

". . . once in a Bustle at the Door about taking coach, when a Child is apt to press too forward, a Beggar-woman, passing by, swept him away; and, after the Coach was gone, the Child was wanted. The Servants ran out several Ways to look for him, and one, by chance, found him in an Alley leading towards Channel-row, in the Hands of the Beggar, who was taking off his Cloaths; so the Child was recovered, but the Woman ran away and escaped Punishment."

Or again:[13]

"When the Committee-house was blown up, he was one that was very active in that Rising, and, after the Soldiers came and dispersed the Rout, he, as a Rat among Joint-Stools, shifted to and fro among the Shambles, and had forty Pistols shot at him by the Troopers that rode after him to kill him. In that Distress, he had the Presence of Mind to catch up a little Child that, during the Rout, was frighted, and stood crying in the Streets, and, unobserved by the Troopers, ran away with it. The People opened a Way for him, saying, *Make room for the poor Child*. Thus he got off. . . ."

Some of his comparisons are striking, as in that of his brother, whose mind breaks and reduces his erudition in Greek literature to a liking for fables and off-color stories:[14] "He seemed as an high flying Fowl with one Wing cut; the Creature offers to fly, and knows no Cause why he should not, but always comes, with a side Turn, down to the Ground." Sleep Roger calls "a short Turn in the other World." Of Francis and Dudley after many years of separation, he writes: "Each was an Indies to the other." Tired counsellors "were as blown Deer"; when Francis contemplates a second marriage: "Bead rolls of Reasons, *pro* and *con*, presented themselves to his Mind"; John at Cambridge, surrounded by undergraduates of good families, is "as merry as a School Boy with a Knot of them, like the Younglings about old Silenus." Even the speech of his brothers he renders dramatically: Dudley with his swearing; John, who liked to say (p. 247) "that of all the Beasts of the Field God Almighty thought Woman the fittest Companion for Man"; Francis on his death-bed, ranting in

[13] *Life of Francis North*, pp. 290-1, *re* Sir Charles Porter.
[14] *Life of John North*, p. 284.

rebellion against opiates and saying (p. 262) "that they thought
all was well if he did not kick off the Cloaths, and his Servant had
his natural Rest; but, all that while, he had Axes and Hammers,
and Fireworks in his Head, which he could not bear."

Roger North finds the English language both too much and
not enough for him. He makes use of the commonest saws and
local proverbs, but he also finds it necessary to coin his own words
from the Latin or to domesticate the French;[15] and the structure
of his sentences becomes frequently unmanageable. "More Squeak
than Wool," or "Squeak and no Wool," he uses to suggest show
without substance; his own writings have very much wool, and
quite a little squeak. There is an early seventeenth century flavor
in his style, with its combinations of incompatible elements and
its complete absence of decorum. Dryden and the Royal Society,
as far as North is concerned, might never have existed. He does
not even like the new handwriting—"as the Fashion now is, un-
cial or semiuncial Letters . . . like Pigs Ribs." His language
smacks of the country squire, almost the yeoman, in such expressions as "one of the greatest Kill-Cows at Drinking," "his Lordship soon became Cock of the Circuit," "he sent them away with
Fleas in their Ear," "he was held at the Long Saw [i.e. kept in
suspense] above a Month," or best of all, "This was Nuts to the
old Lord," meaning that the old lord was greatly pleased.

Roger North thinks, as well as writes, with the independence
of a country gentleman. Unexpected flashes, disillusioned or humorous, abound:[16]

"Men are not honest by Principle, but by Interest, and Fear
that relates to it."

"It is well known that the Merchants abroad are too much
given to the Bottle; and many come home as very Sots, as if they
had never gone abroad."

"It was ordinary for pickpockets to travel the circuits; nay, I
mean not the lawyers, but literally such."

[15] "Gree" for manner, *Francis*, p. 9; "Orage," *Francis*, p. 90; "Fourbs" for
scoundrels; "Emportment" for passion, *Francis*, p. 188; "Brigues" for faction;
"Goust" for taste or liking; "Historiette," more than once, for anecdote; "funest";
"Managery" for company or organization; "debonairtie."

[16] *Life of Dudley North*, p. 150 and pp. 64-5; *Autobiography*, p. 136; *Life of
Francis North*, pp. 262 and 49.

"People will ever be fond of Doctors, as Popish Zealots are of Saints, and think that the Power of Life and Death is in their Hands."

". . . he, with the rest of his Brethren, by Methods too well known, got very drunk."

Or, realizing the power of associational thought, Roger counsels a man of affairs to transact his various businesses in separate rooms, for[17] "if they lie in several Rooms . . . upon the very Entrance into the Room, the Walls, and meer Form of Things lying about, bring the Business into one's Mind, and make an artificial Train of Thinking." And finally:[18]

"We know that there is a pleasure in mere action as such, witness the usual running and play of boys, who will not walk on the ground if a rail be near, but they must walk on the top of that."

This independence of thought is paralleled in his vocabulary. If there is no word, Roger North finds it necessary to invent one. The result is often disconcerting. If "pervivacious," "wittified Ladies," "to reluct," "a summiss Voice," "univocal," "Ubiquitarian," and "Parentele" are fairly easy, "clancular," "retund," and "exility" call for a classical training plus imagination. Frequently only the context saves the reader, so that he will see that a boy who has stuffed himself on apples has displayed "this ingordigiousness of fruit," and will realize that "Politicones" are only politicians, that "expensive Accounts" are expense accounts, and that to "cohibite" and to prohibit are the same.

Language is fluid to Roger North; and the same mind that thronged with images and metaphors uses words with the suggestiveness and the overtones of a poet. Many of his phrases have the double meanings and the ambiguity that twentieth century experimentalists have been trying to infuse into prose. "Degenerous" in Roger North means at one time ungenerous and at another degenerate; the "rigid" water of the Hellespont in which Dudley swims seems to be frigid, gelid, and nearly solid; "timidous" telescopes timid and timorous; "effrontuously" conveys a manner of presumptuous effrontery.

[17] *Life of Dudley North*, p. 182.   [18] *Autobiography*, p. 73.

For Roger North, like Jonson's Spenser, "writ no language." He produced the memorials of the Norths, written in the family *patois*. They are intimate. All the brothers were most content when they were engaged in private domestic concerns. Francis was never happy as Chancellor, nor John as Master of Trinity; and Dudley preferred singing at a workbench to acting as Sheriff of London. "But now," writes Roger,[19] "we have our Merchant, Sheriff, Alderman, Commissioner, &c. at home with us, a private Person, divested of all his Mantlings; and we may converse freely with him in his Family, and by himself, without clashing at all against any Concern of the Public. And possibly, in this Capacity, I may shew the best Side of his Character."

Perhaps Roger North—somewhat "timidous" himself—did not enjoy the responsibilities of being executor for so many dead brothers and dead friends. In the new and not entirely congenial eighteenth century, he turned for comfort to the recording and revision of the early careless days, giving free play to his grotesque stylistic inventions and his shrewd philosophy, and building up, with evident love and longing, his reminiscent picture of a family in which all of the sisters were virtuous, and all the brothers valiant.

At the opposite pole in style from the eccentric Roger North stands Edward Gibbon. Like Boswell's, Gibbon's style reveals with crystal clarity whatever he wishes to reveal. But there are differences: Boswell is at his best in the pure recording of externals and of speech; Gibbon in the neat phrase that catches motive or character. Boswell is notable for his scrupulous preservation of scenes that seem a collection of un-retouched photographs; Gibbon's six self-portraits are carefully posed. The author creates them out of sheer delight at beholding himself in the limpidity of his own style. The very number of attempts that he made to set down his life, and the finish he has given to each, show how seriously he regarded these self-portraits. The last service he must render to the age was to leave it the memorials of one of its three great historians. He ranked himself, with ostenta-

[19] *Life of Dudley North*, p. 194.

tious modesty, below Hume and Robertson; he might therefore be surprised to see how his fame outtops theirs. The amateur of biography may be permitted to wonder how much of Gibbon's fame rests upon his own recorded life rather than upon his history. How many people, for instance, know how and where Gibbon began and finished the *Decline and Fall of the Roman Empire* who know neither how nor where the Roman Empire fell?

One of the causes for Gibbon's clarity in portrayal may be found in his carefully trained temperament. Worldly, urbane, luxury-loving, skeptical, materialistic, witty, self-satisfied, and self-centered, Gibbon is in many ways an epitome of the eighteenth century as it is popularly understood. The kernel of his whole autobiography may be found in the famous phrase which caps his one love-affair, the "strange alliance" to which his father would not give consent: "I sighed as a lover, I obeyed as a son."[20] In such an epigram it is hard to imagine the lover, easy to suspect the motives of the son, and impossible not to admire the stylist. The complacency with which Gibbon records the impression he believes he has made upon the "virtuous heart" of Mademoiselle Curchod is disagreeable; yet he does not regret this indiscretion of his youth, less because of Mademoiselle Curchod's tenderness and passion and wit than because he has paid court to one who later had the ability to make a splendid marriage with the rich and powerful Monsieur Necker.

In complete self-absorption, Gibbon keeps his journal for thirty years, recording his progress and discoveries, for he is determined to make a place for himself in the eyes of the world, a place of dignity and comfort and reputation. This ambition requires rigid training and sacrifice on his part. Such instinctive actions as his youthful embracing of Roman Catholicism are disciplined out of his nature, particularly because his father, upon whom he is financially dependent, imposes a long exile in Protestant Switzerland as opportunity for penance and reformation. Again, his father's approval and allowance weighs more with him than his own feelings for Susan Curchod. The obedience of the dutiful son is tested most excruciatingly in Gibbon's acceptance of his father's

<hr>

[20] pp. 83-4, World's Classics ed., 1935.

second marriage, since a stepmother means a divided estate, but disapproval of a stepmother may mean no estate at all. Later in his life, he loyally supports a government whose policies he cannot entirely approve, thereby winning a lucrative post as a Lord Commissioner of Trade. For patience and prudence do not go unrewarded, and Gibbon was never without a competence.

Gibbon's career is sometimes considered a beautiful example of mediocre abilities producing a monumental work because of unswerving attention to a single end. That end, however, was not his Roman history, but the establishment of his own fame. He essayed politics, but his voice, presence, and temper did not fit him for oratory in the House of Commons; he served for several years as officer in the Hampshire militia, but Gibbon was not designed for a "wandering life of military servitude." He was not cut out to be a statesman or a soldier, a lover or a saint. Even as a man of letters, Gibbon's career was not clear to him from the start. He published an essay on the study of literature, but he wrote it in French. He contemplated a life of Raleigh and read voluminously in source materials. Yet (pp. 119-20) "Excepting some anecdotes lately revealed in the Sidney and Bacon Papers I know not what I should be able to add. My ambition (exclusive of the uncertain merit of style and sentiment) must be confined to the hope of giving a good abridgement of Oldys. . . . My best resource would be in the circumjacent history of the times, and perhaps in some digressions artfully introduced, like the fortunes of the peripatetic philosophy in the portrait of Lord Bacon."[21] He pondered writing the history of Florence under the Medicis, and for a long time turned over in his mind the history of the liberty of the Swiss. Then came the Italian tour in 1764. As he records in his journal his eighth and ninth visits to the Gallery in Florence

[21] Gibbon was always interested in biography. The last project he contemplated was a series of lives or characters of Englishmen from the time of Henry VIII to the present, illustrated with portraits; his own sharply incised sketches of William Chillingworth and Pierre Bayle in his autobiography show how well he could have filled the rôle of biographer; and he mentions in his memoirs, frequently with judgments upon them in their capacity as biographers, Anthony Hamilton, the Chevalier Taylor, Cornelius Nepos, Simon Ockley, Bishop Lowth, Middleton, Mallet, la Bléterie, Dr. Maty, Dr. Birch, Le Clerc, Oldys, Walpole, Hume, David Dalrymple, Bishop Thomas Newton, Whitaker, and Hayley.

in July, and with the usual eighteenth century interest in personality makes brilliant notes on the characters of the Roman emperors as deduced from their sculptured busts, a new and great idea is shadowy in his mind, and he writes (p. 150): "C'est un plaisir bien vif que de suivre les progrès, et la décadence des arts, et de parcourir cette suite des portraits originaux des maîtres du monde." Again, in Florence in August, with something of the spirit of a prophet dreaming on things to come, he marvels at the library which Magliabecchi had managed to accumulate and adds (p. 156): "Mais que ne pouvoit une vie très longue dont tous les momens n'avoient qu'un objet unique?"

Finally, at Rome, the sole end which filled the moments of his life for the next twenty-three years crystallizes in his mind. The cadenced sentence is a familiar one (p. 160):

"It was at Rome, on the 15th of October, 1764, as I sat musing amidst the ruins of the Capitol, while the barefooted friars were singing vespers in the Temple of Jupiter, that the idea of writing the decline and fall of the city first started to my mind."

The ambition of most individuals is greater than their accomplishment, but Gibbon's determination and patience led him to complete a magnificent structure that far outstripped his first project. He planned to record the decay of the city, and lived to write the decline of the empire; he hesitated a twelvemonth over terminating his history with the third volume, the fall of the Western Empire, and then picked up the indefatigable pen to write the final three quarto volumes. The completion of his history occasions one of the most celebrated passages in biography (p. 205):

"I have presumed to mark the moment of conception: I shall now commemorate the hour of my final deliverance. It was on the day, or rather night, of the 27th of June, 1787, between the hours of eleven and twelve, that I wrote the last lines of the last page, in a summer-house in my garden. After laying down my pen, I took several turns in a *berceau,* or covered walk of acacias, which commands a prospect of the country, the lake, and the mountains. The air was temperate, the sky was serene, the silver orb of the moon was reflected from the waters, and all nature was silent. I will not dissemble the first emotions of joy on recovery of my freedom, and, perh'aps, the establishment of my fame. But my pride was soon humbled, and a sober melancholy was spread over my mind, by the idea that I had taken an everlasting leave of an old and agreeable companion, and that whatsoever might be the future date of my *History,* the life of the historian must be short and precarious."

When his task was over, his life was over. His position in society and in the world of letters was established; he had a few faithful friends who made no exacting demands; his house and his library at Lausanne, where he "ranked with the first families," seemed preferable even to the dinner-tables of Paris and London where he had "so long conversed with the first men of the first cities of the world." There was no more to be desired. Yet at the end a loneliness descends upon him which he did not guess at in his earlier years. He imagines different ladies of his acquaintance, one after one, as his wife: this one would give dignity to his table; another is lively and entertaining; three others would be excellent, respectively, as mistress, as nurse, and as economist and housekeeper. "I feel, and shall continue to feel, that domestic solitude, however it may be alleviated by the world, by study, and even by friendship, is a comfortless state, which will grow more painful as I descend in the vale of years" (p. 252). The loneliness echoes in his other letters to Lord Sheffield (p. 246): "Since the loss of poor Deyverdun, I am *alone*; and even in Paradise, solitude is painful to a social mind." It attains final form in his autobiography (p. 215):

"I feel, and with the decline of years I shall more painfully feel, that I am alone in paradise."

Gibbon has shaped his life as he would have it. "We suffer or enjoy the effects of our own choice" (p. 255). The last picture discloses what he has patiently and painfully made of himself: a famous writer grown old alone in a fine house.

Gibbon built up his fame as historian in two ways—by exacting and thorough study, and by a no less exacting cultivation of style. "Style," he writes (p. 1), "is the image of character"; and in his autobiography this dictum seems well borne out. There is nothing accidental about his self-revelation. Each sentence is designed and finished, as a swordsmith might make a rapier of perfect heft and balance after many trials and discardings. His friend and editor Lord Sheffield has joined together his autobiographical writings in a single connected narrative; but it is worth remembering that Gibbon considered this work important enough to record it in six separate versions, as if experimenting in style and scope.

"The style of an author should be the image of his mind," he repeats (p. 177), "but the choice and command of language is the fruit of exercise." "Ease, correctness, and numbers" (p. 204) he bears in mind in his memoirs no less than in his history. He scrutinizes critically the rhythms and proportions of his sentences no less than their sentiments. "It has always been my practice to cast a long paragraph in a single mould, to try it by my ear, to deposit it in my memory, but to suspend the action of the pen till I had given the last polish to my work" (p. 185). This practice in writing the history is evident also in the autobiography; its fine turns of phrase may be found, in rough or finished form, in his journal and letters. Thus, to Lord Sheffield, in the troublous year 1790, he writes of Edmund Burke (p. 249): "I admire his eloquence, I approve his politics, I adore his chivalry, and I can forgive even his superstition." The sentence is one which he will not willingly let die, but in his *Memoirs* he sacrifices epigrammatic point to prudence and precision by changing the last clause to: "and I can almost excuse his reverence for church establishments." And his lively interest in Roman sculpture, which occasioned in his journal keen observations on the physiognomy of the Roman emperors, is compressed to a formal phrase in his *Memoirs* (pp. 148-50): "In the Gallery, and especially in the Tribune, I first acknowledged, at the feet of the Venus of Medicis, that the chisel may dispute the pre-eminence with the pencil."

If there is something affected and faintly ludicrous about this last expression, it is because there was something affected and ludicrous in the man who wrote it. There are stories that suggest that Gibbon lisped in Latinisms. In his own autobiography, the sublime style is made sometimes ridiculous when it clothes ordinary events, just as the famous historian and conscious man of the world seem oddly embodied in Gibbon's very short, paunchy figure, with his snub nose and undeveloped face. He is the eldest child—"From my birth I have enjoyed the right of primogeniture" (p. 19)—and he regrets the death of his only sister, whom he remembers as "an amiable infant." The brother-and-sister relationship, especially if they do not marry, appears to him "of a very singular nature. It is a familiar and tender friendship with a female, much about our own age; an affection perhaps softened by the secret influence of sex, but pure from any mixture of sensual desire, the sole species of Platonic love that can be indulged with truth, and without danger" (p. 19). And the sorrow he may have felt on the death of his father is hidden beneath verbal draperies in the sentences (p. 175): "My grief was soothed by the conscious satisfaction that I had discharged all the duties of filial piety. As soon as I had paid the last solemn duties to my father, and obtained, from time and reason, a tolerable composure of mind, I began to form a plan of an independent life, most adapted to my circumstances and inclination."

Gibbon's self-detachment results in occasional funny allusions to himself in such phrases as "As soon as the use of speech had prepared my infant reason for the admission of knowledge" (p. 21) or the pompous "I cannot forbear to mention three particular books, since they may have remotely contributed to form the historian of the Roman empire."[22] But sometimes this arranging himself for a pen portrait gives faithful and rare objectivity. Not every one dares to speak of himself as Gibbon does: "Gibbon is old, and rich, and lazy."[23] Such playful and frank sentences occur frequently in his letters to his friends and suggest the difference in tone between his letters and his more formal *Memoirs*. For although Lord Sheffield writes that in Gibbon's *Memoirs* (p. 321), "He has described himself without reserve, and with perfect sincerity," nevertheless part of the sincerity comes from the evident reserve of their style, a reserve which, when Gibbon

---

[22] p. 75. Self-satisfaction, almost a universal requisite for autobiography, is evident throughout Gibbon. He introduces a reference to himself from the *Bibliotheca Historica* of Meuselius because the book may not be common in England; the citation begins: 'Summis aevi nostri historicis Gibbonus sine dubio adnumerandus est" (p. 212). And as a young man in Switzerland he writes characteristically to his aunt (p. 76): "though I am the Englishman here who spends the least money, I am he who is the most generally liked."

[23] From a remark of Gibbon's to Lord Sheffield, quoted from p. xviii, J. B. Bury's introduction to Gibbon's autobiography.

appeared before the world, he deliberately assumed. "The style of an author should be the image of his mind." The dignity of his sentences reflects the dignity that he strove for, the dignity which would not permit him ever to mention in thirty-two years his painful and fatal disablement even to his greatest friend, the dignity which caused him to withdraw from London to Lausanne at the height of his fame because his income was insufficient to support him in England in the manner he wished.

"Before I could break my English chain, it was incumbent on me to struggle with the feelings of my heart, the indolence of my temper, and the opinion of the world, which unanimously condemned this voluntary banishment. In the disposal of my effects, the library, a sacred deposit, was alone excepted. As my post-chaise moved over Westminster Bridge, I bade a long farewell to the 'fumum et opes strepitumque Romae'" (p. 200).

The periodic sentences, the clauses interjected in such a manner as to make the reader pause and admire the concord of parts, the carefully calculated phrasing, combine in Gibbon to reveal dignity and polish. As in classic architecture, the sense of dignity and repose is achieved by the exact balance of member against member, of part against part, so that the harmony of the whole depends upon recurrences that are no less pleasing because they are predictable:

"In every state there exists, however, a balance of good and evil. The habits of a sedentary life were usefully broken by the duties of an active profession: in the healthful exercise of the field I hunted with a battalion, instead of a pack; and at that time I was ready, at any hour of the day or night, to fly from quarters to London, from London to quarters, on the slightest call of private or regimental business" (p. 106).

In such sentences the sense is perfectly clear, but the reader and the author are equally fascinated by the delicate adjustment of words, as if they were weighed against each other in a complicated mechanism of large and little scales. Elegance of expression may lead toward verbosity and the fatal flow of words.[24] In the following sentence, for instance, interest in the manner of ex-

[24] Gibbon notices this fault in himself in the last two volumes of his history.

pression crowds out almost completely the simple underlying thought (p. 176):

"Yet I may believe, and even assert, that in circumstances more indigent or more wealthy, I should never have accomplished the task, or acquired the fame, of an historian; that my spirit would have been broken by poverty and contempt, and that my industry might have been relaxed in the labour and luxury of a superfluous fortune."

But in general, Gibbon adapts to "the other harmony of prose" Pope's technique in the heroic couplet. His exact balance allows him to emphasize whatever word he desires, to make his thought admirably clear, to give wit and point to his observations of life. With Gibbon the turn of a phrase takes the place of passion, and he lives in his pen. Many of his best sentences owe their epigrammatic finish to his use of balance (p. 174): "Each year multiplied the number, and exhausted the patience, of his creditors." Or (p. 33): "I arrived at Oxford with a stock of erudition that might have puzzled a doctor, and a degree of ignorance of which a schoolboy would have been ashamed." Other sentences of the *Memoirs* depend upon alliteration, obvious or subtle, for their effects (p. 43): "Flattery is the prolific parent of falsehood." Or upon alliteration plus a rhythm which is not far from verse (p. 85): ". . . steeped in port and prejudice among the monks of Oxford."

Gibbon is a late Augustan poet who has turned to prose. His interest in the technique of expression, his consciousness of style, his sensitivity to words both in their rhythmical arrangement and in the shades of meaning they can assume in various parts of a sentence, make his admiration for Pope easily understandable. His philosophy of life is hardly inspiring; his career was indeed dull; nothing ever happened to him because he spent his life in making it certain that nothing ever would.

"The present is a fleeting moment, the past is no more; and our prospect of futurity is dark and doubtful" (p. 220). Yet in a world which he can so conceive, Gibbon creates for himself an assured place as the result of the labor of "twenty happy years." If his nerves "are not tremblingly alive" (p. 219), even that he may consider a blessing, and write as corollary: "my literary temper is so happily framed, that I am less sensible of pain than of pleasure." He is frank in his self-satisfaction. He makes the happiness he does not find. He is spacious in the possession of an adequate fortune and the knowledge of centuries.

In the history of biography Gibbon is an important figure, for he showed what too few biographers had realized, that care in composition may make the record of an uneventful life aesthetically satisfying. He has given his own exemplification of *Le style c'est l'homme*. He has refined to the level of art his own quiet existence among folios; he has dressed his own nature to such advantage that it shines out as true wit; and in his style, which was his life, the dignity and the polish, the brilliance and the reserve of the eighteenth century, are not allowed to perish.

William Mason, no less than North and Gibbon, is important in English biography because of his style. His "Life of Gray" shows that he had, in addition, a sense of form and organization that is rare in English biography. Little more can justly be said in his praise. Mason as a biographer has been too highly valued, largely because of James Boswell and of Thomas Gray himself. Boswell in the opening pages of the *Life of Johnson* speaks highly of the *Memoirs of Gray* and professes to follow Mason's method of including his subject's letters. And, indeed, the principal charm of Mason's production is that Gray wrote most of it. The wit, the personality, the intimacy, and most of the well turned phrases—these are Gray, not Mason. Editors, notably John Mitford and Mrs. Paget Toynbee, have shown conclusively that Mason changes Gray's original words or omits familiar sentiments and colloquial expressions; the alterations are usually for the worse.[25] Mason's own presence in the biography, in the form of footnotes and digressions, is sometimes annoying. It does not help the reader when Mason, not appreciating Gray's sportive fancy in a letter to his close friend Gilbert West, notes: "This thought is very juvenile";[26] or when he calls attention with an

[25] See Mark Longaker's detailed discussion in *English Biography in the Eighteenth Century*, 1931.
[26] *The Poems of Mr. Gray. To which are prefixed memoirs of his life and writings*, 1775, 2d ed., p. 14. 1st ed. 1774.

asterisk to (p. 345) "An excellent thought finely expressed"; or when he devotes five or six pages (pp. 251-6) to a discussion of his own tragedy *Caractacus*. It is, moreover, disconcerting to find that Mason's practice did not square with his principles. His theory is salutary and well expressed (pp. 1-2):

"A reader of sense and taste never expects to find in the memoirs of a Philosopher, or Poet, the same species of entertainment, or information, which he would receive from those of a Statesman or General: He expects, however, to be either informed or entertained: Nor would he be disappointed, did the writer take care to dwell principally on such topics as characterize the man, and distinguish that peculiar part which he acted in the varied Drama of Society."

Mason is aware also how infrequently biographers make their portraits distinctive. In justifying the inclusion of Gray's correspondence, he takes issue with "the cautious and courtly Dr. Sprat," who had objected to including informal letters in his *Life of Cowley* (1668), and adds (p. 4, note):

"Such readers as believe it incumbent on every well-bred soul never to appear but in full dress, will think that Dr. Sprat has reason on his side; but I suspect that the generality will, notwithstanding, wish he had been less scrupulously delicate, and lament that the letters in question are not now extant."

In the light of such frank and brave statements, Mason's own bowdlerizing and reducing of Gray to elegant and insipid English is the more remarkable. He assumes the episcopal manner of Dr. Sprat himself when he apologizes for the triviality of the youthful Gray's correspondence with West in the following sentences (pp. 5-6):

"But as this is the earliest part of their correspondence, and includes only the time which passed between Mr. Gray's admission into the university and his going abroad, it may be reasonably expected that the manner rather than the matter of these letters must constitute their principal merit; they will therefore be chiefly acceptable to such ingenuous youths, who, being about the same age, have a relish for the same studies, and bosoms susceptible of the same warmth of friendship. To these I address them; in the pleasing hope that they may prompt them to emulate their elegant simplicity, and, of course, to study with more care the classic models from which it was derived."

And Mason is distinctly abandoning his expressed principles when he,publishes the letters to Horace Walpole,[27] "omitting, though with regret, many of the more sprightly and humourous sort, because either from their personality, or some other local circumstance, they did not seem so well adapted to hit the public taste."

Yet a final judgment must allow that in spite of minor defects, Mason's *Memoirs of Gray* are well composed. The principles upon which the book is organized are luminously stated; the language is dignified; the connections are skilful and usually concise; the divisions give structure and perspective to Gray's career; Gray's friendships and numerous scholarly, antiquarian, literary, and scientific interests are not slighted; the explanatory notes for obscure references in the letters and the careful descriptive table of contents are so well handled as to seem innovations in life-writing; and Mason's avowed editorial design—"I have never related a single circumstance of Mr. Gray's life in my own words, when I could employ *his* for the purpose"—successfully transforms Gray's letters, projects, and fragmentary poems into one of the most pleasing of eighteenth century autobiographies.

One further stylist remains—Oliver Goldsmith. In one of his conversational pronouncements, Doctor Johnson termed Mason's style fit only for the second table, but for Goldsmith he reserved almost unrestrained encomiums. Introducing his own life of Thomas Parnell, Johnson wrote:

"The Life of Dr. Parnell is a task which I should very willingly decline, since it has been lately written by Goldsmith, a man of such variety of powers, and such felicity of performance, that he always seemed to do best that which he was doing; a man who had the art of being minute without tediousness, and general

---

[27] p. 16, note. John W. Draper in *William Mason, a study in eighteenth-century culture*, 1924, makes the point that although modern critics censure Mason for altering Gray's letters at all, contemporaries scored him for not altering or omitting more freely.

without confusion; whose language was copious without exuberance, exact without constraint, and easy without weakness."

In spite of such praise, few readers of Goldsmith remember that he wrote biographies, and even fewer are aware that his biographical works are comparable in bulk and number to Izaak Walton's. The parallel between Walton and Goldsmith is more than mechanical: their genial dispositions, their casual handling of facts, and their instinctive artistry bring them close together. Both are biographers by chance rather than by choice. The death of Sir Henry Wotton led Walton to write the life of John Donne, which he presents in deprecatory fashion, lamenting the loss of Wotton's abler pen; the press of circumstance first compels Goldsmith to pick up his biographical pen and give London, in 1758, *The memoirs of a Protestant, condemned to the galleys of France, for his religion. Written by himself.*[28] Of this somewhat perfunctory translation Goldsmith evidently thought so little that he allowed, or suggested, its publication as the work of "James Willington." The account itself, dealing with the suffering and heroism of Huguenot galley-slaves at the beginning of the century, is crammed with adventure.[29]

Goldsmith's next attempt in the biographical field was also a potboiler—the fragmentary *Memoirs of M. de Voltaire,* written in 1759 and published in part in the *Lady's Magazine* in 1761. Poorly proportioned, bewildering in chronology, breaking off in the midst of an extended account of Voltaire's Prussian visit, the life is nevertheless of some value for its account of the Frenchman in England and for its charming anecdotes and style.

Goldsmith's facility led Dodsley in 1763 to contract with him for a two-volume *Chronological history of the lives of prominent persons of Great Britain and Ireland.* This series of *English Lives,* as the project was called later, was never completed; but two extended studies—*The life of Henry St. John. Lord Viscount Bolingbroke,* and *The life of Thomas Parnell*—were published in 1770, and show, as did his first attempts, Goldsmith's haste, his inaccuracy, and his grace.

---

[28] 2 vols. The original, by Jean Marteille of Bergerac in Perigord, was published in Rotterdam in 1757. Repr., ed. Austin Dobson, 1895.

[29] Considered more fully in Chap. IV.

The reputation of Goldsmith as a biographer must therefore rest very largely upon a single work, *The life of Richard Nash, Esq., late master of the ceremonies at Bath. Extracted principally from his original papers,* and first published in 1762. This, again, seems to have been an occasional piece, for the long-lived Beau Nash had died within the year. Goldsmith, however, takes more pains with his work, and is particularly careful to vouch for his own integrity and to proclaim a revolt against the life-and-amours school for scandal to which his subject might so readily have lent itself. The *Life of Nash* has close affiliations with Johnson's *Life of Savage* which preceded it by almost twenty years. Both show a clear understanding of the biographical function, a regard for lucid narration, an uncompromising respect for truth as the writer sees it, and a tendency to draw moral conclusions from the career of an individual.

"The reader," Goldsmith writes in his *Advertisement,*[30] "will at least have the satisfaction of perusing an account that is genuine, and not the work of imagination, as biographical writings too frequently are." And in the Preface:

"The following Memoir is neither calculated to inflame the reader's passions with descriptions of gallantry, nor to gratify his malevolence with details of scandal. The amours of coxcombs and the pursuits of debauchees are as destitute of novelty to attract us as they are of variety to entertain; they still present us but the same picture—a picture we have seen a thousand times repeated. The life of Richard Nash is incapable of supplying any entertainment of this nature to a prurient curiosity. Though it was passed in the very midst of debauchery, he practised but few of those vices he was often obliged to assent to. Though he lived where gallantry was the capital pursuit, he was never known to favor it by his example, and what authority he had was set to oppose it. Instead, therefore, of a romantic history filled with warm pictures and fanciful adventures, the reader of the following account must rest satisfied with a genuine and candid recital compiled from the papers he left behind, and others equally authentic; a recital neither written with a spirit of satire nor

---

[30] 2d ed., 1762, quoted from Cunningham's reprint, 1900, Vol. VII, p. [51].

panegyric, and with scarcely any other art than that of arranging the materials in their natural order."

Yet art, which Goldsmith here disclaims, is shown in the temper which he consistently maintains. If he is not satiric, as he assures us, he is at least detached and superior. Something of the irony of the modern biographer may be detected, given more seriousness in Goldsmith by his careful scrutiny of the rise and fall of a figure with whose interests and ambitions the biographer cannot fully sympathize. "The pains he took in pursuing pleasure," Goldsmith observes in the Preface (p. 53), "and the solemnity he assumed in adjusting trifles, may one day claim the smile of posterity." And again (p. 54):

"Had it been my design to have made this history more pleasing at the expense of truth, it had been easily performed; but I chose to describe the man as he was, not such as imagination could have helped in completing his picture: he will be found to have been a weak man, governing weaker subjects, and may be considered as resembling a monarch of Cappadocia, whom Cicero somewhere calls 'the little king of a little people.'"

For this original and artistic conception of his subject, clearly stated at the outset and followed through to the end, Goldsmith deserves the praise accorded to a pioneer. The Preface contains other interesting biographical concepts, showing plainly the influence of Plutarch, whom Goldsmith reputedly edited in a new five-volume abridgment in the same year (1762).[31] It contains the following paragraphs, which may be taken as one of the best manifestos of the new tendency toward intimate rather than pompous biography, which finds other champions in Goldsmith's friends Doctor Johnson and James Boswell (p. 55):

"History owes its excellence more to the writer's manner than to the materials of which it is composed. . . . whether the hero or the clown be the subject of the memoir, it is only man that appears with all his native minuteness about him; for nothing very great was ever yet formed from the little materials of humanity.

[31] Note also Goldsmith's critical theories as stated in the Preface to this edition of Plutarch, quoted in Chap. VII.

"Thus no one can properly be said to write history but he who understands the human heart, and its whole train of affections and follies. Those affections and follies are properly the materials he has to work upon. The relations of great events may surprise, indeed; they may be calculated to instruct those very few who govern the million beneath; but the generality of mankind find the most real improvement from relations which are levelled to the general surface of life, which tell—not how men learned to conquer, but how they endeavored to live—not how they gained the shout of the admiring crowd, but how they acquired the esteem of their friends and acquaintance.

"Every man's own life would perhaps furnish the most pleasing materials for history, if he only had candor enough to be sincere, and skill enough to select. . . . There are few who do not prefer a page of Montaigne or Colley Cibber, who candidly tell us what they thought of the world and the world thought of them, to the more stately memoirs and transactions of Europe, where we see kings pretending to immortality, that are now almost forgotten, and statesmen planning frivolous negotiations, that scarcely outlive the signing."

This new attempt of Goldsmith's toward the truth, avoiding alike adulation and scandal, allows him at times to be witty, as in his note to the second edition (pp. 57-8):

"Since the publishing of the first edition of this book notice has been taken in some of the newspapers of Mr. Nash's leaving the university without discharging a small debt which he owed to the college where he was placed [Jesus, Oxford], and which stands on their books to this day. This is a circumstance which we were informed of before the publication of our former edition; but as our business was to write the life of Mr. Nash, and not to settle his accounts, it seemed to us too immaterial to deserve any particular notice; besides, had we paid any regard to this, we ought also to have taken some notice of another anecdote communicated to us, which was, that when he was sent from college he left behind him a pair of boots, two plays, a tobacco-box, and a fiddle, which had engaged more of his attention than either the public or private lectures."

The life itself centers on Nash as *arbiter elegantiarum* at Bath, as gamester and as lover—"Wit, flattery, and fine clothes, he used to say, were enough to debauch a nunnery" (p. 85)—on his entourage at the height of his career as the glass of fashion. Then, loading his palette with darker tones, Goldsmith draws the biography to a close with a picture of the gloomy and frantic octogenarian (pp. 123-4) in which Goldsmith's achievements in pathos and moralizing seem more certain and moving than in comparable scenes in *The Vicar of Wakefield* or—may it be hazarded? —in *The Deserted Village:*

"He was now past the power of giving or receiving pleasure, for he was poor, old, and peevish; yet still he was incapable of turning from his former manner of life to pursue happiness. The old man endeavored to practise the follies of the boy: he spurred on his jaded passions after every trifle of the day; tottering with age, he would be ever an unwelcome guest in the assemblies of the youthful and gay, and he seemed willing to find lost appetite among those scenes where he was once young.

"An old man thus striving after pleasure is indeed an object of pity; but a man at once old and poor, running on in this pursuit, might excite astonishment. To see a being, both by fortune and constitution rendered incapable of enjoyment, still haunting those pleasures he was no longer to share in; to see one of almost ninety settling the fashion of a lady's cap, or assigning her place in a country-dance; to see him, unmindful of his own reverend figure, or the respect he should have for himself, toasting demireps, or attempting to entertain the lewd and idle—a sight like this might well serve as a satire on humanity; might show that man is the only preposterous creature alive who pursues the shadow of pleasure without temptation."

(p. 127) "For some time before his decease nature gave warning of his approaching dissolution. The worn machine had run itself down to an utter impossibility of repair; he saw that he must die, and shuddered at the thought. His virtues were not of the great but the amiable kind; so that fortitude was not among the number. Anxious, timid, his thoughts still hanging on a receding world, he desired to enjoy a little longer that life, the miseries of which he had experienced so long. The poor unsuccessful gamester husbanded the wasting moments with an increased desire to continue the game, and to the last eagerly wished for one yet more happy throw. He died at his house in St. John's Court, Bath, on the 12th of February, 1761, aged eighty-seven years, three months, and some days."

Samuel Johnson himself could not surpass the judgment of Nash that comes as summary (p. 141):

"To set him up, as some do, for a pattern of imitation is wrong, since all his virtues received a tincture from the neighboring folly; to denounce peculiar judgments against him is equally unjust, as his faults raise rather our mirth than our destestation. He was fitted for the station in which fortune placed him. It required no great abilities to fill it, and few of great abilities but would have disdained the employment. He led a life of vanity, and long mistook it for happiness. Unfortunately, he was taught at last to know that a man of pleasure leads the most unpleasant life in the world."

The biography ends with Nash's letters against gaming and with two extravagant epitaphs. Goldsmith throughout often strays afield when a tempting anecdote lures him; he judges personally, sometimes melodramatically, the actions of his hero. But he breathes into his lay-figure a sense of life, and he writes at all times with clarity and beauty. "The Duchess of Marlborough," he says wittily (p. 97) "seems to have been not a much better writer than Mr. Nash; but she was worth many hundred thousand pounds, and that might console her." What Goldsmith himself lacked in material wealth, he made up in his powers of writing; and in the field of biography, particularly in his *Life of Nash,* Doctor Johnson's judgment still holds for the naïve ridiculous Irishman: *Nihil quod tetigit non ornavit.*

Johnson changed the course of English biography by his written and spoken observations even more than by his own practice. To an appreciable extent he imposed upon his contemporaries his view of life and his theories as to how lives should be recorded. The lives of individual human beings were of prime interest to him. He saw them under very few delusions. Biography was his favorite division of literature because it treated of actual individuals; his standard for measuring biographies was faithfulness to experience. "The genius of Johnson," Walter Raleigh says,[32] "might be said to consist in an unfailing instinct for the realities of life." How this instinct operated when literature was in question is well stated by Professor Joseph Epes Brown:[33]

"Literature must be tested by a direct appeal to experience, by its truth to human nature, by its effect upon man's mental, emotional, and sensory faculties. And to aid us in determining and applying such tests reason is called to the aid of experience. This is not the subjective approach of the Romanticist critic who appeals to his own personal reaction to a work. It is rather truly classical, in that it is an appeal to general human nature which is 'always the same.' "

"Experience" and "reason," though they may seem at times antithetical, are unfailing criteria in Johnson's thought. "General human nature" is always present: the moral base of his art rests on such an assumption; his belief in the value of lowly lives springs from it. But the "direct appeal to experience" is no less present, and accounts for his insistence upon truth in detail.

"He paid an almost superstitious regard to exact truth in narration, not from care for his own reputation for veracity, but from a passionate interest in the science of human life, which would be immensely advanced if men would but record their feelings and experiences with minute care."[34]

In spite of the simplicity of his reiterated views on biography, it may therefore be said that his attitude was comprehensive. He reconciled in his own mind the older ethical tradition of biography with the eighteenth century curiosity for *minutiae*. Virtue and truth both, perhaps, were only parts of knowledge; and one of his finest sayings is:[35] "All knowledge is of itself of some value. There is nothing so minute or inconsiderable, that I would not rather know it than not." Truth and didacticism combine when Johnson writes to Charles Burney, one biographer to another:[36]

[32] *Six Essays on Johnson,* 1910, p. 37.
[33] *The Critical Opinions of Samuel Johnson,* 1926, pp. xxii-xxiii.
[34] Raleigh, *ibid.,* p. 70.
[35] *Life of Johnson,* Oxford ed., 1934, Vol. II, p. 357. Johnson to Boswell, 14 April, 1775, Good Friday.
[36] Raleigh, p. 86.

"We must confess the faults of our favourite to gain credit to our praise of his excellencies. He that claims, either in himself or for another, the honours of perfection, will surely injure the reputation which he designs to assist."

The fullest statements of Johnson's biographical credo are to be found in the *Rambler*, Number 60, and the *Idler*, Number 84. Although they are well known, they were so frequently held up as authority and quoted at such length that their substance, at least, merits analysis by paragraphs. The *Rambler* for October 13, 1750, maintains:

1. Our emotions are moved by imaginative identification with others.

2. Histories, tragedies, and romances cannot therefore easily move ordinary men like ourselves.

3. Biographies, on the other hand, become useful and delightful to ordinary men.

4. A general history is not of much use to a private individual.

5. An account of *anyone's* life, however, is useful, for all our lives are *essentially* the same.

6. The record of a quiet life—be it of scholar, merchant, or priest—may be valuable even when it is not diversified by incidents.

7. A national figure is nevertheless a fit subject for biography; but his life must be described personally, privately, minutely, not as a record of state affairs.

8. "Many invisible Circumstances," or minute actions, are of more biographical significance than public affairs: witness the erratic gait of Catiline, the punctuality of Melanchthon, and De Witt's care of his health and negligence of his life.

9. Most biographers are ill informed of the nature of their task, and do not transmit a man's real character.

10. Minute facts in recent biographies sufficiently demonstrate this.

11. Antiquarian biography is difficult, for if it is hard to describe accurately a living acquaintance, it is much harder to describe a man distant in time.

12. Yet contemporary biography is equally difficult, for it is hard to achieve impartiality.

The essay ends with warnings of the dangers of uniform panegyric:[37]

" 'Let me remember, says Hale, when I find myself inclined to pity a Criminal, that there is likewise a Pity due to the Country.' If there is a Regard due to the Memory of the Dead, there is yet more Respect to be paid to Knowledge, to Virtue, and to Truth."

The famous fifth paragraph of this essay must be quoted in full:

"I have often thought that there has rarely passed a Life of which a judicious and faithful Narrative would not be useful. For, not only every Man has in the mighty Mass of the World great Numbers in the same Condition with himself, to whom his Mistakes and Miscarriages, Escapes and Expedients would be of immediate and apparent Use; but there is such an Uniformity in the Life of Man, if it be considered apart from adventitious and separable Decorations and Disguises, that there is scarce any Possibility of Good or Ill, but is common to Humankind. A great Part of the Time of those who are placed at the greatest Distance by Fortune, or by Temper, must unavoidably pass in the same Manner; and though, when the Claims of Nature are satisfied, Caprice, and Vanity, and Accident, begin to produce Discriminations, and Peculiarities, yet the Eye is not very heedful, or quick, which cannot discover the same Causes still terminating their Influence in the same Effects, though sometimes accelerated, sometimes retarded, or perplexed by multiplied Combinations. We are all prompted by the same Motives, all deceived by the same Fallacies, all animated by Hope, obstructed by Danger, entangled by Desire, and seduced by Pleasure."

The *Idler* essay for November 24, 1759, is even more assured of the practical utility of intimate biography because it deals with those fundamental faculties, senses, and emotions that are the same in all men:[38]

"Those relations are therefore commonly of most value in which the writer tells his own story. He that recounts the life of another, commonly dwells most upon conspicuous events, lessens the familiarity of his tale to increase its dignity, shews his favourite

[37] Quoted from the 1751 folio collection of the *Ramblers*.
[38] Quoted from the 2-vol. 1761 ed., pp. 178-83 in Vol. II.

at a distance decorated and magnified like the ancient actors in their tragick dress, and endeavours to hide the man that he may produce a hero.

"But if it be true which was said by a French Prince, That no man was a Hero to the servants of his chamber, it is equally true that every man is yet less a Hero to himself. He that is most elevated above the croud by the importance of his employments or the reputation of his genius, feels himself affected by fame or business but as they influence his domestick life. The high and low, as they have the same faculties and the same senses, have no less similitude in their pains and pleasures. The sensations are the same in all, tho' produced by very different occasions. The Prince feels the same pain when an invader seizes a province, as the Farmer when a thief drives away his cow. Men thus equal in themselves will appear equal in honest and impartial Biography; and those whom Fortune or Nature place at the greatest distance may afford instruction to each other."

But a new theme has here been introduced: the superiority of autobiography to biography; and in the succeeding paragraphs Johnson explains the reasons for his preference:

"The writer of his own life has at least the first qualification of an Historian, the knowledge of the truth; and though it may be plausibly objected that his temptations to disguise it are equal to his opportunities of knowing it, yet I cannot but think that impartiality may be expected with equal confidence from him that relates the passages of his own life, as from him that delivers the transactions of another.

"Certainty of knowledge not only excludes mistakes but fortifies veracity. What we collect by conjecture, and by conjecture only can one man judge of another's motives or sentiments, is easily modified by fancy or by desire; as objects imperfectly discerned, take forms from the hope or fear of the beholder. But that which is fully known cannot be falsified but with reluctance of understanding, and alarm of conscience; of Understanding, the lover of Truth; of Conscience, the sentinel of Virtue.

"He that writes the Life of another is either his friend or his enemy, and wishes either to exalt his praise or aggravate his infamy; many temptations to falsehood will occur in the disguise of passions, too specious to fear much resistance. Love of Virtue will animate Panegyrick, and hatred of Wickedness imbitter Censure. The Zeal of Gratitude, the Ardour of Patriotism, Fondness for an Opinion, or Fidelity to a Party, may easily overpower the vigilance of a mind habitually well disposed, and prevail over unassisted and unfriended Veracity.

"But he that speaks of himself has no motive to Falshood or Partiality except Self-love, by which all have so often been betrayed, that all are on the watch against its artifices. He that writes an Apology for a single Action, to confute an Accusation, or recommend himself to Favour, is indeed always to be suspected of favouring his own cause; but he that sits down calmly and voluntarily to review his Life for the admonition of Posterity, or to amuse himself, and leaves this account unpublished, may be commonly presumed to tell Truth, since Falshood cannot appease his own Mind, and Fame will not be heard beneath the Tomb."

Whether or not autobiography is generally better than biography is less important here than Johnson's basing his arguments upon the importance of absolute veracity, and his understanding of human psychology in showing why the truth is ordinarily so hard to attain.

These two papers by Johnson were extremely popular;[39] but their doctrines were not universally understood. Johnson himself wavered on the advisability, for the moralist, of telling the whole truth;[40] and many of his readers were unable to accept complete frankness as a biographical ideal. Thus, William Kenrick opens his account of the life and writings of Robert Lloyd:[41]

" 'He that writes the life of another,' says the Idler, 'is either his friend or his enemy, and wishes either to exalt his praise or

---

[39] It is worth remembering that the *Rambler* was in its 11th edition by 1789, its 17th by 1816. These papers are quoted, moreover, or paraphrased, in the *Annual Register* for 1759, Vol. II; Goldsmith's abridged *Plutarch,* 1762; Boswell's *Corsica,* 1768, and his *Johnson,* 1791; the *Beauties of Johnson,* 1781, 6th ed. by 1782; the anonymous life of William Blackstone, 1782; the anonymous 1785 life of Johnson [by William Shaw?]; Joseph Walker's *Irish Bards,* 1786; Gilbert Wakefield's *Memoirs,* 1792; the autobiography of John Henry Prince, 1807.

[40] cf. his remarks on Parnell and Addison, quoted later in this chapter under the discussion of Boswell.

[41] 1774, p. [v].

aggravate his disgrace.' This is a strange assertion, and would be much stranger if it were true."

Yet after assuring the reader that in spite of Doctor Johnson, William Kenrick will achieve impartiality, the author proves Johnson's point by forgetting his indifference and displaying his enthusiasm and generosity.

Twenty or thirty years after publishing his general biographical theories, when Johnson put them in practice on a large scale in the *Lives of the Poets,* the public seemed still unprepared for them. They were accustomed to panegyrics or defamatory pamphlets; but serious biography that exposed the faults and weaknesses of its heroes roused opposition, and more than one life was composed to refute Doctor Johnson by whitewashing the monument over a dead poet.[42] The summary of the ten volumes of the *Lives* in the *Monthly Review* for 1782[43] expresses the feelings of many intelligent contemporaries:

"Through the whole of his performance the desire of praise, excepting in the case of some very favourite author, is almost always overpowered by his disposition to censure; and while beauties are passed over 'with the neutrality of a stranger and the coldness of a critic,' the slightest blemish is examined with microscopical sagacity. The truth of this observation is particularly obvious when he descends to his cotemporaries; for whom, indeed, he appears to have little more brotherly kindness than they might have expected at Constantinople. And so visibly does the fastidiousness of his criticism increase, as his work approaches to a conclusion, that his Readers will scarcely forbear exclaiming, with honest Candide, What a wonderful genius is this Pococurante! Nothing can please him!"

Yet Johnson had his champions. Arthur Murphy in his *Life of Johnson* (1793) defends him from the charge of malignity against Milton; and Robert Anderson in 1795[44] appraises the *Lives of the Poets* as justly as any critic since. The most sym-

---

[42] cf. the *Swift,* 1784, of Thomas Sheridan, who accuses Johnson of a "strong bias" and "gross imputations"; Wakefield's *Gray,* 1786; Graves's *Shenstone,* 1788; and Hayley's *Milton,* 1796.

[43] Vol. 66, pp. 126-7. cf. also the autobiography of Thomas Newton, who, writing in 1781, is disappointed by the spleen and malevolence in Johnson's *Poets.*

[44] Pref. to Vol. I of his *British Poets.*

pathetic understanding of Johnson's convictions, outside the circle of his immediate friends, is to be found in an unknown "W.R." who wrote an *Advertisement* before Thomas Adam's *Private thoughts on religion* (1795). W.R. writes:

"To the honest heart, the penetrating mind, and powerful intellect of Dr. Johnson, the world is indebted for a superior method of Biography. The persons whose characters he has described are introduced to our acquaintance without any flattering disguise, and made known to us as completely as if we had enjoyed a domestic intimacy with them. And it may be observed, that his own character has been described with equal fidelity, and that posterity will view him exactly as he appeared to those who had daily access to him, when he was alive.

"Some, indeed, who dislike this honest dealing, affect to lament the injury done to the character of Dr. Johnson, by the unguarded communications of his friends and particularly by the Publication of his 'Prayers and Meditations.' Yet this book was published by his own direction, and even the peculiarities, in his devotional exercises, which may be called superstitious, were permitted to appear without any care, on his part, to excuse or conceal them."

Doctor Johnson's *Prayers and Meditations* (1785) show his Christian ethical purpose, his truthful presentation of the *minutiae* of daily consciousness, and his belief that the two are not incompatible:[45]

"Easter Day. April 22, 1764. Having, before I went to bed, composed the foregoing meditation, and the following prayer; I tried to compose myself, but slept unquietly. I rose, took tea, and prayed for resolution and perseverance. Thought on Tetty, dear poor Tetty, with my eyes full."

The man who could commission George Strahan to publish such passages after his death, with their quotidian bareness, their stark sincerity, their implicit realization of the importance of petty events and the littleness of even the greatest, was the same man who wrote the noble sermon on the death of his wife, and the last *Rambler* paper, and the dialogues in *Rasselas*.

[45] 1785 ed., p. 47.

Both the strength and the weakness of Johnson's capacity for seeing eternity in a grain of sand are evident in his autobiography up to his eleventh year. In justice to Johnson, however, one must remember that this fragment was not intended for publication, and that he would probably have consigned it to the flames with the rest of his memoirs in manuscript if Francis Barber had not conveniently managed to mislay it. His small silver cup, his speckled linen frock, his drunken uncle and coarse, good-natured aunt are set down exactly as he remembers them across the great gap of time.[46] Such memories contribute to his stock of harmless pleasure, and the exact record of facts may have diverted his mind from its congenital melancholia.

"I remembered [from the period when he was in his third year] a little dark room behind the kitchen, where the jack-weight fell through a hole in the floor, into which I once slipped my leg. I seem to remember, that I played with a string and a bell, which my cousin Isaac Johnson gave me; and that there was a cat with a white collar, and a dog, called Chops, that leaped over a stick: but I know not whether I remember the thing, or the talk of it."[47]

Latin moods and tenses frighten the infant Samuel (pp. 22-3):

"My mother encouraged me, and I proceeded better. When I told her of my good escape, 'We often,' said she, dear mother! 'come off best, when we are most afraid.' She told me, that, once when she asked me about forming verbs, I said, 'I did not form them in an ugly shape.' 'You could not,' said she, 'speak plain; and I was proud that I had a boy who was forming verbs.' These little memorials sooth my mind."

Such records are precious stuff, and Johnson can easily use a boiled leg of mutton as the prologue to speculation on the influence of sorrow in enlarging the mind.[48] But as Johnson himself had pointed out, a small detail is not significant merely because it is small, and it is hard to conceive what we learn of importance from Johnson's record that when he was only a few weeks old

[46] Certain passages are quoted in Chap. VII to illustrate the biographical treatment of childhood days.
[47] 1805 ed., p. 16, and note on pp. 16-17.
[48] Quoted in Chap. VII.

(p. 10), "an inflammation was discovered on my buttock. . . . It swelled, broke, and healed."

Johnson's interest in biography was extraordinary, even for the eighteenth century. He talked biography, thought biography, and to an extent which is often forgotten, wrote biography.

Reading through Boswell's *Life of Johnson,* one is amazed to see Johnson's constant awareness of the personalities of others. Again and again he wins his verbal victories by an *argumentum ad hominem.* This he could never have accomplished if he had not studied closely almost every person with whom he came in contact. His brief verbal sketches of characters and careers, even of the most unimportant persons, are acute. Like Boswell, he collected human specimens as a botanist collects plants; but he had more of the Linnaean genius for their classification than his young friend from the North. He thought in biographical terms even in the times of his greatest sorrow. Part of his sermon on the death of his wife is an attempt to preserve the essentials of her spirit; he advises Bennet Langton on the death of his uncle to assuage his sorrow by writing a memorial of Peregrine Langton; and his own grief on the marriage of Mrs. Thrale finds outlet in a parallel from biography. His emotion is deep—"The tears stand in my eyes."—but as he writes to her his letter of renunciation he cannot help recalling the Archbishop of Saint Andrew's pleading with Queen Mary as she turns back to England, standing in the midst of "the irremeable stream that separated the two kingdoms," holding her bridle and begging her to return. "The Queen went forward.—If the parallel reaches thus far, may it go no farther."[49]

Johnson's biographical projects are numerous. Among others, he planned a life of King Alfred, a new collection of the lives of the philosophers, and editions of Plutarch and Walton. But apart from such uncompleted schemes, and apart from the *Lives of the Poets,* Johnson's biographical productions are still respectable in number and quality. From his early years in London he steadily wrote—principally for periodicals—short biographies on the most

[49] *Letters to and from the late Samuel Johnson. . . . Published . . . by Hester Lynch Piozzi,* 1788, Vol. II, p. 377.

varied subjects. They ranged from the obscure young Continental scholar John Philip Barretier (1744) to Frederick the Great (1757), from the Italian historian Father Paul (1738) to the Dutch scientist Boerhaave (1739), from Richard Savage, adventurer and poet (1744), to literary recluses such as Sir Thomas Browne and Roger Ascham (1756 and 1761), from the sea-captains Blake and Drake (1740) to the bookseller Edward Cave (1754). All of these were composed before Boswell knew Johnson; some before Johnson was thirty years old. Such lives as these, written at fairly regular intervals over a score of years, though they were usually hasty sketches, contain much that is characteristically Johnsonian. Not one of them lacks its sentences of salty wit or broad vision. Each of them shows that although biography must record fact, it need not disregard style and intelligence. Such a sentence as this, written in 1740, has already the Johnsonian ring:[50]

"For to prolong Life, and improve it, are nearly the same. If to have all that Riches can purchase is to be rich, to do all that can be done in a long Time, is to live long, and he is equally a Benefactor to Mankind, who teaches them to protract the Duration, or shorten the Business of Life."

His massive sentences give dignity to his amused Olympian tone:[51]

"To review this towering regiment was his [Frederick William's] daily pleasure, and to perpetuate it was so much his care, that when he met a tall woman, he immediately commanded one of his Titanian retinue to marry her, that they might propagate procerity, and produce heirs to the father's habiliments."

". . . the eyes of all scholars, a race of mortals formed for dependence, were upon him. . ." (p. 20).

"Princes have this remaining of humanity, that they think themselves obliged not to make war without a reason" (p. 64).

Any chance circumstance in the life of a private individual may strike from Johnson sudden speculations on the lot of man. Roger Ascham's poverty leads him to question the rôles of justice and luck in the ordering of the world; Ascham's death brings a

[50] *An account of the life of John Philip Barretier*, 1744 ed., p. 2.
[51] *Memoirs of Charles Frederick*, 1786, p. 3. Written 1757.

glancing reference to human existence, in which much is to be endured and little to be enjoyed:[52]

"Whether he was poor by his own fault or the fault of others, cannot now be decided; but it is certain that many have been rich with less merit."

"Roger Ascham died in the fifty-third year of his age . . . and who can determine, whether he was cut off from advantages, or rescued from calamities?"

Johnson wears his philosophy lightly. His best remarks are often no more than parentheses in his narrative; their underlying seriousness, comprehensiveness, and profundity may easily be passed over. The place of leisure in a career, the analysis of motives for personal antipathies, the often mistaken zeal of friends, the relation between the contemplative and the active life, are all touched upon in a single sentence in the *Life of Ascham* (p. v):

"His favourite amusement was archery, in which he spent, or, in the opinion of others, lost so much time, that those whom either his faults or virtues made his enemies, and perhaps some whose kindness wished him always worthily employed, did not scruple to censure his practice, as unsuitable to a man possessing learning, and perhaps of bad example in a place of education."

Perhaps the best of his early biographies, always excepting the *Life of Savage,* is his life of Sir Thomas Browne. Sympathetically though ironically done, it is in Johnson's best style, and proportionally contains more of his brilliant generalizations from an individual experience than either the *Savage* or the *Lives of the Poets.* Johnson, who prided himself upon his introductions, opens this life with a paragraph which allies biography with philosophy, psychology, and literature, rather than with historical annals, antiquarianism, or science:[53]

"Though the writer of the following Essays seems to have had the fortune common among men of letters, of raising little curiosity after his private life, and has, therefore, few memorials preserved of his felicities or misfortunes; yet, because an edition of a posthumous work appears imperfect and neglected, without

---

[52] *The English works of Roger Ascham,* 1761, p. xv.

[53] *Christian Morals: By Sir Thomas Browne,* 1756, pp. i-ii.

some account of the author, it was thought necessary to attempt the gratification of that curiosity which naturally inquires, by what peculiarities of nature or fortune eminent men have been distinguished, how uncommon attainments have been gained, and what influence learning has had on its possessors, or virtue on its teachers."

The conclusion of the *Browne* is no less worthy in showing Johnson's understanding of the components of biography, and also Johnson as a "great Christian moralist":[54]

"The opinions of every man must be learned from himself: concerning his practice, it is safest to trust the evidence of others. Where these testimonies concur, no higher degree of historical certainty can be obtained; and they apparently concur to prove, that BROWNE was A ZEALOUS ADHERENT TO THE FAITH OF *CHRIST,* THAT HE LIVED IN OBEDIENCE TO HIS LAWS, AND DIED IN CONFIDENCE OF HIS MERCY."

Between the introduction and the conclusion, supported by and related to the narrative of Browne's progress, are such observations as follow, the mellow fruit of experience and meditation (pp. v, ix, xxx, xlix and l):

"It is, however, to be lamented, that those who are most capable of improving mankind, very frequently neglect to communicate their knowledge; either because it is more pleasing to gather ideas than to impart them, or because to minds naturally great, few things appear of so much importance as to deserve the notice of the publick."

"Of these animadversions [Sir Kenelm Digby's on Browne's *Religio Medici*], when they were yet not all printed, either officiousness or malice informed Dr. Browne; who wrote to Sir Kenelm with much softness and ceremony, declaring the unworthiness of his work to engage such notice, the intended privacy of the composition, and the corruptions of the impression; and received an answer equally gentle and respectful, containing high commendations of the piece, pompous professions of rever-

---

[54] The phrase is from Joseph Epes Brown's *Critical Opinions of Samuel Johnson,* 1926, p. xlii. The quotation which follows is from *Christian Morals,* 1756, p. lxi.

ence, meek acknowledgments of inability, and anxious apologies for the hastiness of his remarks.

"The reciprocal civility of authors is one of the most risible scenes in the farce of life. Who would not have thought, that these two luminaries of their age had ceased to endeavour to grow bright by the obscuration of each other. . . ."

". . . he mentions many other restrained methods of versifying, to which industrious ignorance has sometimes voluntarily subjected itself."

"It is observable, that he who in his earlier years had read all the books against religion, was in the latter part of his life averse from controversies. To play with important truths, to disturb the repose of established tenets, to subtilize objections, and elude proof, is too often the sport of youthful vanity, of which maturer experience commonly repents. There is a time, when every wise man is weary of raising difficulties only to task himself with the solution, and desires to enjoy truth without the labour or hazard of contest."

". . . pride is a vice, which pride itself inclines every man to find in others, and to overlook in himself."

To those who hold that Johnson was incapable of appreciating the wild irregularities of the romantic spirit, the following sentence is a partial answer (p. lv):

"But his innovations are sometimes pleasing, and his temerities happy: he has many "verba ardentia," forcible expressions, which he would never have found, but by venturing to the utmost verge of propriety; and flights which would never have been reached, but by one who had very little fear of the shame of falling."

Johnson's humor, his psychological subtlety, and his art are apparent in a single paragraph in which he discusses Browne's belief that his own life partakes of the miraculous. Particularly notable is Johnson's incidental review of Browne's career by mentioning his past travels. Such summaries, which do much to unite a biography around a living figure when they are not introduced too obviously, are rare indeed in eighteenth century biography (pp. xii-xiii):

"A scholastick and academical life is very uniform; and has, indeed, more safety than pleasure. A traveller has greater opportunities of adventure; but Browne traversed no unknown seas, or Arabian desarts: and surely, a man may visit France and Italy, reside at Montpellier and Padua, and at last take his degree at Leyden, without any thing miraculous. What it was, that would, if it was related, [according to the *Religio Medici*] sound so poetical and fabulous, we are left to guess; I believe, without hope of guessing rightly. The wonders probably were transacted in his own mind: self-love, co-operating with an imagination vigorous and fertile as that of Browne, will find or make objects of aston-ishment in every man's life: and, perhaps, there is no human being, however hid in the crowd from the observations of his fellow-mortals, who, if he had leisure and disposition to recollect his own thoughts and actions, will not conclude his life in some sort a miracle, and imagine himself distinguished from all the rest of his species by many discriminations of nature or of for-tune."

Johnson's not too kindly wit and his beautiful sense of propor-tion find adequate exercise in his discussion of Browne's *Garden of Cyrus* (p. xxv):

"In the prosecution of this sport of fancy, he considers every production of art and nature, in which he could find any decus-sation or approaches to the form of a Quincunx; and as a man once resolved upon ideal discoveries, seldom searches long in vain, he finds his favourite figure in almost every thing, whether natural or invented, antient or modern, rude or artificial, sacred and civil; so that a reader, not watchful against the power of his infusions, would imagine that decussation was the great business of the world, and that nature and art had no other purpose than to exemplify and imitate a Quincunx."

For penetration and truth, his critical observations upon Browne's style and subject matter are comparable to his judg-ments, more than twenty years later, in the *Lives of the Poets*. Yet to single out the witty and significant sections in the *Life of Browne,* to mention the passages that show insight or art or moral seriousness, is practically to reproduce the biography in full.

If this is true for one of his lesser known works, what can be said of the *Life of Savage,* written from a full and indignant heart, or of the *Lives of the Poets,* the mature work of the seventy-year-old philosopher? The generosities of his youth were poured into the *Life of Savage;* the reflections of his whole life into the prefaces to the poets. "Because he had seen much of life," Raleigh justly observes,[55] "his last and greatest work, *The Lives of the Most Eminent English Poets,* is more than a collection of facts: it is a book of wisdom and experience, a treatise on the conduct of life, a commentary on human destiny."

It is enough to observe again that Johnson stands as the most important figure in the development of eighteenth century English biography. Many biographers were taught by him to prize their art highly and to see its scope and purpose clearly.[56] He is a central figure in the art of biography in that he summed up in himself the tried past and the experimental present. He insisted upon the moral purpose of biography; but its ethical function was not to be rendered ineffectual by failure to make the moral spring naturally, organically, from the individual life considered. He therefore insisted upon the importance of keeping the eye on the object: absolute truth was requisite, and truth could only be secured by the observation and record of the essential details, no matter how minute they might be. This part of his theory and practice was most frequently and easily misunderstood. Too many of his followers and admirers failed to realize that Johnson maintained that the small detail should be selected with unusual care because it must be *significant.* He himself was a master, the greatest in English biography, at drawing the general truth from the individual fact. In biography, no less than in his other writings, Johnson shows his "sound conception of the relation of literature to life."[57] In a particular sense, nothing human was

---

[55] *Six Essays on Johnson,* 1910, p. 26.

[56] Johnson's influence is apparent, e.g. in most of his own biographers as listed in the bibliography; in such works as Anna Williams's *Emperor Julian,* 1746; John Hawkesworth's *Swift,* 1755; Joel Collier's *Musical Travels,* 1774; Herbert Croft's *Edward Young,* wr. 1780 and inserted in the *Lives of the Poets* (Croft even deserted law for the Church because of Johnson's influence); Thomas Sheridan's *Swift,* 1784; Charles Burney's *Handel,* 1785, and *Metastasio,* 1796; Christopher Hunter's *Christopher Smart,* 1791; James Keir's *Thomas Day,* 1791; Robert Bisset's *Edmund Burke,* 1798; and in many of the writings of Fanny Burney, Vicesimus Knox, Anthony Pasquin or John Williams, Edmund Malone, George Chalmers, Thomas Davies, and John Watkins.

[57] W. B. C. Watkins, *Johnson and English Poetry before 1660,* 1936, p. 13.

alien to Johnson, for he believed, and in his writings was able to demonstrate, that men are essentially one, with the same hopes, fears, and desires. No matter what might be the arabesques, the variations and improvisations played by each individual, Johnson brought out the underlying and unvarying themes. For the specific art of biography Johnson exemplifies, completely and profoundly, the classic doctrine that art reveals the Universal in the Particular.

Such a conception of the purpose and possibilities of biography made it indeed a dignified form of literature, upon which Johnson himself was willing to expend his best stylistic efforts. At the end of his *Life of Johnson* Boswell gives specimens to show the influence of Johnson's style upon other writers. In the writing of biography also, Johnson's manner found many imitators. Generally, his followers could copy his style no more successfully than they could equal the strength of his thinking. As they use his balanced sentences and his copious triple Ciceronian phrases, Walpole's criticism of Johnson's "triptology" seems more understandable, and "the learned gambol of a lettered elephant" becomes among his followers less learned and more elephantine. Johnson's style had no permanent or beneficial effect, then, upon English biography. It was fitted only for the powerful mind of Johnson himself. When we read the works of his admirers and imitators, we feel that as far as style is concerned, Doctor Johnson taught little fishes to talk like whales. If those who came after him had been able to write with equal finish and think with equal force, English biography might easily have become, as Johnson already envisioned it in his mind, of greater value than the novel and the drama.

One of Johnson's most refractory pupils was Mrs. Thrale. She married the music-master Piozzi not only without his approval but without his knowledge. If he could not make her accept his own moral beliefs, he had difficulty also in teaching her to speak and write with exact truthfulness. Yet she did print, for instance, Johnson's letters of bitter disappointment, even when they reflected upon her own conduct; and in spite of Boswell's repeated cavils at her inaccuracy, Mrs. Piozzi may be freed from the charge of deliberate misrepresentation. She suppresses (as Boswell himself suppresses) material in accordance with her own best judgment. Frequently she distorts a scene, but almost invariably the distortion is caused by her own definite, if somewhat limited personality.

"When we went into Wales together," she writes,[58] "and spent some time at Sir Robert Cotton's at Lleweny, one day at dinner I meant to please Mr. Johnson particularly with a dish of very young peas. Are not they charming? said I to him, while he was eating them.—'Perhaps (said he) they would be so—to a *pig.*'" Johnson's habitual desire to keep his friends from using words in slipshod fashion here becomes (as it evidently seemed to Mrs. Thrale) a boorish and almost insulting remark. Their two tempers differed widely. New peas, not Doctor Johnson, were charming to Mrs. Thrale. The hostess at Streatham was annoyed by his slopply, uncleanly, awkward bulk and his uncouth gestures and breathings. Certainly, more than any other of his biographers, she presents him as a bear let loose in a drawing-room, a creature who, whatever were his mental qualities, was physically repulsive. Throughout her *Anecdotes,* Mrs. Thrale treats him as her husband's friend rather than her own; it was Mr. Thrale's idea that Johnson should have a room in their house; she knows Johnson liked Thrale more than he liked her; she admits (p. 77) that eighteen year's acquaintance made her impatient with him; and she suggests (pp. 292-4) that after Thrale's death she gave up her house at Streatham and retired to Bath largely because she found the Doctor a burden.

In view of their temperamental antipathies and the misprision bred by long familiarity, Mrs. Piozzi's picture of Mr. Johnson— she does not call him Doctor—is surprisingly good. It is lively, and gives the impression of faithfulness. "A story," Johnson had told her (p. 116), "is a specimen of human manners, and derives its sole value from its truth." The Johnson that is given in her anecdotes is a man of irritating idiosyncrasies but of comprehensive mind and complete benevolence, as seen by a fastidious, selfish, witty, and intelligent woman. Her very lack of indis-

---

[58] *Anecdotes of the late Samuel Johnson,* by Hester Lynch Piozzi, 1786, 2d ed., p. 63.

criminate hero-worship, her decided personality, and her sex
brought out traits in Johnson that were hidden from Boswell and
that the lover of Johnson would not willingly resign. Her stories
give him a warmth and a worldliness that is often lacking in
Boswell's oracular Doctor (pp. 27-8):

"Mr. Johnson caught me another time reprimanding the
daughter of my housekeeper for having sat down unpermitted in
her mother's presence. 'Why, she gets her living, does she not
(said he), without her mother's help? Let the wench alone,' continued he. And when we were again out of the women's sight
who were concerned in the dispute: 'Poor people's children, dear
Lady (said he), never respect them: I did not respect my own
mother, though I loved her: and one day, when in anger she
called me a puppy, I asked her if she knew what they called a
puppy's mother.'"

He can joke almost brutally about his own good deeds (p. 51):

". . . when Murphy joked him the week before for having
been so diligent of late between Dodd's sermon and Kelly's prologue . . . Dr. Johnson replied, 'Why, Sir, when they come to me
with a dead stay-maker and a dying parson, what can a man
do?'"

His great gift of compassion never came out more clearly than
in such a chance remark as this (pp. 84-5):

"He loved the poor as I never yet saw any one else do, with an
earnest desire to make them happy.—What signifies, says some
one, giving halfpence to common beggars? they only lay it out
in gin or tobacco. 'And why should they be denied such sweet-
eners of their existence (says Johnson)? . . . Life is a pill which
none of us can bear to swallow without gilding; yet for the poor
we delight in stripping it still barer, and are not ashamed to shew
even visible displeasure, if ever the bitter taste is taken from their
mouths."

Johnson confides in Mrs. Thrale even his early affairs of the
heart, telling her of his affection for Molly Aston (p. 158):

"I asked him what his wife thought of this attachment? 'She
was jealous to be sure (said he), and teized me sometimes when
I would let her; and one day, as a fortune-telling gipsey passed
us when we were walking out in company with two or three

friends in the country, she made the wench look at my hand, but soon repented her curiosity; for (says the gipsey) Your heart is divided, Sir, between a Betty and a Molly: Betty loves you best, but you take most delight in Molly's company: when I turned about to laugh, I saw my wife was crying. Pretty charmer! she had no reason!' "

There is a fine picture of Doctor Johnson riding miles on end after the hounds on Mr. Thrale's old hunter (pp. 206-7):

"He was however proud to be amongst the sportsmen; and I think no praise ever went so close to his heart, as when Mr. Hamilton called out one day upon Brighthelmstone Downs, Why Johnson rides as well, for ought I see, as the most illiterate fellow in England."

We may thank Mrs. Piozzi for telling us that Johnson had light gray eyes (p. 297). She has a faculty for catching external details and making them droll (pp. 237-8):

"Indeed it was a perpetual miracle that he did not set himself on fire reading abed, as was his constant custom, when exceedingly unable even to keep clear of mischief with our best help; and accordingly the fore-top of all his wigs were burned by the candle down to the very net-work. Mr. Thrale's valet-de-chambre, for that reason, kept one always in his own hands, with which he met him at the parlour-door when the bell had called him down to dinner, and as he went up stairs to sleep in the afternoon, the same man constantly followed him with another."

And with rather a tolerant proprietary air she tells of his chemical laboratory at Streatham, where, when the Thrales had gone to London, he almost annihilated their children, their servants, and himself.

"Stories of humour," she observes (p. 240), "do not tell well in books," but Johnson's wit, which keeps better than most, frequently flashes in her anecdotes. Rough answers his remarks generally are, but they are always saved by sense and humor (p. 187):

" 'Dear Doctor (said he one day to a common acquaintance, who lamented the tender state of his *inside*), do not be like the spider, man; and spin conversation thus incessantly out of thy own bowels.' "

Her serious estimates of Johnson's fundamental character may stand unchallenged even today, for Mrs. Thrale was too intelligent not to prefer justice to pique and prejudice in her final summaries. "Had I given," she writes (pp. 219-20),

"anecdotes of his actions instead of his words, we should I am sure have had nothing on record but acts of virtue differently modified, as different occasions called that virtue forth: and among all the nine biographical essays or performances which I have heard will at last be written about dear Dr. Johnson, no mean or wretched, no wicked or even slightly culpable action will I trust be found, to produce and put in the scale against a life of seventy years, spent in the uniform practice of every moral excellence and every Christian perfection, save humility alone, says a critic, but that I think *must* be excepted. He was not however wanting even in that to a degree seldom attained by man, when the duties of piety or charity called it forth."

Like Boswell, she insists that Johnson was greater than any book that might be written about him; she conveys the impression of a noble, proud, expanded mind, of which her anecdotes can merely preserve imperfectly certain fragments (p. 240):

"The cork model of Paris is not more despicable as a resemblance of a great city, than this book, *levior cortice,* as a specimen of Johnson's character. Yet every body naturally likes to gather little specimens of the rarities found in a great country; and could I carry home from Italy square pieces of all the curious marbles which are the just glory of this surprising part of the world, I could scarcely contrive perhaps to arrange them so meanly as not to gain some attention from the respect due to the places they once belonged to.—Such a piece of motley Mosaic work will these Anecdotes inevitably make: but let the reader remember that he was promised nothing better, and so be as contented as he can."

And her final judgment is (p. 306): "The mind of this man was indeed expanded beyond the common limits of human nature, and stored with such variety of knowledge, that I used to think it resembled a royal pleasure-ground."

Nor does she overestimate her performance or believe that her picture of Johnson is complete or final. The Johnson she knew was an old man in a kindly and luxurious haven at Streatham, and Mrs. Piozzi realizes this (pp. 243-4):

"I saw Mr. Johnson in none but a tranquil uniform state, passing the evening of his life among friends, who loved, honoured, and admired him: I saw none of the things he did, except such acts of charity as have been often mentioned in this book, and such writings as are universally known. What he said is all I can relate; and from what he said, those who think it worth while to read these Anecdotes, must be contented to gather his character. Mine is a mere *candle-light* picture of his latter days, where every thing falls in dark shadow except the face, the index of the mind; but even that is seen unfavourably, and with a paleness beyond what nature gave it."

The whole volume is not only buoyant and amusing, but artistic in its absolute concentration on Johnson and its unhesitating conception, well integrated, of his character. Johnson lives again in brief scenes, a witty man remembered by a witty woman; for we may say for Mrs. Thrale, as she said for Boswell, that a long head is better than shorthand.

Sir John Hawkins wrote, in a sense, the "official" biography of Johnson: that is, he was chosen to write the life that preceded the collected edition of Johnson's works. His production has many faults. It is poorly proportioned; it includes long quotations from Johnson's fabricated Parliamentary debates, boring material dug up from the files of the publisher Edward Cave, digressions on Chesterfield, the antiquaries and the novelists, until one feels that everyone and everything except Johnson is receiving attention. More serious than the lack of style and organization is Hawkins's attitude towards his subject. His vanity, snobbery, and pettiness made him the worst person in the world to interpret Johnson. The digression on Goldsmith alone (pp. 415-21) sufficiently betrays Hawkins as mean-minded and unimaginative. His ungenerous intolerance as opposed to Johnson's profound sympathy can best be shown by one of his anecdotes, in which Johnson solicits Hawkins, diplomatically but without success, for financial aid for a ne'er-do-well. Hawkins consents to interview the wife of this dancing-master, imprisoned for a small debt:[59]

"I heard her story, and learned from it, that all the merit of the fellow lay in his heels, that he had neither principle nor discretion, and, in short, was a cully, the dupe of every one that would make him drunk. I therefore dismissed her with a message to Johnson to this effect: that her husband made it impossible for his friends to help him, and must submit to his destiny. When I next saw Johnson, I told him that there seemed to be as exact a fitness between the character of this man and his associates, as is between the web of a spider and the wings of a fly, and I could not but think he was born to be cheated. Johnson seemed to acquiesce in my opinion; but I believe, before that, had set him at liberty by paying the debt."

Although Hawkins reveals his character on almost every page, he seems never conscious of what he is revealing. He obviously felt that his dull galleries of portraits, each tagged with his positive moral judgment,[60] were contributions to the culture of his time.

Granted that Hawkins was a most disagreeable man and no artist, the importance of his *Life of Johnson* has nevertheless been undervalued. Just as Marlowe's lustre is dimmed by his proximity to Shakespeare, so Hawkins always suffers by comparison with Boswell. The six hundred pages of Hawkins's *Life* make it one of the fullest of all literary biographies before Boswell; even a partial failure in the difficult pioneering task of assembling the documents that compose the life of a writer deserves praise. Hawkins's method is chronological, eclectic, antiquarian. He utilizes a variety of sources, from Johnson's own diary to Dr. Brocklesby's account of Johnson's last days. Furthermore, Hawkins's plan is really the prototype of Boswell's: through one central figure the culture of an age is to be reflected. No less than Boswell, Hawkins writes a "life-and-times."

[59] *The works of Samuel Johnson, LL.D. Together with his life . . . by Sir John Hawkins, Knt.*, 1787, Vol. I of 11 vols., p. 405.

[60] Only his judgment on the immorality of Fielding comes as a relief, as much in the twentieth century as in the eighteenth.] ι ε ϯο Ωλαʋϩϧᴇγ

Although James Boswell never admits it, he was deeply influenced by Hawkins. Boswell's repeated and almost uniformly hostile references to his predecessor make his work in one sense no more than a refutation on a grand scale of what he considered an erroneous earlier interpretation. He follows Hawkins closely, therefore, if only to catch him in a slip or an uncharitable judgment. Boswell's great enemy shapes, to an extent generally underrated, Boswell's great work.[61] The genealogy of Boswell's *Johnson* cannot be fully traced, therefore, if this black sheep among its ancestors, the heartily detested Sir John Hawkins, is neglected.

Mrs. Thrale speaks of the nine rumored biographical productions concerning her friend and permanent house-guest. Actually, Johnson had more lives than a cat. It would be useless to consider in detail the elegies, odes, and travesties which his life and death inspired, the anonymous biographies and characters, the jests, *bon-mots,* table-talk, deformities, and beauties, the derivative lives and anecdotes, the partial sketches and reminiscences preserved separately or as parts of other memoirs. As early as 1786 Joseph Towers was writing:[62] "Innumerable anecdotes have been published of him, his most minute singularities have been recorded, and his virtues, and even his weaknesses, laboriously displayed, by those who lived with him on terms of the most perfect intimacy." And Robert Anderson, in his readable, just, and derivative *Life of Johnson,* echoes what all the world knew when he says:[63]

"The events of the life of Johnson, who has written the lives of so many eminent persons, and so much enriched our national stock of biography, criticism, and moral instruction, have been related by friend and foe, by panegyrists and satirical defamers, by the lovers of anecdote, and the followers of party, with a

[61] It is amusing to see, for instance, that although Boswell had in his own rough notes the rhyme of Master Duck (which he had direct from Mrs. Porter in Johnson's presence), he uses Hawkins's version, modified, in his *Life.* Boswell had recorded in his notes that the poor duck was one of a brood of 13; Hawkins says one of 11; Boswell's *Life* says one of 11. For fuller discussion, see Aleyn Lyell Reade's *Johnsonian Gleanings,* Vol. III.

[62] *An essay on the life, character, and writings of Dr. Samuel Johnson,* 1786, p. 1.

[63] 1st ed. 1795; quoted from 1815 Edinburgh ed., p. 1.

diligence of research, a minuteness of detail, and a variety of illustration, unexampled in the records of literature."

One of the essays, however, deserves to be singled out. Arthur Murphy, who knew Johnson longer than either Mrs. Thrale or Boswell, and who asserts he was present at the first meeting of each of them with Johnson, did not publish his *Essay on the life and genius of Samuel Johnson* until 1792. It is not a long work, but it affords a picture different from all its predecessors. Murphy has absorbed and easily reflects Johnson's opinion that a full and truthful presentation of human life constitutes a moral document (1793 ed., p. 2):

"In reviewing the life of such a writer, there is, besides, a rule of justice to which the publick have an undoubted claim. . . . The lights and shades of the character should be given; and, if this be done with a strict regard to truth, a just estimate of Dr. Johnson will afford a lesson perhaps as valuable as the moral doctrine that speaks with energy in every page of his works."

Murphy's estimate of his friend is favorable, if occasionally cynical. Some traits of Johnson's he portrays more successfully than any of his competitors. In spite of his own tendency toward melancholia, for instance, Boswell does not seem able to transfer to the reader Johnson's black despair. Murphy does better (p. 81): "In his sixtieth year he had a mind to write the history of his melancholy; but he desisted, not knowing whether it would not too much disturb him." Murphy quotes aptly a translation of a Latin poem written by Johnson on the completion of his Dictionary, betraying his melancholy. In 1766, Murphy records, the Thrales find him on his knees, praying not to lose his reason. And what a glimpse into depths the reader gets from the phrasing (p. 122):

"For many years, when he was not disposed to enter into the conversation going forward, whoever sat near his chair, might hear him repeating, from Shakespeare,

'Ay, but to die . . .'
and from Milton 'Who would lose
For fear of pain, this intellectual being!'"

"The history of a death-bed is painful," Murphy writes (p. 135). Murphy's account of Johnson's death, which is more painful than Boswell's, may also more nearly approximate the effect upon his contemporaries of Johnson's final struggle.

The many biographies of Johnson demonstrate that biography is an art rather than a science. The same material, the same incidents, the same anecdotes, are handled by many writers, but the resultant portraits of Johnson are not the same. Contemplation of the strong and steady figure of Johnson becomes a means to reveal the character of each of his biographers. Among the arts, biography is no exception to the general rule that the personality of the creator must in some manner disclose itself. Depersonalized biography is a dead thing; most of the mechanical accounts intended simply to convey information and facts are themselves eclectic, derivative from more vital if biased narratives in which the emotions and interests of the biographers themselves are involved. Mrs. Piozzi and Sir John Hawkins and Arthur Murphy and Joshua Reynolds and Lord Macaulay and Thomas Carlyle write about Johnson, but they reveal themselves. And this is no less true with the best of Johnson's biographers, James Boswell. Boswell has sometimes been considered a lucky blunderer, unconscious of what he was achieving; sometimes as a kind of machine for listening, observing, and recording. But Boswell as a conscious artist, who presents not so much a final as a vital picture of his friend, and whose interpretation is colored by his own life, deserves more attention than he has received.

"No one," says Johnson, "is so fit to be a man's biographer as the man himself." The autobiographer, he believed, might surpass the biographer in truthfulness, and therefore in worth and interest. Yet the most famous single work among all biographies and autobiographies is Boswell's *Life of Johnson*. This is the more remarkable because, great as were Boswell's gifts for biography, his potentialities for autobiography might be considered even greater. He possessed in a superlative degree the first requisite of the autobiographer—an overwhelming interest in himself. It is the most famous of all English biographers who says: "In reality, a man is of more importance to himself than all other things or persons can be."[64] Critics have always seen that the *Life of Johnson,* like so many of the greatest biographies, is really a double portrait. But until the vast stores of Boswelliana were removed from Malahide Castle and given to the world, Boswell as the writer of his own life was not, because he could not be, rightly valued. The magnificent eighteen-volume edition published by Lieutenant Colonel Isham, with the brilliant introductions by Mr. Geoffrey Scott and Professor Pottle, is a fit presentation of Boswell the autobiographer. Few people will care to dispute that no one, in any age or nation, has left, such a complete and satisfactory record of his own life as has Boswell.

How is it possible that this most successful of autobiographers, who diligently and conscientiously cultivated his own ego, is also the most successful biographer? A partial answer makes explicit one of the assumptions on which this present volume is based: that the distinction between biography and autobiography is merely formal. In spite of the weight of Johnson's authority, one cannot finally determine whether the biographer or the autobiographer is the more impartial. Nor is it more than a wide generalization to assume that autobiography is subjective, biography objective. Exceptions will immediately occur to everyone, and soon the theorist is tangled in such clumsy phrases as objective autobiography and subjective biography. A man who writes his own life may have different material to draw upon and may adopt a different tone from the man who writes the life of another. But two biographers of the same man may vary equally in their sources and in their interpretations. It is disputable that a man best understands himself or can best record and make clear his experiences. Among moral codes "Know thyself" is by no means the easiest to realize. The conscious, subtle analysis of personality has developed over a period of centuries; its difficult discoveries have been made exclusively neither by professed biographers nor autobiographers; and the methods of revealing character, once disclosed, have been practised by biographers and autobiographers alike. Furthermore, the talent for recording and analyzing one's own experiences is akin to the talent for recording

[64] *The Hypochondriack,* No. 66, 1928 ed., Vol. II, p. 258.

and analyzing the experiences of others. Boswell's unending effort to perfect himself in setting down his own life, an effort which began as early as his eighteenth year and ended only shortly before his death, may be considered the principal cause of his success in recording the life of Johnson. We return, then, to the conviction that the difference between the two forms of writing is chiefly technical, often no more than a question of personal pronouns.

There is, however, a more particular reason why this genius at autobiography should have produced the most celebrated of biographies. In a peculiar sense which could not be fully grasped before the publication of the Isham Papers, Boswell's *Life of Johnson* is actually a fragment of his own autobiography. Technically, of course, its *disjecta membra* are scattered through his own journals, small fractions among his diverse interests and friendships. But in a more fundamental sense, Johnson was a part of Boswell's personal life: the huge embodiment of his aspirations.[65] This is not to say that Boswell has merely created a shadowy figure of fulfilled desire. Those clear eyes and that limited commonplace understanding would have found it as unnecessary to falsify as it was unnatural. Apart from his own convictions of the necessity of minute exactitude, Boswell had a mind neither original nor powerful enough to distort actual events to fit a preconception or a spiritual need. But in Samuel Johnson, by a stroke of luck for himself and for the world, Boswell found a personality which satisfied his moral instincts so completely that he could devote himself to it without reserve. The juggler of Notre Dame performed his tricks before the statue of Mary; Boswell, as his unique tribute to his mentor, centered upon Johnson those unsurpassed powers of observation which almost alone distinguish the Laird of Auchinleck from *l'homme sensuel moyen*. Boswell had met and known more famous and more influential men than Johnson; his tenacity would have made it possible, perhaps, for him to have recorded the life of one or another of them as fully as he did for Johnson.

[65] cf. also, in his *Tour to Corsica,* Boswell's use of Paoli almost as a fetish for his own ardor and love of spirited virtue.

But he chose Johnson because Johnson was a part of himself, the ideal part. There is no need to dwell upon their differences, many of them superficial. The most important one, of course, is their disparate mental statures. The underlying resemblances between Boswell and Johnson, however, are many. The two of them fitted together pleasantly in many of their interests and prejudices: in their regard for rank and family, their Christian orthodoxy, their profound ethical preoccupations, their love of literature and society. Johnson was Boswell as he would like to have been. Boswell could admire the certainty in Johnson which he himself would never possess, just as he could admire Johnson's strong will. Neither was free from the deadly sin of gluttony, yet when Johnson realized the harmful effect of drinking upon him he could forego drink, an exercise of will which all the resolutions Boswell ever made never accomplished. And if we may believe Boswell on such a point, Johnson's early life in London—but only his early life—was not without sexual irregularities: here again Boswell saw and approved the better, but followed the worse. One distinction between them reflects honor upon them both. Johnson, who in most matters practised self-control, was sympathetic enough to realize that there may be a divergence between principles and practice; Boswell, who could not achieve perfection, never accepted what would have been for him such a comfortable answer.

This intense moral seriousness was their greatest bond. Yet they were united through their temperaments as well. Throughout his life Johnson was racked by melancholia and its attendant inertia. Boswell in this respect also seems no other than Johnson on a smaller scale. The *Life of Johnson* leads one to forget too readily that its author also wrote the seventy essays that make up the *Hypochondriack,* or that his periods of lassitude and despair were so overwhelming and crescent that many sections of his journals are painful to read. Johnson gave heart and hope to a wavering, at times a desperate, young man; he taught him from his own experience how to subdue the nightmare imaginings and black negation of melancholia; so that even after Johnson is gone, as death and discouragement and failure crowd closer around Boswell, he manages, in marshalling his memories, to outsoar the shadow of his night. The days and the months which he spent with Johnson, his *alter ego,* his conscience and his consolation, were among the happiest of his life; these periods of buoyancy were naturally reflected in the biography. Yet to think of Boswell as perpetually in good spirits is as erroneous as to think of Johnson as perpetually melancholy. Both were constitutionally subject to moods of deep dejection, just as both possessed a compensating abundance of sociability, humor, and spirits so high that at times they verged upon hysteria. If Johnson's wit and satire are more powerful than Boswell's, again it is probably a difference of degree, for the cast of their minds was here much the same.

Among their similarities, that which is most immediately important to this chapter was their enthusiasm for biography. "The biographical part of literature," said Johnson,[66] "is what I love most"; and Boswell's whole life and works show this liking just as certainly. Both of them saw the past and the present as a series of specific happenings to specific persons. Both of them thought biographically: Johnson founded his moral generalizations on the basis of experiences in the lives of individuals; Boswell felt that the pure event itself, minutely observed and faithfully recorded, was a solace. The exhibition in any form of human individuality, the impact of one irreplaceable personality upon another, gave him delight; and when such high moments of existence occurred, Boswell became eyes, ears, and a memory. What was heard, what was seen, sufficed. "Give us as many anecdotes as you can," said Johnson to the young adventurer,[67] and Boswell brought back the *Tour to Corsica.* "Truth is essential to a story," Johnson remarked,[68] and Boswell ran over half London to verify a date. Johnson maintains that there has rarely passed a life of which a faithful record would not be interesting; Plutarch asserts that trifling events may reveal character more than the greatest battles; and Boswell braves the ridicule he foresaw would follow in order to be specific about men

[66] Vol. I, p. 425; year 1763. References are to L. F. Powell's revision, 1934 ff., of G. B. Hill's edition of the *Life of Johnson.* The date for more important quotations is usually included, to facilitate the use of other editions.

[67] Feb., 1766; Vol. II, p. 11.

[68] March 16, 1776; Vol. II, p. 433.

who would otherwise have been forgotten, and in order to present life as it is lived—as a succession of *minutiae,* apparently unrelated, and often without significance when considered singly. Johnson, one of the great artists and probably with Carlyle the best critic in English biography, as he is certainly the most influential, found in Boswell an apt pupil. Here again one seems made for the other. There is no precept of Johnson's regarding the practice of biography, no far-reaching, deliberate generalization or terse dogma thrown out as passing comment, which Boswell does not illustrate in writing his *Life of Johnson.* He is the disciple who surpasses his master; or more precisely, the author whose practice brilliantly exemplifies his mentor's theories.

As a single illustration, let us consider Johnson's passionate regard for truth as it affects Boswell. Boswell's scrupulous accuracy is a commonplace—largely because he confides to his readers at the very outset of his biography how much trouble this virtue of exactitude has caused him—but it is not generally realized how much of this complacency in truth-telling Boswell built up for himself from the utterances of Johnson. It is no more than poetic justice that the greatness of Doctor Johnson in the eyes of most of the world, his littleness in the opinion of a few, may be directly due to his positive and often repeated insistence, in Boswell's presence, upon truth. Johnson instructing Boswell in truth, as they cross the Thames in a boat on March 16, 1776, to land at the Temple-stairs, is characteristic. "The value of every story," Johnson said, "depends on its being true. A story is a picture either of an individual or of human nature in general: if it be false, it is a picture of nothing. . . . ——— (naming a worthy friend of ours,) used to think a story, a story, till I shewed him that truth was essential to it."[69]

And immediately following this disquisition, Boswell himself, so seldom given to direct moralizing, observes: "The importance of strict and scrupulous veracity cannot be too often inculcated." This generalization is succeeded by referring again to his great exemplar: even in Johnson's "common conversation the slightest circumstance was mentioned with exact precision. The knowl-

[69] Vol. II, pp. 433-4. Boswell's journal shows that Bennet Langton is the friend who is referred to.

edge of his having such a principle and habit made his friends
have a perfect reliance on the truth of every thing that he told,
however it might have been doubted if told by many others." Still
thinking in biographical terms, Boswell proceeds to illustrate this
specific statement by means of an incident still more specific—
Johnson's story of the gentlewoman who offered him money for
assisting her to cross the street, a story which if told by most people
would have been thought an invention. Even here Boswell re-
fines to the last detail of precision: the gentlewoman is not just
a gentlewoman, but a gentlewoman "somewhat in liquor," the
coin is a shilling, and the street is Fleet-street.

Writing to Doctor Johnson on August 30, 1776, Boswell rather
proudly shows his master in veracity how exact he can be in recording details (Vol. III, p. 91):

"For the honour of Count Manucci, as well as to observe
that exactness of truth which you have taught me, I must correct
what I said in a former letter. He did not fall from his horse
. . . his horse fell with him."

And in 1777, when Johnson laughs at a story Boswell tells him,
Boswell goes out of his way to mention that Johnson "had a
thorough dependance upon the authenticity of my relation without any *embellishment, as falsehood or fiction* is too gently
called."[70] In the next year, Boswell checks Mrs. Thrale for making
a trivial error in recalling a story. "I presumed to take an opportunity, in presence of Johnson, of shewing this lively lady how
ready she was, unintentionally, to deviate from exact authenticity
of narration."[71] The next morning at the breakfast table at
Streatham, poor Mrs. Thrale is given a lecture, or "a very earnest
recommendation," by Boswell's preceptor himself, to which Boswell pays heed with the eager complacency of a favorite pupil.

"Our lively hostess, whose fancy was impatient of the rein,
fidgeted at this, and ventured to say, 'Nay, this is too much. If
Mr. Johnson should forbid me to drink tea, I would comply,
as I should feel the restraint only twice a day; but little variations
in narrative must happen a thousand times a day, if one is not
perpetually watching.' JOHNSON. 'Well, Madam, and you

[70] Sept. 1777; Vol. III, p. 209.
[71] Vol. III, pp. 226-30, *passim.* March 29-30, 1778.

ought to be perpetually watching. It is more from carelessness about truth than from intentional lying, that there is so much falsehood in the world.'"

Boswell follows his little dialogue on "strict attention to truth, even in the most minute particulars," by quoting from a review by Johnson:

"'Nothing but experience could evince the frequency of false information, or enable any man to conceive that so many groundless reports should be propagated, as every man of eminence may hear of himself. Some men relate what they think, as what they know; some men of confused memories and habitual inaccuracy, ascribe to one man what belongs to another; and some talk on, without thought or care. A few men are sufficient to broach falsehoods, which are afterwards innocently diffused by successive relaters.'"

And he ends the section by mentioning Johnson's influence upon his friends, an influence which is most marked upon Boswell himself:

"He inculcated upon all his friends the importance of perpetual vigilance against the slightest degrees of falsehood; the effect of which, as Sir Joshua Reynolds observed to me, has been, that all who were of his *school* are distinguished for a love of truth and accuracy, which they would not have possessed in the same degree, if they had not been acquainted with Johnson."

A fair specimen of Boswell's carefulness occurs under date of April 25, 1778, when Boswell records how he secured a list of Johnson's own writings. In a single paragraph, such phrases as "an exact catalogue . . . an imperfect list . . . pretty good reason to suppose was accurate . . . written down in his presence . . . enumerated each article aloud . . . the evidence for its exactness . . . got him positively to own or refuse . . . obtained certainty so far . . . other articles confirmed by him directly . . . made additions under his sanction"—show Boswell's unceasing care to secure absolute authenticity. Boswell's exact recording is such that when Johnson says, on April 17, 1778 (Vol. III, p. 306): "I shall be sixty-eight next birth-day," we feel, not that Boswell has been careless in his dates, but that he has faithfully recorded Johnson's own error of more than a year.

On the subject of truth, Johnson's utterances to the very last have a noble ring. "Sir," he said, during the last of those Good-Friday visits to which Boswell looked forward for annual enlightenment, purification, and strength—"Sir, you should not allow yourself to be delighted with errour."[72]

The proselyte, in his devotion to the ideals of a great teacher, may surpass his leader in strictness;[73] and Boswell's zeal for truth comes close to fanaticism. On the thirteenth of June in the last year of Johnson's life (Vol. IV, p. 305), "We talked of the casuistical question, Whether it was allowable at any time to depart from *Truth*?" and Johnson, no mean casuist himself in the game of conversation, sets up hypothetical situations in which a lie may be allowable. Such circumstances would be rare, in his opinion, for even to a sick man the truth should be told:[74] "You have no business with consequences; you are to tell the truth." Yet Boswell is not convinced that any exceptions should be made, and, one may judge, would feel he should tell an assassin in which direction his intended victim has fled. "I cannot help thinking," he writes (p. 306),

"that there is much weight in the opinion of those who have held, that Truth, as an eternal and immutable principle, ought, upon no account whatever, to be violated, from supposed previous or superiour obligations, of which every man being to judge for himself, there is great danger that we may too often, from partial motives, persuade ourselves that they exist; and probably whatever extraordinary instances may sometimes occur, where some evil may be prevented by violating this noble principle, it would be found that human happiness would, upon the whole, be more perfect were Truth universally preserved."

One of the last letters Johnson ever wrote encourages his friend Doctor Burney in the pursuit of truth:[75]

[72] April 18, 1783; Vol. IV, p. 204.

[73] cf. Boswell's continuing to think that the compliment to Garrick—"His death eclipsed the gaiety of nations,"—was "hyperbolically untrue" even after Johnson's explanations. April 24, 1779.

[74] From Boswell's journals we learn that Boswell departed from this principle and veiled from Johnson the opinions of the Scottish physicians regarding Johnson's lingering fatal illness.

[75] Nov. 1, 1784; Vol. IV, p. 361. cf. his remarks to Malone, under 1781, dated March 15, 1782; Vol. IV, p. 53.

"Of the caution necessary in adjusting narratives there is no end. Some tell what they do not know, that they may not seem ignorant, and others from mere indifference about truth. All truth is not, indeed, of equal importance; but, if little violations are allowed, every violation will in time be thought little; and a writer should keep himself vigilantly on his guard against the first temptations to negligence or supineness."

Boswell, near the conclusion of his biography, repeats a remark of Doctor Johnson's first published in the *Tour to the Hebrides*: "There is something noble in publishing truth, though it condemns one's self." When, in this same passage (Vol. IV, pp. 396-7), Boswell speaks of his own "sacred love of truth," he is still using his words with care.

That Boswell's practice was guided by Johnson's precepts is crystal clear. The passage from which the last two quotations have been drawn is that in which Boswell reveals that in his early life in London Johnson had sometimes been overcome by his amorous propensities. Whatever pain such a passage may have caused Fanny Burney or the lovers of elegant and discreet biography, Boswell must have suffered more; for as he writes he is giving evidence against a friend, exhibiting "a shade in so great a character," and, most painful of all, making his own ideal less certain and shining. The long preamble, the cautious, hesitating phrases, show the serious struggle he went through. He protects and defends Johnson's reputation with warmth and earnestness, but he will not protect him by keeping back the truth. "From the regard to truth which he inculcated," therefore, though "with all possible respect and delicacy," he sets down what he knows.

Boswell's passion for truth is not only intense but limited in conception. Truth to him is external and particular. Living as he does so much on the surface of things, believing as he does that the little facts and actions are enough in themselves, the possible relativity of truth could hardly disturb him.[76] His is not the mind of Donne or of Browning or of Shakespeare. His standard is exacting, for he insists upon an almost mechanical perfection. Other men's records of Johnson do not satisfy him. Thomas Tyers "was not sufficiently attentive to accuracy"; the arch-

[76] Yet cf. *The Hypochondriack,* No. 10.

villain Sir John Hawkins retails a story that "is altogether without foundation"; in a long and interesting passage he animadverts with concern "on the inaccuracies of Mrs. Piozzi's 'Anecdotes'" (Vol. IV, pp. 340-7), though he notes that "however often, she is not always inaccurate"; the upshot of his "altercation with a Lady, who seems unwilling to be convinced of her errors" is a lengthy footnote which presents, on the trivial question of the exact recipient of certain light verses of Johnson's, all of the evidence against Miss Anna Seward's attributions; and because of his "firm regard to authenticity," he will not insert in his work the account of the Quakeress Mrs. Knowles triumphing, as she would have it, over Johnson. Indeed, Boswell is never more the lawyer successfully marshalling evidence that will overwhelm his opponents, than in those workmanlike footnotes in which he examines the statements of his rivals.

Boswell is no less exacting with himself. This most detailed of all biographies is filled with laments and apologies for not being able to record more completely the conversations of one evening or the happenings of one spring (April 10, 1775; Vol. II, p. 350):

"I must, again and again, intreat of my readers not to suppose that my imperfect record of conversation contains the whole of what was said by Johnson, or other eminent persons who lived with him. What I have preserved, however, has the value of the most perfect authenticity."

Boswell subjects each witness to cross-examination, and presents the most trivial statements as if made upon oath (Vol. IV, pp. 307-8): "On Monday, June 14, and Tuesday, 15, Dr. Johnson and I dined, on one of them, I forget which, with Mr. Mickle . . . and on the other with Dr. Wetherell." Who but Boswell or Mistress Quickly could have said "I forget which"? And in reproducing Johnson's letter of March 21, 1782, to Mr. Hector (Vol. IV, pp. 146-7), Boswell displays in a footnote an awful respect for scholarly accuracy that might satisfy an American graduate school:

"A part of this letter having been torn off, I have, from the evident meaning, supplied a few words and half words at the ends and beginnings of lines."

Again and again he tried the patience and braved the anger of Johnson himself in order to verify or disprove a story.[77] His recordings of dates, his exact references to authorities, and his precise presentation of evidence Boswell makes into an art. Recent critics of Boswell have justly emphasized the skill with which he weaves together into a coherent pattern threads of evidence which he must have picked up over years. He makes, to take one example, a general statement: "No man was ever more remarkable for personal courage" (Vol. II, p. 298; 1775). He qualifies this assertion by excepting Johnson's "aweful dread of death, or rather, 'of something after death,' " and tries to justify or explain this fear. The rest of the paragraph is devoted to instances of Johnson's natural courage. The first story is apparently derived from Beauclerk; the second is unattributed; the third illustration Boswell has from Langton; the fourth comes from Johnson himself; the fifth is direct from Garrick; and the sixth from Thomas Davies. The paragraph is introduced into the chronological context after reproducing Johnson's letter in answer to "Ossian" Macpherson's threat—"I hope I shall never be deterred from detecting what I think a cheat, by the menaces of a ruffian"—and the whole is brought to a close by the return to the original episode, when Johnson provides himself with an oak stick as a weapon of defense against Macpherson. This action on Johnson's part is connected with the Davies story by a neat repetition of *motif,* so that the oak staff, which contemporary critics of Boswell had used to ridicule overminute biographical records, becomes in Boswell's hands a symbol for corporal prowess and intrepidity, and a token of Boswell's own dexterity as a biographer.

The authentication of statements[78] is practised by Boswell so continuously that, although it may pass without conscious notice on the part of the reader, it gradually induces a feeling of complete confidence. The mirror, we believe, is being held up to

[77] cf. Vol. III, pp. 194-6, for Sept. 22, 1777; or his gathering the list of Johnson's writings; or his continual attempts to collect material regarding Johnson's early life.

[78] cf. George Mallory, *Boswell the Biographer,* 1912, p. 249, where, after analyzing Boswell's discussion of the question of Johnson and his pension, Mallory concludes: "The mere number of names [five] consulted is sufficiently

nature; and we experience fully one of the great pleasures of reading biography—the sense of participating in actual events. Boswell has learned from Johnson, more easily than did their friend Langton, that "the value of every story depends on its being true," and concentration upon accuracy to the smallest detail produces such complete reliance upon Boswell's dependability in the mind of the reader, that he may say, "I would not take this from report. It *is*."

In the last chapter of this volume, the assertion is made that among the Platonic ideals of the Good, the Beautiful, and the True, eighteenth century biography gives a new significance to the last of the three; and here, too, the *Life of Johnson* stands as the finest example of the attempt to attain truth. To some extent, such an ideal may decrease artistic beauty in that Boswell's *magnum opus* tends to reproduce faithfully the formlessness of life itself. Furthermore, Boswell is aware of the difficulty of relating the record of truth to the inculcation of virtue. Johnson saw too clearly to equate the true and the good in human affairs. Yet two such lovers of virtue as Johnson and Boswell must inevitably attempt to reconcile their fidelity in recording imperfect human actions with their belief in the ethical value of art. Briefly, their reconciliation is this: the dispassionate presentation of faults as well as virtues even in the greatest men, is a more powerful encouragement to the imitation of noble lives than is the delineation of faultless heroes, since unattainable perfection tends to discourage the aspirations of the ordinary mortal. The best expression of this conviction in the *Life of Johnson* occurs in Malone's notes of an interview with the Doctor:[79]

"I then mentioned to him that some people thought that Mr. Addison's character was so pure, that the fact, *though true,* ought to have been suppressed [i.e. Addison's reclaiming by legal process a loan he had made to Steele]. He saw no reason for

imposing. Boswell in fact was collecting evidence for a case. He must examine all the witnesses: also he must examine them in such a way that the truth might be discovered." cf. also Boswell's discussion of Savage's parentage, in which Boswell is at his legal best. (Year 1744.)

[79] Year 1781; Vol. IV, p. 53. The argument that biographers, following the example of the Scriptures, should record imperfections, is familiar in the eighteenth century. See Chap. VII.

this. 'If nothing but the bright side of characters should be shewn, we should sit down in despondency, and think it utterly impossible to imitate them in *any thing*. The sacred writers (he observed) related the vicious as well as the virtuous actions of men; which had this moral effect, that it kept mankind from *despair*, into which otherwise they would naturally fall, were they not supported by the recollection that others had offended like themselves, and by penitence and amendment of life had been restored to the favour of Heaven.'"

Boswell adds that this paragraph is "of great importance," and, indeed, he turns over the question more than once. On September 17, 1777 (Vol. III, pp. 154-5), Johnson tells Boswell that mentioning great men's vices in biography may be ill advised, since "more ill may be done by the example, than good by telling the whole truth."

"Here was an instance of his varying from himself in talk; for when Lord Hailes and he sat one morning calmly conversing in my house at Edinburgh, I well remember that Dr. Johnson maintained, that 'If a man is to write *A Panegyrick*, he may keep vices out of sight; but if he professes to write *A Life*, he must represent it really as it was:' and when I objected to the danger of telling that Parnell drank to excess, he said, that 'it would produce an instructive caution to avoid drinking, when it was seen, that even the learning and genius of Parnell could be debased by it.' And in the Hebrides he maintained, as appears from my 'Journal,' that a man's intimate friend should mention his faults, if he writes his life."

Here is a respected moralist speaking to a professed biographer; and in those two September conversations of 1773 and 1777, Johnson fixed the nature of his own immortality. "If he professes to write *A Life*, he must represent it really as it was." "A man's intimate friend should mention his faults, if he writes his life." Johnson gave his follower such certainty of himself and his method that Boswell can break out in scorn against those who, he thinks, accuse him of "kindly" taking care to draw Johnson's weaknesses and prejudices from their dread abode. "This is the common cant," he writes (Vol. III, p. 275; 1778), "against faithful Biography. Does the worthy gentleman mean that I, who was taught discrimination of character by Johnson, should have omitted his frailties, and, in short, have *bedawbed* him?" From his own master, then, Boswell comes to value truth highly and to believe that truth gives biography its ethical importance as a guide to life.[80]

Johnson also repeatedly stamped with his approval the record of minute details and of domestic life. To such opinions Boswell, who listened to everything, listened with a more than Boswellian eagerness. Hearing Johnson talk on biography, Boswell could readily have said,

> "Phoebus repli'd, and touch'd my trembling ears."

Johnson's encouragement meant much to him:[81]

"I mentioned that I was afraid I put into my journal too many little incidents. JOHNSON. 'There is nothing, Sir, too little for so little a creature as man. It is by studying little things that we attain the great art of having as little misery and as much happiness as possible."

At the Thrales Boswell suggests that Sir Robert Sibbald, whose autobiography he intends some time to publish, returned to the Protestant faith because he found the rigid fasting prescribed by the Roman Catholic church too severe for him. Mrs. Thrale objects. "I think," she says (March 31, 1778; Vol. III, p. 228), "you had as well let alone that publication. To discover such weakness exposes a man when he is gone." But Johnson, defending Boswell, replies: "Nay, it is an honest picture of human nature. How often are the primary motives of our greatest actions as small as Sibbald's." Similar thoughts occur in Johnson's letter to Bennet Langton on the death of his uncle:[82]

---

[80] cf., for a different ethical effect which may be secured in biography, Boswell's own opinion (Vol. IV, p. 198) that "Family histories, like the *imagines majorum* of the Ancients, excite to virtue."

[81] July 14, 1763; Vol. I, p. 433.

[82] May 10, 1766; Vol. II, p. 17. cf. Johnson's jocular superiority to the mention of all Milton's residences by his biographers, a remark which did not keep Boswell from recording 17 London residences of Johnson (Oct. 10, 1779; Vol. III, p. 405); also the remark Dr. Maxwell makes regarding his interesting Johnsoniana, inserted by Boswell (1770; Vol. II, p. 117): "The very *minutiae* of such a character must be interesting, and may be compared to the filings of diamonds."

"I hope you make what enquiries you can, and write down what is told you. The little things which distinguish domestick characters are soon forgotten: if you delay to enquire, you will have no information; if you neglect to write, information will be vain."

Johnson's tendency to see the world biographically rather than historically, to emphasize domestic life rather than politics, is apparent in remarks to Joseph Baretti that seem modelled on Plutarch's famous critical dictum:[83]

"I will not trouble you with speculations about peace and war. The good or ill success of battles and embassies extends itself to a very small part of domestick life: we all have good and evil, which we feel more sensibly than our petty part of publick miscarriage or prosperity."

In the narrowest and humblest life, Samuel Johnson could find interest. He felt he could write the Life of a Broomstick;[84] and he bursts forth in protest against one of the critical platitudes of the century:[85]

"Somebody said the life of a mere literary man could not be very entertaining. JOHNSON. 'But it certainly may. This is a remark which has been made, and repeated, without justice; why should the life of a literary man be less entertaining than the life of any other man? Are there not as interesting varieties in such a life? As *a literary life* it may be very entertaining."

Appreciation for individuating details in the lives of common people Johnson possessed to a remarkable degree; his brief oral characters or biographies were so compressed and clear that Boswell imbedded them in his *magnum opus*; and Boswell may have been encouraged in his own biographical technique as he listened to Johnson's *biographiolae* of the nameless physician in the Leeward Islands, of the Reverend Mr. Charles Congreve, or of the gentleman who made two fortunes in the East Indies.[86] The portrait of Congreve, a clergyman, in Boswell's own manner,

---

[83] Dec. 21, 1762; Vol. I, p. 381.   [84] 1775; Vol. II, p. 389.

[85] April 20, 1781; Vol. IV, p. 98.

[86] March 21, 1776, Vol. II, p. 455; March 22, 1776, Vol. II, p. 460; 1776, Vol. III, p. 20. In a note to the Congreve sketch in the revised Hill edition, Johnson's letter to Hector is quoted, in which occurs a phrase which may give a philosophical basis for Johnson's interest in, and many of his theories of,

could not have been improved by Boswell himself (although, of course, one may argue that he has already touched up the miniature he gives us). Johnson is speaking to his friend Mr. Hector:

" 'He obtained, I believe, considerable preferment in Ireland, but now lives in London, quite as a valetudinarian, afraid to go into any house but his own. He takes a short airing in his post-chaise every day. He has an elderly woman, whom he calls cousin, who lives with him, and jogs his elbow, when his glass has stood too long empty, and encourages him in drinking, in which he is very willing to be encouraged; not that he gets drunk, for he is a very pious man, but he is always muddy. He confesses to one bottle of port every day, and he probably drinks more. He is quite unsocial; his conversation is monosyllabical: and when, at my last visit, I asked him what a clock it was? that signal of my departure had so pleasing an effect on him, that he sprung up to look at his watch, like a greyhound bounding at a hare.' "

After giving such evidence of Johnson's discrimination, Boswell is expressing the admiration of one artist for another when he writes (April 5, 1776; Vol. III, pp. 20-1):

"Very few men had seen greater variety of characters; and none could observe them better, as was evident from the strong, yet nice portraits which he often drew. I have frequently thought that if he had made out what the French call *une catalogue raisonnée* of all the people who had passed under his observation, it would have afforded a very rich fund of instruction and entertainment."

It is indeed ironical that the man whose weakness as a critic of poetry lies in his implied belief that poetry must directly express general truths in generalities should emphasize so forcefully, in the theory and practice of biography, the significance of the little fact. "A man," Johnson tells Boswell (April 3, 1776; Vol. III, p. 8), "is to guard himself against taking a thing in general," and Boswell took the precept to heart.

In 1743 Johnson writes contemptuously of those frivolous biographers who "supply from invention the want of intelligence,"

biography: "Time cannot always be defeated, but let us not yield till we are conquered."'

and who under the title of biography "publish only a novel,
filled with romantick adventures, and imaginary amours."[87] And
thirty years later, "I have as good a right," says Johnson, mocking
Sir John Dalrymple's imaginative style as a historian,[88] "to make
him think and talk as he has to tell us how people thought and
talked a hundred years ago, of which he has no evidence. All history, so far as it is not supported by contemporary evidence,
is romance." Boswell justifies his own hostility to interpretative
biography by relying again upon Johnson (1781; Vol. IV, p.
135):

"In autumn he went to Oxford, Birmingham, Lichfield, and
Ashbourne, for which very good reasons might be given in the
conjectural yet positive manner of writers, who are proud to
account for every event which they relate. He himself, however,
says, 'The motives of my journey I hardly know.'"

Again and again Boswell praises in his friend those qualities
which are evident in his own work. He speaks of Johnson's
"accurate description of real life" and "his nice observation of the
mere external appearances of life." Even more important in the
understanding of Boswell is his very fine analysis of the qualities
that made Johnson excel in biography (1754; Vol. I, p. 256):

"To the minute selection of characteristical circumstances,
for which the ancients were remarkable, he added a philosophical research, and the most perspicuous and energetick language."

The first phrase here suggests the practice of Plutarch, whom
Boswell and Johnson both admired. Johnson planned to edit
Plutarch with notes, and to write "Lives of Illustrious Persons,
as well of the active as the learned, in imitation of Plutarch"
(Vol. IV, p. 382); Boswell refers to him at the beginning of
the *Life of Johnson,* and quotes, in Greek and translation, Plutarch's dictum on the significance to the biographer of "an action
of small note, a short saying, or a jest." This admiration was
steady throughout Boswell's life: his portrait of Paoli in the
Journal of a Tour to Corsica is obviously and successfully modelled on Plutarch, so that popular opinion that the Corsican
patriot had lived two thousand years after his time rests not

---

[87] 1744; Vol. I, p. 165.
[88] Boswell's *Hebrides,* ed. Pottle and Bennett, 1936, p. 392.

only upon Paoli's own character but upon Boswell's portrayal of it. The *Life of Johnson* itself is neo-classical in its emphasis upon the life of man in this world; its concentration, under its temporal particularity, upon the unchanging problems of man; its cool, hard, objective view of the world; its moral and intellectual preoccupations; its giant hero. Boswell himself liked to think of his work as a modern Odyssey, the story of which, said Johnson, "is interesting, as a great part of it is domestick."[89]

Just as Izaak Walton had affinities with the medieval writer of saints' lives, so Boswell and his hero Johnson in many important respects are kin to Plutarch, and exemplify in biography, what critics have found for all other branches of literature in the eighteenth century, the neo-classic spirit.

This argument, which began with the great influence of Johnson upon Boswell and shifted to parallels in their thought and practice, must end with a reservation that restores to Boswell a certain independence. In Macaulay's caricature and in much subsequent criticism, Boswell is considered as little better than a fool, with no mind of his own. The *Life of Johnson,* so natural and clear, is interpreted as artless and accidental. Critics have too frequently maintained that Boswell owes everything to Johnson, that he succeeded because he had a great subject—forgetting that Johnson and even greater men have been made the little heroes of innumerable second-rate biographers. In the light of the evidence now available, Boswell can no longer be underestimated so flagrantly. Boswell was more than a mirror and a mimic. He had a certain Scotch stubbornness in maintaining his beliefs even against powerful opponents. Johnson's high-Tory fulminations against the Colonies pained Boswell but did not shake his confidence in the justice of the American position; the skepticism of the dying Hume, although Boswell realized the superior intellect of the philosopher who had influenced him as a young man, disturbed but did not destroy his own Christian convictions; on the question of male or female heirs to the Auchinleck estate, he capitulated to his strong-minded and frigid father, the opinions of Johnson and his friends, and the

[89] May 1, 1783; Vol. IV, p. 219.

interests of his own daughters, only after a long and painful siege.

It would therefore indeed be surprising if, regarding the form of writing for which he showed genius—the recording of the lives of actual men—Boswell had no opinions of his own. Johnson, for instance, advised Boswell to keep a journal, but Boswell had been keeping a journal for years before he met Johnson. The early records in the Boswell Papers show the exact recording of events, scenes, and even conversations that he brought to perfection in the *Life of Johnson*. Boswell was born a biographer. But he was also born an affectionate social being, with a father whose evident contempt for his son made him unsure of himself, so that he was continually seeking approval. Johnson was important to Boswell as a biographer because Johnson strengthened him in his natural bent, set a precious stamp of critical approval upon Boswell's instinctive practice, and gave him the confidence he lacked.[90] Boswell is thinking with satisfaction of his own projected *magnum opus* when he records such sayings of Johnson's as:

". . . nobody can write the life of a man, but those who have eat and drunk and lived in social intercourse with him."

(March 31, 1772; Vol. II, p. 166.)

"They only who live with a man can write his life with any genuine exactness and discrimination; and few people who have lived with a man know what to remark about him."

(March 20, 1776; Vol. II, p. 446.)

Johnson, therefore, determines the manner of his own biography by giving heart to Boswell in his own convictions: by encouraging his younger friend in his devotion to truth, by suggesting that even a sympathetic interpretation is made more effective by

[90] cf. Boswell's "Ever mindful of the wisdom of the Rambler, I have accustomed myself to mark the small peculiarities of character."—*Corsica*, 1923 ed., p. 64. cf. also Geoffrey Scott's analysis of Malone's encouragement of Boswell in *The Making of the Life of Johnson*, Vol. VI in the *Private Papers of James Boswell from Malahide Castle*. Reference to this 18-vol. ed. in succeeding notes will be abbreviated to *Isham Papers*, since Boswellians owe more to the man who deliberately made them public than to the place where they were fortuitously preserved.

fidelity in shading, by expressing his belief that minute, and auto-biographical, and domestic details are the essence of biography. Boswell meditates upon Johnson's chance sayings, his remarks in letters, his varied biographical productions; following his own method, Boswell assembles these bits into a mosaic of coherent pattern; and in the familiar opening pages of the *Life of Johnson* he presents a theory of life-writing which is mature, consistent, and assured.

A comparison of the bibliography of this volume with an index to Boswell's *Johnson* furnishes additional proof that Boswell is an authority in his field. Close to one hundred biographers or biographies are specifically mentioned, ranging from the ludicrous autobiography in false rhymes of Bet Flint the prostitute to the many references to the biographer of Bacon, the "acute and elegant" Mallet. The leading antiquaries and encyclopedists are all there—William Oldys, George Chalmers, Andrew Kippis, Thomas Flloyd, James Granger, John Nichols, Thomas Birch, David Dalrymple, and Joseph Towers. The writers of dignified historical biography—Robert Watson and William Tytler and Lord Lyttelton and Thomas Carte and Mark Noble—are appraised by Johnson or by Boswell. Earlier biographers such as de Thou and Plutarch and Bishop Burnet and Izaak Walton, win their praises. Yet neither Johnson nor Boswell overlooks peripheral and ephemeral productions, or forgets the eccentrics of their times, whose lives are still entertaining. The extraordinary Mrs. Rudd, the mysterious Psalmanazar, the Reverend Mr. Villette, Ordinary of Newgate, Sixteen-string Jack the highwayman, "the celebrated Mrs. Bellamy," the Reverend Dr. Dodd who was hanged for forgery—all play their rôles in the *Life*. Johnson's judgments show enthusiasm for and wide reading in biography. He illustrates a point by citing from memory evidence in the autobiographies of Mrs. Manley and John Dunton (April 10, 1783; Vol. IV, pp. 199-200); Thicknesse's *Travels* are "entertaining" and "a true book in his intention" (April 3, 1778; Vol. III, p. 235); Boswell asks Johnson if he will not allow that Cibber's *Apology* is well done and Johnson answers: "Very well done, to be sure, Sir" (May 15, 1776; Vol. III, p. 72). If Johnson is aware of the *Biographia Britannica* and the contributions of its various editors, he is also aware of the accounts "of the criminals hanged yesterday" (April 25, 1778; Vol. III, p. 318). Boswell also has gone far afield in his reading and is generally charitable in his judgments. He praises the frankness of the then unpublished life of Sir Robert Sibbald; he calls to the reader's attention "an admirable paper upon the character of Johnson" (1784; Vol. IV, p. 426) written by Dr. Horne, which might otherwise be neglected; John Nichols is a "worthy and indefatigable editor"; "my friend Dr. Kippis" is judicious and distinct; "my friend Mr. Courtenay" describes Johnson's facility of composition "admirably"; William Seward the anecdotist is well known "for his literature, love of the fine arts, and social virtues"; the *Modern Characters from Shakespeare* are "admirably adapted"; and Mason's *Memoirs of Gray* have been held in inordinate esteem largely because of the importance Boswell attaches to them in the introduction to the *Life of Johnson*. Such genuine love of a subject must have been infectious. When Boswell, on October 16, 1769, entertains at dinner Johnson, Reynolds, Garrick, Goldsmith, Murphy, Isaac Bickerstaff, and Tom Davies, the majority of the company were already, or soon became, biographers. Doctor Johnson was their great leader; adapting his own words on Goldsmith, one may say of Johnson, *Nemo quem tetigit vitas non scripsit*. Boswell and Johnson were as well versed in the history of biography as any men of their time, and Boswell's eclectic *Life of Johnson* is truly the flower of eighteenth century lives. It consciously copies the best traits of many predecessors; and represents, in a single work, the best that had been thought and said about biography.

Boswell's solution of the various problems discussed in other chapters of this volume would require a book in itself. It would be interesting, for instance, to collect the obvious and the profound ethical pronouncements of Doctor Johnson, to notice with what astonishing frequency they occur, and to determine, if it were possible, the moral impact of the work as a whole. It would be interesting to scrutinize Boswell's claim to impartiality, to show by comparison with Boswell's journals and the accounts by others to what extent he has changed, softened, or omitted actual episodes that reflect unfavorably upon the character of

Johnson in order to estimate the effect of their altered forms in the biography. It would be interesting to consider the relation of Boswell's *Life* to the anecdotes, *bon-mots,* and jest-books so popular during the period, and to speculate on the extent to which the record of witty utterances, which are usually both more memorable and more stinging than other sayings, contributes to the impression of Johnson as a frightening Great Bear. And it is, of course, a temptation to point out what Boswell has *not* put into his *Life of Johnson,* or to mention in what respects Boswell's picture of Johnson differs from one's own. But this discussion of the *Life of Johnson* will be limited to Boswell's use of conversation, his handling of scene, the style and structure of his work, and the reasons for his attack upon Mrs. Piozzi and Sir John Hawkins.

No one is more aware than Boswell himself, that his great contribution to the art of biography is the record of conversation. No one, moreover, could have been more conscious of the difficulty of his task. If it is true that conversation is the breath of life, it is also true that it lasts no longer than a breath, and Boswell was always agonizing over its preservation. His serious, extended attempt to set down in exact detail the memorable conversations he has heard is without a rival, almost without a competitor. He begs the reader to supply imaginatively the intonations and mannerisms of Johnson's utterance. He testifies that what he records, though not complete, is authentic. Among the many duels which Boswell was on the verge of fighting, he seems to have come closest to bloodshed with Lord Macdonald, most of whose insulting remarks he passed over, but whose slur on the authenticity of Johnson's sayings as reported in the *Tour to the Hebrides* wounded Boswell to the heart.[91] Comparison of the *Life of Johnson* with Boswell's recently published loose notes and his rough and finished journals, demonstrates effectively his fidelity. No one but a pedant could demand greater accuracy. In the *Journals,* if he has not been able to remember the exact word that occurred in some conversation, he has left a blank. Naturally, when he wrote up such notes into a literary narrative, he must either supply words or omit whole sentences, and this seems permissible to

[91] cf. *Isham Papers,* Vol. XVI.

anyone who realizes that a human being is not a dictaphone. He has omitted certain sections, even those which illustrate Johnson's character, because they reflect upon himself; but such self-protection, as he learned from the ridicule which followed the publication of the *Tour to the Hebrides,* was necessary, and he had made clear his procedure in this regard in the dedication of the *Life.* He does not give Johnson's original phrase for "amourous propensities," he omits Johnson's illustration of what he considers foul language, he does not include Johnson's reputed answer in "plainest bawdy" to Garrick's question as to the greatest pleasure in life,[92] and he passes over Johnson's physiological description of the certain way to maintain female chastity. Such silences are rare. And only a fanatic for the whole truth will forget that there is a valid difference between a dignified biography and casual conversation between adult males.

Certain critics, particularly George Birkbeck Hill and R. W. Chapman, have pointed out the liberties Boswell takes with his raw material in shaping it into artful and finished anecdotes. Two sayings of Johnson, for example, are recorded in *Boswelliana:* "He is like a man attempting to stride the English Channell"; and "It is setting up a candle at Whitechapel to give light at Westminster." In the *Life* these are condensed into a single comparison: "Sir, it is burning a farthing candle at Dover to shew light at Calais." Such striking changes may well be emphasized to combat the idea, popularized by Macaulay, that Boswell is a mere reporter; it is pleasant to realize regarding Boswell that "He was not afraid to be an artist, and to let his knowledge and genius 'Johnsonize' what was necessarily raw material."[93] Yet when the rough journals and the finished *Life* are compared, it is indeed surprising to see for what extended sections the raw material differs from the final product only in polish. The essentials of Johnson's talk are preserved, in the same way, perhaps, that a fine portrait painter surpasses a photographer in fixing the salient traits of his subject. Boswell was a born mimic;

[92] It is interesting to note that Professor Pottle, *Isham Papers,* Vol. X, p. 173, note, corrects what seems overemphasis, in the brilliant work of his predecessor Geoffrey Scott, upon Boswell's bowdlerization of himself.

[93] *Boswell's Note Book 1776-1777,* with an introduction by R. W. Chapman.

for imitating the familiar conversation of Johnson, Hannah More gives the palm to Boswell over such a formidable competitor as David Garrick;[94] and the man who could amuse a theater audience by mooing like a cow entertains posterity by the more difficult feat of talking like Johnson.

"A page of my Journal," writes Boswell with considerable satisfaction,[95] "is like a cake of portable soup. A little may be diffused into a considerable portion." The portable Johnsonian soup with its authentic flavor is not the only variety which Boswell concocted. He practised the art of writing dialogue from his young manhood:

"This Creature had forgot to put sugar in my Cup. Lady K. observed it, and with a pleasing sensibility of look, 'What (says she) I suppose there is so much sweetness *there* (carelessly stirring the tea, but with her eyes beaming full upon mine) that there is no need of Sugar.' "

Such an extract might almost be used as proof that Boswell was born Boswell, for it was written when he was twenty-two and before he had encountered Johnson.[96] It occurs in his "Journal of my jaunt, Harvest, 1762," in which most of his distinguishing traits are already evident. The young Scot already approves of the thousand good things spoken offhand in the *"Menagina"* (as he then called it), which he was to refer to in the final footnote to his *Life of Johnson;* he has a warm admiration for Johnson which his friends and teachers cannot shake; he can give vivid and distinct pictures of himself after his falls from horseback; he retails in dialogue form an anecdote about Pope and adds: "I have a pleasure in hearing every story, tho' never so little, of so distinguished a Man." He records and shares Adam Smith's pleasure in distinctive little biographical details "when he read that Milton never wore buckles but strings in his shoes" (pp. 106-7); and he has observed human character so closely that he can imitate David Hume "amazingly well." "Indeed," he adds (p. 135), "it was not an imitation but the very Man."

[94] *Dr Johnson his friends and his critics,* George Birkbeck Hill, 1878, p. 188.
[95] *Hebrides,* 1936 ed., p. 165. The "portable soup" image he uses in at least two other instances.
[96] *Isham Papers,* Vol. I, p. 63.

Facility at reproducing extended dialogues seems instinctive with him. When, on December 24, 1767, he writes his friend William Temple an account of his wooing of the cold Miss Blair, he suddenly interjects a parenthesis—"(Temple, you must have it in the genuine dialogue.)"[97]—and continues his letter by reproducing his conversation with "the Princess." Boswell not only recorded dialogue himself but was the cause of the record in others. He is thus able to reach beyond himself in time and space, and bring Johnson's living words from years before Boswell knew him, or from places where Boswell never penetrated. The Reverend Mr. Thomas Warton communicates "his conversation while at Oxford" in 1754; Doctor Adams furnishes a dialogue for 1748; Doctor Burney contributes some vivacious Johnsonian talk; and even the serious and lanky Bennet Langton does his dutiful best to Boswellize as he tells us that "before dinner he said nothing but 'Pretty baby!' to one of the children."[98] Boswell himself does not often make his sublime friend so ridiculous. He must have compressed his dialogue to its essence, for the longest evening or day of talk recorded would not run to more than minutes on the stage. He selects; when the great Johnson nods, Boswell does not feel that he must record at length, as some of the biographers of actors did record,[99] repetitions, loose phrases, and platitudes. Only rarely does Boswell water his portable soup until it becomes:

"JOHNSON. 'No, Sir.'

BOSWELL. 'How so, Sir?'

JOHNSON. 'Why, Sir. . . .'"[100]

Boswell finds speech so necessary in giving life to a scene that he even creates dialogue when the exact words could not possibly have been remembered, as in his version of the infant Samuel in petticoats learning a collect from the prayer-book,[101] a story which comes to Boswell from Mrs. Lucy Porter who had it from Johnson's mother. Yet when his observation is direct, Boswell is

[97] *Letters*, ed. C. B. Tinker, 1924; Vol. I, p. 139.

[98] Vol. I, pp. 271-4; Vol. I, p. 186; Vol. I, pp. 328-30, and Vol. I, p. 397; the Langton quotation from G. B. Hill, *Dr Johnson his friends and his critics*, 1878, p. 276.

[99] See Chap. I.   [100] April 18, 1783; Vol. IV, p. 206.

[101] 1712; Vol. I, pp. 39-40.

unsurpassed in conveying the sense of completeness and truth. One can never cease marvelling at the capacity that could record for page after page such pure and uninterrupted conversation as that, for instance, of the dinner of April 3, 1778. Only the most rigorous practice and the most astonishing natural ability could have made it possible.

Many of Johnson's good remarks and arguments on important topics were deliberately extorted from him by his biographer. Boswell at times consciously plays the rôle of the inquiring reporter, and he continues even when he knows it may displease Johnson. "Langton told me," he records in his Journal,[102] "he said when they were in the coach, 'When Boswell gets wine, his conversation consists all of questions.'" At Doctor Johnson's house on October 26, 1769, a pretty large circle being present, Boswell's recorded share in the conversation during the evening consisted of twenty questions fired pointblank at Johnson, four remarks which had the effect of questions, and only three observations of his own. After the company had gone, Boswell continued to plague the Doctor with questions on the subject, so hateful to Johnson, of the approach of death, until Johnson called to him sternly at his departure, "Don't let us meet to-morrow." "I am allways," Boswell admits to himself,[103] "studying human nature and making experiments."

One of the greatest scenes in the *Life of Johnson*—the dinner with Wilkes—was engineered by Boswell as an experiment in clashing personalities, for he had a keen sense of drama. And certainly in the selection and arrangement of those scenes in Johnson's life which he has preserved for us, his dramatic sense also guided him. The question of the "influence" of the drama upon the *Life of Johnson* cannot be answered simply. Boswell, as his journals show, was fond of the theater; he attended often, not only in London but in provincial towns. He had as his own friends the reigning artists in comedy and tragedy, Sam Foote and David Garrick. Talk in London frequently turned upon the

---

[102] April 10, 1775; *Isham Papers*, Vol. X, p. 204.

[103] *Isham Papers*, Vol. VII, pp. 36-7. Journal for 1765-1768. George Mallory in "Boswell, the biographer," 1912, has an interesting chapter on Boswell's laboratory method of creating artificial situations and asking provoking questions to see how Johnson will behave.

stage; he met Johnson through that unsuccessful actor and more successful theatrical biographer Tom Davies; he writes critical strictures on Mallet's tragedy of *Elvira;* he tries his hand at writing prologues; like an actor himself, he struts in fine clothes at the Stratford celebration; he knows Shakespeare as an intimate friend, so that *Macbeth* may comfort him when he is feeling unusually the Scot, and *Hamlet* flatter his melancholy, and "Mark Anthony" help him to see himself as the great but erratic lover. The eighteenth century piqued itself on its knowledge of Shakespeare; and it cannot be doubted that the dramatist must have influenced current conceptions of human life, when so many of the men of the time think of themselves in Shakespearean parallels—when Boswell conceives his first meeting with Johnson in terms of Shakespearean actors, so that he himself becomes Hamlet, Davies Horatio, and Johnson the awful and expected Ghost; or when Johnson himself on his deathbed can break out despairingly to his physician, "Can'st thou not minister to a mind diseas'd," and Doctor Brocklesby answer readily and aptly "from the same great poet:

'. . . therein the patient
Must minister to himself.' "[104]

Boswell, moreover, leaned naturally towards the theatrical. He was conscious of his own extreme poses; he liked to attitudinize; and he relished any situation which gained dramatic significance through conflicting personalities. Like the professional dramatist, he values the big scene, and in recording it he adapts for the printed volume almost all the effects which might be secured on the stage. The conversations are usually written as they would be set down in a printed play. Stage directions are given, such as:[105]

"JOHNSON. '. . . I am afraid I may be one of those who shall be damned.' (looking dismally.) DR. ADAMS. 'What do you mean by damned?' JOHNSON. (passionately and loudly) 'Sent to Hell, Sir, and punished everlastingly.' "

This is the script of an actable play. How, or when, or why Boswell came to realize that he should suggest the surroundings and

[104] Dec. 1784; Vol. IV, p. 400.
[105] June 12, 1784; Vol. IV, p. 299.

the physical appearance of his actors cannot be determined.[106] Yet his method here did become clear in his own mind.'

Talking to Lord Kames in 1778 about biography, he writes:[107] "I agreed it should be dramatick. The great Art of Biography is to keep the person whose life we are giving allways in the Reader's view." If the purpose of biography is to reproduce a life, then the biographer must in some manner succeed in making his hero corporeal and in suggesting the world in which he lived. The "history of his times" is not enough; a man lives in houses more continuously than he lives among ideas. Actions and dates do not constitute a life; disembodied statistics, an exact, colorless chronicle, even the most precisely recorded speeches and thoughts if not attached to a person, will not produce the illusion necessary to a good biography. Every individual existence takes place in a body which fills space and moves through it, and which is related to the physical as well as the psychological world. No completely successful biographer can disregard this truth. Because very few biographers of the eighteenth century consciously or unconsciously lived over again, visually and aurally, the lives of their subjects,[108] Boswell's pioneering achievements in these respects should have full weight.

Perhaps the most interesting point about Boswell's art which recent studies and the *Isham Papers* have made it possible to establish is that Boswell normally painted in his figures and background when he wrote the *Life of Johnson,* not when he jotted down his rough notes or made them into his finished journals. Regarding the physical description of the young Johnson at Birmingham, for instance, Boswell's notes read: "He was then by no means a pleasing figure. He had his own hair lank, & opening behind."[109] In the *Life,* Boswell touches this up and makes an arresting picture (1735; Vol. I, pp. 94-5):

". . . his appearance was very forbidding: he was then lean and lank, so that his immense structure of bones was hideously striking to the eye, and the scars of the scrophula were deeply visible.

---

[106] cf., e.g., his already highly developed narrative of tea with Lady K., written in 1762 and quoted earlier in this chapter.

[107] *Isham Papers,* Vol. XV, p. 268.   [108] cf. Chaps. I and VII.

[109] *Boswell's Note Book 1776-1777*; ed. R. W. Chapman, p. 10.

He also wore his hair, which was straight and stiff, and separated behind: and he often had, seemingly, convulsive starts and odd gesticulations, which tended to excite at once surprize and ridicule."

Here Boswell adds to Miss Porter's description permanent physical traits in Johnson which he had himself observed. In talking with or thinking about a friend, each one of us has his image before us, but Boswell was a great enough artist in biography to realize that he must continually reintroduce the *figure* of Johnson to his readers, so that an acquaintance might by process of constant association become a familiar friend. The physical descriptions of Johnson in the *Tour to the Hebrides* and at the conclusion of the *Life* are well done; but far finer and subtler art is to be found in these constantly recurring impressionistic pictures of Johnson as he moves through life. Boswell gives us a full album: the near-sighted young Samuel coming home from school and stooping down on hands and knees to take a view of the street-gutter; Johnson when Boswell first calls upon him, with his brown, rusty suit, his "little old shrivelled unpowdered wig which was too small for his head," shirt-neck and knees of his breeches loose, black worsted stockings ill drawn up, and unbuckled shoes by way of slippers; Johnson in the act of gratifying his fierce appetite, when "the veins of his forehead swelled, and generally a strong perspiration was visible"; the fine landscape-with-figure when Boswell looks back upon his friend on the shore at Harwich (August 6, 1763; Vol. I, p. 472):

"As the vessel put out to sea, I kept my eyes upon him for a considerable time, while he remained rolling his majestick frame in his usual manner: and at last I perceived him walk back into the town, and he disappeared."

So the pictures continue, vivid vignettes triumphantly realized, to the last glimpse Boswell ever had of his friend, in which physical actions help to interpret the deep emotions within (June 30, 1784; Vol. IV, pp. 338-9):

"He asked me whether I would not go with him to his house; I declined it, from an apprehension that my spirits would sink. We bade adieu to each other affectionately in the carriage. When he had got down upon the foot-pavement, he called out, 'Fare you well;' and without looking back, sprung away with a kind of pathetick briskness, if I may use that expression, which seemed to indicate a struggle to conceal uneasiness, and impressed me with a foreboding of our long, long separation."

Such a passage contains evidence in itself that it was written retrospectively, and it is astonishing to find, in contrast to the fullness of Boswell's notes of what he heard, how scanty were Boswell's jottings of what he saw. This may mean that he knew he could trust his visual memory more fully than his memory for conversation. It arose partly, moreover, from his long association with Johnson and his friends; when Boswell calls on a stranger—on William Pitt or Rousseau or Mrs. Rudd—he carefully records their appearance. But it also means that he is quite aware of the difference between the functions of a formal biographer and of the keeper of a private journal, and that when he takes up his pen to record the *Life of Johnson* he has resolved to convey it pictorially and dramatically.

A few further illustrations win a place here. Boswell records in his notebook:[110] "He said it was liberal & noble in Dr Adams to say he was above his mark; & that the Dr had told him he was the best Scholar he ever knew come to Oxford." The last half of Johnson's statement Boswell introduces as direct discourse in a paragraph regarding Johnson's wide reading when he was young; the rest of it becomes—the italics are mine:[111]

"[Dr. Adams] said to me at Oxford, in 1776, 'I was his nominal tutor; but he was above my mark.' When I repeated it to Johnson, *his eyes flashed with grateful satisfaction,* and he *exclaimed,* 'That was liberal and noble.' "

Again, comparison with Boswell's journals show that the following "stage-setting" and producer's cues are added in the *Life* to what was in the original Ashbourne Journal the bare notes for a dialogue on immortality:[112]

---

[110] Ed. R. W. Chapman, 1925, pp. 20-1.

[111] Vol. I, p. 57 and p. 79. Geoffrey Scott, in *The Making of the Life of Johnson,* 1929, illustrates further the transformation of original notes in narrative form into direct dramatic discourse.

[112] cf. Chapman, p. 23; *Life,* Vol. III, pp. 199-200. Sept. 23, 1777.

"While Johnson and I stood in calm conference by ourselves in Dr. Taylor's garden, at a pretty late hour in a serene autumn night, looking up to the heavens. . . .

"He talked to me upon this awful and delicate question in a gentle tone, and as if afraid to be decisive." [The *Note Book* adds: "I was much pleased with this mildness."]

Boswell also adds to this passage in the *Life* the state of his own feelings, occasioned by one of his rare realizations of the passage of time (Vol. III, p. 198):

"This evening, while some of the tunes of ordinary composition were played with no great skill, my frame was agitated, and I was conscious of a generous attachment to Dr. Johnson, as my preceptor and friend, mixed with an affectionate regret that he was an old man, whom I should probably lose in a short time."

As an extended example of Boswell's visual reconstruction of a scene in Johnson's life only after he has become his biographer, the famous Wilkes dinner should be examined in the *Life* and in the *Journals*.[118] The dialogue for this masterful bit of biographical dramatization is fairly complete in the journals, so that Boswell has little to do except fill it out and transpose some parts that are out of temporal or logical sequence. The setting and the action, however, are inserted by Boswell the biographer only in his three-dimensional *Life*. Dramatic suspense is built up before the reader is brought to that "much-expected Wednesday." Johnson "buffeting his books," Boswell flying down the stairs to obtain Mrs. Williams's consent, Johnson roaring "Frank, a clean shirt!" Boswell with Johnson in the hackney-coach, exulting "as much as a fortune-hunter who has got an heiress into a post-chaise with him to set out for Gretna-Green," Johnson muttering "Too, too, too" under his breath, Johnson sitting down upon a window-seat and pretending to read, Wilkes's assiduous attention to Johnson at table in helping him to some fine veal: "Pray give me leave, Sir:—It is better here—A little of the brown—Some fat, Sir—A little of the stuffing—Some gravy—Let me have the pleasure of giving you some butter—Allow me to recommend a squeeze of this orange;—or the lemon, perhaps, may have more

[118] See *Isham Papers*, Vol. XI, pp. 283, 7; *Life*, May 15, 1776, Vol. III, pp. 64-79.

zest," and Johnson's reply: " 'Sir, Sir, I am obliged to you, Sir,'
. . . bowing, and turning his head to him with a look for some
time of 'surly virtue,' but, in a short while, of complacency,"
Wilkes holding a candle to show a fine print of a beautiful female
figure and pointing out the elegant contour of the bosom with
the finger of an arch connoisseur—all of this, which is Boswell at
his best, is not the product of the mythical Boswell with goggling
eyes jotting down notes even while he is at table; it is Boswell
the artist with an extraordinary visual memory and a sense of the
dramatic. When Garrick takes off Johnson by "squeezing a lemon
into a punch-bowl, with uncouth gesticulations, looking round
the company, and calling out, 'Who's for *poonsh?'* "[114] Johnson
is before us no less through the art of a great biographer than
that of a great actor. In dramatic presentation, in the noting or
explaining of psychological states, and particularly in the visualization of motion, gestures, and facial and vocal expressions, the
publication of Boswell's papers shows that Boswell depended in
his *Life* upon his "long head" and his artistic sense much more
than has previously been supposed.[115] That he conceived his *Life*
pictorially, possibly even in terms of the stage, is evident from a
letter Boswell wrote to Bishop Percy in February 1788:[116]

"It appears to me that mine is the best plan of biography that
can be conceived; for my readers will, as near as may be, accompany Johnson in his progress, and as it were see each scene as it
happened."

After reading the *Life,* one is tempted to laugh at Boswell's
feeling of inferiority to his great friend in the power of observing
and describing physical objects. Possibly Boswell was thinking
only of inanimate nature; and there may have been some reason
for him to submit with humility and admiration to Johnson's
correction that such-and-such a mountain was *not* a perfect cone
in shape. Boswell is not a landscape artist, but a portraitist, who

[114] March 1776; Vol. II, p. 464. cf. "woonce" for "once" in the *Journals,* etc.

[115] Yet even in the *Journals* Boswell could experiment with his impressionistic
descriptions, as when, while they are watching a funeral by torchlight, he
repeats to Wilkes a cutting remark Hume had made against Wilkes and his mob,
and then records: "he grinned abashment, as a Negro grows whiter when he
blushes."—*Isham Papers,* Vol. XII, p. 229.

[116] *Boswell the Biographer,* George Mallory, p. 231.

presents a series of sketches with a few selected realistic details. Economy in suggesting actuality is one of Boswell's most admirable qualities as an artist. He presents republican simplicity without the loss of a word, as he describes securing his passport at Corte:[117]

"I was much pleased with a beautiful, simple incident. The Chancellor desired a little boy who was playing in the room by us, to run to his mother, and bring the great seal of the kingdom. I thought myself sitting in the house of a Cincinnatus."

The talent for compressed naturalistic anecdote was his. "I remember," he writes,[118] "the phrase of an English common soldier, who told me, 'that at the battle of Fontenoy, his captain received a shot in the breast, and fell, said the soldier, with his spontoon in his hand, as prettily killed as ever I see'd a gentleman.'" Of this, and a host of similar microscopic stories in Boswell, one may say that it is as prettily told as ever one heard an anecdote. Johnson out of breath as he tries to push a large dead cat over a waterfall with a long pole may afford a picture more faithful than dignified, but it is consciously recorded as "a small characteristick trait" in what Boswell rightly calls "the Flemish picture which I give of my friend."[119] Hogarth himself, who thought the gesticulating Johnson was "an ideot" when he first met him in Richardson's house, and who painted Johnson's cousin Parson Ford, could not have suggested Johnson's idiosyncrasies with more spirit and humor than does Boswell. Reynolds, in his paintings of his good friend, even in the magnificent portrait done in 1778, does not surpass Boswell in the presentation of Johnson's essential nobility and force.[120] The paintings, miniatures in enamel, etchings, drawings, mezzotintos, seals, Roman heads, casts from Nollekens's bust and copper-pieces struck at Birmingham, which Boswell lists so carefully,[121] taken all together cannot compare with Boswell's own single biographical portrait. For biography has this advantage over painting: that it moves through time, and, if the biographer is at all skilful, he can suggest his

---

[117] *Tour to Corsica*, 1923 ed., p. 23.   [118] *Corsica*, p. 98.

[119] Sept. 22, 1777; Vol. III, p. 191.

[120] cf. Boswell and Reynolds in talk together, April 29, 1778, Vol. III, p. 332, in which each talks of his own art in terms of the other's.

[121] 1784; Vol. IV, pp. 421-2, note.

hero's various moods and appearances as he goes through life, while the painter is necessarily limited, except in some esoteric sense, to the portrayal of a moment.

When the structure of the *Life of Johnson* is considered, the stern critic should supplant the enthusiastic Boswellian. The style, though adequate, is not distinguished; the *Life* is, as its sources indicate, the expansion of rough notes into clear English; and its great merit is that the writing seldom comes between Johnson and the reader. Ordinarily the style is as unpretentious as that of a private diary. This matter-of-fact tone makes the occasional embellishments from the classics seem out of place, yet part of our annoyance at the Latin and Greek quotations may be the tribute of an age of ignorance to an age of learning. But the structure of the *Life* itself is open to serious criticism.

Considered purely as a work of art, the *Life* is probably too long. It may seem uncharitable to ask the ox to diminish to the size of the frog; certainly the frequent "Selections" from the *Life of Johnson* afford no solution, for they show only that the work as written profits little by compression, and moves nearly on a level throughout. But any book which is so popular as a bedside volume, to dip into at odd moments, may be suspected to be better in small pieces than as a whole. Here again Boswell may resemble the Dutch painters with their fine brushwork and attention to detail rather than the Italians with their noble designs. Boswell's art lies in the organization of the smaller bits of the mosaic; not in assembling them or relating them to one another. The chronological arrangement, for instance, he uses as a purely formal element in organization; there is little sense of the passage of time, of the youth of the young Johnson or the age of the old, of the changes in Johnson's character (so that he mellows or becomes more intolerant or recovers his health or falls into years of despondency), of hope for the future or backward glances upon the past.

Boswell distrusted interpretative and imaginative biography. But interpretation and imagination are qualities of the artist, and Boswell's *Life* gains as a record of fact sometimes at the expense of art. Instead of creating Johnson himself, it affords material from which Johnson may be created by an imaginative act. Boswell, it is true, quotes his subject's letters copiously, and his use of the *Prayers and Meditations* which Johnson himself wished published does much to reveal Johnson's own mind. But Boswell himself rarely attempts to penetrate into the mind of his hero. He is willing to record even when he does not understand—as in the scene where Johnson sets the echoes ringing from Temple Bar to Fleet Ditch with his laughter—but he cannot, or he will not, make a consistent attempt to see life through Johnson's eyes. Looking at a man from the outside is not necessarily the equivalent of truth; and a book cannot with precision be called *The Life of Samuel Johnson* when it is written more as personal recollections, as an expanded journal, as anecdotes, letters, and gleanings from a hundred disparate sources. In this sense also, the work may be considered in essence as part of Boswell's autobiography —very fine in itself, but not described with complete accuracy as the *Life of Johnson*. Geoffrey Scott has shown the extent to which the *Life* has been worked up from Boswell's journals. As a result, it partakes of the nature of a diary; daily events are observed perfectly, but the scope is limited by the sufficiency of each day unto itself, and Boswell is ill at ease in the rare instances when he attempts to see Johnson's life as a whole[122] and to give significance to the complete career of his tremendous companion.

The myopic focus may also account for the repetitions that mar the work. Boswell may be right in believing that the tiniest truths in Johnson's life should be preserved, but there is little excuse for preserving them twice.

Beautifully executed as individual episodes are, the connections of parts of the narrative, when they are not entirely omitted, are often faulty Boswell's year-by-year scheme of chronicling goes by the board when, with ingenuous openness, he fills in a blank or meager period in Johnson's life with a collection of anecdotes furnished by one of their friends. The fortuitous associations of one paragraph with its successor sometimes savor of the after-

---

[122] His character sketch at the end is, of course, very fine. Even here, however, it is characteristic that he draws upon Clarendon and Bayle to help him in his task; and one might maintain that Reynolds, to mention one friend, is more aware than Boswell of significant and subtle traits in Johnson's character.

dinner speaker, or the stream-of-consciousness novelist. Within the episodes themselves, the compression of conversation to its essence necessitates the omission of the connectives in small-talk, so that the reader jumps from one majestic pronouncement to another, like a man in seven-league boots on the tops of the Alps.

The proportions of the book are not true to Johnson's own life, and cannot give a completely faithful picture of him. One cannot believe that Johnson lived half of his significant life in the last eight years out of a career of seventy-five; yet the last half of Boswell covers that period. Less than one tenth of the work is devoted to the first half of Johnson's life. Naturally, much of this faulty proportioning comes, not from carelessness or indifference, but from ignorance, sheer ignorance, of parts of Johnson's progress and of his nature. Boswell is writing principally from personal observation of his friend, whom he did not meet until Johnson was in his fifty-fourth year. Boswell's own figure, his letters and troubles and legal cases and opinions, cannot have occupied such an important place in Johnson's career as they do in his biography.

This stricture leads to the point that Boswell's *Life of Johnson* is poorly proportioned, considered as an absolute work of art, precisely because it was created as a particular book for particular circumstances.[123] It is Boswell's last word on Johnson after his friends and enemies have spoken of him at length. Consequently much of it is in the form of correction or authentication of already well known stories, or of disputes with rivals whose interpretations of Johnson were then before the public. At a time when Johnson's complete works were appearing in many volumes, when his *Lives of the Poets* were being read and re-read, when anybody's wit was collected under the title of *Johnsoniana*, and

---

[123] For the connections, influence, and reputation of Boswell's work in eighteenth century biography, cf. William Kenrick's *Epistle to James Boswell*, 1768 (satiric); Peter Pindar's *Epistle*, 1786 (satiric); *Living authors of Great Britain*, 1798, Vol. II, pp. 138-9 (hostile); James Keir's *Thomas Day*, 1791, pp. 1-2 and 107 (hostile); Miss Brooke's *Life of Henry Brooke*, 1792 (imitative); *Biographia Britannica*, Vol. V, 1793, in *Corrigenda* (favorable); George Chalmers's *Thomas Ruddiman*, 1794, p. 274 (imitative); Robert Bisset's *Edmund Burke*, 1798, *passim* (imitative); Robert Anderson's *British Poets*, 1795, Vol. XI, p. 779 (fair appraisal); and *The biographical mirror*, 1795, by which time Boswell takes his place among "eminent and distinguished persons."

when the Beauties and even the Deformities of his writings were
gathered together, any new composition of his gave superiority to
its publisher. Boswell proclaims that his work comprehends
"various original pieces of his composition, never before published," just as he asserts that the whole will exhibit "a view of
literature and literary men in Great-Britain, for near half a century," even though the connections between some of his figures
and Johnson are of the slightest. Both of these objects as expressed
on the title-page, together with a third—Johnson's "Epistolary
Correspondence"—make the task of a coherent and artistic *Life*
more difficult. Johnson was seldom an inspired letter-writer, but
Boswell publishes even his dullest notes; and the many long legal
arguments constructed by Johnson for Boswell and recorded so
proudly—on lay patronage, and corporal punishment by school-
masters, and vicious intromission, and the difference between a
physician and a doctor of medicine, and municipal elections, and
inheritance, and censure from the pulpit, and slavery—are heavy
monuments to what is already plain enough without them:
Johnson's facility in arguing on any subject and his deep friendship for the heir of Auchinleck.

Boswell's repeated attacks on Sir John Hawkins and Mrs.
Piozzi give at first glance an air of unnecessary acrimony to his
work. Doctor Johnson seems at times a kind of Scylla who gives
birth in his biographers to a horde of little monsters that snarl
and snap at each other, as well as at their parent. Boswell's personal pride was unquestionably wounded by his predecessors.
Hawkins's contemptuous disregard of "Mr. James Boswell, a
native of Scotland," Mrs. Piozzi's unfair exaggeration of his
method of note-taking, Fanny Burney's dislike and her unwilling-
ness to reveal to him *her* Doctor Johnson, roused his resentment.
In the remarks directed against Hawkins and Piozzi his love of
truth seems to waver, for though their portraits of Johnson are
inferior to his, they are not so bad or so malicious as he implies.

Yet there is a deeper and more honorable reason for his bitterness against them than mere personal pique: his loyalty compelled
him to rescue the memory of his friend from detraction. Johnson's greatness, he felt, must not be distorted by the petty ungenerous mind of the pompous little knight or by the rancor and

irritation of the lively lady who had once been his friend. Indignation against the betrayers of friendship lies back of his references to the "dark uncharitable cast" of Hawkins's biography or "the slighter aspersions" of Mrs. Piozzi, which make her account of him "unfavourable and unjust." To counteract their lack of charity Boswell summons a cloud of witnesses, and the support of such old friends of Johnson's as Langton and Reynolds and Mrs. Lucy Porter gives the seal of authority to his work.

For the final impression left by Boswell's *Johnson* is that it is a magnificent tribute of friendship. A small event may illustrate a character; and Boswell's fidelity to the Great Lexicographer may be seen in his insistent devotion to his own "characteristick" spelling because Johnson had said English words "should always have the Saxon k added to the c."[124] When Boswell speaks of himself as "a faithful biographer," he is thinking of devotion to his friend as much as faithfulness to the truth. His propensities for hero-worship made him love truth largely because in his mind Johnson stood for truth. Boswell craved and received the affection of Johnson; he repaid it after death. The literary dictator who would journey to Harwich to see his new friend off for the Continent could write twenty years later: "I consider your fidelity and tenderness as a great part of the comforts which are yet left me."[125] "Your kindness is one of the pleasures of my life, which I should be sorry to lose," writes Johnson, and Boswell replies: "I do not believe that a more perfect attachment ever existed in the history of mankind."[126] Johnson did all he could to give his vacillating young follower steadiness and strength. In a touching passage of the *Journal,* too intimate to be included in the *Life,* Johnson gives Boswell parting advice that shows his judgment and his care for his friend:[127]

"Don't drink. 'Tis as important for *you* as 'To be or not to be': To be in one's wits or not. . . . Every man is to take existence on the terms on which it is given to him. Yours is given to you on condition of your not using liberties which other people may.

124 1780; Vol. IV, p. 31. Langton's notes.
125 July 26, 1784; Vol. IV, p. 379.
126 Feb. 18 and 24, 1777; Vol. III, p. 105.
127 *Isham Papers,* Vol. XI, p. 289; May 16, 1776.

Don't talk of yourself or of me. . . . Don't make yourself and me a proverb. Have no one topick, that people can say, 'We'll hear him upon it.' "

Yet Boswell and Johnson have become a proverb. The Anglo-Saxon spirit of thane and ring-giver survives in the eighteenth century. To his passion for truth and his assiduity in ascertaining it, Boswell added "fidelity and tenderness" for his friend. The last words of the *Life* are "admiration and reverence." And of the three qualities of a good biographer—truth, diligence, and love—Boswell has shown once again that the greatest of these is love.

The craving and the capacity for affection dominated Boswell's life. "The sound and perfect human being," he writes,[128] "can sit under a spreading tree like the Spaniard, playing on his Guitar, his mistress by him, and glowing with gratitude to his God. Music, Love, adoration! There is a Soul." His affectionate nature helps in explaining his weaknesses as well as his virtues, and in reconciling the "contradictory qualities" in his own character, which he recognized in that of his friend.[129] Unsure of himself, he longed for the approval and admiration of others. He wishes to identify himself with their lives. He could correct his conduct more readily by thinking of himself as "the friend of Paoli" or "the friend of Johnson" than by remembering that he was Boswell *tout simple*. The journals show clearly enough that there were two sides to his character—the preacher and the sinner; yet the moralist preached love and the sinner demanded it. It is not therefore wholly inconsistent that after adoring the three wise men of Europe—Johnson, Rousseau, and Voltaire—in 1763 and 1764, he should cross the Alps in 1765 and fall under the spell of three graces among the Italian ladies. The Boswell who can mercilessly record against himself his sordid encounter with "a βιγ φατ Wχορε" is the same man who confesses his slip to his wife and is so disturbed by her grief that he resolves to make up to her by "μοστ αφεκτιουατε αττευτιου".[130] The maker of resolutions is as much Boswell as the breaker of them, and one

---

[128] *Isham Papers*, Vol. VII, p. 114.
[129] 1784, penultimate paragraph; Vol. IV, p. 426.
[130] *Isham Papers*, Vol. XII, p. 137; Feb. 27, 1777.

must accept for Boswell himself his defense of Johnson: "Let the profane and licentious pause; let them not thoughtlessly say that Johnson was an *hypocrite,* or that his *principles* were not firm, because his *practice* was not uniformly conformable to what he professed."[131]

Boswell was an actor. He imitated his father, and Doctor Johnson, and even the Rock of Gibraltar. Chameleon-like, he could take on the color of his surroundings. With Pitt he was the defender of liberty; with Margaret Rudd he was the gentleman about town. After his first strong impregnation with the Johnsonian aether, he writes to Zelide—he is just twenty-four—reminding her that "Believe me, God does not intend that we should have much pleasure in this world" and that she must guard herself against "ungoverned vivacity."[132] His interview with Rousseau leaves him all noble emotion, so that he records his tears on parting with the comment: "This I retain as a true Elogium of my Humanity."[133] Yet a few months later, immediately after his stay at Ferney, he is acting as Voltaire might have acted in the face of human stupidity:[134]

"This morning, as the Maid was lighting me to my chaise, the candle went out. I gravely said, 'Apportez le comme il est,' as if it's going out had made little odds. She did so for sometime and would have continued, had not I burst out a-laughing at her amazing simplicity."

He observed the great in order to satisfy the moralist in him by imitating them. Yet his friendliness and sociability extended to all human types; his curiosity was insatiable, and nothing is more Boswellian than his disarming remark:[135] "If it were not liable to ridicule, I would say that an acquaintance with the language of beasts would be a most agreeable acquisition to man, as it would

[131] 1784; Vol. IV, p. 396.
[132] *Letters,* C. B. Tinker, ed., Oxford, 1924; Vol. I, pp. 48 and 52. cf. also Johnson's remark about a "woman preaching" with this extract from the *Tour to Corsica,* 1923 ed., p. 11: "In particular, I was struck to find here a small copy from Raphael, of St Michael and the Dragon. There was no necessity for its being well done. To see the thing at all was what surprised me."
[133] *Isham Papers,* Vol. IV, p. 117; 1764.
[134] *Isham Papers,* Vol. IV, pp. 146-7; Jan. 5, 1765.
[135] *Tour to Corsica,* 1923 ed., p. 43.

enlarge the circle of his social intercourse." In talking to Rousseau about his own highly developed art of imitating people, Boswell says of himself:[186] "I was a kind of Virtuoso. When I espied any singular character I would say, 'It must be added to my collection.'" Boswell's extraordinary capacity for observing other people is even more fully brought out in his journals than in his life of Johnson. It is a far cry from Johnson's thunder to the voice of a child, but Boswell's inimitable clarity seems to suggest the very intonation of his daughter's voice as he records:[137]

" 'Suppose,' said I, 'Veronica, when you come to Heaven, you do not find me there. What would you do?' Said she: 'I would cry, "Angels, where's my Pappa?"'' She said this with such an enchanting earnest vivacity, as if she had really been addressing herself to the *celestial Ministers,* that I was quite happy. 'But,' said I, 'suppose they should let you see me walking upon wild mountains and shut out because I had not been good enough?' Said She: 'I would speak to GOD to let you come in.' I kissed her with the finest fondness. The brilliant light shone into my very soul. I was all hope and joy. . . . And may not her prayers to GOD avail much for me yet?"

The scene typically ends with Boswell's affectionate heart full to overflowing. To a man of such warm emotions, the cold reserve of his father was incomprehensible:[138] "It is strange to see such a niggardliness of fondness," he writes. In the journals of this warm and inquisitive spirit, children, dour Scotch aristocrats, criminals about to be hanged, philosophers, statesmen, country-wenches and Thayendanegea the Mohawk chieftain—all alike are displayed in his gallery.

But his greatest portrait is the portrait of himself. He has cultivated the art of exact recording so assiduously that it seems a natural product, and one can easily forget that the whole is deliberate—an unending self-scrutiny. Not only does Boswell accept the comparison of a journal to a looking-glass, but he carries it further: "as a lady adjusts her dress before a mirror, a man adjusts his character by looking at his journal."[139] Boswell does not present a flattering likeness of himself; though he is

---

[186] *Isham Papers,* Vol. IV, p. 113.   [137] *Isham Papers,* Vol. XII, p. 181.
[138] *Isham Papers,* Vol. X, p. 259.   [139] *Life,* Vol. III, p. 228; March 31, 1778.

vain, he is not proud. He records all the stinging criticisms his servant Jacob makes of him and then writes of Jacob: "I admired him."[140] He inserts whatever he hears about himself, the bad as well as the good. Few of his enemies could have told Boswell of any weaknesses in his character which he did not know. After setting down the disgraceful scene in which he returns home drunk, breaks his walking stick and the chairs in the dining-room, and throws things at his wife, he says of himself: "What a monstrous account of a Man!"[141] And elsewhere he writes:[142]

"There is an imperfection, a superficialness, in all my notions. I understand nothing clearly, nothing to the bottom. I pick up fragments, but never have in my memory a mass of any size. I wonder really if it be possible for me to acquire any one part of knowledge fully." '

Self-knowledge, at least, he attained. He saw himself, as he saw his fellows, objectively. This trait split his nature in two, so that he is artist and moralist on one side, impulsive, warm-hearted animal on the other. Such a dual nature may be seen, I believe, in his trick of writing his rough journals in the second person: Boswell the moralist is judging and admonishing the irrepressible "you" who slips and stumbles so often. Boswell is prisoner at his own bar. Divided personality seems also to account for the journals themselves. Whether they were meant for eventual publication is doubtful. But Boswell's instinct as artist, his moral passion for truth, could not be satisfied merely with living. "My tables! Meet it is I set it down" was his constant instinctive response to any incident in his life. The journals give, in Geoffrey Scott's fine phrase, "the patient tale of Boswell's acts and hopes and humiliations, set down for his own solitary view."[143] He was his own audience; and one of his most significant remarks is: "Sometimes it has occurred to me that a man should not live more than he can record."[144]

---

[140] *Isham Papers,* Vol. VII, p. 37.   [141] *Isham Papers,* Vol. X, p. 260.
[142] *Isham Papers,* Vol. XI, p. 45; Dec. 22, 1775.
[143] "The Making of the Life of Johnson," *Isham Papers,* Vol. VI, 1929, p. 67.
[144] *The Hypochondriack,* ed. Margery Bailey, 1928, Vol. II, p. 259; No. 66, "On Diaries."

This is almost to say that the end of life is art, that experience itself serves only to furnish raw material for the recorder. And the ideal of this art that devours life, in Boswell's journals as in his biography of Johnson, is the exact and complete truth:[145]

"It is a work of very great labour and difficulty to keep a journal of life, occupied in various pursuits, mingled with concomitant speculations and reflections, in so much, that I do not think it possible to do it unless one has a peculiar talent for abridging. I have tried it in that way, when it has been my good fortune to live in a multiplicity of instructive and entertaining scenes."

His conception of journalizing his life is so exacting and insistent that he breaks out in despair with:[146] "I have regretted that there is no invention for getting an immediate and exact transcript of the mind, like that instrument by which a copy of a letter is at once taken off." And again:[147] "It is impossible to clap the mind upon paper as one does an engraved plate, and to leave the full vivid impression." And yet again:[148]

"The great lines of characters may be put down. But I doubt much if it be possible to preserve in words the peculiar features of mind which distinguish individuals as certainly as the features of different countenances. The art of portrait painting fixes the last; and musical sounds with all their nice gradations can also be fixed. Perhaps language may be improved to such a degree as to picture the varieties of mind as minutely. In the meantime we must be content to enjoy the recollection of characters in our own breasts."

Boswell's artistic ideals, like his moral standards, were so severe that his practice never satisfied him. Yet surely no one has come closer to engraving his mind upon paper than did Boswell. Nothing is too small for him. All the velleities and whims of his consciousness are recorded. The *Tour to the Hebrides* presents him lying awake and imagining a spider crossing the dark room and crawling up his cot. The journals abound in such trifles, for those

---

[145] *The Hypochondriack*, Vol. II, p. 259. See also, for Boswell's notions that relate to biography, Nos. 10, 35, and 70 in Professor Bailey's excellent edition.
[146] *ibid.*
[147] *Isham Papers*, Vol. X, p. 196. Journal for 1774-1775.
[148] Diary for October 19, 1775. Quoted from Scott's *Making of the Life of Johnson*, p. 17.

"who think much and minutely . . . know well of what little parts the principal extent of human existence is composed."[149]

We know Boswell, therefore, as he studies chemistry intently on the close-stool; as he dreams that his child is dead, sees the worms in the flesh, and then the bones; as he and his wife lie awake all night for fear he may have to fight a duel; as he confides to Doctor Blair his warm effusions; as he composes for his brother the oath to stand by the heir of Auchinleck with heart, purse, and sword; as he confesses, "I own I love nonsense," or decides that he has bottles of champagne in his head which are every now and then poured out. The beautiful volumes of the *Private Papers of James Boswell* reveal him fully, giving hitherto undiscovered lights .and shades in his child-like personality. Though even this great collection is fragmentary, it shows Boswell at his best, for he is natural and informal and lucid. His insistence upon truth justifies itself in his practice. *Tout comprendre c'est tout pardonner* is borne out by the effect upon the reader of this amazing feat in self-revelation; and Boswell has done more than he may ever have planned by increasing our knowledge of human capacities.

[149] *The Hypochondriack,* Vol. II, p. 258; No. 66, 1783.

CHAPTER VII

THE TREND OF BIOGRAPHY

"Knowledge drawn freshly and in our view out
of particulars, knoweth the way best to particulars
again."
—BACON, *The Advancement of Learning.*

THIS final chapter has three purposes. As a whole, it will attempt to summarize and tie together the diverse details of the preceding chapters. Historically, it will note the trend of biography during the century, basing its observations upon contemporary references to a particular biography, upon the demand, immediate or steady, for a biography as indicated by its various editions, and upon the fashions in biography as shown by the prevalence of lives of any definite type. Critically, it will present the technique and theory of biography as developed during the century, its extensions and experiments and successes.

To reduce to simplicity the multiplicity of biographies mentioned in this book requires a departure from the truth. Any generalization which is here made could be refuted by judicious selection of materials from the bibliography. Although generalizations can do no more than approach truth, it may be of some use to fit together these hundreds of pieces into a rough pattern; for the colors in this great mosaic of biography are not the same in all its parts, and many of the tones are caught up and reflected by other pieces in the design.

Looking at all the lives written during the century, one may say that biography during the eighteenth century became increasingly subjective in its emphasis, detailed in its manner, and democratic in its choice of heroes. The traditional religious and didactic purpose of earlier biographers is now supplemented on the one hand by curiosity, which at its best takes the form of the pursuit of truth for its own sake, and on the other hand by a greater trust in emotions and instinct. More briefly, the standards of biography came to be determined not only by the conscience, but by the intellect and by the heart.

On somewhat less positive evidence one may assert that biography became more subtle and sure in its mental analysis; that style came to be considered as of greater importance; that the simple interpretation, the moral purpose, the obvious bias of eulogy or satire were viewed with increasing mistrust; and that at the end of the century the sense of biographical form was almost submerged under a deluge of collected anecdotes.

Fairly safe also is the observation that the eighteenth century Englishman, living in the most social and worldly age in English history, took a lively interest in his neighbor and thereby encouraged the development of biography as in no other century. And. one may say with certainty that the eighteenth century, however conservative may have been many of its forms and traditions, was in biography a period of experimentation and discovery, so that the possibilities of recording a life convincingly, faithfully, and vividly, were notably increased. In the art of biography, the eighteenth century is the High Renaissance. The belief that "The proper study of mankind is man" had its inevitable effect upon the recording of individual lives, and biography, in infinite forms and new hybrids and admirable single specimens, came to its finest flower.

§ I

Certain trends, of course, remain fairly steady during the entire .century. A tendency, for instance, toward documentation and toward encyclopedic and antiquarian collections was already present in the last half of the seventeenth century and even earlier; the tradition of Leland and Pits, of Fuller and Anthony Wood, is carried past the turn of the century by such antiquaries as Prince and Strype, and later regularized, methodized—one may say nationalized—by such scholars as Birch, Oldys, Collins, and Kippis. Before the seventeenth century had closed the great French encyclopedist Bayle had shown the world how to subjoin to a bare biographical account footnotes that rendered its authority unquestionable; such jungles of ill-digested source-material tended to destroy biography as an art. The numerous English adaptations of Bayle's methods, however, in Jeremy Taylor and the other dictionary-makers and in individual works by various disciples,[1] kept biographers continually conscious of the necessity for truth and for that solidity which arises only from thorough knowledge.

No less than the antiquarian spirit, the desire to collect many biographies in a single work remains unwavering throughout the century, though it would have been hard to predict what particular group was to appear next. Who could prophesy, for instance, that between 1704 and 1795 collections would appear chronologically for such classes as great seventeenth century Frenchmen, English reforming divines, Roman Catholic saints, Roman poets, English Baptists, Roman Catholic priests martyred in England, popes, royal and noble authors, Protestant reformers, living English authors, painters, English poets, physicians to the time of Harvey, engravers, Scripture characters, and the orators of the British Parliament?[2] Nor could one generalize, from a series such as this, as to the reasons for such collections, except to say that they satisfy inquisitive, or devotional, or controversial instincts.

The stream of Christian biography also flows undiminished during the century. Individual lives of great spiritual beauty, regardless of their particular creed, inspired biographers to record them as a legacy to the world, as they have always done. But in the main, the strong current of religious conviction and enthusiasm which gave such nobility to the ecclesiastical biography of the seventeenth century flowed, in the first part of the eighteenth century, through the Quaker autobiographies, and later on, through the Methodist journals. In this veering of the current, the theological subtlety and the intellectual vigor of the seventeenth century divines disappears or becomes vulgarized; the evangelical emotional element, in compensation, increases. The

---

[1] See particularly, in the Bibliography, William Harris, John Jortin, Samuel Knight, John Lewis, Oldys, Schomberg, Des Maizeaux, and Clayton.

[2] The years and authors for these collections, respectively, are 1704, J. Ozell; 1709, R. Burton; 1727, C. Fell; 1733, L. Crusius; 1738-1740, T. Crosby; 1741-1742, R. Challoner; 1749-1768, A. Bower; 1758, H. Walpole; 1759, R. Rolt; 1762, W. Rider; 1770, M. Pilkington; 1779-1781, S. Johnson; 1780, J. Aikin; 1785, J. Strutt; 1793, T. Robinson; 1795, A. Pasquin. See also Chap. IV.

democratic quality which marks the century leaves its impress upon ecclesiastical biography: one cannot read the biographies of Friends and Wesleyans without feeling that within a hundred years religious ardor passed from the seminaries of Oxford and Cambridge to the artisans, journeymen, and apprentices. These two outstanding Quaker and Methodist movements seem economic as much as religious. It is as if the middle classes—merchants, shopkeepers, and craftsmen—growing in dignity and self-respect and power and seriousness, had developed a religious expression of their own.

The unquestionable predominance of the Quakers and Methodists in biography does not mean that other communions are biographically barren. The English Baptists have their general historian in Thomas Crosby; Edward Calamy and Daniel Neal act as general Protestant historians for the Nonconformists and the Puritans; the Roman Catholics have such assiduous apologists and biographers as Thomas Phillips, Charles Fell, Alban Butler, and Richard Challoner. Presbyterian biography tends to become an exercise in Scottish patriotism. The Church of England is comparatively silent; most of the Anglican biographical productions confirm the torpor and languor which is commonly attributed to the Church in this period: only a political issue, such as the Sacheverell trial or the Bangorian controversy, can draw forth biographical pamphlets; the most energetic theological reasoners of the time, within or near to the Anglican fold—men such as Samuel Clarke, Thomas Emlyn, William Whiston, and Joseph Priestley—tend to be independent, Unitarian, Arian, or Deistic. The orthodox Anglican biographer of the period, finding the present times uninspiring and even uninteresting, erects his monument of piety by means of antiquarian research, as if the great days of the Church of England were already in the past.[3] An Izaak Walton in the eighteenth century would have had to look far to find such subjects within the Church of England as Hooker, Donne, Herbert, and Sanderson.

Vulgar curiosity, as well as antiquarian and religious interests, persisted steadily throughout the century. The professional hack-

---

[3] See John Lewis, John Walker, and William Gilpin.

writers, under the leadership of Defoe, learned to turn out almost overnight biographical tracts concerning the latest scandal, trial, or execution, giving the common reader repeated pleasant shocks under the guise of preachments against the seven deadly sins. During the last half of the century, possibly responding to the influence of such men as Rousseau and Sterne, these crude biographical thrillers were made more subtle, so that the life of any one man was felt to be worth recording precisely to the extent that it varied from the lives of all others. Idiosyncrasy became a virtue; and instead of profiting from the examples of destructive vices in others, the reader of biography was now advised to laugh at their crotchets. This marks a genuine shift in fashion: from naïve accounts of horror to amused and superior narratives of eccentricity. But curiosity regarding others runs through them all, from the autobiography of Thomas Tryon, vegetarian, astrologer, and preacher of health and cleanliness to housewives at the beginning of the century (1705), through the female soldier Hannah Snell in mid-century (1750), to the 103-year-old Sergeant Macleod (1791) or the indomitable rogue and village-father Blind Jack of Knaresborough (1795) at the end. One biographer accounts for the continued popularity of such lives in plausible fashion:[4]

"Used to contemplate in ourselves and others, human nature, as cast in common molds, we view its eccentricities with the mixed emotions of astonishment and pleasure."

Just as the lives of criminals had their greatest vogue during the first third of the eighteenth century, so the life-and-adventures and the life-and-loves types were at their peak during the same period.[5] They are descended from other types of literature rather than from biography. The life-and-adventures group has close affiliations with the picaresque novel and with the accounts of exploration, voyaging, and geography; the *vie-et-amours* stems from the French romance of the seventeenth century. In the first third of the century, the two groups become conventional and stereotyped. They move in the steps of a formal minuet, following accepted patterns. As the century goes on, fiction or near-

[4] Joseph Berington, *History of the lives of Abeillard and Heloise*, 1787, p. 121.
[5] See Chaps. II and IV.

fiction becomes less prevalent. The patterns are kept, but actual events and careers afford the illustrations. Thus, *Robinson Crusoe* is replaced by Isaac James's account of Alexander Selkirk (1800), and *Captain Singleton* by David Lowellin's adventures in Africa (1792), if, indeed, Lowellin himself is not a fiction; the clever but imaginary *Travels of Edward Brown* (1739) gives way to the more nearly authentic but equally exciting *Travels of Count de Benyowsky* (1789).

Similarly, the artificial accounts of amorous intrigues, usually set in historical courts or centered upon one historical figure, written by Eliza Haywood, Penelope Aubin, Madame D'Aulnoy, or Mrs. Manley, are supplanted by the detailed love-affairs of the actresses and toasts of London, the biographies or autobiographies of Charlotte Charke, Constantia Phillips, George Anne Bellamy, Sophia Baddeley, Sarah Gooch, or Mary Robinson. The current persists, in other words, but it takes a new direction toward the individual and the actual.

Women had a virtual monopoly in recording the affairs of the heart. In the conventional school of *le jeu de l'amour et du hasard* there are really only two authorities among the male biographers of the first third of the century: Anthony Hamilton, who wrote the memoirs of the Count de Grammont (1714), and Alexander Smith, who issued and reissued (1715-1730) his stock of stories as the school of Venus, the history of cuckolds, of celebrated beauties, and of famous jilts, and the secret amours of the British nobility. It is possibly even more remarkable that the century is practically barren in accounts of deep and tender love. The seventeenth century can supply many such stories, and the nineteenth; but they are rare in eighteenth century biography. Boswell's failure to understand fully the relationship between Johnson and his wife may be taken as typical. Most of the lives written in the period disregard love entirely, as they disregard, to a surprising extent, all personal relationships and accounts of friends and family. In a long biography, the writer will refer, in a casual sentence, to a wife; or the reader will be surprised to find him living with his second wife before anything has been said of the death of the first; or marriage will bulk large because it is a business matter of dowry and of industry on the wife's part. When affairs of the heart are not overlooked entirely, they are described in swollen, artificial terms, as if sentiment had been experienced by the writer only while reading some French romance or listening to some heroic drama of the Restoration. The merciless and exact analysis of passion is more frequent, particularly under the influence of the numerous memoirs translated from the French;[6] in the detailed record of passion, native English style, Lady Anne Vane's memoirs (1751) and Elizabeth Steele's *Sophia Baddeley* (1787) are noteworthy. The English public evidently valued the accounts of genuine self-sacrificing love, as is shown by the biographical variations on the story of Abelard and Heloise, or the great popularity of Susanna Dobson's *Petrarch* (1775). But Heloise and Petrarch lived long ago and far away; and it is indeed remarkable that the second half of the century, which set such value upon emotion and invented for itself new brands of sentiment, could so rarely touch in its recording of lives the noble devotion and love of John Wesley or William Godwin, or even the dreaming tenderness of Mary Robinson.

§ 2

English biography is for the most part self-contained. Foreign influences touch its great bulk but lightly, and often indirectly. Thus, it is possible to maintain theoretically that the worship of individual force and genius which characterized the Italian Renaissance eventually made itself felt in England and contributed to the increase in autobiography in the seventeenth and eighteenth century. But the direct influence of Italian letters or thought upon English biography is negligible.[7] The safest generalizations which may be made with regard to foreign influences are briefly these: Greek and Roman literature (often through French sources) helped English biographers to attain an often incongruous grand style, led them astray from the biographical

---

[6] See Chaps. II and III, and Bibliography.

[7] Italy nevertheless furnished English biographers and translators with materials that blended the exotic and the historic. cf. Gordon's *Alexander VI and Caesar Borgia*, 1729; Farneworth's *Sixtus V* (tr.), 1754; Nugent's *Cellini* (tr.), 1771; Caraccioli's *Clement XIV* (tr.), 1776; Roscoe's *Lorenzo de' Medici*, 1795; Noble's *Medici*, 1797; and Tenhove's *Medici* (tr.), 1797.

ideal in copying historians or annalists such as Tacitus, Livy, and Caesar, and afforded them in Plutarch a model much admired and frequently imitated. Spanish literature, through the English novel or romance, contributed to the development of picaresque biography and to the recording of sensational, cunning, or sordid lives in the first half of the century.[8] French memoirs noticeably strengthened the belief in the importance of the individual, and of sentiment in the life of the individual; and helped to teach biographers and autobiographers to observe psychological states without fear and without distortion. Greater truth, clarity, subtlety, and subjectivity, therefore, came from France, infiltrating into English life in editions of important French biographical materials which were immediately turned into English and read with avidity. At the end of the century, the German influence made itself felt in the increasing prevalence of biographies of emotion and sentiment.[9]

Dignity and, seemingly, the approval of the years were given to biography by choosing Latin mottos for title-pages and chapter-headings. Sometimes these afforded a philosophy to the biographer—a central core of belief around which he could shape his interpretation of human life. Sometimes they were little more than decoration. Some of the favorite devices, culled from Vergil, Ovid, Lucretius, and Cicero, were:

"Sequor non passibus aequis. . . ."

"Et genus et proavos, et quae non fecimus ipsi,
Vix ea nostra voco. . . ."

"Tantum suadere Religio potuit. . . ."

and particularly:

"Ne quid falsi dicere audeat, deinde; ne quid veri non audeat."[10]

[8] See Chaps. II and IV. Also F. W. Chandler's *Literature of Roguery*, 1907, 2 vols.

[9] cf. Baron Trenck, 1788; Lavater, 1795; and Kotzebue, 1800; and the influence of Goethe upon Godwin's *Mary Wollstonecraft*, 1798; and contrast with the earlier debonair French spirit of the Baron de Pöllnitz, 1737 and later; or of most lives of Frederick the Great.

[10] This last, for example, from Cicero's *De Oratore*, Book II, is quoted in Phillips's *Pole*, 1764; the life of John Owen, 1721; Coke's and Moore's *John Wesley*, 1792; *Memoirs of the life and misfortunes of Mr. Pless*, 1731; and in numerous other biographies.

Very often a rakish pamphlet or a raffish collection will be given a false air of dignity by some Latin tag on the title-page, as, for instance:

"Dicique beatus
Ante obitum nemo, supremaque funera debet."[11]

"Hoc est
Vivere bis, Vitâ posse priore frui."[12]

"Felix, quem faciunt aliena pericula, cautum."[13]

The culture and polish of the early eighteenth century, with Londoners conscious of the new Rome on the Thames and the new Golden Age, led to a demand for a more detailed knowledge of the antique models in philosophy and literature. Matthew Towers (1744) and Ralph Schomberg (1769) issue derivative accounts of Horace; Schomberg writes a learned life of Maecenas (1766) and a critical dissertation on Pindar; Homer's life and writings are surveyed by Ozell (1712), Pope and Parnell (1715), Thomas Blackwell (1735), and Robert Wood (1775). Xenophon's *Memorabilia* lies back of translations or lives of Socrates by E. Bysshe (1712), John Gilbert Cooper (1750), and Sarah Fielding (1762). George Stanhope's translation of Boileau's life of Epictetus goes through five editions by 1741, and T. M. Gibbs translates de Gomberville's generalized *View of human life, according to the Stoic philosophy* (1721). Other figures, from Hesiod to Petronius and the apostate Emperor Julian, also have their biographers. Lives of the Roman poets, the ancient philosophers, the emperors and the empresses, translations of Diogenes Laertius and Suetonius as well as original compilations, appeared, and the *Biographia Classica* ran through many editions.[14] Middleton's life of Cicero (1741) was one of the most influential and respected biographies of the century, and we may still accept the opinion of Vicesimus Knox when he says that Middleton "has

[11] *A character of the life of the Earl of Orford*, 1745.

[12] *The memoirs of Michael Clancy*, 1750.

[13] *Anecdotes, bon mots, and biographical sketches, of the most remarkable highwaymen*, 1797.

[14] e.g., 1740, 1750, 1777, 1778.

given us a most accurate account of one of the greatest men that ever lived, in a style truly classical and manly."[15]

In their conception of England as Neo-Augustan, eighteenth century biographers issued a number of lives of Romans or Greeks whose careers supposedly paralleled those of important figures in contemporary life. Thus *The life of Aristides, the Athenian; who was decreed to be banish'd for his justice* (1714) appears at a time when the banishment of Bolingbroke was in every man's thought. The life of Belisarius (1713), the great conqueror who fell into disgrace, called Marlborough to mind. Richardson Pack's adaptation of the life of Atticus from Cornelius Nepos (1719) narrates the life of a close friend of such successive rulers as Silla, Caesar, Antony, and Octavius, who kept himself alive to the advanced age of seventy-seven largely because he would not participate in politics; it is written in order to lend support to England's new king, to point out to the Tories their folly, and to counsel moderation to the Whigs. *The Heir Apparent: or, the life of Commodus* (1789), the wastrel successor to Marcus Aurelius, piously disclaims any reflections upon the present Prince of Wales. Such biographies, invariably controversial, were kept anonymous. The reason for such caution is not difficult to see in such a savage attack, for instance, as *Rufinus: or an historical essay on the favourite-ministry under Theodosius the Great* (1712), published just at the sharp turn in Marlborough's career. The author assures the reader (p. 3): "I meddle not with modern Instances"; but no one, least of all the Duke of Marlborough and his Duchess Sarah, was blind to the implications of his conclusion (pp. 43-4):

"If the Poet has been prophetical, and the Vices of Rufinus's Age are again flourishing in ours: If the insatiable Avarice here described should be found in one, the dark and designing Temper in another, the Female Impetuosity and Love of Revenge in a third, then this Translation is seasonable."

One of the later mixtures of the ancient and modern world is the anonymous *Life of John Wilkes, Esq; in the manner of Plutarch* (1773). This is a subtly caustic attack on the idea that "the Voice of the People is the Voice of God" (p. 36), written

---

[15] *Essays moral and literary,* 1782, Vol. II, p. 51; No. 94.

by an anonymous scholar-politician. Although few facts are given, the author manages to convey fairly successfully a hostile view of Wilkes's career. Plutarchian generalizations, digressions, and philosophizing are well copied, and England is mixed neatly with Greece (pp. 12-13):

"And now being full of expectation, and solely bent on the welfare of the public, he consulted an oracle how he should soonest arrive at the Summit of all Political Glory.—The Pythian replied, that he must renounce his constituents at Aylesbury, and make the opinion of the Londoners, the rule and guide of his life. The decrees of fate are irresistible."

In discussing tyranny versus popular government, and established religion versus free thought, the author draws illustrations from the lives of Cicero, Maecenas, Pericles, Lycurgus, and Nero; Plutarch and Tacitus are quoted; and instead of a Plutarchian double parallel, the frontispiece has a quadruple parallel, for above the caption "These are thy Gods O Britain" are engravings of Wat Tyler, Alderman Beckford, Jack Cade, and John Wilkes, the last two represented as cross-eyed.

Much of the effectiveness of such a satire depends upon the familiarity of the public with the original author parodied. The defamer of John Wilkes made no mistake in assuming a widespread knowledge of Plutarch in the eighteenth century: Dryden's translation came out in five, six, or eight volume editions in 1702-1711, 1716, 1727, 1758, and 1763; John and William Langhorne's translation, issued in six volumes in 1770, had reached its seventh edition by 1798; an epitome of Plutarch appeared in 1713; a pleasant condensation, probably by Goldsmith, in five volumes in 1762; and an abridged selection for use in schools in 1800. Sometimes individual lives by Plutarch are translated,[16] and sometimes attempts are made to supplement his roll of illustrious Greeks and Romans.[17]

[16] e.g., *The history of Julius Caesar. Newly translated from the original Greek of Plutarch*, 1771.

[17] *The life of Scipio Africanus, and of Epaminondas; intended as a supplement to Plutarch's Lives*, 1787, tr. fr. the French of de la Tour by R. Parry, 2 vols. Thomas Rowe's *Lives of several ancient and illustrious men omitted by Plutarch*, 1728. cf. also Andrew Thevet's (1676) or Dacier's earlier translated supplements to Plutarch.

Plutarch's striking invention of parallel lives in pairs, implicit in the controversial biographies mentioned earlier in the chapter, is frequently explicit in eighteenth century imitations. The histories of "those two great opposites, Edward Earl of Clarendon, and Bulstrode Lord Whitlock" in the lives of the English Lords Chancellors (1708, 2 vols.), Edward Jesup's lives of Picus and Pascal, to which is subjoined a parallel (1723), Joseph Spence's *Parallel; in the manner of Plutarch* (1757) between an Italian and an English scholar, Jerom Alley's *Comparative view of the lives of Henry the Fourth of France, and William the Third of England* (1789), and John Gillies's parallel between Frederick of Prussia and Philip of Macedon (1789)—all derive from Plutarch in structure and inspiration. To a modern reader, the parallel between Chesterfield and Doctor Johnson by William Hayley (1787) is probably of most interest. Plutarch's conception of collecting lives as exemplifications of good and bad moral conduct encourages such derivative productions as Thomas Mortimer's six volumes of *The British Plutarch,* frequently reprinted; and the *Revolutionary Plutarch* and *The Female Revolutionary Plutarch* at the turn of the century. Plutarch as a political thinker, a defender of the golden mean, was taken as a symbol of liberty and republicanism by such patriots as Dumouriez[18] and Paoli; and possibly the best example, though the subtlest, of the influence of one great biographer upon another is to be found in the exalted Plutarchian sketch of a great man in the service of a great political idea—Boswell's portrait of Pascal Paoli in his *Journal of a tour to Corsica.*[19]

Much of the English familiarity with the men of Greece and Rome, as might be seen by tracing the sources of the classical biographies mentioned above, comes to England from France, and marks only one of the debts of English biography to the French. Some of the finest examples of antiquarian research centering biographically upon a single figure were rendered accessible to

[18] *The life of General Dumouriez,* 1796, Vol. III, p. 428 and elsewhere.

[19] 1768. For Plutarch's influence on other biographers, see Goldsmith's *Nash,* 1762, Hurd's *Warburton,* 1794, or Hume's advice to the historian Robertson (quoted later in this chapter), in A. Stewart's *Robertson,* Vol. I, pp. xl-xli.

the English public in translations from the French.[20] The French savants taught the English—or could have taught them—that to be erudite one need be neither dull nor clumsy. More important, the French writers of memoirs presented some masterly political studies seen through the eyes of an individual—analytical commentaries of the type the greatly respected de Thou made popular, known in England through the works of Clarendon and Burnet, and imitated by Hervey and Walpole. In the continued translations of Philippe de Commines (1712, 1723), in Voltaire's *Frederick, Charles of Sweden,* and *Age of Louis XIV,* in Duclos's history of Louis XI (1746), and in the memoirs of Cardinal de Retz (1723, 1774), of de Fleury (1743), of Guy Joli (1775), and of the Duc de Sully,[21] statecraft becomes a fine art practised by the heroes of biography.

Even in dealing with great historical events, the French writers, in spite of their flair for analysis and generalization, never forgot that the individual is the reality; history, or the state, an illusion. From this realization, in fact, spring "memoirs," that literary form which the French invented. At the outset "memoirs" meant in practice history seen through one pair of eyes while it was unfolding. The good memoir-writer never suffered from the historian's delusions of omniscience or impartiality. Thus the French editor of the *Memoirs of Maximilian de Bethune, Duke of Sully* (1757) says (p. ii): "his character [that of Henry IV] must be fixed by his letters and conversation; the passions are better displayed by a single word, related as it was spoke, than by all the art which a historian can use. This idea of memoirs is quite answered by those of Sully." As a result, many of the longest memoirs and biographies of the period, although they contain invaluable historical material and deal with momentous national events, rarely waver in their biographical focus upon a great figure. Justamond's four-volume translation of *The private life of Lewis XV* (1781) begins with the observation (p. 2):

"We shall not go out of our way to prove the utility of private memoirs; this is too philosophic an age to call it in question, and

20 cf. Burigny's *Grotius,* 1754; Sade's *Petrarch,* 1775; la Bléterie's *Emperor Julian,* 1784; and Fénelon's *Philosophers,* 1726.
21 1756. Six editions appeared within the next twenty-two years.

the multitude of similar publications that have been favourably received, shew how much they are now preferred to large historical collections . . . we set aside the dignity and grandeur of the Monarch, and shew nothing more than the man."

An even better exemplification of history as a by-product of genuine biography—and indeed, one of the best of all historical biographies—is Madame de Motteville's *Memoirs for the history of Anne of Austria,* translated in five volumes in 1725. A French gentlewoman and companion to the Queen is writing, which almost insures that the ensuing memoirs will be at once personal, courtly, and psychological; that the occasional general reflections made with finesse will not detract from the personal history; and that a final sympathetic double-portrait will be left of a great Queen Regent and her conscientious and spirited son Louis XIV. The author says in her preface:[22]

"Other Historians will not fail to tell Posterity the Grand Events of her Time; but I thought it necessary to add the Particulars of her Private Life. . . . I have interspersed in her History, some of her Speeches, Thoughts and Actions, which deserve to be known to the whole World, and which would never have seen the Light if I had not immediately committed them to Writing."

By far the most important contribution of the French to English biography is their psychological sensitivity. It is hardly too much to say that the French biographers made England aware of new areas of consciousness. Where in English literature, before his time, can a temper be found comparable to that of Cardinal de Retz in his cool, disillusioned, cynical, and unashamed self-revelation? Yet his *Memoirs,* which ran through seven editions on the continent within a year from publication in 1717, were of great influence in England steadily from the time of their translation by P. Davall in four volumes in 1723.

"As for my part, Madam," he writes,[23] "I don't pretend to any Merit in my Morals for being sincere with you; for I find so great a Satisfaction when I give you an Account of all the Windings and Turnings of my own Heart, that I act more from a

22 Vol. I, pp. xiii-xiv.   23 1723 ed., Vol. I, pp. 60 and 1-2.

Principle of Pleasure, than from the Reason of the thing it self, when I keep so religiously close to Truth."

"Yet I am resolv'd to discover to you the most minute Particulars of my Life, from the time I began to know my self; and that, without the least Reserve or Disguise."

And no one could wield a more merciless scalpel than de Retz, as he cuts open his life with the detached professional interest of a modern psychologist, and shows himself to be a cold-blooded combination of Cardinal Wolsey and Lord Clarendon—clear-seeing, practical, sensual, worldly, brave, diplomatic, and cunning; running through many magnificent fortunes, and living a dangerous life on the splendid scale of a prince of the world.

Small wonder that a character such as Lord Chesterfield should consider de Retz as the best writer of memoirs. The worldly Cardinal, and other Frenchmen of similar genius, did more than any other force to upset and disturb British sanctimoniousness, which finds moral justifications for every act, turns every sinning autobiographer into a self-made saint, and cannot even publish the cheap, rough, sensual or brutal lives of bawds, cutpurses, or convicts without insisting upon an ethical purpose which is not there.

Not only the dry clarity of de Retz and La Rochefoucauld, and the penetration of Pineau-Duclos, but the wit and apt phrasing of truth in Voltaire's autobiography, the powerful and original emotions of Rousseau's writings, and finally the generous over-welling sentiments of the French Revolution[24] became the common property of the biographers. Particularly in the lives of the great ladies of France, though they may vary from the libertine Ninon de Lenclos to the mystic Madame Guyon, delicacy in psychological observation is carried to such a pitch as to make one believe that there is a real distinction between the masculine and the feminine mind.[25]

La Beaumelle's *Life of Madam de Maintenon,* translated in 1753 and 1760, may be taken as representative of the French spirit

[24] See the lives of the republican and liberty-loving Dumouriez, Brissot, Madame Roland, *The Five Men* [= the Directorate], *Revolutionary Plutarch, Female Revolutionary Plutarch,* Louvet, and Latude. All of these are 1787 or later in date.

[25] See la Motte, la Vallière, Motteville, Maintenon, Ninon de Lenclos, Roland, Guyon, d'Aulnoy. cf. also Chap. III.

and discoveries which were gradually absorbed into English biography. "You will find in it," the Epistle Dedicatory promises (1753, p. vi), "the Marvellous of Romance, the Truth of History, and abundance of little Facts serving to confirm important Truths." This description, which serves to account for the popularity of French memoirs in England, is well carried out. The ensuing biography is written with apparent authority and insight; motives are clarified; the mainsprings of complicated actions are simply indicated; the historical details of a great age are artistically subordinated to the life of a single woman, who moves from childhood to old age. Convincing interpretation—"the abundance of little Facts serving to confirm important Truths"— appears in details of her childhood under her mother's careful training (1753, pp. 21-2):

"A Fire having broke out in the House they occupied in America, and the Daughter crying at the Misfortune, she severely checked her, saying, 'Is the Loss of a House worth crying for?' Madam de Maintenon, who sometimes related this passage, used to add, 'I should have had a great deal more scolding, had my Mother known that I did not cry for the House, but for my Doll that perished in the Flames.'

"Under the Eye of this excellent Mother she could not fail of making a rapid Progress: She made her read Plutarch's Lives, and accustomed her early to think solidly."

The same conception of character recurs in the account of her spiritual problems when she was a young girl in a convent, significant adumbrations of her future piety, charity, and continual moral scruples (p. 27):

"What displeased her most, was that Tenet which excludes from eternal Life all that are not within the Pale of the Church: She often said to them [the Nuns], 'I will turn Catholic, provided you don't oblige me to believe, that my dear Aunt Villette is to be damned:' A Clause proving at once the Goodness of her Heart and the Rectitude of her Mind."

The twin vignettes of her and her husband the comedian Scarron are fine psychological interpretations (pp. 63-4); and the life is full of clever turns of thought, as in Madame de Maintenon's estimation of Ninon de Lenclos (p. 120):

"She was too grateful not to love her, too nice not to detach herself insensibly from her, too judicious to despise her, too virtuous to esteem her."

Such evidence of care, art, and truth in the interpretation of character lies also in the arrangement of material, as when a discursive chapter, which is nevertheless necessary for a full understanding of Maintenon's attitude, is introduced with (p. 143):

"While Madam Scaron, in the Rue des Tournelles, is minding her spiritual Concerns, or improving her Mind, let us take a View of what is doing at that Court where she was, one Day, to reign, and see how many Hearts Louis XIV. tried, before he found one worthy of his own."

The analysis of the King's emotions is given with a superb confidence and authority which English biographers had not yet learned to imitate with assurance (pp. 256-7):

"The King's Heart was cruelly racked: He gave himself up to Fontanges by Inclination; Reflection led him to Maintenon, and Habit brought him back to Montespan. Each of them wanted him entirely to herself. . . . Louis was all at once struggling with the Caprices of Love, the haughty Freaks of Jealousy, the Austerity of Morality, the Queen's Grief which he guessed at, and the Checks of his own Conscience."

And the weighing of motives is done with a convincing sureness of touch (Part II, 1760, p. 35):

"We must not, however, imagine, that it was merely to gratify Montespan, that Madam de Maintenon employed her Interest to obtain her so large an Allowance; that were falling into one Extreme to avoid another. No, Madam de Maintenon knew that Montespan was too avaricious to spend at such a Rate, and therefore considered the greatest Part of what the King allowed her as so much laid by for his Children [there were eight] by that Lady, whom Madam de Maintenon passionately loved, both because they were his, and because she had reared and educated them."

So the story of Maintenon's life, with its piety, benefactions, prudence, wisdom, and genuine love of Louis, continues sympathetically; and if at times the modes of thought or expression seem artificial or faintly false to a modern reader, he must not forget that this new care to make psychological interpretation full, clear, and deep was not an old art in France, and in England marked an invaluable innovation.

This section on French influence may well close with mention of a similar sympathetic and subtle appraisal, Citizen Corancez's *Anecdotes of the last twelve years of the life of J. J. Rousseau* (1798). The influence of Rousseau's own new ways of feeling, which have been touched upon in earlier chapters, and which by indirect or hidden ways did so much to establish a new spirit in biography, is everywhere present in Corancez's work. This little book is built around a clearly stated theme, but the theme is individual, not general; it applies to Rousseau alone. The sharp, direct observation of the romantics, rather than general traditional assumptions, gives such a biography its breath of being (pp. 5-6):

"I wish to lay open his inmost soul to my readers, that they may thus be enabled to judge for themselves of the spring of all his actions. They will see that when he was *himself*, if I may be allowed such an expression, he possessed a singular simplicity of character, approaching even that of infancy; for he had all its ingenuousness, gaiety, kindness and especially its timidity. When he was a prey to the agitations of a certain unhappy humour which seemed to circulate with his life-blood, he was then so different from himself that he inspired not anger, nor hatred, but rather pity; such, at least, was the sentiment with which I long beheld him."

Such a brief glimpse as the following does much to illuminate Rousseau's character (pp. 23-4):

"I have stated that he possessed a simplicity bordering on the character of infancy. On going to see him, one day, I found him joyful, walking up and down his chamber with large strides, and proudly eyeing every thing that it contained. 'All these are my own,' said he.—(It should be observed, that this all consisted of a bed with coarse cotton curtains, a few straw-bottomed chairs, a common table, and a scrutoire of walnut-tree.) 'How were they not your own yesterday?' said I, 'I have long seen every thing that is here in your possession.'—'Yes, Sir,' rejoined he, 'but I was in debt to the upholsterer for them, and it is only this morning that I completely paid him off.' He seemed to enjoy his few articles of furniture with much more real satisfaction, than the wealthy proprietor, who frequently knows not the one half of what he possesses."

The convincing analysis is held together by Corancez's repeated interpretation of Rousseau's eccentric career as dominated by a unique ruling passion—his illusion of persecution (p. 51):

"I cannot give a more just idea of his character, than by saying that he realized to my mind the possible existence of Don Quixote, to whom he bore a most marked resemblance. Each of them had a string of peculiar sensibility. When touched, it vibrated, in the one, to knight errantry, and all the extravagancies which accompanied it; and, in the other, it resounded with enemies, conspiracies, general coalitions, vast plans to destroy him, &c. When this string ceased to vibrate, the minds of both regained their natural tone."

In spite of a disappointing literal translation, the little volume affords a fascinating study of the approach of madness; and Boswellian fidelity in catching conversation and motion in detail is capped by a clear interpretation of character which ordinarily lay outside Boswell's range (pp. 57-8):

"I had long observed a striking change in his appearance; he was often in a state of convulsive agitation, which so distorted his features that I scarcely knew them, and imprinted on the whole of his figure, an expression truly horrible. In this state, his view seemed to embrace the immensity of space; his eyes appeared to see every thing at the same moment, but in fact they saw nothing. He turned round upon his chair, and flung his arm behind it; and thus suspended, it assumed the vibratory motion of a pendulum."

The little biography draws to a close with the burial of its hero, recorded in a scene which gives a new importance in biography to sentiment and setting, and which comprises an admirable retrospective conclusion (pp. 86-7):

"The interment took place on the same evening, during the finest moonlight, and the most serene sky. Think, reader, what were my feelings, as I entered the aisle with the body.

"The place—the brightness of the moon—the stillness of the air—the man himself—the transactions of his life—his uncommon destiny—the end which awaits us all—passed in melancholy succession through my mind. But, what it dwelt upon longest, and with most complacency, was the thought that the unfortunate Rousseau, at length reposed in peace,—dearly purchased it is true, but which there was no hope of his attaining in this life."

The *Anecdotes* are not unworthy of Rousseau himself; and after the fearless scrutiny of human foibles, of irrational genius, even of insanity, the reader is left with a greater sympathy and understanding of human nature and an increased admiration for both Rousseau and his biographer.

French biographers throughout the century, in summary, did their part in increasing the English understanding of human nature and of the art of recording a human life;[26] their influence was steady and diverse, even in the hands of translators whose morals were obviously too correct, and whose English not enough so.

French biography—coupled with English drama, the newly developed English novel, and the growing Romantic spirit, each of which has called for a separate chapter—extended the range of English biography in the eighteenth century. New matter in human experience became part of man's conscious life; and new techniques for rendering life-histories more amusing, more vivid, more faithful in the re-presentation of an individual existence, were discovered or adapted from allied forms of literature. English biography became more subjective.

§ 3

The second great shift in emphasis during the century was caused by the democratization of biography. Before 1700, kings

---

[26] Sporadic instances of French influence are not mentioned in the survey here presented. The debt of *The English Theophrastus: or, the manners of the age. Being the modern characters of the court, the town, and the city*, 1702, to La Bruyère, Saint Evremont, and La Rochefoucauld is therefore omitted from the text; as are such instances as the debt of Walpole to Saint Simon and the Duchess of Orleans in his *Reminiscences*, 1788; the influence of Madame de Sevigné's letters upon the autobiography and letters of Mary Granville, Mrs. Delany, who died in 1788; the influence of Bayle's method upon the *Biographia Britannica*. The influence of the French *éloges* is discussed later in this chapter. See also Chap. V.

and churchmen were almost exclusively the subjects for life-writing. They were presented not because they were important as individuals, but because the king was the symbol of the state and the saint was the symbol of the future state. When the life of a private man was set down, usually he belonged to a great family; for the information of descendants in that family his career, conceived as part of a genealogical record, was put in writing.

But the Civil Wars destroyed the conception of a stable church for the entire state, so that careers magnificent and significant as Anselm's and Becket's—even Cranmer's or Donne's or Hooker's—were no longer recorded. The Civil Wars likewise opened a rift between the aristocracy and the middle classes; the Bloodless Revolution of 1688 and the events of the Hanoverian succession, equally bloodless and almost more of a revolution, took away much of the importance from the king and his courtiers. A hundred years had wrought a great change. The genuine admiration for Elizabeth and the adulation of James was extended to Charles I; so that the immensely popular pseudo-autobiography of the martyred king, the *Eikon Basilike,* did indeed set up the royal image almost to be worshipped as a saint. This portrait, compared with Pope's picture of George II in his *Epistle to Augustus,* is Hyperion to a satyr. Nor in the eighteenth century will one find contemporary family-histories comparable in number or quality to those of the preceding hundred years. The lives of the Carys, of Colonel Hutchinson, of the Duke and Duchess of Newcastle; the aristocratic tone of Evelyn's *Margaret Godolphin,* and even, one may say, of Walton's biographies, die out; Roger North's *Lives of the Norths,* with its pride in birth and its family solidarity, seems already a throwback to an earlier age; and the family histories are principally antiquarian, as if the great lords and ladies were manifestations of a past long dead. Carte's massive life of the Duke of Ormonde in three folio volumes (1737) is typical; but it is also typical that Thomas Carte must quarry his giant figure out of seventeenth century documents.

If the lives of Strafford and Laud, with their fanatic devotion to political and religious ideals, may be taken as typical of the seventeeth century, the biographies of Robert Walpole are characteristic of the eighteenth. And Walpole even in his own time was known to stand for peace because it contributed to commercial prosperity. The eighteenth century was not shaken to its foundations by a civil war; it was, however, thoroughly upset in its own mind by the South Sea Bubble.

The commercial middle-classes—yeomen, shopkeepers, artisans, merchants, and housewives, all those who could afford an evening at Vauxhall, a trip to Scarborough, or the season at Bath—were assuming an importance they had never assumed before. The expanding metropolis, the greater leisure of various classes of people, and the growing insistence upon education, created a demand for more and more reading matter, suited to an audience which became increasingly bourgeois in character. The eighteenth century is marked by the vulgarization of literature. Common curiosity about one's neighbor made this new literary field extremely propitious for the development of biography. That much discussed institution the coffee-house need be mentioned in this study only because it satisfied the need for a place for gossip and the painless transfer of information, at a cheap price, open to all. Many straws show which way the wind was blowing. The growth of places of public amusement—of Ranelagh and Vauxhall—the spending of fabulous sums, ultimately supplied by the pleasure-seekers themselves, on such a structure as the Pantheon or such a watering-place as Bath, the development of cheap books and of new means of disposing of them, such as Lackington outlines in his memoirs—all these betoken the increase of democracy and the new uses for communal wealth. The growing importance attached to money in itself may be deduced from such varied phenomena as the amazing mania for gambling prevalent in all classes, the making of forgery a capital offense, as if money had suddenly become the lifeblood of the nation, and the unfortunate elevation of economics to the rank of a science with Adam Smith's *The Wealth of Nations*.

Democracy and commerce had their effects upon biography. First of all, life as a problem in economics may be seen in the money-centered biographies of such men as Elwes, Lackington, Thomas Guy, Hutton, Simon Mason, and Aldermen Barber and Barnard. Second, collections of biographies for almost every class imaginable might be profitably published,[27] from Quakers to sea-captains, Puritans to thief-catchers, botanists to "eccentric characters": now all men were becoming equally interesting in their own rights. Third, the sensationalism of biography at the beginning of the century, its tendencies toward triviality at the end, are partially due to the change in the reading public. More and more, men wrote to make a profit out of writing, and the biographies of crime and lust, the accounts of current cynosures in the public eye, journalistic competence in getting the latest crimes immediately before the public, tales of the sordid, the brutal, and the grotesque, the appeal to curiosity—these were found to pay. Biography was in consequence adulterated to gratify the common taste of the common reader. Fourth, the lives of the most insignificant of mortals were elevated to the dignity of permanent record. It is indeed an innovation of the century that a twenty-six-year-old nobody should record his life only because he has been transported to the Colonies for seven years for robbery; that the life of a pious servant-girl in France, to whom nothing except her death ever happened, should be widely read; that a nameless household drudge should write, almost from the parish workhouse, her own detailed story of starvation and scourgings; and that the wastrel son of Irish Quaker parents should believe all the world was eager to hear of his debts and mistresses and his final attempt to get out of a spunging-house by giving false information as to who set fire to the dockyard at Portsmouth.[28] The humble classes no longer needed to feel humble; their lives were now read with interest not by their superiors, but by their peers.

A good example of this recording of lives unimportant by almost any conceivable standard is Matthew Bishop's own account of his *Life and adventures* (1744). Although his sponsor finds it necessary to apologize for publishing the account of "one in his Sphere," Bishop himself does not beat about the bush with reasons for writing. He assumes that everything he does is enthralling. He joins the navy in 1701, and **one** would judge from

---

[27] cf. Chaps. III and IV.

[28] Respectively: William Green, p. 1774; Armelle Nicolas, 1710, 1754, 1772, 1796, and probably in other editions; *Lamenther*, 1771; Joshua Dudley, 1772.

his account that everyone from the captain to the common sailors depended upon him. Life at sea, however, proves too slow for Bishop. He determines to join the land forces and insure a decisive victory for Marlborough on the Continent. He is so naïve in his self-confidence that, when the godfather of the girl he hastily marries between campaigns tries to shoot him, he is not so much frightened as hurt in his feelings. He takes French leave of his new bride, but he honors her with one of the poetic effusions that he complacently displays in his autobiography. These lines afford a fair sample (p. 119):

> "The Thoughts of parting fill my Eyes with Tears,
> And rend my Heart with tender, anxious Fears
> For You, to whom I ever shall be true;
> But yet my Queen expects my Duty too.
> Her Service now has called me aside,
> And of the two I must neglect my Bride."

When he had returned from the navy, he had learned that his father had died of a broken heart. Yet he is quite willing to tell his mother that he is leaving again, and when she begs him not to take from her her last prop, he writes (p. 84): "Her tender Expressions and the word Father cut me to the Heart, and no one can imagine the Torture I endured. It was then I found that I was of two Natures, having degenerated from a Heart like a Lion to a melting Heart. I strove to hide my Grief from my Mother by going into Kent." Certainly there will be little self-criticism in an autobiographer who is so affected because his mother is heartbroken at his departure that he departs. Matthew Bishop is always in the right, always brave, self-satisfied, and mystified because the world has not yet rewarded him for his great services. An entertaining chapter is afforded when he shows how by great drinking-bouts and greater self-assurance, on a march from Oxford to London, he recruits half of England for service in Flanders.

When he is fighting abroad, "Give me leave," he says (p. 178), "to explain my own Nature and Disposition. When I faced my Enemies, instead of being intimidated as most Men are, at the first Appearance, I was always animated." His effrontery is so complete that it ceases to be irritating and becomes amusing; the reader can enjoy his many fine *genre* pictures of war as seen by the common soldier. He writes of Oudenarde and Malplaquet, of the sieges of Douai and Lisle; he even goes on an expedition to Canada. But he does not bother with political or military theory; he is content with history and war as it is lived, so that he gives his reader a succession of scenes in which he and a few companions or adversaries appear as large foreground figures— Jordaens or Jan Steens of battle.

In over six years of absence, he writes his wife only three times. In the last three years he does not write her at all. Yet when at last he returns unexpectedly, he is grieved and wronged to learn that years after hearing a report of his death she has married again. His uncle advises him not to injure her by revealing his presence, for she is pregnant. Surpassing Enoch Arden, with his uncle's connivance he calls upon her wearing a wig as a disguise; she recognizes him, swoons, and is put to bed in a serious state (p. 271):

". . . the Jaws of Death had taken Hold of her, for she continued in that deplorable Condition three Days, and then expired. But from the Hour that it happened, to half an Hour before she gave up the Ghost, her Senses were almost lost. Yet just before her Glass was run, she said, my Dear, forgive me and all is well. Then she closed up her Eyes, and went off like a Lamb.

"I could not help bewailing my unhappy Fate, and wishing I had never been born; as I was the Occasion of her Death. How can I account for this, though there was no Ill meant by me?"

Such self-reproach and speculation do not last long, however, and he is soon happy in quarreling with her second husband, during all of which he was "as cool as a Lamb" (p. 270)—his favorite comparison. So he writes for her memory another of his poems, a six-line epitaph beginning (p. 273):

> "Unhappy Woman by Relations led,
> Thou innocently didst corrupt my Bed,"

and makes his way, accompanied by "my little Boy," to "the Place of my Nativity," Deddington in Oxfordshire. There, though he records truly enough that (p. 273) "my Nature is strenuously inclined never to be easy any longer than I am in Action," the biography ends with his trying to drive away thoughts of his dead wife by projecting a long composition, dignified by many Biblical examples, to show "the true Character of an honourable Soldier." It is not difficult to imagine whom Matthew Bishop imagined as his model.

Such a biography shows life justifying itself by its own vitality. In spite of its amusing character, it would not merit such extended notice if it were not typical of a large new class of English life-writers and of their confidence that any life may be worthy of record, a confidence which with qualifications was shared by no less an authority than Samuel Johnson.[29]

Many of these lives, moreover, were published for a new and special reason: for the profit of and at the expense of the auto-biographer himself. Autobiography thus becomes a kind of closet-drama, in which, if the hero can sufficiently amuse or horrify or entertain his audience by strutting and fretting before high heaven, he hopes to be amply rewarded. Colley Cibber's and Connie Phillips's apologies must both have been money-makers; they led to many imitations by such figures as Charlotte Charke and George Anne Bellamy. Whether or not this exploitation of one's own personality was always financially profitable is difficult to determine; that it was frequently practised, however, the title-pages testify. Most of the autobiographies "printed for the author" never reached a second edition; but their subscription lists were often long enough to show the diligent canvassing of London or of the provincial towns in which they were issued.[30]

[29] For further lives of the bourgeoisie, see Thomas Tryon, merchant and Pythagorean, 1705; Henry Lampe, Quaker apothecary, 1711; Ambrose Barnes, merchant and alderman of Newcastle, 1716; James Fretwell, Yorkshire dissenter, 1739; William Stout, Quaker ironmonger and grocer of Lancaster, 1744; Simon Mason, a failure in business, 1754; Jane Cooper, maid-servant, 1764; John Barnard, self-made alderman and knight, 1776; Thomas Aram, merchant sailor, 1776; Thomas Hollis, dilettante and antiquarian, 1780; John Law, Scottish financier, 1721 and 1791; Thomas Firmin, merchant philanthropist, 1791 reprint from 1698 edition; John Metcalf, eccentric road-contractor, 1795; William Hutton, bookseller, 1798; and John Haime, soldier in the Queen's Regiment of Dragoons, 1799. Some of these are discussed in Chaps. III and IV.

[30] Specimen titles: *Journal of the life of Thomas Story,* 1747, a Quaker, the expenses of publishing which were to be defrayed out of his estate, Newcastle-

Dublin was either exceptionally warm-hearted, or exceptionally crowded with impecunious autobiographers, for a disproportionate number of these commercial autobiographies were issued in that city. Captain Dudley Bradstreet (1755) closes his life-and-adventures with an account of his methods of securing subscribers. He seems to have been successful, for within two years he has issued a second volume, which contains a list of subscribers filling a dozen pages and which promises still a third volume. Henry Grace (1764) closes his story of hardships as a captive to American Indians by calling to mind that though a soldier, he has no pension from the government, that he knows no trade, and that he cannot work well as a day-laborer because of a wound in his right arm.

"On these Considerations," he writes (p. 56), "I submit my Case, with the many Distresses I have gone through, and my present melancholy Situation, to the Consideration of the Humane and Benevolent, hoping for some Relief; and any Favours received, will be acknowledged with the utmost Gratitude, By their Distressed Humble Servant, Henry Grace. Finis."

The compiler of the life and gallant exploits of Sergeant Donald Macleod, who goes Swift's old soldier Creichton considerably better by dictating his memoirs in his hundred-and-third year (1791), mentions his many sons and daughters (p. 80), "of whom, the eldest, by the present wife, is a mantua-maker, in pretty good business, in Newcastle. Perhaps this intimation may have the good effect that is certainly intended." Such begging by means of biography is astonishingly common. One unique biographical tract exists in the form of a poem, which its author peddled in cheap pamphlet form from door to door. And Jane Elizabeth Moore is quite explicit as to the results she wishes to effect in

upon-Tyne; *The Female Soldier: or, the surprising life and adventures of Hannah Snell*, 1750, issued in parts; *The life and distresses of Simon Mason, apothecary*, [1754] Birmingham; *Memoirs of Capt. Peter Drake*, 1755, Dublin, with four pages of subscribers' names in double columns; *The life and uncommon adventures of Capt. Dudley Bradstreet*, 1755, Dublin; *The real story of John Carteret Pilkington*, 1760; *The life and sufferings of Henry Grace*, 1764, Reading; *Memoirs of Peter Henry Bruce*, 1782, printed for his widow; *Memoirs of the life and gallant exploits of Serjeant Donald Macleod*, 1791; and *Memoirs of a printer's devil*, 1793, Gainsborough.

publishing her *Genuine memoirs*. Her introductory rhymes end:[31]

> "Near twenty years in wedlock's union bound,
> The heroine of this piece I now am found,
> And trust e'er volumes three, are well dissected,
> My candid friends will 've healed the part affected."

So that no one may misunderstand her meaning, she appends a footnote to the last couplet: "By a full supply of subscriptions." Charlotte Charke even uses her autobiography, published in weekly parts in 1755, to call public attention to her sister Marples's "neat, well-accommodated house of entertainment . . . which she opened last Thursday, the 20th instant [March 1755], in Fullwood's Rents, near Gray's inn."[32]

The most sordid commercial traffic in men's lives is glimpsed in a scene in Captain Peter Drake's *Memoirs* (1755), which Drake himself published in Dublin in order to make money. At one time in his career, Drake, an adventurer and soldier, had had sentence passed against him and some companions for high treason. His captain, who is condemned to death and eventually executed, is attended during his last days by Paul Lorrain, the chaplain and ordinary of Newgate. Lorrain wishes the captain to supply him with his life, last words, and repentance, which he intends to publish as a routine commercial venture. But the captain has already given this usual composition of celebrated criminals to another. Thereupon Lorrain becomes very angry, and Peter Drake observes (p. 157): "by this it seems, the Ordinary of Newgate has his Perquisites more at Heart than the Souls he prays for."

Biographies were so widely read during the eighteenth century that they became a real force for effecting various ends. Thus Major John Bernardi issues his autobiography (1729) in an attempt to secure his release from Newgate, where he is confined for treason; Johnson writes a life of William Dodd in a fruitless effort to gain a reprieve from the death-sentence against Dodd for forgery; Cruden publishes his *History of Richard Potter* (1763) in order to save the life of his subject, condemned to

---

[31] 1786. Vol. I, "Index."   [32] pp. 88-9, 1827 reprint.

death for fraud, and is so successful in arousing interest that Potter's execution was delayed for a fortnight and afterwards the sentence was commuted to transportation; Boswell's account of the patriot Paoli is said to have secured for the Corsican his generous pension from the English government.

In such instances, the potentialities of biography to accomplish practical ends were exploited in the interests of justice and humanity; but its sinister possibilities, likewise, were not neglected. If the secret history of the eighteenth century could be laid open, an interesting essay on the biographer as blackmailer might be written. John Carteret Pilkington, perfecting a technique which his mother had done so much with, betrays the subscription-beggar's menace of slanderous reminiscence. Lord Carteret, after whom he is named, does not appear in the long list of subscribers, and his supposed pettiness and meanness is therefore embroidered at length; nor is Pilkington at all sparing of anyone who has offended him. Before the century was over, the practice had become so common that the *Monthly Review* in 1787,[33] with the instances of Mrs. Bellamy (1785) and Steele's *Sophia Baddeley* (1787) immediately in mind, may write, with as much truth as satire:

"The success of Mrs. Bellamy's memoirs hath, no doubt, paved the way for these relative to her *professional* sister; and here too, as in the former publication, many are the *names* introduced, and many the reputations that are 'hack'd and hew'd,' past all mending.—But, Ladies, you should consider that if this practice continues, the cause of *pleasure,* your *sacred* cause! must, in consequence, greatly suffer. Ye priestesses of Cyprus, who will then dare to sacrifice at your altars? 'Gallants, beware! look sharp! take care!' For, sooner or later, *all will out*; and then, brothers, uncles, fathers, aye and grandfathers too, will stand exposed, as in these volumes, and pointed out by the finger of scorn, and the eye of ridicule.

Spectatum admissi risum teneatis?

Adad! even REVIEWERS themselves may not be safe!"

[33] Vol. 77, pp. 83-4.

To give the last turn of the knife, some of these biographies (such as Letitia Pilkington's and George Anne Bellamy's) were issued serially or in successive parts or volumes, so that veiled threats in early issues might later become open slander, unless the guilty or innocent person crossed the proper palms with the proper silver in order to keep his name out of print.

§ 4

Certainly biography as a weapon for blackmail is far different from biography conceived as the guide to life, the branch of literature which is more useful than philosophy because it teaches by example rather than by precept. The earlier moral conception of biography split into fragments in the eighteenth century. To some extent it was gradually replaced by a subtler ethical creed which believed in understanding human frailties and in exercising a more urbane tolerance, rather than in making simple and violent judgments. To some extent, also, it persisted in the religious biographies of the century. But to a very large extent, it was supplemented by biography designed purely to satisfy curiosity, to answer, without moral predispositions of any sort, the simple question, "What happened?" Probably this shift from didacticism to sheer inquisitiveness was caused partially by the shift in the reading public. With the exception of the definite but limited groups of evangelical Christians, the middle class demanded two things only of their biographical reading: it must entertain and it must convince. The odd, the topical, the shocking, the titillating, the unique—these afforded entertainment; and the hack-writers did their diligent best to see that no biographical subject was overlooked, either in the past or the present, that might gratify the taste of the curious. But mere fantasy, or the formal play of wit, did not satisfy the eighteenth century reading public. The taste trained to enjoy an artificial mode, which delighted in the Tudor dramatic romance, or the formal French novel of sentiment, or the Restoration heroic drama, formed no part of the cultural equipment of the burghers: they demanded that the lives they read should seem true to experience. Authors secured this sense of actuality by presenting figure, date, hour, and place, the exact fact, the concrete detail of every sort, and the sources of their information. At the beginning of the century, this technique was largely used by the novelists in order to give verisimilitude to their productions;[34] the novelists themselves may have learned it from the genuine and artless biographical accounts of the seventeenth century. As the century progressed, however, the mania for exact and minute detail became more and more marked; so that together with the increasingly subjective and democratic nature of biography, its greater dependence upon detail affords the last of the three fairly safe generalizations on the biographical trend. Memoirs, as opposed to formal general histories, were widely accepted and popular in England because they presented historical events convincingly—that is, as seen in all their small particularities through the eyes of a single beholder. And the blend of the entertaining and the convincing produces the most characteristic form which biography assumes during the last half of the century: the anecdote.

As then understood and practised, the anecdote is a short, actual incident, with a beginning and an end but very little middle, artfully told and usually witty. It is an apothegm that has been lived, a jest in biographical form. Most anecdotes are designed to illustrate character or merely to entertain; they usually do not have, for instance, the moral purpose of the medieval *exemplum*. They are unsuccessful if they seem either fictitious or pointless. Naturally enough, anecdotes as here defined occur in biography before the eighteenth century. Thomas More, with his evident dramatic sense in his *Richard III*; More's own son-in-law, that early Boswell, William Roper; Izaak Walton himself in narrating the best sallies of his witty friend Sir Henry Wotton— these writers and others produce true anecdotes. Even in such a stately history as Mallet's life of Lord Bacon (1740), with its balanced periods of pure Johnsonese, anecdotes occur, as in the story of Bacon's father who dies, saying to a servant who has let him sleep in a draft: "Thus, by your civility I lose my life." But the astonishing point is what a small part of any biography before 1750 falls into this definite form, and what a large part of a great many biographies after 1750 is given over to anecdotes.

---

[34] See Chap. II.

For some reason the anecdote is closely connected with the theater. Possibly the cause lies in that the typical actor is not interested in didactic seriousness. Possibly he is cleverer at catching the characteristic and amusing in human personalities. Possibly he has learned from dramatic writing the art of organizing and effectively pointing a short scene. Or possibly the important moments in the life of a comedian are just those instances which readily shape themselves into jests and anecdotes. At any rate, in biographical writing before 1750, there are few exceptions to the statement that only in the lives of actors, and even more exclusively, only in the lives of comedians, are anecdotes collected consciously or systematically.[35] The *Comical exploits and adventures* of Jo. Hayns (1701), told with local color in dialogue, and with an attempt to suggest the emotions of its characters, is an interesting early example of a life conceived as a succession of anecdotes; Hayns's encounters with various Dulcineas in the papally licensed bagnios of Rome and the seraglios of Turkey, though even his biographer admits that they "savour'd a little too much of the Libertinism," are at times funny. The *Life and pleasant adventures of the late celebrated comedian Mr. James Spiller* (ca. 1729) has as its principal title: *Spiller's Jests*, and reveals its hero, in a series of trivialities, as (p. 37) "a good-humour'd Fellow and a most facetious Companion."

The connection between the stage and anecdotal biography is further illustrated in such later biographical productions as Letitia Pilkington's *Jests* (1759); William Cooke's *Memoirs of Samuel Foote, Esq. with a collection of his genuine bon-mots, anecdotes, opinions, &c* (1805); *The life of Mr. James Quin, comedian* (1766), followed by *Quin's Jests; or, the facetious man's pocket-companion; Aristophanes, being a classic collection of true Attic wit, containing the jests, gibes, bon-mots, witticisms, and most extraordinary anecdotes of Samuel Foote* and other characters (1778), which also contains the life of Foote; and Anthony Pasquin's *The life of the late Earl of Barrymore. Including a history of the Wargrave Theatricals, and original anecdotes of eminent persons* (1793). Joseph Haslewood reflects a sentiment

[35] cf. the lives of Hayns, 1701; Spiller, *ca.* 1729; Wilks, 1732; and Booth, 1733. Also cf. Chap. I.

which the eighteenth century shared and illustrated, when, in his *Secret history of the Green Rooms* (1790), he neglects criticism of various actors' abilities on the grounds that it would be appreciated only by Londoners who had seen these performers, and concentrates in compensation on anecdotes, for a good anecdote is universal. Nor is Haslewood ashamed of his authentic, frank, and entertaining memoirs of the actors and actresses in the three Theatres Royal. "We indulge," he says (Preface p. ix), "an honest pride in contributing our *mite* to the treasures of BRITISH BIOGRAPHY."

What one remembers from these biographies, and from the lives of other actors and actresses, of David Garrick and Mrs. Bellamy, is principally anecdotal; and even Boswell,[36] if he has not learned his art directly from his reading in the drama and from his associations with the theater, closely parallels the technique of telling and pointing up a story which the lives of actors had gradually perfected. Owing much to Boswell himself is one of the best anecdotal biographies of the century—Samuel Burdy's life of the stalwart Reverend Philip Skelton (1792), staging his adventures among the wild Irish in a series of rough, humorous scenes of action.

One of the earliest realizations of the growing prevalence of anecdotes comes in a review of Walpole's *Royal and noble authors* in the *Annual Register* for 1758:[37]

"There never was a time in which anecdotes, especially literary anecdotes, were read with greater eagerness than they are now. Such reading suits extremely well with the spirit of indolent curiosity and learned loitering, which is so much the character of these times. The present work is certainly one of the best of that kind. . . . It were to be wished that the author had indulged himself less in points and turns."

But points and turns are the essence of a good anecdote. As moral purpose loses importance, artistic presentation gains importance; your good anecdotal biographer will take great care with his striking scene, his lifelike phrasing, and his deft ending. Here is

[36] See Chap. VI.   [37] Vol. I, 1791 ed., p. 475.

the speech of one hero, whose principal claim to fame is that
he dived off Westminster Bridge:[38]

" 'D—n my eyes,' said he, 'when I was stripping to *buff,* there
was a decent woman kept looking at me at all the time; I'll be
d—'d if she was not a modest woman for all that, but she would
not stir, nor take her eye off me, till I had pulled off my breeches,
and then she fainted away.' "

Philip Thicknesse, one of the best *raconteurs* of his time, tells
many stories of Gainsborough that catch his temper in action as
exactly as a high-speed camera records a high-jumper:[39]

"I suppose he did not die, worth a tenth part of what he might
have been possessed of, had he been a worldly minded man; a
Humourist he certainly was, but in the most pleasant cast of
that character, for when a certain rich citizen was sitting to him
with his five guinea new powdered bob wig on, the *chap* looked
so *rum,* and sat so very *pretty,* that poor Gainsborough found it
impossible not to burst out in a fit of laughter, and while he was
wishing for some occasion to plead his excuse, the Alderman desired him not to overlook the *dimple in his chin*; no power of
face could stand that;—Gainsborough burst forth in laughter,
threw his pencil upon the ground, and said d—n the dimple in
your chin, I can neither paint that nor your chin neither, and
never touched the picture more."

One of the most gifted biographers of the time, who was fully
aware of the fashions in biography, utilizes anecdote skilfully
in his account of the life of a dissenting minister:[40]

"His sensibility in receiving a civility was equal to his delicacy
in conferring one. In the early part of his life, when he was very
poor, a person thought he had conferred an extraordinary favour
on him, by obtruding on his acceptance an old suit of black
clothes. Robinson was one day dining at his table. 'Mr. Robinson,'
said the donor, 'I never saw you look so much like a gentleman.'
'Sir,' replied Robinson, 'I cannot afford to look like a gentleman:' then taking the butter-boat, he emptied it on the clothes,

[38] *The life and political opinions of the late Mr Samuel House,* 1785, p. 11.
[39] *A sketch of the life and paintings of Thomas Gainsborough* [1788], pp. 42-3.
cf. also his *Memoirs and anecdotes of Philip Thicknesse,* 2 vols., 1788.
[40] George Dyer, *Memoirs of the life and writings of Robert Robinson,* 1796,
pp. 140-1.

and immediately going out, he stripped himself, and putting on his own clothes, he took his leave."

These examples were both written during the heyday of the anecdote—the last two decades of the eighteenth century. At this time, in fine turns of phrase, in solid sense back of the keenest wit, Samuel Johnson was the acknowledged master. Around his name at this period, witticisms, bon-mots, and anecdotes gathered as naturally as satyrs around Silenus, or anonymous tracts around the name of Defoe.[41] In the early nineties it was even possible for a young Oxonian to collect "from Boswell, Piozzi, Hawkins, Baretti, Beauclerk, Sir Joshua Reynolds, and other gentlemen in the habits of intimacy with the Doctor," :"The witticisms, anecdotes, jests, and sayings, of Dr. Samuel Johnson," and to add to them "A great number of jests, in which the most distinguished wits of the present century bore a part."[42] An anecdote can now be told without wasting a single word:

"A gentleman who introduced his brother to Dr. Johnson, was earnest to recommend him to the Doctor's notice, which he did by saying, 'When we have sat together some time, you'll find my brother grow very entertaining.'—'Sir, (said Johnson) I can wait.' "

Or, when Johnson was crossing the Thames in a boat, at a time when the boatmen vied with each other for supremacy in vituperation:

". . . a fellow having attacked him with some coarse raillery, Johnson answered thus, 'Sir, your wife (under pretence of keeping a bawdy-house) is a receiver of stolen-goods.' "

The rage for anecdote had grown up within a period of thirty years. It is interesting that three typical retailers of anecdotes, each excellent in his way—Joseph Spence, Sarah Duchess of Marlborough, and Dr. William King—though they wrote re-

---

[41] See, of course, the anecdotes in Boswell, Mrs. Piozzi, and Fanny Burney, as well as in his minor and anonymous biographers listed in Bibliography. cf. also *The beauties of Johnson*, 1782; *The deformities of Johnson*, 1782; *Johnsoniana*, 1785; and *Memoirs . . . containing . . . several interesting anecdotes*, 1785.

[42] J. Merry, 1791. pp. 31 and 32 for the anecdotes quoted below. Merry gets the two stories from Boswell (see 1924 Oxford ed. *Life of Johnson*, Vol. II, pp. 348 and 351). Boswell gets them from Langton. Anecdotes rapidly become communal property.

spectively in 1728-1737, 1737-1742, and 1761, did not attain publication until 1820, 1788, and 1818. *Real characters, and genuine anecdotes* (1769) affords an early use of the term on a title-page; and Walpole, in his *Anecdotes of painting in England,* issued in four volumes between 1762 and 1771, consciously chooses this title instead of "The lives of the English painters" because, he says, there are so few good English artists and the materials for their lives are so sketchy.[43] "Anecdotes," then, became the usual title for a kind of *biographie manquée,* in the same way that "memoirs" frequently indicated informal, or fragmentary, or haphazard, historical collections. And although Walpole's supple wit really produced a series of biographies under the diffident headings of "Anecdotes," in the hands of less gifted authors there was always the danger that the anecdotal method of recording a life would lead to mere rhapsody and froth. John Nichols is probably the worst offender in this respect, though he is conscious of his weakness—"claiming, indeed, some merit on account of intelligence, but not the least on the score of arrangement or composition."[44]

In the last decade of the century, miscellanies of odds and ends, loosely grouped around a central figure, became popular under the title of *-ana*.[45] They were, of course, almost without biographical organization other than their connections, sometimes very tenu-

[43] See his Preface, Vol. I, p. vi.

[44] *Biographical anecdotes of William Hogarth,* 1781. See also Nichols's *Anecdotes of Bowyer,* 1782; his "historical notes and memoirs of the author" before William King's *Works,* 1776, and before Welsted's *Works,* 1787; his "notes, biographical and historical" before an eight-volume collection of poems, 1780-1782; his compiled anecdotes of Hogarth, 1798; and his many sporadically published volumes of *Literary anecdotes.* In all of these he seems modestly to be drawing a distinction between a compiler or antiquarian and a genuine biographer; he is merely collecting materials to serve for future biographers.

[45] *Anecdotes, historical and literary,* 1793, explains in the Preface that this collection is "like the various French *Ana."* Topics vary from "Greenland Poetry" to "Ash-Wednesday." William Seward's *Anecdotes of some distinguished persons,* 5 vols., 1795-1797, appeared initially as "Drossiana" in the *European Magazine* for 1789 and admits its debt to Brotier's *Paroles memorables;* Seward's *Biographiana* appeared in 1799, 2 vols.; C. H. Wilson, editor of 1804 ed. of *Walpoliana,* mentions *Addisoniana,* 1803, *Swiftiana,* 1803, [Henry] *Brookiana,* 1804, as well as *Walpoliana,* 1799. At the beginning of the century, Curll had published several volumes of *-ana,* such as *Atterburyana,* 1727, and *Whartoniana,* 1727, which are pointless jumbles beneath contempt.

ous, with their titular subject, and the workmanship or the delight in artistry of the anecdotist sometimes tended to disappear.

Most interesting of them all is *Walpoliana,* two brief little volumes edited in 1799 by John Pinkerton, who opens his Preface with:

"This little lounging miscellany aspires to the singular praise of being beneath all criticism:

For who would break a fly upon the wheel?

It is, in most instances, a mere transcript of literary chit-chat, sent to the press in the original careless and unstudied expression. Horace Walpole was not one of those who regard conversation as an exercise of gladiatorial talents, or who study moral maxims, and arrange bons-mots, to be introduced into future colloquies."

What follows is as careless as his quotation above from Pope, as cavalier as the glancing hit at Johnson's conversation. But from this very attitude of carpet-slippers and dressing-gown, this prizing of trifles because they are trifles, something very delicate may spring, as in Pinkerton's accompanying *Biographical sketch, in fugitive crayons, of Horace Walpole.* Especially good here is the *Character,* which proceeds largely by giving "a private rainy day of Horace Walpole." Fine touches are introduced: his "favourite little dog, the legacy of the Marquise du Deffand, which ease and attention had rendered so fat that it could hardly move," and which sits by him "on a small sofa"; his tea-drinking "out of most rare and precious ancient porcelain of Japan"; his perpetual ice-water at his elbow; his talk from five until two in the morning on his sofa, with the "snuff box of *tabac d'etrennes,* from Fribourg's" beside him; his going for walks bareheaded, his gout, affability, and sensibility, his being "subject to the caprices of Colomb, his Swiss valet-de-chambre"; his visits to his *chère amie* Mrs. Clive in her cottage on his estate; his "what the French term *le fleur d'esprit,* the product of a brilliant fancy, and rapid association of ideas, joined with good sense"; "his goodness" in playing whist with the blind old Duke of Montrose; his proposals of marriage, when he inherited his title at the advanced age of seventy-four, to each of the two charming young sisters he had loved and cajoled and protected for so long.

"Even in trifles his taste for enjoyment was elegant and learned: the pots of tuberose, or of canary heliotropes, the papers of orange flowers, that perfumed his chamber, were luxuries rather feminine" (Vol. I, p. xlix).

In the fine lines of such portraits, in the biographers of Johnson, and particularly, of course, in Boswell, the use of anecdote and of minute detail amply justifies the fashion that spread so rapidly at the end of the century. Certain of the collections dealing with great foreign princes were particularly well done.[46]

But critical rebellion against such a novel and seemingly purposeless form of biographical writing was soon to develop, when anecdotal groupings could be published to show the opinions of a coxcomb or the exploits of a blind man, to gratify the spite of a disappointed butler, to inculcate virtue in youth, to illustrate contemporary politics, to issue a shuddering warning against lust and uncleanness, and to record the maunderings of a printer's devil or the bon-mots of highwaymen.[47] In writing his *Poetical and congratulatory epistle to James Boswell, Esq. on his Journal of a tour to the Hebrides* (1786), Peter Pindar is undoubtedly

[46] See Jacob Staehlin's *Original anecdotes of Peter the Great*, 1788, giving the sources for each anecdote, a fine example of the pure and proper anecdote; *Characteristic anecdotes, tending to illustrate the character of Frederic II of Prussia*, by B. H. Latrobe, 1788; and *Interesting anecdotes of Henry IV. of France, digested into chronological order, and forming a complete picture of the life of that amiable and illustrious hero. Translated from the French*, 1792, with sources at the end of each anecdote.

[47] Titles, respectively: *Memoirs of the life of Gilbert Wakefield*, 1792; *The life of John Metcalf, with many entertaining anecdotes of his exploits*, 1795; *Original anecdotes of the late Duke of Kingston and Miss Chudleigh*, by Thomas Whitehead, 1792; *Anecdotes, bons-mots, and characteristic traits of the greatest princes, politicians, philosophers, and wits of modern times . . . calculated to inspire the minds of youth with noble, virtuous, generous, and liberal sentiments. By the Rev. John Adams*, 1789; John Almon's *Anecdotes of William Pitt*, 1791, 3 vols., and his *Biographical, literary, and political anecdotes*, 1797, 3 vols.; *Biographical anecdotes selected from history sacred and prophane*, 1795; *Memoirs of a printer's devil; interspersed with pleasing recollections, local descriptions, and anecdotes*, 1793; *Anecdotes, bon mots, traits, stratagems, and biographical sketches, of the most remarkable highwaymen, swindlers, and other daring adventurers . . . both cautionary and entertaining*, 1797.

exercising a satirist's prerogative to exaggerate when he assures that "ambitious Thane" (p. 3):

> "Thou, curious scrap-monger, shalt live in song
> When Death hath still'd the rattle of thy tongue,"

and when, after ludicrously rhyming Boswell's most trivial or absurd anecdotes, he sums up his case (p. 9):

> "Rare anecdotes! 'tis anecdotes like these,
> That bring thee glory, and the million please!
> On these, shall future times delighted stare,
> Thou charming haberdasher of small ware!"

But Peter Pindar is not alone in observing or criticizing the writers of anecdote. In a single year, 1788, the three following excerpts from biographies show that the use of anecdotes in life-writing had become a storm center, and that many of the thunderbolts were aimed at the towering figure of Johnson or his circumambulating biographers:

"The public is at present so much in the habit of bearing with persons afflicted with the biographical cacoëthes, and especially with publishers of anecdotes and confidential letters, that I may perhaps hope for an extension of the like indulgence to me."[48]

"But a rage for anecdotes of every kind seems to distinguish the present age: and the colour of Dr. Johnson's coat, his oaken staff, his inordinate love of tea, and his flatulencies, are listened to with patience and complacency."[49]

"The author of the subsequent account professeth a departure from the customary mode of detailing puerilities of thought, expression, or habit. Such puerilities are but too prevalent, even where intellectual greatness most abounds; and it surely is becoming the office of candour to veil, rather than exemplify, the weaknesses of our nature."[50]

The rise of the anecdote, therefore, until it is flourishing enough to bear the brunt of bitter attacks, has as corollaries the develop-

---

[48] Translator of B. H. Latrobe's *Anecdotes of Frederic II*, 1788.

[49] Richard Graves, *Recollections of William Shenstone*, 1788, Advt., p. vii.

[50] *An authentic detail of particulars relative to the late Duchess of Kingston*, 1788, pp. 1-2, which descends, in spite of this opening, to the most scandalous anecdotes.

ment of humor, wit, and style in telling a story, and the growing general appreciation of minute detail in the recording of a life. The anecdote itself seems to have become popular when sheer inquisitiveness supplanted didacticism as a reason for writing biography.

Though the anecdotist and the antiquary may seem far apart, curiosity inspired the latter as well as the former. His question is still: "What happened?" Dignified by scholarship and by the centuries that separate the biographer from his subjects, the antiquarian collections, the succession of biographical encyclopedias, and the long-buried lives reconstructed by patient search were called into being by the same interest in one's fellow creatures that dictated the lives of footpads, freaks, and travellers.[51]

One interesting consequence of this non-moral curiosity as the motive for life-writing is that truthfulness became, in fact as well as in repeated avowals, a criterion for biography. Now that the biographer has no longer an ethical case to demonstrate, which he has adopted in advance, he can afford to tell all that he knows. At an earlier period, biographers had suppressed or distorted or emphasized details in order to point the desired lesson; they could view with contempt the writer who brought in intimate details in the life of his hero, or with indignation the rebel who mentioned his weaknesses or vices. Now, however, the peculiarities and foibles may be the reasons for public interest in a man's life. The character-sketch of any hero in a medieval saint's life could be substituted for that of almost any other, for holiness did not vary from man to man. But the eighteenth century sought not the general in biography, but the particular, not the similarities in Chesterfield and Johnson, but their differences. And if Columba, Cuthbert, Odo, and Dunstan alike possessed fortitude, patience, humility, charity, and the rest, no one in England but Samuel Johnson went through London touching every other lamp-post, twitching spasmodically, collecting orange peel, or muttering "too-too-too" under his breath. Accuracy in presentation is the standard which remains when the didactic drive diminishes; and many a biographer of the period finds his chief artistic pleasure

51 See Chap. IV.

in presenting an impartial, exact, and detailed account of his subject.[52]

The enthusiasm for truth has a noble ring throughout the century, so that consciously expressed, it tends to become an adequate moral principle in itself. "The following Sheets," writes one biographer,[53] "contain nothing that is not to the best of the Author's knowledge strictly true; nor is the Truth ever heightned or exaggerated for the sake of moving the Passions, or pleasing the Imagination. The End aimed at was, to represent things as they really are."

"Indifference, with respect to persons, and Impartiality, with regard to facts," are another biographer's watchwords;[54] and William Godwin, with his fanatical zeal for truth, even sets up in glowing words a goddess of Historical Impartiality.[55] The old ethical ideal may be blended with this stern regard for truth, as in Mallet's *Life of Bacon,* whose career, of course, would test the best of biographers (1740, pp. 1-2):

"The antient Egyptians had a law, which ordained, that the actions and characters of their Dead should be solemnly canvassed before certain Judges; in order to regulate what was due to their memory. No quality, however exalted, no abilities, however eminent, could exempt the possessors from this last and impartial trial. To ingenuous minds this was a powerful incentive, in the pursuit of virtue: and a strong restraint on the most abandoned, in their career of vice. Whoever undertakes to write the life of any person, deserving to be remembered by posterity, ought to look upon this law as prescribed to him. He is fairly to record the faults as well as the good qualities, the failings as well as the perfections, of the Dead; with this great view, to warn and improve the Living."

---

[52] As examples of this sincere quest for impartiality, see: Ambrose Philips's *Life of Archbishop John Williams,* 1700; John Campbell's *Memoirs of the Duke de Ripperda,* 1740; David Mallet's *Life of Francis Bacon,* 1740; Thomas Sharp's *Archbishop John Sharp, ca.* 1735?; *The life of Belisarius,* 1759; James Yair's *Life of Servetus,* 1771; William Kenrick's *Robert Lloyd,* 1774; William Enfield's *Biographical sermons,* 1777, pp. 159-60; William Godwin's *William Pitt,* 1783; Thomas Adam's *Private thoughts,* 1795; George Dyer's *Robert Robinson,* 1796; Richard Phillips's *Public characters of 1798.*

[53] See in list given in preceding note, J. Campbell, 1740, p. xv.

[54] W. Kenrick, above. 1774, Preface.   [55] *Pitt,* 1783, Introduction.

In mid-century, the *Monthly Review,* in noticing the fourth volume of the *Biographia Britannica,* cogently states the ideal of impartiality as applied to the great collections:[56]

"To rescue, therefore, the characters of the Great and the Worthy, from misrepresentation; to place their actions in a proper point of light; to determine the share of merit or demerit due to each; appears to be one intention of this work."

Even where it is most difficult to hold the scales even—in the biographies of contemporaries—the ideal of impartiality is strenuously upheld:[57]

"No attachment to any particular set of men or opinions, no prejudices against men in place, no prepossessions in favour of men out of place, no bias towards any controverted points of theology, no personal antipathies, no malevolent exaggerations, no invidious disposition to detract from acknowledged virtue or merit, have influenced, in whole or in part, the conduct of the Projector and Conductors of the Work."

As usual, the ubiquitous figure of Doctor Johnson is an accepted leader in this quest for truth. The Advertisement before the *Private thoughts* of the Reverend Thomas Adam pays him deserved tribute,[58] for he had already sustained repeated attacks for belittling the characters and works of many of the poets whose lives he wrote:

"To the honest heart, the penetrating mind, and powerful intellect of Dr. Johnson, the world is indebted for a superior method of Biography. The persons whose characters he has described are introduced to our acquaintance without any flattering disguise, and made known to us as completely as if we had enjoyed a domestic intimacy with them. And it may be observed, that his own character has been described with equal fidelity, and that posterity will view him exactly as he appeared to those who had daily access to him, when he was alive.

"Some, indeed, who dislike this honest dealing, affect to lament the injury done to the character of Dr. Johnson, by the unguarded

---

[56] Vol. 17, p. 578, year 1757.
[57] Richard Phillips, *The public characters of 1798,* 1799, p. ix, Preface. Printed in italics.
[58] 1795, York, 2d ed. Signed "W.R."

communications of his friends, and particularly by the Publication of his 'Prayers and Meditations.' Yet this book was published by his own direction, and even the peculiarities, in his devotional exercises, which may be called superstitious, were permitted to appear without any care, on his part, to excuse or conceal them."

Such certain and sincere respect for truth, which echoes throughout the century, does not preclude by any means satirical and panegyrical biography. The above quotation from Adam, for instance, follows the expressed regret that modern biographies should be so flattering in tone; and the age of satire was certainly not without exemplars in the field of biography.[59] Satire, indeed, even degenerated into open slander; for after the repressions of the press under the Stuarts and Cromwell, a reaction set in. It was possible in the eighteenth century to publish with impunity almost any accusation, and the best men were open to the vilest calumny. An attack called forth a defense; the libellers generated apologists; and from the controversy and the acrimonious replies truth sometimes emerged.[60]

But although satire and panegyric, mudslinging and white-washing, continued seemingly unabated in spite of the frequently expressed ideal of impartiality, one important change fortunately did take place: the biographer is now quite fully aware of his own inclinations. He, and other biographers, and his readers as

[59] A representative but far from complete list is: *The religious impostor, Dr. William Salmon* [1700?]; *Life and actions of St. Whigg*, 1708; *True and faithful account of the death of Tom. Whigg*, 1710; Bisset's *Modern fanatick*, = Dr. Sacheverell, 1710; *Life, death and character of Mr. Daniel Burgess*, [1713]; *The life of Lavinia Beswick, alias Polly Peachum*, 1728; John Jackson's *Life of [Daniel] Waterland*, 1736; *The Life of Captain John Porteous*, 1737; *Methodism and enthusiasm fully display'd*, the life of George Whitefield, 1743; *Memoirs of Magopico*, 1761; *Authentic memoirs of the Countess de Barre* [= Dubarry], 1771; *Musical travels through England. By Joel Collier*, 1774; *Memoirs of the late Edw. W——ly M——tague*, 1779; *Characters of the present most celebrated courtezans*, 1780; *Life and amours of Lady Ann Foley*, [1786?]; *Memoirs of the late pious and rev. Gabriel D'Anville*, 1787; Benjamin Goosequill's [= J. M. Adair's] *Philip Thicknes*, 1790; *Memoirs of Antonina*, = Marie-Antoinette, 1791; *Memoirs of Mrs. [Elizabeth] Billington*, 1792; Jesse Foot's *John Hunter*, 1794; Charles McCormick's *Edmund Burke*, 1798; Henry Hunter's *Catharine II*, 1800.

[60] Discussed in Chap. IV. See also, in Bibliography, Bolingbroke, Pole, David, Billington, Rudd, Richard III, Marlborough, Robert Walpole, Burke, Hypatia, Hume, Chesterfield.

well, realize that the human individual, try as hard as he may, is almost necessarily prejudiced.[61] More and more frequently one comes across critical analyses of a biographer's position, such as the following explanation of Hacket's distortion of his subject Archbishop Williams, in a biography the authenticity of which had passed unquestioned in the seventeenth century:[62]

"His Lordship's [Hacket's] commendable Gratitude to his Great Patron Williams, has made him so very studious of Embellishments for his Life, that I can liken the Lord Keeper, as represented by him, to nothing so properly as to the Statue of some Ancient Hero, so beset with Trophies and Ornaments, that the Comliness and just Proportion of the Image underneath is scarce discernable at first sight."

The particular form of the funeral sermon may serve as an instance. Just as in the preceding century, these sermons continued to be published with a character or brief account of the deceased usually appended. But their unescapable attitude of *de mortuis nil nisi bonum* and their professional stereotyped nature kept most of them from attaining the nobility and sincerity of Samuel Johnson's sermon written in memory of his wife. The eighteenth century saw clearly that the funeral sermon, even with its accompanying sketch, was no substitute for biography, for the tone of the writer or preacher was pre-determined. At the beginning of the century one biographer writes of "the Abuse of Funeral Sermons"; he considers their original design so much perverted that "in many Instances they are A Scandalous Satyr, both upon the Preacher himself, and upon the Dead Man: Who (meerly) for his Noble Legacy [to Mr. Parson] is made a Saint; for which Reason many think Funeral Sermons unlawful."[63] And at the end of the century another biographer, after an attack on all funeral sermons and especially on those published by the Wesleyans, writes:[64]

[61] See Johnson's strong statement of this principle, quoted in Chap. VI.

[62] Ambrose Philips's *John Williams,* 1700, Preface.

[63] John Dunton, *The Hazard of a Death-Bed-Repentance,* 1708, p. 8.

[64] *Autobiography of Thomas Wright,* wr. 1795-1797. 1864 ed., p. 217.

"Sir, in your funeral talk I'm griev'd,
So very much is said;
One half will never be believ'd,
The other never read."

The search for truth has led, therefore, to the most difficult realization of all—though it is never completely clear or frequently expressed during the century—that the biographer and his reader must both be aware of his attitude and possible prejudices toward his subject. These attitudes are varied. Pasquin and Topham are as conscious entertainers as are stage magicians; Colley Cibber and George Anne Bellamy are professional apologists; Calamy and Wesley are compilers and editors with Christian purposes; Oldys or Malone are dispassionate recorders. Even more clearly, the partisan biographer realizes that he traffics in applause or libel. Panegyrics, for instance, flourish during the period, and the newly introduced French form of the *éloge* is frequently practised; but this is done with the consciousness that the writer is exercising within the limits of a particular art form, and not with the mistaken belief held by earlier writers that the panegyrist and the biographer were essentially the same.[65] These panegyrics were monuments to, not statues of, the dead; they were formal exercises in commemoration by antiquaries, men of letters, rhetoricians, and scientists. And there is little danger that eulogy and biography will be really confused, for instance, in a production that is published with the title of *The life of General James Wolfe, the conqueror of Canada: or, the elogium of that*

[65] Illustrative of the development of *éloges* and panegyrics are: *Characters historical and panegyrical*, translated from Perrault of the French Academy by John Ozell, 1704, 2 vols.; John Provoste's *Panegyrical essay* on the Duke of Gloucester, 1701; *Memoirs of literature . . . Vol. I. For the Years 1710. and 1711*, 1712, which includes French *éloges* in translation; *The magistrate and the Christian, exemplified in Sir Thomas Abney*, by Jeremiah Smith, 1722; Fontenelle's *éloge* of Isaac Newton, preceded by its translation as *The Panegyrick*, 1728; William Kenrick's *Monody to the memory of Frederick Prince of Wales*, 1751; John Fothergill's *Peter Collinson*, 1769, read before the Society of Physicians, as the *éloges* were read before the French Academy in tribute to deceased members; Thomas Henry's *Albert de Haller*, 1783, "compiled, chiefly, from the Elogium spoken before the Royal Academy of Sciences at Paris"; *Transactions of the Royal Society of Edinburgh*, 4 vols., 1788-1798, with the Scottish equivalent of the "professed panegyric on every one of the 'Members, after his death" which had become so popular abroad; Anthony Pasquin's *Memoirs of Warren Hastings*, 1793.

renowned hero, attempted according to the rules of eloquence (1760). The author is conscious of "the Novelty of the Composition, rarely attempted among us."

§5

Many biographers of the century, indeed, no longer primarily concerned with the ethical lessons of their writings, became increasingly concerned with their art. If the Good is no longer the sole ideal of biography, more importance may be attached to the True and the Beautiful. A neat example is furnished by George Dyer in his preface to the *Memoirs of the life and writings of Robert Robinson* (1796, p. iv):

". . . my eye has been fixed on Robert Robinson. . . . As he diversifies his pursuits, I diversify my chapters. The only questions with me of importance, are, Have I, on the whole, preserved the truth of character, and yet maintained something like unity of design? If so, I have accomplished all that was intended."

No moral purpose is stated here; but the preoccupations with truth and with art are evident. The artistic questions of prose style, of form, and of the exact reproduction of personality, engross the biographer and account for the numerous biographical experiments in life-writing which the century produced.

When the purpose of biography was purely ethical or utilitarian, writers might disregard prose style. But now that its primary purpose is often to furnish entertainment, conscious stylists become more common. Sir John Pringle, for instance, who wrote the elogium of General Wolfe, finds the taking of Quebec less fascinating than the tinkering with his own sentences:[66]

"Hark! what Shouts of Joy rend the Sky whilst Britons cry VICTORY! The neighbouring Mountains send back the Sound; Quebec hears it, chilled with Horrors; the Indian Nations stand astonished: But alas! this Joy, so full of Confusion for the Enemy; so sweet a Source of Pleasure for Britons, is soon marred with Bitterness. Britons see, with Sorrow painted on their down-cast Faces, their General breathing his last; they count over, with

[66] 1760, pp. 2-3. For highly wrought or self-conscious styles, see also *Memoirs of the life of Elizabeth Cairns,* 1762; James Nassau's *Josiah Tomkins,* 1774; Joseph Cornish's *Thomas Firmin,* 1780; William Godwin's *William Pitt,* 1783.

Regret, his honourable Wounds; and while they bathe them with their Tears, they cannot help thinking, that, that Victory must be inestimable, which required for its Purchase the Blood of so great and so good a General."

And occasionally the expression may become so mannered and eccentric that the result is closer to the poetry of Gerard Manley Hopkins than to normal autobiography:[67]

"I have long agoe when I was a child found the lord awakening my conscience, & shaking the foundations of my soul with strange & strong confusions, convictions, & convulsions, wherby my woeful doleful & undone estate by nature was discovered. I saw my selfe graceles, christles, & therby hopeles & helples."

The quotations in this study, however, are sufficiently extended to afford a brief anthology of eighteenth century prose styles in biography and to show their variety. A few additional remarks here may suffice. The eighteenth century prized a "nervous," "elegant," "perspicuous," "pure," or "manly" style, cultivated so intensively since the days of Dryden that correctness had become an art. Middleton's *Cicero* (1741) was valued almost primarily for its style; Gibbon was aware that he could add to Oldys's voluminous collections on Raleigh only the dubious merit of style; and Alexander Bicknell writes a new life of Alfred the Great (1777) because he finds "the antique style and circumlocution of Sir John Spelman" unfortunate, and evidently thinks his own manner of writing is "nervous and comprehensive." Many of the biographies of the eighteenth century, then, and particularly the lives of famous historical figures, were recorded in the clear dignity of Augustan prose. The novelists also, when their style was easily imitated, had some influence.[68] Laurence Sterne, for instance, taught an informal, flowing, conversational style to biographers, which as modified in the hands of William Cobbett, is thoroughly delightful. But it must also be admitted that many a biography has been pulled completely to pieces by imitating Sterne. Certain biographers, such as John Wesley and Henry Hunter—evidently because of their own pulpit experience—were

---

[67] Autobiography of the Rev. Oliver Heywood, 1630-1702, pub. 1882-1885, 4 vols., Vol. I, p. 134.
[68] See Chap. II.

masters of a limpid oral style that catches the persuasive intonations of a human voice. And even an anecdotal biographer such as Mrs. Piozzi, no less indebted to funeral sermons and eulogies for her style than to Italy for her final image, brings her work to a conclusion in ecclesiástical rhythms. Doctor Johnson's life, she writes:[69]

"passed in the practice of refined morality, ending in a death which attested the purest faith; what remains but to reflect, that by that death no part of Johnson perished which had power by form to recommend his real excellence; nothing that did not disgrace the soul which it contained: like some fine statue, the boast of Greece and Rome, plastered up into deformity, while the casts are preparing from it to improve students, and diffuse the knowledge of its merit; but dazzling only with complete perfection, when the gross and awkward covering is removed."

Recording the attempts to impose form upon biographical materials would be tedious. Frequently this was done by concentrating on a single action or a simple thesis;[70] sometimes by a balanced comparison or contrast between two or more figures. The parts of a life were integrated chronologically—by sections dealing with definite successive periods—or psychologically—by chapters treating the hero's various interests, accomplishments, abilities, or traits. A few writers tried to suggest a future unknown to their readers by creating scenes of suspense. Conversely, when future events were well known to the public but unknown to the actors whose lives were being narrated, some writers secured artistic effects by the use of irony. And in rare instances, retrospective passages were introduced, so that the various links in a whole career might be made into a chain. It is indeed curious that memory and anticipation, which play such important rôles in human life, were no more exploited than they actually were by the psychologically alert experimentalists of the century.[71] Studies in the psychological stuff from which biography is made, experiments in new techniques, and the inclusion of new types of heroes, also marked the period.[72]

---

[69] *Letters to and from the late Samuel Johnson,* 1788, 2 vols., Vol. II, p. 390.
[70] See Chap. V.　　　　　　　　　[71] See, however, Chaps. III and V.
[72] See the first six chapters.

A more faithful reproduction of the diversity of experiment in the century might result from disconnected notes than from a neat analysis with no loose threads hanging. An impression of the century may be conveyed, for instance, by saying that its ten successive decades produced: a biography whose chapters alternated between a career as it was lived and the same career as it should have been lived (John Dunton's *Life and errors,* 1705); the life of an aristocratic roué told as a joke by his two nephews (*Memoirs of the life of Count de Grammont,* 1714); a sympathetic, indirect presentation of Thomism by narrating the parallel lives of a Renaissance Italian scholar and a French philosopher (Jesup's *Picus and Pascal,* 1723); a collection of the lives of khalifas, Soltans, and Wazirs extracted from the most authentic Oriental chronologers (*The lives and memorable actions of many illustrious persons of the Eastern nations,* tr. by George Sale, 1739); the lives of the professors of Gresham College written in order to show the advantages accruing to the public from the philanthropy of the founder of the college (John Ward, 1740); the autobiography of the "bottle-conjurer," an adventurer who lived on the gullibility of the public, even in this last published piece of effrontery (*The life and uncommon adventures of Capt. Dudley Bradstreet,* 1755); the life of a great musician consciously designed only "to give the Reader those parts of his Character, as a Man, that any way tend to open and explain his character as an Artist" (John Mainwaring's *Memoirs of Handel,* 1760); an attack upon the hypocrisy of certain Christians and a defense of atheism ostensibly presented as an apology for the life of David Hume (*An apology . . . with a parallel between him and the late Lord Chesterfield,* 1777); the life of Lucian presented in the form of a dialogue between him and Lord Lyttelton in the Elysian fields (Thomas Francklin, before his 2-vol. ed. of Lucian's *Works,* 1780); the life of a Wesleyan author printed entirely as notes subjoined to several of the principal traits in his *Portrait of St. Paul,* whose character is supposedly comparable to his own (Joshua Gilpin's account of John William de la Flechere, 1790).

These examples have been chosen with no principle other than that of showing the persistence of biographical experimentation in every decade of the century. It was a time of exploration in life-writing, rather than of fixed tradition; and novelty of theme or presentation was an advantage rather than a drawback in any biographical piece. Even John Wesley, the lives of whose followers fall into one of the most easily recognizable patterns of the time, presents to the public the journal of a seventeen-year-old girl with evident satisfaction because of its unique character:[73]

"Among the innumerable Novelties which have appeared in the World, within half a Century, I do not remember to have seen the Experience of a Child written by herself."

And Horace Walpole apologizes for his unusual grouping of the lives of royal and noble authors by demonstrating that collections have been made on even odder principles:[74]

"Some years ago nothing was more common than such divisions of Writers. How many German, Dutch, and other heralds, have marshalled authors in this manner! Balthazar Bonifacius made a collection of such as had been in love with statues: Ravisius Textor, of such as have died laughing: Vossius, of chronologers: Bartholinus, of physicians who have been poets. There are catalogues of modern Greek poets; of illustrious bastards; of translators; of Frenchmen who have studied Hebrew; of all the authors bred at Oxford, by Antony Wood; and of all British writers in general by Bale, Pitts, and Bishop Tanner."

The best justification for such biographies collected for a limited class Richard Pulteney prefixes to his lives of English botanists. All flower-lovers, he thinks, should have not only "an acquaintance with the Philosophy of Vegetables" but with those who have made this unusual science possible:[75]

"In tracing the progress of human knowledge through its several gradations of improvement, it is scarcely possible for an

[73] *An extract of Miss Mary Gilbert's Journal*, 1768, "To the Reader."

[74] *A catalogue of the royal and noble authors of England*, 1758 ed., Vol. I, Advt., pp. ii-iii.

[75] *Historical and biographical sketches of the progress of botany in England*, 1790, 2 vols., Preface, p. x. In botany alone, cf. also Derham's *John Ray*, 1760; Duncan's *John Hope*, 1789; Thomas Martyn's *John Martyn*, 1770; and Mason's *Thomas Gray*, 1775. As far as "experiment" is concerned, the first of these seems written for an encyclopedia, the second was delivered as the Harveian Oration at Edinburgh, and the third was prefixed to its subject's remarks upon the Aeneid.

inquisitive and liberal mind, of congenial taste, not to feel an ardent wish of information relating to those persons by whom such improvements have severally been given: and hence arises that interesting sympathy which almost inseparably connects biography with the history of each respective branch of knowledge."

Indeed, whenever a class in society seems to have been neglected by biographers, someone is ready to illustrate its peculiarities, virtues, qualities, and problems, in grouped biographies or in the career of a single individual. "There is another advantage that attends this kind of writing," announces the biographer of one of His Majesty's Justices of the Peace,[76]

"which renders it still more curious, useful and entertaining; and that is, that it shews us what kind of abilities are requisite in different professions; and in this respect, the following pages may boast of somewhat new. We have the memoirs of many able statesmen, great captains, gallant seamen, and indeed, of almost all professions, but the memoirs of a magistrate, the life of a justice of the peace, has scarce hitherto appeared, and yet it will be found, that this, like all other characters, requires particular talents, and that the qualities which render a man capable of shining therein, are not so common, or so trivial, as many people imagine."

Various professions developed an evident *esprit de corps* in the eighteenth century, and learned to take care of themselves very well biographically. The physicians achieved memorials through concerted effort;[77] the scientists through individual memoirs;[78]

[76] *Memoirs of the life and times, of Sir Thomas Deveil, Knight,* 1748, anon., p. 2.

[77] See John Aikin, *Biographical memoirs of medicine,* 1780, and *Specimen of the medical biography of Great Britain,* 1775; the lives evidently supported by or demanded by the medical profession, such as John Freind, 1750; Richard Mead, 1755; Asclepiades, 1762; Nathan Alcock, 1780; John Fothergill, 1782; Messenger Monsey, 1789; Benjamin Hutchinson's *Biographia Medica,* 1799; the memorials read before medical societies, such as those by John Fothergill or S. F. Simmons. The Society of Physicians and the Royal Society of Edinburgh (for men of learning) were of particular importance in establishing such published memorials for their members.

[78] cf. John Saunderson's *Nicholas Saunderson,* 1740, the blind professor of mathematics; William Whiston's memoirs, 1749; Henderson's *James Ferguson,*

the painters and admirals had immortality thrust upon them.[79]

In the collecting of biography William Oldys made a noble experiment in setting up standards of impartiality, scientific completeness, and documentation. The idea of completeness, however, can be carried too far, and the experiments of the young Scot David Stewart, Earl of Buchan,[80] and of the London publisher John Nichols,[81] if they had been carried out on the scale on which they were conceived, would have filled several museums to overflowing with Scottish and British biography alone. In the edition of the *Biographia Britannica* which died of its own distention in the last decade of the century, the individual articles were so long that several of them were issued separately as complete biographies.[82] Lives which originally appeared in magazines were sometimes reprinted separately,[83] in their original form or expanded. And the development of periodicals themselves, the systematic recording of current affairs and comments on current personalities in newspapers, journals, and magazines, was not without influence upon biography. Such publications as the *Gentleman's Magazine* or the *Monthly Review* not only reviewed biographies but published their own brief life-sketches and obituaries, thereby increasing, or creating, the demand for timely and

1773, a self-made scientist; Stewart's and Minto's *John Napier*, 1787, inventor of logarithms; Joseph Priestley's autobiography, *ca.* 1795, discoverer of oxygen.

[79] See Richard Graham's *Eminent Painters*, 1716; Vertue's *Hollar*, 1745; J. Buckeridge's *Modern Painters*, 1754; Walpole's *Anecdotes of painting*, 4 vols., 1762-1771; Walpole's *Engravers*, 1763; Matthew Pilkington's *Dictionary of painters*, 1770; William Beckford's *Extraordinary painters*, 1780; Richard Cumberland's *Spanish Painters*, 1782; Strutt's *Dictionary of engravers*, 1785; Thicknesse's *Gainsborough*, 1788; Malone's *Reynolds*, 1797; Ireland's *Hogarth*, 1798.

For seamen, see the collections by Campbell, 1742-1744; Berkenhout (*post* 1779); Kent, 1785; Charnock, 1794; the anonymous *Lives of the admirals*, 1787-1788; Martin-Leake's lives of Admiral Leake and Captain Martin [*ca.* 1750]; and Kippis's *Captain Cook*, 1789.

[80] cf. his Advertisement to *An account of John Napier*, 1787. Also his *Fletcher of Saltoun*, 1792, and his *James Thomson*, 1792. cf. Sir David Dalrymple's attempt at Scottish biography, beginning with separate lives.

[81] cf. Bibliography, especially his 10-vol. *Bibliotheca Topographica Britannica*, 1780-1790.

[82] cf. Richard Gough's *George Greg*, 1789, and *John Fastolff*, 1793; Gregory's *Thomas Chatterton*, 1789; Gough's *Nicholas Ferrar* (*ca.* 1793); and earlier, Arthur Onslow's *George Abbot*, 1777, reprinted "with some additions and corrections."

[83] See, e.g., Samuel Johnson's brief periodical lives, in Bibliography; or Matthew Maty's memoirs of Dr. Richard Mead, 1755, expanded from the *Britannic Journal*.

exact biographical information. By the end of the century this
resulted in such productions as the *Annual necrology for 1797-
1798*—"intended to be continued annually"—and *The public
characters of 1798,* which actually was continued, and which constitutes a forerunner of the modern *Who's Who.* An offshoot of
this last series of volumes contains a short item which shows the
ultimate limit which biography might reach:[84]

"Found hanging by his garters, Mr. Griesdale, a dealer in coals
near Bishopsgate-street. He is said to have laid in a large stock of
coals the day before the thaw."

Neither the living nor the dead were safe, and now, not even the
humble. No flowers were allowed to blush unseen, no gems to remain in dark, unfathomed caves; and the short but simple annals
of the poor appeared monthly, annually, systematically, in the
Wesleyan Magazine, the *Arminian Magazine,* and the *Biographical Magazine.*

The variety continues. Biography is used as a scheme for begging; biography is written as a series of letters, as a parallel
within a dialogue, as a proof that the spendthrift is more useful
to society than the miser; and as a defense of English genius
while France was echoing to the fall of the Bastille; biography is
composed in rhyme.[85] When Arabia and India are exhausted,[86]
Persia still remains, and Persian poems may be quoted in the
original Persian characters.[87] And when there are no more men
to write about, then the ambitious author may still turn to animal
biography and regale his readers with "Authentic anecdotes of the
lives, manners, and economy" of quadrupeds, birds, and worms.[88]

When all the demands of the reading public have been exploited, there is still the juvenile audience to fall back upon; for
now not only the women and the burghers, but the children as

[84] *The historical, biographical, literary, and scientific magazine,* for November
1800, p. 4.

[85] cf., for these respective innovations, Henry Grace, 1764; John Hill, 1752, or
Lord Orrery, 1752; William Hayley, 1787; Pasquin's *Barrymore,* 1797; *The genius
of Albion,* 1790; Jane Elizabeth Moore, 1786, *Index.*

[86] cf. Chap. IV.

[87] See J. H. Hindley's "Sketch, biographical and literary, of Abu'l-Taieb al
Motanabbi," in *Oriental Collections,* 1797.

[88] The Reverend William Bingley's *Animal Biography,* 1804, 3 vols., 2d ed.

well have learned to read. The development of biography designed for the youth of England is one of the noticeable characteristics of late eighteenth century life-writing.[89]

It would seem safe to say, therefore, that the eighteenth century mind turned easily and naturally to biography. The art of life-writing, moreover, was elastic and experimental throughout the century. The subjects considered suitable for biography increased, the materials that were held to form any individual life came to be more complex, the manners of presentation took on greater variety, and the audience for which it was designed became larger.

§ 6

But were its innovations and enlargements of permanent value? In considering this question, one might take certain ever-present problems of the biographer and briefly consider how they were handled in the eighteenth century. How, for example, did the writers conceive the portals of life, the gates of birth and death? Was the period of youth unimportant, or was it connected significantly with maturer years? How were history and biography adjusted to one another? Did these biographers conceive a career as a series of pictures? Did they attempt to reproduce the faces and bodies of their heroes, the scenes and backgrounds of a life? How did they handle the element of time, which should differentiate a biography from a character-sketch? What experiments were made in suggesting the approach of age, the weight of years, the ripening or changing of personality, the increasing distance of the past?

All these questions are important. The answer to any one of them might fill a volume. Discussion here can be no more than suggestive and cursory, a few remarks on a few salient writers.[90]

An anonymous biographer tells two little stories of the youth of John Churchill, who became the Duke of Marlborough.[91] At the

[89] cf. Chap. V. Also Goldsmith's *Plutarch*, 1762; the *British Plutarch*, 1776; William Heckford, 1787; the *British Nepos*, 1798; Elizabeth Helme, 1799; Mrs. M. H. Pilkington, 1799; Mavor's *Plutarch* for schools, 1800; and Mrs. Cummyng's *Juvenile biography; or, lives of celebrated children*, 1801.

[90] An attempt to answer some of them more fully has been made in Chap. VI for the most important lives of the century.

[91] *The history of Prince Mirabel's infancy, rise and disgrace*, 1712, pp. 5-6.

age of six he tries to revive a companion struck dead by lightning. But that is not all:

"In the same Year, approaching too near the Cage of a Vultur which was kept in the Court-yard of the Dome, and thrusting his Hand into the Cage in derision, the Vultur being throughly vex'd, and hungry withal, seiz'd his Hand in one of her Talons, which was in some measure defended by a thick Glove he had on: The brave Youth no ways shock'd at the Danger of this Assault, pluck'd a tame Pigeon out of his bosom, and lur'd the ravenous Bird from the Prey he had under his Claws with so cheap a sacrifice, 'till he found an Opportunity to disengage himself.

"These Events how trifling soever they may seem, and not worthy to be rank'd amongst the stupendous Actions of his advanc'd Years . . . were sure Prophecies of a Mind not easy to be disturb'd by any Appearances of Danger, and never to be broke by the most pressing Menaces of Fate."

Such stories may or may not be true. The important point is that just as Parson Weems records his invented story of the young George Washington and the cherry tree at the other end of the century, this biographer details the episode of the vulture because he knows the public accepts and enjoys stories that show future traits exemplified during the childhood of some great man. Of the same sort is an anecdote told by an adventurer, traveller, and reckless soldier; the eighteenth century public could be certain that the autobiography that followed would be that of an impetuous military man:[92]

"One Day that my Father shut me up in a Chamber for I know not what Fault, after I had quite tired my self with bawling and thundering to no Purpose at the Door, I was in such a Rage that I pluck'd off a good deal of my Hair, and knock'd my Head against the Wall to such a Degree, that when they came and open'd the Door, they found me all over bloody, my Head almost bald, and full of Bumps."

[92] *Memoirs of the Count* [*Claude*] *de Forbin*, 1731, p. 4. For other such adumbrations of future conduct, see Gilbert Langley, 1740, and Jacob Boehme, 1780. cf. also Boswell's *Johnson*.

Such a belief was expressed as conscious theory. Thus, Dr. John Fothergill writes in his *Essay on Alexander Russell*:[93]

"In infancy, almost in the period of youth and adolescence, many traits are often observable, that strongly mark the future character of the man. The relation of incidents, of no consequence in themselves, viewed in this light, affords us satisfaction, when we recollect them as the early presages of future worth."

And John Aikin, in setting down the principles governing his *General Biography,* which appeared in eight volumes between 1799 and 1813, states in his Preface that he has taken particular care to inquire for each subject into *"the manner in which he was first formed to his art or profession,* with the gradations by which he rose to excellence." The first phrase in this quotation he considers of sufficient importance to set off in italics.

John Mainwaring states convincingly his belief that genius manifests its particular bent in infancy:[94]

"And here it may not be unpleasing to the reader, just to remind him of the minute and surprising resemblance between these passages in the early periods of Handel's life, and some which are recorded in that of the celebrated monsieur Pascal† ["†Tycho Brahe is another instance of the like kind."], written by his sister. Nothing could equal the bias of the one to Mathematics, but the bias of the other to Music: both in their very childhood out-did the efforts of maturer age: they pursued their respective studies not only without any assistance, but against the consent of their parents, and in spite of all the opposition they contrived to give them."

A realization of the importance of the *minutiae* that mark the beginnings of great men's lives is furnished by the anonymous *Memoirs of the life of John Lord Somers* (1716), which ends a defense of trivial anecdotes of early life by saying: "For this Reason it is, that we lament the want of Memoirs of the Life of my Lord Somers from his Youth to his Manhood." In spite of such lamentations, the eighteenth century is not destitute of satisfying accounts of childhood. For these amusing or senti-

---

[93] 1769, p. 362 in Fothergill's *Works,* 1783, Vol. II.
[94] *Memoirs of the life of George Frederic Handel,* 1760, p. 6. See also Burney on Handel later in this chapter, and cf. Bicknell's satire on Burney's belief.

mental recollections, the autobiographers, naturally enough, are almost solely responsible; and in the stories told by Samuel Johnson and William Cobbett (1796); the miniatures of boyhood by James Lackington (1791), William Hutton (1798), and John Dunton (1705); the reveries and dreams of Henry More (1710), John Nelson (1749), and John Manton (1797); the effusive memories of Kotzebue (1800) or Mary Robinson (1800); the full-length portraits of *jeunes filles en fleur* given by Madame d'Aulnoy (1715) and Madame Roland (1796); the lives of those who died young, such as the ten-year-old Prince William Henry (1789),[95] the pious prodigy Christlieb Von Exter (1709), and *Juvenile biography; or, lives of celebrated children* (1801)—in these and others, an importance was given to childhood in biography which foreshadows, however dimly, the exalted intuitions which Wordsworth was soon to express in poetry.

The quotations given above indicate that occasional biographers conceived character to be organic rather than static, and wished to show the minute gradations, the infinite small changes through which the man emerged from the child. The idea that the child is father to the man, that our days are bound each to each, found further expression elsewhere; and the importance of the formative early years on the future development of character is thus stated by one biographer:[96]

". . . the character of the future man is marked essentially by the impressions he receives during his state of childhood, when the mind is of a more plastic and yielding texture, and takes its modes of thinking and acting from those precepts and examples which are presented most strikingly before the eye."

Roger North achieves a subtle and seemingly modern bit of self-analysis when he tries to trace the reasons for his intense loyalty to the Crown back to a childhood which he cannot even recall to consciousness:[97]

[95] Illustrations from all the above biographies have been quoted in earlier chapters. Consult Index.

[96] *An affectionate tribute to Dr. John Fothergill,* by W. Hird, 1781, p. 20.

[97] *The autobiography of the Hon. Roger North,* 1887, p. 19. cf. the suggestion of the anonymous author of *The life of Commodus,* 1789, that this Emperor's brutality and love of boxing was caused by his mother Faustina's sucking blood from the wounded arm of a favorite gladiator before Commodus was born.

"And I cannot to this hour discover or tell from what spring this humour arose, unless it were that universal alacrity which was upon the King's return [Charles II], while I was a very boy; the discourse of which, though not much minded by me, might sink and make an impression so as to determine my early inclination, and that goes a great way in the future conduct of life. . . . Such little accidents, when placed on men that come forwarder in the world than I could pretend to, have great influence in the great revolutions and troubles of the world."

Such sensitivity and such conscious theorizing about the importance of childhood and its imperceptible changing into youth and manhood are by no means the common property of eighteenth century biographers. Many—one is tempted to say most— of the life-writers treated their heroes as static, almost as if their subjects had been born as dignified and important old men. Even Boswell himself cannot be totally freed from such an accusation. Little sense of life, and no sense of childhood, will result from a biography that can state: *"Mr* Samuel Medley was born,"[98] or from another that records: "When he was only about seven or eight years old he was desired by his mother to write her some lines. . . . *The Doctor obeyed.*"[99]

Also, of course, not every writer of the century was willing to accept the importance attached by the above biographers to childhood. Alexander Bicknell, for instance, satirizes Charles Burney's convictions by narrating the early experiences of his musician-hero Joel Collier, who, like Burney's and Mainwaring's Handel, gives precocious evidence of his future abilities:[100]

". . . whilst I was yet in coats, I took vast delight in pinching the tails of the Parson's litter of pigs, and would listen to their various notes and tones from the f sharp of the whine of the least of the family, quite down to the b flat of the boar himself."

And another biographer dismisses childhood as unimportant, though possibly his is a case of sour grapes:[101]

[98] *Memoirs of the late Rev. Samuel Medley, compiled by his son,* 1800, p. 63.
[99] *Memoirs of the Rev. Isaac Watts,* 1780, p. 5.
[100] *Musical travels through England. By Joel Collier, Organist,* 1774, pp. 3-4.
[101] L. D. Campbell's life of Hugh Boyd, before Boyd's *The Indian Observer,* 1798.

"With the circumstances attending his childhood, I am not at all acquainted, nor indeed if I was, could they be interesting to any reader. An uniformity of incident pervades infant life. We have but few instances of the dawn of genius, in that period of existence."

Yet in spite of such occasional attacks upon the narration of youthful experiences in biography, childhood was treated ordinarily as a necessary part of the account of a career, if only material from this period could be found. At times childhood was considered as a token of future greatness; at times as the tender April of life when a character was just beginning to take shape; at times sentimentally, as a magic land that can be reentered only in memory; and very frequently, without conscious theory, as an additional period that illustrated the delightful variety of human experience. The moments of birth and death were occasionally regarded as parts of a wider scheme, and their significance seen *sub specie aeternitatis:*[102]

"On Tuesday he received the Sacrament, from the Hands of the Bishop of Salisbury and Doctor Clark his Parish Minister, and on Wednesday Mrs Goodiere his House Keeper coming into his Room, he seriously asked her, what it was to bring a Child into the World? she answered, a pain that surpasseth imagination: and so it is also to get out of it says he, how vain is this World, and yet what a struggle we have to part with it."

Such questioning of the worth of life is as transient as it is serious. Rarely found in biography is such a passage as the following, in which a deist and playgoer speculates on the death of his Christian hero, in a letter to a friend who seems to be a skeptic:[103]

"Look down thou blessed spirit!—But I forget; with you, the invocation of saints is more than even a poetic licence.—And now, my friend, admitting sovereign perfection to preside over human affairs; If there does exist, as surely all nature attests, a power above us, who delights in virtue; must not the righteous man triumph in death? Can it be other than a new birth, to a more exalted state of life, to a more consummate felicity, than

---

[102] *The life and character of Charles Duke of Shrewsbury*, 1718, pp. 33-4.
[103] *Sermons . . . by the late Rev. James Duchal*, prefatory life, anonymous, pp. xxx-xxxi, 1765.

the heart of man can now conceive? Virtue is the perfection of our highest powers, the image of Divinity within us! matured by discipline, it is necessarily related to objects, 'beyond this visible diurnal sphere'—to the Supreme Being himself, the Supreme Good! Can it then, in its most finished state, in the article of dying, be quenched in eternal darkness? If so, all moral order is subverted; and Chaos is come again! Abstracted from supernatural testimony, this single phenomenon of the good man's exit from the present transitory scene, by appointment of the great Master of the Drama, reflects, one would think, such light of evidence, as nothing can put out, but that folly which has forfeited the joyful hopes of Immortality; or cogitations dark as Erebus—at least, it should seem that there is nothing, in all the magazine of metaphysics, so satisfactory against the fear of extinction, in Death!"

Such speculation seldom occurs. The deaths of Voltaire and of Hume afford forensic battlegrounds for believers and skeptics. Death is infrequently envisioned as anything other than an accidental terminus to life. Few biographers conceive of it dramatically or causally, as, say, the approach of Nemesis, or of a physician healing long pain; it is conceived neither as port after storm, nor as mysterious terror, nor as the purposed end of a pilgrimage, nor as a vantage-point from which a last survey and farewell may be taken. Death is merely the fortuitous and conventional circumstance that indicates to the biographer that his job is done. This common failure to find moral or artistic significance in death gives a beauty which may be no more than relative to such a passage as the following:[104]

"He used often to say, That if he were to chuse a Place to die in, it should be an Inn, it looking like a Pilgrim's going home, to whom this World was all as an Inn, and who was weary of the Noise and Confusion in it. He added, that the officious Tenderness and Care of Friends was an Entanglement to a dying Man; and that the unconcerned Attendance of those that could be procured in such a Place, would give less Disturbance. And he

[104] David Wilson's account of Archbishop Robert Leighton, prefixed to Leighton's *Works*, 1758, p. xxvi. cf. Shenstone's and Johnson's similar sentiments.

obtained what he desired, for he died at the Bell Inn in Warwick-Lane."

The great exception, of course, to this usual blindness to the significance of death, is the positive faith expressed in the experiential Christian biographies. Here the general speculations of Young's *Night Thoughts* and Gray's *Elegy* become highly personalized and hopeful convictions. To the Quakers, and even more to the Wesleyans, life was a preparation for death, and death itself only the gateway to eternal life. This belief makes the death scene in a Methodist biography by far the fullest and most important of the whole work. The subject is always joyful on the point of death, never afraid; usually he sings hymns during the final week; his friends gather round and are encouraged and made joyful themselves by his dying remarks, his exclamations, and his Biblical quotations which are treasured in such exact detail. Death has here become of such tremendous import that the preceding years and decades of life can be dismissed in a few pages or sometimes omitted altogether. Death, in other words, is not only of equal importance with life, as in the "brief account of the life and death" of Barbara Walker (1777) or of Mrs. Sarah Brough (1781); it is of sole importance, as in the "short account of the death of Mrs. Mary Hutton" (1777) or of Mrs. Anne Thornton (1799). And its significance is obvious in such a title as *Faith triumphant, exemplified in the death of Mrs. T——* (1782). It is, moreover, of great value to fellow-believers, and the *Short account of the death of Elizabeth Hindmarsh, who died Sept. 6, 1777; in the twenty-first year of her age* goes through four editions by 1789.

The act of dying can be of such dramatic and inspiriting finality as to cause John Wesley himself to write:[105]

"I am sensible, it is the method of almost all Writers, to place the Character of a man at the conclusion of his Life. But there seems to be a particular reason for varying from the usual practice in this place. The death of Mr. Fletcher (hardly to be paralleled in the present century) was so uncommon a display of the power and goodness of God in behalf of his highly-favoured Servant,

---

[105] *A short account of the life and death of the Rev. John Fletcher*, 1786, pp. 160-1.

that it is not proper for any thing to come after it. It must needs therefore close the whole account."

The didactic importance of a Christian death was so widely accepted that it caused a commercial biographer, with no obvious religious interests, to write of the popularly accepted belief that Johnson's horror of death persisted to the last: "The tremulous manner in which Dr Johnson died, has, in my idea, been more detrimental to the general interests of Christianity, than any other event appertaining to a single individual."[106] In the medieval saint's life, death comes as a glorious culmination; to Samuel Johnson, in spite of his Christian belief, death is terror, and life must be clutched at and lived to the last gasp. Apart from the religious journalists and a few rare moralists in life-writing, death is not conceived as having any logical, psychological, or philosophical connection with a hero's life; and though there is a kind of unescapable natural drama about the last scene in a man's progress from the cradle to the grave, so that one does not easily forget Johnson's terrible last quotations from Shakespeare, or Sterne's agonizingly operatic "Now it is come!" or Major-General Lee's "Stand by me, my brave grenadiers!" or Sophia Baddeley's sordid end in Edinburgh, or the death of Richard Savage in prison, nevertheless, the eighteenth century biographer does little to render artistically significant or final, under "the great Master of the Drama," his hero's last leave-taking from the stage of life.

The eighteenth century performed a useful service by completing the separation of history from biography. In spite of the differentiation between the two forms which such writers as Francis Bacon and John Dryden had insisted upon, the seventeenth century tended to blur them; indeed, until the century was nearly over, "historian" or "historiographer" was the usual designation for the biographer, and the word biography itself did not appear in England until after the Restoration. Writers labored under the impression that an individual career must be made worthy of a reader's attention by the inclusion of great historical events. Or again, the materials for a life would be so scanty that

---

[106] Anthony Pasquin's *Eccentricities of John Edwin*, 1791, 2 vols., Vol. I, p. 318.

they could be rounded out into a volume only by filling in the historical background, whether or not it was relevant. Quite naturally, therefore, when the eighteenth century came to consider each individual as of worth and importance, when it developed an insatiable passion for small anecdote, and when the available records for biography were measurably increased, biography became distinct from history. Although the eighteenth century theorists still granted to history the greater dignity, they came to feel that biography had the greater usefulness.

The persistence of the old attitude can be marked occasionally. "This History," one writer frankly declares,[107] "is entitled *The Life of the King of Prussia;* yet it is neither confined to the Conduct of that Prince only, or to the Period of his Existence." Another writer of an individual life boasts:[108] "In a word, we have omitted nothing that might give an exact idea of the state of Europe for these fifty years past." Still a third biographer ingenuously writes of his hero:[109] "As I find nothing particular recorded of him before he became Batchelor of Arts, only in general of his application to his studies, and great proficiency in them, I shall endeavour to fill up this chasm, from the beginning of the Century to the Year 1521, with a view of the age in which he was born."

The most painful, and at times ludicrous, attempt to ride simultaneously the two steeds of history and biography is Joseph Berington's *The history of the lives of Abeillard and Heloisa* (1787).

"In writing the present history," Berington says (Preface, p. vii), "I had then more in view, than the bare delineation of the two principal characters: but of these I have never lost sight. . . . At any time, how little connection has the life of a literary man, and much less that of a cloistered nun, with the schemes of politicians, and the feats of warriors?"

This question of incongruity the biography does little to solve. The breathtaking transitions make even the Reverend Mr. Berington uncomfortable (p. 57):

---

[107] *The life and actions of Frederic III,* 1759, Introduction.
[108] *The life of James Fitz-James, Duke of Berwick,* 1738, anon. tr., Preface.
[109] Glocester Ridley's *Nicholas Ridley,* 1763, p. 3.

"From the contentious scenes of war and politics, on which the pride of history loves to dwell, I return, with pleasure, to the more humble walk of biography. Thus the traveller, who, on the glacieres of Grindelwald o Chamoigny, has contemplated nature in her sublimest horrors, sinks to the vale below with gentler emotions, where he meets the creeping woodbine and the purling stream."

In these attempts to give weight and dignity to his story by the intrusion of general history, he achieves a climax when, after he has narrated the lurid incident of Abelard's emasculation, his sense of duty leads him to a truthful anticlimax (p. 94):

"While the business, I have described, engaged all the attention of the Parisians, nothing very interesting occurred in the affairs of Europe."

Yet these examples are exceptional; and quite painlessly, almost unconsciously, the eighteenth century drifted into the habit of writing a biography as if it were the life of a single individual and not a history of the world. The theoretical distinction between the two is best stated with Gallic precision in the translated preface to the Abbé Prévost's *History of Margaret of Anjou* (1755, pp. 4 and 10, Preface, Vol. I):

"My first remark is, that the design of a particular history being only to make known the actions, qualities, dispositions and manners of a person of either sex, all the public events that are the materials of a general history, ought not to be introduced, unless they are interwoven with those which we undertake to relate."

"It is peculiar to a particular history, that it admits of circumstantial relations that would appear puerile in a general history; and that to the nobleness of this species of writing may be joined all that is agreeable in the most personal and private memoirs. Here nothing is little, nothing despicable, that serves to give us a more perfect knowledge of the principal characters."

All of this means, of course, that the biographers are conceiving more realistically their function of re-creating an individual life. Their subject must be presented as a three-dimensional individual, occupying particular space and living in particular time. To the biographer, the hero is not so much a part of the history of the world as the history of the world is a part of the hero. He himself, his surroundings, and the events in his existence, must be realized concretely.

One illustration of this change lies in the growing importance attached to the portraits, verbal or linear, of individuals. The eighteenth century is the age of Reynolds and Gainsborough and Hogarth, of Lawrence, Raeburn, and Opie. Nor is it fantastic to trace parallel developments in technique, manner of treatment, purpose, and achievement between biography and painting. Interest in a person's physical traits and mannerisms is developed notably during the eighteenth century. Physical descriptions, though common enough in earlier biography, are for the most part wooden and unsuccessful; they bear generic resemblances to one another, much like Elizabethan portraits, or the second-rate paintings of Stuart courtiers. Only gradually did it become conventional to include a portrait engraving of an author even before his collected works.

Contrast this seventeenth century lack of interest with the eagerness of the latter part of the eighteenth century: in 1743, in two enormous and costly folio volumes, appeared *The heads of illustrious persons of Great Britain, engraven by Mr. Houbraken, and Mr. Vertue.* To accompany the portraits, Thomas Birch drew up lives and characters in a Procrustean two-page documented biography for each. In 1769 this work was eclipsed by James Granger's *A biographical history of England, from Egbert the Great to the Revolution: consisting of characters disposed in different classes, and adapted to a methodical catalogue of engraved British heads. Intended as an essay towards reducing our biography to system, and a help to the knowledge of portraits.* The two volumes of this work, bound as four, contain portraits and anecdotes for twelve classes of people, from kings and queens to "Poets and other ingenious Persons," "Painters, Artificers, Mechanics, and all of inferior Professions," and even "deformed Persons, Convicts, &c." Before the end of the century, in adaptations, imitations, extensions, and modifications, many similar collections of portraits with accompanying biographical notes had

appeared.[110] At least two of these collections show that the compilers were consciously trying to publish paintings and drawings
which had not hitherto been reproduced,[111] and one of them was
evidently planned to be continued periodically.[112] One compiler,
John Chamberlaine, anticipates certain modern biographers in
his belief that character may often be read in a man's face. He
shows this preoccupation not only in the general plan of accompanying reproductions of Holbein's portraits with "biographical
tracts," but in casual remarks such as this regarding Sir Thomas
More's son John:[113]

"It has been said, that he laboured under an intellectual weakness from his infancy, and the report has originated in a great
measure from the character fancied to be expressed in his portrait. . . . To the opinion founded on the picture, not to mention
the uncertainty of physiognomical conclusions, it may be fairly
answered, that it is in a great degree contradicted by the evidence
of the portrait itself, for who would paint a fool with a book in
his hands, and in an attitude of deep study?"

If in the above passage Chamberlaine blows hot and cold about
the Platonic correspondence between inner and outer man, he
is more characteristically assured in such a phrase as that which
accompanies the drawing of Thomas More's father Sir John
(Number 32):

"Not much has been delivered to us respecting his character.
. . . The portrait, however, to which this little tract is annexed
affords a strong presumptive evidence in his favour—it is surely
the head of a wise man, and Holbein's pencil has seldom been
accused of infidelity."

110 cf. John Chamberlaine's *Imitations of original drawings by Hans Holbein
. . . with biographical tracts*, 1792; *The biographical mirrour, comprising a series
of ancient and modern English portraits*, 1795, by F. G. Waldron, in 3 vols.;
H. N. Williams's *Biographical sketches of eminent persons, whose portraits form
part of the Duke of Dorset's collection at Knole*, 1795; John Pinkerton's *The Scot-
ish Gallery; or, Portraits of eminent persons of Scotland . . . with brief accounts
of the characters represented*, 1799; John Adolphus's *The British cabinet; containing portraits of illustrious personages, engraved from original pictures: with
biographical memoirs*, 1799-1800, 2 vols.
111 Waldron and Adolphus.
112 Adolphus.
113 1792; Number 34.

This belief that character may be read in the face and actions is frequently assumed by biographers. Thus, a Baptist historian writes:[114]

"As to his person; his countenance express'd the innocence, as well as greatness of his soul. It had nothing of that perplexity, which a confus'd or a vitious mind often throws upon the face; but always appear'd with that sweet calm, which springs from inward peace, and satisfaction of mind."

And John Elliot writes of Dr. Fothergill:[115]

"The person of Dr. Fothergill (says Dr. Hird) was of a delicate, rather of an extenuated make. His features were all character. His eye had a peculiar brilliancy of expression; yet it was not easy so to mark the leading trait, as to disengage it from the united whole. . . .

"His dress was remarkably neat, plain, and decent, peculiarly becoming himself; a perfect transcript of the order, and, I may add, of the neatness of his mind."

Jesse Foot, moreover, conveys his jealous and mean-spirited interpretation of Dr. John Hunter (1794) by means of a personal description in which realistic detail produces the effect of a hostile character-sketch (pp. 285-6):

"His person was about the middle stature: he was rather robust, but not corpulent: his shoulders were broad and high, and his neck remarkably short: by the exertions—which he constantly made, after the manner of something like a cough,—he seemed as if he solicited,—to set the circulation of blood a going. His features were hard,—cheeks high,—eyes small and light,—eye lashes yellow, and the bony arch protruded. His mouth was somewhat underhung. He wore his hair curled behind. His dress was plain, and none of the neatest. He was frequently seen to smile in conversation—but it was generally provoked, from a ridiculous, or a satirical motive."

At the end of the century, as the amateur and anecdotal spirit tended to prevail, a few biographies were presented as tentative or half-finished sketches—dilettante portraits by dilettantes. Thus

---

[114] Account of John Gale's life before his *Sermons*, 1726, p. xviii, probably by Thomas Crosby.
[115] Life, before Fothergill's *Works*, 1781, p. xviii.

John Pinkerton presents his unique study of Horace Walpole (1799) as a *Biographical sketch, in fugitive crayons*. And Philip Thicknesse defends his successful attempt to catch life and spirit by means of quick, inspired strokes by saying:[116]

"This is a hasty sketch of my departed friend and his family, written in one day and finished in one respect only, like his best pictures, *i.e.* at *one sitting*, for I think the finest head he ever painted, was that of his nephew, Mr. Dupont, and that was never touched but once, and that once the work of one hour."

In attempts, therefore, to copy the methods of painting, in a belief that character may be read from features and mannerisms, and in a growing interest in descriptions or portraits of its heroes, eighteenth century biography begins to realize that life is lived largely in the world of the senses; it becomes more visual—even, if the term may be used, more corporeal.

If the actors in eighteenth century biography are sharply described, the background against which they act is no less vividly realized. Quotations in earlier chapters sufficiently illustrate this ability to paint a scene—the views in London and on the road from France of the spy and furtive fugitive William Fuller; the exact detail in the pictures of adventurous action given by James Wyatt; Fawcett's idyl of rejoicing in the family circle of the Reverend Oliver Heywood; John Carteret Pilkington's staged scenes of Irish life in a smoke-thatched cottage in Cork or in a country castle; the night scenes (in which suppression of detail seems to increase emotion) of Mary Robinson, or Corancez, or Lavater; William Cobbett's exceptional powers of visualizing his life as a child, a youth, and a man. That such a knack at sketching in background could be consciously admired is shown by the following contemporary praise of Mrs. Pilkington, after her characterization has been favorably noticed:[117]

"The same Kind of Commendation is almost every where due to the scenecal Parts of her Narration; for this Lady being blest with a brisk Imagination, and a retentive Memory, describes things not as she would have them, or as she thinks they will

---

[116] *A sketch of the life and paintings of Thomas Gainsborough*, 1788, p. 49.
[117] *The parallel; or, Pilkington and Phillips compared*, 1748, p. 15.

please, but as they really happened; and thus without attending to it, she takes a much better Method than if she had put her Abilities to the stretch. Her Ideas fall upon the Paper just as they rose in her Mind, and the Reader sees Things as she saw them, and therefore sees them as they were."

This gift of realizing background—consciously or unconsciously, and not necessarily by direct description—is important to the biographer. Even in Boswell, in spite of his own belief that he had no power to describe physical objects such as mountains or buildings, the most memorable passages are associated with a room, a street, an inn, or are made vivid by some gesture, expression, or action of one of his cast of characters.

Most of the famous passages in biography are, literally, scenes. One need go no further than Gibbon's autobiography, in which the two best-known paragraphs present the moments of the inception and the completion of the *Decline and Fall*. But if the background for these moments is taken away—the Temple of Jupiter amidst the ruins of the Capitol in one instance, and the moonlit night in the summer-house of the garden at Lausanne in the second—the moments themselves lose their significance and beauty. What is true for Gibbon (who, like Boswell, had no extraordinary power at natural description) is true for his contemporaries.

Nor need the scene be unusual or picturesque to call forth this power of sharp suggestion. Experience Mayhew (1727) skilfully handles the local color of Martha's Vineyard in his struggles with the Sagamore Sachims and Pawwaws of that island to win "Indian Converts"; but Thomas Wright (1795-1797) is equally adept at the descriptions in his autobiography of more homely scenes, such as Lower Blacup Farm, or a plum-tree that he remembers from childhood, or his last sight of his grandmother. One remembers the ungainly bulk of Doctor Johnson on horseback against the wild moorlands of the Western Islands; but one also remembers him in the back-parlour of Mr. Tom Davies's shop the day when Boswell first met him. Far-away places and strange scenes are described successfully when Robert Drury recounts his escape from the Madagascar tribes (1729), or Henry Grace tells of three years' privation among Canadian Indians

(1764), or Philip Thicknesse (1788) makes the reader share with him an ambush by wild negroes in Jamaica. But not less successful than these pictures of African rivers and Jamaican jungles is Mrs. Delany's picture of the English country-seat in which she spent the best years of her girlhood:[118]

"The Farm is a low house, with very good, convenient room in it, the outside entirely covered with laurel, the inside neat furnished with home spun stuff, adorned with fine China and prints. The front of the house faces the finest vale in England, the Vale of Evesham, of which there is a very advantageous view from every window: the back part of the house is shaded by a very high hill which rises gradually; between lies the garden, a small spot of ground, but well stocked with fruit and flowers. Nothing could be more fragrant and rural: the sheep and cows came bleating and lowing to the pales of the garden. At some distance on the left hand was a rookery; on the right a little clear brook run winding through a copse of young elms (the resort of many warbling birds), and fell with a cascade into the garden, completing the concert. In the midst of that copse was an arbour with a bench, which I often visited, and I think it was impossible not to be pleased with so many natural beauties and delights as I there beheld and enjoyed around me."

The following account of a quarrel and reconcilation between friends is given in full, because in it (and many similar instances could be found in the century) the wall of a summer-house seems to play almost as active a third rôle in the drama as did the wall in Bottom's production of Pyramus and Thisbe. The value of exact detail in background and action may be appreciated by imagining how little would be left of Shenstone's personality if the whole incident were passed over with a general statement about his irascibility, his pride, and his forgiving temper:[119]

"We were one day engaged in a warm debate, in which, I think, I had the upper hand, and drove my antagonist to a painful dilemma; and with exultation pursued my advantage so far,

---

[118] *The autobiography and correspondence of Mary Granville, Mrs. Delany*, 3 vols., 1861, Vol. I, pp. 17-18. Wr. 1740 and later.

[119] *Recollection of some particulars in the life of William Shenstone*, 1788, probably by Richard Graves, pp. 37-9.

that Mr. Shenstone grew angry; and our trifling dispute terminated on each side in a sullen silence, which as Mr. Shenstone
would not vouchsafe to break first, I, from a youthful spirit of
independence, disdained to submit; so that, although we ate and
drank together, this pouting humour continued, and we never
spoke to each other for near two days. At last, as I was never
much addicted to taciturnity, and it was pain and grief to me to
keep silence, I wrote upon the wall, in a summer-house in the
garden [at Harborough], a line from Anacreon:

'θέλω, δέλω μανῆναι.'

Which I translated,

'I will, I will be witty.'

Under this Mr. Shenstone wrote this distich:

'Matchless on earth I thee proclaim,
   Whose *will* and *power* I find the same.'

This produced a reply on my side; that a rejoinder on his;
till, at last, the ill-fated wall was scribbled from top to bottom;
which the next morning was succeeded by a laugh at each other's
folly, and a cordial reconciliation."

Informal in style, these reminiscences are charmingly written.
The wine-parties and cliques at Pembroke, Shenstone's first falling in love, his opinions and his friends are all lightly touched
upon. The descriptions are unusually good, from such an integration of background and characters as that quoted, to the more
extended account of Shenstone's landscaping and his work on his
cascades at Leasowes, or to the following impressionistic sketch of
London, with a closeup of the disreputable publishers' domains
(pp. 94-5):

"At London every object, from the highest to the lowest, and
the most obvious, struck Mr. Shenstone with amazement. The
theatres, the coffee-houses, the Mall, the public gardens, were
scenes of uncommon amusement to a man of reflection and an
active imagination.

"He lodged in Fleet-street, where he had a back·view into
Black-friars, and where was then (and probably may still be) a
kind of magazine or manufactory of dying speeches, bloody mur-

ders, rapes, and robberies; songs and ballads, political, satirical, comical, and tragical, and all the various effusions of those learned gentlemen who write from a better motive than the love [of] fame."

Similar in his gift for suggesting a background by a few selected impressions is Silas Told, who thus describes the crowd that gathers to see a public hanging:[120]

"There was a very crouded concourse, among whom were numberless gin and gingerbread vendors, accompanied by pick-pockets and whores, of almost every denomination in London; in short, the whole scene resembled a principal fair, rather than an awful execution."

Yet in such a scene as this, the lens is no longer completely true and clear. The reader feels that the personal judgment and moral convictions of the Methodist biographer shape to some extent what his eye sees; and that possibly this picture of the gallows has some of the imaginative quality of Bunyan's Vanity Fair.[121] And indeed some of the most vivid scenes in eighteenth century biography are realized by writers in whom intensity of vision, rather than accuracy of observation, is remarkable. Their scenes are done in the manner of Rembrandt rather than Vermeer, of El Greco rather than Velasquez.[122] Note, for example, how the following idyl of townsfolk dancing on the green at Pontivy gains effectiveness from the revulsion of the now reformed sinner who narrates it:[123]

"For upon the Lord's-Day the Idolatrous Papists, after their Mass was over in the Morning, and some other unreasonable

[120] *An account of the life, and dealings of God with Silas Told,* 1786, p. 102.

[121] The gruesome anecdote that follows the above description narrates how the body of the criminal Lancaster was cut down, carried away by "the surgeon's mob," captured by eight sailors who learn of the hanging from "an old woman who sold gin," carried around London for a lark, and finally thrown discarded on a doorstep—his mother's. The story seems true; it is vivid; but its melodrama is used definitely to further the purposes of a reformer. John Wesley, telling the same story, interprets the action as the charitable recovery of the body by friends of Lancaster's mother.

[122] cf. subjective biographies, *passim,* in Chap. V.

[123] *The life of the Reverend Mr. Geo. Trosse,* 1714, p. 7. cf. "Some brief memoirs of the life of David Hall," 1758, a Quaker, who beards a dancing-master, who speaks against Christmas celebrations, and whose father, also a Quaker, refuses to tailor gay clothes even for his customers.

and superstitious Services in the Afternoon, would go out of the Town, (very near the Castle) and there the Young Men and Maidens were wont to dance upon the Dove, which was a Rising Ground before the Castle. They danc'd together in a Ring, Two of them leaping in the midst, and when they had shewn their Activity, they would call other Couples out of the Ring to do the like. Of this foolish, indecent, and dangerous Exercise We were the pleas'd Spectators."

And Thomas Story, who catches motion and setting with the utmost fidelity, nevertheless colors and vitalizes his pictures because of his Quaker convictions. When the young Peter of Russia is learning about Western civilization in England, Story waits upon him and presents him with books to help him understand the Society of Quakers. Peter's question, "Of what Use can you be, in any Kingdom or Government, seeing you will not bear Arms and fight?"[124] is recorded, but is brushed aside as not worth a serious answer. In the same fashion, when in his preaching all over the kingdom he comes at last to Oxford, "that old Seat of the Power of Darkness, and Subtilty of the sensual and earthly Wisdom of this World," Story tells how the undergraduates bait him while he is haranguing them, interrupting him with "several great Floods of Laughter, more forced than natural . . . in the Times of their loud Cachinations, they most nearly resembled a Flock of Geese of any thing I could compare them to."[125] Yet though he presents faithfully the actions and words of others, the beliefs of the Czar of Russia or of the young men of Oxford never penetrate into his own individual world: he thinks he has done them some good, and he writes his long journal as a kind of self-communion in which the external world appears as a shifting phantasmagoria where the clear outlines, the brilliant lights, and the deep shades are without other than pictorial significance.

However they may be viewed, with fidelity, or reminiscent sentiment, or almost as hallucinations, sharply realized scenes add immeasurably to biography; for without such background, the most cleverly reconstructed character is left in a condition in

[124] *A journal of the life of Thomas Story*, 1747, p. 124.
[125] *ibid*., pp. 715-16.

which his life was not lived—a disembodied spirit, with a name, perhaps, but with no local habitation.

Yet the conscious analysis of the ingredients which might enter into life-writing—the physical descriptions of the hero, the influence of his surroundings or his awareness of them, the rigidity of his character or its gradual development or its sudden wilful deflection—was almost wholly lacking in the eighteenth century. With regard, for instance, to the temporal element of life alone, practically no observations are to be found. A few instances are mentioned in the text and bibliography in which a biographer has suggested the effect of the passage of the years over some character,[126] so that the reader is conscious of the seven ages of man, acquires a sense of the hero or heroine gradually becoming an old man or woman, or realizes the striking event which changes a whole personality or career. But far too frequently it is assumed that a single character-sketch adequately describes a man from the days of the colic to the days of the gout. The age of reason insisted upon simplification; and simplification, destroying the complex individual, was destructive to naturalistic biography. When divisions of a man's life were made at all, they were usually chronological, as if the important epochs in a man's life began with a new year, or the death of a monarch, or the assumption of some office or title. The sense of man as a creature living in, and destroyed by, time, is acknowledged only by a few worn phrases—from the cradle to the grave, or from birth to burial.

§ 7

The paucity of critical theory and its entire absence concerning some of the most important functions of the biographer are counterbalanced to some extent by the eagerness with which critics embraced, and the assiduity with which they repeated, certain ideas. This chapter has so far proceeded first by generalizing concerning the trend of eighteenth century biography as it appears to the modern reader, and second by some attempt to appraise its successes or failures in dealing with certain funda-

[126] See Mary Robinson, Sophia Baddeley, Madame Roland, William Hutton, Roger North.

mental problems in biography. There yet remains to consider how eighteenth century biography appeared to eighteenth century eyes, to what extent their conscious theories were developed, and what trends seemed notable to contemporary critics.

The close of the seventeenth century had witnessed, in such writers as Bishops Sprat, Fell, Hacket, and Burnet, the attempt to elevate biography to the plane of history by recording only matter of great dignity and national import. This attempt at monumental, decorous biography persists at the beginning of the eighteenth century, even at the time when the journalists and publishers are destroying it with their sensational biographical tracts. Thus, Abel Boyer writes of his *Memoirs of the life and negotiations of Sir W. Temple* (1714, p. 418):

". . . my Design is to represent and record his publick, not his private Life; and to avoid what I ever accounted a Fault in Biographers, the raking into minute Domestick Passages, exposing Privacies to publick View."

The most powerful champion of discreet biography is Addison, whose remarks on the difficulties of good biography and the requisites for producing it, and whose contempt for Curll and the tribe of scandalous biographers, are worth noticing at some length. Elegance, impartiality, and accuracy are his watchwords; freedom from bias seems more important to him than fulness of detail or closeness to the subject:[127]

"Gratian, among his Maxims for raising a Man to the most consummate Character of Greatness, advises first to perform extraordinary Actions, and in the next Place to secure a good Historian. . . .

"The Misfortune is, that there are more Instances of Men who deserve this kind of Immortality, than of Authors who are able to bestow it. Our Country, which has produced Writers of the first Figure in every other kind of Work, has been very barren in good Historians. We have had several who have been able to compile Matters of Fact, but very few who have been able to digest them with that Purity and Elegance of Stile, that Nicety and Strength of Reflection, that Subtilty and Discernment in the Unravelling of a Character, and that Choice of Circumstances for

[127] *The Freeholder* for Friday, April 20, 1716; Number 35, single sheet.

enlivening the whole Narration, which we so justly admire in the antient Historians of Greece and Rome, and in some Authors of our neighbouring Nations. . . .

"There is a Race of Men lately sprung up among this sort of Writers, whom one cannot reflect upon without Indignation as well as Contempt. These are our Grub Street Biographers, who watch for the Death of a Great Man, like so many Undertakers, on purpose to make a Penny of him. He is no sooner laid in his Grave, but he falls into the Hands of an Historian; who, to swell a Volume, ascribes to him Works which he never wrote, and Actions which he never performed; celebrates Vertues which he was never famous for, and excuses Faults which he was never guilty of. . . . what can we expect from an Author that undertakes to write the Life of a Great Man, who is furnished with no other Matters of Fact, besides Legacies; and instead of being able to tell us what he did, can only tell us what he bequeathed. . . .

"The Truth of it is, as the Lives of Great Men cannot be written with any tolerable Degree of Elegance or Exactness, within a short Space after their Decease; so neither is it fit that the History of a Person, who has acted among us in a publick Character, should appear till Envy and Friendship are laid asleep, and the Prejudice both of his Antagonists and Adherents be, in some Degree, softned and subdued. . . . It were happy for us, could we prevail upon our selves to imagine, that one, who differs from us in Opinion, may possibly be an honest Man."

To Addison, then, posterity becomes the sole judge, and, as if reversing Johnson's dictum before it was known, Addison holds that no one can know the truth about a man who has known him well enough either to love or hate him.

Addison was not the only critic who attacked the inflated and often misnamed biographical productions of the popular biographers. In order to issue a volume that would touch upon the man of the hour and the topics of the day, the Grub-street writers had two courses open to them. They could either include extraneous material already in print or accessible to all—such as news items of Marlborough's campaigns, culled from the gazettes and sold as a life of the Duke; or poems published in various miscellanies issued as part of the life of some author recently deceased; or last wills and testaments as soon as they were made public. Or they could swell the number of pages with invented stories. Only the most naïve of readers could have been completely hoodwinked by such proceedings. Soon these discursive pseudo-biographies were common enough to sustain parody, as in *The life of Mr. John Dennis . . . not written by Mr. Curll* (1734), whose anonymous author ironically remarks (pp. 4-5):

"Being to write the Life of Mr. John Dennis, some will wonder perhaps why we dwell thus long upon the Excellencies of another; but our Design in this, is to give the more delectable Entertainment to our courteous Readers, and likewise to follow the Mode and Fashion of the present Times, and, as far as our poor Abilities will permit us, to imitate the admired Writings of some of the choice Spirits of the Age, who do endeavour so much to vary from the Subject they first set out upon as, many times, almost, and sometimes quite to forget it."

Even more cogent criticism of the formlessness of Curll's publications is to be found in the *Remarks on 'Squire Ayre's Memoirs of the life and writings of Mr. Pope. In a letter to Mr. Edmund Curl.* The author tells Curll that it appears wonderful to him[128]

"that you did not, as you might assuredly, with equal Justice, introduce Memoirs of the Life, &c. of every Friend, and every Enemy of Mr. Pope's; and by that Means, have swelled your Work into twenty Volumes in Folio: And I cannot but think, this Example of your's will be of notable Use to another Writer, of much your Stamp, the Ordinary of Newgate; who has already found the Way of stretching his Accounts of wretched Creatures, under his Care, to second, and third Parts; and may, by following your Method, swell 'em into fifty, but [= by?] adding only to his Detail of the Culprits Crimes the whole Lives and Characters of his Judges and the Jury."

"Nay, you have, in one Instance, even outgone this large Allowance [of comparing the subject's quoted verses with the verses of other writers], bringing in, by Head and Shoulders, a

[128] 1745, pp. 22-3 and 37.

Dialogue from the Craftsman, for no other Reason in the World but because it was not Mr. Pope's. Here lay an ample Field, indeed, for enlarging your Work to whatever Dimensions you might think convenient; for by a Parity of Reason you might have call'd in all the Authors of the World to your Assistance."

Little defense, of course, was made or could be made for such frankly commercial ventures as the lives of highwaymen or the secret histories of great figures. Robert Burton, one of the most assiduous of these booksellers and compilers, issued a biographical *florilegium* with the explanation that "in this Age . . . a great many . . . have not Patience to read large Histories."[129] And the Gentleman of Norwich who wrote the life of his school-fellow Christopher Layer, from his birth to his execution for high treason (1723), merely notes—what the publications of the century certainly bear out—that "egregiously remarkable" acts are sure to excite attention and win popularity. He cites the lives of Sally Salisbury, Madame de Maintenon, Titus Oates, the Duke of Marlborough, Cromwell, Ravaillac the murderer of Henry IV, and Masaniello; and ends his catalogue (for he has presented a statement of fact rather than a justification of sensational biographies):[130]

"Mary Magdalen was as Popular in her jovial Harlottry as she was in her Christian Tears; Saul for his Persecution of the Gospel, as Paul for his Propagation of it; King David for his Adultery as for his Repentance; and his Son Solomon for his innumerable Follies, when he acted them, as for his immense Wisdom when he corrected them."

The criminals themselves realized the difference between a tale of horror and a biography; the condemned Eugene Aram submits the account of his life to the Reverend Mr. Collins with the words (1759, p. 32):

"I always believed any Relation of my Life of no Manner of Importance or Service to the Public, and I never either had any Temptation or Desire to appear in Print. The Publications ushered to the World, which I ever had little Concern for, and have

---

[129] *Unparallel'd varieties: or, the matchless actions and passions of mankind,* 1728, 4th ed., "To the Reader."
[130] Introduction, p. v.

as little now, by Persons in my Situation, always appeared to me only calculated for the Advantage of the Press, and for the Amusement of a very idle Curiosity."

The clearest presentation of the antagonism between the biographical ideal and the commercial exploitation of horrors comes in Lord Lyttelton's witty twenty-eighth Dialogue of the Dead, between Plutarch and a Modern Bookseller. Plutarch is surprised to find that booksellers dictate to authors what is to be written, and that the inculcation of morality is no longer the purpose of literature. The bookseller replies that he has lost money on an edition of Plutarch, and continues:[131]

"That work which repaired the loss I sustained by the costly edition of your books, was, *The Lives of the Highwaymen:* but I should never have grown rich, if it had not been by publishing *the lives of men that never lived.* You must know, that though in all times it was possible to have a great deal of learning and very little wisdom, yet it is only by a modern improvement in the art of writing, that a man may read all his life and have no learning or knowledge at all, which begins to be an advantage of the greatest importance. . . .

"*A secret history,* in which there is *no secret* and *no history,* cannot tempt indiscretion to blab, or vanity to quote; and by this means modern conversation flows gentle and easy, unincumbered with matter, and unburthened of instruction. . . .

"I tell you, our women do not read in order to live or to die like Lucretia. If you would inform us, that a *billet-doux* was found in her cabinet after her death, or give an hint as if Tarquin really saw her in the arms of a slave, and that she killed herself, not to suffer the shame of a discovery, such anecdotes would sell very well. Or if even by tradition, but better still, *if by papers in the Portian family,* you could shew some probability that Portia died of *dram-drinking;* you would oblige the world very much; for you must know, that next to new-invented characters, we are fond of new lights upon ancient characters; I mean such lights as shew a reputed honest man to have been a concealed knave; an illustrious hero a pitiful coward, &c."

---

[131] *The works of George Lord Lyttelton,* 1774, pp. 514-16. First ed. of these dialogues, 1760; 4th by 1765.

Fortunately for biography, neither the cold and formal ideal of Addison nor the sordid practice of the commercial booksellers prevailed. Biography developed during the eighteenth century largely because its writers came to believe that absolute truthfulness was essential and that this could be secured only by the preservation and inclusion of exact, minute, personal detail. That the actual is of more avail than the fictitious in impressing a moral lesson is affirmed in the preface to D'Argens *Memoirs of the Count Du Beauval* (1756). The English translator informs the reader that the Marquis D'Argens has attached his invented anecdotes to "the real Names of Persons, who have been remarkable in Life; conscious that we pay a more strict Attention to the Occurrences that have befallen those who enter within the Compass of our Acquaintance, or Knowledge, and if a Moral ensues from the Relation, it is more firmly rooted in the Mind, than when it is to be deduc'd from either Manners or Men, with whom we are entirely unacquainted." If such feigned truth is better than fancy, how much superior is actuality to this attempted verisimilitude! More and more the eighteenth century came to share Johnson's opinion that truthfulness is essential to a good story. Sometimes this passion for truth takes the form of an attack on panegyric.[132] Sometimes it encourages the most minute antiquarian research, or promotes the record of contemporary lives at a time when errors may still be corrected by publicity.[133] The profession of impartiality on the part of the biographer is so frequent that it may even be satirized. "It is also customary for biographers," one of them writes,[134]

"to tell their readers what a biographer is. To expatiate upon the importance of his business. To inform them what qualities he ought to possess. And, finally, to assure them that he is, in every respect, perfectly well qualified for the very arduous task; being entirely divested of prejudice or favour, candid and im-

[132] Thomas Haweis's *William Romaine*, 1797, pp. 9-10.

[133] cf. Robert Bisset's life of Edmund Burke, 1798, p. 3: "No one individual can know *all* the facts which may form the materials of an entertaining and useful life. *Variety of narratives,* if authentic, impartial, and not trivial, will tend to the great ends of biography." Also Richard Phillips's *Public characters of 1798,* 1799, which justifies the record of contemporary lives on five scores.

[134] J. A. Colet's life of Wesley, 1791, pp. 3-4.

partial, willing to sacrifice friendship to truth: that personal regard, and even the ties of blood, weigh nothing with him, when opposed to his duty and respect to the public."

Absolute faithfulness in representing life came to be almost the ethical ideal of eighteenth century biography.[135] This sense of exact truth may best be conveyed through the small anecdote scrupulously recorded. Such anecdotes, mixing the useful and the sweet, at once effective in suggesting character and delightful in themselves, were developed in eighteenth century biography almost as if they were manufactured wholesale. On such a scale, naturally enough, the introduction of the anecdote into biography could not escape critical comment; and whether or not to use anecdotes, in fact, becomes one of the most frequently debated questions in critical theory.[136] Thomas Warton, writing in 1772, speculates regarding the causes for the development of such detailed life-writing:[137]

"Biographers, in the pursuit of information, are naturally betrayed into minute researches. The curiosity of the reader is seldom proportioned to that of the writer in this species of composition. Every incident, relating to a favourite character which the mind has long contemplated with attention, acquires importance. On these principles we may venture to found a plausible excuse, for the many trifling discoveries, and intricate discussions of insignificant circumstances, with which personal history so much abounds."

The best defense of the value of minute traits and episodes is to be found in the *Monthly Review* for 1800, in a discussion of the unsatisfactory memorials of deceased members of the Royal Society of Edinburgh:[138]

"The materials for this biographical part, looking to the interest which they can excite, appear to us scanty and inefficacious; and we have to wish that the little which was to be said had been said in a different manner. We would willingly exchange the

---

[135] See Chap. V.

[136] cf., as early as 1758, the *Annual Register*, Vol. I, 1791 ed., p. 475, quoted earlier in this chapter.

[137] *The life of Sir Thomas Pope*, 1772, Preface, p. [iii].

[138] Vol. 31, New Series, p. 2.

general terms and long phrases, which seem to involve virtues and talents that were splendid and various, for distinct instances of goodness, and evident specimens of mental ability; we would resign abstract designations, in order to gain sensible images. As the lives are now written, we might venture to say, without fearing any very severe retort for want of feeling and judgment, that the perusal of them has made us neither merrier, wiser, nor better; and that characters, so obscurely pourtrayed, impress the mind for a moment faintly and confusedly, and then leave it without a clear object of admiration or a specific model of imitation."

Although some reviewers were sympathetic toward the anecdote, although some biographers invoked the authority of Plutarch to sanction their small sayings and trivial actions, and although the public as a whole showed its approval of and delight in anecdotal biography, nevertheless a great weight of critical opinion was hostile to this new development.

One of the earliest effective attacks is to be found in the *Monthly Review* for 1758:[139]

"As the business of biographical writing, however, consists principally in the art of *compiling,* the seeming facility of the employment, has induced many laborious drones to commence biographers, who have neither been blest with genius, taste, or learning. They have collected materials without discernment, put them together without order, and commented upon them without judgment.

"These industrious drudges, equal to any fatigue themselves, seem to imagine that their readers can never be tired. Their writings are like old women's stories, in which we do not lose a single *How d'ye do?* They, no doubt, think it the office of a faithful historian, not to omit the most trivial anecdote; and they often insult our patience with tedious relations, as uninteresting as if they were to acquaint us—That on such an hour, of such a day, in such a year, the Hero of their endless tale sat down, to pair his nails."

[139] Vol. 19, p. 386. Review of Jortin's *Erasmus*.

But it is at the end of the century, and as a result, one might say, of the biographical productions that cluttered the grave of Doctor Johnson, that the indignation against trivial anecdotes grows most warm. The most complete criticism occurs in an essay by Vicesimus Knox, "On the character of Dr. Johnson, and the abuse of biography,"[140] from which the following remarks might be selected:

"Biography is every day descending from its dignity. Instead of an instructive recital, it is becoming an instrument to the mere gratification of an impertinent, not to say a malignant, curiosity. There are certain foibles and weaknesses, which should be shut up in the coffin with the poor reliques of fallen humanity. Wherever the greater part of a character is *shining,* the *few blemishes* should be covered with the pall.

"I am apprehensive that the custom of exposing the nakedness of eminent men to every eye, will have an unfavourable influence on virtue. It may teach men to fear celebrity.

". . . this biographical anatomy, in minutely dissecting parts, destroys the beauty of the whole; just as in cutting up the most comely body, many loathsome objects are presented to the eye, and the beautiful form is utterly disfigured."

The distrust of anecdotes is not always so philosophically argued. One biographer, before presenting one of the most scandalous of pseudo-biographies, laments hypocritically:[141]

"This is an age when the prying eye of curiosity penetrates the privacy of every distinguished person; neither the living nor the dead escape. The most trivial pursuits of the one, and the former table-talk of the other, are exposed and narrated, with all the pomp of importance, by some officious hand, engaged to furnish anecdote for the world."

At the very end of the century Dugald Stewart, in an attempt to stem the tide of anecdotal biographies, presents a powerful argument which is worthy of serious consideration but which had not previously been advanced:[142]

---

[140] *Winter evenings: or, lucubrations on life and letters,* 1790, 2 vols., 2d ed., Vol. I, pp. 106-8.

[141] *Life and memoirs of Elizabeth Chudleigh, Duchess of Kingston,* 1789, p. 2.

[142] *Account of the life and writings of Thomas Reid,* 1802, pp. 142-3. Reid died in 1796.

"I recollect few, if any anecdotes, of Dr REID, which appear to me calculated to throw additional light on his character; and I suspect strongly, that many of those which are to be met with in biographical publications, are more likely to mislead, than to inform. A trifling incident, it is true, may sometimes paint a peculiar feature better than the most elaborate description; but a selection of incidents really characteristical, presupposes, in the observer, a rare capacity to discriminate and to generalize; and where this capacity is wanting, a biographer, with the most scrupulous attention to the veracity of his details, may yet convey a very false conception of the individual he would describe."

Stewart, therefore, attempts to convey a general impression of his subject's character, "instead of retailing detached fragments of conversations, or recording insulated and unmeaning occurrences." One final adverse criticism of anecdotes is worth recording, since it points out, much as Vicesimus Knox had done, that anecdote is not far from gossip, and gossip is never far from malice:[143]

"The greatest and the best of men have their blemishes and failings: whether it is for the benefit of society to scrutinize too nicely into these may well be doubted; to expose the inmost recesses of the closet to the rude eye of the public, especially when it is done with ill-nature, is not to be justified, let the writers of anecdote plume themselves upon it as much as they will. Truth is sacred, but it is not necessary that every insignificant truth should be proclaimed with sound of trumpet to the whole world."

There is, however, one argument for the inclusion of trivial detail that has not yet been mentioned. If, for the most part, men's lives are essentially the same, then the record of an obscure tradesman or harmless drudge may be of as great interest as that of a conquering general. And though any incidental happening in the life of an individual may be of no absolute value, nevertheless, if it illustrates the life and thoughts of the reader, if it strikes home to men's business and men's bosoms, then it should by all means be included. Here the criterion is not the uniqueness or splendor of any event, but its applicability to the

---

[143] Thomas Martyn's life of his father John Martyn, before his *Dissertations upon the Aeneids,* 1770, Preface, p. ii.

lives of many men. The argument is really democratic; it appealed to crescent classes in the eighteenth century; it had been used in modified form in earlier times to justify the lives of contemplation rather than of action; it is based upon a belief that the lives of others may help us to live our own, and that therefore the life that is closest to the average man's will be of greatest value if recorded.

More than any other man, Doctor Johnson is responsible for giving shape to this doctrine that the life of any individual, faithfully recorded in its minute details, is of service to the world, because all men are in essence alike, and are capable of profiting from the errors and triumphs of their brothers.[144] A few parallel formulations of this belief, however, are necessary to show its prevalence. One of the best of the defenses of private life is the anonymous *Memoirs of the life and times, of Sir Thomas Deveil* (1748), which opens:

"There seems to be no kind of writing more in favour with the present age, than memoirs, or accounts of persons who have distinguished themselves in the world, by arms or arts, by wit or learning, in a civil, military, naval, or commercial capacity . . . however people may differ in their public stations; in their private characters, in their virtues and vices, inclinations and aversions, they stand much upon the same foot, and it gives the ordinary rank of mankind, no small pleasure to find, that so it is; and that how different appearances soever men wear, yet follow them close, enter with them into their cabinets, or, which is still more, into their private thoughts, and the dark recesses of their minds, and they will be found pretty much upon a level."

The witty sentences of the anonymous satirist who wrote the *Memoirs of Magopico* contain more than a shred of truth:[145]

"Great and manifold are the advantages to be reaped from the tribe of matter of fact writers, whether historians, biographers, gazettists, memoirists, journalists, or anecdotists. Dead men are thus made alive again, so far as needful, without having their rest broke; a man gets a view of all that is to be seen in the physiognomies of many men of past generations, who, though

144 See Chap. VI.
145 1761, 2d ed., Chap. IX, "The praise of history."

they wore their periwigs of a different make from ours, yet breathed the same vital air, drank the same whisky-punch, and ate the same bread and butter, as we do."

Best of all is Thomas Martyn's defense of the truthful record of everyday life:[146]

"To read of kings, generals, and statesmen; of wars, battles, and the intrigues of politics; is delightful to the bulk of mankind, for the same reason that romances were once so bewitching: because they are above their level, and therefore answer the same purposes with giants and enchanted castles."

The eighteenth century, however, as he points out, has changed all that:

"The lives and actions of illustrious warriors and statesmen have ever been esteemed worthy the attention of the public: but this age has been the first to enter the more private walks of life, to contemplate merit in the shades, and to admire the more silent virtues. Dazzled with the glare of military talents, or caught in the intricacies of state politics; the world seldom condescended to look upon literary accomplishments even of the highest order; but wholly disdained the study of common life, and those characters which it would be of the most general use to be acquainted with, because they lie most open to imitation."

Critical theory, therefore, here and particularly in the two famous essays of Doctor Johnson—the *Rambler* Number 60 and the *Idler* Number 84[147]—has caught up with English biographical practice. In no other nation had the lives of humble individuals received as much attention as in England. Edmund Calamy in 1725, writing of the "Lives of persons eminent for learning or piety," justly observes:[148] "we have a greater Number of such Lives in our own Language, than most other Nations: Perhaps I might truly say, than any one." And the great French biographical encyclopedist Niceron praises the English for their lives of illustrious men of letters:[149] "Il n'est gueres de Sçavant de cette

[146] Life of his father John Martyn, 1770, before *Dissertations upon the Aeneids*, p. i.

[147] cf. Chap. VI.   [148] *Memoirs of Increase Mather*, 1725, Preface.

[149] *Memoires pour servir à l'histoire des hommes illustres dans la république des lettres*, 1727. Preface to Vol. I, p. a iiii; originally this appeared in 43 vols. issued from 1727 to 1745.

Nation un peu illustre, dont on n'ait écrit la vie, qui contient aussi souvent un abregé de ses Ouvrages, & un détail exact de tout ce qui peut y avoir rapport." Largely because of the English passion for the private and the minute as opposed to the historical and the overpowering, autobiographies in general and lives of literary figures in particular came to be highly valued, since these forms were peculiarly adapted to the conveying of intimate observations of human life. Doctor Johnson again gives his critical sanction to autobiography, and many of the writers of the time prefer it to pure biography. "Mr Gray, the poet, says Horace Walpole, has often observed to me, and with justice, that if any man was to form a book of what he has seen and heard himself; this alone *must*, in *whatever* hands, prove a most useful and entertaining one."[150]

And William Houstoun writes:[151]

"Of all History I have always had the greatest Pleasure, Satisfaction, and Edification from *Memoirs of Lives,* especially when wrote by the Persons themselves, from Caesar's Commentaries to Colley Cibber's Life; for it is impossible, even for the best Limner, to draw a just Picture to the Likeness, unless the Original is the Object of his Senses. It is true, all Actions in human Life, especially the glorious Transactions of the Great, are the Object of our Senses, but none know the original Source and secret Springs of those Actions and Transactions but the Actor himself. I must own, that Vanity, which every mortal is possessed of, more or less, naturally leads us to be partial to ourselves; but this is sufficiently counter-balanced, by Honour, Sincerity, and Truth, and, in my humble Opinion, every Man of tolerable Understanding, with common Honour and Honesty, is the fittest Man to write his *own Memoirs*; for he certainly knows more of himself, than others can possibly know of him."

[150] Quoted from *Memoirs of the life of the Rev. Dr. Trusler,* 1806, p. 4. This saying by Horace Walpole is used as a motto in Pinkerton's *Walpoliana,* 1799.

[151] *Dr. Houstoun's memoirs of his own life-time,* 1747, p. 8. cf. Gilbert Wakefield's *Memoirs,* 1792, which holds autobiography superior to biography, quotes the *Idler,* No. 84, in support of this statement, and cites the autobiographies of Herbert, Lilly, Whiston, Clarendon, and Cibber.

The great popularity of the lives of authors is explained by one writer:[152]

"It is an old observation, that we are no sooner interested by the writings of an author, than our curiosity is awakened for his history, his fortune, and his character."

And more fully by Thomas Amory:[153]

"When persons have distinguished themselves in the learned world, and especially by Writings, in defense and recommendation of religion and virtue; it is natural for those who read and value their works, to be inquisitive as to their private characters, and the principal circumstances of their lives. . . . We are desirous of knowing, whether the principles of truth, and rules of goodness, which their writings recommend, were properly exemplified in their conduct."

When even the lowliest scribbler came to have his biographer, a rebellion broke out against the custom. "Biography," Sir William Young observes,[154]

"taken in its narrow and proper acceptation, seems to be ill applied, and to lose much of its essential interests, its use, and its amusement, when engaged in the barren service of *men of letters*. A few stories of ingenuity in early youth, of premature talents, and of their early application to some branch of science, form the first set of scanty materials. At a more advanced period of life, we are told of literary disputes, of compliments between students in the same class, and of friendships and of enmities which go no further than paper-love, and paper-war; and these fill up the ordinary measure of their days.

"This sameness, this still-life, so unfit for public representation, appears a necessary result from a first principle [i.e., the hero's consecration to study or literature]."

Yet authors insist upon writing of fellow-authors, which explains (p. 4) "the many learned '*lives without adventures*' which are daily published." Sir William Young's cavils need not be taken too seriously, however, for they are followed by his own life of

---

[152] *Catalogue of five hundred celebrated authors of Great Britain*, 1788, Preface, p. v.

[153] Life of George Benson, before Benson's *History of Jesus Christ*, 1764, p. iii.

[154] Life of Brook Taylor before Taylor's *Contemplatio Philosophica*, 1793. Introduction, pp. 1-2.

the learned recluse who was his grandfather. Horace Walpole makes a similar apology, and follows his epigrammatic observations with a similar life of an obscure Cambridge don. "The deep or extensive learning of a man of letters," Walpole writes,[155]

"is but a barren field for biography. His notions are speculation; his adventures, enquiry. If his studies fermented or consolidated into compositions, the history of his life commonly proves but a register of the squabbles occasioned by his works, of the patrons he flattered, of the preferments he obtained or missed. The dates of his publications and their editions form the outlines of his story; and frequently the plans or projects of works he meditated are taken to aid the account; the day of his death is scrupulously ascertained:—and thus, to compose the life of a man who did very little, his biographer acquaints us with what he did not do, and when he ceased to do any thing."

The most unmistakable evidence that biography was considered seriously by critics and writers is the continual realization throughout the century of the difficulties of producing a satisfactory life. Again and again, theorists and biographers state the ideal requirements, and show that standards of life-writing were continually being debated and reduced to rule and discarded. The repeated and public avowal that biography is not a species of scribbling to be undertaken lightly, but that it has its own rules, ideals, and requirements must, of course, have done much to improve the writing of lives. Doctor Johnson is not alone in pointing out the difficulty of getting the requisite material for a life. The writers of the time lament because the important intimate details of their heroes' careers are lost in antiquity, or because no one remembers or has recorded the stories of childhood and youth. Yet such sad cries show a clearer knowledge that personal and minuscule details are the life-breath of biography; furthermore, a realization of their regrettable absence in the records of the past makes it more likely that they will be preserved in the memoirs and journals and biographies of the

[155] *Works,* 1798, 5 vols., Vol. II, p. 341, *The life of the Reverend Mr. Thomas Baker . . . written in 1778.*

present and the future. "The early events of an illustrious character," Doctor Burney writes,[156]

"are generally as obscure and fabulous, as the first years of an ancient and powerful empire. For Biographers, notwithstanding the title they assume, seldom draw from the life; nor, till an illustrious personage has been some time deceased, do enquiry and conjecture begin to busy themselves in tracing incidents, describing situations, and delineating characters. And hence, by procrastination, the whole becomes little better than a mere *fancy-piece.*

"If it were possible, however, to know, in detail, the youthful exploits of an Alexander, or a Caesar; the first poetical effusions of a Homer, or a Virgil; the dawnings of reason in a Newton, or a Locke; or the primary fermentations and expansions of genius in a HANDEL, they would afford great gratification to human curiosity, which delights in seeing by what minute gradations, or gigantic strides, men gifted with uncommon powers, begin their journey to the Temple of Fame."

If Doctor Johnson's opinions seem to lie behind his friend Burney's remarks, they are no less evident in George Chalmers's observations at the opening of his life of Defoe:[157]

"It is lamented by those who labour the fields of British biography, that after being entangled in briars they are too often rewarded with the scanty products of barrenness. The lives of literary men are generally passed in the obscurities of the closet, which conceal even from friendly inquiries the artifices of study, whereby each may have risen to eminence. And during the same moment that the diligent biographer sets out to ask for information, with regard to the modes of life, or peculiarity of character belonging to writers who have amused, or instructed their country, the house-keeper, the daughter, or grand-child, that knew family traditions, drop into the grave."

Yet even when the evanescent and perishable stuff out of which biography is created exists in plenty, a successful biog-

[156] *An account of . . . Handel,* 1785, pp. 1-2, *Sketch of the life of Handel.* cf. William Harris's *Thomas Manton,* 1725, in which Harris laments the necessity for writing biographies at too great a distance from the subject, and cites as examples Walton's *Hooker* and Calamy's *John Howe.*

[157] 1785 ed., p. [i].

raphy is still not easily produced. The essential requisites for a good biography, as Gilbert Wakefield sees them, are:[158] "events not wholly unimportant, nor unconnected with the political or literary transactions of the times, related in a style perspicuous, nor yet void of ornament, with the confidence of integrity, and the simplicity of truth." Significant material, stylistic competence, and truthfulness in presentation are not given to every writer of biography even when he possesses the best of intentions. With regard to the question of fidelity of portraiture alone, too often, as one antiquary observes:[159]

"A Biographer seems to be by profession A Writer of Panegyric; as it is a strong predilection in favour of some particular character, that generally determines him in the choice of his subject: Praise therefore being the fixed object of his plan, he often makes a sacrifice of truth without scruple, to his partiality for a friend, or his gratitude to a benefactor."

The *Monthly Review* for 1799 points out, in a discouraging analysis, the obstacles to the production of a good biography:[160]

"Of the many who have engaged in communicating to the world the lives of those whose fortunes or merits have entitled them to its notice, perhaps fewer have excelled than in any other branch of literature. Some have collected facts which they committed to paper without order or selection; others have selected facts, but with the sinister intention of consigning their subject to unmerited infamy, or of bedecking him with undeserved praise. Some have been impartial, but have been indolent in research, and destitute of discrimination; while many have brought to their task impartiality, industry, and good sense, but have wanted taste, learning, and skill in composition, to illustrate and adorn the subject on which they wrote."

In regard to the style and the form of biography, few critical discussions exist in the eighteenth century. An individual biographer may exercise considerable skill in dividing his hero's life into periods; or he may affirm, and try to illustrate, that both variety and dignity are necessary in the actions of his hero if

---

[158] *Memoirs of the life of Gilbert Wakefield*, 1804, p. 6. First issued in 1792.
[159] Benjamin Pye's *Life of Cardinal Reginald Pole*, 1766, p. ix, Preface.
[160] Vol. 30, New Series, pp. 241-2.

his biography is to be pleasing; or he may believe that biography is an easy art which requires only "a talent for arrangement"; or he may wish only to give to a rough earlier account the merits of uniform narration and simplicity of style; or he may decide to herd all his notes into the back of the book in order to make an uninterrupted narrative.[161]

Yet such experiments in style and form are sporadic and without great influence. It is of little importance in the history of biography, for instance, that an ambitious young writer is so worried about "The Design" of his work that he assures his reader:[162] "The Stile which the Author uses, is such in every Place as the Subject seems to require, concise tho' circumstantial in the historical Parts, diffus'd and declamatory in the Recapitulation, and close and unaffected in the occasional Reflections." It is hardly more important, though it is more interesting, to hear of speculation as to the type of career which would make a good biography:[163]

"Biography would always engage the passions [which makes narrative pleasing], if it could sufficiently gratify curiosity: but there have been few among the whole human species, whose lives would furnish a single adventure; I mean such a complication of circumstances, as hold the mind in an anxious yet pleasing suspense, and gradually unfold in the production of some unforeseen and important event; much less such a series of facts, as will perpetually vary the scene, and gratify the fancy with new views of life."

If such implicit requirements for a well shaped and interesting biography had caught hold and been regarded by other writers, they might deserve greater consideration; but actually such speculations were no more than casual remarks, swallowed up

[161] The references are, respectively: Thomas Milles's *Life of Isaac Milles*, 1720, p. 73; Joseph Cornish's *Life of Thomas Firmin*, 1780, Preface; Theophilus Smart's *Authentic memoirs of Captain Paul Jones* [1779], p. 3; P. Peckard's *Memoirs of Nicholas Ferrar*, 1790, p. xv; *Memoirs of Thomas Comber*, 1799, by his great-grandson Thomas Comber.

[162] John Gilbert Cooper, *Life of Socrates*, 1750, p. viii.

[163] Quoted from *Monthly Review*, Vol. 7, p. 374, for 1753. Reprinted in John Hawkesworth's *The Adventurer*, 3 vols., 1794, Vol. I, p. 28, "Of the different kinds of narrative." Hawkesworth was the biographer and friend of Johnson.

and lost without a trace in the conventional theories and the unthinking practices of the century.

This section of the chapter has tried to mention the most striking new thoughts in critical theory—not to record again the traditional opinions. It is not so important, for example, to record the generally expressed belief that biography serves a utilitarian purpose as it is to show a biographer breaking away from that belief with the satirical introductory drollery:[164]

"Biography, in sooth, is a study, the which will make wise men nought the worse, and leave fools just where it found them." Or again, the difference in temper between the century that read Augustine's and Bunyan's confessions and the century that read Rousseau's and Sterne's may be sketched in a sentence:[165] "So delicate is the pleasure, so superior to defending, is the dignity of confessing, one's follies, that the wonder is to see so few capable of it." Such a light remark as this is indeed indicative of a shift in biographical theory: curiosity and eccentricity supplant didacticism; so that by the end of the century one biographer diffidently hopes that no great harm will come from his serious biography even in this age of "light, gay, and amusing" books;[166] and another writer apologizes for intruding religious biography upon an age that esteems the brilliant and the entertaining, the records of amorous intrigues, political machinations, fashionable vices, unprincipled statesmen, tyrants, and free-thinkers.[167] If Handel, Raphael, Shakespeare, or Newton may be praised for their peculiar excellences, he goes on, "why then, in the philosophy

[164] *Memoirs of Magopico*, 1761, 2d ed., Editor's Proem, p. [3]. One might mention, however, an instance in which biography was of immediate practical usefulness in curing eyestrain: "my Eyes did not see as usual, but dazzled after an aukward Manner. . . . At this Time I met with an Account, either in Conversation, or Writing, that Mr. Boyle had known of a Person who had new whited the Wall of his Study or Chamber, upon which the Sun shone, and used to read in that glaring Light, and thereby lost his Sight for a Time, till upon hanging the Place where he studied with Green, he recovered it again; which was exactly my own Case, in a less Degree, both as to the Cause and the Remedy."—*Memoirs of William Whiston*, 1749, pp. 20-1.

[165] John Cleland's *Memoirs of a coxcomb*, 1751, p. 1.

[166] John Smith's *Saint Columba*, 1798, Preface, p. vii.

[167] P. Peckard's *Nicholas Ferrar*, 1790, pp. 1-2 and 253-4. For the conscious trend toward the more frivolous and curious aspects of biography, see Semple, Thicknesse, Prince, Pasquin, or Rolt. Also see Chaps. III and V.

and practice of Religion alone should peculiar eminence be stigmatized with sarcastic censure?" A hundred years earlier such a defense of ethical or religious biography would have been unnecessary; it would have been almost unthinkable.

To take another example of convention and revolt in biographical theory, William Burton is following centuries of tradition when he writes:[168]

"Two of the principal inducements to record the lives of those, who by their distinguish'd merit have done honour to mankind, are, to reflect that honour on their memory, and to excite posterity to a noble emulation."

Here is biography in its old form, playing its dual rôle as memorial to the dead and example to the living. But the new spirit of the times takes the last judgment out of the power and province of God and gives it to the contemporary reader. The biographies of the great, one theorist observes with acuteness and originality, afford the sole means of dealing out justice to those whom it would have been dangerous to offend while they were alive. "Posterity," he continues,[169] "has a Right to have such Truths transmitted to them fairly, and private Men may be allow'd to look behind the Scenes, when the Play is over, and there's no Danger of disturbing the Actors in their Parts." A bit more grim in their implications of public judgment of the most private circumstances are these paragraphs:[170]

"It was customary among the antient Egyptians, to try before a public tribunal, the characters of their princes and great men after death. At these trials of the dead, the living were allowed, without incurring danger from punishment or revenge, to bring forward their accusations in proof; and if the deceased was found guilty of having led a vicious, irregular, or useless life, his body was refused a place in the catacombs, the rites of burial, in a more private way; or a sentence, stigmatizing his character, was passed and entered against him upon record by the judges.

[168] *An account of the life and writings of Herman Boerhaave,* 1743, p. [1].
[169] *Memoirs of Andrew-Hercules de Fleury,* 1743, p. 2.
[170] *The life and memoirs of Elizabeth Chudleigh, Duchess of Kingston* [1788], p. [5].

"Though no such formal mode of trial exists in this country, yet the art of printing, and the liberty of the press, have established what virtually amounts to the same; for in these times, not only every person eminent for rank or virtues, but all, whose characters have been remarkable, or whose genius has been distinguished in arts, sciences, and professions, as well as those whose lives have been notorious for villany, debauchery, or folly, are after their decease, brought to an ordeal, to receive judgment from public opinion; and every action is investigated and determined upon, by a scrutiny equally circumspect as that carried on against the defunct by the Egyptian jurists.

"At the bar of this court stands, the character of Elizabeth Chudleigh. . . ."

If the democratic and skeptical principles of the century are apparent in such a conception of biography, the growing consciousness of the reality of the individual as opposed to the phantoms of the state or society, is evident in this critical defense of biography:[171]

"No species of writing combines in it a greater degree of interest and instruction than Biography. Our sympathy is most powerfully excited by the view of those situations and passions, which, by a small effort of the imagination, we can approximate to ourselves. Hence Biography often engages our attention and affections more deeply than History. We are more concerned by the display of individual character than of political measures, of individual enjoyment or suffering, than of the prosperity or adversity of nations. Even in History, the biographical part often interests us more than any other. We consider some one personage with more attention and concern than a whole people. Our sympathetic feelings accompany Epaminondas, not the Thebans, at Leuctra and at Mantinea—Hannibal, not the Carthaginians, at Cannae and at Zama."

And the beliefs in original genius, in distinctive personality, and in knowledge of human capabilities as a good in itself are all im-

[171] Robert Bisset's *Biographical sketch of the authors of the Spectator*, 1793, Preface, p. [vii].

plicit in such a sentence as the following from the translations of Condorcet's *Life of Voltaire*:[172]

"Every circumstance relating to such a man promotes the study of the human mind; with which we cannot hope to become acquainted if we do not observe its properties as they exist in those to whom Nature has been prodigal of her riches and her power, and if we do not seek in such minds what they possess in common with others, and in what they are distinguished."

Such statements are rare in the eighteenth century, because in biography as in other branches of literature, critical theory usually lags far behind practice and is only slowly, painfully, gropingly built up. Yet the century was undeniably fascinated by the possibilities of biography. Of its three great historians, we find one— Edward Gibbon—contemplating various biographical schemes to the end of his life, and Hume writing to Robertson in an effort to turn the grave and sublime historian from his considerations of America, India, Scotland, and the Holy Roman Empire under Charles V to more frivolous biography:[173]

"You see that in Plutarch the Life of Caesar may be read in half an hour. Were you to write the life of Henry the Fourth of France after that model, you might pillage all the pretty stories in Sully, and speak more of his mistresses than of his battles. In short, you might gather the flower of all Modern History in this manner. The remarkable Popes, the Kings of Sweden, the great discoverers and conquerors of the New World; even the eminent men of letters, might furnish you with matter, and the quick despatch of every different work would encourage you to begin a new one. If one volume were successful, you might compose another at your leisure, and the field is inexhaustible. There are persons whom you might find in the corners of history, so to speak, who would be a subject of entertainment quite unexpected; and, as long as you live, you might give and receive amusement by such a work."

Certainly, among the biographers themselves, the citation of precedents for their productions and the numerous surveys of

---

[172] 1790, 2 vols., Vol. I, p. 2.
[173] Quoted from Alexander Stewart's *Life of William Robertson*, 1820, Vol. I, pp. xl-xli.

what had already been done show a lively and continued interest.[174]

It is not too much to say that the eighteenth century, engrossed in this world, in social relations, and in the individual, thought in biographical terms. Such interest in personal human life almost necessarily resulted in a varied series of biographical productions, and in more than a few works of the first rank. "When is biography interesting?" asks a reviewer at the close of the century, and he answers his own question:[175] "—when it excites curiosity by reporting the little things of great men; rouses attention by splendid events and busy scenes; elevates affection by tales of distress or goodness; excites to virtue by records of eminent excellence; raises mirth by witty sayings and humorous anecdotes; or when it enlarges knowledge and corrects judgment by profound remarks and curious criticisms." Such a broad conception of the functions and effects of biography could be made only in an age of achievement and vitality. Its varied demands are not satisfied so fully either in the seventeenth or the nineteenth century; in the eighteenth century, biography was in full flower. This book will have served its purpose if it suggests that Boswell and Johnson do not stand alone; that even the addition of such names as Roger North and Edward Gibbon and William Mason will not make the roster of important eighteenth century biographers complete; and that the eighteenth century, for originality, art, and truth to human experience, is the golden age of English biography. If the theory is at all tenable that at least a part of Shakespeare's greatness comes from his birth as one among many Elizabethan dramatists, then Johnson and Boswell—the best in English biography—may be explained in part by remembering that they lived in a time when writing biographies was a natural pastime and a national art.

[174] cf., e.g., Nathanael Parkhurst's *William Burkitt*, 1704, which cites precedents from Homer to Bishop Burnet; Oldys's remarkable critical and historical sketch of biography before the *Biographia Britannica,* 1747; Berkenhout, 1777; the critical analysis of its predecessors before the first volume of *A new and general biographical dictionary,* 1761; Vicesimus Knox's very interesting "Cursory thoughts on biography," Number 94 of his *Essays moral and literary,* 1782.

[175] *Monthly Review,* Vol. 31, New Series, p. 2. 1800.

The classical and medieval theories of the stable social and religious order in which man was a subordinate part had not yet been completely supplanted by the introspective individualism of the Romantics. For a short period during this transition, man as an individual, and the world in which he lived, were both realities. Out of this fortunate moment, reflecting the interplay of old and new conceptions, rose the biographies of the eighteenth century in vigor and variety that have not been surpassed.

INDEX

INDEX

NOTE: This index includes all the names mentioned in the text

(1) of biographers before 1800,

(2) of subjects of biographies before 1800, and

(3) of sources of, or influences upon, these biographies.

It also includes the few unusual titles of biographies (in italics) when such biographies could not easily be found by reference to subject or author.

Names of later editors and critics are here omitted, but may in some cases be found in the Bibliographical Supplement.

For a review of subject matter, consult the detailed descriptions given in the Contents.

A footnote reference is indicated by an *n*. after the page number.

Numbers in italic type indicate the pages of principal entries.